MW00475387

PARLIAMENT AND CONGRESS

Parliament and Congress: Representation and Scrutiny in the Twenty-First Century

William McKAY and Charles W. JOHNSON

OXFORD
UNIVERSITY PRESS

OXFORD
UNIVERSITY PRESS

Great Clarendon Street, Oxford OX2 6DP

Oxford University Press is a department of the University of Oxford.
It furthers the University's objective of excellence in research, scholarship,
and education by publishing worldwide in

Oxford New York

Auckland Cape Town Dar es Salaam Hong Kong Karachi
Kuala Lumpur Madrid Melbourne Mexico City Nairobi
New Delhi Shanghai Taipei Toronto

With offices in

Argentina Austria Brazil Chile Czech Republic France Greece
Guatemala Hungary Italy Japan Poland Portugal Singapore
South Korea Switzerland Thailand Turkey Ukraine Vietnam

Oxford is a registered trade mark of Oxford University Press
in the UK and in certain other countries

Published in the United States
by Oxford University Press Inc., New York

© Charles Johnson and William McKay 2010

The moral rights of the authors have been asserted
Database right Oxford University Press (maker)

First published 2010

All rights reserved. No part of this publication may be reproduced,
stored in a retrieval system, or transmitted, in any form or by any means,
without the prior permission in writing of Oxford University Press,
or as expressly permitted by law, or under terms agreed with the appropriate
reprographics rights organization. Enquiries concerning reproduction
outside the scope of the above should be sent to the Rights Department,
Oxford University Press, at the address above

You must not circulate this book in any other binding or cover
and you must impose the same condition on any acquirer

British Library Cataloguing in Publication Data

Data available

Library of Congress Cataloging in Publication Data

Data available

Typeset by SPI Publisher Services, Pondicherry, India
Printed in Great Britain
on acid-free paper by
CPI Digital

ISBN 978–0–19–927362–1

1 3 5 7 9 10 8 6 4 2

This book is dedicated with respect and affection to
our friends
Betty Boothroyd, formerly Speaker of the House of Commons,
and
Kieran Coughlan, Clerk of Dáil Éireann

Preface

Kenneth Bradshaw and David Pring published their classic study of Parliament and Congress in 1972. An updating chapter had to be added to a second edition only nine years later. Over the past quarter of a century, change in Washington and Westminster has continued and indeed accelerated. This work is not therefore an updating of Bradshaw and Pring, but an entirely new view of the two legislatures, sometimes more optimistic than theirs, sometimes not. We have tried, like them, not to replicate the standard reference works—*House Practice* and *Senate Procedure* for Congress and Erskine May's *Parliamentary Practice* for Westminster—a temptation the more easily resisted since we ourselves respectively edited two of the most recent editions. Within limits—and with suitable caution as no doubt befits even former parliamentary officials—we have now and again made judgements on developments in the legislatures.

Change is equally certain in the future, both in Washington and Westminster, and the direction of change is always unpredictable. An account such as this can be only a snapshot. For example, as this work was being completed, the House of Commons was struck by the tsunami of public criticism generated by newspaper reports of Members' expenses claims. Fundamental changes in aspects of the House's work far beyond administration and accounts will surely follow. Yet however keenly the need for reform may presently be felt, the House of Commons is not dysfunctional. The past three or four decades have witnessed changes probably more radical than in any past age. It would be a pity if a new agenda were allowed to crowd out that already before Parliament, in which much has been achieved. A comparable evaluation of the extent of changes in the Congress during the same forty-year period will reveal similar acceleration, and with mixed results when measured for institutional quality.

Because this is not intended to be a standard textbook, we have chosen not to overload it with references illuminating particular events. As Sir Thomas Erskine May (Clerk of the House of Commons between 1871 and 1886) himself remarked about his magnum opus, 'the citing of precedents at length makes a work very long'. It will not, we believe, be difficult for readers to locate the details of a proceeding to which we have referred.

We are immensely grateful to our respective former colleagues—that they are far too many to enumerate in no way diminishes our gratitude—for assistance in the preparation of our account. The Congressional Research Service and the House of Commons Sessional Returns Office were sources for valuable institutional information, as were the Offices of House and Senate Parliamentarian and the Office of House General Counsel. Of course, the responsibility for the text remains wholly with us.

William McKay
Charles W Johnson

September 2009

Table of Contents

List of Abbreviations

C & AG	Comptroller and Auditor General
CAA	Congressional Accountability Act
CBO	Congressional Budget Office
CG	Comptroller General
COSAC	Conference of European Affairs Committees
CR	continuing resolution
CRA	Congressional Review Act
CSPL	Committee on Standards in Public Life
DHS	Department of Homeland Security
EU	European Union
FISA	Foreign Intelligence Surveillance Act
GAO	Government Accountability Office
HR	House of Representatives
IG	Inspector General
IT	information technology
MEC	Members' Estimate Committee
MPC	Monetary Policy Committee
NAO	National Audit Office
NASA	North American Space Agency
NLRB	National Labor Relations Board
NPO	National Parliament Office
OMB	Office of Management and Budget
OTA	Office of Technology Assessment
PAC	Political Action Committee
PBR	Pre-Budget Report
PL	Public Law
POST	Parliamentary Office of Science and Technology

RfR	Request for Resources
S&I	surveys and investigations
SSRB	Senior Salaries Review Body
TARP	Troubled Assets Relief Program
VAT	Value Added Tax

Table of Cases

1

Introduction

Separation of powers

Any comparative analysis of the British and United States systems of government, and the influences of one upon the other, should from an American perspective at least, begin with an examination of the Federalist Papers, a series of essays written by Alexander Hamilton, James Madison, and John Jay in 1787 in contemporaneous criticism of the Articles of Confederation and in defence of the proposed Constitution as it had been forwarded to State conventions for ratification. They were published under the pseudonym Publius in New York City newspapers in an effort to win ratification of the New York convention. The Federalist Papers have attained abiding importance as a statement of a political philosophy of constitutional government. Of the central themes of the Federalist ('federalism', 'checks and balances', 'separated powers', 'pluralism', and 'representation') all describe a divided, balanced, and limited governmental system intended for the ultimate protection of sovereignty of the governed people under a written Constitution. The original empowerment as it bears upon the contemporary role of the legislative branch of the national government as a participant in this structure will be a central focus of this work.

The embodiment of 'federalism' in the US Constitution begins with the conferral in Article I, section 1 of all those legislative powers granted (in section 8) to the national Congress. The Constitution then proceeds in the 9th and 10th Amendments to protect the respective sovereignties over non-enumerated rights to the States or to the People. Section 8 therefore enables legislative power over various aspects of public affairs while not claiming to confer total legislative power. The people as ultimate sovereign retain certain specific freedoms from legislative encroachment in areas of speech, assembly, religion, press, and petition in the 1st Amendment.

While Madison did not believe in the total equality of the three branches of government, but in legislative supremacy—'In republican government the legislative authority, necessarily, predominates' (Federalist no. 51)—he acknowledged that the branches were to be allowed a 'partial agency in and control over the acts of the other' (Federalist

1

no. 47). The term 'checks and balances' does not textually appear in the Constitution itself but is utilized sparingly in the Federalist Papers more often to explain limitations within the legislature in defence of bicameralism than among the branches of the entire constitutional system. The term 'checks and balances' is derived from the philosophy of 'mixed government', a classical notion applied to the British system at the time of formulation of the US Constitution based on aristocratic assumptions of a vertical alignment of classes which seeks a social equilibrium by arming the different orders of society—the monarch, the aristocrats and the people—with a means to check each other.[1]

The concept of separation of powers calls for a division of forces in terms of function where governmental entities do not speak for different segments of society, but rather for efficiency's sake address different tasks of the whole society. As Madison suggests in Federalist nos. 62 and 63, a Senate is needed to give government sufficient credit with foreign powers, not that the Senate will represent a different class in America, one commanding respect abroad, but rather a body sitting for a longer period, one renewed by staggered elections, giving the continuity necessary for commitment to treaties and an international order. The whole House of Representatives can be voted out of office every two years, thus ensuring accountability to the electorate, not only for the House but for the whole government (since the House originates control of the purse strings of the whole government). The Senate, by contrast, supplies a different function, a steadiness of aspect, a predictability in the eyes of foreign powers—qualities proper to the Senate in making treaties and confirming ambassadors.

For Madison, separation also meant a mutual check between the two Houses, wherein the Senate does not speak for an aristocracy over against the people but for the 'national character' or reputation that Senators are pledged to uphold (Federalist no. 63) while Representatives will with the people on their side at all times be able to bring back the constitution to its primitive form and principles (Federalist no. 62). A Senate as 'a second branch of the legislative assembly distinct from and dividing the power with a first' must be in all cases a salutary check on the government.

Madison gives a third reason for the separation of powers beyond efficiency and the balancing of constitutional values against each other, namely legitimacy. In Federalist no. 10 he says that the concentration of all power in one place is the very definition of tyranny. This was a commonplace of constitutional theory in the aftermath of Britain's two revolutions in the seventeenth century. The restoration of a constitutional monarch involved the limiting of sovereignty to preclude absolutism. The king remained sovereign but had to observe the general rule that 'no man is allowed to be a judge in his own cause' (Federalist no. 10). The king's power as executive was 'separated from the judicial application of the law by disinterested courts... As a king is prevented from becoming a tyrant by the separation of executive and judicial functions, so a popular tyranny must be avoided by a separation of powers... In England the king himself was a segment of society, with the nobility and commoners in a "mixed government".' In America the sovereign was to be 'the whole body of the people'. Once the sovereign people have spoken through the Legislature, the same people speak in theory through the Executive that enforces and the Judiciary that applies the laws.

In the United States, the relative constitutional 'looseness' between the Legislative, Executive, and Judicial branches is assured not only by the textual separate conferrals of power in Articles I, II, and III of the Constitution, but further by the prohibition against the simultaneous holding of incompatible offices in more than one of the three branches, contained in Article I, section 6, clause 2 of the Constitution. This restriction is explicitly applicable to Members of both Houses of Congress, and is coupled with a prohibition against Members of Congress holding any office created by law or emoluments of which are increased during their terms.

Indeed, James Madison proceeded to analyse in Federalist no. 47 the peculiar distribution of the conferred 'mass of power' among the constituent parts of the government envisioned in Articles I, II, and III of the Constitution, and to contrast it with the British Constitution as follows: 'On the slightest view of the British Constitution, we must perceive that the legislative, executive and judiciary departments are by no means totally separate and distinct from each other.'

The Founding Fathers saw clearly the need to avoid the shortcomings of the contemporary British Constitution, with its organic development, pragmatic approach to problems and institutions based on a society distinct from theirs. They were men of the Enlightenment, with a clear view of the need to proceed on the basis of reason and a horror of the arbitrary power lurking in unwritten constitutions to the detriment of the individual citizen. Notwithstanding such fundamental difference, it is not difficult to account for such similarity as exists between the two legislatures. American independence was won from the British, but the men who gained their political freedom in the 1770s could hardly avoid modelling some part of their new Congress on Westminster. There were two reasons for that. The British Parliament was the only credible example, even if it sometimes indicated only what had to be avoided. France, America's ally in winning independence, was no help—when the first Congress convened, even the beginning of the end for the *ancien régime*, the fall of the Bastille, was still four months in the future. Secondly, the thirteen Colonies themselves derived their polities for the most part directly from England, and many of the men who created the US Constitution were veterans of colonial legislatures.

A shadow of the relationship of earlier days may still be traced today. Before new Rules are adopted at the beginning of each successive Congress,[2] one of the foundations on which the procedure of the House of Representatives depends is that set out in Thomas Jefferson's *Manual of Parliamentary Practice*. The *Manual* was compiled when Jefferson was President of the Senate between 1797 and 1801, and his sources are exclusively British. Some are collections of parliamentary debates, incorporating Speakers' rulings; also included are the Commons Journals, demonstrating how that House extricated itself from difficulties over the centuries (and which came into play in connection with a vexed procedural question raised by the intended impeachment of President Clinton; see page 515). Others are legal tracts touching on Parliament. Several are works written specifically (some by Clerks) to describe in detail how Westminster worked. The book which drew highest praise from Jefferson was the work of the contemporary Clerk of the House of Commons, John Hatsell. He was a Northamptonshire gentleman, who, though he bought the position of Clerk in 1768, became the most professionally effective holder of that office for well over half a century. His *Precedents of Proceedings in the House of Commons* became a standard textbook. However abundantly Washington has developed and flourished from these beginnings, its roots are in the soil of Westminster.

There are also cases where, in relatively minor aspects, British parliamentary practices dead or dying on their home soil were adopted by the early Congress. Congress has retained and developed them; Parliament has abandoned them. Two short examples will illustrate the phenomenon. First, Conferences to adjust disputes between the Houses are a regular part of Congressional affairs (see pages 448–61). By 1778, the last British Conference of a kind modern Senators and Congressmen would recognize was a generation in the past (in 1740), and there was only to be one more, in 1836. Secondly, the 'previous question', a means of avoiding a decision on the matter under discussion (with the ironic penalty that if it fails in that end, it will accelerate that decision) still exists on Capitol Hill and at Westminster. The form in which it is put, once common to both legislatures, has however changed at Westminster—by the addition of the word 'not'[3]— and though flourishing on Capitol Hill the procedure is moribund at Westminster.

There is no separation of powers where, as in Britain then and now, the Executive is represented in and depends for its continued existence on the support of the Legislature. As a result, however close the original models, their development took quite separate tracks. The development of the British Parliament—and the Commons in particular— since American independence has fallen into several phases, beginning with a House which saw itself as an institutional opposition to the Crown and procedure as its principal weapon. The next stage was a long era in which governments acquired and retained a near-monopoly of the initiative in bringing forward business, with which went control of time, and the weakening of the House's scrutiny function. The twentieth century tightened the screw of government on the Commons still further. The present situation demonstrates a retreat from these strong positions. Government has surrendered some prerogative powers hitherto unchallengeable by Parliament, conceding to the Houses (for example) authority to commit armed forces into action, and both Houses have revived— or perhaps more accurately developed for the first time—credible instruments for scrutinizing the Executive. The time–business relationship remains critical—the balance between the need, within constitutional limits, for the government to secure its business and for the Houses adequately to debate proposals coming before them. Where it will come to rest, even temporarily, is for the future.

Congressional and parliamentary powers

With certain exceptions, and uniquely among parliamentary bodies in the world, the two Houses of the United States Congress have co-equal legislative (law-making) powers and functions, as both Houses must pass bills in the same form during the constitutional term of a Congress (two years) before presentment to the President for enactment into law (Article I, section 7). The only exception with respect to origination of legislation is confined to the authority of the House of Representatives (the House more closely representing the electorate) to originate revenue bills (a prerogative extended to the origination of appropriation bills by traditional insistence of the House though not conferred textually by Article I, section 7).

Beginning about the time of the Glorious Revolution of 1688–90, the House of Lords in Britain has yielded political primacy to the Commons. The nineteenth- and early twentieth-century expansion of the franchise naturally reinforced the trend. The origins of the financial authority of the lower House as against the upper are medieval in origin, and though occasionally challenged the Commons always successfully defended its predominant right to tax the people and vote aids and supplies to the Crown, subject only to the simple concurrence of the Lords. The Parliament Acts 1911 and 1949 went further by removing from the Lords the right to reject Money bills. Contemporary debate over the composition of the Lords, involving as it does the diminution and perhaps disappearance of the non-elected element, may institute a period of rebalancing in which the Commons may have to return to some of the old battlegrounds.

Other House and Senate responsibilities which are conferred by Article I of the Constitution in addition to their primary law-making function will be analysed and compared in later chapters of this work. These functions involve quasi-judicial responsibilities and include the sole prerogative of the House of impeachment (presenting accusations or charges recommending removal from office for high crimes and misdemeanours) of civil Officers of the United States, while the Senate exclusively sits as a court to try impeachments wherein a two-thirds vote is required for removal of the impeached Officer. As a later chapter shows, impeachment in the UK—at any rate in its traditional form—is both dead and unnecessary.

Additional quasi-Legislative or quasi-Executive political prerogatives of the Senate shared with the Executive as granted in Article II, section 2 of the Constitution include, respectively, ratification by a two-thirds vote of treaties made by the President with the advice and consent of the Senate, and advice and consent by majority vote to Executive and Judicial nominations by the President (see Federalist no. 66).

The 'advice' role of the Senate with respect to negotiation of treaties and particularly regarding confirmation of nominations, has been the subject of much contemporary analysis. This has evolved in the treaty context by the emergence of Congressional–Executive agreements such as international trade agreements enacted into statutory law pursuant to 'fast track' authority—a bargain (a mechanism incorporated into law) between the President and Congress whereby the President gives both Houses greater input into the substance of an international agreement in lieu of a treaty in return for assurances that as an exercise in each House's rule-making authority, Congress will either accept or reject the agreement in a short time and with no amendments.

In the context of confirmation of nominations, the role of the Senate to 'advise' the President as to his judicial nominees, either before or after their formal submissions, and the guarantee of direct majority votes on 'consent' to nominations once presented and reported from committee, has been drawn into question. 'Filibusters' of certain nominees have caused delays and in some cases the inability of the Senate to vote directly on a number of Presidential nominations. Both of these issues highlight the evolutionary nature of the constitutional roles envisioned for the Legislative and Executive branches in a modern setting of complexity and of extreme partisanship, especially regarding lifetime appointments to an 'independent' Federal judiciary with final authority to interpret the constitutionality of enacted law.

Parliamentary interest has brought both nominations and treaties on to the British parliamentary agenda, and as pages 71 and 76–7 will show, appreciable progress has been made. For obvious constitutional reasons, Congressional authority in these matters will remain greater than that of Parliament, but the speed with which an activity regarded as speculative a decade or so ago has become real may indicate how quickly an idea can move if it is flowing with a tide.

There is a unique role of the House and Senate respectively, under the 12th Amendment to the Constitution, to count in joint session the electoral votes cast for President and Vice President, and then for the House to proceed to elect a President and the Senate to elect a Vice President where no candidate has received a majority of electoral votes. This political role imposed on Congress to elect the Executive where Electors chosen by the various States have been unable to do so was circumvented by the Supreme Court decision in *Bush v Gore* (531 US 98 (2000)) and is discussed in greater detail in the chapter on Basic Constitutional Distinctions at page 18.

Courts and Acts

The judicial review role of the Federal Judiciary in determining the constitutional validity of Acts of Congress was not a function textually conferred upon the US Supreme Court in Article III of the Constitution beyond the extension of the Judicial power to all cases arising under the Constitution. Rather it was conferred through litigation by the Supreme Court itself in the landmark case of *Marbury v Madison* 1 Cr (5 US) 137 (1803). Alexander Hamilton in Federalist no. 78 had anticipated the issue of judicial review of Congressional Acts as follows:

> If it be said that the legislative body are themselves the constitutional judges of their own powers and that the construction they put upon them is conclusive on the other departments it may be answered that this cannot be the natural presumption where it is not to be collected from any particular provisions in the Constitution. It is not otherwise to be supposed that the Constitution could intend to enable the representatives of the people to substitute their will to that of their constituents. It is far more rational to suppose that the courts were designed to be an intermediate body between the people and the legislature in order, among other things, to keep that latter within the limits assigned to their authority. The interpretation of the laws is the proper and peculiar province of the courts. A Constitution is, in fact, and must be regarded by the judges as a fundamental law. It therefore belongs to them to ascertain its meaning, as well as the meaning of any particular act proceeding from the legislative body.

While not as historically significant as determinative of the basic separation of powers among the three branches of the Federal government, the Supreme Court decisions in *Naturalization Service v Chadha* 462 US 919 (1983), discussed in greater detail in the chapter on Legislation at page 473, and in *Bowsher v Synar* 478 US 714 (1986) helped redefine that doctrine as between the Legislative and Executive branches for the modern age. In 1985, Congress passed the Balanced Budget and Emergency Deficit Reduction Act, also known as the Gramm–Rudman–Hollings Act, which set a cap on the amount of deficit spending Congress could undertake between the years 1986 and 1991. Any resulting cuts were to be implemented by the Comptroller General, an official heading the Government Accountability Office independent of the Executive departments, who while appointed by the President and confirmed by the Senate can be removed from the job only by impeachment or by a joint resolution of both Houses of Congress, and not merely at the will of the President.[4] The assignment to such an official of a basic Executive branch function to execute a law once enacted was held to violate the separation of powers doctrine envisioned in Articles I and II of the Constitution.

The evolution of the doctrine of separation of powers in the USA will be further discussed in a variety of contexts in this work. The chapter on the Four Houses will examine treaties and international agreements, and confirmation of nominations at pages 59, 72. The entire chapter on the Power of the Purse (pages 225–306) will focus on the respective priorities of the Legislative and Executive branches in raising and spending revenues. The chapter on Scrutiny and Oversight includes a case study of War Powers at page 000. The chapter on Legislation at page 381 will treat initiatives in proposing and approving or vetoing legislation, and will analyse the Chadha decision as it relates to Congressional review of Executive decisions and line-item veto provisions enacted into law. The chapter on Privilege and Contempt at page 478 will approach separation of powers relating to contempt of Congress and to Impeachment.

One modern manifestation of shifting Legislative, Executive, and Judicial responsibilities under separation of powers merits mention at this point. The American body politic has become increasingly polarized, as indicated by the inability of a politically closely divided Legislative branch, even with guidance from an elected Executive, to resolve certain questions of human morality when presented in a legal 'privacy' context, including abortion, death, and sexuality. The Federal courts have become the arbiters of these issues in the context of cases presenting the denial of liberty without due process under the 14th Amendment. Some would argue these are questions more appropriately reserved to the elected branches. In partial reaction, the Congress has been urged to exercise its constitutional authority under Article III (to create and prescribe the jurisdiction of inferior Federal courts) to limit Federal court jurisdiction over certain types of cases where court decisions have resulted in a trend not politically popular. These efforts, for example to limit Federal court jurisdiction over cases regarding the Pledge of Allegiance or over the 'Defense of Marriage Act' are modern manifestations of separation of powers issues.[5] To date, there appears to be no direct legislative or judicial precedent for modern 'court stripping' proposals which have passed both Houses and have been enacted into law. If enacted those laws would have been subject to scrutiny by the Federal courts as a separation of powers or Equal Protection Clause matter, but that did not prevent the House from passing legislation in those areas in the 109th Congress, as a political reaction to some 'activist' Federal judges.

Congress's involvement in the Terri Schiavo case in 2005 was an extraordinary example of a Legislative branch mandate requiring Federal court involvement in what had traditionally been a matter of State law—an essentially moral question of privacy involving the right to die. The unprecedented response of Congress, returning to session upon joint leadership recall during an extended (Easter) recess to pass what was essentially a private bill directing a particular Federal court to re-examine an issue (the forced reinsertion of a feeding tube) despite prior exhaustive State and Federal court review, brought a new level of intrusiveness by Congress into a matter of private litigation. It demonstrated an extreme expansion of legislative involvement in a matter traditionally separated and delegated to the Judicial branch. The chapter on Legislation will discuss private bills, including the Schiavo bill in March 2005, and its expedited passage in both Houses, including its superficial draft as a public bill in order to qualify for programming under suspension of the rules in the House.

British courts have long confined themselves to interpreting the statutes which emanate from Parliament. A century ago, a court was so anxious not to pass one iota beyond the confines of statute in passing sentence in a capital case that the judge sent for the Roll of Parliament, the medieval manuscript of (in this case) a fourteenth-century Act, to establish whether at a critical point the original contained a comma. Even the House of Lords in its judicial capacity, then the highest civil court in the UK, did not presume to weigh statute against some external canon, in effect to go beyond interpretation and to determine whether the statute itself was valid. A recent case, commented on at pages 512–3, raised however an intriguing issue of the validity of a statute passed under the accelerating procedures of the 1949 Parliament Act (see page 64). It was argued that the Commons acted improperly in enacting the 1949 Act under the procedures of the 1911 Parliament Act. The 1949 Act was not therefore good law (it was said) and by extension the statute passed with its help was invalid. Alternatively and less apocalyptically, the court was not determining the validity of either Act but simply construing the true meaning of the 1911 Act. In the end, the dust settled and nothing previously believed to be statute law ceased to enjoy that status. But some of the obiter remarks of the Law Lords contemplated 'constitutional fundamentals' which even 'a sovereign Parliament acting at the behest of a complaisant House of Commons' could not abolish. In any case, it was observed, parliamentary sovereignty is just a construct of the common law: another 'construct of constitutionalism' could be envisaged. When there are added to these straws in the wind the consequences of the decisions of the European Court and the European Court of Human Rights, one may discern a possible future challenge to the concept of the sovereignty of Parliament unexampled since the Houses' common lawyers saw off the prerogative in the seventeenth century.

Themes

A major emphasis of this work so far as the contemporary Congress and Parliament are concerned will be an evaluation, including comparisons, of its transparency, fairness, and deliberative capacities. This will be approached in part as an examination of the extent to which scrutiny of government, debates, amendment processes, and availability of measures follow standing rules and traditional practices. This work will demonstrate a circumvention of those cornerstones of legislative practice, especially in the House of Representatives, by a variety of Majority leadership-initiated procedures designed to assure the retention of a partisan voting majority, as well as to enhance the certainty of time and issue, the minimization of minority rights, and political 'cover' for Majority Members, all at the expense of a more open, informed, and deliberative process. While this work will develop constitutional matters of separation of powers, checks and balances, and Federalism, it must be remembered that the history of the United States scheme of government has not been static, as it reflects 'separate institutions sharing functions, and even competing for predominant influence in exercising them...as fundamental to national decision making'.[6]

In Parliament, significance is given to the steady recovery of authority by the Houses over the past thirty years or so—never enough for the media, and short of what radical reformers might demand, but by comparison with parliamentary history, very significant. At the head of the column are select committees. As their agendas became more heavyweight—and therefore more potentially party political—committees have naturally found it much harder to make decisions on the evidence alone. Such strains are unlikely to diminish, but the system as a whole and its individual committees have accumulated both experience and respect. Only a few years ago, no one could have imagined a Prime Minister subjecting himself to cross-questioning by a committee of backbenchers, in full view of the public and the media, on any politically sensitive current topic of the committee's choosing, across the whole breadth of his administration's concerns, and in as much depth as a very large committee could handle. A great deal remains to be done. Committees are independent sources of expertise but not yet of central political authority, without which they are constantly at risk of marginalization. The next step will depend on wider developments, and specifically whether governments show themselves willing in future to engage in dialogue with rather than dominate the House of Commons.

When the details of the origins and operations of the two principal legislatures in the Anglo-Saxon tradition have been teased out and their many differences explained, it would be a pity to lose sight of how much they have in common. A comparison in the sporting world comes to mind. Any spectator can see that Rugby Union football as played in and between the nations of the UK and far beyond and football (to which outside its homeland the adjective American is applied) have much in common. The goalposts have the same peculiar shape, the ball is oval, and the method of scoring is broadly similar. The ball is carried over the goal-line to score in either game, and it hardly matters that in the UK the ball has to be grounded and in the USA it does not. There are of course more significant differences acquired over time which clearly mark off one from the other. The skill and spectacle of a quarter-back passing with complete accuracy to a player running at top speed many yards in front of him is one of the glories of the American game: by contrast, if the ball is thrown forward in the slightest degree in rugby it is an offence which instantly stops the action. (One might add that the UK should cherish the absence of 'fund-raising' commercial time-outs which also stop the action, an analogy some might apply to the comparative attention paid in the two countries to money in politics.) So it is with Congress and Parliament. In their origins they are closely related and that proximity is still visible; but their development has been different, according to the political framework within which each is set.

Notes

1. Since evolved by law to assure the sovereignty and supremacy of Parliament.
2. This is distinct from the practice at Westminster where the rationale of Standing Orders is to bridge the gap between Parliaments.
3. The common original formulation of the previous question was 'That the question be now put.' At Westminster, the original version had to be changed in the 1880s from 'be *now* put' to 'be *not now* put', for fear of a confusion with the recently devised closure procedure.
4. 31 USC 702–3.

5. To date the only recent 'jurisdictional stripping law' passed by both Houses and signed into law, denying Federal Courts jurisdiction to hear *habeas corpus* petitions filed by foreign combatants, was held unconstitutional by the Supreme Court in *Boumediene v Bush* 553 US 000 (2008). This decision, while confined to the constitutional proscription against the suspension by Congress of the writ of *habeas corpus*, indicates that the Supreme Court remains the ultimate arbiter of denials of Federal court jurisdiction by the political branches.

6. Walter Oleszek, *Congressional Procedures and the Policy Process* (6th edn, 2004), 4.

2

Basic Constitutional Distinctions

This chapter deals with fundamental constitutional difference between the USA and the UK in the context of their respective legislatures, particularly in the areas of federalism in the US, parliamentary sovereignty and statutory devolution in the UK, and UK membership of the European Union.

Congress and the States

The ratification of the Constitution to a significant extent defined the lines of authority between the State and Federal governments. In recent years, the Supreme Court has decided several cases which address this historical relationship between the Federal government and the States. These 'Federalism' cases include Congressional power under the Commerce Clause and the 14th Amendment; constitutional limits on Congressional powers, such as the 10th Amendment; and State sovereign immunity under the 11th Amendment.

States may generally legislate on all matters within their territorial jurisdiction. This 'police power' does not arise from the Constitution, but is an inherent attribute of the States' territorial sovereignty. The Constitution does, however, provide certain specific limitations on that power. For instance, a State is relatively limited in its authority regarding the regulation of foreign imports and exports or the conduct of foreign affairs. Further, States must respect the decisions of courts of other States and are limited in their ability to vary their territory without Congressional permission. Also, the Supreme Court has ruled that States have limited power to burden inter-state commerce.

The powers of the Congress, while limited to those enumerated in the Constitution by the 10th Amendment, have been interpreted broadly, so as to create a large potential overlap with State authority. For example, Article I, section 8, clause 18 provides that 'the Congress will have power...to make all laws which will be necessary and proper for carrying into Execution the foregoing Powers and all other Powers vested by this Constitution in the Government of the United States, or in any Department or Officer thereof'. Early in United States history the Supreme Court found that this clause enlarges rather than narrows the powers of Congress.

Congress has broad financial powers, including the power to tax and spend in order to pay debts and provide for the common defence and general welfare of the United States. The Congress also has the power to borrow money, and to appropriate money from the United States Treasury. The purposes for which Congress may tax and spend are very broad, and are not limited by the scope of other enumerated powers under which Congress may regulate. On the other hand, Congress has no power to regulate 'for the general welfare', but may only tax and spend for that purpose.

The Congress also has broad authority over the commercial interests of the nation, including the power to regulate commerce, to establish bankruptcy laws, to coin money, to punish counterfeiters, to establish Post Offices and post roads, and to grant patents and copyrights. Regulation of inter-state commerce covers all movement of people and things across State lines, including communication and transportation.

The Congress has wide powers over citizenship, including the power to define the circumstances under which immigrants may become citizens, and to protect the rights of those persons who have citizenship. The 14th Amendment gives the Congress the power to enforce the guarantees of that Amendment, including the right to due process and equal protection. This power extends specifically to the power of Congress to protect the rights of citizens who are at least 18 to vote regardless of race, colour, previous condition of servitude, or sex. The Congress is also empowered to regulate the time, place, and manner of Federal elections. The Congress has the power and authority to purchase and administer property, and has power over those jurisdictions which are not controlled by States, such as the District of Columbia and the territories. Congress is limited by the 5th Amendment, however, in the taking of private property without compensation. The Congress has numerous powers related to war and the protection of the United States and its sovereign interests.

While the Commerce Clause of the Constitution is the basis for a significant portion of the laws passed by Congress and represents one of the broadest bases for the exercise of Congressional powers, the Supreme Court in *United States v Lopez* 514 US 549 (1995) held that the Gun-Free School Zones Act of 1990, which made it a Federal offence for 'any individual knowingly to possess a firearm at a place that the individual knows, or has reasonable cause to believe, is a school zone,' exceeded the authority of Congress, because the Act neither regulated a commercial activity nor contained a requirement that the possession was connected to inter-state commerce. In so ruling, the court has suggested new limits to Congress's legislative authority. The court had developed an expansive view of the Commerce Clause relatively early in the history of judicial review. Chief Justice Marshall wrote in 1824 that 'the power over commerce is vested in Congress as absolutely as it would be in a single government' and that the influence which their constituents possess at elections are the sole restraints on this power. However, the issue in most of the early Supreme Court Commerce Clause cases dealt not with the limits of Congressional authority, but on the implied limitation of the Commerce Clause on a State's ability to regulate commerce. It has been suggested that the Commerce Clause should be restricted to the regulation of 'selling, buying, bartering and transporting'. In fact, much of the Federal legislation approved of by the Supreme Court early in the twentieth century did relate to such issues, while at the same time the court struck down a series of Federal statutes which attempted to extend commerce regulation to activities such as 'production', 'manufacturing', or 'mining'.

Starting in 1937, however, with the decision in *NLRB v Jones & Laughlin Steel Corporation* 301 US 1 (1937), the Supreme Court held that Congress has the ability to protect commerce from burdens and obstructions which 'affect' commerce transactions. In the NLRB case, the court upheld the National Labor Relations Act, finding that by controlling industrial labour strife, the Congress was preventing burdens from being placed on inter-state commerce. Thus the court rejected previous distinctions between the economic activities such as manufacturing which led up to inter-state economic transactions, and the inter-state transactions themselves. By allowing Congress to regulate activities which were in the 'stream' of commerce, the court set the stage for the regulation of a variety of other activities which 'affect' commerce. Subsequent court decisions found that Congress had considerable discretion in determining which activities 'affect' inter-state commerce, as long as the legislation was 'reasonably' related to achieving its goals of regulating inter-state commerce. Thus the court found that in some cases, events of purely local commerce (such as local working conditions) might, because of market forces, negatively affect the regulation of inter-state commerce, and thus be susceptible to regulation. The court has also held that an activity which in itself does not affect inter-state commerce could be regulated if all such activities taken together in the aggregate did affect it.

The *Lopez* case was significant in that it was the first time since 1937 that the Supreme Court struck down a Federal statute purely based on a finding that Congress had exceeded its powers under the Commerce Clause. In so doing, the court revisited its prior cases, sorted the commerce power into three categories, and asserted that the Congress could not go beyond these three categories: (1) regulation of channels of commerce; (2) regulation of instrumentalities of commerce; and (3) regulation of economic activities which 'affect' commerce.

Within the third category of activities which 'affect' commerce, the court determined that the power to regulate commerce applies to intra-state activities only when they 'substantially' affect commerce. The court in *Lopez* spoke approvingly of earlier cases upholding laws which regulated intra-state credit transactions, restaurants utilizing inter-state supplies, and hotels catering to inter-state guests. The court also recognized that while some intra-state activities may by themselves have a trivial effect on commerce, regulation of these activities may be constitutional if their regulation is an essential part of a larger economic regulatory scheme. Thus the court even approved what has been perceived as one of its most expansive rulings, *Wickard v Filburn* 317 US 111 (1942), which allowed the regulation of the production of wheat for home consumption.

The court in *Lopez* found, however, that the Gun-Free School Zones Act fell into none of the three categories set out above. It held that it is not a regulation of channels of commerce, nor did it protect an instrumentality of commerce. Finally, its effect on inter-state commerce was found to be too removed to be 'substantial'. The court noted that the activity regulated—the possession of guns in school—neither by itself nor in the aggregate affected commercial transactions. Further, the statute contained no requirement that inter-state commerce be affected, such as that the gun had been previously transported in inter-state commerce, nor was the criminalization of possession of a gun near a school part of a larger regulatory scheme which did regulate commerce. Finally, the court indicated that criminal law enforcement is an area of law traditionally reserved to the States. Consequently, Congress did not have the authority to pass the Gun-Free School Zone Act.

It should be noted that the *Lopez* court purported to be limiting, but not overruling, prior case law which had supported an expansive interpretation of the Commerce Clause. Consequently, most existing Federal laws, which have traditionally been drafted to be consistent with this case law, would arguably survive constitutional scrutiny even under *Lopez*. However, in at least one significant case, the Congress passed a law, the Violence Against Women Act, which seemed to invoke the same concerns that the court found in *Lopez*. In *United States v Morrison* 529 US 598 (2000) the court noted that unlike traditional statutes based on the Commerce Clause, the activity in question (gender-motivated violence) had nothing to do with commerce or an economic enterprise.

In *Gonzales v Raich* 545 US 1 (2005) the court rejected the argument that a narrow class of activity being engaged in—the intra-state, non-commercial cultivation and possession of cannabis for personal prescribed medical purposes pursuant to valid State (California) law—did not have a substantial impact on commerce. The court held that even if an activity were local and not commerce, it might still be regulated by Congress if it exerted a substantial economic effect on inter-state commerce, that is, the aggregate effect on the illegal market for marijuana, and frustration of the Federal interest in eliminating commercial transactions in the inter-state market based on impact on supply and demand.

The 14th Amendment provides a significant source of Congressional power, as section 5 provides that the Congress has the power to legislate to enforce the amendment restricting States from depriving citizens of 'life, liberty or property' without due process of law or from depriving them of equal protection of the laws. The Amendment represented a significant shift of power in the Federal system, as the Constitution was limited to establishing the powers and limitations of the Federal government. Those Amendments ratified immediately after the Civil War—the 13th, 14th, and 15th—dramatically altered this regime by subjecting a State's control over its own citizens to oversight by either the Federal judiciary or the Congress. The most significant impact of the 14th Amendment has been its implementation by the Federal courts, as State legislation came under scrutiny for having violated due process or equal protection. The Congress has also exercised its power under the Amendment to address issues such as voting rights and police brutality.

The scope of Congress's power under the 14th Amendment has been in flux over the years. In *Katzenbach v Morgan* 384 US 641 (1966) the court held that section 5 authorized Congress not just to enforce the provision of that Amendment as defined by the courts, but to help define its scope by 'appropriate' legislation consistent with the 'letter and spirit of the Constitution', the rationale being that Congress had the ability to evaluate and address factual situations which it determined might lead to degradation of rights protected by the 14th Amendment. Subsequently the reach of the *Katzenbach* case has been limited by *Oregon v Mitchell* 400 US 112 (1970), where the court struck down a requirement that the voting age be lowered to 18 for State elections. As

18-year-olds are not a protected class under the 14th Amendment, the court found that Congress was attempting to create, rather than protect, rights under that Amendment. Generally, the scope of the enforcement power under section 5 has been adjusted by a series of Supreme Court opinions which either evaluate the 'congruence and proportionality' between the injury to be remedied and the law adopted to that end, or are based on another provision of the Constitution which restricts Congress's power. For instance, the 11th Amendment and State sovereign immunity generally have been held to prohibit individuals from suing States for damages under Federal law. However, the Supreme Court has also held that Congress can (where a pattern of discriminatory or improper State intrusiveness is found) enact 'proportional and congruent' remedial or preventive laws which abrogate State sovereign immunity under the 14th Amendment, meaning that litigants suing States will have to find a basis there for Federal legislation in order to defeat an 11th Amendment defence of State sovereign immunity. The proper enactment of Federal law under the Commerce Clause does not necessarily empower suits in Federal court against States unless the enactment is based on factual findings by Congress demonstrating a compelling need for protection against State (as contrasted with local government or private) activity under the 14th Amendment. In some of the cases testing the relationship between these constitutional provisions, the court has determined that neither the Commerce Clause nor the 14th Amendment empowerments permit Congress to overcome the 11th Amendment restriction on the judicial power of Federal courts against lawsuits against a State brought by a citizen of another State, while in others significant evidence of a long and extensive history of discrimination by the States may be sufficient to justify a Federal law allowing redress against the States.

The 11th Amendment and State sovereign immunity provide an example of the complicated interaction between the powers of Congress, the State, and the individual. The basic issue is the extent to which individuals can sue States under Federal law, and the answer depends in part on the law under which the suit is brought, whether the State has taken action to make itself amenable to such law, and what relief is being sought. While the text of the 11th Amendment seems limited to preventing citizens from bringing diversity cases against States in Federal courts, the Supreme Court has expanded States' sovereignty further. The 11th Amendment was adopted as a response to the case of *Chisholm v Georgia* 2 US 419 (1793) wherein two citizens of South Carolina had sued the State of Georgia to recover a Revolutionary War debt. The court had held that the Article III grant of diversity jurisdiction to the Federal courts over suits 'between a State and citizens of another State' had authorized the suit even without that State's consent. The States were outraged that such a suit could be brought in Federal court, having been promised by the drafters of the Constitution that States would not be sued by their (debtors) creditors in Federal courts. Thus the 11th Amendment was adopted almost immediately following the *Chisholm* decision to ensure that a citizen could not sue under Federal diversity jurisdiction without a State's permission.

In *Hans v Louisiana* 134 US 1 (1890) the Supreme Court expanded the 11th Amendment to reach beyond diversity jurisdiction cases to bar suits by citizens in Federal court against their own States without a waiver of sovereign immunity. State sovereign immunity means that a State must consent to be sued in its own court system. This concept is based on early English law, which provided that the Crown could not be sued in English courts without its consent. The doctrine of sovereign immunity was in effect in the States which were in existence at the time of the drafting of the Constitution, and the court in *Hans* answered in the negative the question whether the grant of jurisdiction to Federal courts under Article III had abrogated State sovereign immunity. Subsequently, the court in *Seminole Tribe of Florida v Florida* 517 US 44 (1996) further restricted Congress's authority, by statute, to abrogate a State's sovereign immunity. The court had found previously in *Pennsylvania v Union Gas* 491 US 1 (1989), that the Commerce Clause plenary power was so broad that of necessity it required the ability to abrogate State sovereign immunity. The court in *Seminole* overruled *Union Gas*, holding that as the 11th Amendment was ratified after passage of the Constitution and Article I, it was a limitation on Congress's authority to waive a State's sovereign immunity which took precedence over the Indian Commerce Clause, but not necessarily over protections in the 14th Amendment which became part of the Constitution after the 11th Amendment. Thus in many cases litigants suing States will try to find a 14th Amendment denial of due process or equal protection of the laws basis for Federal legislation enacted pursuant to section 5 in order to defeat an 11th Amendment defence. In *Alden v Maine* 527 US 706 (1999), the court even extended the sovereign immunity to suits brought against a State in a State's own courts, prohibiting an abrogation by Congress despite the 11th Amendment's literal application only to the Federal courts. In that case the court declared sovereign immunity to be a 'fundamental postulate of the Constitutional design not amenable to Congressional abrogation'. The same reasoning that prohibited these suits from being brought in Federal court, a deference to the 'respect and dignity' of State sovereignty, led the court to conclude that it would be anomalous to allow such cases to be brought instead in State court.

Even where the 11th Amendment and State sovereign immunity are not at issue, the court in *Morrison* decided that the 14th Amendment did not establish a sufficient basis for a Federal law (creating a Federal private right of action for victims of gender-motivated violence) which does not appear to have a constitutional basis elsewhere in the Constitution (the Commerce Clause in that case being found inapplicable). The court has long held that the 14th Amendment permits Congress to regulate States, but not individuals. In *Morrison*, the court held that the test of 'congruence and proportionality' to the injury to be prevented and the means adopted to that end did not permit Congress to establish a private right of action against individuals engaging in the violence itself, rather than against State officials.

The 10th Amendment provides that 'powers not delegated to the United States by the Constitution, nor prohibited by it to the States, are reserved to the States respectively, or to the people'. While this language would appear to represent one of the clearest examples of a Federalist principle in the Constitution, it has not significantly limited Federal powers. In *Garcia v San Antonio Metropolitan Transit Authority* 469 US 528 (1985), the Supreme Court overruled *National League of Cities v Usery* 426 US 833 (1976) by ruling that most disputes over the effects on State sovereignty of Federal commerce power legislation are political questions and that the States should seek relief from Federal regulation through the political process.

Then in *New York v United States* 505 US 144 (1992), the court addressed the question of how the 10th Amendment limits the process by which the Federal government regulates the States. The court found that although the Congress had the authority under the Commerce Clause to regulate low-level radioactive waste, it could only do so directly without requiring the State legislatures to perform the regulation of disposal at the risk of taking title to such waste were it not to enact regulations. In effect, the Congress had sought to 'commandeer' the legislative process of the States, which was not a power envisioned in the Constitution. In a subsequent 'commandeering' case, *Printz v United States* 521 US 898 (1997), the court extended the 10th Amendment's restriction to Congressional attempts to regulate a State's Executive branch officers, by declaring invalid a Federal statute requiring State officials to conduct background checks on prospective handgun purchasers. More recently, in *Reno v Condon* 528 US 141 (2000), the court suggested that the Federal law mandate in question could properly provide 'substantive regulation' of State activities but could not seek to control the manner in which State legislatures or executives regulate private parties.

Although the Federal government is prohibited from commandeering either the Legislature or Executive branch of a State, such is not the case with State Judicial branches. The Constitution (Article VI, clause 2) provides that 'the Constitution and the Law of the United States...shall be the Supreme Law of the Land; and the Judges of every State shall be bound thereby'. Therefore State courts must follow Federal law even if it overrides State constitutions or laws.

The status of States in the Federal system has been enhanced by the cited recent Supreme Court opinions. Although the court has not scaled back the Federal government's substantive jurisdiction significantly, it has to some extent prevented the expansion of Congress's power under the Commerce Clause and under section 5 of the 14th Amendment, and it has created a variety of obstacles as to how these powers can be executed, forbidding the Congress under the 10th Amendment from commandeering the authority of State Legislative and Executive branches, and limiting the authority of Congress to abrogate State sovereign immunity. Ultimately, however, Congress under the Supremacy Clause may require the enforcement of its laws in both State and Federal court.

The preceding discussion of Federalism in the American constitutional system as contrasted with the British system of parliamentary supremacy and sovereignty demonstrates the constraints which a written Constitution containing specific legislative empowerments, and with reservations of power to other levels of government, as ultimately interpreted by an independent judiciary, imposes on the Federal legislature. These limits on authority cannot be superseded by enactments by Congress, short of proposed amendments to the Constitution itself and the cumbersome process of ratification by three-fourths of the State legislatures.

Electoral count and election of President and Vice President

Both the House and Senate formally participate in the process by which the President and Vice President are elected. Congress is directed by the 12th Amendment to receive, and in joint session to count, the electoral votes certified by the States. If no candidate receives a majority of the electoral vote, the House is directed to elect the President, and the Senate is directed to elect the Vice President.

The House has on two occasions, in 1801 and in 1825, proceeded to elect a President where no candidate had a majority of electoral votes.[1] Both Thomas Jefferson and John Quincy Adams were chosen after prolonged debate and repeated ballots in the House. Under both the original constitutional provision and the 12th Amendment, balloting was by States, with each State having one vote. Under the procedures governing the electoral count as enacted in 1887 and codified in 3 USC section 1–19, certificates identifying electors are prepared and transmitted to the Archivist. The Electors of each State meet and vote on the first Monday after the second Wednesday in December every four years (approximately one month following the election), the 'Electoral College'. The certificates are transmitted to the President of the Senate. When addressing a dispute over the election of President and Vice President in the State of Florida, the Supreme Court indicated its view of a section of the statute addressing a State's ability to determine controversy or contest as to the appointment of electors.[2] Ultimately, the Supreme Court found that the Florida Supreme Court had violated the Equal Protection Clause of the 14th Amendment by ordering certain counties to conduct manual recounts of the votes without establishing standards for those recounts.[3]

The electoral count occurs in a joint session of the two Houses in the House Chamber on 6 January succeeding every meeting of electors. Federal law provides the procedures for the count[4] which are joint rules of the two Houses and govern procedures both in the joint session and in each House in the event the two Houses divide to consider an objection. The President of the Senate (the Vice President who has himself several times been a candidate for President and has announced the result) presides over the joint session.

An objection to the counting of any electoral vote must be in writing and signed by a Member and a Senator. In that event, the joint session divides, and the objection is considered by each House in separate session. The Act of 1887 prescribes the procedure to be followed in debate after the two Houses have separated.[5] If either the House or the Senate rejects the objection, the presiding officer directs the tellers to record the votes as submitted. The joint session also divides to consider any 'other question arising in the matter', and again the presiding officer (the sitting Vice President) may be called upon to make procedural rulings as on the effect of disagreement between the two Houses.

Where no candidate receives a majority of all electoral votes cast, as would have been the case if the joint session in 2001 had not counted Florida's electoral votes, then the 12th Amendment requires that the House of Representatives should proceed to elect the President from among the three candidates receiving the most electoral votes, each State having one vote as determined by a majority of its delegation with two-thirds of the States constituting a quorum. The Senate voting per capita must likewise proceed to elect a Vice President from between the two highest candidates, a majority of all Senators being necessary to a choice.

In *Bush v Gore*, the Supreme Court spared the Congress and the nation the potential application of the 12th Amendment, as Vice President Gore in the wake of that court decision conceded that his opportunity for a recount had been denied and prevailed upon all Senators to refrain from filing a written objection which would have triggered a division of the two Houses (an objection having been filed by House Members). That might have led to a disagreement between the two Houses as to the counting of the Florida certificates (the Houses then having different party majorities assuming the Vice President's vote in the evenly divided Senate to break a tie), and potential rulings by him as presiding officer, all of which could have presented a profound conflict of interest for him. The fact that the Florida Supreme Court had only ordered a partial manual recount in certain counties as requested by Gore, rather than a complete recount, permitted the Supreme Court majority to articulate an 'equal protection of the laws' violation under the 14th Amendment while at the same time cautioning Federal courts not to consider the decision a precedent. Had the political nature of the controversy been permitted to play out as contemplated by the 12th Amendment, and assuming the lack of an electoral majority (270 electoral votes), at least twenty-eight State delegations in the House had Republican majorities and presumably would have elected Bush as President. The uncertainty facing the nation of preparation for an Executive branch transition underlay the court's decision. Also, interlocutory issues to be resolved between 5 and 20 January (including the openness of meetings by State delegations and the method of voting, would have demanded attention in special rules adopted by the House in the 107th Congress organized only three days previously. The vote required on those questions, whether by Members per capita or by State delegations, would likewise have needed to be addressed before the votes for President were taken.

Parliamentary sovereignty and statutory devolution

That the legislature should be unlimited in its law-making authority by any codified constitution, recognized convention, or judicial rulings, unable to bind its successors and freely capable of undoing any of the works of preceding Parliaments, has been for centuries an axiom of law making in the UK. Separation of powers and checks and balances there may in practice be, but none of these is protected by legal instruments or made particularly difficult to change or supersede. It is unthinkable—or it was until recently (see page 513)—that the validity of legislation made by the British Parliament should be subject to judicial intervention. The observation of John Ley, a nineteenth-century Clerk of the Commons, remained apposite: 'the House can do what it likes. Who can stop it?' Speculation concerning the possibility of entrenching present or limiting future legislation, or of confining the law-making power within common-law principles, ethical demands, or political values could be left to academic lawyers: Parliament got on with the practical work of legislation. These peaceful days are ending and John Ley's question is no longer rhetorical. One of the Law Lords observed recently: 'step by step, gradually but surely, the English principle of the absolute legislative sovereignty of Parliament which Dicey derived from Coke and Blackstone is being qualified'.[6]

The most obvious challenge to sovereignty as hitherto understood is the law-making power of the European Union and the enforcement authority of the European Court of Justice. The most acute aspect of the problem, which arises when the UK Parliament makes law later found to be inconsistent with EU law, together with other aspects of Parliament's response to the existence of a law-making authority for the UK located in Brussels, is dealt with at pages 22–40.

Another limitation on the action of Parliament springs from the Human Rights Act 1998. The minister in charge of a government bill must, before its second reading in either House, certify in writing that its terms are compatible with the European Convention on Human Rights or that, though he cannot do so, the government intends nevertheless to press on with its bill. Moreover, the courts are instructed by the 1998 Act to read and give effect to UK primary and secondary legislation in a way compatible with rights under the Convention 'so far as it is possible to do so'. They are thus implicitly free to do so in a way which overrides any different meaning which Parliament may have intended that the text being interpreted should bear. In the last resort, if a higher court cannot reconcile legislation with Convention rights, it may not strike down the statute but will make a declaration of incompatibility, which will not however affect the validity and operation of the law. Any court may annul secondary legislation, provided that its provisions are not a necessary consequence of a statute. If in the course of legal proceedings enacted legislation is found to be incompatible with Convention rights, there is a fast-track procedure to amend or repeal the offending primary legislation (for which see pages 472–3). At the time of enactment, the Lord Chancellor said that Parliament 'may, not must, and generally will' legislate if the courts find a statute incompatible with human rights.[7]

If there are any practical—even if not legally entrenched—limitations on the powers of Parliament which may be compared with the situation of Congress, they derive from neither UK membership of the European Union nor from the Human Rights Act, but go back much further.

The Acts which created the parliamentary Union of 1707 between Scotland and England were intended to incorporate both countries in a single new State. Over the centuries since then, however—despite all the common history—the ghostly apparition of two separate nation-states may occasionally still be glimpsed. The Union settlement, extinguishing two Parliaments and creating one new legislature for two nations, can be represented as run-of-the-mill legislation only by a stretch of the imagination. What therefore is the status of the parallel Acts of Union, one English, the other Scottish? Do they approach the character of 'constitutional' documents? They contain no clear declaration of superior constitutional status, no entrenching provision or special procedures for amendment. The belief that they have a status above and beyond 'ordinary' law has been found exclusively in Scotland, where however it has manifested itself at intervals for some 300 years. Its most significant appearance was made in 1953 when the most senior Scottish law officer conceded in the highest Scottish court that certain parts of the Union settlement 'could not' be changed by subsequent legislation of the UK Parliament. The principal Scottish judge reserved his opinion on the validity of certain UK legislation where it might be found contrary to provisions of the Acts of Union. The most authoritative constitutional lawyer in Scotland agreed more recently that there were fundamental provisions which could not be altered by Parliament.[8] How any real-time battle over this ground would be resolved will depend on prevailing political circumstances. All that can be said otherwise is that these considerations might prove to be a potential limitation on the fullness of Westminster's sovereignty with respect to Scotland, or at least a constituent element in any political disputes which might arise out of national tensions within the UK.

The status of the Union legislation was not however at issue when, in the most far-reaching constitutional changes for two centuries, the Parliament at Westminster created, in statutes exactly like any other, the Scottish Parliament, the National Assembly for Wales, and the Northern Ireland Assembly. The striking phrase with which the Scotland Act 1998 begins, 'There shall be a Scottish Parliament,' brought into being a body able to make laws for Scotland in all areas not reserved by the Act to Westminster or incompatible with European Union law or obligations. The Scottish government is responsible to the Scottish Parliament, as ministers are to the Parliament at Westminster. Yet parliamentary sovereignty emerged from the devolution settlements entirely unaffected. The sovereignty of the UK Parliament was not abridged because the same section of the Scotland Act which devolved the law-making power also stipulated that 'this section does not affect the power of the Parliament of the United Kingdom to make laws for Scotland'. In practice, Westminster has not to date used its override powers in defiance of the Parliament in Edinburgh. Indeed, it has frequently legislated for Scotland in other than reserved areas, at the request of the Scottish Parliament and in the interests of avoiding unnecessary distinctions in the law prevailing in different parts of the UK.

The Scottish Parliament consists of 129 Members, returned for constituencies (see below) or on eight regional lists. The subject areas wholly reserved to Westminster are, for example, the Crown, foreign affairs, defence, immigration and nationality, and the civil service. Areas in which some matters are devolved and others reserved include fiscal, economic, and monetary policy (where the balance is very much in favour of reserved authority), data protection, and insolvency. The boundaries of devolved authority may of course change if, following a recent high-level study, the Westminster Parliament is persuaded to amend the Scotland Act.

The Wales Act 1998 set out an entirely different basis of devolution for that part of the UK, though the overriding power of Parliament to make law for Wales remained, just as it did for Scotland. Most noticeably, Welsh devolution did not originally separate the Legislative and the Executive. The National Assembly for Wales consisting of sixty Members exercised the statutory powers previously in the hands of the Secretary of State for Wales. Nearly a decade later, fundamental changes to enhance the powers and standing of the Assembly were made by the Government of Wales Act 2006. The National Assembly may legislate in a number of broad fields, including agriculture, economic development, the environment, and highways. In other fields, the Assembly's power is restricted to 'matters' within the field: examples of fields so limited are education, health, and local government. The areas of the Assembly's legislative competence may be extended by a procedure involving the assent both of the Assembly and—critically—the UK Parliament. Four such Legislative Competence Orders were subject to this procedure in 2007–8. National Assembly legislation takes the form of Measures, which have effect in Wales in the same way as Acts of the UK Parliament. Subordinate legislation made by Welsh ministers is subject to approval or disapproval by the National Assembly.

Devolution to Northern Ireland has not followed as relatively smooth a course as in Scotland or Wales. Despite the fact that a bicameral Parliament existed in Northern Ireland from the 1920s to the 1970s, the modern history of devolution in the Province is intimately bound up with successive political crises and troubles there. Development of power-sharing—a term which included the allotment of ministerial posts in proportion to party/community representation and the need for certain resolutions in the legislature to command cross-community support—was fitful. In 1998 however, following talks involving the British and Irish governments and political parties in Northern Ireland, an agreement to restore legislative powers was endorsed in a referendum. The Northern Ireland Act 1998 provided for an Assembly of 108 Members, with full power to make laws in areas transferred to that body, including health, education, social security, and the environment. Section 5(6) of the Act provided, on the Scottish and Welsh model, that the power of the UK Parliament to make laws for Northern Ireland was not affected.

Certain matters are excepted from devolution and remain with Westminster. They include defence and national security, nationality, and the appointment of the judiciary. There is also a category of reserved matters—criminal law, public order, and the police, for example—which with the consent of the Secretary of State following cross-party agreement in the Assembly may be transferred to that body. In early 2009, preparations were being made for the transfer of police and justice matters. The Assembly was suspended in 2002 but resumed sitting in the spring of 2007.

The devolution settlements contain within themselves an element of parliamentary disequilibrium the more acute the greater the freedom of action conferred on the devolved bodies: in short, the problem principally concerns the Scottish settlement. This is the notorious West Lothian question,[9] which asks why Scottish Members at Westminster should be able to vote on (for example) education in England, perhaps thereby altering the party balance prevailing among Members for English seats, when the latter (and Welsh and Northern Irish Members) cannot vote on Scottish education, which is devolved to the parliament in Edinburgh. Attempts to find a stable solution have concentrated on the creation of an English quasi-parliament not separate from but within the UK body at Westminster, arranging to disqualify non-English votes in certain circumstances on legislation relating exclusively to England. No proposal has found favour across all parties, for obvious political reasons. Moreover, the technical problem of identifying bills or clauses in bills which have no consequences beyond England has not been solved. In any case, if the temporary disqualification of non-English Members is not restricted to second or third readings of bills (as has been suggested) but extends to committee stage—where nevertheless the detailed work is done—there might be no end to the chaos such an arrangement might visit on legislative procedure.

Constitutional division of power, constantly subject to judicial interpretation, is a very different animal from statutory devolution, in which the details of the distribution of legislative authority are still unsettled. In the first, there are complex and well-tried provisions for amending the Constitution so as to adjust the respective powers of Congress and the States. In the second, while there are statutory provisions in the settlements for resolving disputes over the *vires* of actions of the devolved legislatures, the respective competences of Westminster and the devolved legislatures are not wholly fixed: and if and when they are to be changed, a simple Act of the Westminster Parliament is all that will be needed. Moreover, in Scotland at least, the party currently in power in the devolved parliament has as a main plank of its policy the demise of the Union within which the devolution settlement was arrived at. The less entrenched constitutional system may therefore have to withstand the greater political strain.

European Union: national accountability and European legitimacy

Some of the domestic legislative and constitutional change since 1972, when the UK joined what is now the European Union (EU) of twenty-seven member states, can be seen as a prolonged adjustment to something approaching a written constitution on the

US model. How far such a development will progress is of course impossible to predict. What is clear is that British membership of what is now far more than a simple *Zollverein*, a customs union, but is not—or is not yet—'one and indivisible', carries with it local constitutional consequences of the first magnitude. These in turn bring with them novel and complex issues of parliamentary scrutiny.

Delivering accountability and scrutiny in complex supranational circumstances is far from easy. The organs of the EU do not resemble any national governmental arrangement. At the head of the tree is the European Council on which all heads of state or government sit. This is a political rather than a legislative body, and takes no legally binding decisions. The Council of Ministers (or rather Councils, since the composition of the Council will vary according to the subject matter under consideration) comprises a representative of each member state. It is the principal EU decision-making body, under procedures which may involve decisions taken exclusively by the Council or in co-decision with the European Parliament. The European Commission is a body with no parallel in domestic arrangements in Washington or London. It is the executive organ of the EU, with a right of initiative in policy,[10] though its proposals can be amended or rejected by the Council and the European Parliament. One Commissioner from each member state sits on the Commission, though the Lisbon treaty[11] provides that after 2014 the Commission is to consist of Commissioners representing only two-thirds of the member States on a rotational basis.

The European Parliament is elected by universal suffrage in all member states. It consists of no fewer than 785 members, though following the ratification of the treaty of Lisbon that number will be capped at 750. The Parliament's law-making procedures are complex, recalling its gradual evolution from an essentially advisory role to partnership with the Council. Nevertheless, the European Parliament 'differs in several fundamental respects from national parliaments: no part of it sustains a government, it does not impose taxes, and it does not initiate legislation'.[12]

In some areas, the organs of the EU have exclusive law-making competence; in others, authority is shared with national governments according to details in treaty provisions; and in still others the member states have supporting authority, where the aims are shared but harmonization of law is not required.[13]

National Parliaments naturally wish to maintain effective scrutiny of their governments' activities on the European stage, which equally naturally leads them into scrutinizing the activity of the EU institutions on which governments are represented. A significant proportion of law applicable in the UK has its origin in the EU. The Houses at Westminster understandably wish to have their views taken into account when that law is made: but the body primarily charged with the oversight of the Commission is the European Parliament. Hence much frustration and sensitivity. For example, the Lisbon treaty—a document which the Lords European Union Committee found 'complicated and inaccessible'[14]—seemed originally to impose on national parliaments a legal duty to contribute to the good functioning of the Union. The Commons European Scrutiny Committee demurred strongly. The phrase 'shall contribute' in the draft treaty, with its implications of central direction, had to be (and was) changed to the normative 'contribute', in order to avoid what was seen as the imposition of a wholly unacceptable duty on a sovereign Parliament; no ambiguity was tolerable.[15]

'...Without further enactment...'

Section 2(2) of the European Communities Act 1972 provides that rights and remedies arising under European Union treaties are 'without further enactment to be given legal effect or used in the United Kingdom'. The treaties which have followed the accession treaty have extended the competences and membership of the Union beyond those initially specified or brought new areas of activity within intergovernmental cooperative frameworks. On one view, the powers enjoyed by the institutions of the Union under the treaties are given to them by the British Parliament, which may if it so decides override or vary their exercise. Thus, if European law under the treaties has priority over law made at Westminster, it is because what is called 'European' law is really (it is argued) part of British law. Other arguments point in quite a different direction. Even before UK entry to the Union, the European Court of Justice (an organ of the Union) had enunciated the principle that the treaties conferred rights and imposed obligations which could be enforced, notwithstanding any contrary provisions in pre-existing national legislation. Reconciliation of the two standpoints, if reconciliation can be achieved, passed to the courts.[16]

British opinion has not found it easy to dispense with traditional notions of the absolute supremacy of statutes passed at Westminster. The most prominent occasion where European law and UK legal conventions collided is the *Factortame* case.[17] It was argued that certain provisions of the UK Merchant Shipping Act 1988 relating to the registration of fishing vessels were incompatible with EU law, because they discriminated against Spanish-owned ships. The British statute was passed well after the UK's accession to the Union, so that the conflict was very acute. The complainants asked for implementation of the statute to be suspended while the European Court of Justice determined the issue of incompatibility. After high judicial consideration in London and in the EU, means were devised within which incompatibilities once identified might be sorted out and the issue of invalidating the 1988 Act was sidestepped. The government made an order which amended the 1988 Act to conform with the ruling. The sovereignty of the UK Parliament remained, but Parliament's position at the centre of law making was undeniably challenged.

Parliamentary scrutiny: the significance of EU legislation

Parliamentary structures as well as the courts have struggled to adapt to the new problems. The parliamentary quandary is how to scrutinize legislation enacted beyond the shores of Britain: and in devising scrutiny processes, it is necessary to avoid slowing further an already sometimes sclerotic EU legislative process, while coping with a mass of material without detriment to effective scrutiny.

Many normal parliamentary means of calling the UK government to account may be employed in a European context—Questions, ministerial statements, or debates. These everyday weapons need to be supplemented, however, by more specific procedures. By the European Communities Act 1972, the British government may implement EU obligations by (unamendable) secondary legislation, even when a bill might otherwise have been expected, and in exercise of certain powers may even choose which of the procedures for secondary legislation—affirmative or negative (see page 469)—is appropriate. The effect on the degree of parliamentary scrutiny of proposals for new law made in this way is obvious. If EU-inspired proposals for changes in UK law cannot be amended, Parliament must, through ministers, influence the proposals while they are still in the EU decision-making machine.

In a manner which echoes some of the developments in the context of secondary legislation (see page 470), preliminary sifting for political and legal significance on the one hand and decision making on selected documents, including proposals for legislation on the other, have been separated. In the Commons, all EU documents (defined for this purpose as proposals for legislation or common strategies or positions under the treaties) are automatically referred to a select committee, the European Scrutiny Committee, composed of sixteen Members, with a government majority. The Committee identifies those documents which are of political or legal importance and decides which merit debate. Before coming to a conclusion, the Committee may engage in a dialogue with the government, seeking further particulars. The process may conclude in oral evidence from the government. On the basis of regular governmental statements, the Committee also monitors the business before the Council, the position taken by UK ministers, and the outcome of Council consideration. Broader stand-alone inquiries into institutional or legal developments in the Union or specific topics are also conducted. These have ranged from Subsidiarity, National Parliaments, and the Lisbon treaty to roaming charges made for the use of mobile/cell phones. Oral evidence is often taken from ministers following meetings of the European Council of heads of EU governments.

All documents referred to the Committee are accompanied by an Explanatory Memorandum under the authority of the responsible UK minister, detailing the effect of the proposal, its legal implications, the timetable, and the stance taken by the government. Each Memorandum is expected to comment specifically on issues of subsidiarity (see page 28). Though by inference excluded from commenting on the merits of the documents which come before it, the committee may report on the reasons for its opinion, and in any case may have to reflect on the merits of a proposal in order to determine its importance and whether further information is required. Going into detail, however, would be expensive in terms of time and might prove too politically divisive to be comfortable.

Some documents will be cleared: some will be held over for further examination or until more details become available; and some will be recommended for debate. For example, the Committee's tenth report of 2008–9[18] recommended two documents for debate in European Committees as raising matters of political or legal importance, deferred a decision on three, and cleared nine. A further twenty-five were not significant enough to warrant a substantive report. One of those which the Committee recommended for debate originated from the Commission and was entitled 'Towards a comprehensive climate change agreement in Copenhagen'. It set out not only commitments already entered into on the reduction of greenhouse-gas emissions by 2020, but with the Copenhagen meeting in mind proposed longer-term policy for developed and developing economies, including such issues as the financing of low carbon development and raising revenue on the global carbon market.

The Committee may recommend EU documents for debate on the floor of the House or in European Committee, though the decision in favour of the former depends for its implementation on the government. In session 2007–8, thirty-five weekly reports on current documents were produced and there were four reports on particular topics, not counting a review of the Committee's work.

Table 2.1 setting out the number of EU documents considered by the scrutiny committee, and the number recommended for debate either in a European Committee or on the floor of the House is to be found in the Annex.

It is understandably important not to isolate European scrutiny work from the mainstream of parliamentary affairs. The upstream activity of the European Scrutiny Committee in Brussels needs to be complemented by parliamentary attention downstream—that is, to the consequences for the UK. To this end, the scrutiny committee may seek the opinion of other select committees on matters before them. The power has been used only sparingly—three times in 2006 and twice in 2007 and in 2008—though it should be added that there are also more informal channels of communication such as the scrutiny committee's practice of sharing its briefing with the departmental select committees, and its recommendations to departmental select committees for lines of inquiry into aspects of strategic or planning documents emanating from the Commission or Council. It may be that the limited flexibility of departmental select committees' work programmes, set against demanding EU timetables, is likely always to put a limit to the practice. Moreover, though examination of Commission policy proposals is part of the core tasks of select committees (see page 374), it seems that it is not always easy for select committees to be aware in good time of what is under consideration. Nevertheless, a start has been made.

Speed is an essential element of effective scrutiny. The scrutiny committee, with its staff of fifteen—relatively large by Westminster standards—can deal with texts within a week, but major developments naturally demand much longer. What is required is a system which assures Parliament of both information on EU intentions and parliamentary time in which to consider them. Under the Lisbon treaty national parliaments are to be given eight weeks to comment on proposals for EU legislation (see below). In the nature of negotiations, however, problems may still arise when hurried, often last-minute, rearrangements are made by the Council. The government issues a written ministerial statement before every Council meeting, confirming the agenda and setting out the UK position. Another statement is made on the outcome. Though matters are improving, the Commons European Scrutiny Committee has described these as variable in quality 'to say the least'.[19] In addition, UK parliamentary officials—the National Parliament Office (NPO)—have been since 1999 permanently stationed in Brussels. The NPO acts as a forward observation post of official activity within the organs of the Union, keeping both Houses at Westminster as up to date as possible with developments, as well as enhancing direct bilateral and multilateral links between national parliaments. This sometimes has unexpected benefits, as when a minister may find himself or herself behind a game that the committee's informants have enabled it to be ahead of.

Parliamentary debate: the merits of EU legislation

A thoroughgoing overhaul of the way the House of Commons handles European legislation was recommended by the Modernisation Committee in 2004–5.[20] Though not all the proposals of that Committee were taken up, the current procedure is intended to over-come two sets of problems then identified. The first was the need to join up the delibera-tions and expertise of the European Scrutiny Committee (and the relevant departmental select committee) with the more political debate in the European Committees. Secondly, it had in the past proved difficult to spark interest in what might have seemed an impor-tant but remote and specialized area, where the time scales were short, there was a lack of continuity and the procedures were unfamiliar. It was hoped the new arrangements would overcome these problems.

In the Commons, documents which the scrutiny committee recommends for further consideration stand referred to one of three European Committees. If the scrutiny com-mittee proposes that the matter ought to be debated on the floor, a motion may be made to disengage this provision.[21] Only the government may move to implement a recom-mendation for debate in the Chamber, but it has never failed to do so where the scrutiny committee has recommended that course. On the other hand, these debates—which are relatively few in number (see above)—may last for only ninety minutes as opposed to two and a half hours in committee, and their timing is a matter for ministers.

Each of the three European Committees of thirteen members considers documents relating to different groups of government responsibilities. There is however no continu-ing membership of these committees: members are nominated for each document or group of documents referred to a committee.[22] Where possible, the Committee of Selection is to nominate at least two members of the European Scrutiny Committee, and at least two members of the select committee whose responsibilities most closely relate to the subject matter of the document under consideration. A further five will be ministers, party spokesmen and whips, an arrangement intended to ensure that a high proportion of those selected are likely to have an interest in the area under discussion. In addition, any Member of the House may attend and speak. These do not have the power to make motions (unless they are ministers) or vote, but they can move amendments.

The committees begin each sitting by hearing one of the appointed members of the scrutiny committee explaining (for five minutes) why that committee found the docu-ment sufficiently significant to refer to a European Committee. There follows, for up to an hour with the possibility of an extension at the discretion of the chairman, a ministe-rial statement, followed by questions without notice. The format of the questioning is more akin to the probing of a select committee than Question Time in the House, a procedure which has attracted the commendation of the scrutiny committee. Finally for a further hour and a half there is a debate on a government motion relevant to the docu-ment, and probably an Opposition amendment to it. The committee's resolution is reported to the House and decided without debate.

In addition to the regular activity of the European Committees, the government has undertaken that two debates will be held annually in Westminster Hall (see pages 55–6) on the Commission annual policy statement and its legislative and work programme.[23]

Proceedings in the Lords are generally similar to and indeed complement those in the Commons, though with some differences of emphasis. The Lords Select Committee on the European Union is the equivalent of the Commons scrutiny committee, but operates not as a unitary body but in seven subcommittees, each with a policy area to cover, though an impressive report on the impact of the Lisbon treaty was the combined work of all these bodies. The Committee is chaired by the Principal Deputy Chairman of

Committees, who also sifts the documents deposited in the Lords, and refers appropriately those which he considers require examination. Lords inquiries are deeper and longer than those in the Commons, but the overall range is necessarily less wide. In addition, the Lords committee may appoint subcommittees to look into particular issues or make reports on broad aspects of EU policy or practice.

For more than a decade, both Houses have had in place a scrutiny reserve resolution, which declares that ministers are not to agree to any European legislation, pre-legislative statements of intention, major proposal under the common foreign and security policy, or cooperation in police and judicial matters unless and until the scrutiny committee (or in the case of documents recommended for debate, the committee and the House) have approved it or agreed that it may proceed without clearance. An exception is made for trivial, routine, or confidential material. If the scrutiny committee is hesitant about granting clearance to a piece of legislation it will seek further and better particulars from the government. Matters are steadily improving: in the year from July 2005 to June 2006, there were thirty-one overrides. In the first half of 2007, however, that figure fell to only five and in the same period in 2008, four. The scrutiny committee has confirmed a significant improvement in departmental practice over the past two years.[24]

Some breaches arise simply because the working timetable of the EU organs is not the same as the sitting pattern at Westminster, and clearance which would otherwise be obtained cannot be had because the Houses and the relevant committees are not sitting. Roughly half the scrutiny overrides in 2006 arose for that reason. Moreover, if special considerations persuade a minister to breach the terms of the resolution and agree to some document without clearance, he or she must explain the reasons without delay, though in practice it will usually be possible for the minister to explain the case to the committee in advance. The Commons scrutiny committee normally calls a minister who overrides the resolution without what the committee regards as good cause to explain his or her actions in a public evidence session. There remains some concern that the scrutiny reserve should be put on a statutory basis, to be sure that it will be observed to the letter. The greater the reduction in the number of breaches, the harder will be the task of those who argue that the resolutions of both Houses should be made more binding by being converted into law.

Subsidiarity and the powers of national parliaments

Where national parliaments particularly resolutely defend their position in EU law making is in the area of subsidiarity. This is the principle that where the Union does not by treaty enjoy exclusive competence, it should take action only when and so far as the objectives of the proposed action cannot be sufficiently achieved by the member states at central, regional, or local level, but can be better achieved at Union level. Decisions, in short, should be taken as close to the persons affected by them as is consistent with equity and efficiency.[25] To date, systematic parliamentary scrutiny of subsidiarity has been informal and voluntary. The Conference of European Affairs Committees (COSAC) on which all the parliaments of the Union are represented, including three members of the scrutiny committee in each of the Houses at Westminster, meets every six months to exchange views and experience on common problems. Since 2005, COSAC's activity has included some reviews of EU legislation for its subsidiarity and proportionality.

The treaty of Lisbon puts new weapons into the hands of national parliaments. There is an arrangement by which, within the eight-week period mentioned above, parliaments may notify the relevant EU organ that they do not consider the draft under discussion respects the principle of subsidiarity. If a third (or in some cases a quarter) of the total number of Chambers is reached, the EU organ must review its decision. Before the opportunity thus offered can be taken up, many difficult questions will have to be solved. They include how the two Chambers should coordinate their action (since each has a separate vote); whether the Chambers can act independently of the government in office; whether the time scale is practical, especially taking account of periods when one or both Houses are adjourned; how the devolved legislatures can be played in; and—most challenging but also most interesting of all—how cross-national alliances of parliaments can be handled.

There are also areas where the arrangement will need to be tested. In no part of the scheme can national parliaments stop a draft going forward: the most they can do is to have the decision to go ahead explained. The Lords European Union Committee pointed to a case in 2007 in the course of the informal COSAC scrutiny of subsidiarity in which fourteen Chambers raised issues, but the package was passed regardless.[26] The Commons scrutiny committee welcomed the proposals regarding the role of national parliaments but thought they could easily be exaggerated. They doubted whether the Lisbon treaty provisions would have much practical difference to the influence presently enjoyed by the British Parliament.[27] Perhaps the conclusions of the Lords scrutiny committee go as far as possible for the present: 'The existence of a sanction gives scrutiny teeth, while making it less likely that the sanction will need to be deployed.'[28]

Notes

1. *Hinds' Precedents*, vol iii, sect 1983, 1985.
2. *Bush v Palm Beach County Canvassing Board* 531 US 70 (2000).
3. *Bush v Gore* 531 US 98 (2000).
4. 3 USC 15–18.
5. 3 USC sect 17.
6. [2005] UKHL 56 at para 104.
7. HL Deb (1997–8) 582 c 1229.
8. *MacCormick v The Lord Advocate* 1953 SC 396; Professor T. B. Smith in *Stair Memorial Encyclopaedia of the Laws of Scotland*, vol v para 349.
9. So named because West Lothian was the constituency then represented by the Member who first drew the issue to public notice.
10. See European Union Committee Twenty-Second Report, Initiation of EU Legislation 2007–8 HL 150, and HL Deb (2008–9) 706 c 585.
11. The Lisbon treaty signed in December 2007 is the latest in a series of such agreements marking institutional change in the Union. The treaty was not ratified until nearly two years later, following a second confirmatory referendum in Ireland.
12. European Scrutiny Committee Thirty-Third Report 2001–2 HC 152-xxxiii-I para 85.
13. EU Regulations are directly binding on member States without any national legislative intervention but will usually need supplementary national legislation. EU Directives leave the form and method of implementing a Union decision to national decision.

14. European Union Committee Tenth Report 2007–8 HL 62-I para 1.8.
15. Third Report 2007–8 HC 16-iii. The problems in this area may be illustrated by the fact that only the English text of the draft had to be altered as a consequence of the change.
16. By the European Communities Act 1972, decisions of the European Court of Justice were made authoritative in British courts.
17. *R v Secretary of State for Transport ex p Factortame* (No. 2) [1990] 2 AC 85; [1991] 1 AC 603.
18. HC 19-ix.
19. Twelfth Report 2007–8 HC 315 para 51.
20. HC 465-i.
21. In addition, a note may appear on the House of Commons Order of Business drawing attention to the relevance of an EU document to any other motion or business, quite separately from the process of scrutinizing the particular document.
22. The European Scrutiny Committee criticized this provision as having a detrimental impact on lobbyists and interest groups who find it difficult to bring their concerns to the attention of the House (Fourth Report 2008–9 HC 156 para 17).
23. HC Deb (2007–8) 471 c 1179.
24. Fourth Report 2008–9 HC 156 para 31.
25. European Scrutiny Committee Thirty-Third Report 2001–2 HC (152-xxxiii-I) para 109. There is a parallel concern with proportionality, where the content and form of Union action should not exceed what is necessary to achieve treaty objectives. The definitions of subsidiarity and proportionality given here are derived from the text of the Lisbon treaty.
26. Tenth Report 2007–8 HL 62-I para 11.34.
27. Thirty-Fifth Report 2006–7 HC 1014 para 68; Fourth Report 2008–9 HC 156 para 29.
28. Tenth Report 2007–8 HL 62-I para 11.50.

3

The Four Houses

The term of a Congress and a Parliament, and the effect on legislation and on Members

The term of a Congress before the ratification of the 20th Amendment on 6 February 1933 began on 4 March of the odd-numbered years and extended through two years. This resulted from the action of the Continental Congress on 13 September 1788 in declaring, on authority conferred by the Federal Constitutional Convention, 'the first Wednesday in March next' to be 'the time for commencing proceedings under the said Constitution'. This date was 4 March 1789. Soon after the first Congress assembled, a joint committee determined that the terms of Representatives and Senators of the first class commenced on that day and must necessarily terminate on 3 March 1791.

The discrepancy between the commencement of terms of Members of Congress on 4 March of odd-numbered years, and the day of convening of regular sessions each year on the first Monday in December pursuant to Article I, section 4 of the original Constitution resulted in a period of nine months during which newly elected Members did not convene. It lasted for 144 years and was rectified by the ratification of the 20th Amendment in 1933. For the first time, the terms of Representatives and Senators, and the specified day for convening regular sessions, coincided under the Constitution. Under the 20th Amendment the terms of Representatives and Senators begin on 3 January of the odd-numbered years, and the convening day is 3 January each year as well. Under section 2 of the 20th Amendment, Congress may set a different day by law for the convening of an annual regular session. Congress has often done so, by law signed by the President, to accommodate a more convenient day in the month of January, taking into consideration the actual calendar day of the week upon which 3 January falls, the length of the prior session if extended into December, and the need to be organized and in session for the count of the electoral vote in joint session on 6 January every fourth year pursuant to the 12th Amendment. In recent laws establishing a date later than 3 January, those laws have reserved to the two Houses a possible earlier assembly from 3 January by joint House-Senate leadership recall.

If a prior session of the Congress remains in session at noon on 3 January, the Speaker or the presiding officer of the Senate as the case may be declares that body adjourned without motion sine die, not needing the consent of the other House. The Constitution permits no extension of a regular session beyond that time, regardless of the two Houses' inability to consent to a final adjournment. If the next session of the same Congress is to begin at noon on that same day (not having set another day by law for convening) the two Houses immediately reconvene following the sine die adjournment.

A joint resolution providing for a convening day other than 3 January enjoys no special privilege for consideration in either House, as to do so would permit the two Houses to expeditiously pass laws enabling them to remain out of session for great lengths of time following the beginning of the terms of new Members, precisely the dichotomy the 20th Amendment sought to avoid. Should Congress enact such a law establishing a late convening day, the only ways for convening earlier than the date set by law would be by a call of a special session by the President pursuant to Article II, section 4 as an 'extraordinary occasion', or by joint leadership recall if that authority had been conferred by the two Houses.

The Legislative Reorganization Act of 1970 provides that unless otherwise provided by Congress, the two Houses shall either (a) adjourn sine die (final adjournment of the session without setting a day certain for reconvening) by 31 July of each year, or (b) in odd-numbered years, adjourn in August until the first Wednesday in September pursuant to a concurrent resolution adopted by roll-call vote in each House, except where a state of war exists. This law suggests a termination of annual proceedings of Congress leaving sufficient time (five months) before the start of the next session, unless the two Houses go on record as desiring to remain in session. The 1970 Act requirement for an 'August recess' each odd-numbered year reflected a guarantee to Members of a summer recess for which they could plan well in advance of that month. Notwithstanding this law, the Congress has not adjourned sine die by 31 July for many years, and the law has been routinely waived by concurrent resolution, thereby permitting the two Houses to continue in session in order to enact necessary fiscal legislation before the end of the fiscal year (30 September). The realization that Appropriation bills must be enacted by that date unless continuing appropriations are enacted to bridge the gap beyond 30 September, together with the unfinished status of much other business, contributes to the unwillingness of Congress to enforce the statutory end-of-July final adjournment date every year.

Clause 6 of Rule XI of House rules provides that all business of the House at the end of one session shall be resumed at the commencement of the next session of the same Congress, in the same manner as if no adjournment had taken place. At first the Congress attempted to follow the rule of the British Parliament that business unfinished in one session should begin anew at the next, but in 1818 a rule was adopted that bills should be continued at the next session of the same Congress after six days, except bills referred to committees. The current rule was adopted in 1860 to permit all business to carry over between sessions of the same Congress.

The Senate has a comparable rule (Rule XVIII), providing that at the second or any subsequent session of a Congress the legislative business of the Senate which remained undetermined at the close of the next preceding session of that Congress should be resumed and proceeded with in the same manner as if no adjournment of the Senate had taken place. Thus both Houses have adopted the same practice requiring introduction and new numbering of bills in each new Congress. The Senate rule reflects its one-third new membership and avoids confusion of carry-over status of bills numbered in the prior Congress, despite the fact that it considers itself a continuing body for the purpose of ongoing application of rules.

Bills finally passed at the end of a term of a Congress may be signed into law by the President even after the constitutional term of that Congress has expired if presented to him in a timely manner (by 3 January), and the President has ten calendar days, not counting Sundays, under Article I, section 7 of the Constitution to approve the bill as law or to veto the bill. A bill so vetoed can be revived in the next Congress only by its reintroduction as a new measure, as the President cannot return the vetoed bill to the new Congress.

At Westminster, most Lords sit for life, whether they acquired the right by heredity or by grant of a peerage for their own life: the bishops have retiring ages (see page 123). The mandate of the Members of the House of Commons expires five years after their election. However, since 1911, when the term of a Parliament was set at five years, no Parliament has been dissolved by the passage of time. Parliament is normally dissolved by royal proclamation. Her Majesty acts on the advice of the outgoing Prime Minister, who naturally chooses a timing considered likely to be most advantageous to the government party at the ensuing general election (see page 123).

A Parliament is divided into annual sessions, each—until recently—strictly separate from any other. A session begins with the State Opening of Parliament, usually in the late autumn, at which Her Majesty informs both Houses, the faithful Commons summoned to attend at the bar of the House of Peers, of the programme of legislation her government intends to lay before Parliament in the ensuing session. Business not completed at the end of that session, which nowadays is usually only days before the State opening of the next, normally lapses and must be recommenced from the beginning in the next session.

This principle has however been modified lately by carrying bills over from one session to the next, partly to accommodate more thorough scrutiny of bills and partly to avoid the undue concentration of legislative work in certain limited parts of the session, which (if it happens) works havoc with the business of whichever House is the second House for a contentious bill (see pages 465–6).

Assembly and organization of the four Houses

At the beginning of each new session in Congress, a quorum call is conducted in each House to establish a quorum, and the President and the other House are notified of that fact. The House then proceeds to elect its Speaker, normally the nominee of the majority party conference or caucus (the Clerk from the previous Congress by tradition taking the Chair until that time). This election must be the first order of business after establishment of a quorum, as pursuant to statute and precedent nominations for election of the Speaker are of the highest privilege, even taking precedence over a question of the privileges of the House relating to the interim election of a Speaker pro tempore pending an investigation of the ethics of a nominee for Speaker. Further discussion of the Office of Speaker will follow later in this segment at page 40 under the position and powers of the presiding officer.

The Vice President presides at the organization of the Senate and administers the oath of office to newly elected Senators. The President pro tempore of the Senate is normally the Senator of the majority party with longest seniority. He is not re-elected in each new Senate unless there is a vacancy in that position or a change in party majorities. The Senate being a continuing body, with only one-third of its membership changing every two years, its presiding officer, party leaders and officers remain the same from Congress to Congress unless newly chosen or elected. House Officers are elected by the House at its organization, as their offices are only re-established by the adoption of rules on that day. While all the Representatives are sworn in en masse by the Speaker following his or her election, their terms having just begun, only the newly elected Senators are sworn, as the remaining Senators' terms have not expired.

The House then proceeds to adopt its standing rules and standing orders governing proceedings for that Congress. The preface to the resolution adopting the rules provides that 'the rules of the House of Representatives of the (preceding) Congress, including applicable provisions of law or concurrent resolution that constituted rules of the House at the end of the (preceding) Congress, are adopted as the rules of the (current) Congress, with amendments as follows...'. This readoption takes cognizance of the constitutional requirement in Article I, section 5 that each House should determine the rules of its proceedings. Thus no prior Congress can bind a new House to its rules, either by resolution or by law, and so provisions intended to transcend the life of a Congress must be re-established as rules of the new House. Before the adoption of formal rules, the House operates under the Constitution and general parliamentary law, which are rules that embody practices of long-established custom to be enforced as if already in effect. The most important order of business conducted under general parliamentary precedents is the resolution itself establishing the rules of the House. The resolution is called up as a constitutionally privileged matter by the Member so directed by the Majority party caucus. The resolution is considered under the hour-rule tradition with its sponsor yielding half the time for debate to a minority Member. The resolution is subject to the motion for the previous question—the primary motion under parliamentary law which if adopted has the effect of foreclosing further debate and amendment to the resolution. The Minority party asks that the motion for the previous question be defeated to enable the Minority to offer an amendment—which is usually characterized as the Minority party's rules alternative. The previous question is nevertheless ordered by a Majority party-line vote as a matter of party discipline. The motion to commit after the previous question has been ordered is given enhanced status as a final Minority motion under House standing rules, and by extension as a matter of precedent even prior to their adoption, and represents a second opportunity for the Minority to offer an amendment to the Majority resolution. No division of the question on the resolution (permitting separate votes on various portions) or on the motion to commit is permitted unless the House has first adopted a special order to that effect. On two recent occasions, divisions of the question were specifically permitted when a new Majority took power in 1995 and again in 2007, in order to permit separate debates and votes on each package of procedural reforms it had touted during the campaign.

The new majority (Democratic) Caucus in the 110th Congress did not fulfil its traditional role of formally recommending a rules package to the House. The language of the resolution adopting the rules was drafted informally by Majority leadership without the participation of the caucus. That fact did not prevent its being offered as a privileged matter by the Majority Leader but is reflective of an unprecedented centralization of procedural power in the hands of the elected Majority party leadership without the imprimatur of the full party caucus.

In recent Congresses, the resolution adopting the standing rules also contains a separate section providing for standing orders which are specific to that Congress (such as the carry-over of enforcement or scoring provisions of a concurrent resolution on the budget adopted in the prior Congress, or the creation of a select committee). Special orders of business may also be included as separate sections to make in order particular measures introduced that very day at the opening of the Congress. This technique is only utilized when the Majority party determines to consider a measure or matter prior to the organization of its Rules Committee, which only springs into existence upon the adoption of the rules and of separate resolutions electing its members. Most recently, this technique has been employed to permit the immediate consideration under expedited procedures of legislation which has been the particular focus of the national election (where political promises of immediate action received extensive publicity) and which may have received some prior attention in, although not finally enacted by, the previous Congress. By this technique, committee deliberation and the normal amendment process are bypassed to accommodate immediate passage, permitting only one Minority option of committal to committee with instructions to report a germane alternative.

A recodification (technical rewriting and renumbering) of all the standing rules of the House was accomplished (in the 106th Congress) in the opening day rules resolution, and was perceived as a non-partisan draft without substantive change because fully vented by those responsible for its preparation. In this manner, the partisan Rules Committee was not called upon to report the codifying resolution.

By contrast, Senate Rule V, cla use 2 provides that the rules of the Senate shall continue from one Congress to the next Congress unless they are changed as provided in these rules. While the Senate can amend its rules at any time by majority vote, Senate Rule XXII provides that two-thirds of Senators must vote to invoke cloture to end debate on any proposal to directly amend Senate rules. Thus it becomes politically difficult to come to a final vote on any proposition directly amending (not merely affecting) Senate rules in the face of a one-third minority determined to continue debate. A subsequent segment of this work examines in detail the cloture procedure generally and the 'nuclear' or 'constitutional' option debated in 2005 with respect to terminating debate on the President's judicial nominations at page 4. It was suggested that at the beginning of each new Congress the ability of the Senate to change its rules by majority vote unencumbered by the cloture Rule XXII was a viable option under the Constitution, but that contention never materialized.

Both Houses at Westminster are in effect continuing bodies, at least in the sense that their Standing Orders—whether regular guidance for the conduct of business or means of continuing consideration of particular public or private bills notwithstanding the sessional break—retain their validity from session to session. Business in connection with Her Majesty's Gracious Speech at the beginning of a new Parliament or a new session is discussed at page 49.

The presiding officers

An eighteenth-century Member of the Commons visiting Capitol Hill today would probably find the American Speakership quite familiar. Sir Fletcher Norton, Speaker between 1770 and 1780, felt free to criticize the government at the bar of the Lords when (as Speaker) presenting a supply bill for the royal assent. The wholly non-partisan role of the modern Westminster Speaker would present something of a puzzle. From about the fourth decade of the nineteenth century, a mantle of absolute neutrality descended on the occupants of the Chair at Westminster. The Lord Speaker and the Speaker are probably the most insulated from party of any in the world (see below). The most careful set of conventions governs their personal conduct within the Palace of Westminster, in order to avoid the least suspicion of partisanship, however unfounded.

On election to the Chair, the Commons Speaker resigns party membership and fights elections without party affiliation, not now opposed by any major party. When Lady Boothroyd, who before her election to the Chair had sat as a Labour Member, fought an election as 'The Speaker seeking re-election'—the customary description—so non-party was her candidacy that during the election she was taken on a tour of the Conservative headquarters in her constituency. The last occasion when a previous Speaker returned to the House at a general election was not re-elected to the Chair was as long ago as 1835. On resignation, a Speaker will also give up his seat in the House, and is granted a peerage.

No Commons Speaker has been relieved of his office on motion since Sir John Trevor was found to have improperly accepted 1,000 guineas from the Corporation of London in 1695. Only three motions have been before the House critical of the Speaker since 1902, none of which was carried. In 2009, Mr Speaker Martin resigned his office, not by virtue of the House's agreement to a critical motion—though one had been tabled—but following sustained allegations in the House and in the press that the system of claims for Members' expenses had been abused (see pages 524ff.), and that the Speaker had failed to lead the House 'out of the mire', as one Member put it. The circumstances were unique—as of course all such events are—but it would be a pity if the practice that direct criticism of the occupant of the Chair may be made only on a temperately drawn motion were weakened.

Such a development would be most serious, for the Speaker's impartial character is vital to the working of the Commons. Without it, that underlying balance and fairness which are the legacy of the pre-modern House and the collective view of every successive House—the inconvenient understanding that there are some things which even the largest majority simply ought not to attempt—would disappear in never-ending wrangles.

The essence of the Commons Speaker's role is to guide the practice and interpret the rules of the House, in the interests of fairness and moderation, within the dominant position over the House's procedure which the rules give to the government.

Despite the completely apolitical character of the office and its occupants, a number of concerns about the background of candidates for the Speakership persisted throughout the latter part of the twentieth century. Should the Speakership regularly alternate between the major parties, or could a change of government justify the new majority in claiming that at the first opportunity the next Speaker should come from their side of the House, regardless of the origin of his or her predecessor? Mr Speaker Clifton Brown was elected to the Chair in 1943, having previously sat as a Conservative Member. In 1945, the announcement of a Labour landslide convinced him that he must prepare to leave Speaker's House. His surprise at being renominated to the Chair was correspondingly great. The details of elections to the Chair since 1945 set out in Table 3.1 in the Annex show how the principle of not ejecting a sitting Speaker has frequently accommodated— eventually—the desire of a party to elect one of its own Members to the Chair.

Notwithstanding that party allegiance did not determine elections to the Chair, party whips on both sides nevertheless had by tradition a practical role to play in facilitating the House's assessment and selection of the candidates most likely to excel in presiding over the House. The ideal, however, was that the House should elect unassuming backbenchers, 'House of Commons men'—or women—of independent mind, who blossomed in the Chair, despite lack of front-bench experience. Consequently, there was repeated anxiety about whips' activity behind the scenes and front-bench influence on the selection of candidates for the office.

Several former ministers have been elected to the Chair. Mr Speaker Hylton-Foster in 1959 was a former Attorney General; Mr Speaker Selwyn Lloyd in 1971, a former Foreign Secretary; and Mr Speaker Thomas in 1976 a former Secretary of State for Wales. Of course, none brought political partiality to his decisions from the Chair, but election of former ministers was a development which, had it become a regular occurrence, risked altering the perceived character of the Speakership. In 2000, however, a dozen candidates sought election, and the ancient procedure, which presupposed no more than one or two contenders for the honour, was rightly criticized for being too cumbersome. Subsequently, long-standing back-bench discontent with front-bench infiltration of business seen as properly none of their concern used the dissatisfaction with the procedures of 2000 to bring forward an entirely new method of election, intended to be secure from the intervention of whips, further buttressing the neutrality of the Speakership.

When the House of Commons meets after a general election, the Speaker's Chair is taken by the father of the House, that is, the Member with the longest unbroken service. If the previous Speaker has been returned to the House, the procedure is that in force in all elections to the Chair before 2000. A Member recognized by the father of the House in the Chair nominates the former Speaker, who then modestly submits his candidacy to the will of the House. The House then takes its decision for or against, with or without a division, and the Speaker-elect (if successful) takes the Chair.

The ballot procedure puts a premium on cross-party support, since each candidate must have between twelve and fifteen proposers, of whom at least three must be of a party other than that of the candidate. It also does everything possible to insulate the election process from front-bench pressure. If there is more than one nominee, the order in which their candidacy is brought to the vote is settled by lot, thus solving a most vexing problem faced by the father of the House in 2000. Each candidate addresses the House, and in successive secret ballots the candidate with fewest votes and any candidate with fewer than 5 per cent of the votes cast drops out. Once any candidate receives more than half the votes cast, the House decides whether to call him or her to the Chair. The first time the procedure was used was not in the wake of a general election but in mid-Parliament in the summer of 2009, on the resignation of Mr Speaker Martin. The new procedure ran smoothly, coping with what was, by the standard of elections other than that of 2000, a multiplicity of candidates.

Some traditional ceremonies were unaffected by the reforms of 2000. A Speaker-elect, however chosen, is gently propelled from his or her place to the Chair by the Members who proposed and seconded him or her, the nominee's formal reluctance a reminder of days when taking the Chair of the House of Commons might involve danger to life and limb—nine Speakers were executed (two on the same day) or died a violent death before the middle of the sixteenth century, though not, it must be said, for their performance in the Chair. The Speaker-elect takes the upper step of the Chair, and returns thanks to the House for the honour bestowed. The Mace, which had been under the Table to signify the absence of a fully constituted House, is laid on the Table, but no business is done and the Mace is not borne before the Speaker-elect as he leaves the House. The following day the Speaker-elect and the House are summoned to the Lords, where the election is reported to Lords Commissioners acting on behalf of Her Majesty, who confirm the Speaker-elect in office. There is no question of interference at that stage with the House's choice: no elected Speaker has met royal disapprobation for nearly 350 years. If the election was held at the beginning of a Parliament, the Speaker then lays claim formally to the ancient privileges of the Commons—freedom of speech in debate, freedom from arrest, freedom of access to Her Majesty, and that the most favourable construction may be placed on the Commons' proceedings. As demanded, these claims are medieval in origin and though they are significant in linking the modern rights of the Commons to those made in their earliest days, privilege law has of course developed far beyond the original scope of the demand (see pages 478ff.).

Within the Chamber, the Speaker is traditionally not only the guardian of order but also the protector of backbenchers (see pages 203–4). Though no Standing Order gives the Speaker his role as guide, philosopher, and friend to the back benches, he is nevertheless always anxious to ensure that equity prevails when the demands on time of the front and back benches conflict, or for example when government unreasonably delays an answer to a backbencher's Question. A grave sin which successive Speakers have often damned from the Chair (and which the new Speaker in 2009 has expressed himself sternly about) is for the government to give important information to the press before releasing it to the House (see page 310). It is the trust placed in the impartiality of the Speaker in all parts of the House which renders more acceptable his or her equally necessary but less welcome duties—the imposition of restrictive provisions of all kinds, cutting off carefully crafted speeches, bringing debate to an end when Members still wish to speak, ruling cherished amendments out of order, or denying them debating time even if they are not.

Relatively few duties are laid on the Speaker by statute. Until recently, it seemed unlikely that Speaker's Conferences, which reviewed administrative aspects of electoral law in a non-party political context, would reappear. The last such Conference was held in 1977, and many of their functions probably now attach more naturally to the Electoral Commission, a standing public body. In 2007, however, the idea was revived, and the following year a Speaker's Conference was set up in the form—as none of its predecessors had been—of a select committee, consisting of up to seventeen Members of the Commons appointed by and under the chairmanship of the Speaker. Its task is to find ways of rectifying the disparity between the representation of women, ethnic minorities, and disabled people in the Commons on the one hand, and the proportion of these categories in the general population on the other. It may consider other associated matters, and has such powers as the House may confer on select committees as the Speaker shall determine.

The Speaker controls many aspects of the services and accommodation of the Palace of Westminster, though much of the day-to-day burden is assumed by the Administration Committee (see page 362). He chairs the House of Commons Commission and its alter ego the Members' Estimate Committee. The first is at the top of the chain of responsibility for the personnel and financial affairs of the House of Commons, including the appointment and conditions of nearly all staff. The second considers the sensitive matter of Members' pay and allowances (see pages 141).

There are three Deputy Speakers, who preside in the House of Commons in the absence of the Speaker, and take the chair in Committee of the whole House in their alternative personae as Chairman and First and Second Deputy Chairmen of Ways and Means. The Deputies, who are drawn from both sides of the House, are elected on a government motion, which attracts none of the formality or the need to secure the confirmation of Her Majesty which attends the election of the Speaker. The new Speaker elected in 2009 put in hand a mid-Parliament election of Deputy Speakers, whose selection would depend not on their 'emergence' from consultation but by a process of election and the Procedure Committee in 2008–9 sought the agreement of the House to the principle that there should be a ballot designed to ensure that the successful candidates reflected the party balance in the House. It was an unexpected and interesting parallel to the developments in the process of electing the Speaker himself, though the role and independence of the Deputies are unlikely to be changed. The Deputies enjoy nearly all the powers of the Speaker in their guidance of debate. Their role in the Chair of the House or the Committee of the whole House is performed with the same scrupulous impartiality as that of the Speaker though unlike him they must fight elections in the interests of the political party to which they belong. The Chairman of Ways and Means is responsible for the supervision of the modicum of private business which comes before the House—once a flood, now only a trickle—and he chairs Business Committees under guillotine orders and Programming Committees under programming orders. He was also recently nominated to the Finance and Services Committee, an interesting administrative addition to what had hitherto been an exclusively procedural role.

The only other Members permitted to take the Chair are those invited by the Chairman of Ways and Means—briefly and in practice no more than once or twice a year—to preside in Committees of the whole House, though not the House itself. Those invited to do so are drawn from the Chairmen's Panel, those Members selected by the Speaker to take the chair in Public Bill Committees. Usually two members of the Panel will be chosen to assist the Chairman and Deputy Chairmen when a Finance Bill is before the Committee of the whole House. Members of the Panel also preside in sittings in Westminster Hall (see page 55).

The position of the Lord Chancellor in the Lords is referred to at page 172. As part of recent changes from which there emerged a Supreme Court to which Members of the Lords hitherto called Lords of Appeal in ordinary have migrated, the Lord Chancellor ceased to be either Speaker of the Lords or head of the judiciary. The most immediate consequence was that thought had to be given to who should preside in the Lords if not the Lord Chancellor. After consideration by two select committees, the Lords decided that their Speaker should be elected by the House. By contrast with the Commons the Lord Speaker is elected by the alternative vote system, including postal votes. The election is confirmed by Her Majesty, though without the traditional ceremony of the confirmation of a Commons Speaker. The Lord Speaker serves for five years and if re-elected may enjoy a second term. The Lords elected their first Speaker in the spring of 2006, selecting Baroness Hayman from nine competing Lords.

There remained the issue of what the role of the Lord Speaker should be. The Lords had always been self-regulating. The Lord Chancellor did not determine points of order, or call Lords to speak. When they spoke, they did not address him. These fundamental considerations are not changed in the new dispensation. While the Lord Speaker represents the House at home and overseas, in the Chamber she 'assists but does not rule' the House, having no power to act without its consent. The Lord Speaker will not call Lords to speak. She may remind Lords of the customary procedure applicable to items of business, usually at the outset (as the Lord Chancellor did not), but she does not thereafter intervene to call attention to irregularities in debate. Other things did change. The Lord Speaker is not a Member of the Cabinet, or indeed of any party: she cannot vote or step aside from the Woolsack to make a speech. She is not the head of the judiciary. The Lord Speaker will preside in Committees of the whole House. Other Lords continue to have a role in the running of the business of the House. For example, the Leader of the House assists at Question Time, the Government Chief Whip advises on speaking times, and the front benches will seek to persuade Lords to keep to them.

There are some respects in which the Lord Speaker resembles the Speaker of the Commons. She chairs the House Committee, the equivalent of the House of Commons Commission (see page 364); she determines whether or not there should be an emergency recall of the House and has power to waive the sub judice rule. She makes preliminary decisions on private-notice questions.

The Chairman of Committees, who is appointed by the Lords at the beginning of every session, is chairman of all other committees unless alternative arrangements are made. He is also first of about twelve Deputy Speakers who assist in presiding over the House. There is also a Deputy Chairman of Committees, who assists the Chairman and chairs the European Union Committee.

In Washington, Article I, section 2 of the Constitution directs that the House shall choose its Speaker and other officers. Thus the Speaker is the first officer mentioned in the Constitution, and the Vice President in the role of President of the Senate is next mentioned. Indeed, the position of Speaker is so exalted in the statutory prominence it plays under the doctrine of separation of powers and succession to the office of President that, pursuant to Article II, section 1, clause 6 of the Constitution ('Congress may by law provide for the case of removal, death, resignation or inability, of both of the

President and Vice President, declaring what Officer shall then act as President'), the law[1] provides that the Speaker shall, upon qualifying and resigning from that office, be the first to act as President. (By comparison, the last British Speaker to succeed to the premiership—of course, in days when political impartiality in the Chair was less of a sine qua non—was Addington in 1801.) Only in the event of the Speaker's not fulfilling that role, does the responsibility devolve on the President pro tempore of the Senate and then on enumerated Cabinet officers in a prescribed order beginning with the Secretary of State. In recognition of the principle that the Speaker is the highest-ranking elected officer listed in the law, that statute provides that should the responsibility devolve upon anyone enumerated below the Speaker or President pro tempore, based upon a temporary vacancy or failure of a Speaker or President pro tempore to qualify, and should a Speaker subsequently qualify, then the new Speaker displaces the Cabinet officer as acting President. The succession law, enacted in its present form in 1948, has been criticized by those who contemplate the possible election of a Speaker not of the same political party as the President and Vice President, or in the wake of a catastrophic occurrence by a potentially unrepresentative House whose entire membership may have been severely diminished, even to the extent of superseding a prominent Cabinet officer of the President's political party and confirmed by the Senate. Nevertheless, the prominence given to the Office of Speaker as an elected officer by the succession statute symbolizes a unique intersection under a system of separation of powers while maintaining the constitutional principle against holding incompatible offices.

The Speaker is the presiding officer of the House and is charged with numerous duties and responsibilities by law and by House rules. As the presiding officer, the Speaker maintains order, manages its proceedings, and governs the administration of its business. The major functions of the Speaker with respect to the consideration of measures on the floor include recognizing Members who seek to address the House, construing and applying House rules, and putting the question on matters arising on the floor to a vote.

Some of the Speaker's responsibilities are truly non-partisan and institutional in nature, and do not reflect political determinations. They include: calling the House to order and announcing her approval of the Journal (subject to a vote of the House); referral of bills and other matters to committees following the advice of the Parliamentarian relating to committee jurisdiction; appointment of Speakers pro tempore and Chairmen of the Committee of the Whole; declaring the House in recess or adjourned to another place or time in event of an emergency; preliminary decisions as to questions of privilege; ruling on all points of order and responses to parliamentary inquiries; maintaining order in debate; and assignment of floor privileges to bipartisan leadership staff. Certain of her impartial decisions are not subject to challenge by appeal, including her determination of the presence of a quorum when a point of order is made, decisions on the outcome of voice votes and counts on division (standing) votes, and the discretionary recognition of Members. The Speaker administers censure by direction of the House, certifies to a US Attorney persons found by the House to be in contempt of House committees, and signs various documents.

By rule since 1989, Speakers (together with Minority Leaders) have had access to the meetings and files of the Permanent Select Committee on Intelligence, becoming ex officio members of that panel in 1995. By law, the Speaker is one of the 'gang of eight' entitled to receive briefings from the President in the most sensitive areas of covert activity. This role, originally conceived as bipartisan, and the partisan controversy it provoked in 2009, are discussed in greater detail in the chapter on Scrutiny and Oversight at page 327.

In all these respects, the Speaker's role as presiding officer is an impartial one, and her rulings serve to protect the rights of the Minority. Because contemporary Speakers are increasingly preoccupied as the political and fund-raising leader of the majority party rather than as presiding officer, the responsibility for assuming an impartial role in the latter capacity during daily sessions falls to her appointed Speakers pro tempore and Chairmen of the Committee of the Whole. Together, these occupants of the Chair, while all Majority party members, have consistently accepted the non-partisan advice of the Parliamentarian and have properly interpreted and enforced the standing rules and special orders of the House in responding to points of order and to parliamentary inquiries. Where appeals have been taken from their rulings, they have seldom been based upon a perceived unfairness of the ruling but rather upon frustration stemming from the political motivation of the majority underlying the rule or order being enforced. (A more detailed discussion of the Speaker's appointment and utilization of the Committee on Rules to bring special orders of business to the House is at page 426.)

When majorities change in the House, as has happened twice in the past twelve years, false expectations of the role of the Chair emerge, as the new Majority tends to rely upon the Chair as its ally, rather than as impartial referee in conducting proceedings, while the new Minority may feel overly aggrieved when rulings forced upon the Chair by partisan special rules adopted by the House do not permit them to exercise a full range of procedural options. Thus the role of the Chair is often not properly understood by many Members, including the party leaderships, and unrealistic expectations or frustrations result in further politicization and diminution of respect for, or manipulation of votes on appeals from, the presiding officer.

In choosing temporary presiding officers, the Speaker selects from members of her own party who have had experience in that role and who are not members of the committee managing the pending business. There are no Deputy Speakers chosen by the House who eschew all partisan debating and voting activity as in the House of Commons. Rather, these occupants of the Chair do vote from the Chair on all pending questions, and do relinquish the Chair on occasion to engage in debate from the floor.[2]

Other aspects of the Speaker's role are more partisan but relatively institutional, including her authority to appoint Members to select and conference committees. In that appointment capacity, the Speaker has political discretion in naming Members while remaining within the established ratios of Majority to Minority Members. With respect to time limits on the referral of bills, her decisions, while not subject to challenge, are somewhat more political than her determinations of committee jurisdiction, since the amounts of time granted to secondary committees often reflect party priorities with respect to agenda setting. By statute, the Speaker has authority to appoint Members and other persons to boards and commissions, which sometimes reflect political considerations. Depending on the law or rule governing the appointment, the Speaker is sometimes required to accept the recommendation of the Minority Leader, but more often is merely guided by those recommendations.

Many matters have been held to be beyond the scope of the Speaker's responsibility under the rules. The Speaker does not, for example: construe the legislative or legal effect of a pending measure or comment on the merits thereof; determine whether Members have abused leave to print; respond to hypothetical questions, render anticipatory rulings, or decide a question not directly presented by the proceedings; determine questions that are within the province of the Chairman of the Committee of the Whole; pass on the constitutional powers of the House, the constitutionality of House rules or of pending measures; rule on the consistency of an amendment with another already adopted; anticipate the availability of amendments not yet offered; rule on the sufficiency of committee reports beyond the inclusion of certain matters required by the rules; construe the political consequences of a pending vote; determine whether a Member should be censured or whether he holds an incompatible office, those all being matters for the House to decide. To venture into any of those areas would presumptively insert the Speaker either into a position for which she has no special expertise or which would cause her to speculate on matters more properly left to debate and determination by the collegial body.

There is perhaps no more fundamental difference between the roles of the US and UK Speakers as presiding officers than their respective responsibilities for the selection of amendments to be considered in plenary sessions. While the standing rules of the House of Representatives require most measures to be first considered in a Committee of the Whole and presumably allow all germane amendments to be offered at some point in the proceedings, the Speaker is not presiding at that stage and does not select amendments to be offered. More often in recent practice, however, special orders of business reported from the Committee on Rules restrict the amendments which may be considered to those specified in the special order. The Speaker has no direct role in the selection of those amendments by the Rules Committee, but through her appointment as party leader of nine of the thirteen members of that committee for the duration of each Congress, she indirectly influences the selection of amendments by making her wishes known to those Majority Members as they meet to propose what amendments shall be made in order to each measure to be considered in the plenary session. Often the Speaker's wishes in this regard are based on partisan political considerations which seek to maximize Majority Party advantage on the framing and outcome of issues, and the immunization of politically vulnerable Members from having to cast difficult record votes. By contrast, amendments selected by the Speaker for consideration in the House of Commons are based on equitable factors such as relevance, balance in party sponsorship and in rotation among individual Members in securing recognition (see page 174). Increasingly, fewer such institutional factors influence the selection of amendments by the partisan majority of the House of Representatives' Rules Committee.

Both with respect to the selection of amendments and to rulings on questions of order generally, there is no regular system of appeal from decisions of the British Speaker, while in the House of Representatives the House is permitted by voting on appeal to be the ultimate arbiter of the correctness of the Chair's rulings (except on totally discretionary matters of recognition and the veracity of vote counts). This distinction reflects an acknowledgement of the essential difference in the political origins of the selection of Speaker in the two Houses, that is, the expectation of Majority party nomination in the USA contrasted with his or her uncontested election to the House of Commons in the case of a returning British Speaker.

The foregoing description of the duties of the Speaker as Chair, contrasted with her responsibilities and origins as political leader of the majority party, demonstrates the dual nature of the office. A balanced performance of those dual roles becomes increasingly difficult where the pressures of time, differences with or advocacy and implementation of (as the case may be) policies of the President, Minority party marginalization, and political fund raising force the Speaker as Majority party leader to minimize her institutional role or to assign it to others.

A recent self-analysis of the responsibilities of the Speaker was articulated by the incumbent of that office in November 2003. During the Cannon Centenary Conference,[3] Speaker J. Dennis Hastert described his seven principles of being an effective Speaker: (1) 'To be good at the job of Speaker, you must be willing to put in the time to be a good listener...to the Members of the House'; (2) 'people expect you to keep your word. You are better off not saying anything than making a promise that you cannot keep'; (3) 'A Speaker must respect the power of regular order...it is important to rely on the committees to do their hearings and markups. I don't like to create task forces to craft legislation'; (4) 'While a Speaker should strive to be fair, he also is judged by how he gets the job done. The job of the Speaker is to rule fairly, but ultimately to carry out the will of the majority. We are not the Senate: the rules of the House, while they protect the rights of the Minority, also insure that the will of the majority of the House will prevail...Sometimes we have a hard time convincing the majority of the House to vote like a majority of the House, so sometimes you will see votes stay open longer than usual. But the hallmark of an effective leadership is one that can deliver the votes'; (5) 'My fifth principle is to please the majority of your Majority. The job of Speaker is not to expedite legislation that runs counter to the wishes of the majority of his Majority. On each piece of legislation, I actively seek to bring our party together. I do not feel comfortable scheduling any controversial legislation unless I know we have the votes on our side first'; (6) 'The Speaker's job is to focus on the House and nothing but the House. That means more than just sitting in the Speaker's chair. It means doing those things necessary to keeping the majority, whether that means fundraising for incumbents or campaigning for challengers'; (7) 'My final principle is my most important principle: never forget who sent you to Congress in the first place—your constituents.'

For the purpose of this work, a commentary on Speaker Hastert's commitment to enforce 'regular order' is appropriate and is developed in greater detail at pages 426–8. 'Regular order' has evolved from the once-traditional and predictable reliance upon standing rules, orders, and practices which presume an 'open' amendment process, into whatever ad hoc process the Majority leadership deems appropriate to assure daily majorities and the retention of a political majority into the next Congress. The Speaker, through her appointment of a majority of the Rules Committee members and her other considerable authorities, ultimately dictates a process utilizing 'structured' rules, including the 'self-executing' authority of the Rules Committee (the ultimate 'task force') to supersede committee work products, and a minimization of individual Minority Members' rights to offer amendments and to participate in conferences with the Senate. Insistence on a return to 'regular order' as traditionally understood and contemplated under standing rules was an integral part of Minority Leader Pelosi's complaint in 2006 about management of the House under her predecessor and her promise to lead a more 'open' House. Upon being elected as the first woman Speaker in the history of the House of Representatives, the new majority proceeded to endorse the more partisan processes followed by her predecessor in the interests of certainty of time and issue, and marginalization of the Minority. The contrast of those positions taken by the Speaker before and after her election was not lost on the Minority, and has further impacted on the institutional respect held for the office on the Minority side of the House. The Rules Committee minority published a document on their website in the 110th Congress entitled '*Wipe-out*'—*a comparison between promises and performance of the Rules Committee's reporting of special orders of business in the two Congresses where majority control shifted*, showing a statistical trend toward even greater diminution of minority procedural options under the Speaker's leadership than those complained of by her in the earlier Congress.

It was telling that at the beginning of the 111th Congress on 6 January 2009, Speaker-elect Pelosi in her traditional acceptance speech made no mention of institutional or procedural fairness, openness, adherence to deliberative thoroughness, and minority protection (a pledge traditionally included in Speakers' remarks) preferring to focus instead on the political need for expeditious action in the face of worsening economic conditions. Combined with her endorsement of a rules package which further diminished the procedural options available to the minority and her ongoing total delegation of the role of the Chair to other Members, she marginalized the importance of her own role as presiding officer.

The Speaker's term of office begins on her taking the oath of office, which immediately follows her election and opening remarks on the convening of the first session of a Congress. The term ends on the expiration of the Congress in which she was elected, unless she has resigned, died, or been removed from office. During the 104th to 107th Congresses, the Speaker's term of office was limited to four consecutive Congresses, but that rule was repealed in the 108th Congress in 2003. The election of the Speaker is by precedent and by statute considered the matter of highest priority at the beginning of each Congress, and whenever a vacancy occurs in the office. In 1997, election of a Speaker was held to take precedence over a resolution directing the House to temporarily elect a Speaker pro tempore where the majority party candidate for Speaker (Newt Gingrich) was the subject of an ongoing ethics investigation into his official conduct. On that occasion, the Clerk's ruling was appealed and sustained by a straight party-line vote, symbolizing a political protest against the incumbent Speaker and not a disagreement with the precedential basis for the ruling of the Clerk.

In the event of a vacancy in the office of Speaker, US House practice requires the immediate election of a new Speaker, but also permits the Speaker to designate a non-public list of Members to preside over the House for the purpose of electing a new Speaker. This rule was put in place after 9/11 so that a sworn Member, rather than the Clerk, would preside over the House during the election of a new Speaker to fill a vacancy. By contrast, at the beginning of a new Congress, the Clerk from the preceding Congress presides over the organization of the House until the Speaker is elected (a procedure inherited from but now changed at Westminster). At that point, the rules have not been adopted and the House has not yet authorized the Speaker to appoint Speakers pro tempore. Following the adoption of rules, however, the Speaker may appoint Speakers pro tempore for up to three days in her temporary absence, for up to ten days in the event of illness, or the House can proceed to elect a Speaker pro tempore if one is necessary for a longer time. The Speaker may with the approval of the House appoint Speakers pro tempore to sign enrolled bills.

A vacancy can be created by the resignation of a Speaker 'upon the election of his successor', as happened in 1869 and again in 1989. On those occasions, the Speaker's letter of resignation prompted an election of his successor, and upon the announcement of the result of that vote, his resignation became effective without specifically having been 'accepted' by the House. Unlike the resignation of other elected House officers, the Speaker's resignation is not accepted by the House. On one notable occasion in 1820, Henry Clay resigned as Speaker and in his letter asked the House to accept his resignation. The House took no action to accept the resignation but immediately adopted a motion to proceed to the election of Speaker. (These precedents thus avoid the possible refusal of the House to accept a Speaker's resignation which would be incompatible with his announced determination that he no longer wishes to serve in that position.)

Precedent in the House indicates that a resolution declaring the office of Speaker vacant can be raised at any time as a question of the privileges of the House. In this regard, such an action is not necessarily viewed as a disciplinary matter, but rather as a political issue somewhat equivalent to a vote of no confidence, having a constitutional underpinning based on the Article I authority of each House to elect its Speaker. This principle was established on 19 March 1910, when Speaker Joe Cannon stated:

> The Speaker does now believe, and always has believed, that this is a Government through parties, and that parties can act only through majorities. The Speaker has always believed in and bowed to the will of the majority in convention, in caucus, and in the legislative hall, and today profoundly believes that to act otherwise is to disorganize parties, is to prevent coherent action in any legislative body, and is to make impossible the reflection of the wishes of the people in statutes. The Speaker has always said that, under the Constitution, it is a question of the highest privilege for an actual majority of the House at any time to choose a new Speaker, and again notifies the House that the Speaker will at this moment, or at any other time when he remains Speaker, entertain, in conformity with the highest constitutional privilege, a motion by any Member to vacate the office of the Speakership and choose a new Speaker; and, under existing conditions would welcome such action upon the part of the actual majority of the House, so that power and responsibility may rest with the Democrats and insurgent Members who, by the last vote, evidently constitute a majority of this House. The Chair is now ready to entertain such motion.

Cannon's exercise of power from the time he became Speaker in 1903 had culminated in the Speaker's assignment of Members to committees, his appointment and removal of committee and subcommittee chairmen, his regulation of the flow of business to the floor as chairman of the Committee on Rules, his referral of measures to committee and his control of floor debate through the power of recognition. His Speakership had come to be described as a case of 'excessive leadership'. On 17 March 1910, a Member offered as a question of constitutional privilege a resolution removing the Speaker as chair and member of the Committee on Rules. Following two days of debate on a point of order that the resolution was not privileged, Cannon sustained the point of order, but was overruled on appeal by a vote of 182:162. The Speaker's ruling was correct under precedents established prior and subsequent to that occasion, to the effect that the rules, once adopted, cannot be changed except by procedures provided therein (reports from the Committee on Rules), and not under the guise of questions of privilege. Nevertheless, an instant coalition of the House had overruled his decision on appeal (as it had also done the previous day on a procedural question, where he had ruled that a census matter took precedence over a 'Calendar Wednesday' call of committees which had been put in place to diminish the power of the Rules Committee—all part of the 'Cannon Revolt'), both successful appeals prompting him to rule a resolution declaring the office vacant to constitute a constitutionally privileged matter at any time. The House rejected the resolution which was then offered at Cannon's invitation, but the precedent was established that the person elected to the Office of Speaker, could in effect, be subject to a vote of no confidence. While the rationale for conferring privilege on such a resolution was to permit an indication of shift in Majority party control of the House, the precedent stands for the proposition that removal of the Speaker for any political reason remains a matter of privilege, and need not be linked to allegations of misbehaviour or to a party caucus determination.

Eighty-eight years later in 1998, the possibility of such a resolution being presented by insurgent Members of the Majority party was publicly discussed. Several dissident Members of Speaker Newt Gingrich's party were dissatisfied by his leadership and believed that a coalition of those Members and virtually all of the Minority party Members could combine to vacate the office. When advised that such an action, if successful, would prompt the respective party caucuses to nominate candidates to fill the vacancy, it became apparent that the majority Republican Conference would renominate Speaker Gingrich. To be elected Speaker, a candidate must receive a majority of all votes cast for or against a candidate, and votes for candidates not nominated are counted. It appeared that Minority Members would vote for their nominated candidate, the Minority Leader, and that most Majority Members would vote for Speaker Gingrich, so that neither candidate would receive a majority unless the dissidents supported the Minority Leader. Their possible support of a third candidate would merely have deprived all candidates of the necessary majority and the vacancy would have continued, and so the effort never materialized.

As the role of the modern Speaker in the House of Representatives is increasingly politicized, with incumbents devoting less time and attention to the institutional aspects of that office, modern Speakers sometimes find themselves more exposed to ethical questions involving their official conduct as the Minority party attempts to build a case of 'a culture of corruption'. The chapter on Ethics and Standards at page 540 documents this focus which began in 1988 ending in the resignation of Speaker Jim Wright in 1989, and continued through the entire Speakership of Newt Gingrich. It has included more recent allegations of ethical negligence or complicity in Speaker Dennis Hastert's handling of ethics charges against a sitting Majority party member, and Speaker Pelosi's deliberate holding open a vote solely to change the result despite a new House rule prohibiting that action by the Chair. Since 1962, only the Speakerships of Carl Albert and Tip O'Neill from 1971 to 1986 escaped allegations of ethical improprieties and resulted in voluntary retirements not occasioned by scandal. Speaker McCormack retired in 1970 following allegations of improper lobbyist influence-peddling through his office, and Speaker Foley in the early 1990s confronted allegations of condoning mismanagement of the House 'bank' and post office. The politicization of the Speakership may well force future Speakers to entrench themselves behind party barriers in order to thwart this kind of attack, or may leave them inevitably vulnerable to those attacks in part due to their own previous complaints against Majority party corruption when in the minority. In any event, resumption of the mantle of Speaker for the whole House becomes more elusive where members of the Minority are unwilling to accept a Speaker who has successfully pressed ethics allegations against the other party in his or her ascendency.

The position of President pro tempore in the Senate, while reflecting some of the institutional responsibilities conferred upon the Speaker of the House, is much more a ceremonial than a political office, to which the majority Senator of the longest continuous service is elected by resolution. That Senator remains in that office from Congress to Congress until his term as Senator expires, unless replaced or upon a shift in party majority. Some non-partisan responsibilities of the Chair inure to the President pro tempore, including the impartial presiding role acting on the advice of the Parliamentarian.

Rule I of the Senate's standing rules provide that the Secretary of the Senate shall preside in the absence of the Vice President and pending the election of a President pro tempore. This situation obtains occasionally when the term of a Senator who has been elected President pro tempore expires and before he is re-elected or another President pro tempore has been elected.

Acting Presidents pro tempore are selected by the President pro tempore for no more than one legislative day from among Senators in the majority party on a rotating basis upon recommendation by the Majority Leader's office and primarily include the most junior Senators (more senior Senators having greater committee responsibilities). Those Senators preside during most of the Senate sessions. In turn, the Chair's consistent first recognition of the Majority Leader on any matter signifies that the political and agenda-setting responsibility falls to that politically elected party Leader and is preserved and promoted by, but not performed in the person of, the presiding officer. (A more detailed discussion of the role of the Majority Leader is contained in the chapter on Legislation at page 415.) When ruling on questions of order, the presiding officer is normally much terser in explaining the basis for his ruling than is the Chair in the House, reflecting the relative importance placed upon the rationale of those rulings as governing precedent in the House. The likelihood of appeals from the Chair's ruling in the Senate has on recent occasion indicated a determination to consider the merits of the underlying question, where there is no Senate panel such as a Rules Committee with jurisdiction to recommend a waiver of points of order to accommodate such consideration. Also, the Senate has erected barriers of points of order requiring super-majority three-fifths votes for waiver in several procedural areas involving the Congressional Budget Act or matters added in conference.

In addition to presiding, the President pro tempore or Acting President pro tempore signs enrolments and announces appointments from the Chair made pursuant to law and rule, although the political responsibility for the appointments is usually that of the Majority Leader. As an indication of the limited responsibilities of the President pro tempore, as a Senator he also normally serves as chairman of one or more Senate standing committees based upon seniority in the Senate.

The State of the Union and the State Opening

Article II, section 3 of the US Constitution requires the President to give to the Congress from time to time Information of the State of the Union, and recommend to their consideration such measures as he shall judge necessary and expedient. The initiative is taken by the President, who informally indicates to House and Senate leadership his willingness to address the two Houses in joint session, normally near the beginning of an annual session in January of each year. As a matter of long-standing custom, the two Houses usually do not begin transacting legislative business at the beginning of a Congress until after the President has delivered his Message, but on two recent occasions, the House has as part of the resolution adopting its standing rules adopted a special order providing for the immediate consideration of a bill introduced that day and symbolizing a campaign priority of the majority party. From the earliest Congresses, 'from time to time' meant 'annual', and in 1913 President Woodrow Wilson re-established the tradition discontinued by President Thomas Jefferson in 1801 by delivering his State of the Union Message in person.

Two statutory requirements for submission of the President's Budget and Economic Report at the beginning of each calendar year combine with the timing of the State of the Union Message to indicate that Congress will defer to the President, especially at the beginning of a new Congress, before it begins legislative business. In fact, the President's budget triggers early hearings in the Appropriations and Budget Committees of both Houses prior to the formulation of Congress's own budget and the consideration of portions of the President's budget in various subcommittees of the Committee on Appropriations. This is discussed in greater detail in 'The Power of the Purse' and in 'Scrutiny and Oversight' at pages 225–306.

When the President indicates that he will address Congress in person, a concurrent resolution is called up as privileged (a matter essential to the organization of Congress) and adopted by both Houses arranging for a joint session in the House Chamber to receive the message. At the appointed hour, the Senate arrives, as does the President's Cabinet, the Supreme Court, and the Diplomatic Corps (previously seated) and represented by the Ambassador ('Dean') with the longest service. The President of the Senate (the Vice President) sits to the right of the Speaker as the higher ranking Constitutional Officer, but in the absence of the Vice President, the President pro tempore sits to the left of the Speaker. The Speaker presides. While the pageantry of the joint session bears no resemblance to the State Opening of Parliament, the speeches are similar in their presentation of political priorities. The President's focus is often more on generic issues than on specific legislative proposals, which he subsequently submits with or without accompanying draft language by written messages during the year. The occasion is much more a message to the nation, televised at prime time during the week and embellished to include the President's welcome to his distinguished guests in the gallery.

Though pageantry is more in evidence at the State Opening of Parliament than at the President's State of the Union Address, the purposes are remarkably similar. At the beginning of a normal session—the first session of a new Parliament is slightly different—Her Majesty proceeds in state, that is, wearing the Crown and attended by officers of state led by the Lord High Chancellor, to the Throne in the House of Lords. Members of that House are already seated in the scarlet and ermine of their Parliament robes. The senior judges are present, and as in Washington the Diplomatic Corps is represented. The Gentleman Usher of the Black Rod is dispatched to the Commons, only to find that the door of their Chamber is slammed in his face, an assertion of defiance dating from more turbulent times. When he gains admittance, he summons the Commons to attend Her Majesty in the House of Peers. The House, led by the Speaker, then walk informally two-by-two to stand at the bar of the Lords—as many as can press in, which is far fewer than the membership of the House—and the Queen reads the Gracious Speech. The text is prepared by the government and contains—among other comments on national and international affairs and an account of royal visits—the programme of legislation for the ensuing session. Her Majesty having prayed 'that the blessing of Almighty God may rest upon [the] labours' of both Houses, the Commons then withdraw. Later in the day Lords and Commons begin debates which last several days on motions to thank Her Majesty for her Gracious Speech. Before they do so, however, both Houses read a bill formally the first time, a further reminder of days when Parliament was determined not to dance to the royal tune but to set its own agenda.

In the not too distant past, the contents of the Gracious Speech were carefully guarded, and while there might be informed speculation in the media there was no advance detail of what the government planned. Later, the speculation became more authoritative and comprehensive, as the consultations undertaken in advance of presentation of legislation became public knowledge. Recent government proposals took this progression to its logical conclusion. While the Speech remains 'the only formal, final announcement of the government's legislative programme and the principal national occasion on which The Queen outlines the programme of her government',[4] before Easter in the parliamentary session preceding that in which the Speech is delivered, the government informs Parliament and the public of the proposals for legislation the Speech is likely to contain. Publication permits wider advance consultation and consideration of how best to use the parliamentary time available for the programme, and there is a report on the outcome of the process, giving details of areas where the government's mind has been changed and those where it has not. It is intended there should be a full day's debate on the draft programme before Parliament rises for the summer. A comprehensive review of the several elements of the programme by the responsible select committees is proposed. The prospect found committee chairmen in two minds. On the one hand, they welcomed a development of existing work on pre-legislation (see pages 463–5); on the other they were reluctant to be 'sucked into' government-originated work at the expense of their own scrutiny priorities.[5]

In 2008, the draft legislative programme contained eighteen bills and three pre-legislative texts.

The Chambers: size and arrangement; access to

That part of the medieval Palace of Westminster which included the Chambers of both Houses was destroyed by fire in 1834. Rebuilding was completed in an ornate mid-Victorian Gothic style just over a decade later. Since then, the interior of the Palace has undergone much internal modification, constrained however by the need to retain architectural and artistic sympathy with the original. After the bombing of 1941, the Commons Chamber was not reoccupied until 1950. A number of adjacent buildings have since been taken over and adapted for parliamentary use, and a large new building, Portcullis House, was constructed on an adjacent site in the 1990s.

The Chambers of both Houses at Westminster are rectangular (see page 51). In both Houses, Her Majesty's ministers and the Lords and Members who support them sit on the right of the presiding officer and the Opposition on the left. By convention, the Cabinet and shadow Cabinet sit on opposite benches nearest the Chair (in the Commons) or the Woolsack (from which the Lord Speaker presides). Unlike the practice in Congress, if after an election the government party changes, a successful Opposition moves to the Lord Speaker's or the Speaker's right. Those parties in Opposition other than the principal Opposition party sit furthest from the presiding officer. In the Lords, two benches are reserved for the twenty-six archbishops and bishops of the Church of England who are members of the House (see page 123), and a significant proportion of the House sit facing the Woolsack on the cross benches, whose occupants are members of no political party. In the Commons, the Mace—which signifies the authority of the House—sits horizontally at the end of the Table furthest from the Speaker: in the Lords the Mace is placed, also horizontally, on the Woolsack.

The Lords Chamber, in the furnishing of which red predominates, is much as it was constructed in the middle of the nineteenth century, dominated by the Throne behind the Woolsack, with a second woolsack for the judges. The Table of the House lies between the front benches. The Bar, at the end of the Chamber furthest from the Woolsack, is railed. The original Commons Chamber, where the benches were green, otherwise originally closely resembled the Lords. When the Commons Chamber was rebuilt after the War, it was still in green but in a simpler and less sombre style than before. The cross benches are vestigial, the Table is immediately in front of the Speaker's Chair, and the Bar is normally indicated only by a line on the carpet.

The rebuilt Commons Chamber has the same dimensions as its burned-out predecessor, with the result that no more than just over half the total of Members of the House can find a seat. This was a deliberate decision, with which Sir Winston Churchill is often associated. It candidly recognizes that the Commons Chamber is rarely full and that oratorical flourishes are usually lost on it. A smaller Chamber is best suited to the conversational style of debate, and the normal number of Members attending—while often the subject of constituency criticism—do not look as sparse as would be the case in a Chamber capable of seating the entire 646. A less expected advantage is that, when the House is full for the Budget or issues of peace and war and Members sit crowded together on the benches, in the galleries, and even on the floor of the aisles, the sense of theatre is overwhelming. But high drama is present in other circumstances too. No one who was present will ever lose the memory of the utterly unbroken silence when the House stood to commemorate the dead of the 9/11 atrocity.

Except as mentioned above, no individual Member of either House at Westminster has a particular place on a bench—there are no individual seats—though in practice retired Prime Ministers, if they retain membership of the House, have tended to sit on the front bench below the gangway which splits each side of the Chamber—that is, further from the Chair. (It was not always so. Winston Churchill's father and the gadfly 'Fourth Party' sat there at the end of the nineteenth century.) On the other side of the House, the leader of the second largest Opposition party usually sits on the bench which is second up from the front, below the gangway.

Lords and Members address their respective Houses from their place on the bench. Such an arrangement confers an advantage on the frontbenchers. They can rest their notes on the dispatch boxes which sit on either side of the Table of the House, lean on them, or assault them—the marks of Gladstone's ring are said to be still visible in the

Commons. Backbenchers have no such physical or oratorical advantage. Since the Chambers are quite steeply raked, the bench in front of a non-ministerial Member does not reach his or her knees, making the delivery of a speech much more of an ordeal. In both Chambers, there is a sound-reinforcement system not involving personal microphones to ensure that speeches are audible in all parts of the House.

Behind the walls forming the long sides of both Chambers, there are division lobbies through which Lords or Members of the Commons walk in order to cast their votes (see page 221).

No person not elected to the Commons, other than officers of the House whose duties demand their presence in the Chamber—the Clerks at the Table and other clerks, the Speaker's Secretary, the Serjeants, Badge Messengers carrying messages for Members, and the Gentleman Usher of the Black Rod when he summons the Commons to attend in the Lords on ceremonial occasions (see page 49)—are permitted on the floor of the Commons Chamber. Civil servants advising ministers are corralled in a box on the government side of the Chamber, with no access to the floor other than by handing notes to those Members who are ministerial aides.

Arrangements are much the same in the Lords Chamber, with the addition that privy counsellors, even if they are not Lords, may sit on the steps of the Throne, which is not technically within the Chamber.

In Washington, both House and Senate wings of the United States Capitol opened in 1857 and contain the current Chambers of the Congress. The House first met in its current Chamber on 16 December 1857 when 234 Representatives from thirty-two States and seven Delegates sat at individual desks. Since 1913, the House has been designed for theatre-style seating. In marked contrast with the two Houses of Parliament, the House of Representatives and the Senate are designed in a semi-circular seating fashion, with all seats facing the rostrum—the Chair of the presiding officer and desks for other officials. A middle aisle divides seating for the two political parties.

In both US Chambers, all Members can be accommodated for seating and for debate. In the House Chamber, there are approximately 648 seats, with 324 on each side of the centre aisle, but with no seat assigned to any Member. Microphones are only available at the two committee tables located on each side and at two lecterns located in the well of the House. The Chair will normally require Members to be at one of the microphones before recognizing them for debate, unless they are merely rising from their seats to object to a unanimous consent request. Members speaking from the table microphones face the Speaker, while Members speaking from the well lecterns face the membership. It is their choice as to which microphone they utilize. The Republican side of the aisle corresponds with the right side of the Chamber facing the rostrum, and the Democratic Members sit on the left side. When majority status changes between the two parties, there is no shift of seating in the Chamber. That is, there is not a permanent Majority and Minority side of the Chamber (as is the case with government and opposition in the Houses of Parliament). On occasion, but with decreasing frequency, Members from one political party informally sit on the other side of the aisle from that designated for their party, if only for a brief time. Debates in either House are seldom well attended, Members and Senators preferring to observe, or have staff observe, on closed-circuit television when they are not directly participating. The Chambers are most often fully occupied by a large portion of the membership during votes, especially during a series of record votes where there is no intervening debate, or immediately following quorum calls where the leadership desires attendance for whipping purposes during important debates.

All voting is done within each Chamber, open to the public, and not in separate adjacent lobbies. While voting totals are displayed electronically outside the Chamber via television monitors during the conduct of each recorded vote, by parties and by the number in favour and opposed, individual votes are not available outside the Chamber until several minutes following the conclusion of the vote. Electronic voting stations are scattered throughout the Chamber and Members may cast their votes from any station, so their seating on either side of the aisle is irrelevant in that regard. Importantly, despite the scattering of voting stations, the whips can immediately ascertain whether a Member has voted and can usually locate him or her unless the Member is determined not to be found during the course of a vote. The five doors of the Chamber and two cloakroom doors are not locked so as not to prevent the departure of a fleeing Member.

With increasing frequency, Members utilize visual displays during televised debate in both Houses, an indication that they are not always debating each other but are addressing an audience outside the Chamber. When displays are utilized from the well lecterns, they are often not visible to the Chair but only to Members viewing from their seats facing the Chair. This arrangement can have unforeseen procedural consequences when possibly unparliamentary materials are displayed which the Chair cannot immediately examine. The use of visual displays will be examined further in the chapter on Procedural Basics relating to debate at page 168.

In the Senate, there are 100 desks assigned to individual Senators with the Majority and Minority Leaders' desks in the first row on either side of the centre aisle, which separates Republican and Democratic sides. As in the House, the desks are in a semi-circle facing the rostrum, the Republicans are on the right side of the centre aisle facing the presiding officer, and the Democrats are located on the left side of the centre aisle. When the party majority shifts after an election, desks are moved from across the aisle to accommodate the new Senators, but as in the House the majority is not always on the same side of the aisle. Each desk is equipped with a lapel microphone to amplify the Senator's words in the Chamber and for televised coverage. Senators speak only from their desks, and face the presiding officer when doing so.

In the House, Members sometimes face each other during direct debate, especially when one of the participating Members is speaking from a lectern in the well. Just as frequently they face the Chair with oblique gestures toward the Member whom they are debating, the usual case when neither Member is in the well with his back to the Chair.

In each Chamber, since all the independent Members have chosen to caucus with one or the other of the two political parties, their seat assignments or choices normally reflect that preference.

As there are no 'back-bench' Members per se in the House or Senate, there are no seats or desks reserved only for ministers or shadow ministers. The closest similarities in the House to the dispatch boxes in the House of Commons are either the lecterns in the well (one on each political side) or the leaders' tables on either of the aisles running obliquely from the well to the rear of the Chamber. Senate leaders have prominent desk assignments in the front row to the immediate left and right of the centre aisle.

In decided contrast to the UK Parliament, standing rules of both Houses permit a variety of other persons on the floor during sessions. This includes committee staffs on the floor (five at any one time in the House) during the pendency of business from their committees, additional leadership staffs, and staffs of individual Members during pendency of their amendments. Rules of both Houses also delineate other persons granted floor privileges, including Members of the other House, former Members, and foreign ministers. By tradition, children of Members under the age of 12 can accompany the Member in the House. House rules prevent unanimous consent requests to permit other persons on the floor, while such unanimous consent requests for staffs of individual Senators are commonplace.

Extraordinary places of meeting

Article I, section 5, clause 4 of the US Constitution provides that neither House may, without consent of the other, adjourn 'to any other Place than that in which the two Houses shall be sitting'. This requirement for consent has been interpreted to apply only beyond the seat of government, which has been, since 1800, the District of Columbia. Therefore either House may sit in another place within the District of Columbia without the consent of the Senate, as they did in 1940 when the roofs of the two Chambers required repair. Again in 1949–50 when the two Chambers were being refurbished, the House convened pursuant to its own order in the Ways and Means Committee room in the Longworth House Office Building and the Senate in the Old Supreme Court Chamber in the Capitol.

Contingency plans for alternative locations within and outside the seat of government for both Houses have been formulated by leadership of both Houses since 11 September 2001, but have not been publicly announced. An anthrax terrorist threat in 2002 nearly prompted a meeting of both Houses in other places within the District of Columbia, but the threat was cancelled prior to the scheduled meeting of the two Houses upon thorough inspection before the next convening. Beginning in the 107th Congress, the two Houses authorized joint leadership recall from an adjournment 'at such place and time as they may designate whenever, in their opinion, the public interest shall warrant it', permitting recall to a place outside the District of Columbia. That authority was expanded in the next Congress and remains current policy to give blanket leadership authority regardless of an adjournment to a day certain. By statute, the President may convene Congress at places outside the seat of government during hazardous circumstances, but that authority has never been utilized.

Neither US House has ever convened for a legislative session outside the seat of government. On two ceremonial occasions, the two Houses gathered pursuant to concurrent resolutions but did not 'convene' or 'assemble' outside the seat of government—in 1989 to celebrate the bicentennial of the US Constitution in Philadelphia, Pa., and in 2002 in New York in Federal Hall, the site of the first Congress in 1789, to honour the victims of 11 September 2001. During neither of these ceremonies was either House in actual session, nor was there a joint session.

In contrast to the Westminster Hall proceedings of the House of Commons (see page 55), the US House of Representatives has never deemed it necessary to establish an additional or concurrent meeting place for the conduct of debate, preferring instead both to rely on traditional committee proceedings or to lengthen periods of time for debate in the House Chamber by 'Morning Hour' debates on Mondays and Tuesdays of each week and by special order speeches to follow legislative business each day, discussed under 'debates' at page 154. The ability of more Members of Parliament to question ministers—to scrutinize government—which has prompted the concurrent Westminster Hall debates has not been a compelling reason for similar debates in either House of Congress. There, the questioning of government occurs at the committee level, with cabinet secretaries appearing before standing and select committees of each House in separate rooms set aside for that purpose. No plenary sessions are considered necessary and a suggestion that there be 'question times in the House' was dismissed in 1992. This will be discussed more extensively at page 347.

In the UK, both Houses are summoned by royal proclamation to meet at Westminster, and from at least the middle of the sixteenth century, they have not—with one exception—sat elsewhere than in the Palace of Westminster. When the Commons Chamber was destroyed by enemy action in 1941, the House occasionally sat in premises close by belonging to the Church of England or in the Lords Chamber, the Lords being accommodated in another part of the Palace. Even in such extremities, Parliament continued to sit in Westminster, the location to which it was summoned.

The Parallel Chamber and other expedients

The critical significance of the time/business balance for the Commons is discussed elsewhere (pages 391, 440, 463ff.). Time is always in great demand but short supply. One of the means by which that balance is tipped to extend the time available in the Commons Chamber is 'the House sitting in Westminster Hall'.[6] In 1999, following a report of the Modernisation Committee, and in the wake of an idea flourishing in the Australian House of Representatives, a 'parallel Chamber' was devised, which all Members may attend. What takes place is a sitting of the House and not of a committee—despite the awkward existential fact that on Thursdays 'the House' sits simultaneously in the Chamber and in Westminster Hall. Sittings in Westminster Hall are held on Tuesday mornings, Wednesday mornings and afternoons, and Thursday afternoons.

The time gained as a proportion of time spent in the Chamber is appreciable and a Table 3.2 giving these and other details relating to Westminster Hall is to be found in the Annex.

The business considered at the sittings in Westminster Hall is deliberately non-controversial, and indeed divisions may not take place. Tuesdays and Wednesdays are usually 'adjournment' debates (see page 80) mostly initiated by backbenchers chosen randomly by ballot, who are answered by a minister. Select Committee reports are debated on six Thursdays, the choice for debate being made by the Liaison Committee (see page 362). A Question Time has occasionally been arranged for Westminster Hall, when Members put to ministers questions on matters which cross departmental boundaries, easier to deal with in the (usually) more relaxed atmosphere of these sittings than in the pressure-cooker of Question Time in the House. This interesting experiment seems to have faltered, however. There were six Question Times in Westminster Hall in 2002–3, two in 2003–4, and none since.

Sittings in Westminster Hall are one of the most ingenious procedural developments among the proliferation of ideas in the past decade. Substantial gains in debating time have been conjured out of nothing. It would make a lot of sense if these advantages were built on and sittings in Westminster Hall were expanded, for example to plug the gaps in the House's scrutiny of delegated legislation (see page 472) even if it remained for the most part uncontroversial, or to take up the Modernisation Committee's suggestion that occasionally Questions with a European theme—crosscutting business par excellence—might be attempted with profit in Westminster Hall.[7] The Procedure Committee thought that a Member who had not received a satisfactory response to a petition he or she had presented (or indeed no response at all) should be entitled to half an hour's debate in Westminster Hall. In the context of these and no doubt other possibilities, the government's preparedness to undertake a review of the work of Westminster Hall is welcome. Members are naturally concerned that the usefulness of Westminster Hall should not be diminished by forcing contested business into the non-partisan atmosphere in what would then be a vain pursuit of more debating time overall. But the benefit so far has been so great that, with due care, the risk might well be worth it.

Broadly the same kind of solution to the problem of augmenting the time available to match increased levels of business has been adopted in the Lords, though in a more thoroughgoing way. In the course of the financial year 2006–7, Grand Committees, which every Lord may attend and in which no divisions may take place, met on fifty occasions. On thirty-four of these they considered stages of bills—including a private member's bill—and on the remainder delegated legislation, and two select committee reports. There was also a Question for short debate (see page 345). The levels of activity in Grand Committees were slightly down in 2006–7 by comparison with previous years, but are vastly above those of a decade ago. In short, particularly in their consideration of legislation both primary and secondary, Lords Grand Committees have advanced a stage further than the Westminster Hall experiment in terms of the range of business considered. It is of course true that proceedings of all kinds are less likely to give rise to divisions in the Lords than in the Commons, but significant progress has been made without sacrificing the principle that such business may not be controversial.

The Lords: mending, not ending

To eyes accustomed to Montesquieu's regard for the separation of powers—what James Madison saw as an 'essential precaution in favor of liberty'—the need to change the constitution of the British upper Chamber was no doubt always self-evident. The Lord Chancellor's role must have seemed particularly anomalous—at one and the same time the presiding officer of one House of the legislature, the head of the judiciary, and a Cabinet minister. Yet there were always sensible arguments in favour of such an arrangement. The triple role entrenched at the heart of government respect for the independence of the judiciary. Was it really such a hostage to fortune if senior judges had a seat in the legislature, provided they were cautious about the topics on which they intervened in debate? They made a collective statement, perhaps prompted by the demands of the

Human Rights Convention in respect of judicial independence, that they would not speak on matters of party political dispute or those likely to come before them on appeal: was this not enough? In any case, the powers of the judges would not be significantly different whether they were the Appellate Committee of the House of Lords or a quite separate Supreme Court. Nevertheless, the present government decided that the judges should migrate from the Lords to a Supreme Court, and that the triple role of the Lord Chancellor should cease. The consequences for the Speakership of the Lords are dealt with at page 40.

The history of the attempts (characterized by bursts of radical change interrupting long periods of inactivity) to tackle the unelected and overwhelmingly hereditary membership of the Lords is separate from change in the nature of the office of Lord Chancellor, though the two issues came together in recent years.

At the end of the nineteenth century, the Lords was composed almost exclusively of hereditary peers—those who had become legislators simply by inheriting titles conferred on their ancestors in past centuries—together with a handful of bishops of the Church of England and even fewer judges, who owed their seats to the fact that the House of Lords retained its medieval character as the supreme court. The long-standing Conservative majority in the Lords never had many inhibitions about rejecting high-profile Liberal bills, and even before crisis point was reached there was growing awareness that the hereditary principle would have to be abandoned or modified to fit contemporary politics. In 1909, the Lords rejected a Liberal Budget, the government's central economic and fiscal programme, which in this case was a particularly radical one. The result was the Parliament Act 1911 (see page 64), the preamble of which openly threatened that the next stage was 'to substitute for the House of Lords as it at present exists a second Chamber constituted on a popular instead of hereditary basis'.

For the next thirty years or so, ideas for reform proliferated without reaching fruition: election of the upper House by the Commons in regional groupings, election of sitting peers by the peerage as a whole, nomination by the government, or any combination of these. Sometimes action did follow. The Lords' power of delay was subjected to tighter time limits in the Parliament Act 1949. In 1958, life peerages were introduced. Several years later, it became possible to disclaim a hereditary peerage for the lifetime of the individual disclaiming.

An attempt in 1968–9 to divide the Lords into those with the right to vote and those who could participate in debate but not vote foundered in the Commons, opposed by an alliance of those who wished to abolish the upper House and those who wanted only very limited change.

By then the House was, in theory, very large: there were some 1,250 Lords, though the active membership was of course much smaller. In 1999, the House of Lords Act was the latest and thoroughgoing attempt at reform (see page 117). Only ninety-two hereditary peers were in future to sit in the House, reducing the size to about 700. There was broad agreement that the Lords should not be able to challenge the elected House and should act as a partner rather than a co-equal: but it was not clear exactly what the future held in terms of the composition or the powers of the upper House.

Whether appointed or elected, there were a number of creative ideas around regarding the future of the Lords—representatives from the nations and regions was one.

There was concern that the independent-minded and informed non-political element which had for decades characterized Lords debates, as life peers and others brought their experience and expertise, should survive reform. Should the presence of Church of England bishops be widened to include other Churches or faith communities? Certainties were hard to find.

As part of the attempt to build consensus, a Royal Commission was appointed, but even after its thorough examination had been published, no universally acceptable pathway through the obstacles had been identified. Nearly everyone could see the case for removing the remaining ninety-two hereditaries; it was not thought necessary to alter the existing balance of authority between the Chambers; and there was general agreement that in some way the make-up of the Lords should reflect the broad political balance in the country. But there was no settled conclusion within as well as between the parties on how members of the Lords should be selected and for how long they should serve.

In 2002, the government tried again, by appointing a parliamentary Joint Committee to consider the options and prepare the way for a parliamentary solution. The Committee carefully presented Parliament with seven options, ranging from a fully appointed Chamber through varying balances to one wholly elected. Early in 2003, the House of Lords opted for a fully appointed second Chamber. The Commons rejected all seven options. In February 2007 a White Paper entitled 'House of Lords Reform' (Cm 7027) attempted to balance the vital principles of Commons primacy and Lords legitimacy. A fully elected upper House might well challenge the first, an all-appointed House might not deliver the second. The government therefore put forward a House of 540, of whom half would be elected for a single fifteen-year term and the other half would be appointed by an independent Commission, 30 per cent party-political and 20 per cent non-political. When the Commons came to consider the scheme, it favoured a House of Lords which was 80 per cent or 100 per cent elected: the Lords themselves preferred a fully appointed House. The earlier stalemate had returned in a slightly different form. Further talks to search for an agreed basis for progress were announced.

A White Paper entitled 'An elected second Chamber' (Cm 7438) appeared in July 2008, reshuffling the familiar cards. There was to be no change in the powers of the upper Chamber: a more assertive second Chamber operating within its existing powers was not seen as a threat to Commons primacy. The remaining hereditaries would go, but the future of life peers was undecided. Peerage itself, however, was to be exclusively an honorary status, without any consequences for membership of the legislature, the upper House of which could not therefore be called the House of Lords. The new upper House should be directly elected, though whether exclusively so or only as to 80 per cent of its membership was not settled. The argument for appointment (by a statutory Commission) was that it would be most likely to preserve the valuable cross-bench character of the House. A third of the elected members would retire each year, and those returned would serve for a single non-renewable term. Even recall ballots on the US model were contemplated.

Wherever the pendulum eventually comes to rest, recent history suggests that some or all of these concepts will feature in the solution—but at this stage it is quite impossible to say which.

Supremacy of the lower Houses

In this segment the focus will be on constitutional or traditional authority of the House of Representatives and of the House of Commons, respectively, to originate revenue and appropriation measures, or money and supply measures, as compared with the prerogatives of the Senate and House of Lords respectively. A more complete discussion in the chapter on the Power of the Purse at page 225 will describe the respective roles of the Legislative and Executive branches in proposing all such measures, as well as comparisons between the two systems as to the deliberative nature of proceedings on those measures in each of the houses.

In Federalist no. 58, Madison examined the proposed relative sizes, compositions, and powers of the House of Representatives and of the Senate and the respective interests of large and small States in sharing powers of a national government. He made the following observations:

> Notwithstanding the equal authority which will subsist between the two Houses on all legislative subjects, except the originating of money bills, it cannot be doubted that the House composed of the greater number of members, when supported by the more powerful states, and speaking the known and determined sense of a majority of the people, will have no small advantage in a question depending on the comparative firmness of the two Houses... a constitutional and infallible source, still remains with the larger states, by which they will be able at all times to accomplish their just purposes. The House of Representatives cannot only refuse, but they alone can propose the supplies requisite for the support of government. They in a word hold the purse; that powerful instrument by which we behold in the history of the British constitution, an infant and humble representation of the people, gradually enlarging the sphere of its activity and importance, and finally reducing, as far as it seems to have wished, all the overgrown prerogatives of the other branches of the government. This power of the purse, may in fact be regarded as the most compleat and effectual weapon with which any constitution can arm the immediate representatives of the people, for obtaining a redress of every grievance, and for carrying into effect every just and salutary measure.

In speculating about the ability of the House of Representatives 'to be as much interested as the Senate in maintaining the government in its proper function' and about the cause of 'the smaller...number and more permanent and conspicuous the station of men in power' (that is, the Senate and the President), Madison suggested that 'to those causes we are to ascribe the continual triumph of the British House of Commons over the other branches of the government, whenever the engine of a money bill has been employed'.

Article I, section 7, clause 1 of the US Constitution provides that 'all bills for raising Revenue shall originate in the House of Representatives, but the Senate may propose or concur with Amendments as on other Bills'. The House has traditionally taken the view that this prerogative encompasses the sole power to originate all general Appropriation bills as well as revenue bills. That view has been acquiesced in over time by the Senate and has specifically been endorsed in Senate Doc 62–872 printed in 1912 as a treatise on 'The Supply Bills' by Senator John Sharp Williams of Mississippi.

In 1787 earlier drafts of the Constitution in the drafting committee had provided that 'all bills for raising or appropriating money ... shall originate in the House of Representatives'. The two terms were used cumulatively to describe 'supply' or 'money' bills, and in the final draft the term was refined to eliminate the words 'or appropriating money' and was confined to 'raising revenue', with the understanding that 'revenue' to the government is money in the Treasury rendered available to the Executive for expenditure for carrying on the government by an appropriation. As explained by Sen. Williams:

> Much of the confusion has grown out of forgetting that in the early history of the country, tax bills and appropriation bills, the conjoint purpose of the two being to raise Government revenue, were provided for in the same Act. The Ways and Means Committee of the House levied a tax and at the same time appropriated the tax in one act, which constituted a budget. Later on, when the magnitude of our governmental machinery began to assert itself, the work was divided (in 1865). Tax bills were left to the Committee on Ways and Means, and bills appropriating the proceeds of taxes were within the jurisdiction of a new Committee on Appropriations. It was not until after this division of labor occurred, that any confusion in public thought ever occurred. Levying a tax and appropriating the money thus raised are two parts of the same act, the object of both of which is to 'raise revenue' for carrying on the Government.

On several occasions the House has returned to the Senate a Senate bill or joint resolution appropriating money on the ground that it invaded the prerogatives of the House. In support of the view that the House has the sole power to originate Appropriation bills, it has been argued that at the time of the adoption of the Constitution the phrase 'raising revenue' was equivalent to 'raising money and appropriating the same'.[8] This argument was countered by a majority report from the House Judiciary Committee in 1881 recommending adoption of a resolution that 'the power to originate bills appropriating money from the Treasury of the United States is not exclusive in the House of Representatives'.[9] Five of the fifteen members of the committee filed dissenting views, recommending that 'section 7 of Article I confers exclusive power upon the House to originate bills appropriating money from the public treasury'. The majority report argued that the distinction between raising revenue and disposing of it after it had been raised was sufficiently obvious to be understood 'even by the commonest capacity', even though at the time of the constitutional conventions there had been an impression that this clause had a much broader signification than its terms implied.

Madison, in Federalist no. 58, regarded the expression 'bills for raising revenue' as synonymous with the term 'money bills', and he examined the use of that term especially with reference to the usages of the British Parliament, where money had long been raised and expended by the same bills. At the time of the formation of the Constitution as well as since, the appropriation of the revenue was in Britain a mere incident to measures by which it was granted to the Crown (through its ministers in the House of Commons) and brought into the Exchequer. The House of Commons claimed and exercised the exclusive right both to raise and appropriate the revenue (in modern practice since 1865 accomplished by separate bills—a coincidental date splitting the work in both legislatures). Thus the majority suggested that with this common usage in mind, the framers could have written section 7 of Article I 'in plain and unequivocal terms' had they intended to confine the origination of Appropriation bills to the House. In the State conventions the debates focused on whether 'money bills' were to be the original prerogative of the House, and refusal to finally use that term in the Constitution indicated to the majority that the House was not given the exclusive privilege.

The minority submitted several counter arguments, that the word 'revenue' meant money received into the Treasury for public purposes, and the words 'raising revenue' must include bills appropriating money to the use of the government, as well as bills providing for levying and collecting taxes. 'This was shown from the English precedents, where the essential act to constitute the money raised revenue was the grant, without which not one dollar could be used for the national expenses.' Various scholarly opinions were cited to show that the phrase 'bills for raising revenue' was the equivalent of 'money bills', which in the British Government at the time of the framing of the Constitution included bills of appropriation. The Minority argued that from the time of the first Congress Appropriation bills had, with few exceptions, originated in the House. By unvarying usage all general Appropriation bills had originated in the lower branch of Congress. Finally the Minority contended that 'the immediate representatives of the people should have the control of the "purse", and the power of originating Appropriation bills was a trust which should be retained'.

In modern practice, the House has successfully maintained its prerogative to originate not only tax and tariff 'revenue' bills, but also general Appropriation bills. On one occasion in 1962, the Senate adopted a resolution asserting that the power to originate Appropriation bills was not exclusively in the House of Representatives, citing the 1881 majority House Judiciary Committee report and calling for the establishment of an appropriate commission 'of outstanding educators specializing in the study of the English language' to submit a recommendation. Beyond this symbolic gesture, however, all general Appropriation bills and continuing Appropriation joint resolutions originate in the House. Since 1962, the Senate has not provoked a confrontation on this matter, as it has not seen fit to insist upon origination by utilization of a Senate number which it messages to the House. Rather, the Senate has often considered introduced Senate-numbered revenue and Appropriation bills, reported from the Senate Finance or Appropriations Committees respectively, in advance of companion House-numbered bills, and has even passed such bills prior to House action, but has not messaged those bills to the House. The Senate has chosen to substitute its Senate-passed language as an amendment in the nature of a substitute for the House-passed measure if and when received in the Senate, and then to table (that is, lay aside) the Senate-numbered bill. In this practical way the constitutional prerogative of origination and the possibility of collateral challenge in the House or in the courts have been minimized. However the Senate, as an essentially co-equal Legislative branch and in fulfilment of its constitutional authority to amend revenue bills, has sometimes been the first House to begin consideration of such measures by conducting contemporaneous committee hearings, filing committee reports and even being the first House to act, while not messaging that action to the House. In the few instances wherein the Senate has seen fit to message a Senate-originated measure to the House, the House, upon discovering the infringement upon its constitutional prerogative, has sometimes merely ignored the Senate measure by leaving it on the Speaker's table or referring it to committee while passing a House measure in lieu thereof. In so doing, the House properly relies on Federal court rulings that the courts will not look behind the bill number to determine the chronological sequence of origination and amendment, nor the germaneness of the Senate-attached language so long as the House-numbered bill is a revenue measure (*Hubbard v Lowe* 226 F 135 (SDNY 1915)).

While any Member may raise the question of infringement by the Senate of the House's prerogative to originate revenue bills as a question of privilege requiring the House's immediate attention under Rule IX, whenever the measure complained of is in the possession of the House, in practice the Committee on Ways and Means and the Committee on Appropriations serve as the watchdogs of the House in order to bring recommendations of return (blue-slip resolutions; see page 242) to the House's attention. Because questions relating to the prerogative of the House to originate revenue legislation involve interpretation of the Constitution rather than House rules, they are decided by the House and not by the Chair. While over 200 years of precedent serve as a guideline as to the type of tax or tariff measure which may be considered a House prerogative, continuing diligence remains necessary. 'User fees' originated by the Senate became a focus in the 1980s, with the House asserting its prerogative to return a Senate measure containing fees assessed on regulated entities where the proceeds to be received were applied to funding a broader range of governmental activities than regulation of the assessed activity itself and took on the character of an 'excise tax'[10] (cf. page 243).

On one recent occasion,[11] where the question was not the Senate's origination but rather a conference committee's insertion of a new tax provision into a general appropriation bill which had originated in the House and upon which conference report the House was acting first, the House by a margin of one vote tabled a question of privilege calling for return of the measure to conference, thereby permitting inclusion of a revenue provision at the conference stage in a non-revenue House bill. The bipartisan effort of the Chairman and ranking minority member of the Committee on Ways and Means to force the conferees to reconsider inclusion of a tax provision was frustrated by Majority leadership efforts to expedite the omnibus appropriation conference report containing it. The measure was subsequently vetoed by the President, and so no collateral challenge was able to be litigated in the courts. The leadership's departure from support of a bipartisan Ways and Means Committee effort was a mere anomaly (it was the first such example in House history), and not necessarily an indication that the House will not henceforth protect its prerogative.

In addition to the availability of Rule IX questions of privilege resolutions permitting matters of highest priority in returning offending bills to the Senate, House rules also interpose points of order against Senate amendments which seek to insert 'tax or tariff' provisions into non-revenue bills originated by the House, or to add appropriation amendments to House measures not containing appropriations. Thus both Article I of the Constitution and the standing rules of the House permit the House to enforce its prerogatives on money bills, but those provisions are not self-enforcing. Where the Senate does arguably transgress the House prerogative on a bill, enactment of which is essential, the conferees are sometimes expected to eliminate the offending provisions in lieu of a formal return to the Senate, with the option that failure to make this correction will permit a question of privilege to be raised prior to House consideration of the conference report containing the matter.

Beyond the textually committed prerogative stated in Article I, section 7 to originate revenue-raising bills, and its traditional extension to general appropriation bills, there is in modern practice no other legislative origination prerogative which the House consistently claims. Assertions in the middle of the twentieth century that the House should originate debt-limit measures have not been pursued in recent years, as in fact the Senate has originated bills to increase the bonded borrowing authority of the Federal government. Debt-limit bills are in essence the antithesis of revenue bills. Bills to increase the statutory debt ceiling represent an acknowledgement that revenues are not sufficient to offset the costs of government, and that money must be borrowed through the issuance of bonds on which interest must be paid to the bondholders. The proceeds from the sale of such bonds are not 'revenue' to the government but represent a loan to the government repayable with interest and so for political expediency the Senate has originated debt-limit measures with no complaint by the House.

Every other legislative measure may originate in either the House or Senate, and to this extent the Senate is a co-equal branch with the House of Representatives. Beyond the question of collective legislative power, differences range in composition, size, rules, practices, and varying unique constitutional responsibilities. Size explains much about why the two Chambers differ. Because it is larger, the 435-Member House is a more structured body than the 100-Member Senate. Whereas Senate rules maximize freedom of expression, House rules show a constant subordination of the individual to the necessities of the whole House as the voice of the national will. Table 3.3 in the Annex makes comparisons of major differences.

To the table the following characterization of the two Houses should be added, based on expanded use of cloture votes and waivers of points of order in the Senate in recent years. The House is essentially a majoritarian institution, permitting virtually every agenda and measure to be adopted by a majority vote with the constitutional exception of the override of a Presidential veto and standing rules exceptions requiring super-majority votes on motions to suspend the rules or to consider tax-increase measures. The Senate requires super-majorities to permit consideration of most matters. It is required by the Constitution to utilize two-thirds majorities for treaty ratification and impeachment trials as well as for veto overrides. By rule, when incapable of unanimous consent consideration, the Senate must obtain a three-fifths vote to permit consideration of bills and amendments as a precondition to majority votes on passage.

There are several unique quasi-legislative or quasi-judicial responsibilities assigned to the Senate in Article I and Article II discussed at pages 66, 72, 510. They include the exclusive role as a court to try impeachments (see segment on Impeachment). Article II, section 2 of the Constitution confers upon the Senate the unique role of ratification of treaties, and advice and consent to Executive and Judicial nominations by the President.

At Westminster, much of the relationship between the Commons and the Lords (as presently composed)—which amounts to the political predominance of the lower House to a degree not found in Washington—is set out in statute or is found in the practice of Parliament. The financial privileges of the Commons are somewhat wider and less contested than are the case in Washington. The details are set out on pages 265ff.

Commons predominance based on statute comes into play when the Lords reject or fail to pass a bill sent to them by the lower House. If there is no majority for compromise, subsequent proceedings are governed by the Parliament Acts 1911 and 1949, which enable bills to be presented for Royal Assent despite the opposition of the upper House. The genesis of the 1911 Act was the 'people's budget' of 1909 and its legislative vehicle the Finance Bill of that year, though in fact the Lords had for a generation chafed at Liberal policies which they disliked, even destroying a bill embodying a central piece of Liberal policy, home rule for Ireland, in 1893.[12] The Lords rejected the 1909 Finance Bill, thereby incautiously carrying the battle on to ground where the Commons felt most secure in their traditional powers—taxation. The government did not back down as they had in 1893. The two general elections of 1910 returned Liberal governments dedicated to reforming the upper House, though in neither had the Liberals an overall majority. The Lords, appalled by the threat to create no fewer than 249 new peers at once, thereby overwhelming the Conservative majority, backed down. The result was the Parliament Act 1911, which permitted the Commons, within certain time limits, to override a Lords refusal to agree to bills (other than bills introduced into the Lords or bills to prolong the maximum duration of a Parliament). In 1949, the Labour government, finding the Lords reluctant to pass into law a bill bringing the iron and steel industry into public owner-ship, secured the amendment of the 1911 Act to reduce its time limits. As the law now stands, if a bill has been passed by the Commons in two successive sessions; if the bill reaches their Lordships at least a month before the end of each of those sessions; if there is a year between the second reading of the bill in the Commons in the first session and its passing in the second; if the bill is in all material respects unchanged in the second session; and if the Lords then reject or by the end of the session have not passed the bill, then the bill may be presented to the Sovereign for the Royal Assent without the consent of the Lords. Since 1911 the procedure has been invoked only infrequently: no more than seven bills have reached the statute book in this way. Four instances however have occurred since 1991.

The Parliament Act 1911 also provided that Bills certified by the Speaker as Money Bills which were not passed by the Lords within a month after being sent to them—provided they were sent at least a month before the end of the session—also might receive Royal Assent without the agreement of the Lords. This procedure is more fully discussed at page 267.

Other significant parts of the relationship between the Houses at Westminster are subject not to statute or parliamentary rules but to political conventions, undefined and forever subtly changing. In May 2006 a Joint Committee on Conventions between the Houses was given a cautious preliminary mandate 'to consider the practicality of codify-ing the key conventions on the relationship between the two Houses...which affect the consideration of legislation in particular'. At the end of the year, the Committee made a thoughtful report. Though issues of membership and powers were not within its order of reference, it recognized that if the Lords acquired an electoral mandate, the conventions would probably have to change. The degree of change would no doubt be dependent on the political authority acquired by a reformed upper House. But definition and codifica-tion of conventions should not even be attempted: all that could be said of them was that we know them when we see them.[13]

The most important informal element in the relationship is the Salisbury–Addison convention. Conservatives in the Lords, in light of the huge Commons majority of the 1945 Labour government, conceded that however large the Conservative majority in the upper House—at that point sixteen Labour peers faced over a thou-sand Conservatives—the Lords would not reject bills which came to them from the Commons and which embodied commitments given by the government in their manifesto at the preceding general election. The concept solved the immediate and indeed middle-term political problem but it was not a timeless panacea, for a number of reasons.

The subsequent exponential growth in detailed proposals contained in manifestos may be said to have changed the basis of the agreement, and made it hard to define a manifesto bill. It can be argued indeed that the convention now covers all government bills, except in the most unusual circumstances, of which the Criminal Justice Mode of Trial (No. 2) Bill 2000 rejected by the Lords at second reading was one. The Liberal (later Liberal Democrat) party was not party to the original convention, which was less material in the immediately post-war Commons where their representation was very much smaller than it became as Liberal Democrat representation grew in size. This aspect of the issue may have been superseded by the silent transformation of the convention into an unwritten agreement between the Houses rather than—or as well as—an inter-party understanding. Finally, it has been argued that the removal of most hereditary Lords from the House necessitated a change in the ground rules irrespective of any future reform of the Lords. Nevertheless, the Joint Committee on Conventions did not recommend substantial change in this convention, limiting themselves to a modest move towards clarification by way of the exchange of Resolutions of understanding between the Houses.

Further development of the relationship between the Houses—even without changes in the composition of the Lords—should be seen against the remarkable change in the political composition of the upper House over the last generation or so. From 1965, the numbers of non-aligned or cross-bench peers grew steadily so that by 1999, when all but ninety-two of the hereditary peers left the House, the Conservatives remained by far the largest group but they no longer had a majority over all other groups combined. As a result of creations since that date, Labour peers are now the largest single political grouping, but they in their turn are still well short of an overall majority. The figures for party and non-party[14] allegiances in the Lords in December 2008 are set out in Table 3.4 in the Annex.

The number of occasions on which the current Labour government was defeated in the Lords has been fairly stable over recent years, and remains—from a government whip's point of view—inconveniently substantial, as appears from Table 3.5 in the Annex.

There have however been no more than fourteen attempts to defeat a government bill on second reading in the Lords since 1970, only six of them successful.[15] The latest instance was the Fraud (Trials without a Jury) Bill in 2007, the first since 2000. A bill sponsored by a Lord who was not a member of the government, the Assisted Dying for the Terminally Ill Bill, was defeated on second reading also in 2007, the first such casualty since 1998.

The present political balance between the Houses is thus both temporary and unstable. If an upper House with a credible claim to a popular mandate and an urge to use it emerges from the current discussions, governments may look back with regret to the level of inter-House disagreement in recent sessions, however greater that may be than a few decades previously. On the other hand, if (as is intended) no party gains an absolute majority in a reformed Lords, the change in the relationship with the Commons may be very limited.

Treaties and International Agreements

Alexander Hamilton in Federalist no. 75 summarizes the rationale behind the decision of the Framers of the US Constitution to involve both the President and the Senate, but not the House of Representatives, in the making of treaties with foreign nations.

> The essence of the legislative authority is to enact laws, or in other words to prescribe rules for the regulation of the society. While the execution of the laws and the employment of the common strength, either for this purpose or for the common defense, seem to comprise all the functions of the executive magistrate, the power of making treaties is plainly neither the one nor the other. It relates neither to the execution of the subsisting laws, or to the enactment of new ones, and still less to an exertion of the common strength. Its objects are contracts with foreign nations, which have the force of law, but derive it from the obligations of good faith. They are not rules prescribed by the sovereign to the subject, but agreements between sovereign and sovereign. The power in question seems therefore to form a distinct department, and to belong properly neither to the legislative nor to the executive. The qualities elsewhere detailed, as indispensable to the management of foreign negotiations, point out the executive as the most fit agent in those transactions; while the vast importance of the trust, and the operation of treaties as laws, plead strongly for the participation of the whole or a part of the legislative body in the office of making them.

Assuming the possibility that a President holding a limited term and acting alone could enter into such a contract with a foreign sovereign and then leave office to become the beneficiary of its terms as a private citizen, Hamilton went on to suggest that 'the joint possession of the power in question by the President and Senate would afford a greater prospect of security, than the separate possession of it by either of them...' but that 'conclusive force argues against the admission of the House of Representatives to a share in the formation of treaties. The...multitudinous composition of the body forbid[s] us to expect in it those qualities which are essential to the proper execution of such a trust. Accurate and comprehensive knowledge of foreign politics; a steady and systematic adherence to the same views; a nice and uniform sensibility to national character, decision, secrecy and dispatch; are incompatible with the genius of a body so variable and so numerous.'

Thomas Jefferson wrote that treaties

> are legislative acts. A treaty is the law of the land. It differs from other laws only as it must have the consent of a foreign nation, being but a contract with respect to that nation...By the Constitution of the United States this department of legislation is confined to two branches only of the ordinary legislature—the President originating and the Senate having a negative. To what subjects this power extends has not been defined in detail by the Constitution; nor are we entirely agreed among ourselves...By the general power to make treaties, the Constitution must have intended to comprehend only those subjects which are usually regulated by treaty, and cannot be otherwise regulated...and also to except those subjects of legislation in which it gave a participation to the House. This last exception is denied by some on the ground that it would leave very little matter for the treaty power to work on. The less the better, say others.

Under the US legal system, international agreements can be entered into either pursuant to a treaty or via executive agreement. The Constitution allocates primary responsibility for entering such agreements to the Executive branch, but Congress also plays an essential role. First, in order for a treaty (but not an executive agreement) to become binding on the United States, the Senate must advise and consent to its ratification by a two-thirds majority. Secondly, Congress may authorize by law Congressional-Executive agreements. Thirdly, many treaties and executive agreements are not self-executing, requiring implementing legislation to permit US bodies to enforce and comply with the international agreement's provisions. The Senate may, in considering a treaty, condition its consent on certain reservations, declarations, and understandings concerning treaty application. If accepted, these may limit or define US obligations under the treaty.

The great majority of international agreements that the United States enters into are not treaties but executive agreements that are not submitted to the Senate for its advice and consent. Congress generally requires by law notification upon the entry of such an agreement. There are three types of prima facie legal executive agreements: (1) Congressional-Executive agreements, in which Congress has previously or retroactively authorized an international agreement entered into by the Executive; (2) executive agreements made pursuant to an earlier treaty, in which the agreement is authorized by a ratified treaty; and (3) sole executive agreements, in which an agreement is made pursuant to the President's constitutional authority without further Congressional authorization. The President's authority to promulgate the agreement is different in each case, as are the respective Congressional roles of the two Houses.

The participation of the House in the treaty-making power has been examined in both Houses since Jefferson's *Manual* was written. The House on several occasions has debated and taken action in carrying into effect, terminating, enforcing, and even suggesting treaties. Those debates were conducted in the nineteenth century for the most part, and are not symbolic of current institutional concerns about the prerogatives of the two Houses. As early as 1796 the House affirmed that, when a treaty related to subjects within the power of Congress, it was the constitutional duty of the House to deliberate on the expediency of carrying such treaty into effect, and in 1816, 1868, and in 1871 the House maintained its position that a treaty must depend on a law of Congress for its execution as to such stipulations as relate to subjects constitutionally entrusted to Congress. In 1887, the House Judiciary Committee concluded that the Executive branch might not conclude a treaty affecting the revenue without the assent of the House. In 1880 the House declared the negotiation of a revenue treaty an invasion of its prerogative, and in 1844 a Senate committee concluded that tariff duties were more properly regulated (by statute) with the publicity of Congressional action than by treaties negotiated by the President and ratified by the Senate in secret.

The conclusion of the Second World War ushered in a greater leadership role for the United States in world affairs. Not surprisingly, this period witnessed a dramatic increase in the number of international agreements entered into, disproportionately more executive agreements (both sole and Congressional) than Article II treaties, due to their efficiency. The Article II treaty process solely involving the Senate has two features which make it a less attractive option for concluding international agreements; a constitutionally prescribed super-majority requirement, and a temporal disjunction between Executive branch negotiation and Senate consent (Senate consent not being constitutionally required during the session of Congress in which the treaty was negotiated and extending indefinitely into the future.)

Since the early days of the Washington administration the Senate's role in treaty making is primarily one of either consent or rejection of a treaty already negotiated by the President, the role of giving 'advice' during the negotiation process having been minimized, with some exceptions where individual Senators have served as negotiators on treaties. This exception has raised concerns about general separation of powers, as Senators may not under Article I, section 6, clause 2 be appointed 'to any civil Office...which shall have been created during their terms'. Also, Senators eventually have to vote on treaties which they may have helped negotiate under the President's authority. Thus Members of Congress often serve as advisers or observers rather than as members of the negotiating delegation, so as not to view that delegation as an incompatible Office.

After a treaty has been signed by the President's delegates, it is transmitted by the President to the Senate, usually with an explanatory message. The Senate's consideration of treaties is governed by Senate Rule XXX. That rule provides for the receipt, referral to committee, plenary consideration, and amendment of proposed treaties.

When a treaty is received from the President, the Senate Majority Leader, in executive session, will ask for unanimous consent to consider the treaty as having been read once, for removal of the injunction of secrecy, and that the treaty be referred to the Foreign Relations Committee. That committee has exclusive jurisdiction over the consideration of treaties. The decision to hold hearings or take action on a particular treaty is usually made by the committee chairman in consultation with the ranking Minority member and the Executive branch. Pursuant to the rules of the Foreign Relations Committee, if no action is taken on a treaty in a given Congress, the treaty remains on the Committee Calendar. For non-controversial treaties, the Committee generally conducts hearings and reports the treaty, along with a resolution of ratification, to the Senate within a year. More controversial treaties may either languish on the Committee Calendar or be reported with the recommendation of numerous conditions, and are referred back to the Committee if not acted on by the Senate by the end of that Congressional session. At times, the Senate, by unanimous consent, has agreed to vote on several non-controversial treaties at once, and consider them as separate votes.

Amendments to the text of the treaty, which may be proposed by the committee or by any Senator during executive session, are in order only prior to the consideration of the resolution of ratification. They are changes in the text of the actual treaty and will require the other parties' consent, and need not be germane unless cloture has been invoked. The cloture provisions of Rule XXII can be applied to treaties, and require the consent of three-fifths of the Senators present and voting. If cloture is invoked, consideration of amendments to the treaty and the resolution of ratification is limited to thirty hours. Amendments to treaties are themselves amendable in the same manner as amendments to bills, and require a majority for adoption. Amendments have become increasingly rare as Senators prefer to attach reservations to the resolution of ratification instead.

Approximately 15 per cent of Article II treaties have been ratified subject to conditions, which fall into one of four categories: reservations, understandings, declarations, and provisos. A reservation is a unilateral statement, however phrased or named, made by a State, when signing, ratifying, accepting, approving, or acceding to a treaty, whereby it purports to exclude or to modify the legal effect of certain provisions of the treaty in their application to that State. An understanding simply represents a statement by the Senate of its interpretation of the text of the treaty and is not intended to modify any terms. A declaration is similar to an understanding in that it merely represents the Senate's view on the subject matter as opposed to a specific part of the text, and is not meant to change the meaning of the treaty. A proviso is a condition that has wholly domestic effect and is often a means of communication with the President on the proper means of implementation.

Because the Senate generally has little involvement in the negotiation of treaties, conditional consent, primarily in the form of a reservation, has become the principal means of affecting the substance of a treaty. Conditional consent occurs only after the parties have come to an agreement on the terms and thus represents an incomplete method of negotiation. If the conditions in any way alter the bargain that was struck, the President must obtain further consent to the condition from the other parties. The reservations made by parties can either be accepted or rejected by the other parties, with such rejection serving as grounds for refusing the entry into force of the treaty.

The treaty process is subject to a variety of criticisms, including temporal uncertainty of proposed treaties languishing indefinitely even beyond the term of a Congress for failure of a super-majority in support, or based on controversy within the Committee on Foreign Relations. The Senate's practice of attaching reservations and understandings has been criticized as contrary to international law and the Constitution. Some multilateral treaties have attempted to prohibit reservations, only to have the Senate make a reservation to that reservation. For non-self-executing treaties, which includes many environmental and human rights treaties, treaty consent must be coordinated with separate implementing legislation, which necessarily involves the House of Representatives. The abandonment of any formalized communication between the President and the Senate before and during the actual negotiation of treaties has contributed to the President's inability to obtain consent after the agreement with the other parties has been reached, and has forced the Senate to adopt the controversial practice of conditional consent. Even though the Constitution specifically calls for the Senate's advice during negotiations, Senate rules and contemporary practice do not require it.

Notwithstanding the decision by the Framers to exclude the House of Representatives from a constitutional role in treaty making, these inefficiencies have led Congress to venture into the area of negotiation of international agreements in the context of international trade. By statute, Congress has empowered both its Houses to engage in negotiations with the Executive branch over the content of international trade agreements before they are submitted to Congress. The Senate has acknowledged by passing such law that the House can be a full partner in preparing international trade agreements, in derogation of the Senate's own exclusive ratification role for treaties under the Constitution. This process was enshrined in the Trade Act of 1974 when it became apparent that the House would need to become a full partner in originating and enacting revenue (tariff) implementing legislation should an international agreement be negotiated. Rather than await a subsequent separate legislative process, the mechanism was devised to cede an exclusive Senate prerogative by including the House in negotiation of trade agreements, and simultaneously, in the enactment of implementing legislation, albeit as part of the same agreement.

   The Constitution grants to Congress the power to 'regulate commerce with foreign nations'. For much of the nation's history, Congress exercised this power to set tariff levels on imported goods, but after the disastrous effects of the Smoot–Hawley Tariff Act of 1930 wherein Congress tried to micro-manage individual tariffs, Congress decided to cede some of its authority to the President in order to facilitate the negotiation of bilateral tariff reductions. This negotiating authority was continually extended by the Congress until 1967, and the system, operating under the umbrella of the General Agreement on Tariffs and Trade, had been fairly effective in reducing world tariff levels. By the Nixon administration, however, a Democratic Congress had become more sceptical of the Republican President's broad authority as international trade agreements shifted from an exclusive concern with tariff levels to the broader problems of non-tariff barriers to trade. Congress reacted by enacting the Trade Act of 1974 which reclaimed some of Congress's authority. Pursuant to a bargain with the President, the Congress would eliminate most procedural hurdles for the President's proposed trade agreements (as a joint exercise in rule making) in return for greater consultation with Congress on the substance of proposed agreements. The basic bargain requires Congress to use its rule-making authority to assure the President that the agreement once concluded with foreign countries must be immediately introduced as a bill, considered with dispatch by the relevant committees but without the opportunity to amend, subject to limited floor debate, and must receive a timely vote. In exchange, the President allows Congress to help formulate the negotiating objectives and ensures consultation and notice with the Congress during the course of the negotiations. Also, either House has the ability to repeal the 'fast-track' bargain by rule-making, a matter more easily accomplished in the House by majority vote on a recommendation from the Committee on Rules than in the Senate where rules changes require super-majority votes to end debate. The specific requirements which assure expedited consideration in both Houses virtually guarantee that there will be no amendments in either House to the bill once introduced by the leadership. Therefore there will not be a need for a conference committee to resolve differences, and the bill will be available for final passage in approximately sixty days. The most obvious advantage is that these agreements require only majority support in both Houses rather than super-majority support in the Senate. The twenty-first century distribution of power by party in Congress and the White House suggests that the Congressional–Executive agreement may be more likely to result in legislative approval than Article II treaties.

   In exchange for this procedural expedition in both Houses, the President agrees to ensure that Congress has an active role in shaping the substance of any agreements. The law authorizing 'fast-track' procedures contains a list of negotiating objectives, both general and specific, and creates a bipartisan group of Congressional Advisers to participate in the formulation of trade policy objectives before negotiations commence, and then in negotiation of the agreement with the foreign government. Because of the constant communication between the Executive branch and key members of both Houses, the opportunities for misalignment between Executive and Legislative branch objectives are minimized. Because of the notice requirement, divergent views on the substance of these agreements will be discovered before the Executive makes a good-faith commitment by signing an international agreement.

   Some have contended as a result of the success of the fast-track procedure in concluding international trade agreements that many other topics of international agreement (including environmental and arms control pacts) should bypass the Senate's 'advise and consent' treaty-ratification process. Others have responded that there are constitutional limits on the extent to which Congress can enact fast-track laws in derogation of the Senate's unique advice and consent role requiring a two-thirds vote. The Supreme Court has never confronted the question of whether some international agreements must be ratified pursuant to the Article II treaty process, but the constitutionality of Congressional-Executive agreements was litigated in lower courts in the context of the North American Free Trade Agreement (NAFTA), and the ability of both Houses to pass NAFTA by a simple majority vote, rather than by a two-thirds vote of the Senate, was upheld by a Federal appeals court relying largely on the expansive scope of the Foreign Commerce Clause empowerment of Congress (*Made in the USA Foundation v United States* 242 F 3d 1350 (11th Cir 2001, cert denied 2001)). The extent to which the Constitution requires that for some international agreements, the Treaty Clause provides an exclusive procedure for treaty approval, or rather is virtually interchangeable with alternative procedures enacted into law, remains unclear under Supreme Court decisions to date, despite the denial of *certiorari* in the *USA Foundation* case. The involvement of the House as a co-equal partner with the Senate in the enactment and implementation of Congressional–Executive agreements exists under current 'fast-track' laws, but can only continue or expand if the Senate acquiesces (as an exercise of the Senate's rule-making authority) by including the House as an equal partner.

At Westminster, the situation is very different. Treaty making and indeed the conduct of foreign policy have always been seen as part of the prerogative, the collection of powers which peculiarly attach to the Sovereign and which at least since 1689 have been deployed on the Sovereign's behalf by ministers. As a result, neither House has a legal claim to approve treaties before they are concluded in the name of Her Majesty. If the effect of a treaty does not require to be carried into domestic law—and the really significant European Union treaties have all been carried into domestic law—there is legally no necessity for either House at Westminster to be involved. In reality however treaties have political consequences, and thus do feature in parliamentary debates, though in many cases only if the government thinks it appropriate to take the initiative. Recently however the government has given ground to parliamentary interest in these matters. Treaties laid before Parliament are now accompanied by an explanatory memorandum. The long-standing convention that where a treaty requires ratification or approval of an earlier draft, no such agreement is given until the text has been laid before Parliament for twenty-one sitting days, to allow parliamentary interest to be expressed, has been enhanced. Copies of treaties subject to the convention have begun to be sent to the relevant departmentally related select committee, with explanatory material, and the government has accepted that if a committee secures the agreement of the Liaison Committee that a debate should be held, time will be made available. Indeed, the government is now prepared to turn the convention into law. Where a treaty or agreement is scheduled to a confirming bill, neither House may amend the text of the treaty, though (presumably with some difficulty with respect to order) amendments may be made to the bill which will modify or qualify the effect of the treaty or agreement. Like pre-appointment hearings, what is proposed is, within UK constitutional proprieties, well worth Parliament's acquisition, though at the most optimistic assessment the influence of the UK Parliament will not equal that of Congress.

Confirmation of nominations

Article II, section 2 of the US Constitution provides that 'the President shall have power to nominate, and by and with the advice and consent of the Senate (by majority vote), to appoint Ambassadors, other public Ministers and Consuls, Judges of the Supreme Court, and all other Officers of the United States, whose appointments are not herein otherwise provided for, and which shall be established by law; but the Congress may by law vest the appointment of such inferior Officers, as they think proper, in the President alone, in the Courts of Law, or in the Heads of Departments'. In *Buckley v Valeo* 424 US 1 (1976) the Supreme Court held that any appointee exercising significant authority (not merely internal delegable authorities within the Legislative branch) pursuant to the laws of the United States is an Officer of the United States and must therefore be appointed pursuant to this clause, and that Congress cannot by law vest such appointment authority in its own officers or require that Presidential appointments be subject to confirmation by both Houses.

Thus the Constitution carves out for the Senate a unique role in confirmation of Presidential appointments which may not be shared by the House through the enactment of a law permitting House participation. The Federalist Papers suggest that the Framers intended a shared responsibility between the Executive and Legislative branches, but limited to that body of the Legislative branch with more experience and stability. As Hamilton wrote in Federalist no. 76:

> To what purpose then require the co-operation of the Senate? I answer that the necessity of their concurrence would have a powerful, though in general a silent operation. It would be an excellent check upon the spirit of favoritism in the President, and would tend greatly to preventing the appointment of unfit characters from State prejudice, from family connection, from personal attachment, or from a view to popularity. And, in addition to this it would be an efficacious source of stability in the administration.

The role the Senate has played in the nomination process has varied depending, in part, upon the relationship between the particular President and Senate elected at that time, although the vast majority of nominees eventually have been confirmed. Over time the Senate has developed a series of informal procedures and practices to deal with the concerns of its Members on nominations. There is the custom of senatorial courtesy, whereby Senators, more often from the same party as the President, might influence a nomination or kill it by objecting to it. This tradition has not been absolute, but has allowed Senators great influence, particularly in the selection of nominees within a Senator's home State, such as for Federal district court judgeships. Senators may have their own nominee or slate of nominees, or they may choose at the point a vacancy occurs on the Federal bench to reserve judgement, preferring to react to the Attorney General's nominees. In any case, their role is crucial, and may become a virtual veto over the President's choice. The extent and nature of this exercise of power varies, some Senators preferring wide consultation with State and local interests, others dictating the choice of a particular nominee. Much of the process is informal and takes place behind closed doors, and differs among States, some having advisory commissions and others having no agreement mechanism at all. Senatorial courtesy can be invoked at any point in the process, as at hearings or on the floor, by a Senator claiming that the nomination was 'personally obnoxious' to him, without necessarily stating the grounds for the objection, or by merely making it known that for a group of nominees Senators were withholding support where the President has not consulted with home-State Senators.

A temporary but potent constraint on the Senate's power to confirm Presidential nominations is contained in Article II, section 2 of the Constitution, which permits the President to fill vacancies in Offices of the United States during 'recesses' of the Senate, that is, periods of adjournment for more than three days. In such event, the President may fill a vacancy for a period ending not later than the end of the next Session of the Senate without the need for Senate confirmation. In Federalist no. 67 Hamilton explains that 'the ordinary power of appointment is confided to the President and Senate jointly, and can therefore only be exercised during the session of the Senate; but as it would have been improper to oblige this body to be continually in session for the appointment of Officers, and as vacancies might happen in their recess, which it might be necessary for the public service to fill without delay', the temporary authority is granted the President. In modern Congresses this has resulted in a reluctance of the Senate to take extended adjournments beyond three days, and rather to conduct 'pro forma' sessions every fourth day during the contemplated period of the recess, in order to prevent the President from making temporary appointments. Presidents have proved themselves inclined to make such recess appointments of particularly controversial nominees to avoid protracted Senate confirmation hearings and filibusters requiring three-fifths votes to surmount. Beyond the next session of the Senate, however, the President must either resubmit that or another nomination for full confirmation proceedings.

For Federal judicial nominations, the Senate Judiciary Committee has developed a tradition of 'blue slips' as a subset of the notion of Senatorial courtesy (a term to be differentiated from the 'blue-slip' resolution utilized by the House to assert its prerogative to originate revenue measures; see pages 62, 242). In the judicial nomination context, it is a document (public on the committee website in modern practice) used to get a home-State Senator's opinion on a judicial nomination. If the 'blue slip' document is not returned by the Senator to the committee, a Senator may thereby block the nominee for unstated reasons. The Chair of the committee determines how much weight to give a Senator's objection to a judicial nominee.

Senators have used the informal tradition of 'holds' to prevent or delay the Senate from acting on a nomination. 'Holds' are also a device available to block or delay action on a treaty or on legislation (see page 421) as well as on nominations, merely by individual Senators telling their party leader that the Senator wants to delay floor action on the matter in question. Prior to the enactment of section 512 of PL 110-81 in 2007, the procedure of a 'hold' was informal and was not mentioned in Senate rules or orders. It gave the Majority and Minority Leaders much discretion in deciding whether to honour a 'hold' and for how long. The request was not known to the public unless the Senator placing the 'hold' announced that information, and the potential complexity of 'multiple and counter holds' permitted unrelated Senate actions to be delayed depending on the insistence of individual Senators reacting to other 'holds' and the honouring of those requests by the two party leaders. The standing order embodied in section 512 now requires Senators intending to object to proceedings on a measure or matter to notify their respective leaders, following an objection to a unanimous consent request on their behalf, that they 'intend to object to proceedings' and the reasons therefor. Those notices are then published in the Record and in Senate Calendars.

As a general proposition, the Senate allows its Members to debate an issue for as long as they desire. This assertion will be further developed at page 197. When opponents of a measure or nomination use this ability to try to prevent final action on the matter at hand, it is called a filibuster. Prior to 1929, action on confirmation of nominations by the full Senate was done in executive (closed) session, open only when the Senate voted to do so.

Until 1949, cloture could not be invoked on nominations and before 1980 this action was attempted only twice. From the 96th Congress (1979–80) to the 102nd (1991–2) cloture was never sought on more than three nominations in a single Congress, but since then this level has been exceeded three times. From 1949 to 2004, cloture was sought on forty-nine nominations, and invoked on twenty-one. Except in the 103rd Congress (1993–4) most of the nominations involved have been judicial. Fourteen of the forty-nine nominations were not confirmed, all of whom were among the eighteen on whom the Senate rejected cloture and could not therefore come to a final up-or-down vote on the nomination itself. Eleven of the fourteen nominations not confirmed were considered during the 108th Congress (2003–4). In the 109th Congress, two nominations were withdrawn and returned to the President where the Senate could not invoke cloture. In the 110th Congress, only one nomination was confirmed following invocation of cloture, and no nominations were rejected by failure to invoke cloture.

Cloture has been sought on four nominations to the Supreme Court. In 1968 a cloture vote on the motion to proceed to consider the nomination of Abe Fortas (an Associate Justice) to be Chief Justice failed, and his nomination was then withdrawn by the President. In 1971, when he was first appointed to the court as Associate Justice, opponents of William Rehnquist successfully defeated a cloture motion but subsequently were not able to reject the nomination. Five years later he was confirmed as Chief Justice, and in 2006 Samuel Alito was confirmed following invocation of cloture.

No limit is placed on the number of times a cloture motion may be attempted on a single piece of legislation or on a nomination. Seven cloture votes were held in 2003 on a controversial Federal circuit court nominee (Miguel Estrada), before he withdrew his name from consideration. This nomination and several others engendered unusual partisan acrimony as the Minority party used the filibuster to challenge the President and his Majority party over who would control the ideological balance of power on Federal courts. In 2005 there emerged a threatened extraordinary procedural option, announced as a possible circumvention by the Majority Leader of the cloture rule with respect to judicial nominations, and variously described as the 'constitutional' option by its proponents or the 'nuclear option' by its opponents. In varying forms, it contemplated a ruling by the presiding officer, to the effect that the Senate's constitutional role with respect to nominations was an 'up-or-down majority vote' to confirm the nomination and was uniquely different from cloture as applied to legislation, where the Senate's amendment power is undeniable. At least with respect to judicial nominations, the presiding officer would rule in response to a point of order that the Constitution contemplated only a majority vote and not the invocation of any super-majority procedural vote in advance thereof, and that the notion of unlimited debate and therefore the need for a cloture petition was inapplicable to the issue of closing debate on the nomination. Assuming an appeal from that decision, the non-debatable motion to table would under Senate rules adversely and immediately dispose of the appeal and of debate thereon. Tabling an appeal upholds the presiding officer's decision and creates the most authoritative type of precedent, one established by vote of the Senate. This precedent could then be used to stop future judicial (and then possibly legislative) filibusters. The description of this strategy as 'nuclear' relates to the likely catastrophic effects of the invocation of such a ruling on future business to be conducted in the Senate by unanimous consent and, as a departure from traditional Senate practice, upon comity in the Senate generally. Opponents also suggested that its use would weaken the Senate's ability to check executive power, and undermine the Senate's traditional respect for minority rights, both in diminution of future prerogatives of potentially different Senate political majorities and minorities.

In May of 2005 negotiations between the Majority and Minority Leaders about implementation of this option in the context of a series of five pending circuit court nominations were discontinued, and the Majority Leader called up one such nomination which had been reported favourably from the Judiciary Committee on a straight party-line vote. Cloture was filed on that nomination and was expected to fail, following which the Majority Leader would invoke the threatened procedural 'nuclear' option. This strategy was forestalled by an announced accord reached by an ad hoc 'moderate' group of Senators, seven from each party, who voting as a bipartisan bloc could determine the likelihood of cloture invocation assuming strict partisan voting by all other Senators. The agreement contained three main features and was to remain in place for the duration of the 109th Congress (to 2006). (It was not renewed in the 110th Congress where Majority party control shifted and the threat of invocation of the nuclear option abated.) In this signed statement, they agreed to invoke cloture on a specified three of the five most controversial Federal appellate court nominees then reported from committee and pending, virtually assuring the three of Senate approval on straight party-line up-or-down votes on confirmation. Those three nominees were confirmed by the Senate and the other two continued to face unbreakable filibusters if they were brought to the floor. Second, the seven Majority Senators promised not to support 'any recommendation to or interpretation of the Rules of the Senate that would force a vote on a judicial nomination by means other than unanimous consent or Rule XXII'—the cloture rule. This feature effectively prevented the Majority Leader from using the nuclear option and protected the minority's right to filibuster, because the fourteen Senators would not vote in the majority to sustain the Chair's ruling circumventing those procedures. In return the seven Minority Senators agreed that judicial nominees 'should only be filibustered under extraordinary circumstances, and each signatory must use his or her own discretion and judgement in determining whether such circumstances exist'. This provision affected the Minority party's ability to mobilize forty-one backers to sustain a filibuster. Third, the accord sent a signal to the President that he should consult with Majority and Minority Senators on prospective judicial nominees under the Article II, section 2 constitutional role given to the Senate to give 'advice' prior to submission of, as well as to consent to, Judicial nominations. The agreement did not relate to Executive branch nominations or to any other use of the filibuster in Senate legislative proceedings.

The durability of this bipartisan agreement remains in question, although a test of its viability is possible in the context of a future Supreme Court nomination. To date the President has submitted three nominations to fill vacancies on the Supreme Court (one

being withdrawn shortly thereafter). The nomination of Federal circuit judge John
Roberts to be Chief Justice was confirmed without the invocation of cloture and pursuant to a unanimous consent time agreement for debate, where his nomination had some
bipartisan support on the Judiciary Committee. A second nomination of Harriet Miers
to be Associate Justice was submitted on 7 October 2005 and then withdrawn on 27
October 2005. A replacement nomination was submitted on 10 November 2005 of Samuel
Alito to be an Associate Justice, and his nomination was confirmed one day after cloture
was invoked on 30 January 2006. In that case the nomination was not considered an
'extraordinary circumstance', at least by the group of fourteen, which would justify their
unwillingness to invoke cloture. Would a nominee 'out of the judicial (or political) mainstream' represent such a circumstance? Would extraordinary circumstances include not
only unusual personal behaviour but also extraordinary ideological positions taken in the
past or during confirmation proceedings? The tenuousness of the agreement itself was
manifest both with respect to its limited duration and to its inevitable invocation of
political considerations in discerning an 'extraordinary circumstance'. The inherent
imprecision of this standard demonstrated that the stakes are always high in confirming
judges to lifetime positions on the Federal bench. Ideological disagreement coupled with
the rising importance of a closely balanced Federal appellate bench have intensified
in the process of advice and consent, resulting in resort to new tactics and new crises, as
the two parties struggle to shape the future of the Federal courts.

No informal procedural agreement as to the invocation of cloture applies within the
contemporary Senate with respect to Executive branch nominations, where Presidential
appointments are necessarily confined to the term of the administration itself. Nor are
there any informal agreements regarding cloture as it relates to the ordinary legislative
responsibilities of the Senate. Thus, absent 'recess appointments' not requiring Senate
confirmation but lasting only for a session, extraordinary three-fifths majorities must
still be called upon to invoke cloture and limit debate to permit up-or-down votes on
any contentious Cabinet or agency appointment requiring Senate confirmation. In the
end, the ability of the Majority party to secure a 'filibuster-proof' sixty-vote super-
majority becomes, in an era of increased partisanship, an important litmus test of
Senate election politics.

There is at Westminster no parallel to the constitutional responsibility of the US
Senate to advise and consent in the appointment of officers in the service of the United
States. British governments long took the view, first that officials owed their loyalty to
the minister who appointed them and it was the minister alone whom the Commons
should hold responsible. Secondly, prior approval of appointments (far less the act of
appointment) was not for select committees, because they were not decision-making bodies. There was no constitutional room for a parliamentary system of advice and consent.

Even in this relatively hostile climate, however, scrutiny of major public appointments made an appearance among the Liaison Committee's core tasks for committees
(see page 374) and the Public Administration Committee[16] came up with a scheme to
give committees an 'explicit though still proportional role' in vetting appointments. A
number of select committees took evidence from senior departmental officials and chairmen of statutory boards very soon after the appointment of these individuals. The
Treasury Committee held hearings (which were strictly speaking more pre-commence-
ment than pre-appointment) with those appointed by the Chancellor of the Exchequer

to the Bank of England's Monetary Policy Committee. examining their personal independence and professional competence.[17]

Over the past decade, however, beginning with the Liaison Committee's seminal report on *Shifting the Balance* in 2000,[18] parliamentary opinion moved clearly in favour of pre-appointment hearings by select committees, and it has prevailed. Early in 2008, in the Green Paper, *The Governance of Britain*,[19] the government itself proposed a non-binding select committee pre-appointment hearing into the suitability of candidates for a list of some thirty appointments, touching also on the appointment process. In specially sensitive cases such as those of the Governor and Deputy Governors of the Bank of England, the hearing would take place after appointment but before the appointee took up post. Not all senior public appointments would fall within the system. Those aimed at were particularly positions where the appointee was required to hold the government to account or to exercise statutory or other powers in protecting the public's rights or interests—senior auditors, ombudsmen, chief inspectors, and regulators, including the regulator of the appointments process. In the month the Green Paper was published, the House of Commons approved the appointment of a Chairman of the Statistics Board who had given evidence to and been recommended by the Treasury Committee.

In elaborating and discussing the government proposals, the Liaison Committee and the Public Administration Committee made suggestions about timetables, conduct of hearings, and criteria for selecting to which posts the procedures should apply.[20] Committees such as the Defence Committee and the Children, School and Families Committee are pressing for more than the government are presently disposed to concede.

However great the advance, it is important to be clear that what is proposed for Parliament is not a parallel to the constitutional responsibilities of the US Senate. Senate hearings are held in a particular political context, the legislature providing a cross-party check on overtly political appointments. In Britain too, the pre-appointment hearing is meant to add political balance to a ministerial decision, and the hearing will have no direct responsibility for the selection of a candidate; but while the ground rules admit questioning on an appointee's political activity in the past, because that may be relevant to his or her independence in the job, questions probing political views (or private matters) are distinctly off-limits. The hearings are to be an expression of public accountability in and through Parliament, following an impartial selection process to ensure that the Executive is properly accountable to Parliament.[21] The outcome of a committee's rejection of a nominee at a pre-appointment hearing is left unclear. The government insisted that a committee's judgement was not binding but considered that rejection should be exceptional. From a purely parliamentary point of view, the hearings will also set the agenda for the relationship between the relevant select committee and the post-holder after appointment.

It was envisaged that a committee should be prepared to undertake up to three pre-appointment hearings a session, and would be under no obligation to undertake any particular hearing. In session 2007–8, while the arrangements were still getting off the ground, there were nine hearings, five of them by the Treasury Committee. The pre-appointment hearings in 2007–8 were supplemented by eleven induction hearings, in which appointees were asked about the main issues facing them and what their priorities were.

Presidential disability and Vice Presidential vacancies

Pursuant to the 25th Amendment to the Constitution, the House and Senate have the duty of determining disputes as to Presidential disability. If the President has declared his own temporary disability or the Vice President and a majority of the Cabinet have so determined, the Vice President acts as President until the disability is removed by the President, unless kept in place by the Vice President and majority of the Cabinet, subject then to a two-thirds vote of both Houses within twenty-one days to continue the disability. Presidents have twice (in 1985 and in 2002) informed the Congress of temporary incapacities and then of resumption of powers and duties.

Where a vacancy in the office of Vice President occurs, the President may nominate a Vice President who must be confirmed by a majority vote of both Houses on separate resolutions. Presidential nominations of Vice Presidents under the 25th Amendment have been twice made and confirmed by separate votes of both Houses (in 1973 and 1974). This confirmation role for the House is the only one contemplated by the Constitution, all other confirmations of Executive and Judicial nominations being the prerogative of the Senate by majority vote.

How a sitting is closed: adjournment from day to day

Article I, section 5 of the US Constitution together with clause 4 of Rule XVI of House rules establish the fundamental precedence in parliamentary procedure of the House of motions to adjourn. Likewise paragraph 1 of Rule XXII of Senate rules establishes the comparable precedence of that motion over all other motions in that body. Both rules provide that the motion shall be non-debatable, and under the Constitution it is only one of two motions (the other being the motion to compel the attendance of absentees) which can be adopted in the absence of a quorum. Thomas Jefferson in his *Manual* states that 'a motion to adjourn simply takes place of all others; for otherwise the House might be kept sitting against its will, and indefinitely. Yet this motion cannot be received after another question is actually put and while the House is engaged in voting.' To permit debate on the motion would obviously destroy its purpose.

The Chair cannot refuse to recognize a Member having the floor for a simple motion to adjourn. A Member must be recognized (obtain the floor) if he insists that he wishes to offer this most preferential motion. The motion is often utilized by opponents of the pending or scheduled business as soon as they can obtain recognition to indicate their momentary displeasure or to bring about a delay in proceedings. The motion seldom prevails unless the Majority leadership offers it or it comes at the end of the business of the day and following special order speeches. When offered, the Chair is required to put the motion to an immediate voice vote. Should the nays prevail on that vote, any Member may object to the voice vote for lack of the presence of a quorum, in which case an 'automatic' roll-call vote ensues on the motion to adjourn. If a quorum of 218 is present or if the voice vote is in the affirmative, the yeas and nays can still be ordered on the motion by the constitutional one-fifth of Members present. The motion not only has the highest precedence when a question is under debate, but with certain restrictions under all other conditions as well. However, the motion may not interrupt a Member who has the floor, and is not in order during time yielded for a parliamentary inquiry. While privileged, it may not be repeated in the absence of intervening business. The motion takes precedence over motions to suspend the rules and reports from the Committee on Rules, but by specific rule only one motion to adjourn is in order, pending a motion to suspend the rules or a special order from the Rules Committee. The motion takes precedence over a point of order of no quorum, since under the Constitution it may be adopted in the absence of a quorum. However, the motion to adjourn may not be made where the House has adopted a special order of business which orders the previous question to final passage or adoption on a pending measure 'without intervening motion'. Nor may it be made in the Senate where that body has entered a unanimous consent order for a recess at the conclusion of the day's proceedings or for completion of specified business 'without intervening motion'. In that event, the special order supersedes and precludes the precedence otherwise given to the motion to adjourn under the standing rules. The motion to adjourn may be made by any Member, Delegate, or Resident Commissioner, including a Minority Member, and is in order at the beginning of a daily session even prior to approval of the Journal. The Chair may declare the House adjourned by unanimous consent when no Member is available to offer the motion. Of course, the motion must be adopted before the House can adjourn from day to day, and so it is moved at the end of business and following scheduled special order speeches which may run no later than midnight (see Procedural Basics at page 154). Frequently at the time the motion is actually made, only the Member making it and the Chair are actually in the Chamber, and it is adopted by voice vote. Neither the House nor the Senate set pre-established times for adjournment, it coming only when there is no further Member to be recognized for any other purpose.

While the motion may not be amended to set forth the day on which the House is to reconvene, the simple motion to adjourn may be preceded at the Speaker's discretion by a non-debatable and unamendable motion provided by clause 4(c) of Rule XVI that when the House adjourns on that day, it adjourn to meet on a day and time certain (not in excess of three calendar days). The latter motion is of equal privilege with the simple motion to adjourn at the Speaker's discretion, and is utilized to change the reconvening time set by standing order for the next session when that cannot be accomplished by unanimous consent. In the Senate, the non-debatable motion that the Senate adjourn to a day certain is in order, is lower in priority than the simple motion to adjourn, and if it changes the daily hour of convening previously established by Senate order requires a quorum for adoption.

In both the House and Senate there is a distinction between an adjournment and a recess, the former ending the daily session and requiring the convening of a new session on a subsequent legislative day, and the latter merely suspending the current daily session until resumption at a subsequent time. In both Houses, a daily adjournment requires the order of business on the succeeding day to begin as provided by the rules and orders of each body, as contrasted with the resumption of unfinished business at the completion of a recess. The introduction and reporting of legislation is foreclosed during the adjournment period, but not during recesses of the House. While the motion to adjourn is of the highest privilege, the declaration of a recess by the Speaker for 'a short time' under clause 12(a) of Rule I is in order when no question is pending, such as when a Member indicates his desire to offer a motion to adjourn but has not yet been recognized by the Chair for that purpose. This use of a recess declaration can foreclose a 'dilatory' motion to adjourn on which the Majority leadership does not wish to conduct a record vote. Such 'short time' recesses have extended for many hours (often overnight) since the Speaker was first empowered with that declaration authority in 1993. Accordingly the utilization of motions to confer recess authority has abated since increased use of declarations by the Chair. The primary purposes of a declaration of recess are to avoid unanticipated motions, to postpone business either until the responsible Members appear on the floor to call up the next legislative matter, to permit longer periods of legislative inactivity to enable Majority leadership to await filing of reports and to plan scheduling with the assistance of Majority caucus or the Rules Committee (to be discussed at length in the legislation chapter), to accommodate a ceremonial occasion, or in the event of an emergency. In the latter case, emergency declarations may be declared even if business is pending.

In the House of Commons, adjournment motions are of several kinds. The days to which the House normally adjourns at its rising are fixed by Standing Order (see page 149), but normally every daily sitting concludes with the making of a motion by a government whip 'That this House do now adjourn.' There follows a short debate—for no more than half an hour—on a matter of which a back-bench Member has given notice, which is answered by a minister (see page 158). By practice, the Chair will not permit a division on the motion, and if at the expiry of the time limit the minister is still on his feet, the Chair will declare the House adjourned until the next regular or otherwise scheduled sitting day. Motions to adjourn over days on which the House would ordinarily sit—mostly 'holiday' adjournments—are put for decision without debate. Dilatory motions for the adjournment of the House or of debate (and their parallels in Committee of the whole House) are dealt with at page 194. Finally, there are substantive motions for the adjournment, which in fact have nothing at all to do with the sittings of the House but permit broad debate on a topic specified on the Order of Business. These motions may not be amended, and while they may be divided on, for the most part they are intended to support an expansive rather than controversial debate. In future, this form may be less frequent, being supplanted by the—more informative but equally unamendable—motion 'That this House has considered [a specified matter].'

Adjournments requiring consent of other House

In neither US House—there is no British equivalent—may an adjournment or a recess extend beyond three calendar days (Sundays excepted) without the consent of the other House, pursuant to Article I, section 5 of the Constitution. While the House can adjourn by motion from Thursday to Monday, or from Friday to Tuesday, the House cannot adjourn from Monday to Friday without the Senate's consent. Sundays are not included in the calculation unless either House has agreed to meet on Sunday as a separate legislative day. The concurrent resolution may set forth the days and times at which the adjournment is to begin and end, but frequently the resolution will provide optional departure dates 'on motion of the Majority Leader or his designee' so as to give each House some discretion in determining the exact period of adjournment. A concurrent resolution may grant the consent of the House for adjournments or recesses of the Senate for periods of more than three days as determined by the Senate during such period, or may grant the consent of the Senate to a day certain, or to any day before that day as determined by the House. In case of disagreement between the two Houses with respect to an adjournment, the President may under Article II, section 3 adjourn both Houses as he deems proper, as he may convene either or both Houses prior to a scheduled reconvening date on 'extraordinary occasions'. Often concurrent resolutions originating in one House and providing only for an adjournment of that House are amended in the other House to provide separate adjournment dates and times therefor, which amendments must be adopted by the originating House. Also contingent unanimous consent request orders are entered in either House for a reconvening within three days if the other House has not by that time messaged its agreement to the concurrent resolution of adjournment for longer than three days. The basic constitutional scheme envisions that neither House should be allowed to adjourn for lengthy periods without the consent of the other, and the role of the Executive is relegated to that of an arbiter where the two Houses cannot agree, or where, once adjourned, either or both Houses must be reconvened on 'extraordinary occasions'. While a number of early Congresses were convened by Presidential proclamation, the last separate session so convened was in the 76th Congress on 21 September 1939, and the last Presidential reconvening of existing sessions of a Congress adjourned to a day certain were on 27 July 1947 and on 20 June 1948. Thus the exercise of joint Congressional leadership recall authority 'where the public interest so warrants' (now conferred as a matter of course in adjournment resolutions), rather than Executive authority 'on extraordinary occasions', is more appropriate in the modern practice to bring the two Houses back into session during lengthy adjournment periods.

Adjournments sine die (literally 'without day' or without setting the date for reconvening in the concurrent resolution) are used to terminate the sessions of a Congress. Since Congress normally completes its work more than three days prior to the constitutional date for the convening of the next session (3 January), in the usual practice adjournment sine die is accomplished by the adoption of a concurrent resolution. Of course, a session terminates automatically at the end of the constitutional term, and if the two Houses are still in session at that time, no concurrent resolution is necessary. Until recent years, sine die adjournments in even-numbered (election) years were normally taken by October (under the assumption that the business of the Congress be completed before Members to the next Congress are elected (on the first Tuesday in November), and usually somewhat later in non-election odd-numbered years. In more recent (105th–109th) Congresses, however, the final sine die adjournment of Congress has come after a 'lame-duck' session following the election of Members to the Congress beginning in January of the subsequent odd-numbered year, while the terms of some defeated or retiring Members and Senators have not yet expired. Senate adjournments to a day certain or sine die are sometimes replaced by 'pro forma' (non-business) sessions of the Senate every fourth day in order to prevent non-confirmable 'recess' judicial or executive appointments by the President which under Article II, section 2 may extend through an entire subsequent session (see page 73).

Sine die adjournment concurrent resolutions are privileged matters in both Houses and are not debatable, and require a quorum for adoption. Once a session of Congress has been adjourned sine die, it may be reconvened pursuant to joint House–Senate majority leadership recall provisions contained in the standard resolution, or by the President under the Constitution 'on extraordinary occasions'. A resolution may specify the particular legislative or calendar day of adjournment or may specify two or more (even indefinite) optional dates, in the latter case effected by a motion of the Majority Leader or his designee. A resolution providing sine die adjournment of a first session may contain a proviso that when the second session convenes, the two Houses may not conduct organizational or legislative business but shall adjourn on that day to a date certain, unless sooner recalled by the leadership. Such a resolution is not privileged since containing an order of business (a prohibition on the conduct of business) for the second session in addition to the sine die adjournment.

Leadership recall provisions contained in adjournment concurrent resolutions are of relatively recent origin. From the 81st Congress until the 91st Congress, no leadership recall provisions were included in resolutions either adjourning to a date certain or sine die. Then in 1970, the House and Senate for the first time adopted an 'August recess' concurrent resolution permitting the Speaker to recall the House if legislative expedience so warranted. That single House recall authority was not again contained in an adjournment resolution until 1998, when the two Houses adjourned sine die on 20 October but also provided for alternative joint leadership recall authority by the two Houses or for a House-only recall by the Speaker ('in the event the public interest warranted it'—that is, anticipated Articles of Impeachment reported from the House Committee on the Judiciary against President William J. Clinton). That recall authority of a 'lame duck' session of the House was exercised by Speaker Gingrich on 17 December 1998, to consider four Articles of Impeachment against President Clinton. Joint leadership recall authority was not exercised pursuant to adjournment resolutions until the 109th Congress on 20 March 2005 when the House was recalled during an adjournment to a date certain (for Easter recess, the Senate having remained in session), to consider a private bill for the relief of Terry Schiavo (discussed at page 7).

Quorums

Once having met, any assembly needs a quorum, a number below which proceedings are not considered properly conducted or decisions valid. In the House of Lords, the quorum for deliberation is no more than three, or in certain divisions, thirty. In the Commons, the rule is equally relaxed. The quorum is a simple forty, though the application of the rule is not as straightforward as that. First of all, it is not necessary for a quorum to be present at the beginning of business: the presence of the Speaker at Prayers 'makes a House'—similar to the rule in Congress where the presence of a quorum at the opening prayer may not be challenged (see below). Nor nowadays can any Member rise in his or her place at any time and demand that the House be counted. The only means by which the absence of a quorum in the Commons can be established is—again as it is in the House of Representatives—when a vote is taken. If fewer than forty Members are in evidence, that is thirty-five voting in the division lobbies, plus two tellers on either side, plus the Speaker or Deputy in the Chair, a quorum is not present. If that happens, the business under discussion stands over to a future day but the sitting continues. The procedure is almost identical in Committee of the whole House, save that if a quorum is found to be absent in a division in Committee, the Chairman leaves the Chair to report the circumstance to the Speaker and the Committee business stands over to the next sitting day. Failure of a quorum in modern practice is really relevant only on poorly attended private Members' Fridays when it may be used in particularly intricate ways in the un-whipped struggle between the backers and opponents of bills.

Article I of the US Constitution provides that a majority of each House shall constitute a quorum to conduct business. This constitutional requirement has been interpreted in both House and Senate to constitute a majority of those Members living and sworn, whose offices have not been terminated by resignation, death, declination, or expulsion or other action of that House. Thus 218 Members constitute a quorum in the House assuming no vacancies, and fifty-one Senators similarly constitute a quorum of that body.

Vacancies are reflected in the number of Representatives and Senators counted as a quorum to do business. The constitutional requirement in Article I that a majority of each House's Members shall constitute a quorum for the conduct of business has been consistently interpreted by the rules and precedents of both Houses to require computation based on the total number of Members living and sworn, and not on the number of Members-elect or on the number of seats (435) established by law. Thus when a vacancy occurs in the House or in the Senate, the denominator of the fraction which determines the presence of a 'majority' is reduced by one (the numerator representing the number of Members actually present whenever the ascertainment of the presence of a quorum is required). The number constituting a majority and a quorum when all 435 Members are living and sworn is therefore 218. When vacancies occur for any reason—death, resignation, expulsion, declinations, or actions by the House or Senate—the number of those present constituting a quorum is correspondingly reduced and is announced to the House.

In the aftermath of the 11 September 2001 attacks in the United States, including an attack on the seat of government, attention focused on quorum requirements and on replenishment of Members in both Houses in the event of massive vacancies or incapacitations. It became clear that deaths of Members created vacancies which in the Senate could be promptly filled by Governor's appointment under the 17th Amendment pending an election, but which in the House under Article I could only be filled by election. It was understood that in the event of catastrophic deaths of many Members, the quorum requirement would be greatly reduced and could become a number so small as to be unrepresentative of the nation. As an extreme example, if 432 Members were known to be dead as the result of a massive attack, only three Members would remain to constitute the House, and two of those would constitute a quorum to elect a Speaker (third in the line of Presidential Succession) and to conduct business until the replenishment of the House by elections conducted under State laws.

This possibility of extensive vacancies in the House has prompted the recent enactment of a law under the Article I authority of the Congress to pre-empt State law relating to the time, place, and manner of elections for Representative. The new law[22] requires States to hold special elections in every district where a vacancy occurs, if more than 100 vacancies are certified to exist at any one time, within forty-nine days of the

certification. This statutory approach was utilized rather than a constitutional amendment which would have permitted appointment (either by a Governor, State legislature,
or the Representative himself as a surrogate) of temporary Members of the House in the
case of vacancies or disabilities of a threshold number of Representatives, pending the
special election of replacements in the event of a vacancy or the removal of disability of
the incapacitated Representative. The House rejected the constitutional amendment
appointment approach by an overwhelming majority of 68:353 on 2 June 2004. The
House Majority believed it essential to maintain the unique basis of membership in
the House, namely election by the people, and not appointment by any other authority.
That new law was meant to supersede any State law otherwise requiring a longer period
than forty-nine days for the conduct of primary and special elections. At this writing this
requirement has drawn little response from State legislatures.

The House also adopted a new rule at the beginning of the 109th Congress, following
a hearing in its Rules Committee in the prior Congress, permitting a smaller number of
Representatives to constitute a temporary majority for the conduct of business in the
event of the certified incapacitation of Members due to catastrophic circumstances, and
following a quorum call lasting at least seventy-two hours during which a full quorum of
a majority of Members living and sworn failed to appear. It was contended that the
House could not validly adopt such a rule absent an enabling constitutional amendment,
as the constitutional requirement for a majority of each House's living and sworn
Members to be present to conduct business could not be changed by a rule of either
House. Indeed, the same clause of the Constitution which requires a majority to constitute a quorum for the conduct of business admits of only two exceptions, that a fewer
number of each House may adjourn from day to day or may vote to compel the attendance of absent Members. The Constitution makes no other exception. While each House
is also empowered in Article I to adopt its own rules, those rules must be consistent with
other provisions of the Constitution and cannot be validly adopted in contradiction
thereof. The House nevertheless proceeded to address the incapacitation issue by a unilateral rules change secure (in the Majority mind at least) in the belief that the Federal
courts would not consider the matter, it being a political issue involving separation of
powers. Alternatively, it was assumed that a collateral challenge to the constitutionality
of such a rule would require a justiciable controversy or case brought by an aggrieved
plaintiff in Federal court, during which extended period of litigation the House quorum
would be replenished by subsequent election, and that any law enacted by a smaller
quorum could be ratified by subsequent proper enactment. Thus, the House on 4 January
2005 chose to adopt a standing rule recommended by the Majority Party conference as
part of a package of rules for the 109th Congress. While the Speaker properly refused to
rule on the constitutionality of that proposed rules change when it was submitted (the
Chair by precedent does not rule on constitutional questions but allows the House to
determine them by voting on the merits of the underlying matter), the House did vote
separately to consider the resolution and, in effect, to endorse its presumed constitutionality. The subsequent (110th) Congress under a new party majority retained that rule
despite previous protestations from its then-Minority leadership.

The Senate, while not presented with the same prolonged quorum requirement as
the House in the event of vacancies, due to Governors' appointment authority, is confronted with a similar dilemma in the event of incapacitations caused by catastrophic

circumstances. In that event the quorum would by rule remain a majority of those Senators living and sworn. At this writing, the Senate has not addressed this issue as a rules change or as a constitutional amendment.

The Constitution does not further define those legislative proceedings that are to constitute 'business' for purposes of the quorum requirement. 'Business' in this context has become a term that, under the House rules and precedents, does not encompass all parliamentary proceedings. For example, the prayer does not constitute business requiring the presence of a quorum under Rule XX, clause 7. Thus the voluntary nature of attendance for the daily prayer in the House has been construed by the Federal courts as an indication that the House by its rules has not constituted an unconstitutional establishment of religion in violation of the 1st Amendment (*Murray v Buchanan* 729 F2d 689 (DC Cir 1983)).

Other parliamentary events not constituting 'business' requiring the presence of a quorum include administration of the oath, certain motions incidental to a call of the House, and the motion to adjourn from day to day. Rule XX, clause 7 specifically prohibits the entertainment of a point of order of no quorum unless a question has been put to a vote. Thus the mere conduct of debate, where the Chair has not put the pending question to a vote, is not under House rules 'the conduct of business' requiring a quorum under Article I, section 5 of the Constitution.

By contrast, the Senate has not adopted such a rule, and 'suggestions of the absence of a quorum' are in order if made by a Senator having the floor and being recognized, even during debate, but may not interrupt another Senator who has the floor. Customarily, the Senate by unanimous consent rescinds an order for a quorum call once another Senator is on the floor to seek recognition, and so quorum calls are mechanisms to bide time until another Senator seeks recognition. Once underway, however, they can be rescinded only by unanimous consent, and a single objection forces the completion of the quorum call and the establishment of a quorum to proceed with business.

In the House, a quorum call once underway following the Chair's ascertainment of an absence of a quorum cannot be rescinded even by unanimous consent, since such a unanimous consent request would constitute business which itself requires the presence of a quorum. Thus the House cannot conduct business after the absence of a quorum has been announced, until a quorum is shown to have responded on a quorum call or on a record vote which simultaneously establishes a quorum.

In both Houses, a quorum is presumed to be present unless the point is properly raised and the Chair actually counts and announces that a quorum is not in fact present or a vote discloses its absence. The presumption of a quorum being present permits many measures to be passed by unanimous consent, voice votes, or other non-recorded votes when in fact fewer than a majority of Members of either House are present, since the Record does not disclose the absence of a quorum which would reverse this presumption. One matter requires votes by the yeas and nays (the recording of each vote by name) under the Constitution—passage of measures in each House over the President's veto by a two-thirds vote of those Members present and voting under Article I, section 7, and on such occasion a quorum must be established by the yea and nay vote and cannot be presumed to be present. House standing rules require the passage or adoption of several measures by the yeas and nays, including general Appropriation bills, budget concurrent resolutions, and conference reports thereon, and motions closing conference meetings to the public, and the failure of a quorum to vote on those matters would vitiate the vote by order of the Chair.

Otherwise, matters requiring passage by two-thirds votes, such as constitutional amendments, motions to suspend the rules, and treaty ratifications in the Senate, need not necessarily be accomplished by yea and nay votes, and the presumption of the presence of a quorum would support final action by voice vote, unanimous consent, or other non-recorded vote. Indeed in the Senate in modern practice, unanimous consent orders are sometimes entered in advance of receipt of official papers from the House 'deeming' a measure to be passed by the Senate once a specified message is received from the House. These deeming orders are unanimous consent accommodations made for Senators at certain times when their actual attendance at the seat of government becomes an inconvenience, for example because the House is yet to act on a measure (such as a revenue or Appropriation bill or conference report thereon which the House must originate), and the Senate leadership does not wish to organize a quorum. Of course, the political certainty of passage of such a measure is whipped and assured in advance in order to obtain unanimous consent, but the avoidance in recent years of independent debate and votes on several major pieces of legislation denigrates the independent role of the Senate and inappropriately signals to the House that the Senate has prejudged and has deemed passed a measure that the House has not yet passed.

A quorum is not required on an affirmative vote on a simple motion to adjourn in either House, but a negative vote requires the subsequent presence of a quorum to proceed with business. That quorum may be shown by the requisite majority voting in the negative on the motion to adjourn.

Until 1890 the view prevailed in the House that it was necessary for a majority of the Members to vote on a matter submitted to the House in order to satisfy the constitutional requirement for a quorum. Under that practice, the opposition might break a quorum simply by refusing to vote. That practice was changed in 1890 with the historic ruling of Speaker Thomas B. Reed, later embodied in the standing rules (clause 4(b) of Rule XX) that Members present in the Chamber but not voting would be counted in determining the presence of a quorum, and that the Chair could instruct the Clerk to record the names of such Members as 'present'. This ruling was upheld by the Supreme Court in *United States v Ballin* 144 US 1 (1892), declaring that the authority of the House to transact business is 'created by the mere presence of a majority'. A quorum of either House may thus be expressed as a fraction in which the numerator is the number of Members who are present and the denominator is the number of Members who are extant. As the issue in *Ballin* was Speaker Reed's method of counting the number of Members present, the decision of the Supreme Court addressed the numerator of this fraction. In dictum the court examined the question 'how shall the presence of a majority be determined?' and observed that, because the Constitution does not prescribe any method for determining the presence of such majority, it is within the competency of either House to 'prescribe any method which shall be reasonably certain to ascertain the fact'.

Arguments that the *Ballin* case justified House adoption of the new rule for reduced quorums based on Members' incapacitation in the event of a catastrophic circumstance are therefore misplaced, since *Ballin* only addressed the propriety of the ruling for establishing physical presence—the numerator of the quorum faction—and did not authorize either House to adopt a rule changing the denominator, the number of Members living and sworn whose terms have not been vacated by resignation, death, declination, or action by the House.

Under the Constitution, each House may establish procedures permitting fewer than a majority of its Members to adjourn from day to day, or to compel the attendance of absentees. Where it is not possible for the Chair to count a quorum or where a record vote, including those present in the Chamber, does not disclose the presence of a majority, the House has a long-established rule permitting as few as a majority of fifteen Members to compel the attendance of absentees. This is accomplished by a motion directing the arrest of absent Members by the Sergeant at Arms (a procedure known at Westminster as the 'call of the House' and last in evidence in the Commons in 1836). In practice, however, this free-standing motion is seldom utilized, since quorums are not required to be present in the House unless the Speaker is putting the pending question to a vote. In that event, another clause (6) of Rule XX provides for an 'automatic' vote by the yeas and nays in the House on any question requiring a quorum for adoption. Under that rule, the Sergeant at Arms is forthwith to bring in absentees and permit them to vote. Compulsory attendance or arrest is seldom used in modern practice, despite the mandatory language of this clause. To make an arrest under this clause, the Sergeant at Arms must have in his possession a warrant signed by the Speaker. Although the Speaker possesses full authority to issue a warrant of arrest, she usually does not do so without specific House authorization.

Members normally respond voluntarily on 'automatic' roll-calls despite the controversial nature of the matter being voted on, if only to vote 'present'. While occasionally protesting an action of the House by a 'walkout', they do not conspire to remain absent to deny the presence of a majority. Most votes in current practice are scheduled to a great extent to accommodate Members' availability at the seat of government and their desire to maximize personal voting percentages. Thus w… e requirement for a majority to be present to conduct business may seem … strictive compared with the Commons requirement that a mere forty … resent to conduct business, the perception of the importance … and party discipline combine to minimize the need for comp… resence of a quorum during the conduct of most business.

Until 1890, a quorum of the Committee … e as in the House. From that date in the Committee of the Who… onduct business has been set at 100 Members (including Delega… oth Congresses) by standing rule. The fundamental purpose of a Co… Whole is to permit the House to conduct preliminary business on a bill un… dited procedures, particularly the five-minute rule governing amendment procedures, subject to ratification of adopted amendments and to final action in the full House. Like the House rule, points of order of no quorum in Committee of the Whole are with one exception restricted to occasions when business of the Committee is being conducted—where the Chair is putting a question to a vote, and not during the conduct of debate. Optional quorum calls are in order once during debate. If the Committee of the Whole following the conduct of a quorum call cannot establish a quorum of 100 Members, it reports that fact to the House which must then establish a full quorum of 218 to proceed with business. As a practical matter, a Committee of the Whole easily establishes a quorum of 100 during the conduct of a vote on an amendment or motion. Because the reduced number only applies to a 'committee' proceeding, the House may constitutionally establish a smaller number without running afoul of the requirement of Article I, while needing a constitutional quorum when acting on recommendations of the Committee of the Whole. Further discussion of quorum and voting procedures in Committee of the Whole will be found at pages 430–3.

The Senate has no comparable rule permitting a smaller number of its Members to constitute a quorum, as it does not have any Committee of the Whole of its Members. In marked contrast to the House, the presiding officer of the Senate has no authority to count to determine if a quorum is present when a Senator suggests the absence of a quorum unless the Senate is operating under cloture; the rules provide that once a Senator makes a point of no quorum, the Secretary shall forthwith call the roll and the presiding officer shall announce the result, unless, by unanimous consent, the quorum call is rescinded. Once the absence of a quorum has been announced by the Chair following a roll-call, the quorum call may not be called off, even by unanimous consent, and no business (other than a motion to adjourn or to compel the attendance of absentees) or debate is in order, until a quorum of the Senators (fifty-one) has responded to the call.

The significance of differences between a two-party and an effectively multi-party legislature

Both countries have in the past operated under a political system comprising two major political parties. While in the UK there has emerged over the past two or three decades a third major political party, the Liberal Democrats, with a significant number of seats in the House of Commons (not to mention other smaller party representations), in the USA there is no formal third political party which has influenced Congressional elections. Rather, there has emerged a larger segment of the electorate which identifies itself as 'independent' and which, depending on State laws permitting independents to vote in primary elections, has had significant impact on the composition of Congress. Of course, Presidential and Congressional elections are separately conducted under Federal and State law, and while the 'coat-tail' effect of a Presidential candidate's popularity on Congressional candidacies is often a factor, the basic separation of powers permits the electorate to make separate selections of a Legislature and an Executive, whether or not there are two or three major parties.

Another similarity, regardless of the number of parties, is that both electorates choose their legislators from single-Member constituencies or districts, as contrasted with any form of proportional representation. The 'first-past-the-post' notion in the UK (other than in the devolved legislatures) is mirrored in the USA, with the exception of those States having laws which require majorities to elect rather than pluralities, thereby requiring run-off elections between the top two where no candidate receives a majority of all votes cast for the office.

Here similarities end, and the essential relevance of a political party's influence in establishing government becomes more direct under the British system. There, a voter's choice of a Member of Parliament is—European elections apart—the only vote cast at the UK level, and the political choices which establish governance are focused entirely through the political party which sponsors the candidates. In practice at a general election the electorate decides which political party is to be in the majority, and from the candidates who successfully stood for that majority party, the Prime Minister and other ministers (the Cabinet) who form the government within Parliament are drawn. The voters decide on a constituency-by-constituency basis which political party, by means of its elected Members and its chosen leaders, is to govern. An elector can choose one party either because he likes its leaders or programme (or particular party candidate for that constituency), or because he dislikes the leaders or programmes of all the other parties. The leader of the party winning the majority of seats in the House of Commons becomes Prime Minister at the invitation of the Monarch and forms a cabinet from members of either House, usually belonging to the same political party. The government can be expected to implement the party programme or manifesto because it is directly backed by the authority of the voters. With more than two parties, the possibility of minority governments exists and potentially leads to coalitions of parties, to compromises on matters of policy, and to a blurring of the electorate's message.[23]

In the United States, the Constitution by separating Executive from Legislature and by establishing a federalist system of State and local governments rules out a national party government as understood in Britain. Elections for President are further deflected into choices for partisan Electors—a composite number of private citizens in each State (based on population of the State in the last census) who are pledged under State law to vote for Presidential candidates in unison (except for Maine and Iowa) for the party candidate receiving a majority or plurality of popular votes in that State. In recent Congresses there has been one independent candidate elected to the House of Representatives (from Vermont), who has chosen to caucus with the Democratic party. In the Senate, one Republican Senator from the same State had previously switched parties by declaring himself an Independent and then caucusing with the Democratic Senators. Over an eight-year period, the typical voter in the United States is permitted to vote for partisan Electors for President and Vice President twice, for Representatives four times, and for two Senators at least once, while the elector in Britain may vote for a Member of Parliament from one of three parties (or from other smaller parties in portions of the UK at least once), and that vote reflects his only choice for a national government and is addressed primarily to the choice of alternative governments.

The American voter is confronted with a wider variety of national and local issues when casting a series of votes for a number of government offices than is his British counterpart. The influence of the two political parties toward these selections is considerable, but is diffused by the variety of organization of each political party—national, State, and local, and the influence of independent voters through their ability to participate in partisan primaries in some States. As expressed by Bradshaw and Pring, 'the business of the parties is, first and foremost, a problem of organization; from the diverse interests, needs and aspirations of fifty States, the concept of a national party has somehow to be nurtured. The complexity and expense of this exercise weight the system heavily in favour of two parties, that is, the minimum number required for a political choice.'[24]

Those two features of the American party system—local or State orientation and a preoccupation with organizational (and increasingly fund-raising) problems—have been given emphasis by the Constitution. Candidates for both Houses of Congress have to be 'inhabitants' of the State when elected, and the choice of a candidate is motivated primarily by his stance on local and regional issues. Spending for Federal elections has been construed as protected free speech by the Supreme Court, against which limits cannot be legislatively imposed. This court interpretation of the 1st Amendment inures to the benefit of the political party able to raise the larger amount in political contributions.

Other observations from the point of view of a political scientist might lend themselves to comparisons as the impact of a two- or multiple-party system on regional and local matters. The notion that the successful political parties in the USA have been able to combine diverse regional and local interests into durable alliances in support of party candidates must be re-examined. The suggestion of Maurice Duverger that US political parties are 'founded on no ideological or social bases...they include elements and doctrines that are completely heterogeneous...fundamentally they are simply organizations for the conquest of political office'[25] no longer fully describes the impact of political parties on Congressional composition or influence. Increasingly, single-issue ideological interests have injected themselves, through campaign financing and voter turnout particularly at primary elections, as formidable groups more inclined to associate with one or the other of the two political parties based almost exclusively on that party's Congressional leadership's willingness to support their relatively narrow legislative agenda (see for example pro-life and pro-choice alliances, gun control groups). To be sure, the division between the two political parties in the House and Senate has been narrow in recent years, and has resulted in close votes on a number of issues decided almost exclusively by party affiliation rather than by coalitions between portions of the two parties depending on the issue being debated. This has resulted from a 'win-at-all-cost' attitude taken, especially by Majority leadership in the House, which has minimized Minority party participation at various stages of the legislative process and has been driven by the determination to govern in order to enhance and in response to (re-) election prospects of party incumbents and other candidates. When this unfolds, as it has, on a strictly partisan basis, the fact that only two political parties are participating in the legislative process and in the attendant and perpetual fund-raising activities virtually assures that coalitions or independent voter influences will be minimized.

The conclusion reached by Bradshaw and Pring that the fundamental purpose of the two political parties in the USA is to unify diverse interests, rather than as in Britain to divide interests and to present them vividly to the electorate for a choice of national government, can be debated. In addition to the caveat that there are now more than two parties impacting on that process in the UK, one must also weigh the notion of the US political party organization in Congress as 'unifying' from the standpoint of winning close votes and re-elections in Congress with the very divisive impact of increased Congressional partisanship on the American body politic. While party unity in Congress, especially in the House, has taken hold in both political parties and has dictated outcomes in votes, fund raising, and elections, the very politicization of the process has had a divisive impact on the electorate when judged by voter turnout and on the participation of independent voters, especially during primary elections where most gerrymandered Congressional seat outcomes are decided.

The impact of two-party versus multi-party composition of the Houses will focus on procedural distinctions between sharing what has to be shared (principally debate time) on the one hand, and authority (Majority party participation at various stages of the legislative process based on a winner-take-all attitude in diminution of the availability of procedural alternatives to one or more Minority party groups within each House). Much of this analysis with respect to the presence of one minority party in each House of Congress is contained in the chapters on Legislation and on Procedural Basics at pages 147, 381, and 433, where the extent to which standing rules, procedures, and practices are impacted by the utilization of special rules in order to minimize the Minority party's participation is discussed in detail. The sharing of time and authority would be markedly different if a third party in either House were able to influence agendas and policy. Such is not the case, and, but for an extraordinary shift in political sentiment giving rise to an effective third political party in the United States, does not appear as a practical alternative.

Beyond the roughly equal division of debate time between the two political parties in the US House, however, is the reality of Majority party dominance in the exercise of authority, including the organization of House, the selection of its officers and employees, and the setting of the legislative and oversight agenda. There are no 'Opposition days' for Minority party motions (beyond a guarantee of one day at committee hearings for witnesses called by the minority party), no Questions to the government in plenary sessions, and no automatic protection to the Minority party to offer legislative alternatives, beyond the motion to recommit a measure with instructions pending final passage. As discussed in greater detail in the chapter on Legislation, the guarantee to the Minority party of the motion to recommit is a protection to the Minority, unique among parliamentary bodies in the world, which cannot be denied by the Rules Committee in a special order of business. It reflects the traditional custom (assured to the Minority since the 'Cannon revolt' against the autocratic rule of Speaker Joe Cannon in 1909) that a final opposition alternative be permitted pending the vote on final passage, and that 'opposition' to the pending bill as the qualification to be recognized to offer an alternative be understood in terms of the Minority party by specific reference to the Minority Leader or his designee in the standing rule. Nowhere in House rules and practices, however, is there an acknowledgement that multiple political parties may play a role in organization and operation, because they have not in the 220-year history of the House. The Speaker has never been called upon to recognize third party leaders for debate, amendments, or motions. There is no allocation of budgetary resources to third party caucuses or committee staffs. While more than two candidates have been nominated for the Office of Speaker, they have not represented a third political party but are independent candidates.

These institutional allocations of time between managers of the two parties have their limits, as where special orders of business from the Rules Committee prescribe an order of consideration of amendments which can be very partisan and can have the overall effect of minimizing the Minority party's ability to offer amendments upon which debate is divided. Beyond the question of availability of time between the two parties, and the absence of a third or of multiple parties to further sub-allocate that time, is the more basic issue of authority to conduct the business of the House and Senate. Organization of committees to conduct the business of the House at various stages has traditionally been based on the ratio between the two parties. Committee and subcommittee ratios are negotiated between the party leaderships at the beginning of each Congress and, with the exception of the House Rules Committee or the equally divided

Standards Committee, reflect that overall ratio. Conference committee ratios, while the prerogative of the Speaker to appoint, generally reflect the overall party ratio as well, but on occasion are rounded to be more balanced in favour of the majority party (for example, 3:2 or 6:4).

The same ratio arrangement is true in the Senate, where all committees except Ethics are composed of a majority from the Majority party, with independent Members being factored into those ratios based on the caucus with which they meet. Minority party membership in that body, unlike the House, has an enhanced status based upon the three-fifths requirement of Senate Rule XXII to invoke cloture to terminate debate on a pending issue and bring it to a direct up-or-down vote. Thus if, as is increasingly the case in a politically polarized Senate, the Minority party assumes a party position in opposition to an issue, it can effectively unify to prevent that issue from coming to a direct vote, assuming that its membership numbers at least forty Senators. This issue is discussed in greater detail at page 437. For the purpose of this analysis the decision-making role conferred on a majority by House rules almost always translates into business being made in order by the Majority party on a party-line 'procedural' vote. In the Senate the power and influence of the Minority party and individual Senators is greatly enhanced through the lack of a germaneness rule, and the threat of a filibuster requiring a super-majority to restrict, and leads to accommodations of alternatives by unanimous consent to avoid those confrontations. Both Houses have become increasingly partisan in recent Congresses if measured by political party positioning in contrast to issue-by-issue coalitions which might potentially involve a third position. Especially in the House, Minority party participation has been minimized even to the extent of being shut out in practical terms.

Legislative staff

Those who work for Parliament itself, in whatever capacity, unlike civil servants, are not servants of the Crown, though by statute parliamentary staff must be 'broadly in line' with the civil service as to complement, pay, and grading. They are appointed and carry out their duties (as opposed to those serving individual Members or Lords) in a wholly non-political manner. Each House has its own staff, though increasingly, in areas such as information technology and estates, it has been recognized that it makes better sense to create joint departments or at least to coordinate working.

Following a recent reconstruction which completed a long process of unification of the six departments of professional staff serving the House of Commons, there are now four Directorates in the House service, each headed by a Director General who sits on a Management Board. The Department of Chamber and Committee Services is responsible for advisory and other services supporting the work of the Chamber and committees—principally the work of Clerks—Hansard, and part of what had been the Serjeant at Arms Department, in charge of security and ceremonial. The House Library metamorphosed into Department of Information Services which also provides information to the public, and the Department of Resources incorporates staff who provide human resources and finance support to the House service and administer Members' pay, pensions, and allowances—the last a function which will fall to the Independent Parliamentary

Standards Authority under the Parliamentary Standards Act. Finally, the Department of Facilities looks after accommodation, the upkeep of the fabric of the Palace, and refreshments and other facilities.

The post of Chief Executive of the House service and chairman of the Management Board is held by the Clerk of the House, who in his statutory capacity of Corporate Officer is also responsible for formal and contractual affairs concerning property and similar matters, the House itself not being a body corporate.

Notwithstanding that there was no equivalent rise in the number of sitting days or in many of the other activity indicators, the increase in the Commons' workload is reflected in the numbers of those employed by and in the House. In the nine years between 1998–9 and 2006–7, staff employed by the House increased in number by some 13 per cent. The 2007–8 total stands at 1,696 (as opposed to 2,694 Members' staff). Most of the increase derives from the development of select committee work and IT requirements. The overall growth over the same period in the number of Members' staff in respect of whom House officials provide payroll services has been much steeper, rising from 1,849 to 2,650, or roughly 44 per cent.[26] Not all of this increase will be directly attributable to a greater legislative and constituency workload, however: some must derive from the fact that as allowances have increased—nearly trebled over the period in question—Members have hired more staff. Changes in methods of working have played their part too, as (for example) the Library makes more information available electronically to everyone and produces fewer customized responses to Members' or other individual enquiries.

The administrative structure of the Lords is very like that of the Commons. The Clerk of the Parliaments (strictly speaking the Clerk of the Commons is Under-Clerk of the Parliaments) is Chief Executive and Corporate Officer, and responsible to him are parliamentary services, corporate services, information services, committees, a financial directorate, another for human resources and security and housekeeping functions. Staffing levels in the Lords are more modest than in the Commons, though there too increased numbers have been a feature of recent years. At 490, the official staffing level of 2007–8 is well over 30 per cent above that of 1998–9. There is no statutory equivalent in the Lords of the House of Commons Commission, but the House Committee (a select committee) bears many of the same responsibilities.

The constitutional authority conferred on each US House to adopt its own rules and elect its own officers is the primary reason that each House administers its own internal affairs, subject to the constitutional requirement that no money can be appropriated except pursuant to law enacted by Congress. Even in that respect, while the Congress annually enacts a Legislative Branch Appropriation Act for the ensuing fiscal year which provides money from the Treasury to operate each House, that bill is enacted under a process wherein each House shows deference to the recommendation of the other with respect to its own internal budgetary needs. Only with respect to 'joint items' such as expenses and administration of entities serving both branches including the Capitol Police, the Architect of the Capitol, and the Library of Congress do the two Houses negotiate differences and reach budgeting and administrative compromises, usually on a bipartisan basis because the accommodations serve relatively non-political employment and security needs of all Members and staff. To that end, many of the support entities serving the entire Congress are staffed by non-partisan officials who are selected in a bipartisan manner. Those principal offices include the Architect of the Capitol, the

Director of the Congressional Budget Office, the Librarian of Congress and its Congressional Research Service, the Office of Compliance, the General Accountability Office, the Office of Emergency Planning, Preparedness and Operation, and the Office of the Attending Physician. Some of these offices are in turn overseen by statutorily created House and Senate leadership entities such as the Capitol Preservation Commission (overseeing the construction of the Capitol Visitors Center) and by committees of each House. While on occasion, partisan pressures emerge which influence the actions of those officials, the above-mentioned entities serving the whole Congress are bipartisan because neither party is unduly advantaged by services which are more administrative than political and which inure to the benefit of all Members.

The internal administration of the House and Senate is facilitated by their elected officers—the Clerk, Chief Administrative Officer, and Sergeant at Arms in the House and the Secretary and Sergeant at Arms in the Senate. Because they are elected by the Majority Members of each House, they have some discretion to appoint employees on the basis of political patronage and not merely as non-partisan administrators. Other officials in the House, however, are by law or rule required to be appointed solely on the basis (non-partisan) of ability to perform the functions of the office. Those officials include the Parliamentarians, the Legislative Counsel (bill drafters), Law Revision counsel (codifiers of enacted law), and Inspector General. Other officials, whose appointments are not explicitly non-partisan such as the General Counsel and Historian, are expected to provide non-partisan services to all Members and staff.

When it comes to the distribution of annually appropriated funds within each House, however, especially within the committee structures, the priorities for allocation become decidedly more partisan. House rules put a cap on the overall number of staff to which each committee is initially entitled by providing that each committee may appoint, by majority vote, not more than thirty professional staff members to be compensated from the funds provided for the appointment of committee staff by primary and additional expense resolutions. Of that number, the Minority Members on each committee are entitled to select and to direct the work of ten professional staff, thereby establishing a two-to-one ratio for the Majority party regardless of the ratio of Members on that committee or in the House overall, and regardless of any past non-partisan employment of staff by that committee. The one-third staff guarantee for the Minority was first adopted in 1995 (at the same time as overall staff sizes for all committees were reduced by one-third), and superseded prior committee staffing practices which in some Congresses only provided one-fourth funding for Minority committee staff. Only the Committees on Appropriations, Standards of Official Conduct, and the Permanent Select Committee on Intelligence are exempt from this requirement. Previous entitlements to at least one separate staff for subcommittee chairman and ranking Minority Members, apart from approval by votes of the Majority and Minority committee Members respectively, have been eliminated to give the full committee chairman and ranking Minority Member more formal authority over all employment decisions, subject to ratification of their respective committee Members and subject to the equitable allocation of Majority and Minority staff resources to subcommittees.

At the beginning of each Congress, at the organizational meeting of each standing committee, that committee's two-year budget is negotiated between Majority and Minority Members and is then introduced in the form of a funding resolution sponsored by the chairman and often the ranking Minority Member. All such resolutions are referred to the Committee on House Administration which consolidates all committees' resolutions within an overall appropriated amount for committee expenses and sub-allocated for each of the two calendar years of that Congress. That recommendation is reported as a privileged funding resolution to the House, normally within the first three months of each Congress. That resolution finances all committee activities except for the Committee on Appropriations, which is separately funded directly from the annual Legislative Branch Appropriations bill and is not required to be reviewed by the Committee on House Administration. This autonomy enables the Appropriations Committee to be relatively free from Majority leadership control over staffing, both in terms of numbers and resulting policy priorities. Otherwise under Majority caucus rules the Speaker appoints six of the nine members of the Committee on House Administration directly without going through the Steering and Policy Committee (just as she directly nominates nine of the thirteen members of the Rules Committee), giving her greater leverage over the operations of those two internal housekeeping committees and indirectly over staffs of the other standing committees.

Additional staff including consultants or contract employees may be employed if the relevant funding resolution provides sufficient resources for their services. The extent to which the chairman and ranking Minority member of the full committee agree to utilize the services of their entire staff in a bipartisan manner varies from committee to committee, but House rules, while permitting the employment of non-partisan committee staff by separate votes of Majority and Minority committee members, clearly contemplate the partisan selection and utilization of committee and subcommittee staff.

While the consideration of the biannual committee expense resolution is privileged when reported from the Committee on House Administration and then susceptible to amendment, the Committee on Rules has recently reported special orders of business 'hereby adopting' by self-execution the funding resolution reported from House Administration without intervening motion, such as a Minority motion to recommit, where the Majority leadership wishes to minimize Minority options. More recently, since funding resolutions must emerge with a one-third funding allocation for all committee minorities, the resolution has been considered by unanimous consent or under suspension of the rules where no amendments or motions to recommit may be offered, but where bipartisan support has been anticipated. As long as the current requirement for one-third Minority staffing is attained in the overall allocation, partisan disputes which characterized earlier Congress over that percentage of allocation and within subcommittees have been minimized.

In the Senate, a comparable rule (Senate Rule XXVI) requiring allocation of at least one-third of committee resources to the Minority mirrors the House committee funding procedures described above, with the additional admonition that staff ratios should reflect the ratios of Senators on all committees. Pursuant to a Senate standing order, all committee funding resolutions on an annual or biannual basis first originate from the respective standing committees, and are then referred when reported to the Committee on Rules and Administration for consolidation with all other funding resolutions and reported as one resolution, covering the period from 1 March until the end of February of the following year. As in the House, this consolidation and adjustment of amounts by the committee on Rules and Administration must be approved by the Senate, and may be augmented by supplemental committee expense resolutions processed in the same way as the primary biannual resolutions.

Records and papers

Article I, section 5 of the US Constitution requires each House to keep a Journal of its proceedings and to publish it, except for matters requiring secrecy. The Journal, and not the Congressional Record, is the official record of the proceedings of each House, and (as in the UK) by law certified copies thereof are admissible in judicial proceedings. 'Proceedings' include the text of all matters voted upon, the recorded votes cast (both in the House and in Committees of the Whole), and any other business which by rule or custom either House determines to have been its proceedings. The Journal records House and Senate actions, and is not a verbatim transcript or even a summary of the circumstances attending those proceedings (that being the province of the body and digest of the Congressional Record discussed at pages 98–101).

Proceedings that are reflected in the Journal (and also in the Congressional Record) include public and private bills, resolutions, and documents introduced and referred under the rules indicating sponsors, number, title (but not full text), and committees of reference, petitions, and memorials which are referred to committees, questions of order arising during proceedings in either House (but not in Committee of the Whole), titles of reports of committees delivered to the Clerk, motions entertained by the Speaker unless withdrawn the same day, motions to discharge when signed by a majority of the total Membership, presentation of conference reports and the disposition thereof, messages from the other House or from the President, unanimous consent or other special orders agreed to by either House, and the names of those Members voting by the yeas and nays or other recorded vote, responding to quorum calls, and those absent or not voting. The Senate Journal contains the same essentials of business, with separate Journals being kept and published for Legislative, Executive, and Court of Impeachment business.

The House, but not the Senate, acts to approve its Journal as the first order of business every day. The Senate sometimes recesses rather than adjourns from day to day and is thus not required to approve its Journal unless it is a new legislative day following an adjournment. In modern practice, the Senate by unanimous consent usually enters an order which approves the Journal in advance while also setting the reconvening time for the next legislative day. Even following an overnight recess, the Senate routinely approves its Journal by unanimous consent because the Journal otherwise accumulates to be potentially read for corrections or approval at the beginning of a new legislative day. In 1986 Rule IV was amended to permit a non-debatable motion immediately following the daily prayer as the first order of business to approve the Journal to date in order to waive the reading and amendments thereof, where a unanimous consent order has not been entered for advance approval.

As a practical matter, however, the House approves its Journal of the previous day on the next legislative day by unanimous consent or by motion either as the first order of business or as a postponed record vote later on, while the Senate by unanimous consent approves its Journal at the end of a legislative day by unanimous consent in 'wrap-up business' which also sets the convening time for the next legislative day.

Pursuant to clause 1 of House Rule I, the Speaker at the convening of each session announces her approval of the Journal (which has been prepared by the Journal Clerk under the supervision of the Parliamentarian). The Speaker's approval of the Journal is deemed agreed to subject to a vote on the demand of any Member. When that demand is made, it is normally to provoke a recorded vote either at that time or later in the legislative day if the vote is postponed at the Speaker's discretion, and not based on any dispute as to the accuracy of the Journal. Because approval of the Journal is the first order of business under the standing rules, the Journal (or a motion to adjourn) becomes the first target for a protest vote or a means of determining a quorum especially since points of no quorum are not in order unless the Speaker is putting a question to a vote. The Speaker can offset this strategy if employed as a Minority tactic by postponing the vote until any subsequent time that legislative day, usually to follow in sequence another vote to be taken in the House so that Members are not called back to the Chamber merely for a Journal vote.

Under modern practice, the reading of the Journal is dispensed with unless the House, following initial rejection of the Speaker's approval, adopts a motion requiring its reading. Amendments to the Journal are then only in order following the reading in full and then only if the House rejects a motion that the Journal be approved as read. The only business which takes precedence over approval of the Journal at the beginning of the legislative day is the motion to adjourn, a question of the privileges of the House, the administration of the oath of office, and the declaration of a recess for a short time at the Speaker's discretion. While each House controls its Journal and may decide what are proceedings, it has been held not in order to amend or strike out a Journal entry setting forth a motion exactly as made, such as by striking out a resolution which was actually considered. Where the House adjourns on consecutive days without having approved the Journal of the previous day's proceedings, the Speaker puts each question in chronological order as the first order of business after the daily prayer on the subsequent day.

At Westminster, there are two parallel records of the decisions—not debates—of both Houses. In the Commons, the daily version is the Votes and Proceedings which at the end of each session is transformed into the second, the Journal, a series nearly complete from 1547. Neither the Votes and Proceedings nor the Journal is approved by the House with or without debate (though the Votes are strictly speaking published only 'after first being perused by Mr Speaker'). In fact, the only dispute in the Chamber over the accuracy of the Votes and Proceedings is half a century in the past. The Lords Journal is known to date from 1461 and is compiled, like the Commons Journal, from the daily minutes of proceedings.

The character of the Journals of both Houses of Parliament is very similar to that of the Congressional Journals. There is no verbatim narrative (except on extraordinary occasions such as the reading of ceremonial messages by the Speaker in the Chair). The formal versions of committee reports are included—that a bill has been reported with or without amendment, or recording a resolution to which a general committee has come; that a bill has been read a second or third time, including intermediate procedural events such as closure, attempted or successful; that a resolution (of which the complete text is given) has been come to, for example approving secondary legislation or programming a

bill; that the House divided on a particular question, with details of the numbers voting—not names, except those of the tellers; that specified amendments have been made,
rejected, or withdrawn in the course of a bill's career in Committee of the whole House;
and that public petitions have been received. Papers laid on the Table by statute or by
order of the House and the fact that select committees have reported are also recorded.
The (theoretical) informality of Question Time in the Commons (see page 337) meant
that until very recently no mention was made in the Votes and Proceedings of Questions
or indeed of statements. Strict procedural purity has yielded to, if not readability, at
least the conveying of relevant information.

Reporting of parliamentary debates began to flourish in the eighteenth century, when
one of those employed to take notes in the Commons was Dr Samuel Johnson. Johnson's
output seems to have consisted largely of what he wished had been said—he later boasted
that he never gave the Whigs the better of the arguments—though it may be hoped that
others were more scrupulous. By the time Charles Dickens the novelist entered the reporters' gallery in the following century,[27] parliamentary reporting was much improved. The
series of reported debates subsequently undertaken exclusively by Luke Hansard and his
company (originally one of several such enterprises) did not however receive public funding till 1878 and was not officially taken under Parliament's wing until 1909.

A complete verbatim account of what is said in either Chamber of Parliament, at
Lords Grand Committees, and at sittings in Westminster Hall is published in the Official
Report (Hansard)—one for the Lords and another for the Commons—appearing in hard
copy and electronically the following day. In addition to speeches in debate and the
exchanges at Question Time, Hansard contains answers given to written questions and
(in the Commons) written statements. A separate Hansard appears for each sitting of a
public bill committee. The record of Lords Grand Committees is included with the
Hansard of proceedings in the House. It is not the practice of Hansard to record (except
by the cryptic reference '[*Interruption*]') remarks interjected by Members who do not
have the floor, if they are not taken up by the Member who is addressing the House.[28]

The Lords and Commons Hansards are prepared by staff of the respective Houses.
What is said in debate is recorded in direct speech, and is a verbatim account though
omitting redundancies, repetitions, and correcting obvious mistakes. The rules admit a
limited degree of correction, principally to put right inadvertent errors of fact by ministers or others providing information to the House, but there is generally no question of
any Lord, Member, or minister adding to the record material not actually spoken in
debate, or being allowed to 'revise and extend' his or her remarks. The principal exception to the rule is the printing in the Lords Hansard of important ministerial statements
made in the Commons.

The reporting of proceedings in select committees of both Houses is separate and is
the contractual responsibility of a company independent of the House, whose connection
with the House goes back two centuries.

The first debates in the Congress beginning in 1789 were published in condensed form
in the Annals of Congress. The Congressional Globe began in 1833 and continued until
1873, when the Congressional Record was first published. The Congressional Record,
which is printed each day when the Senate or House is in session, consists of sections
devoted solely to the proceedings of the Senate and to the proceedings of the House
respectively. There is also a section entitled 'Extensions of Remarks' for the inclusion of

matters presented by Senators and Representatives for printing but which are not part of the proceedings of either body and are not necessarily concerned with legislation. In practice, this section consists primarily of material inserted by Representatives, as Senators' remarks are more often included in the body of the Senate Record. There is also a section entitled 'Daily Digest', which is printed in the back of each day's Record as a summary of committee meetings of both Houses and of action taken by the two Houses, with references to the appropriate pages in the body of the Record.

The Congressional Record is governed by statutory provisions and by both joint and supplemental separate rules as to its format and content.[29] Control over the arrangement and style of the Record is vested in the Joint Committee on Printing. Neither the Speaker nor the House may order changes in the type size or printing style without the approval of the Joint Committee.

Despite statutory and joint rules intended to enforce common discipline in both Houses, current practices of the two Houses diverge widely with respect to the reporting of their respective proceedings and the inclusion of additional matter. At the beginning of the 104th Congress, House rules were amended to require a substantially verbatim account of remarks made during debate to be published in the Record, subject only to technical, grammatical, and typographical corrections authorized by the Member making the remarks. Unparliamentary remarks may be deleted only by permission or order of the House, and these verbatim requirements are explicitly made standards of official conduct.

Prior to that time to 1994, both Houses followed Joint Committee on Printing rules requiring 'bulleting' of inserted matter in the Record, where no part of the remarks was actually uttered in debate. A black dot bullet would so indicate at the beginning of the inserted matter. Members could revise their remarks which were actually uttered in a substantive way if permitted by either House to do so, and those revisions would not be distinctively shown in the Record. Currently in the House under the verbatim requirement imposed in 1995, any substantive change is shown in a distinctive type style subsequent to, and not in lieu of, the remarks actually uttered. In no event are the actually uttered remarks removable by the Member. Only if remarks are ruled unparliamentary by the Chair, can uttered remarks be deleted and then only if the House so determines by unanimous consent or motion. The uttered remarks complained of are reported to the House by the Reading Clerk. If ruled out of order and deleted from the Record at the point where uttered, they remain in the Record in the context of the Chair's ruling for precedential purposes to document the basis for the ruling (pages 190–1 contains a more detailed explanation of these procedures). Because a departure from the verbatim requirement in the House may be treated as an ethics issue, Members have been reluctant since 1995 to revise their uttered remarks in a substantive way under the modern practice. The Speaker has even publicly instructed the Official Reporters of Debates to adhere strictly to the verbatim requirement of House rules. Included in that admonition has been the Speaker's ruling that no remarks uttered by a Member not 'under recognition' by the Chair, even though in fact audibly uttered, will be printed in the Record. Such unrecognized interruptions—for example, where the Member under recognition has not yielded to another Member or where utterances are made beyond the time for which recognized by the Chair—are not considered proper debate and are not transcribed by the Official Reporters of Debates. This practice generally reflects the non-inclusion in Hansard of remarks uttered from a 'sedentary position' in the House of Commons (see above).

Unlike the Senate, no colloquys between two or more House Members may be inserted in the Record as if actually spoken or even in a distinctive type style, but must either be actually uttered verbatim or must appear as separate statements and not as colloquys. In this respect the Senate is far more tolerant of insertions of colloquys in the Record 'as if actually uttered'. On a recent occasion (21 December 2005) an eight-page colloquy involving several Senators on the issue of lawsuits brought by enemy combatants in Federal courts was inserted in the body of the Senate Record as if actually spoken, even including such exchanges as 'I see that my colleague, the senior Senator from South Carolina, is also on the floor', 'If I might interrupt...', and 'Mr President, I see that we are nearing the end of our allotted time'. That colloquy was subsequently cited in court proceedings as legislative history showing the intent of Congress in a case contesting the constitutionality of military tribunals, and was only subsequently disclosed in press accounts to have been a wholly inserted 'colloquy' with little value as 'legislative history'. Despite that obvious embarrassment, the Senate took no action to correct the Record or to more strictly enforce a verbatim standard.

In addition, while the Senate has supplemental rules requiring material non-germane to pending Senate business to be 'bulleted', that requirement is routinely ignored by Senators' or leadership staff's private requests made to the Record Clerk to carry such material 'live' in the Senate proceedings. Also, Senators are privately permitted to revise their remarks upon request to the Record clerks. The Senate Procedure Manual on page 652 reads as follows: 'A Senator in making a revision of his remarks is not supposed to make any substantial changes therein. (He has no rule of the Senate for guidance.)' An egregious example of 'leave to print' in the Senate includes the 'deeming' of measures to have been considered and passed by unanimous consent—often several measures under one unanimous consent request—together with insertions of statements and colloquys by Senators 'as if spoken'. Thus the Senate Record itself does not even show such deemings to have occurred by unanimous consent, but only carries the deemed proceedings as if they had in fact occurred. The only notice to the observer in such unanimous consent situations is that the number of the bill is recited by the Senator making the request and the title of the bill is read by the Clerk, but not the text of the bill or amendments deemed adopted thereto. Nevertheless all these deviations from strict rules on verbatim reporting are permitted by unanimous consent or by private requests from individual Senators in order to facilitate Senate business and to accommodate absent Senators. Beyond televised coverage, observers of such Senate proceedings are left to read the Congressional Record the following day to discover what measures may have passed and the reasons therefore. Information immediately available internally to the Senate includes unofficial lists and summaries in the cloakrooms and an electronic website accessible only within the Senate.

The Congressional Record contains the text of all measures voted on in the two Houses, as well as the debates thereon, and in this form is markedly different from Hansard which includes only the parliamentary debates and ministerial answers to written questions, and the text of motions and amendments, but not the text of statutory measures themselves. Absent authority to 'revise and extend' by unanimous consent, Hansard, unlike the Congressional Record, does not include remarks not actually uttered or any other inserted extraneous material, and is for that reason a more accurate indicator of actual proceedings.

In the US House, the insertion of any extraneous material beyond two Record pages in length requires House approval of a preliminary estimate of cost and insertion 'notwithstanding that stated estimate'. Members may include statistical and other supporting material as extensions of their own remarks if logically an expansion thereof and not in the form of other supporting documentation emanating from another source (for example, articles or speeches of another person) without those extensions being considered 'extraneous' and therefore requiring an estimate of additional cost.

The printed format of the Congressional Record (since 1989) and of Hansard are available in electronic form to readers on the calendar day following utterance or insertion. A statute enacted in 1993 requires the Superintendent of Documents to 'provide a system of online access to the Congressional Record'.[30]

Media coverage

The first effort to link the US Congress and broadcasting occurred in 1922 when Rep. Brennan introduced a resolution to allow radio coverage of House proceedings. The measure was not adopted, and not until the late 1940s was the idea revived. Television, having arrived as a mass medium by then, was allowed by the Senate in 1948 to cover hearings of the Senate Armed Services Committee. Since few Americans had television receivers in 1948, it was not until the early 1950s that televised Congressional hearings generated any viewer interest. Two televised hearings during the 1950s in the Senate drew public attention. Hearings conducted by the Senate Special Committee to Investigate Organized Crime in Interstate Commerce brought the faces and words of notorious mobsters into US homes via network television. Then the hearings of a Senate Committee on Government Operations subcommittee investigating alleged communist infiltration of the US Armed Forces, known as the Army–McCarthy hearings chaired by Wisconsin Senator Joseph McCarthy, drew national attention.

Two decades later, in 1973, the Senate Select Committee on Presidential Campaign Activities conducted what became known as the Watergate hearings. Evidence of misdeeds by President Richard Nixon led the next year to House Judiciary Committee hearings on Articles of Impeachment. Nearly all public deliberations of both of these committees were televised gavel-to-gavel by votes of the respective Houses. The House had amended its rules effective in 1971 to permit committees to televise their hearings, and three years later on 22 July 1974 extended that authority to coverage of all committee meetings as well, on the eve of the Judiciary Committee's meetings to mark up Articles of Impeachment of President Nixon.

Serious attention to television coverage of actual Congressional floor proceedings began in 1973 with the formation of the Joint Committee on Congressional Operations, which was charged with examination of means by which Congress could better communicate with the American public. The House responded eight years sooner than the Senate in the actual implementation of gavel-to-gavel coverage of proceedings.

Anticipating an impeachment trial of President Nixon in 1974, the two Houses made tentative provisions for the first live television coverage of their respective proceedings. Just prior to Nixon's resignation in August, the House adopted a resolution reported from the Committee on Rules permitting television and radio coverage of floor impeachment proceedings. The Senate following the resignation tabled a resolution reported from its Committee on Rules and Administration which would have permitted coverage of a Senate trial. Several months after Nixon's resignation made a trial unnecessary, the Senate took advantage of those preparations to telecast Nelson Rockefeller's 19 December swearing in as Vice President—the first coverage of Senate floor proceedings.

Prior to the 95th Congress, the rules and precedents of the House did not permit public radio and television broadcasts of House proceedings, including committee sessions (except for anticipated impeachment proceedings in August 1974 which never materialized). In 1977, the House adopted a resolution directing the Committee on Rules to investigate the impact on the safety, dignity, and integrity of House proceedings, of a test authorized by the Speaker under his general control over the hall of the House for the audio-visual broadcast of House proceedings within the Capitol and Office Buildings. Shortly thereafter the House adopted a resolution reported from the Committee on Rules to provide a system of closed-circuit viewing of House proceedings and for orderly development of a broadcasting system. The House quickly decided the contentious question of coverage (by in-house staff or by network cameras) by enacting a limitation in the Legislative Branch Appropriation Act for 1979 providing that 'no funds in this bill may be used to implement a system for televising and broadcasting the proceedings of the House pursuant to H.Res.866 under which the cameras in the Chamber purchased by the House are controlled and operated by persons not in the employ of the House'. The networks had lobbied to be permitted to provide the coverage, concerned that control by the Speaker would minimize network flexibility on camera angles and placement. Speaker O'Neill's endorsement of that limitation on funding reflected, however, the proper concern that only 'proceedings' of the House be responsibly covered, and not side-bar events or conversations in the Chamber not officially part of those proceedings.

Under House Rule V, the Speaker directs the unedited audio and visual broadcasting and recording of all the proceedings of the House, including periods of voting. Broadcasts are made by closed-circuit television in House offices and have been made available to the news media and to cable television systems. The C-Span public service television company has agreed to carry (by satellite signal financed by cable companies and available to all carriers) all House and since 1986 all Senate proceedings on separate cable channels, although its coverage has in recent years been embellished by descriptive captioning and simultaneous split screen coverage of editorial analysis or other public events. Broadcasts made available under the rule may not be used for political or commercial purposes. Thus incumbent Members are not permitted to use televised proceedings to promote their candidacies.

In 1977, the Senate took a half-step toward media coverage by allowing radio broadcasts of the 1978 debates on the Panama Canal Treaty. A rules change was introduced in 1981 by the Majority Leader to authorize permanent live coverage of Senate floor proceedings. That position was opposed by influential Senators who argued that it would lead to more, longer, and less relevant speeches, to more posturing by Senators, and to even less useful debate and efficient legislating, and that Senate proceedings with many intermittent quorum calls were less conducive to continuous coverage than were House proceedings. By early 1986, Senate leaders were concerned that the lack of television coverage was transforming the Senate into the nation's forgotten legislative body. House

Members were becoming more visible than Senators to their constituents. Thus the Senate voted to begin a three-month trial period, with live national coverage to begin on 2 June 1986. Senate coverage has not been discontinued since that date.

A positive result has been increased access to ongoing floor debates in Senate and House offices, allowing Members and staff to monitor them and to better prepare for participation. Some would contend that the quality of speeches has improved in both Houses with the advent of television and with utilization of charts and graphs to support arguments. Others would counter that spontaneous and interactive debate has been adversely impacted, as Members are focused on addressing a television audience (including evening news segments) and are less inclined to yield to each other for full debate. This trend is discussed in greater detail at pages 155–6 and 163–8.

Pursuant to his authority to control broadcast coverage, Speaker O'Neill directed the Clerk in the 98th Congress on 10 May 1984 to immediately implement periodic wide-angle television coverage of all 'special order' speeches at the end of legislative business with captions at the bottom of the screen indicating that legislative business had been completed. That episode and the resulting recriminations in the House are discussed in greater detail in the chapter on Procedural Basics at page 155. The Speaker's order of wide-angle coverage reflected an awareness of the increasing influence that televised coverage of House proceedings was having on the American viewing public. He defended his order on the ground that viewers had been misled to perceive the simulated 'debates' to constitute actual business of the House. The wide-angle coverage of special order speeches, often showing an otherwise empty Chamber, lasted through subsequent Congresses until the 103rd Congress in 1993, when it was replaced by a policy of Speaker Foley which directed that television coverage would not 'pan' the Chamber during such post-legislative business, but would be accompanied by a caption run at the bottom of the screen to show that legislative business had been completed for the day (that is, that the viewing audience should not expect a large number of Members to be present in the Chamber). Currently, special order coverage periodically includes camera angles depicting all the Members engaging in debate but does not emphasize the emptiness of the Chamber.

Generally, televised coverage of House and Senate proceedings has reduced the spontaneity of debates, and the willingness of Members to debate with each other directly. Instead, Members increasingly use prepared speeches together with visual aids such as charts, graphs, and photographs to make a debating point to a television audience. Together with the drastically increased use of special order resolutions from the Committee on Rules which limit the amendment process and which restrict 'pro forma' amendments so that time may not be separately sought by opposing Members, television has had a negative impact on the quality of debates and on the likelihood that debates may influence votes. In addition, so-called 'one-minute speeches' at the beginning of the legislative day, and 'special order speeches' following legislative business until midnight, are not always debates between Members but rather represent political messages intended to be communicated to the viewing public. One-minute speeches are often staged by leadership 'theme teams' at the beginning of each day whereby Members are recognized to deliver partisan party messages which may have no relationship to the agenda for that day and which, if unduly personalized, set an unfortunate tone for the up-coming business. Prior to televised proceedings, 'special order speeches' following legislative business (the equivalent of adjournment debates in the UK) were fewer and did not involve the use of visual aids, since Members could insert their remarks in the Record and did not need to take up the time of the House, and when conducted were sometimes real debates among Members.

House rules now require and do not merely permit all committee meetings and hearings to be available for radio and television broadcasting, unless closed to the public, if a television network (usually C-Span) wishes to provide the coverage. A majority of House and Senate committees have their own internet computer websites which separately convey their proceedings with robotic coverage provided by committee staff rather than by accredited camera technicians. As a component of this coverage, those committees sometimes provide in-house coverage which does not normally extend beyond the precincts of the House Office Buildings.

There has not been the same criticism of televised coverage of committee hearings and meetings as there has been of the loss of spontaneity of plenary House and Senate floor proceedings, since in committees the rules of procedure are not as easily utilized to prevent individual Members from meaningful participation. Committees are not as free to adopt restrictive rules by motion-governing proceedings as is the House, and committee members generally employ the 'five-minute rule' either in the interrogation of witnesses or at the amendment stage to more fully participate in proceedings, whether or not the proceedings are televised.

The constant '24/7' electronic media competition for instant political news reporting and analysis and Members' responses to those pressures have compelled Members and Senators to enhance their office press capabilities in recent Congresses as network, cable, and local stations compete for instant information. Also, the use of television interviews and advertisements to wage political campaigns, and the cost to Members' campaign funds of advertising, encourage Members to actively seek free media coverage wherever possible. The inevitable posturing that results from such media coverage detracts from the quality and the importance of committee and floor debates in decision making. While the prohibition in House rules against the use of televised House and committee proceedings for political purposes discourages direct Member use of House proceedings in political advertisements, it encourages some Members either to posture during debate, assuming televised news coverage of their remarks, or to respond off the floor via news coverage and to use that coverage for political purposes.

The entry of television cameras into Parliament (in the Lords in 1985 and the Commons in 1989) has not had the far-reaching effect of the televising of Congress (page 103). Whether recent years have witnessed a significant fall in the standard of debate is a matter of opinion, but even if that were so it would be hard to pin the blame principally on the cameras. Indeed, apprehension about the stifling effect of cameras on the spontaneity of debate has turned out to be misplaced. Whatever view is taken of the standard of debate, its conversational tone has survived and the understanding that debate ought to be an exchange of ideas is still alive even if as an aspiration from which performance falls short. What has probably diminished attendance in the Chamber is not television but the uncertainty of being able to speak to one's amendments in programmed proceedings on legislation. The only behavioural change has been 'doughnutting', when Members deliberately place themselves in shot around the colleague who has the floor and try to give the impression that their rapt attention and supportive cries represent the response of the whole House. (The ingenious phenomenon of reverse-doughnutting, as colleagues are seen ostentatiously to leave the immediate vicinity of the Member called, is less frequent.) Nor in Parliament could the occupant of the Chair have done what Speaker Tip O'Neill did in 1984 to alter the kind of shots permitted (page 168). Editorial rules of coverage are under the control of a committee in each UK House. The rules are intended to ensure a 'full, balanced, fair and accurate account of proceedings', which respects the dignity of the Houses and presents Parliament as a working body and not a palace of varieties. Nothing which is not a proceeding may be broadcast—disturbances in the gallery, for example—and there are rules about filming Members other than those in possession of the floor. Guidelines further guard the use which can be made of excerpts from the tapes of parliamentary debates. All these are subject to the oversight of an officer of both Houses.

The signal is produced by an independent operator contracted to a private company on the board of which Parliament and broadcasting organizations are represented, and which is chaired by a nominee of the Commons Speaker. The operating company provides the signal to television companies. There is also a closed-circuit broadcast within the Palace. The public sessions of committees may be broadcast live or recorded without the specific agreement of the committee, except in the case of the Standards and Privileges Committee.

Working papers

The daily working papers of the Commons are complex. As a simple guide, however, they are divided into those printed on blue paper, which are notices given of or relating to business to be taken on a future day, and those on white paper, which are either current business or records of proceedings.

The Order of Business (on white paper) contains details of the bills or other orders which the House is to consider that day, the questions for oral and written answer, and details of committee meetings. Forthcoming business is added, that intended for debate in the following week or so with dates for its consideration, some simply listed without a settled date. Amendments to bills which are under consideration appear with the Order of Business. With some exceptions, such as Urgent Questions, raising matters of privilege and ministerial oral statements (pages 156, 500), no substantive business can be taken if notice has not been given in the House's papers.

On blue paper are to be found the Questions to ministers and amendments to bills offered in Public Bill Committees or on the floor of the House, which have been tabled the preceding day and are for consideration on a day later than that on which they first appear in print. Among this category are Early Day Motions, which are texts tabled by Members with a view to drawing the matter to the attention of colleagues and the public rather than securing time for debate. Many touch on issues of broad concern, such as the ethics of animal research or the deployment of the armed forces: others raise constituency issues, congratulating the local soccer club or opposing the closure of a hospital department.

Lords business papers begin with the business scheduled for the day of issue, and continue by setting out business arranged for specified future days, motions, and

Questions tabled but for which no day has been assigned, Questions unanswered beyond the normal period for reply, committee meetings, the Minutes of the previous day, and bills and statutory instruments in progress.

Thomas Jefferson acknowledged the importance of order respecting papers by the admonition in his *Manual* that 'the Clerk is to let no journals, records, accounts or papers be taken from the table or out of his custody'. Despite the advent of the electronic age, the rules, practices, and traditions of both US Houses require 'official papers' which certify to the authenticity of actions taken. The Clerk of the House and the Secretary of the Senate are the elected officers responsible for the accurate preparation and transmittal of the official papers which must accompany every message between the two Houses. As in the UK Parliament, the two Houses communicate and coordinate their activities by sending formal messages to each other. Despite depictions of those actions by televised proceedings and electronic facsimiles, these signed messages constitute the sole source of official information regarding actions taken by the other House. On rare occasion, anticipatory or 'deemed' House or Senate action is by unanimous consent made contingent upon receipt by the Clerk or Secretary of a message from the other House transmitting the official papers in a prescribed form in order to avoid waiting for the message (such as 'deeming' a bill not yet passed by the Senate in an amended form to be sent to conference upon receipt by the Clerk of a message to that effect). For the most part action awaits, as it should, actual receipt by messenger. Present rules permit the receipt of messages by the appropriate agents for either House whether or not that House is in session. The refusal of one House to receive a message from the other is a breach of comity and may present a question of privilege. A message from one House requesting the return of official papers in order to correct an error is presented as a matter of privilege both in the House making the request and in the other House from which the return is requested, and may be disposed of either by unanimous consent or by motion. Such a request is not privileged, however, where the official papers are correct but rather a substantive change is contemplated—it not being a proper substitute for a motion to reconsider which can only be made while the originating House is in possession of the papers.

Prior to passage or adoption in either House, a bill or resolution will not bear any signature other than that of its original sponsor. The Clerk retains the original signed copy of all introduced measures, and printed copies are sent to committees. Committee reports accompanying bills and resolutions are not required to be accompanied by a covering letter or signed by the chairman or other Member filing them with the Clerk, but the official 'engrossing' copy of that measure, as amended or not from its introduction, is stamped by the Clerk upon its filing and remains the official copy establishing the basis or eventual printing as a House- or Senate-passed measure. Additional identical copies of accompanying reports are simultaneously filed for transmittal to the Government Printing Office for printing as House or Senate reports. Once a measure passes the House or Senate, it is printed as an 'engrossment' on distinctive coloured paper—blue for the House and white for the Senate, reflecting all the amendments adopted prior to final passage, and any technical and conforming changes the clerks may have been authorized to include by unanimous consent order of either House.

Amendments between the Houses are likewise printed as engrossments, either as numbered amendments changing portions of text or as amendments in the nature of a substitute striking out all after the enacting clause and inserting new language. Such amendments are certified by the Clerk or Secretary and accompany the original measure in messages between the Houses for all subsequent proceedings.

Conference reports represent compromises recommended by managers of the two Houses and submitted to each House in an effort to resolve differences. Unlike measures reported from standing committees, they are signed by at least a majority of the managers appointed by the presiding officers of each House and those signature sheets accompany the other official papers for final action in both Houses. Original signatures are essential to conference reports because they are the only evidence of final approval in each conference committee, where each House has one vote on final endorsement of the report and where votes are not otherwise recorded or dispositive of the resolution of separate issues committed to conference. These working papers are printed as reports and also in the Congressional Record, and are accompanied by joint statements of the conference managers which are similarly signed by a majority of the conferees from each House.

Two recent instances demonstrate the importance of the sanctity of official papers and the possibility that a determined and misguided leadership can subvert or compromise this basic institutional protection to achieve a political end (even while remaining subject to a subsequent collateral ethics challenge as a question of privilege). At the end of the first session of the 109th Congress in December 2005, the Majority Leader of the Senate, accompanied by the Speaker of the House, importuned the staff director of the House Appropriations Committee (who was about to file in the House a conference report containing the requisite number of signatures) to insert language into the report which had not been agreed to by the conferees when they signed the signature sheets, and without the knowledge and consent of the conferees. The conference report subsequently was considered and adopted in the House on the same day pursuant to a special order reported from the Rules Committee waiving all points of order. In the Senate, no point of order was raised and the conference report was adopted and signed into law by the President.[31]

The second irregularity occurred when the House adopted a conference report on the 'Deficit Reduction Act' which read, in pertinent part, '13' relating to a Medicare provision. Two days later, the Senate, by operation of a rule permitting 'extraneous matter' in a budget reconciliation conference report to be removed on a point of order, rejected the conference report and instead amended the original House-passed amendment to the Senate bill, intending that its amendment should read, in pertinent part, '13', just as the House-passed conference report had read. By inadvertence, the Senate's engrossment of its amendment read, in pertinent part, '36' (having the effect of reducing the Medicare cost by $2 billion). The best evidence of the content of the Senate amendment is the engrossment of that amendment in the official papers in the Senate's resulting message to the House. Therefore the Senate's final action became, in pertinent part, '36' as it was messaged to the House. The Senate did not ask the House to return the papers so that it could correct its depiction of its final action. The House, its leadership having knowledge of the error in the Senate message, nevertheless utilized the Rules Committee to report a special order concurring in the Senate amendment which it had in its possession, and therefore its final action read, in pertinent part, '36'. This was done in the House to avoid a separate vote on any request by the Senate for return of the message, or subsequently on any concurrent resolution correcting the final enrolment. The final version passed by a 216:214 vote. The Senate Enrolling Clerk in preparing the final enrolled parchment then changed the number '36' back to '13' without the authority of either House, as would normally have been ordered by a concurrent resolution correcting the enrolment. Rather, the Senate Secretary's inexplicable preparation of the final version was then certified as true and presented for signature by the Speaker and President pro tempore, and then by the President into law. This sequence reflected the Secretary's determination to correct the error which she had earlier committed but which had not been properly corrected by a return of official papers or by a concurrent resolution.

A collateral challenge to this impropriety was made by the House Minority Leader in the form of a resolution raising a question of the privileges of the House, also alleging in the preamble the earlier impropriety of leadership change in the text of the conference report prior to filing. The resolution called on the Committee on Standards to investigate 'the abuse of power surrounding the inaccuracies in the process and enrolment of the Budget Reconciliation legislation cleared for the President on 1 February 2006'. The resolution was laid on the table without debate by a straight party-line vote on 16 February 2006.

There followed a series of lawsuits filed in Federal courts, including one brought by Minority Members of the House, challenging the enactment of a variety of provisions in that Deficit Reduction Act on the ground that both Houses did not pass the bill in the same form as required by Article I, section 7 of the Constitution. In defence of the validity of the enactment of that law, the Justice Department cited the Supreme Court case of *Field v Clark* 143 US 649 (1892) for the proposition that the courts will not as a matter of separation of powers look behind the signatures which certify the true enrolment of the measure. At this writing, several of those lawsuits have been dismissed by Federal district courts, including *Public Citizen v Clerk of the U.S. Dist. Ct. for D.C.* 451 F Supp. 109 (DDC 2006). That opinion cited *Field* for the proposition that under the 'enrolled bill rule' the legislative process must have some clearly defined endpoint—an authoritative statement of what was agreed to by each House of Congress. The enrolled bill constitutes such a statement, as indicated by the signatures of the certifying officers. Plaintiff attempted to limit the scope of *Field* by arguing that the enrolled bill rule merely excluded Congressional Journals as appropriate evidence for deciding bicameral passage issues. However, the dismissing district courts considered the language of that case to be much broader, essentially incorporating any proceedings, reports, or bill drafts prior to the final version authenticated as the enrolled bill. Thus the court reaffirmed that the enrolled bill is 'complete and unimpeachable' evidence of the Acts of each Chamber. In weighing the relative probabilities of violating the bicameral requirement, the court reasoned that 'the dangers of opening the door to evidence of unknown reliability' were far greater than the risk that the enrolled bill, for whatever reason, did not reflect the true intentions of Congress. In *United States v Munoz-Flores* 495 US 385 (1990) the Supreme Court refused to overrule or significantly narrow the holding in *Field*. The court noted that even the Congressional Record, a comprehensive source of Congressional deliberation, was not free from ambiguity. In short, the court concluded that the rationales for the enrolled bill rule 'remain valid today'.

The rules and practices of both Houses continue to require printing of measures at various stages of consideration. Nevertheless most documents are currently prepared for printing in electronic format so as to expedite availability. To date, however, the rules of neither House reflect alternatives which would permit electronic transmittal and availability of bills and reports to suffice to permit consideration within certain time layover requirements. That is left to the Rules Committee in recommending waivers of points of order (based on some electronic availability). Where the Government Printing Office is responsible for printing errors, it assumes the cost of reprinting the bill or report as a 'star print'. Where the error is that of the sponsor or committee staff, however, and is shown in the print, it must be corrected by amendment. Technically, all measures when filed become the property of the House and, when received and numbered, cannot be withdrawn from its possession.

House Rule VIII provides that upon notification to the House that a judicial or administrative subpoena or judicial order for the production or disclosure of any document relating to the official functions of the House has been received by a Member, officer, or employee, and upon a determination that its issuance is a proper exercise of court jurisdiction, is material and relevant, and is consistent with the privileges and rights of the House, there shall then be compliance with the subpoena by the Member, officer, or employee served. Under no circumstances may transcripts of executive sessions be disclosed or copied. If that person is advised by General Counsel that the privileges of the House or of the Member prevent production, the Speaker informs the House of that fact. This rule, originally added in 1981, serves as a replacement for what was previously an ad hoc response to each service of process, and presumes that the Clerk will furnish certified copies of the requested documents upon determination of propriety and absent a resolution of the House to the contrary. The establishment of the Office of General Counsel, coupled with the adoption of Rule VIII, has in modern practice streamlined the process for responses to requests for House records and has minimized although not eliminated the likelihood of ad hoc responses by the House to individual requests.

The Senate has not amended its rules to provide for an overall procedure for responding to subpoenas for Senate records. There—with fewer Members, officers, and employees—responses remain basically ad hoc with the Office of Senate Legal Counsel advising as to whether the Senate should adopt a privileged resolution authorizing compliance in each particular case. Most often, such business is accomplished by unanimous consent in the 'wrap-up business' at the end of each legislative day with bipartisan leadership approval and does not necessitate separate consideration and voting.

In Parliament, the prohibition in Article IX of the Bill of Rights 1689—that proceedings in Parliament are not to be 'impeached or questioned' in any other court (see pages 484–5)—would be the basis on which court orders for production of papers would be resisted, unless what was intended was simply reference without challenge. When recently the subject matter of the material sought was relevant to a commercial case, however, the Commons agreed to make available to parties to an action certain papers of select committees responsible for administrative matters, though they otherwise fell within the definition of proceedings.

Since 1880 the House of Representatives has had a rule archiving 'non-current' records of the House (as distinguished from those of an individual Member). In 1989 the rule (VII) was amended into its current form to provide for systematic archiving and retrieval of such records. It requires the transfer of all 'non-current' committee records from the chairman of each committee and each House officer to the Clerk at the end of each Congress for delivery to the Archivist of the United States for preservation. Such transferred records remain available for public use if previously available to the public. If investigative or other hearing records have been received in closed committee sessions or are personal data relating to a specific living person and would be an unwarranted invasion of personal privacy, they remain inaccessible for fifty years from date of existence or sooner if ordered by the House. All other non-public archived House records remain inaccessible for thirty years. The Clerk of the House is authorized to make further determinations of non-availability if in the public interest or to protect the privileges of the House, subject to an order of the House or retrieval by order of the relevant committee. Arrangements regarding both Houses at Westminster are very similar.

The Senate has no comparable rule on archiving and retrieval, considering itself a 'continuing body' with ongoing committee functions and relying upon ad hoc committee determinations of 'non-current' status for archiving. The Senate can consider privileged resolutions to address particular cases and requests as the need arises.

Public access to official information of all kinds has been a matter of great concern in recent years. In 1966, Congress fashioned various statutory arrangements for realizing public access to Executive branch information. It was believed that Congress made much of its own deliberations and proceedings subject to public observation, largely published its records, and that Congress was otherwise constitutionally authorized to engage in information restriction. For example, the Constitution explicitly permits each House of Congress discretion to keep portions of its Journal of proceedings secret, as well as disallowing in the Speech or Debate Clause the questioning of Members of Congress, including staff, in 'any other place' regarding official business. By extension, the combined constitutional protections of Congressional secrecy at the discretion of each House, the empowerment of rule making with respect to committee records, and the Speech or Debate privilege, enabled Congress to refrain from legislating public access to Congressional documents, and did not make the Freedom of Information Act applicable to the Legislative branch. The Executive departments and agencies were the principal object of government information access reform laws. The Congressional Accountability Act enacted in 1996 by its terms acknowledged that, while attempting to legislate against employment discrimination by Members of Congress, it could not permit public access to information in contradiction of the Speech or Debate clause.

The UK Freedom of Information Act 2000 defined Parliament as a public authority subject to the provisions of the Act, save where release of information would infringe parliamentary privilege, inhibit the giving of advice, or prejudice the effective conduct of public affairs. Lords and Members holding information in their individual capacity are not caught, but the administration of both Houses is within the scope of the statute. Before the introduction of the bill for the Act, a series of parliamentary committees insisted that Parliament should not be 'a statute-free zone' and should be covered so far as its administrative functions were concerned. The relevant authorities in both Houses released figures for the take-up of allowances by individual Members voluntarily in 2004, but the move satisfied neither Members, who felt that without explanation and understanding of the system they risked being pilloried for profligacy, and enthusiasts for freedom of information who demanded further and better particulars. A private Member's bill was introduced in 2006–7 to remove Parliament from the list of public authorities and exempt Members' correspondence from the principal Act. The bill made progress but failed to reach the statute book. There followed, a year or so later, initially by leak, the publication of the details of allowances claims, which so overwhelmed Members, politically and personally (see page 142).

The number of requests dealt with under the Freedom of Information Act has grown appreciably in recent years, principally driven by interest in Members' allowances, from 141 in financial year 2005–6 to 173 in 2006–7 and 2,463 in 2007–8. To date, only a handful of exemption certificates have been given, most of them in the area of privilege.

Notes

1. 3 US Code 19.
2. A scholarly detailed discussion of these respective modern roles of the Speaker and Speakers pro tempore is contained in The Cannon Centenary Conference: *The Changing Nature of the Speakership*, held on 12 November 2003 (House Doc 108–204) and was occasioned by the 100th anniversary of the defining speakership of Joseph Cannon which began in 1903.
3. H Doc 108–204.
4. *The Governance of Britain*, Cm 7170, para 102.
5. Select Committee on Modernisation of the House of Commons, First Report 2007–8 HC 81.
6. In reality, it sits in a large committee room off the Hall.
7. Second Report 2004–5 HC 465-I para 83.
8. S Doc 62–872, 'The Supply Bills'.
9. *Hinds' Precedents*, vol ii, sect 1500.
10. Speaker's jurisdictional statement of 3 January 1991, Rec p 64.
11. 27 July 2000, Rec p 16565.
12. W. S. Gilbert, in the comic opera *Iolanthe* first produced in 1882, satirized such noble political gesturing: 'When Wellington thrashed Bonaparte, as every child can tell | The House of peers throughout the war | Did nothing in particular | And did it very well.'
13. First Special Report 2005–6 HL 189, HC 1151 para 8.
14. These details ignore Lords who have leave of absence. Twenty-three Law Lords were members until the Supreme Court legislation came into force. There are twenty-six archbishops and bishops of the Church of England.
15. Joint Committee on the Conventions First Special Report 2005–6 HL 265-I, HC 1212-I paras 35 and 95.
16. Fourth Report HC 2002–3 165-I para 108.
17. The Committee subsequently called an appointment to the MPC into question, but the government refused to take any notice: Treasury Committee Seventh Report 1999–2000 HC 520I and Seventh Special Report 1999–2000 HC 859. In 2007, following what was called an Introductory Hearing, the Science and Technology Committee expressed reservations about the chairman of a Research Council, who had however been in office for some time (Eighth Report from the Science and Technology Committee 2006–7 HC 746).
18. First Report 1999–2000 HC 300 para 24: and in particular in this context see First Report 2002–3 HC 558 para 13.
19. Cm 7170.
20. Public Administration Committee Sixth Special Report 2007–8 HC 515.
21. See Public Administration Committee Third Report (2007–8) HC 152 and Liaison Committee First Report (2007–8) HC 384.
22. PL 109-55: 2 USC 8.
23. K.A. Bradshaw and D.A.M. Pring, *Parliament and Congress* (1971), 11.
24. Ibid 12.
25. Maurice Duverger, *Political Parties* (1964 edn), 210.
26. Not all Members' staff work in the Palace of Westminster.
27. Sir Courtenay Ilbert, Clerk of the House at the beginning of the twentieth century, recorded his belief that Dickens contributed more to the House than accurate shorthand. The rule of anticipation,

that a less effective proceeding should not be allowed to take place if the effect would be to block off a more effective one, was—Ilbert claimed—first recorded in Dickens's novel *Little Dorrit*.

28. The most famous intervention not recorded happened the day before war broke out, Saturday 2 September 1939. Though help had been promised to Poland, no announcement was made by the Conservative Prime Minister of any ultimatum to Berlin. Another round of appeasement was suspected. As Arthur Greenwood rose to speak for the Labour Opposition, a right-wing anti-appeaser (accounts vary as to who it was) shouted across the Chamber to roars of Conservative support, 'Speak for England, Arthur.' On another occasion, the House rocked with laughter at an aside of Winston Churchill not found in Hansard. In 1938, at the height of Neville Chamberlain's appeasement policy, the Colonial Secretary, in a speech about British-mandated Palestine, made a pious reference to Bethlehem, 'where the Prince of Peace was born'. 'Good Heavens,' said Churchill, not altogether *sotto voce*, 'I never knew Neville was born in Bethlehem.' (John Field, *The Story of Parliament* (2002), 253.)

29. 44 USC 901-10.

30. 44 USC sect 4101.

31. The inserted matter provided liability protection for drug companies from cases involving consumers injured by avian flu vaccine, and was included in the Defense Appropriation conference report for fiscal 2006.

4

Representatives, Members, Lords, and Senators

Numbers in the four Houses

Section 2 of the 14th Amendment to the United States Constitution provides that 'Representatives shall be apportioned among the several States according to their respective numbers, counting the whole number of persons in each State, excluding Indians not taxed'. Article I, section 2 of the Constitution requires that 'the actual enumeration shall be made...within every subsequent term of ten years, in such manner as they (Congress) shall by law direct'. Only Congress can by law change the total number of seats in the House, and Congress has enacted a law[1] providing that after each fifth Congress (ten years) from the first session of the Eighty-Second Congress (in 1941) the President shall transmit to the Congress a statement showing the whole number of persons in each State as ascertained under each subsequent decennial census of the population, and the number of Representatives to which each State would be entitled under an apportionment of the then existing number of Representatives (435) by the method known as the method of equal proportions, 'no State to receive less than one Member'. Under current Federal law, such a statistical model is used to determine the number of Representatives to which such State is entitled. The equal proportions method chosen by Congress has been upheld under the Constitution and was intended to reach, as closely as practicable, the goal of 'one person, one vote'. The Federal courts have also recently upheld a counting methodology utilized by the Census Bureau in the most recent (2000) decennial census known as 'imputation', which was distinguished from the methodology of 'sampling' prohibited by Federal law[2] in census counts for Congressional reapportionment. The method of apportioning seats in the House is vested exclusively in Congress, and neither States nor courts may direct greater or lesser representation than that allocated by Federal law. Apportionment under the 'equal proportions' method is complex. The problem is to allocate a finite number of seats (385, after each State has received one) among fifty States of widely varying population, where no seat can be shared between two

States, and where the principal aim is to allot each seat to as nearly as practicable an equal number of constituents. The allotment is accomplished by dividing the population of each State by the geometric mean of successive numbers of Representatives ($n \times [n-1]$, where n is the number of the seat). For example, the population of State A is first divided by $2 \times (2-1)$ to establish its priority value for a second seat, then by $3 \times (3-1)$ to establish its priority value for a third seat, and so on. Priority values are computed for all the States, for successive numbers of seats, and then all the values are listed in descending order. If State A has a very large population, its claims for a second, third, and more seats will be listed ahead of the claim of State B for a second seat, if State B is sparsely populated. Thus the 385 seats are allotted to the States whose priority values are the first 385 on the priority list.

The Constitution requires the apportionment of seats based on the number of 'persons' in each State as discerned by the decennial census. This requirement includes the counting of citizens, and also legal and illegal aliens, in each census for the purpose of apportionment, and has the effect each decade of redistributing Congressional seats more heavily weighted toward States such as California which have a disproportionate number of immigrant non-citizens, and not merely based on population shifts of citizens.

Since the admission of Alaska and Hawaii to statehood, the total membership of the House of Representatives has remained fixed by Federal statute at 435 seats. That number had initially been set in 1913 when the United States expanded to forty-eight States, but was temporarily set at 437 when the United States expanded to fifty States in 1959 and 1960, and reverted to 435 in 1963, the effective date of the reapportionment under the 18th decennial census.

The Constitution in Article I, section 3 originally provided that 'the Senate of the United States shall be composed of two Senators from each State, chosen by the Legislature thereof... and each Senator shall have one vote'. When the 17th Amendment to the Constitution was ratified in 1913, that provision was superseded to require instead that Senators should be chosen by the people from each State, and that the people entitled to vote for the office of Senator in each State should be the same electors who are qualified under State law to vote for the most numerous branch of the State legislature. The size of the Senate expanded from ninety-six Senators, its size since 1913 when the forty-eighth State (Arizona) was admitted to the Union, to ninety-eight and then to 100 when Alaska and Hawaii became States in 1959 and in 1960, respectively.

The Commonwealth of Puerto Rico, the District of Columbia, and the Territories of the Virgin Islands, Guam, American Samoa, and the Northern Mariana Islands, not being States, are not entitled to voting representation in either full House of Congress. Congress has at various times passed Federal laws empowering the District of Columbia, and those current and predecessor Territories and the Commonwealth to elect non-voting Delegates to the House of Representatives, but not to the Senate. For Puerto Rico, the office is that of the 'Resident Commissioner' who uniquely serves a four-year term in the House, unlike Representatives and Delegates who serve two-year terms by the Constitution or pursuant to law.

The Office of Delegate from a Territory was first established by ordinance of the Continental Congress and confirmed by a law of the first Congress in 1789. That law recited that Delegates from the Territory Northwest of the Ohio River should be elected by the territorial General Assembly to the 'Congress', with a seat in Congress and the right to debate but not vote. A Territory or District must first be organized by law before the House will admit a Delegate. The current Offices were chronologically established as follows: the Resident Commissioner from Puerto Rico in 1917, the Delegate from the District of Columbia in 1970, the Delegates from Guam and the Virgin Islands in 1971, the Delegate from American Samoa in 1978, and the Delegate from the Northern Marianas Islands, with Delegates elected to the House in the Congresses beginning after those years.

Delegates and the Resident Commissioner are not Representatives from States. Their offices are created by Federal law, and under Article I of the Constitution cannot be counted for the purposes of apportionment of seats or toward the number necessary for the establishment of a quorum, nor are they empowered to cast votes in the full House on any matter. Delegates have been empowered by House rules and enabling statutes to participate fully in committee proceedings in standing committees to which they are elected by the House, and that empowerment is not inconsistent with the constitutional restriction since committee decisions are not final but are only advisory to the House. Delegates are permitted the full privilege of debate in the plenary session of the House, including the right to make or object to any unanimous consent request or to make any motion except the motion to reconsider (as that motion presumes a vote on the prevailing side of an issue in order to qualify), and to introduce bills or resolutions to the same extent as Members. Delegates' committee assignments are recommended by the party caucus or conference to which they belong.

In the 103rd Congress (and again in the 110th Congress), the Democratic party majority adopted a rule permitting the four (now as of 2009, five) Delegates and the Resident Commissioner from Puerto Rico to vote in the Committee of the Whole House on the State of the Union. The Committee of the Whole was fashioned by Jefferson in his Manual to be a procedure comparable to the British Committee of the whole House and designed to expedite debate and amendment options under the five-minute rule but subject to ratification by the full House of any adopted amendment. The fact that all five were members of the majority party did not escape the attention of the Minority leadership, who sued in Federal court in 1993 seeking injunctive relief against the implementation of this rule as an unconstitutional diminution of their Representatives' voting rights in the full House. The two Federal courts considering this case agreed that it was justiciable—that a case or controversy existed and that plaintiff Members had standing to bring the suit (claiming diminution of their votes)—but determined on the merits that the House rule was constitutionally valid as virtually 'meaningless', reserving to the full House the immediate and automatic ability to reconsider any vote in the Committee of the Whole where the collective count of Delegates' votes was decisive to the outcome. The rules change had been inspired by the Delegate from the District of Columbia, who uniquely represented constituents required by Federal law to pay Federal taxes but who were unrepresented by a vote in the full House. The fact that their constituents varied widely in number and did not pay Federal income tax was ignored, as the Majority party empowered all its Delegates (and permitted them to preside as Chairmen of the Committee of the Whole) for an entire Congress. This rule was immediately repealed when the party majority (having no Delegates) shifted in 1995. It was readopted again in 2007 after a contentious debate.

Some would argue that a constitutional amendment would be required to enfranchise electors from any of these constituencies in either House. In fact, the House in 1967 passed a constitutional amendment creating a Representative for the District of Columbia in the House, but the Senate never voted on that joint resolution in the 90th Congress and it was not proposed to the State legislatures. Legislation in the 109th and 110th Congresses was proposed to enact into Federal law an enlargement of the House of Representatives by two seats in order to give the District of Columbia a voting Representative (presumably Democratic), and to give the State of Utah—the State identified by the last census as next deserving another district based on population growth—a presumably offsetting (Republican) additional seat. In justification for the creation by statute of full voting representation for the District, the committee report in the 109th Congress[3] contended that constitutional authority for Congress to enact such a law existed based upon the overriding power given to Congress in Article I, section 8, clause 17 over the District as the seat of national government, and upon court cases enabling Congress to treat the District as a State for the purpose of a variety of Federal laws and constitutionally protected rights. The contention was that Congress can provide for the general welfare of citizens within the District of Columbia by any act of legislation, such as treating the District as a State, and that the District Clause contains no limitation on Congressional powers because there is nothing in the Constitution which prevents Congress from treating the District as a State. This argument, generally unsupported by case law, was propounded despite the clear creation in Article I of the House of Representatives as consisting of Representatives elected by people from the several States, with each State entitled to at least one seat. The Supreme Court recognized in *Hepburn v Ellzey* 6 US 445 (1805) that Congress and not the courts can treat the District as a State for some purposes, and in *National Mutual Insurance Co. of D.C. v Tidewater Transfer Co.* 337 US 582 (1945) relying on *Hepburn*, held that although the District is not defined as a State for the purpose of Article III, other provisions of the Constitution do not prohibit Congress from treating the District as a State for the purpose of granting diversity jurisdiction in Federal courts to District residents. An extension of this argument to empower Congress by law to consider the District as a State for purposes of voting representation in the House does not necessarily withstand constitutional scrutiny. Six of the nine Justices in the Tidewater case authored opinions which rejected the proposition that Congress's power under the District Clause was sufficient to effectuate structural changes to the political structures of the Federal government. To date, no other case law supports such an expansion of Congress's authority. The issue remains unresolved, first due to lack of Senate action and a Presidential veto threat in 2008, and then due to Senate linkage in 2009 of the voting representation issue with a provision on gun control in the District of Columbia—a Senate-passed bill on which the House has taken no action at this writing.

By comparison with the House of Commons and the lower Houses of several Western European countries, the House of Representatives is on the one hand slightly smaller, though for the same reason each of its Members represents a great many more electors. Table 4.1 in the Annex will illustrate the point.

In the House of Commons, unlike the House of Representatives, the number of seats does not remain more or less fixed as population growth inexorably increases the size of the electorate of each. After the Second World War, the membership of the House of Commons stood at 640, was then reduced to 625, reached 651 after the general election of 1983, and now stands at 646. As is explained below, it is the interplay of population growth with the broad aim of successive governments of equalizing the size of constituencies which largely accounts for these figures. Over the years, suggestions have regularly been made that the House would operate more efficiently with fewer Members (and it probably would, if practical concerns were given priority over political and representational interests) but for obvious reasons the proposal has never been greeted with much enthusiasm at Westminster, though it was aired in the recent crisis over Members' expenses.

Even after partial reformation, the House of Lords remains non-elected. The attempts made over the past decade or so to construct a broad consensus over the powers of the upper Chamber have not yet borne fruit. It may be a temporary delay to catch breath, but—given the history of Lords reform—it is equally possible that the intermediate stage now reached will endure (see pages 57–8). Progress has however been made in reducing the number of Lords of Parliament from the 1,200 which was reached a generation ago, when it was wittily observed that the Lords was unique among legislatures, being kept efficient by the persistent absenteeism of a majority of its Members. In 1999, the House of Lords Act was the first stage in a thoroughgoing attempt to tackle the related problems of size, power, and composition. (Some voices were heard calling for the Lords to be ended and not mended, but unicameralism was not widely supported.) The right of all but ninety-two hereditary peers to sit in the House of Lords was extinguished. At a stroke, the Lords was reduced to a Chamber of roughly 700 (but has subsequently grown by about another fifty). The average daily attendance in 2008 was 411. The bishops remained (but the Law Lords departed for the Supreme Court in 2009). This was however intended to be only an interim settlement. Many important decisions remained to be taken. The size of the new House was one of them. Most opinions backed a House of 300 to 600—at the upper end still quite a large Chamber by international standards.

One of the possibilities was an elected or partly elected upper Chamber, completely separating peerage as a rank from membership of that House. At that point, many in the Commons were suspicious that an elected or even partly elected Lords could not help challenging the political primacy of the Commons. Yet in 1924, no less a politician than Winston Churchill remarked:

> If we are to leave the venerable if somewhat crumbled rock on which the House of Lords now stands, there is no safe foothold until we come to an elected Chamber.[4]

Others feared that, failing election, an appointed House would be reluctant to bite the hand that appointed it, rendering it unable to take up a revising—or any other—role with credibility. The complicated history of attempts to alter the composition and powers of the Lords, as well as perhaps to introduce some element of popular election, is dealt with at greater length at pages 57–8.

Constituencies and districts: the Lords and the Senate

The rules which govern the division of the British electorate into constituencies are based on statute law, and are applied by four impartial Boundary Commissions, one for each of England, Scotland, Wales, and Northern Ireland, all four presided over ex officio by the Speaker of the Commons.[5] Every eight to twelve years the Commissions conduct a general review of all constituency boundaries, making proposals for change, including the creation of new constituencies by the division or amalgamation of existing ones.

In the UK, as in the USA, it is envisaged that, so far as possible, the size of the area in terms of population which is represented by one elected Member should be similar to that represented by the others. This apparently simple aim has been extremely hard to achieve. In the first place, the Boundary Commissions undertake general reviews only every eight to twelve years. General reviews are also time consuming in themselves. There are interim reviews but they are not intended to update boundaries so as to match changes in population distribution. Inevitably therefore constituency boundaries for a general election may rest on outdated statistics. Moreover, the arithmetical accuracy of the aim is modified principally by respect for existing local authority boundaries, in which context it should be recalled that Britain has (it is said) more administrative boundaries than the rest of Europe put together. Other circumstances to which the Boundary Commissions have regard include informal patterns of living, day-to-day and historical associations, and the obvious inconveniences in changes in settled arrangements, however otherwise sensible. The principle that each vote, wherever cast, should have equal weight in determining the national outcome, is in practice secondary.

In addition, undertakings given in 1944 about the preservation of the numbers of seats in Scotland and Wales—modified subsequently in the former case[6]—have combined with growth in the electorate of England relentlessly if slowly to increase the number of constituencies. The system also builds in expansion of constituencies in response to population changes such as recent movement out of cities. Labour seats in the inner cities—which continually leak population to the suburbs and country areas where the Conservative vote tends to be stronger—may have quite small electorates.

Across the UK as a whole, the resultant imbalances have been shown to be appreciable, as demonstrated in Table 4.2 in the Annex. Put another way, there are roughly five times as many electors in the largest English constituency (Isle of Wight, 104,000) as there are in the smallest in Scotland (Na h-Eileanan an Iar—Western Isles, 21,000) and the rationale for both sizes is exactly the same—the desirability of not dividing island communities. The largest constituency in Scotland has not many more voters more than the smallest in England. This is a world away from the American courts' pursuit of strict equality of districts.

Wherever responsibility rests, the independence of the redistribution process is carefully guarded. Recommendations for change made by the Boundary Commissions must be put to the government, who then lay Orders before both Houses giving effect to the proposals. Governments have the opportunity to interpose their will between the recommendations of the Commissions and their implementation in law, but they have never done so directly.[7] Party views are of course put to the local public inquiries conducted by independent lawyers on behalf of the Commissions, which consider the fittest way to interpret the Commissions' guidelines locally, and the parties are very well aware of the electoral consequences of one outcome as against another. But leaving aside parliamentary consideration, the decision rests with the experts on the Boundary Commissions.

By contrast with the position in the UK, the US Supreme Court has ruled that congressional districts must be as equally populated as practicable (*Wesberry v Sanders* 376 US 1 (1964)) and that variances in population among Congressional districts within a

State may be considered de minimis only if they cannot practicably be avoided. By Federal law, each State entitled to more than one Representative shall establish a number of districts equal to the number of such Representatives, and Representatives shall be elected only from the single-Member districts so established. However, after any reapportionment, until a State is redistricted in a manner provided by its own law, an earlier enacted (and not specifically repealed) Federal law permits the election of some Members to be 'at large' (that is, by voters in the entire State) but States usually enact new State law creating, as the case may be, additional or fewer districts, in time to meet the requirement that Representatives be elected only from the new single-Member districts and to avoid 'at large' elections.

The Constitution in section 4 of Article I reserves to State legislatures the authority to draw district boundaries within each State by empowering State legislatures to prescribe 'the times, places and manner of holding Elections for Senators and Representatives' while reserving to Congress the authority to make or alter such regulations. To date, Congress has not chosen to enact Federal law drawing Congressional districts in any State, thereby allowing the State legislatures to perform that function. By tradition, State legislatures redraw Congressional districts once, based on decennial reapportionments resulting from the census, to last for ten years until the next census and it is done in the two-year period immediately following the census. There is no constitutional or Federal law provision, however, restricting any State legislature from redrawing Congressional district lines more than once in a decade, and Texas and Georgia legislatures twice in the same decade passed State laws, the second time after new State legislatures were elected in mid-decade after 2000, to redraw Congressional district lines in a manner more compatible with the political realignment of parties in the legislature. In 2006, the Supreme Court in *League of United Latin American Citizens v Perry* 548 US 399 (2006) (the so-called Texas redistricting case) upheld the constitutionality of mid-decade redistricting, ruling that neither the Constitution nor Congress have stated any prohibition of mid-decade redistricting to change districts drawn earlier in conformance with a decennial census. This politically charged effort in Texas had ramifications which were reviewed by the Supreme Court both because of its mid-decade timing and for compliance with racial equality requirements under the Voting Rights Act of 1965. Whether this case opens the floodgates to partisan gerrymandering in mid-decade in other States remains to be discovered. Suffice it to say that the politicization of reapportionment, facilitated by the precision of computerized gerrymandering relying on up-to-the-minute voter registration, has in recent years had considerable impact on the drawing of district lines by State legislatures at the behest of party leadership, and on the resulting emergence of many more 'politically safe' districts where the political ideologies of successful candidates in primaries are inclined to be more pronounced and to receive greater support. In turn, the willingness of State legislatures to delegate the reapportionment responsibility to non-partisan commissions has been minimal, with nineteen States having enacted legislation creating various forms of advisory commissions, but only one State (Iowa) having authorized a non-partisan commission to directly draw Congressional district lines. Congress has not pre-empted this area, being collectively content with (and the creature of) the political arrangements made at the State level with their complicity. Ultimately, collegiality and moderation within the House is impacted by the politicization of reapportionment responsibilities at the State level.

The 'great compromise' of the Founding Fathers at the Constitutional Convention between the large and small States (needing ratification by nine of the original thirteen State Constitutional Conventions) is reflected in Article I of the Constitution which constructed a Congress with two Houses of approximately equal legislative authority and originally comprised one House chosen by the voters and the other House chosen by the State legislatures in equal numbers per State (amended in 1913 to require election of Senators by the people directly, unless temporarily appointed by Governors to fill vacancies). The Constitution also provides for Congressional elections separately from Presidential elections (although election day every four years coincides pursuant to Federal law), and for different terms of office, and thus imposes an electoral plan which mandates not only a separation of powers between the Legislature and Executive but also at least a partial separation of the constituencies electing persons to those offices. This hybrid enfranchisement of the people, the State legislatures, and the Electoral College reflected a reluctance to confer all voting power directly upon the people. This is in radical contrast with the concept of parliamentarianism, where the Executive branch is within the Legislature and consists of ministers who are for the most part elected from separate single-seat constituencies to the House of Commons, and who then organize themselves within the majority party into ministries which perform the executive function to execute laws enacted by the Legislature and signed into law by the Monarch. A further distinction between the two systems acknowledges that while in Congress both Houses are elected by the people, only the Members of the Commons are elected in the British parliamentary system. The absence of a hereditary Monarch under the United States Constitution underlies the most basic distinction between a democratically elected republic (representative) form of government and a partially elected, partially appointed parliamentary monarchy.

Terms of the mandates, vacancies, and resignations

Under Article I, section 2 of the US Constitution, the terms of all House of Representatives Members are limited to two years, and under section 1 of the 20th Amendment, begin at noon on 3 January of the odd-numbered year following the election on the first Tuesday of November in the even-numbered year (the day prescribed by Congress by law) and expire at noon on 3 January of the following odd-numbered year. Prior to the ratification of the 20th Amendment in 1920, pursuant to the action of the Continental Congress in 1788 in declaring, on authority of the Constitutional Convention, 'the first Wednesday in March next to be the time for commencing proceedings under the said Constitution', House and Senate terms began for two- and six-year respective terms on 4 March 1789, and a joint committee assembled by the first Congress determined that House terms must necessarily end on 3 March 1791. There was an obvious chronological discrepancy between the terms of office for Members and the original constitutional days for the convening of regular sessions of Congress on the first Monday in December each year under Article I, section 4 of the original Constitution, since Members' terms would not begin until March and the Congress would not regularly convene until the following December. The 20th Amendment, ratified in 1920, coincided the beginning of Representatives' and Senators' terms with the required convening day for the annual regular session on 3 January of each odd-numbered year, although that Amendment delayed the beginning of the Presidential term for seventeen days until 20 January every fourth year, to enable a newly elected and convened Congress to organize, to count the Electoral vote for President and Vice President pursuant to the 12th Amendment. The 12th Amendment requires separate electoral votes for each office, replacing the original requirement that the second-place finisher become the Vice President, and requires the House to proceed if necessary to separately elect a President (one vote per State delegation) and the Senate to elect a Vice President if no candidate receives a majority (now 270) of electoral votes.

Terms of Senators likewise begin at noon on 3 January but are for six years unless they are the result of elections called to fill the unexpired terms of vacated Senate seats. As there are two Senators from each State, the Constitution has always required the staggering of terms by 'classes' so that two Senators are not elected from the same State for the same term. When the 17th Amendment was ratified in 1913, a new provision was added to authorize State Governors to fill vacancies in Senate seats by appointment, until such time as a special election is held pursuant to State law but in no event beyond the six-year term contemplated for the 'class' of that Senate seat. Thus if vacancies occur early in a six-year term, a Governor may fill the vacancy until State law requires the holding of an election—usually coinciding with a general election for the House in November of an even-numbered year—to fill the seat for two or four years. If the vacancy occurs late in the term, the appointment normally covers the remainder of the unexpired six-year term.

In both the House and Senate, vacancies may occur by reason of death, resignation, declination to be sworn, or by action of either House in declaring the seat vacant by failure of the Representative or Senator-elect to be truly elected, to meet the constitutional qualifications for office, or by expulsion. Unlike the Senate, where temporary appointment by the State executive is permitted, membership in the House can be achieved only by election. This requirement embodied in Article I, section 2, clause 4 directs the Governor to issue 'writs of election' when a House vacancy 'happens'. At that point, the Governor calls a special election pursuant to State law unless the vacancy occurs so late in the two-year term as to make it impracticable to conduct a special election in addition to the general election set by Federal law for the first Tuesday in November in each even-numbered year. In that event, special elections for the unexpired term from November until 3 January of the odd-numbered year are often called to coincide with general elections to the next Congress.

On one recent occasion in 1994 a State law in Oklahoma required the Governor to 'appoint' a Member-elect, elected to the next Congress, beginning in 1995, to also fill a vacancy in the existing Congress, which vacancy did not actually happen until the week following the election. The Governor had been unable to call a special election based on a known vacancy to coincide with the general election on that occasion, as the vacancy did not occur until the week after election day in November 1994. Only then did a sitting House Member, elected to the Senate to fill a vacancy there, formally resign his seat in the House the week after the general election upon being certified as having been successfully elected to the Senate. This unusual and arguably unconstitutional State law, which deemed the election to the next Congress to be also an election to the current Congress requiring the appointment based on a contingent vacancy, should have been more critically scrutinized by the House. The House permitted the 'appointed' Member-elect to be sworn but referred the question of the final right to the seat for the unexpired term to its Elections Committee. No report was made on the propriety of that special 'election' during the remaining two months of that Congress, and the matter was mooted when that Congress terminated.

On another occasion, an Oklahoma law specially enacted after a letter of prospective resignation had been received from a House Member enabled the Governor to call and conduct a special election to fill a 'vacancy' which had not yet actually occurred, as the Member's resignation from the House was prospective to a day subsequent to election day but was considered irrevocable under State law. For the State Governor to take cognizance of a prospective resignation, he must have assurances that there is no possibility of withdrawal or modification, but even this likelihood should not permit the conduct of an election where the vacancy has not yet 'happened' on that day. This type of special election to fill a prospective albeit certain vacancy has been replicated under some other States' laws, but most States wisely have not enacted laws to address these anomalous situations. In each case the State tries to balance the constitutional requirement that a vacancy must exist with the desire to leave a vacancy in place for as brief a time as possible. States normally prefer to promptly enable special elections, preceded by primary elections, and to minimize the expense of conducting those elections.

Notwithstanding these isolated anomalies, the process to create and then fill vacancies in both Houses has its basis in the Constitution, which leaves it to the State Legislatures and Executives to perform their duties under State law. A Member properly submits his resignation to an official designated by State law and simply informs the House of his doing so, the latter communication being satisfactory evidence of the resignation. Usually the State Executive declares the vacancy to exist in the event of a resignation, death, or declination. Where the House has created the vacancy by expulsion, exclusion, or judging the election result, the State must first be informed by the House of that fact. Vacancies need not be accepted by the State Executive or by the House to be effective, but must be irrevocably communicated by the Member. The resignation is solely the option of the Representative or Senator, since the Governor and the House have not chosen the Member in the first place.

A resolution of either House declaring a seat vacant may be used where the person elected is unable to take the oath or to decline the office due to an incapacitating illness. On one occasion in 1983, the Attending Physician of Congress documented the physical condition of a Member-elect who was comatose even prior to the election and unable to present herself to take the oath of office for an extended period. The House, by declaring the seat vacant by a majority vote, was (as stated in the resolution itself) judging a constitutional qualification of the Member-elect, namely the requirement that she take the oath of office as prescribed by law. The resolution was not treated as an expulsion (a punishment requiring a two-thirds vote), but rather as a judgement of the constitutionally prescribed qualifications for office. Even if sworn, a Member can be unseated by majority vote if later found not to have been validly elected or not to have qualified under the Constitution.

If a Representative or Senator resigns directly to the State Governor, as is the customary practice and the requirement under most State laws, the House or Senate is thereupon notified and no action by either House is needed to 'accept' the resignation.

By precedent, if the Representative resigns directly to the Speaker, the Speaker may be given the authority to notify the State Governor of the vacancy. Although a resigning Member may specify that his resignation take effect in the future, there is doubt as to the validity or effectiveness of a resignation which does not specify its effective date. Where the resignation is addressed to the incorrect State official, it is invalid and is revoked by a subsequent resignation properly addressed with a future date certain. Resigning Members have on occasion made their resignations effective on a future date following the anticipated date of a special election to fill the vacancy which would be created, but such resignations are only valid if irrevocable and not if based only upon the election of their successor without specifying a specific date.

'Vacancies' beyond elections, qualifications, or disciplinary matters will also be treated in the context of incapacitations in the event of catastrophic circumstances, and the impact on quorum requirements in each House. One unique aspect of the creation and existence of a vacancy relates to the office of Speaker. This process is discussed in detail at page 45. Vacancies on committees will be discussed at pages 370–1.

Once elected, a Member of the House of Commons serves until the dissolution of the Parliament, whenever that may be (other than in the unusual event of his or her being expelled; see page 127). By statute, a Parliament ceases to exist on a day five years later than that on which Her Majesty summoned it to meet, but such a full-term Parliament, ceasing to exist by the passage of time, is very unusual. More normally, a Parliament will come to an end on a date fixed in a proclamation of dissolution—which simultaneously sets a date for the assembly of the new Parliament—made by Her Majesty on the advice of the Prime Minister. Prime Ministers may be forced into dissolution by defeat or serious loss of confidence in the House of Commons (as in 1979) or they may choose to dissolve at the date which they believe most favourable to their prospects of success.

In practice, roughly four-year Parliaments are becoming the norm (which will of course make it easier to argue for four-year fixed-term Parliaments). Since and including 1945 there have been seventeen general elections, and only three (in October 1951, March 1966, and the second of 1974) have been held significantly sooner than four years after the previous election. Whether sufficient of the royal prerogative remains to enable Her Majesty to deny a Prime Minister the right to a dissolution, for example when he or she cannot command a majority in a 'hung' Commons but the Sovereign thinks another politician might do so without the need for a further general election, is a mystery of the British constitution. There is simply insufficient modern experience on which to base a judgement.

The mandate of a Member of the House of Commons expires on the issuing of the proclamation of dissolution of Parliament. Membership of the Lords is not similarly interrupted by dissolution. The latter begins with the issue of letters patent by the Sovereign creating the peerage, followed by a writ of summons to attend the House. Life peers are now principally those nominated by political parties as 'working peers', some non-political nominations by the Appointments Commission (which also vets the party appointments), nominations made by Prime Ministers at the time of dissolution or resignation, and a limited number of senior public or parliamentary servants, the latter including retired Speakers of the Commons. There is no age of retirement for life peers. The twenty-six bishops and archbishops of the Church of England sit until they retire from ecclesiastical office, though the archbishops then usually receive life peerages. The remaining ninety-two hereditary peers sit until the next stage of reform is completed—whenever that may be (see page 58)—with occasional vacancies being filled by a system of by-elections in the party or cross-bench constituencies from which the surviving hereditaries were originally elected.

A Member of the Commons who wishes voluntarily to give up his or her seat does not simply inform the Speaker or the electorate. In earlier years, leaving the service of the Crown in Parliament voluntarily was seen as in some sense dishonourable, so that for centuries Members who give up their seats have been required to do so by deliberately disqualifying themselves. Even today, they seek and are granted an office of profit under the Crown—an automatic disqualification—in the shape of the entirely notional office of steward or bailiff of Her Majesty's Chiltern Hundreds of Stoke, Desborough, and Burnham, or of the manor of Northstead. It is a transparent legal fiction, but the procedure is simple and straightforward. The office is granted and the disqualification becomes effective at once. The Chief Whip of the party which held the seat will—at a time of the party's own choosing, though by convention within three months of the vacancy—move that the Speaker 'do issue his warrant to the Clerk of the Crown to make out a new writ for the electing of a Member to serve' in the constituency, 'in the room of Mr X who since his election hath accepted the office' which carries the disqualification. For the most part, such proceedings are formal, but on occasion the motion for a new writ has been the occasion of party dispute, and elaborate procedural ingenuity has had to be deployed by the Clerks so that the House did not, by defeating the motion for a new writ, inadvertently make it impossible for the by-election to be held for many months. (These proceedings are governed by the general rule that a motion once defeated may not be brought forward again the same session, failing a substantial change in circumstances.)

Deaths of sitting Members are announced by the Speaker to the House, and the machinery for the necessary by-election is put in motion as described above. A similar announcement of the death of a Lord is made in the upper House.

Qualification and disqualification

The approach to disqualification for membership of the two legislatures is essentially similar, for obvious historical reasons. By contrast with UK practice, however, where disqualification is not in any way entrenched, generally applicable rules regarding disqualification for membership of either House of Congress can be only those enumerated in Article I of the US Constitution. The Supreme Court ruled in *U.S. Term Limits v Thornton* 514 US 779 (1995) that neither Congress nor the States were capable of adding to those qualifications by law, by State constitution, or by action of either House in judging the elections or qualifications of its Members. Section 2 of Article I establishes only three qualifications for Representatives in the House, the first two of which need only be met before being sworn in. Representatives must be at least 25 years old, and citizens of the United States for at least seven years when taking the oath of office. They must also be inhabitants of the State when elected. In the Senate under section 3 of Article I, each Senator before being sworn must be at least 30 years old, a citizen of the United States for at least nine years, and an inhabitant of the State when elected.

A fourth qualification must be added, namely the ability and willingness to take the oath of office to support the Constitution, as required by Article VI of the Constitution for all Representatives and Senators, State legislators and executive and judicial Officers of the United States and of the several States. State law recall mechanisms would not withstand constitutional scrutiny. States may not enact recall constitutions or laws as a means of adding to those enumerated qualifications so as to enable electors to challenge Members' political or personal performance during their terms.

Congress may not exclude by majority vote a Member-elect by judging the sincerity of his willingness to take the oath of office (*Bond v Floyd* 385 US 116 (1966)), or by adding to the enumerated qualifications spelled out in the Constitution. The power of exclusion is derived from the right of each House to determine the qualifications of its Members, whereas the power of expulsion stems from its authority to discipline Members for misconduct. In 1870 a Member-elect was excluded by majority vote of the House for corruption on the ground that he sold appointments to the Military Academy. This precedent was relied upon by the House in 1967 where, after an investigating committee recommended that a Member-elect be fined and censured for improperly maintaining his wife on the clerk-hire payroll and for other improper use of public funds for private purposes, the House by majority vote determined instead to impose a stronger penalty—to exclude him by denying him his seat. The Supreme Court found that such an exclusion (understood by the House on that occasion to only require a majority vote although in fact receiving more than a two-thirds affirmative vote), was not a sanction to be invoked in cases involving the misconduct of a Member. The remedy of exclusion is only available for failure to meet the constitutional requirements of Members as to age, citizenship, and residency (*Powell v McCormack* 395 US 486 (1969)). This case is further discussed in the subsequent chapter on Ethics and Standards at page 519 as a landmark decision leading to the establishment of an ethics process in the House.

Disqualifications for failure of Members-elect to meet other constitutional requirements may also be grounds for exclusion by majority vote. For example, section 3 of the 14th Amendment disqualifies Representatives and Senators-elect (and other Federal and State-elected officers) from holding that office where, having previously taken the oath, the office holder has engaged in insurrection or rebellion or given aid and comfort to enemies thereof, unless by a two-thirds vote of each House Congress removes that disability.

Article I, section 6 of the Constitution prohibits the holding of 'incompatible offices' by Representatives and Senators by stating that 'no person holding any Office under the United States shall be a Member of either House during his continuance in Office'. This restriction has as its basis the separation of powers between the Legislative, Executive, and Judicial branches of the Federal government and between the Federal, State, and local governments, and it serves as a valid basis for exclusion or vacating a seat by majority vote by either House where a Member is found to hold another governmental office which he will not relinquish at the time he is sworn. This is a matter for each House to determine. The fact that in contemporary Congresses several Members also have Reserve Military Commissions has not been considered to be a disqualifying incompatible 'office' where the matter has not been publicly raised. Where Governors have been elected to either House, they are not sworn, even though their terms may have begun, until they resign the incompatible office or that term of office has expired. By precedent, offices have been held 'incompatible' where they involve the exercise of Legislative or Executive power, and where the office holder receives compensation.

In the UK, statute has codified and brought up to date a range of common law disabilities for election to the Commons of very long standing. It is therefore within the power of a single Parliament to change the law on disqualification, and indeed the principal Act is frequently brought up to date without further legislation, simply by Orders made by ministers and approved by the Commons.

At the time of election—there is neither qualifying period of citizenship nor residence requirement—a Member must be 18 years old, not an alien, not otherwise disqualified, and not a member of the House of Lords. Membership of the Commons is not permitted to any civil servant whether full-time or part-time including ambassadors, to members of the regular (but not reserve or emergency) armed forces, or to most policemen. There are a great many miscellaneous disqualifications arising from membership of statutory bodies—regulatory or executive boards such as the Electoral Commission or the Boundary Commissions themselves—whose members are appointed by the Crown. Most professional judges are not qualified to be elected. Those who have been found guilty of treason, or detained in prison for more than a year for any offence are *ipso facto* disqualified. A bankruptcy restriction order has the effect of voiding an election or vacating a seat. Equally, conviction for certain corrupt electoral practices will result in disqualification. There is a statutory procedure for unseating a Member who is mentally ill.

It occasionally happens that a Member elected for the first time discovers with horror that he or she is under a statutory disqualification by virtue of a minor offence which had escaped notice. The Commons has authority to direct that such disqualification be disregarded. Instances of this kind are rare, but not unknown.

A further disqualification provision is that no more than ninety-five holders of paid ministerial offices are entitled to sit in the Commons at any one time. Ministers receiving salary and appointed after the limit is reached may not sit and vote until the numbers have returned to ninety-five.

If a candidate is found guilty by an election court of corrupt or illegal electoral practices, he or she is thereby disqualified from being elected to the House of Commons for five years (in the case of a corrupt practice) or three years if illegal practice has been established. A sitting Member found guilty of corrupt or illegal practices by a criminal court is similarly disqualified, though there are provisions for the sentence not to take effect for three months to permit an appeal to be disposed of, provided that in that period the Member may not perform any of his or her functions as a Member.

In the Lords, disqualification rests only on aliens, those under 21, Lords in bankruptcy, and those convicted of treason. There is no procedure for suspending membership by reason of incapacitating mental illness.

Members of the House of Commons legally qualified to sit, and returned at an election must—like Representatives and Senators—swear an oath before taking their seats. In Westminster the oath is one of allegiance to Her Majesty. It is an offence punished by the vacation of the seat if a Member crosses the bar of the House without taking the oath. When in 1997 Sinn Fein members were returned for constituencies in Northern Ireland and were unwilling to take the oath on political grounds, the Speaker limited their access to parliamentary facilities and their call on salaries and allowances. Their ability to represent their constituents was explicitly protected by the arrangement. An appeal against the Speaker's decision reached the European Court of Human Rights, which concluded that the obligation to take the oath did not contravene the Convention on Human Rights. In March 2005, the House suspended the payments under the 1997 decision, but in February 2006 financial assistance and allowances for members of parties who choose not to take their seats was restored, and funds roughly analogous to Short Money (see below) were added.

Expulsion

Expulsion from the legislature can be viewed either as a punishment for very serious offences or in the context of unfitness to serve the people in a legislative capacity. For that reason, the text here should be read in conjunction with what is said at pages 529, 544 in the context of Ethics and Standards.

Involuntary departure from the Commons—other than at a general election—is rare. The reason is not legal but political. Expulsion is a weapon which majorities at Westminster have learnt to handle with care. In the eighteenth century, the celebrated John Wilkes was three times expelled, but since he sat for one of the most nearly democratic constituencies in the country, he was able to show succeeding generations how electoral success after expulsion could be a means of defying an oppressive House. At Westminster, the key element in expulsion is however not so much punishment as a general sense of the offender's unfitness to continue to sit in the Commons. Some of the offences which in the past led to expulsion were more dramatic than those likely to be encountered today. They included rebellion, corruption in public office (including a Speaker), contempt of the House, and 'having behaved in a manner unbecoming an officer and a gentleman'. The last expulsion from the Commons was in 1955, following a conviction for fraud. The Lords may not permanently exclude by expulsion someone who had received a writ of summons, but their Committee for Privileges has recommended that two Lords be suspended from the service of the House for a period shorter than a Parliament[8] and legislation which might empower the Lords to expel has been foreshadowed (see page 530).

Expulsion is the only punishment that is expressly contemplated in the US Constitution. Of Senate expulsion cases in history, fifteen Senators have been expelled: one in 1797; and fourteen during the Civil War for 'support of rebellion'. More recently (in 1982 and in 1995) two Senators have resigned before apparently certain expulsion action by the Senate, one who had been convicted of bribery in the ABSCAM investigation and the other for sexual misconduct. Of twenty-nine House expulsion cases, five Representatives have been expelled, three during the Civil War. The most recent expulsions were in 1980, following conviction for receiving a bribe in an FBI sting operation (another Member having resigned before expulsion), and then in 2002, following a Member's conviction on several counts of corruption. In both cases the court transcript became the main body of evidence considered by the Committee on Standards of Official Conduct. (See chapter on 'Ethics and Standards', pages 517–46.)

Elections and election contests

Though at the time of American Independence the right to determine disputed elections was a jealously guarded privilege of the House of Commons, once the franchise began to be enlarged and statute had standardized the qualification to vote across the country as a whole, the House surrendered to the courts the resolution of the outcome of controverted or corrupt elections. In fact the earliest attempts to eliminate partiality actually preceded American Independence, but it was not until a century thereafter that the argument was won and the transfer of jurisdiction achieved. The current law is contained in a statute of 1983, by which two judges chosen from the benches in the appropriate part of the UK—England and Wales, Scotland or Northern Ireland—hear petitions complaining of irregular elections or corrupt practices. The determination of the election court is certified to the Speaker, who will inform the House, and the House will take steps to carry the election court's decision into practice, either seating the proper candidate or ordering a new writ after an election has been declared void. The procedure is unusual though not unknown: there have been about half a dozen cases which reached an election court in the past half-century.

The House of Commons retains the notional right to determine questions affecting the seats of Members not arising out of controverted elections. Until very recently, at the opening of every session the House agreed to some rather antique resolutions about how certain aspects of these matters would be dealt with. In particular, the resolutions dealt with the situation where there was an equality of votes in a constituency, or where a Member was returned for more than one seat. A third threatened the severest action by the House against those who procured a return by bribery. A recent Procedure Committee report pointed out however that double or equal returns have been settled by other means for more than half a century, that the last case of a Member returned for more than one place was in 1910—in a constituency no longer in the UK[9]—and that statute law had quite superseded parliamentary jurisdiction regarding electoral corruption. All three resolutions have now been suppressed, and with them has gone much of what notionally remained of the House's right to determine electoral oddities.

In the Lords, the Committee for Privileges considers claims of peerage which, before the recent reforms (see pages 57–8), carried with them membership of the House. Since peerage and an automatic right to a seat in the upper House have been separated by the House of Lords Act 1999, the Committee's decisions are correspondingly restricted in their effect.

Just as Article I, section 5 of the US Constitution makes each House the judge of the qualifications of its Members, so also are they made the ultimate judges of the elections and returns of their own Members. Therefore, where the conduct of election officials or of candidates and their agents constitutes fraud or illegal control of election machinery, or a recount reveals the inability to determine the correctness of the election result, the House or Senate may void an election and refuse to administer the oath to a Member-elect. This authority allows the House or Senate to deny the right to a seat without unlawfully depriving a State of its right to equal representation in the House.

It is clear that only voters (electors) in States may elect voting Representatives and Senators to the Congress, since those two Houses are described as being 'composed' of

Representatives and Senators respectively (see also pages 115–6). It is also clear that the Constitution not only grants the States power over election procedure, but also delegates to them the power to prescribe the qualifications for voters for both the House and Senate. Voters must possess those qualifications requisite to vote for the most numerous branch of the State legislature under State law. However, variations among the States in regard to the qualifications of electors have been greatly diminished through constitutional amendment, through judicial decisions, and through Federal legislation. The franchise has been extended to all citizens, male and female, regardless of colour, race or creed, or wealth, who are at least 18 years of age. The right to vote in primaries, which are an integral part of the elections process, to register as voters, and to vote without discrimination, intimidation, or threats have been ensured by civil rights legislation spanning from 1870 to the present. The courts have been active in invalidating State statutes and practices which deny the right to vote or which discriminate unreasonably.

As nearly all the laws governing the elections of Representatives in Congress are State laws (Article I conferring upon the States the authority to regulate the time, place, and manner of Congressional elections subject to supervening Congressional regulation), the relationship between State laws, their enforcement and interpretation, and the ultimate authority of each House to judge elections has often raised questions of the applicability and binding effect of State law. Although Congress has the absolute power, as affirmed by numerous decisions of the Supreme Court, to fashion a complete code for Congressional elections, Congressional regulation has been directed largely towards the failure of the States to ensure the regularity of elections under their own State law and to the failure of the States to adequately protect the voting rights of all citizens entitled to vote. The actual mechanism of holding Congressional elections is the province of the States. In judging the elections and returns of its Members, the House has usually deferred to State law on the procedure of elections, on recount remedies and the validity of ballots, and on the functions of State election officials. However, the House determined early that the certificate of a State Executive issued in strict accordance with State law does not prevent independent examination of the votes by the House and a reversal of the return. When the question concerns not the acts of election officials (where voters' intent may still be discerned), but the act of the voter in giving his vote, the House has had more difficulty deciding whether to defer to State law or to make independent judgement as to the intent of the voter.

With respect to Congressional and other primary elections, the Supreme Court in the case of *California Democratic Party v Jones* 530 US 567 (2000) ruled that it was a violation of a political party's 1st Amendment right of association for a State to mandate that political parties use a 'blanket' primary to choose their candidates. Under such laws, 'closed primaries' in which only a political party's members could vote on its nominees, were changed to permit ('blanket') each voter's ballot to list every candidate regardless of party affiliation and allow the voter to choose freely among them, forcing several States (California, Washington, and Alaska) to change their blanket primary systems in order to permit non-party voters in primaries to vote for only one party's candidates. Until that case, those States permitted non-party voters to pick one candidate for each office on the ballot without regard to party lines. Only the candidates with the highest votes by party for each office advanced to the general election, as the respective party's nominee. Now, State laws requiring the 'open primary' permit voters to pick candidates regardless of their own party registration, but only to choose among candidates from a single party of the voter's choice. Only the State of Louisiana has a non-partisan blanket primary system where voters can choose any candidate from any political party in the opening round of voting. If one candidate wins a majority of votes cast, that candidate is declared the winner, and a general election run-off is not held. If no candidate wins a majority, the top two vote-getters, regardless of party affiliation, move on to the general election on the first Tuesday in November as required by Federal law. In Congressional races, that has several times pitted two candidates from the same party who were the top vote-getters under 50 per cent against each other, so that the main two political parties were not represented in the run-off.

The content, form, and disposition of ballots used in Congressional elections are generally regulated by State law. The only Federal requirement is that such ballots be written or printed, unless the State has authorized the use of voting machines. In judging election contests, the House must on occasion gain access to the ballots cast and determine whether they were properly included within or omitted from the official count taken by State authorities. House committees investigating contests, or investigating election irregularities or fraud, may be granted authority to impound ballots within the custody of State officials. In judging the validity of ballots, the House or its committee relies on State statutes regarding ballots and on State court opinions construing those laws. The general rule is that laws regulating the conduct of voters and the casting of votes are mandatory in nature and violations thereof invalidate the ballots cast, particularly where the voter's intent cannot be clearly ascertained. Laws regulating the functions of election officials are directory in nature and in the absence of fraud the officials' conduct will not vitiate ballots, even if they are subject to criminal sanction for the breach complained of. The House may order its own recount of the votes cast, without regard to State proceedings, under Article I, section 5 of the Constitution, but by precedent it has not assumed authority to order a State or local elections board to undertake a recount.

To facilitate the resolution of election contests in the House, Congress has enacted a Federal Contested Election statute which provides an alternative means of presenting election contests for committee and then plenary disposition in the House, while permitting the Member-elect possessing a certificate of election as determined under State law to be presumptively seated, with the question of final right to the seat referred to the Committee on House Administration under prescribed regulations. This statute sets forth the procedure by which a defeated candidate may have his claim to a seat adjudicated by the House. The statute provides for the filing of notice of contest and other proceedings, for the taking of testimony of witnesses, and for a hearing on the depositions and other papers filed with the Clerk. The contest is heard by the Committee on House Administration or a sub-panel thereof. Acting on committee reports, the House, by privileged resolution, then disposes of the case by declaring one of the parties to be entitled to the seat. Of course, this statutory scheme—for which there is nothing comparable in the Senate—is not a total substitute for the authority of each House to judge its Members' election by whatever method it may choose in a given situation, but rather is a convenient alternative which acknowledges a presumption in favour of the candidate with credentials and which permits the district to be represented pending a subsequent investigation. Thus, Members' elections may be challenged in either House when the Member-elect presents himself to be sworn, and the House may refer the matter to committee while initially seating the certified Member. This is the normal disposition of the question of 'prima facie' seating of the Member-elect holding the certificate, based upon the presumption of regularity and the desire of the House to permit the district to be represented pending protracted proceedings both in State courts and in the House committee.

On one occasion in 1985, the House when it convened declared that neither candidate for an Indiana seat was entitled to be seated pending a committee investigation, although one candidate held a certificate of election. The House referred both the question of prima facie and final right to the seat to committee. This action was ostensibly based on a precedent in 1961 involving another election to the House from the same State (Indiana), but was distinguishable as in that earlier case the certificate of election received by the Clerk had been 'impeached' by other documentary evidence from State officials received by the Clerk. The Majority Leader in bringing the challenge in 1985 improperly cited the earlier case as a valid precedent, resulting in the refusal of the House to temporarily seat either candidate although one of them possessed an unimpeached certificate of election. In both cases, the House committee conducted its own complete recount, and recommended to the House that the non-certified candidate be declared elected and finally entitled to the seat. In both cases, the House as it convened immediately overcame the presumption of the regularity of State law, even in the second instance without having yet established its own evidentiary record of any irregularities sufficient to overcome the presumption of prima facie seating of the certified Member-elect. In both cases, the certified Member-elect was from the Minority party, the recount took several months, and the ultimately seated Member was from the Majority party. This extraordinary example of the exercise of majority power to prevent the certified Minority Member from being temporarily seated pending an investigation created a prolonged sense of unfairness in the minds of the then Minority, which sentiment extended well beyond the Congress in question. Following the shift in 1995 of majority control of the House, this lingering resentment manifested itself in a year-long election contest in 1999, instituted under the statute by a defeated incumbent Majority Member. The House refused to dismiss the contest for many months following a committee investigation which determined the Minority party (certified) Member to have been finally elected. While this comparison demonstrates the difference between proceedings under the statute, where the certified Member has taken the oath and prima facie seating is not challenged, and the more egregious 1985 case of prima facie challenge where neither candidate was initially seated, it also symbolizes the institutional impact of perceived unfairness by the Majority in judging elections of Members, and the unfortunate precedential effect such perception can have on subsequent election challenges. These two anomalous cases, in 1985 and in 1999, belie the general pattern that the House in judging the elections of its Members has proceeded fairly without regard to party status of the certified Member.

In the period from 1933 to 2008, there were 109 contested election cases. Many of these cases involved an allegation of fraud and other election improprieties. Of these cases, a vast majority were resolved in favour of the contestee (the candidate who was originally declared the victor and seated). Since the Federal Contested Elections Act of 1969 was enacted, most cases have been dismissed because the contestant failed to sustain the burden of proof by a preponderance of the evidence necessary to overcome a motion to dismiss. In the 110th Congress, an election contest was initiated under the statute in an extremely close election which involved the alleged inoperability of electronic voting machines and a disproportionate 'under-vote' for candidates for Congress in certain precincts, as compared with candidates for other offices on the ballot. On opening day, the Member-elect who had been certified was permitted to be temporarily seated pending the outcome of litigation in a State court and upon a filed complaint triggering an investigation by the Committee on House Administration, to be conducted under the Contested Election statute. It was understood that a finding of irregularity in the State court could result in sufficient uncertainty to allow the court to recommend that the House declare a vacancy to permit a special election, where no paper trail existed to trace the 'under-votes' allegedly not counted by computer technology. The House returned to the presumption of regularity by the temporary seating of the certified candidate and by avoiding a resort to specific action on opening day. The committee's proceedings under the statute would be conducted without prejudice to the final seating of either candidate. In 2008, the committee and the House dismissed the contest where the investigation, utilizing the General Accountability Office, could not trace the lost electronic votes as having been cast for either candidate.

While the Senate has no comparable statute governing election contests, it has, in judging the elections of its Members, also conducted a complete recount resulting in the declaration of a vacancy and the ordering of a new election. In 1974, a Senator-elect was certified as having been elected from New Hampshire by two votes. He had also been appointed to fill the unexpired term of his predecessor, who had resigned to permit an early appointment by the Governor to increase seniority status over other newly elected Senators. When the Senate convened in January 1975, it determined not to seat either candidate and after an investigation declared the seat vacant in August of that year. The same candidate who had lost the 1974 election was elected in a special election later that year for the unexpired term to 1980 (*Wyman v Durkin*). Because only one-third of the Senate is elected every two years, it has not been considered necessary to enact a statute or to adopt special Senate rules governing election contests brought in that body, the Senate preferring to judge the elections of its Members on an ad hoc basis when individual challenges are brought before it.

Campaign practices and finance

The Supreme Court has affirmed that the power of Congress to make regulations for holding elections extends to every phase of the election process, including campaign practices. Until 1972, campaign practices in Congressional elections were governed by the Corrupt Practices Act of 1935, as amended. The Federal Election Campaign Act of 1971 repealed that Act and established a new and comprehensive code for campaign practices and expenditures with provisions for investigations and enforcement. The 1971 Act required reports on campaign contributions and expenditures to be filed with the Clerk by candidates for election to the House and designated the Clerk as 'supervisory officer' of the Act in relation to House elections, with duties as to investigations, enforcement, and referral to prosecutors of violations of the Act. The Federal Election Campaign Act Amendments of 1974 imposed new limitations on campaign contributions and expenditures, modified reporting requirements under the Act, provided for public financing of

Presidential nominating conventions, and created a new Federal Election Commission to investigate and enforce compliance with the Act. The Supreme Court in the case of *Buckley v Valeo* 424 US 1 (1976) ruled that while contributions limitations imposed by the Act were within the power of Congress, certain of the spending limitations imposed by the Act violated the 1st Amendment of the Constitution as an infringement on freedom of speech. The Supreme Court has been urged to reconsider that decision as it impacts on Congressional inability to impose overall spending limits, as well as limitations of candidates' personal funds and independent expenditures. The fundamental question remains whether expenditure of money for campaigns is a form of speech which Congress is powerless to restrict by law. In the meantime expenditures for Congressional candidacies have increased to extraordinary levels in an effort both to meet costs of campaigning (primarily television costs) and to accumulate campaign 'war chests' to discourage potential opposition. This has necessitated constant activity by incumbent Representatives and Senators to raise campaign funds and in many cases to distribute them to colleagues and to leadership Political Action Committees (PACs) to the detriment of the availability of time for constitutionally mandated legislative and oversight responsibilities.

While corporations and labour unions are prohibited by law from contributing directly to political campaigns, they remain free to establish voluntary PACs, often administered by their own compensated lobbyists, whereby their employees and members are importuned, although not compelled, to contribute to raise and distribute campaign funds for Members of Congress. The practice of 'bundling', whereby lobbyists as individual contributors to campaigns are limited by law in the amount of their contributions but are free to collect contributions from other like-minded contributors and combine them as one fund-raising effort, has been restricted by Public Law 110-81. At this writing, that law represents the most recent successful effort by Congress to address certain lobbying practices. It also incorporates internal Senate rules changes which mirror similar House rules adopted by the House in the 110th Congress with respect to gifts, travel, and staff conduct.

The role of some lobbyists as both contributors to and facilitators and managers of Members' campaign funds is linked by some public-interest groups to improper gifts from lobbyists to Members of Congress and their staffs. Recent statistics demonstrate the increasing extent to which lobbyists are serving as principal fund raisers for lawmakers they are trying to sway. Federal Election Commission records show seventy-one lawmakers listed as lobbyists in 2007 as treasurers of their re-election or PACs. In 1998, the number had been fifteen. The increase is attributed to the sharply rising costs of political campaigns. This raises the question of whether lawmakers who rely on lobbyists become beholden to them, and thus more willing to help their clients. While some have advocated that registered lobbyists be banned from raising money for Members, others would only require them to disclose when they host fund-raising events for politicians. Many lobbyists also raise funds for specialized funding organizations called leadership PACs in order to help fellow party members in close election races. Under Federal election rules, incumbent Members cannot donate more than $4,200 per election cycle from their own re-election coffers to the campaign of any colleague, but can funnel as much as $10,000 per election cycle from leadership PACs to another campaign. In practice, such financial support from politically secure lawmakers for the re-election efforts of vulnerable colleagues often translates to reciprocal support, such as leadership races within Congress. When Republicans took over the House in 1995, about ninety Members operated leadership PACs, which together raised a total of $28 million. In a more recent election cycle in 2004, more than 300 leadership PACs took in $127 million, according to the Federal Election Commission.

The 1974 Act has been amended several times, in 1976, 1979, and 2002, and prohibits union and corporate contributions, imposes limits on individual, interest group, and political party contributions to candidates and committees involved in Federal elections for President and Congress, and requires public disclosure of contributions and expenditures by participants on a regular basis. Within this framework, a dual system of finance has evolved: (1) a Presidential system, funded in large measure from public monies, with concomitant, voluntary limits on campaign expenditures; and (2) a Congressional system, funded solely by private donations and free of circumscriptions on campaign spending since *Buckley* (see page 133). The Act distinguished between expenditures—money spent to communicate election messages (which cannot be limited by Congress under the 1st Amendment)—and contributions, money given to others (candidates, parties, or PACs) to make expenditures for election messages. Current contribution limits can generally be described as follows: on individuals, $2,400 per candidate per election; $10,000 per year to State party; $25,000 per year to national party; $95,000 aggregate in Federal contributions per two-year election cycle; on parties, $35,000 from national or senatorial committees to general election candidates, indexed all but State party limit for future inflation.

Other Federal laws codified in the Criminal Code (title 18) bear on campaign practices, including laws prohibiting bribery, a candidate's promise of employment, solicitation or receipt of political contributions from Federal employees (Hatch Act), solicitation of political contributions in Federal buildings, or from Federal contractors, and contributions from corporations or labour unions to Federal campaigns. All are within the power of Congress to regulate by law the manner of elections to Congress, in addition to many State laws on those subjects. The chapter on Ethics and Standards at page 517 will discuss in further detail the 'sovereignty' of Congress, and of Parliament, to permit other branches of government to investigate, prosecute, and adjudicate misconduct of public officials, including Representatives and Senators, while maintaining the separate constitutional responsibilities of judging the elections and the conduct of its Members.

In the UK, the most significant change in the monitoring and development of electoral law has been the creation of the Electoral Commission. From the 1970s, party funding had been a topic of public debate. Secrecy promoted suspicion. There was concern over the lack of information on the origin of large donations and the possibility the money could buy access to ministers. Pressure built up on parties to disclose the details of donations, in particular those from overseas. The much-disputed issue of State funding of political parties was never far away. Debate was intensified by the widespread concern about 'sleaze' in the early 1990s (see page 523). In general, it became clear that, whatever the way ahead, it needed to have cross-party backing if it was to be effective.

In 1998 the Committee on Standards in Public Life (see page 524) concluded that the law regarding political donations needed to deliver more transparency, a greater assurance that there could be no secret influence over policy formation, and a generally higher level of public confidence in the political process. The competing claims of free speech were weighed, but—in contrast to the US experience—were found less persuasive than the need to reinforce public confidence in as unimpeachable a political process as could be secured.

The Electoral Commission created by the Political Parties, Elections and Referendums Act 2000 was the response of the government of the day. The Commission registers parties, without which accreditation their candidates may not participate in elections (though it remains possible to stand for election as an Independent); monitors and publishes significant donations; regulates spending by parties on their campaigns; reports on the conduct of elections; and advises those who conduct and participate in elections.

For most national and local elections, political parties must register with the Commission, thereby bringing themselves under its regulatory and financial control. In March 2008, 412 parties were registered, though only about a quarter of that number contested parliamentary seats in the general election of 2005. Statements of accounts must be presented to the Electoral Commission annually.

In 2007, British political parties received £56.5 million in donations. Donations of more than £200 to a registered party or £50 to a candidate may be accepted only if the donor falls within a category which is limited to individuals registered to vote in the UK, or UK-registered parties, companies, trade unions, or similar bodies: the connection with the UK is critical, and the rules in that respect were tightened by a further statute in 2008. Support in kind comes within the regulation as much as cash donations. Donations of £5,000 and above to party headquarters and £1,000 to constituency associations or parties are reported to the Commission by the parties at quarterly intervals—which become weekly intervals in a general election period—and published. Records must be kept of donations of £200 or more. The aim of the Electoral Commission is to encourage smaller contributions from a larger number of people, to ensure that no single source of funds has undue influence on a party, and to see that the system neither entrenches the status quo nor stands in the way of new parties.

Subsequently there were political squabbles over compliance with the new rules at a detailed level, followed by wider concern that the requirements for declaration did not cover soft—or indeed any—loans to parties. Police investigations, a specially constituted official inquiry, and select committee attention have been engaged by accusations that peerages have been conferred in return for, or at least in close connection with, contributions to party funds. Electoral law was tightened in 2006. Loans and other credit facilities were brought within the reach of the regulatory arm of the Electoral Commission, and at the end of 2007 British political parties had accumulated £36.5 million in new and outstanding borrowing.

The days when general elections were simply a matter of constituency contests between individuals are long gone. Whatever difference to the outcome may sometimes be made by a very good or an indifferent local candidate, general elections are fought at national level by mass parties with a national message. The Act of 2000 therefore limits party campaign expenditure at that level, allowing £30,000 for each Westminster constituency contested, or £810,000 in England, £120,000 in Scotland, and £60,000 in Wales, whichever is the greater. In the 2005 general election, campaign expenditure (which is defined in some detail by the Act of 2000, and includes things like broadcasts, advertisements, transport, leaflets, and rallies) on the part of the three largest parties in Great Britain amounted to roughly £40 million, broken down as set out in Table 4.3 in the Annex.[10] These sums are hardly to be compared with the levels of expenditure in the

USA. It has been reported that the mid-term senatorial contest in Pennsylvania in 2006 cost as much as the Labour national campaign in the UK in 2005.[11]

A separate regime sets limits for the candidates in each constituency. In county constituencies, a candidate may not spend more than the aggregate of £7,150 plus 7p for each person on the electoral register. In elections in borough and burgh constituencies, the sums are £7,150 and 5p. In 2005, the total spent in Great Britain was £14 million, each candidate (including those unsuccessful) spending on average £4,000, well within his or her limit. All relevant expenditure is channelled through the party election agent, as a means of monitoring the control. Not later than five weeks after the election, the agents in each constituency must return to the Commission an account of expenditure (and it is a criminal offence to have exceeded the limits) including all payments made by the agent, money contributed by the candidate from his own resources to meet the costs of the election, and donations accepted of more than £50.

A further responsibility of the Electoral Commission is the disbursement of a fairly modest amount of resources for 'policy development' by parties (seven are eligible) which have won at least two seats in the Commons. This is intended to assist them in working up the ideas which will feature in the party manifestos, but may not be used for routine or campaign expenditure.

Policy Development funds are to be distinguished from 'Short Money' which opposition parties in the Commons have received since 1975 to assist them in the discharge of their responsibilities in the House of Commons. The sum received is £12,793 for every seat won plus £25.55 for every 200 votes cast. £141,000 is divided between the parties for party business (including research and parliamentary staffing) and travel and associated expenses, with £595,999 set aside for the office of the Leader of the Opposition. In the Lords, a parallel system of grants began in 1996, in which the amounts payable are fixed, known as 'Cranborne money'. The purpose of the schemes is clear, and serious abuse is unlikely. On the other hand, accountability is—perhaps inevitably—cloudy, and the political point-scoring to which some of these arrangements periodically give rise suggests that the present dispensation may be no more than a temporary resting place.

Compensation and allowances

The vast difference in the geographical spread of the USA and the UK and the disparity between the size of Congressional districts—let alone States—on the one hand and parliamentary constituencies on the other, are reflected in the levels of financial support given to those elected (or appointed) to serve in Washington and Westminster. Whether these differences in weight and character of workload wholly explain the wide gap between levels of financial support to legislators on either side of the Atlantic is a matter on which doubtless there will be many views: but that such a gap exists is obvious. Ten years ago, it would have been even more cavernous.

Article I, section 6 of the US Constitution provides that 'the Senators and Representatives shall receive a compensation for their services, to be ascertained by law, and paid out of the Treasury of the United States'. The 27th Amendment to the Constitution was proposed on 25 September 1789, but not ratified by the legislatures of three-fourths of the States (thirty-nine) until 7 May 1992. It provides that no law varying the compensation for the services of the Senators and Representatives shall take effect 'until an election of Representatives shall have intervened'. To quell speculation over the efficacy of a ratification process spanning two centuries, the House in 1992 adopted a concurrent resolution declaring the ratification of the 27th Amendment, and the Senate adopted a similar concurrent resolution. Congress has by law provided for automatic cost of living increases for Federal employees, including Members of Congress, which take effect every year unless prohibited by Act of Congress. The Federal courts have upheld the validity of this law as not in contravention of the 27th Amendment, since the law has been in place since 1989 and the salary adjustments emanate from that law, and not from any new law enacted prior to an intervening election (*Boehner v Anderson* 809 F Supp 138 (DDC 1992); affd 30 F 3d 156 (DC Cir 1994)). Thus Senators and Representatives received a 3 per cent cost of living adjustment which increased their salaries to $174,000 beginning 1 January 2009, based on the formula in the 1989 Act (and therefore not running foul of the 27th Amendment because not based on any law newly enacted prior to the next election of Representatives. The 27th Amendment was intended to prevent Congress from enacting new law increasing their own compensation with an effective date prior to their (re)election, so that constituents would be aware of that enactment when voting for an incumbent Member who stood to benefit. Congress by law denied itself any cost of living increase in 2010 in the wake of the financial crisis in 2009, thereby negating application of the 1989 formula for one year.

The Ethics in Government Act of 1989 which provided the automatic cost of living adjustment also limited permissible outside earned income to 15 per cent of Senators' and Representatives' salary ($25,830 in 2008), and prohibited certain types of outside earned income altogether. Representatives and Senators are allowed to deduct, for income tax purposes, living expenses up to $3,000 per annum, while away from their Congressional districts or home States. Representatives and Senators are eligible to participate in the Federal Employees Health Benefits Program and may select from among several health benefit plans. Participation is on a voluntary, contributory basis. They are eligible to participate in the Federal Employees Group Life Insurance Program, the coverage of which is determined by a formula based on the coverage elected. Various options are available to Representatives and Senators regarding participation in the Civil Service Retirement System and the Federal Employees Retirement System, with minimal benefits vesting after twenty years of federal service and accelerated to fully vest at 80 per cent of salary after thirty-two years of service. Participation in the Medicare portion of Social Security is mandatory for Members and staff, but they do not participate in the retirement pension portion, being instead covered under one of the Federal retirement plans mentioned above.

Representatives have one allowance available to support them in their official and representational duties to the districts from which they were elected. This allowance is the Members' representational allowance, comprising three individual allowances, each of which has a separate authorized dollar limit, and all of which are by law disclosed to the public in printed detailed quarterly Chief Administrative Officer's reports, and on order of the Speaker beginning in 2009, online. This is in marked contrast to the allowances for Members of the House of Commons, ranging from housing and mortgage allowances, to food and other purchase allowances and travel allowances which caused so much controversy in 2009 (see below).

The personnel allowance component is the same for each Member. The office expenses (including travel) and mail allowance components have a base of $194,980 adjusted by differences in the distance between a Member's district and the seat of government for the mileage allowance, the cost of office space in the district, and the number of non-business addresses for the mail allowance. In calendar year 2009, the Members' representational allowances ranged from $1,722,242 to $1,391,370. These allowances are authorized in law, are appropriated annually under the heading 'salaries and expenses' and are regulated and adjusted by the Committee on House Administration which need not be approved by the full House by separate votes. All such House allowances are reported in the quarterly Statement of Disbursements of the House.

The personnel allowance is available for employment of staff both at the seat of government and in the District offices. Each Representative is entitled to an annual personnel allowance of $922,350 in 2009 for no more than eighteen permanent employees. As many as four additional part-time employees do not count against the limit. House employees' salaries were capped at $172,500 in 2009, Senate personal staff salaries at $169,659, and Senate Committee staff salaries at $171,315.

While the basis for all of the allowances discussed in this chapter is established by law enacted by both Houses, each House is deferential to the other in their formulation and regulation. Senators have three official allowances for personnel and official office expenses. They are the administrative and clerical assistance allowance, the legislative assistance allowance, and the official office expense allowance. The first and third of these vary and are governed by State population, distance from the seat of government to home State, and committee-authorized limits. Totals of $1,926,936 were available in States with population under 5 million up to $3,170,602 in States above 28 million populations. The legislative assistance allowance is a set amount for all Senators. The total amount available to a Senator is the sum of the two personnel allowances and the office expense allowance. In 2009, the total of the three allowances available for Senators ranged from $2,758,000 (Delaware) to $4,417,000 (California) depending on the size of the State, its distance from Washington, DC, and the number of mailing addresses for franked mail. All funds made available to each Senator for the three allowances can be interchanged by the Senator, subject to regulations issued by the Committee on Rules and Administration. As is true for House allowances, they may not be used to defray any personal political or campaign-related expenses, and are reported quarterly for public inspection.

Each House has a constitutionally designated presiding officer—the Speaker (salary set at $223,500 in 2009), and the Vice President, whose compensation in 2009 was established by law at $227,300. They are entitled to comparable retirement and health benefits prescribed by law, and to official office expense allowances. For the Speaker, these allowances are in addition to any allowances received as a Representative. Elected party leaders in both Houses receive compensation greater than other Members (at $193,400 in 2009) but below the levels of the presiding officers, as well as separate allowances commensurate with their leadership responsibilities.

These amounts taken together may suggest that Members of Congress are generously compensated for their services. Comparisons with private sector compensation are seldom persuasive or relevant. The Constitution itself in the 27th Amendment acknowledges the political reality of the persons receiving them, and in effect requires transparency to avoid a short-term conflict of interest. Other political factors in setting compensation levels include comparisons with Federal judicial salaries—the prevailing Congressional view linking the two at the same level, although the Chief Justice of the Supreme Court annually reminds Congress in his written 'State of the Judiciary' message of the pressing need to attract new Federal judges with higher salary levels, free from the political constraints that limit what Congress will provide for itself. While the Constitution prohibits Congress from diminishing the salaries of Federal judges (to prohibit undue influence on judicial decisions), there is no requirement that judicial salaries be increased at any time.

Political attempts to limit salary adjustments for Congress are sometimes linked in introduced legislation to perceptions of legislative performance, such as levels of national debt or deficit. These adjustments have never become law. Annual attempts to restrict the availability of appropriated funds to pay increased Congressional salaries are normally unavailing, since Congress has enacted a permanent appropriation to pay compensation of Members, thereby rendering attempts to limit the annual availability of appropriated funds ineffective or in violation of House rules against changes in existing law when added to annual appropriation bills. The Ethics in Government Act of 1989 linked an annual 'cost of living' adjustment formula for Congressional salaries to ethics rules changes prohibiting or limiting outside sources of income in order to restrict conflicts of interest competing for Members' time and attention. The reality of Members' maintenance of two residences—in their Congressional districts and at the seat of government, assuming a full-year legislative schedule—continues to justify a compensation level above those prevailing in many Congressional districts although often viewed as overly generous by some critics.

In the UK, payments and travel expenses were intermittently made to Members of the medieval English House of Commons but they seem to have ceased about the end of the seventeenth century. Pressure for their reintroduction began in 1780—just about the time Article 1, section 6 of the US Constitution provided for payment to Senators and Representatives—and continued until success was achieved in 1911. There was a significant up-rating after the Second World War, when in addition a modest daily allowance became payable. Since then the basis on which salary and allowances are founded has changed several times. Ideally, the salary and allowances of Members of the elected House ought to be set at levels which are modest but sufficient, their comparability with other walks of life and their appropriateness to the task which Members perform independently and expertly determined. Perhaps inevitably, however, it has been difficult to construct a basis for these payments which commands universal approval.

Even when parliamentary salaries have been linked to a single external comparator—a specific grade in the civil service, for example—and despite a series of triennial expert reviews by the Senior Salaries Review Body (SSRB) beginning in 1971, until very recently the final decisions remained with the House itself. What these decisions were depended in practice on a number of competing factors. Feeling on the back benches usually favoured upward movement, or at least cherry-picking of what left the SSRB as a balanced and nuanced package. Downward pressure was exerted by the government, not always wholly successfully. A generally sceptical public opinion was frequently fuelled by a normally hostile press. For the most part, governments managed to persuade the

House to follow the SSRB's proposals with or without some adjustment, but there have been occasions when feelings have run so high that governments have had to yield to back-bench dissatisfaction. In 1996, for example, the SSRB recommended an increase of 26 per cent: the government countered with 3 per cent: and the House preferred the SSRB figure. Ministers could always have blocked an effective increase in public expenditure attributable to enhancement of parliamentary salaries by refusing to exercise their prerogative to make the necessary spending motion (see page 264): but equally, that might have given rise to an embarrassing defeat.

In 2008, following an SSRB report, the government grasped the nettle and declared that it was inappropriate that Members should in future settle their own pay and conditions: 'a significant constitutional reform', the Leader of the House called the proposal. A further review was set up to look into how this end might be achieved. Perhaps significantly, not only was any new and independent mechanism for pay-setting to have regard to the need to maintain the support and trust of the public and Members, but it should take account of government policy on public sector pay and its inflation target. On consideration of the latter report, the House agreed that in future Members' salaries should be annually up-rated by a figure equivalent to the median increase for a range of public sector groups, without formal approval by Members. The salary of a Member is £64,766 with effect from 1 April 2009.[12] The SSRB notifies the Speaker annually of the appropriate level of increase, which is then implemented. They will normally conduct a full-scale review of Members' salaries only at the beginning of every Parliament. Following enactment of the Parliamentary Standards Act, Members' salaries will be paid by the independent authority created by the bill.

The Speaker receives an annual salary of £144,520, the same as that of a Cabinet minister. The Speaker's salary is—uniquely—fixed on the Consolidated Fund: all other parliamentary remuneration—by contrast with Congressional practice—is paid from money voted annually. The Chairman of Ways and Means receives £106,136, the same as a senior non-Cabinet minister, and the other Deputy Speakers £101,126, slightly more than a junior minister. All figures include the element attributable to salary as a Member. On the same basis, the Leader of the Opposition has a salary of £138,383. Whips on both sides of the House receive salaries ranging from the Government Chief Whip's total of £144,520 to £91,390 for assistant government whips and the Opposition Deputy Chief Whip.

Pensions for Members of the Commons were introduced in 1964. Currently, the Parliamentary Contributory Pension Fund is a final-salary scheme deriving its income from the deduction from Members of 5.9, 7.9, or 11.9 per cent of their pay, according to whether the rate of accrual is one-sixtieth, one-fiftieth, or one-fortieth, with government contributions of nearly 29 per cent of the Fund's income making up the balance. The normal age of retirement is 65 and the minimum 50: retirement from the House earlier than 65 will reduce the payment. There are survivors' benefits.

Long before the hostile public response to publication of Members' expenses claims in the spring of 2009, it was clear that there were many problems in the system of allowances claimable by Members in connection with their parliamentary duties. Members' personal circumstances and their widely differing ways of going about parliamentary and constituency work—both of which change over time—inevitably meant that the rules had to be complex and their application, within reason, flexible. Yet flexibility was just what the system lacked, since the rules were contained in a series of resolutions of the House, some of them so out of date as to require heroic interpretation to meet changing conditions. For obvious reasons, government legislation took priority, making it difficult to find time on the floor for updating and revising resolutions. Until about 2001 sleeping dogs were allowed to lie. Raising financial limits in existing allowances and creating new ones was no doubt an approach more congenial to successive governments keen to avoid the headlines greeting increases in parliamentary salaries. Against that background, it seems that allowances—which the SSRB more accurately called reimbursements—imperceptibly came to be thought of as entitlements within the relevant financial limit.

The most acute difficulties arose with the Additional Costs Allowance, under which Members could claim assistance with the cost of renting or purchasing accommodation other than their principal residence, or incurring hotel or similar costs: 441 Members claimed for a second home in London and 148 for a second home elsewhere, according to latest figures. Claims could arise for food, utility bills, local taxes, mortgage payments, security, and maintenance on their nominated second home. In the latest figures available, the average claim was nearly £20,000 a year.

Despite the torrent of criticism in 2009 over expenses, the fact is that there had been considerable change. In 2004, the House of Commons Commission—the statutory responsibilities of which did not extend to allowances—was ingeniously turned into a select committee, the Members' Estimate Committee (MEC) charged with codifying and keeping under review the public funding of Members' work, modifying it 'as the committee thought necessary in the interests of clarity, consistency, accountability, and effective administration, and conformity with current circumstances'. The MEC advised the Speaker when requested in particularly difficult cases. In January 2009, the MEC was strengthened by the transformation of what had been an informal advisory group into the Members' Allowances select committee, on which the government did not have a majority. That Committee advised the MEC, approved practice notes, and determined the application of the rules in hard cases.

Outside the House, too, thought was given to the reimbursement/allowance system. The SSRB's 2007 report drew attention to the need for improved transparency in order to meet public concern, though it had received no substantial evidence of abuse. Several adjustments to the system were proposed. Early the following year the government moved and the House agreed to refer nearly all these recommendations to the MEC. Almost immediately thereafter, a high-profile case concerning staff payments came before the Standards and Privileges Committee (see page 528), and the MEC concluded that a root-and-branch examination of the current system was required. The Committee reported in the summer of 2008.[13] They recommended a robust new system of practice assurance involving regular financial health checks on records kept and procedures used in Members' offices, using external teams covering a quarter of all Members each session and the whole House in the course of a Parliament. The National Audit Office (NAO) would make a sampling check on claims paid. All expenditure would require to be receipted: there would be no lower limit. The Additional Costs Allowance (now the Personal Additional Accommodation Expenditure Allowances: see below) should become an overnight expenses allowance with a maximum budget, on the basis of itemized reimbursement and a flat daily subsistence. If the MEC had had its way, there would have been no more claims for furniture or household goods on second homes and no question of Members' retention of increased capital value of property when they moved from accommodation which had been supported from public funds. The House, on a free vote in July 2008, clearly thought this went too far. The government's motion implementing the proposals was amended to provide only that there should be a rigorous system of internal audit, rejecting the proposal that all claims, however small, should require to be receipted. It turned out to be an unwise decision.

In January 2009, the MEC recommended that, in addition to the work of its own audit committee, there should be external audit by the NAO, internal audit assisted by an external partner, and (as the government had proposed) an internal operations assurance unit, advising Members, reviewing evidence for claims, maintaining standards, and enforcing compliance. This would amount to 'a proportionate system which would enable Members' allowances to be audited, and to provide a suitable level of assurance regarding their use'. A trial for a full-scope NAO audit had '[given] no serious grounds for concern about Members' use of their allowances'.[14]

In mid-2008, the House authorities had lost an action under Freedom of Information legislation to limit the accessibility of Members' expense information (see also page 110 for an attempt to amend the Freedom of Information Act so far as it affected Parliament), and soon after the MEC's report, the government brought forward proposals which would have nearly doubled the number of categories of published expenditure in the House's Publication Scheme. A full-scale NAO audit of expenses was to be conducted, putting the Commons on a footing with other public authorities. The limit for unreceipted claims was reduced to £25, leaving only 1 per cent of refundable purchases in that category. A new set of principles for expenses claims clearly stated that claims should be above reproach, and advised Members to avoid purchases which could be seen as extravagant or luxurious. Pressure was not eased, and in April the Prime Minister asked the Committee on Standards in Public Life to examine Members' expenses. The House of Commons welcomed the move and reduced the non-receipted claims limit to zero. Other changes were made which are referred to at page 525.

Such measured progress ended when in early May 2009 a national newspaper published full details of all Members' expense claims. Public outrage ensued. On the basis of the published information, some Members seemed to have straightforwardly broken the rules; others, including very senior Members, were presented as having made claims within the letter but not the spirit of the rules, counter to the more austere principles mentioned above; some Members refunded payments to which criticism attached but others did not; the rules were denounced as too vague and their interpretation too relaxed. When the dust settles, spurious or doubtful claims may indeed stand revealed, but it should be remembered that the great majority of Members were not affected by the stories. Nevertheless, the immediate uproar was rightly described by the shadow Leader of the House as 'the most serious and revolutionary shift in popular opinion and in the reputation of Parliament in our lifetime'.[15] Pressure arising from the predicament in which the House found itself caused the Speaker to resign (page 36). Pending the report of the Committee on Standards in Public Life (CSPL), expected in the autumn of 2009, interim measures were put in place on the proposal of the MEC. Among them were limitations on the types of expenditure which could give rise to a claim in respect of other than principal dwellings. Mortgage interest claims were capped and the designation of what was a principal residence could be changed only in exceptional circumstances.

All past claims for the additional costs allowance over the previous four years would be looked into, and arrangements would be made for repayments in appropriate cases. No changes were to be made to any other allowances until the CSPL reported.

At the same time, the Prime Minister proposed a very radical solution, that Parliament should '[switch] from self-regulation to independent external regulation'[16] to be set out in statute.

The Parliamentary Standards Act of July 2009 made a number of important changes to the existing arrangements—fewer, however, than were originally intended by the government. Some of these will be discussed under Ethics and Standards (pages 523ff.) and Privilege and Contempt (page 486): here the focus is on the future of parliamentary allowances in the Commons. (Curiously, despite the term 'Parliamentary' in its title and in that of the Authority it creates, the Act does not affect the House of Lords, though changes are likely subsequently be made to arrangements there.) The Independent Parliamentary Standards Authority is charged with the responsibility of drawing up and maintaining a scheme of allowances paid to Members. The scheme will define the kinds of expenditure and the circumstances in which allowances are to be payable in future, the conditions on which they are paid and the limits on the sums involved. The scheme is to be laid before the House but, unlike the Code of Conduct under the Act (see page 526), no provision is made for its approval by the Commons. The chairman of the Authority and the four members are appointed by Her Majesty on an Address by the House of Commons, to which the Speaker (who makes the original nominations) will have given his assent. There are particular specifications concerning the background of three of the four members. One must be a retired judge, one an auditor, and one a former Member of the House. Other than the last, no member of the Authority may have sat in the Commons in the previous five years. The Speaker is to be advised in his nominations by a committee including the Leader of the House of Commons, the chairman of the Standards and Privileges Committee, and five backbenchers appointed by the Commons.

The Authority will be responsible for setting the ground rules for investigations of Members in cases where payments have been made to Members which should not have been allowed or where the Code of Conduct may have been breached by a failure to register a relevant interest. The investigations are to be carried out by a Commissioner appointed under the Act. If irregularity is proved, the Commissioner refers the matter to the Standards and Privileges Committee for disposal in the usual way, the penalties including apology to the House, with or without suspension and withholding of salary, and even in appropriate cases—none of which has yet arisen—expulsion.

After two years following the Act's entry into force and at similar intervals thereafter, key provisions will expire unless extended by statutory instrument approved in draft by the Commons (see page 469). Even before then it is possible that the forthcoming report of the Committee on Standards in Public Life, the remit of which is at least cognate with those matters, may propose further changes to the regime.

On the assumption that the new regime will to some degree resemble the old, the existing arrangements are as follows.

The Personal Additional Accommodation Expenditure—which replaced the allowance most heavily criticized in the expenses crisis—is set at £24,222 for each Member each year. It is intended to meet the cost of staying overnight away from home (whether 'home' is designated as in London or in or near the constituency) and now covers rent, interest arising from mortgage arrangements, utilities bills, and local taxation.

Costs of staff employed by a Member wholly and exclusively for the purpose of his or her parliamentary duties are met from House administration funds, up to a maximum of £103,812 for each Member in 2009–10. The staff must be able, qualified, and actually doing the job for which they are paid. There are standard contracts (between the staffer and the Member, and not the House administration), and pay ranges are aligned with what would be received for similar jobs outside the House. The employer is the Member, who selects the employee and is responsible for compliance with the demands of employment law. As part of the reforms referred to above, however, the House decided in April 2009 that in future Members' staff are to be employed by the House itself, though selected and managed by the individual Member. The House of Commons Commission has been asked to consider how best to implement that decision.

For Members who represent constituencies in Greater London (definition of which for this purpose was among the changes made in April 2009), where costs of all kinds are higher than elsewhere, there is a London Costs Allowance of £7,500.

Administration and Office expenditure may be claimed up to a maximum of £22,393 a year, to provide accommodation and office facilities—equipment, furniture, supplies, security, and telephones—for Members and their staff other than in the Palace of Westminster.

Travel costs by rail, sea, or air arising from parliamentary (including constituency) business are met from public funds, whether a Member uses his or her car or public transport (or even bicycle). Limited travel to and from institutions and capitals in member States of the EU and candidate countries, recently extended to national parliaments of member States of the Council of Europe, may also be repaid, and there are some allowances for travel to London for Members' spouses and children.

The Communication Allowance of up to £10,400 annually is intended to cover Members' contacts with their constituents where these are of a representative and not a party political nature. It covers the cost of such things as newsletters, advertising advice sessions, and development of websites.

Finally, there are resettlement grants of between 50 and 100 per cent of salary, dependent on age and length of service, for those who retire from the House at a dissolution, and a winding-up allowance of up to £42,068 to settle accounts which arise after a Member's parliamentary duties have ended whether by death, defeat, or retirement. These were criticized by the SSRB in 2007 and the matter is evidently to be revisited by the CSPL in 2009.

The system in the Lords varies from that in the Commons in one central respect. Lords receive no salary, but are reimbursed for expenses incurred in attendance at the House and its organs at a maximum overnight rate of £174 or a day rate half that. Secretarial allowances and additional cost allowance are paid up to a daily maximum of £75. Other allowances parallel arrangements in the Commons, such as that for travel to and from the EU. The Prime Minister has asked the SSRB (see page 139) to review financial support for the Lords, to increase accountability, enhance transparency, and reduce costs.

Staff and assistance

In addition to limits on allowances for Members' staff, including a limit of eighteen on the number of full-time employees at salary limits as described above, the Code of Conduct for the House of Representatives specifically prohibits the employment of spouses by Members, Delegates, and the Resident Commissioner from Puerto Rico, as well as committee employment of any spouse of a member of that committee. This anti-nepotism prohibition was added in 2001 to restrictions which already precluded the employment of persons who did not perform duties commensurate with compensation received. This rule is in contrast with the system in the House of Commons which permits the employment of spouses if they perform their duties (see page 528). In the USA, to avoid this conflict, spouses are sometimes employed by colleagues of Members under various reciprocal arrangements.

The Code of Conduct also states that Members may not discriminate in employment on the basis of sex, race, religion, age, marital or parental status, or national origin, but may take into consideration the domicile or political affiliation of the employee.

Members' staff (one at a time) may be present on the floor of the House only when amendments offered by that Member are under actual consideration (see Chapter 3, The Four Houses, at pages 53–4).

The Congressional Accountability Act of 1995 established employment rights for Congressional employees comparable to those of other public and private sector employees. To enforce those employment rights an Office of Compliance was created in that law comprising five individuals appointed jointly by the Speaker, the Majority Leader of the Senate, and the Minority Leaders of the House and Senate. The office has regulatory, enforcement, and educational responsibilities under the Act, and was intended to minimize employment grievance lawsuits brought in other forums. A General Counsel is appointed by the Chair of the Compliance Board to exercise the authorities of the Office.

As long as employees complete their official duties required by the Member and for which the employees are compensated from public funds, they are generally free to engage in personal, campaign, or other non-official activities. The broad prohibition against campaign activity by Executive branch personnel, known as the 'Hatch Act', does not apply to Congressional employees. While a Congressional employee may not make a campaign contribution to his or her employing Member, 'contribution' for this purpose does not include volunteer activity. Thus they may participate in partisan campaign activities while not being solicited by their employers for campaign contributions.

The US criminal code makes it unlawful to solicit or to receive any political contribution in any building where Federal employees work, which includes the US Capitol and Congressional office buildings. Thus Congressional employees must engage in campaign fund-raising activities only off the premises, and must forward contributions unexpectedly received in the Member's office to a political campaign committee located elsewhere.

There are a variety of other restrictions on Congressional employees' political activities separately explained in House and Senate Ethics Manuals republished in 2008. The effort in this segment is limited to an outline of authorized staff support for Members both in terms of financing, limits on numbers of personnel, and on permissible range of official activities. Comparable restrictions on committee staff are discussed in the segment on committees. There is a dichotomy between the importance of public service and the temptation of employees to become former employees and to enter the 'revolving door' into the lobbying industry. Factors include greatly increased remuneration and access to their former employers and to campaign contributions. The discussion earlier in this segment of these potential intersections, if not conflicts, of interest between Members, their staffs, lobbyists, and campaign contributions again highlights the potentially insidious impact of the cost of campaigning on the time and inclination of all involved to focus on matters of public policy.

At Westminster, there are no political constraints on Members' staff as there are on staff employed by the Houses: the former are not within civil service pay and pension schemes and the latter are. Members' staff are however automatically enrolled in a group pension scheme to which the Commons administration makes a contribution equivalent to up to 10 per cent of salary. General employment law applies to Members' staff, and the House generally submits to the jurisdiction of the courts. In other cases—which are a growing number—statute has in terms overridden any relevant parliamentary privilege in matters of employment.

Notes

1. 2 USC 2a.
2. 13 USC 195.
3. H Rep 109–593, part 1.
4. Quoted in HC Deb (2006–7) 463 c 452.
5. It had been intended that the functions of the four separate Commissions should be transferred to the Electoral Commission (see page 135) but no action to that effect has so far been taken, and the Committee on Standards in Public Life in its Eleventh Report 2007 Cm 7006 thought the change should not be made.
6. The number of Scottish seats was reduced from 70 to 59.
7. In 1969–70, the government of the day wished to delay implementation of redistribution to beyond the forthcoming general election, arguing that this was sensible in the light of impending major changes in local government. Political and legal pressure, arguing that the government was really trying to avoid a redistribution which would not be favourable to them, compelled the Prime Minister to abandon the plan in that form. He brought the orders implementing the recommendations before the Commons, and then invited his party to vote against them. The general election proceeded, as the government had originally wished, on the existing constituency basis. Similarly, it has been argued that another government speeded up a review in the 1990s, because it believed the outcome would be to its advantage.
8. Lords Committee for Privileges, First Report 2008–9 HL 87, and Second Report HL 88-I.
9. Cork City and Cork County.
10. Source: The Electoral Commission.
11. *The Times*, 6 October 2006.
12. The UK figure for basic salary—comparison of the full package is much more complicated—is not too far out of touch with other North and West European legislatures. France, Belgium, the Netherlands, Sweden, and Finland have salaries at roughly the same level. Salaries in Germany and the Irish Republic are about a third higher than the UK figure, those in Spain are half, and those in Italy double (*The Times*, 12 May 2009).
13. Third Report 2008–9 HC 578-I.
14. Members Estimate Committee, First Report 2008, Revised Green Book and Audit of Members' allowances, HC 142.
15. HC Deb (2008–9) 492 c 1507.
16. Ibid c 1505.

5

Procedural Basics

The general background

At the time of American independence, the Founding Fathers had a legislative model in some senses to follow, in others to avoid. Procedure in the British House of Commons had developed as a vehicle for expressing hostility to—or at least suspicion of—the Crown. Antique forms and ceremonies were lovingly cherished in short sessions not dominated by government legislation, backbenchers were free to initiate business unhindered by limits on debating time or much insistence on relevance, and there was a presumption in favour of delay rather than progress. Governments could not always count on securing the modest amount of legislation which they brought forward. Private bills, for the benefit of individual localities or enterprises, were more numerous than public bills.

Subsequently, in the nineteenth and for most of the twentieth centuries, British governments with lots of public business and increasingly disciplined back-bench support, pruned the old baroque procedure, stepped up the legislative work rate. New procedures were devised to compress the growing workload into the more or less unchanged time available—in other words, to curtail debate, and lay hold on most available time for the government. Party discipline pressured backbenchers into progressively surrendering their rights to bring business of their choice to the floor at a time of their selection. Increased insistence on relevance in debate drastically diminished their opportunities for which the growth of Question Time was no substitute.

The right of Members at large to intervene in any debate was not of course directly diminished, but they have lost ground in two ways. There is now only limited opportunity for them to bring matters to the floor;[1] and indirectly the insistent pressure of business on time has given rise to expedients which may severely ration their speaking time. Furthermore, majorities prevail. A minority may always express its dissatisfaction by voting, but if they choose to do so the time spent in dividing may make further inroads into what is left for debate.

As a result, the Opposition and (a long way behind) private Members now occupy what is available after the government has appropriated most of the time (though the balance is not quite so skewed as this might suggest; in 2007, on fifty-nine of 155 sitting days non-governmental business had priority).[2] The official Opposition has Opposition days (see page 309): jackpots for backbenchers, such as urgency debates, are very rare indeed. Overall constraints on time are not uniquely aimed at backbenchers, but it is governments alone which have available to them procedural means of relaxing the pressure in order to secure their business. It is the demand for the successful completion of the government's aims which underpins many contemporary procedures. Yet here as elsewhere, the wind is beginning to change.

The Modernisation Committee in the Commons declared recently that 'Parliament must make its procedures more open and engaging if it is to encourage greater activity in the House... The parliamentary role of a Member is pivotal and should not be marginalised'. Backbenchers, the Committee thought, should be given greater opportunity to initiate business.[3] Hence the introduction of topical debates and topical Questions (see pages 156, 341). Shorter, more focused debates would, the Committee hoped, be better attended and would afford more opportunity for such procedure to be back-bench initiated. If time for backbenchers' substantive motions were restored (the procedure was suppressed in 1992), perhaps in Westminster Hall, private Members would benefit further—though to be frank, such debates before their abolition never threatened to set the Thames on fire. Moreover, what has not much featured in the consideration of these good things is the possibility that sustained scrutiny work, on the floor or in Committee, might be diminished by the desire to discuss matters of topical—which may also mean passing—interest.

Thomas Jefferson wrote in his *Manual* (quoting in part the Commons Clerk, John Hatsell) with respect to the necessity for procedural rules that 'whether these forms be in all cases the most rational or not is really not of so great importance. It is much more material that there should be a rule to go by than what that rule is; that there may be a uniformity of proceeding in business not subject to the caprice of the Speaker or captiousness of the members. It is very material that order, decency and regularity be preserved in a dignified public body'. Further discussion of procedure as applicable to legislative business is contained at page 381.

In the USA, at the beginning of each Congress there are no standing rules in place which govern the proceedings of the House, as Article I of the Constitution leaves it to each House to adopt its own rules. The adoption of rules is the first order of business following the election of Speaker. In the interim, the House is governed by the Constitution and by 'general parliamentary law'—that body of precedent which traditionally serves as guidance for proceedings pending the adoption of formal rules. While the motion–amendment–disposition sequence is properly descriptive of 'general parliamentary law', only one Member (normally the Majority Leader) is recognized to offer and control debate on the resolution adopting the standing rules and orders. That Member first recognized possesses the parliamentary ability to cut off amendment and further debate by offering the motion for the previous question which has the same high priority under general parliamentary law as it has under House standing rule and which is normally adopted as a 'procedural' vote commanding party loyalty. Interlocutory motions, for example, to refer the resolution for study, are in order but may be laid on the table without debate. The Minority party seeking to propose its own rules changes is relegated to the motion to commit with instructions to amend, a motion which likewise derives its

precedence under general parliamentary law from prior usage. It is a motion traditionally utilized by the Minority caucus to propose its alternative rules changes and is a
guaranteed protection to the Minority notwithstanding the adoption of a motion otherwise cutting off amendment. The motion to commit is, however, traditionally rejected by
the Majority as a party 'procedural' matter.

Jefferson then speaks of an 'arrangement of business', suggesting that despite the
power of discretionary recognition being conferred upon the Speaker so as not to precisely bind her as to what matters shall be first taken up, unless the House on a question
decides to take up a particular subject, 'a settled order of business is necessary for the
government of the presiding person, and to restrain individual Members from calling up
matters...out of their just turn'. This sampling of Jefferson's notions of arrangement of
business reflects the basic parliamentary premise that a measure or matter must first be
brought up for consideration in either House by motion or by order before it can be
debated, amended, and decided upon. The authority to determine the order of consideration is no longer merely the Chair's discretion, for in both US Houses, but especially in
the House of Representatives, rules, customs and practices are in place which restrict an
unfettered exercise of discretion and instead require the order of business, and therefore
the question of consideration, to be established by the House either by standing rule,
special orders of business or unanimous consent orders.

Sittings

Both Houses at Westminster sit on more days a year than most though not all comparable legislatures. Their work rate is roughly equal, as may be seen in Tables 5.1 and 5.2
in the Annex.

For many years, the Commons had an uncomfortable if deserved reputation for sitting very late into the night, as governments moved regularly to prolong the sittings
beyond the moment of interruption—the 'normal' time for ending a sitting (see page
157). That was thought to be the only way a government could get all its business
through and an Opposition grind down a government's resolve. The cost of this political
arm-wrestling was sometimes the ill health or even early death of Members on both
sides. The electorate could never see the point, but within the House the suggestion that
there might be a better way of doing things was long shouted down as politically feeble.
More recently, however, there has been a sea change. The sight of doctors checking
whether Members in ambulances in New Palace Yard were still alive so that their vote
could be recorded may have changed minds. On average the House of Commons sat just
over an hour beyond the moment of interruption in 2004-5, just under in 2005-6, half an
hour in 2006-7 and 37 minutes in 2007-8. The House's public reputation has however
only begun to be credited with these significant changes.

Comparable statistics for the US House and Senate, while available in whole numbers
of days and hours of session in a given year, are not as informative as the statistics
shown above, because many of the 'legislative days' of session were in fact 'pro forma
days when either or both Houses met and would adjourn following one-minute and
special-order speeches, without conducting legislative business. Many of those pro forma

days, for example on a fourth consecutive calendar day (not counting Sundays), were necessitated by lack of concurrent resolutions permitting adjournments for more than three days, as required by the Constitution. As well, the Senate often meets pro forma during extended holiday recesses in order to prevent the President from making 'recess' appointments to executive or judicial positions permitted under Article II, section 2 of the Constitution not requiring Senate confirmation (where the President is determined to avoid Senate advice and consent for up to one yearly session of Congress). Nevertheless, the days of session (and hours for the House) from the 109th and the 110th Congress are shown in Table 5.3 in the Annex at page 552 to demonstrate an increase in days of session during a Democratic Congress.

Motions in Congress

Prior to a discussion of the order of business in each House of Congress it is helpful to analyse the decision-making process in more general parliamentary terms as a continuum of motions or orders which enable consideration, followed by periods of debate and variations of an amendment process, culminating in a decision. Measures and matters can be considered in either House when a Member is recognized for that purpose by the Chair in a number of ways: by motion, by the Chair's designation pursuant to a special order of business, by a call of a calendar, or pursuant to a unanimous consent request.

A measure or matter may become the business of either House by way of a Member being recognized to offer a motion or to call up the matter pursuant to a previously entered order. In certain circumstances the Chair may 'lay before the House or Senate' an item of business either at the invitation of the Majority Leader or without an initiative from the floor being necessary. The distinction between a motion and a 'call up' is relevant in that the former requires a vote for adoption, whereas the latter automatically places the question before the House unless properly challenged by a Member immediately raising the question of consideration. In the Senate, the motion is usually in the form of the 'question to proceed'. Either initiative has the effect, if not properly challenged, of bringing the matter to the immediate attention of the respective House for disposition. Motions are utilized for a variety of purposes because they are specifically provided for by rule. Some motions are free-standing in that they can be offered independently of a matter to be considered and address the basic question of whether the House shall conduct any business on that day. Primary among such motions is the motion to adjourn which enjoys the highest privilege and is decided without debate or amendment. Motions for a call of the House, to set a date to which to adjourn, or to authorize the Chair to declare a recess are likewise independent of a pending measure or matter and are not debatable. but are by rule totally within the discretion of the Speaker.

Most motions however, pertain to the consideration or disposition of business. Some are original motions, such as the motion that the House resolve into the Committee of the Whole to consider a particular measure. That motion is not debatable and is not subject to the question of consideration, since a vote on the motion itself determines whether the measure is to be considered. Its precedence as 'privileged' (meaning that the

Chair is constrained by rule to recognize for that purpose) depends on whether the measure to be considered is in order under a standing rule or under a special order of business adopted by the House. Such 'main' or 'original' motions do not depend on the pendency of an underlying measure, but rather accomplish both the pendency of that business and at least preliminary debate thereon. Other such commonly utilized original motions include motions to suspend the rules and pass a measure, motions to discharge a committee pursuant to a discharge petition, or a vetoed bill once referred, noticed motions to instruct conferees, and motions to send a matter to conference or to dispose of amendments between the Houses.

In the Senate the order of business is to a large extent determined by unanimous consent requests or motions to proceed made by the Majority Leader or his designee, who enjoys the right of first recognition by the presiding officer whenever he seeks to call up a measure or matter. In the Senate the motion to proceed is normally debatable wherever applied. Unless the Senate has previously entered a unanimous consent order requiring the consideration of a measure or matter at a prescribed time, or a statute makes the motion privileged on a certain matter (in which event there is no motion to proceed), the motion is fully debatable and requires a three-fifths vote to invoke cloture (limit debate) thereon. This basic difference from the House means that the Senate as a more 'deliberative' body often debates the question of whether to consider a matter and requires a super-majority to limit debate in order to come to a direct vote on the motion to proceed, even prior to debate on the underlying matter itself. The larger size of the House suggests that body should decide the priority of its business without debate. The purpose of the rule permitting any Member to demand that the question of consideration be put would be defeated if preliminary debate were allowed. To that end, the House adopted a rule in 1803 that 'all questions relating to the priority of business shall be decided by a majority without debate'[4] in order to prevent obstructive debate and allow a majority of the House to prioritize its business.

Other parliamentary motions are secondary or incidental to a measure or matter already under debate and only operate to change or dispose of that matter. In the House, Rule XVI, clause 4 establishes the basic priority of motions when a matter is under debate, beginning with the non-debatable motions to adjourn (which also has the highest priority even if no matter is pending), to lay on the table (final adverse disposition), or for the previous question (to cut off debate and amendment), followed in order of precedence by the debatable secondary motions to postpone the pending matter to a day certain, to refer, to amend, and to postpone indefinitely. Motions must be in proper form (in writing if demanded) and are only in order upon recognition. The Chair ascertains the proper order for recognition by inquiring: 'For what purpose does the gentleman rise?' By this query the Chair determines a correct order under the rules and practices before actual recognition is conferred, especially where more than one Member seeks recognition.

In the Senate, Rule XXII, clause 1 establishes an order of precedence of motions very similar to House Rule XIV, clause 4 as follows:

> When a question is pending, no motion shall be received but to adjourn; to adjourn to a day certain, or that when the Senate adjourn it shall be to a day certain; to take a recess; to proceed to the consideration of executive business; to lay on the

table (all the above motions not debatable); to postpone indefinitely; to postpone to a day certain; to commit; and to amend, which several motions shall have precedence as they stand arranged.

The only difference between the House and Senate rule is the reverse priority given to the two motions to postpone, the absence of the motion for the previous question in the Senate, and the consideration of Executive business in the Senate. In lieu of the motion for the previous question, clause 2 of rule XXII reflects the more deliberative nature of Senate rules toward assuring the protection of individual Senators' debating and amendment rights by providing that a majority cannot close debate. That rule provides that the motion to invoke cloture is available only if adopted by three-fifths of the Senate. The cloture motion is further discussed in the chapter on Legislation at page 437, and in this chapter at page 200.

The motion to lay on the table enjoys a high priority in both Houses, but its use in the Senate to dispose of amendments is more frequent than in the House. In both Houses, the motion is not used simply to put aside a pending matter (as is the question of consideration), but rather to finally and adversely dispose of it without debate or after some debate. It takes precedence over the motion for the previous question in the House, and when applied to a pending amendment has been held to carry the entire underlying bill to the table with it. Thus the motion to lay on the table is not normally applied to amendments in the House or in its committees, since the same majority which has allowed the underlying bill to be considered does not want to adversely dispose of it merely by tabling a troublesome amendment. The House is better able to control the flow of amendments by enforcement of the germaneness rule or by the motion for the previous question, the adoption of which forecloses subsequent amendments. The Senate does not permit the motion for the previous question so that a majority cannot foreclose the right of individual Senators to offer amendments. However, the motion to lay on the table is often applied directly to amendments once offered, since by standing rule (XVII) it does not carry the underlying measure with it and may be applied without debate at any stage of the pendency of the amendment. In both Houses, the motion to lay on the table can only be applied to measures or matters which are under debate or consideration, and so the question of consideration must first be decided in the affirmative for the matter to be pending.

All motions must be stated by the Chair or read by the Clerk before they can be debated, modified or amended, or voted on. Motions, measures or matters may be withdrawn in either House from consideration as a matter of right by their proponents without unanimous consent during their reading or prior to a decision or amendment thereon, which in the House includes the ordering of the previous question. A motion or resolution may be withdrawn in the House if an amendment has been offered to it but prior to adoption of the amendment. Once the previous question is ordered or the yeas and nays are ordered, unanimous consent is required to withdraw a motion or measure.

As a general principle, modifications of a pending motion or measure, if in order at all, must be separately approved by the House. There is one narrow exception to this principle, that a Member having the right to withdraw a motion before a decision is made thereon and to immediately thereafter re-offer it, has the resulting right to modify the motion without approval of the House. In most cases, however, the right of withdrawal and re-submission in a modified form does not exist, because the modification has not been noticed in compliance with rules, or because the change requires unanimous consent approval, or because the modifier is not guaranteed the right to immediate recognition to re-offer the motion, amendment, or measure. Similar leeway for the withdrawal of a measure in the Senate exists prior to some action being taken on the motion or measure. Somewhat greater leeway exists for modifications to pending measures or amendments by the proponent as a matter of right without unanimous consent unless the Senate has taken an action on the underlying matter, as the Chair's power of recognition is not in practice as severely constrained as in the House.

In the House, the question of consideration may be raised whenever a measure or matter is first called up, unless the procedure utilized is one which already assures consideration and thereby prevents the question of consideration from being voted upon. Rule XVI, clause 3 provides that when any motion or proposition is entertained, a Member may demand that the question be put: 'Will the House now consider it?' This rule, adopted in its present form in 1880, permits the House by simple majority vote to refuse to consider business at that particular time. The question itself is not debatable, as to permit debate on whether to consider would defeat the purpose of the question. When demanded, the question of consideration must be determined in the affirmative before any debate on the measure begins or secondary motions may be offered. Conversely, it is too late to raise the question of consideration once debate has begun or secondary motions have been offered.

The daily framework

Debate time in the House of Representatives is subdivided into various segments on a daily basis, and its conduct and length depend on the application of various standing rules, unanimous consent standing orders, statutes, special orders of business, and traditional practices, in addition to the Chair's inherent power of recognition. The approach taken in this segment will be to analyse each aspect of debate as it unfolds chronologically on a typical legislative day, acknowledging that some forms can be more properly described as collegial 'debate' among Members than other forms of speech making aimed at a real or imagined television audience.

The ability of Members to address matters not on the daily legislative agenda is facilitated by allowing 'one-minute speeches' at the beginning of most days and five-minute 'morning-hour speeches' on Mondays and Tuesdays, followed by 'special order speeches' (somewhat akin to 'adjournment' debates) at the end of the legislative day, respectively. None of these procedures is specifically provided for in the standing rules, and their use is permitted by long-standing custom based on the underlying assumption that the Speaker will recognize for unanimous consent requests from individual Members to address the House, or will recognize Members from lists submitted by the Majority and Minority Leaders pursuant to unanimous consent standing orders of the House. A typical day in the House normally begins with recognition of Members for 'one-minute speeches', a practice which is totally within the Chair's discretion and which may be limited, postponed or curtailed entirely by the Speaker on a given day, depending on the press of business. Pre-business speeches were limited to one minute in length beginning in 1937 and were affirmed as standard practice in 1945. Beginning in 1984, the Speaker announced a policy of alternating recognition between the two parties, and since that time has often announced a limit on the number of speeches he will entertain prior to the legislative business, thereby deferring remaining requests until the end of legislative business prior to 'special order speeches'. From time to time in contemporary Congresses, the respective leadership offices have organized 'theme teams' to occupy many of their party's one-minute time slots, in order to emphasize a political message which is sometimes relevant to the scheduled legislative business but which often sets a provocative tone resulting in a partisan atmosphere carrying over to the legislative business. Were it not for the televised coverage of those speeches, which began in 1978, they would be far fewer in number, since opposing Members are seldom on the floor to engage in collegial debate but rather for their own speeches on another subject. The Speaker will not recognize for unanimous consent requests for more than one minute or for second speeches by the same Member on the same day. This restriction may be circumvented if another Member under recognition is willing to yield an unspecified portion of his one minute to a Member who has already spoken. On a typical legislative day the Majority leadership will have approximated the time it wishes to be available for such speeches before legislative business begins, all in an effort to predict certainty in time and issue throughout the day while accommodating some individual Members at the outset. Thus the Speaker will announce a limit on 'one-minute speeches' as 'ten per side', and additional Members will be accommodated only at the end of the legislative business and prior to five-minute or then longer 'special order speeches'. Apart from the 'theme team' efforts of the party leaderships, the subjects of these speeches is virtually limitless, but must be conducted in accordance with the rules applicable to all debates, avoiding personal references to other Members, the President, Vice President and to Senators, while permitting the use of displays (charts, graphs and photographs, but no electronic portrayals) to augment the speech.

Morning-hour debates, as distinguished from morning-hour business (a seldom-used 'calendar' for the consideration of a small class of reported bills) were instituted in 1994 as part of a unanimous consent standing order, the primary purpose of which was to terminate 'special order speeches' at the end of the day at midnight. To offset unavailable time after midnight, the leaderships agreed on earlier convenings (ninety minutes) on Mondays and Tuesdays of each week for 'morning-hour debates', wherein Members selected by the party leaderships would be recognized for up to five minutes, to speak on a subject of their choosing, alternating between the parties, during which period no business could be conducted and following which the Chair would declare a recess until the regular convening time for that day. In this format, the Speaker was required to recognize Members listed by the party leaders and was not free to exercise discretion as by unanimous consent.

The final segment of non-business debate regardless of topic is the 'special order speech' period at the end of legislative business each day. It may not extend beyond midnight. This segment takes two forms, the first for five minutes or less per Member by unanimous consent of the House, alternating between the parties and available to any Member without limit on numbers, until midnight. Members who utilize a five-minute special order may not then be listed for longer special orders by their leaderships, but may participate where other listed Members yield to them. Unanimous consent requests for such speeches may not be entered more than a week in advance, to avoid pre-scheduling earlier than the week in question—an abuse allowing Members to schedule five-minute special orders weeks or months in advance corrected in 1994 by the standing order of the House. The primary purpose of that order was to place responsibility in the party leaderships for prioritizing Members' contemporaneous control of this televised debate time, leaving them free to impose additional conditions so as to take advantage of a party message—the first hour being set aside for the party leader or his designee, while allowing leaders to impose limits on Members seeking to monopolize the remaining time. Only two hours of time per party is allocated, with the midnight cut-off and alternation of the first hour between parties on consecutive legislative days.

Only infrequently will the viewer observe bipartisan participation in a given special order speech, since the allocated time is by the party leader and the Member controlling the time is free to yield or not to other Members. Most often, the time is allocated so that a series of Members from the same party can utilize displays and engage each other in colloquys to present an uninterrupted political message, but seldom will spontaneous debate involving Members in disagreement materialize unless the controlling Member and his leadership are willing to so engage. This format utilizes the camera focused only on the Member speaking, while running a crawl at the bottom of the picture explaining that legislative business for the day had concluded.

It was not always so. When unedited televised proceedings began in 1978 under the direction and control of the Speaker but requiring 'gavel-to-gavel coverage', meaning from convening to final adjournment, the camera portrayed only the Member under recognition but did not indicate that legislative business had been completed. There gradually developed, especially on the 'back benches' of the Minority party, a recurring technique utilizing rhetorical questions and gestures to suggest that true debate was underway. This prompted Speaker Tip O'Neill on 12 May 1984 to order the cameras to 'pan' the Chamber by wide-angle coverage during special order speeches. This order, which took the Minority totally by surprise, resulted in a series of recriminations in debate with the participating Members and the Minority Leader accusing the Speaker of improper conduct. When the Speaker took the floor to defend his order as within his authority and in response to 'the lowest thing he had ever seen in all his thirty-five years in politics'—namely the rhetorical use of gestures and questions in debate to falsely depict the presence and reluctance of other Members—his words were 'taken down' as unparliamentary and ruled out of order as a personality against the Member to whom addressed (Rep. Newt Gingrich of Georgia who later became Minority Whip in 1992 and then Speaker in 1995). The Chair's ruling, made by a Speaker pro tempore (Rep. Moakley, Mass.), a close personal friend of Speaker O'Neill, was made particularly difficult by Moakley's personal conviction (expressed privately to the Parliamentarian) that Speaker O'Neill had in fact been truthful in his remarks and was therefore in order. He agreed to rule the remarks out of order as a personality toward Rep. Gingrich only when advised that the Chair should not attempt to discern the truth of the language complained of, as to do so would set an incorrect precedent permitting the use of personalities against other Members if 'true'. It marked the first time since 1798 that a Speaker himself had been ruled out of order in debate. Nevertheless, his order for wide-angle coverage of special orders persisted until 1994, when a return to close-up coverage of the Member speaking was made part of the standing order also covering morning-hour debates and recognition for special orders until midnight entered by unanimous consent.

This watershed incident has been credited for the 'martyring' of Newt Gingrich and his Minority back-bench colleagues and for contributing to his eventual ascendancy to a leadership position and to the Speaker's chair after forty years of continuous Minority party status. It symbolizes the perception, if not the reality, of the importance of televised coverage of proceedings of the House, whether or not those proceedings are legislative in nature or are mere speech making. While there may be a very small number of consistent viewers of House or Senate proceedings, the news organizations are free to take portions of those debates for both local and national news coverage (although Members may not use those debates for commercial or campaign purposes). Often one-minute or special order speeches will be motivated by a local television station's willingness to carry that Member's 'debate', if 'newsworthy'.

The Speaker takes the Chair in the House of Commons on Mondays and Tuesdays at half-past two; on wednesdays at half-past eleven; on Thursdays at half-past ten; and on Fridays at half-past nine. (The House sits on Fridays only to consider private Members' bills unless an order to vary that arrangement is made.) On days other than Fridays, the House will, after prayers, usually spend an hour on Question Time, including Prime Minister's Questions for half an hour on Wednesdays and topical questions (see pages 337ff.). With the Speaker's agreement—obtaining which is by no means a formality—a Member may, after the end of the regular period for Questions, ask an urgent question of which it was not possible to give printed notice. There may follow a ministerial oral statement on a matter of public interest or government policy, on which Members may ask questions within an informal limit of about a further hour.

One of the products of the recent emphasis on topicality is the institution of topical debates, which take place in government time approximately weekly. The choice of subjects is made by the government after consultation with other parties and representations by backbenchers. A minister moves the open motion that the House has considered a specified matter which must be of regional, national or international importance, must not have been previously debated and must be a matter of public policy and concern. The minister may speak for ten minutes, an Opposition spokesman for a further ten minutes and a representative of the third largest party for six minutes, either following the opening speech or before the wind-up. Other speakers may be time-limited. The entire debate comes to an end, generally without a vote, after ninety minutes. The procedure is still experimental, and a review is expected to report shortly.

If the rest of the day is to be given over to a single piece of business, a second reading for example, proceedings are opened by a minister, followed by an official Opposition spokesman, then a Member from the Liberal Democrats and perhaps the chairman of the most relevant select or party committee. Thereafter back-bench Members are called by the Chair, alternately from one side and the other, until twenty or thirty minutes before the moment of interruption—ten o'clock on Mondays and Tuesdays, seven o'clock on Wednesdays, six o'clock on Thursdays and half-past two on Fridays.

The art of the Chair, the persuasive powers of the whips, the general expectation that a debate should normally be concluded before the moment of interruption, and the imposition of time limits on speeches (see page 203) combine to ensure that as many backbenchers are called as time will allow. The last backbencher knows that he or she must sit down leaving sufficient—but not generous—time for the front benches to wind up before the moment of interruption. The moment of interruption is just that—the time when the Speaker breaks in to put an end to the debate. Reaching the moment of interruption is not however necessarily followed by taking the decision to which debate was leading, unless the House has made an order to that effect. Ordinarily, that outcome must be stage-managed. When the last backbencher has resumed his or her seat, about forty minutes or less before the moment of interruption, spokesmen for the main parties will make their concluding speeches. The whip on the government front bench must ensure that the minister—who intervenes last—speaks right up to but does not continue past the moment of interruption. He will do this if necessary by literally pulling at the coat-tails of a colleague borne headlong on the flood of his own eloquence. Should the minister go on beyond the critical hour, the business would be lost, at least for that day, and the Chief Whip would be seriously displeased.

Stage-management sometimes breaks down. Miscalculation may shorten the time available for the wind-ups. The minister may sit down several minutes before the critical moment, allowing an Opposition gadfly to seize the opportunity to 'talk out' the business—a tactic doubtless then countered by a government motion to closure the debate. Alternatively, a backbencher who has the floor may not sit down to permit the front benches to conclude, but with political malice aforethought will go on speaking through the moment of interruption, in order to ensure that no decision can be taken. Again, closure is the standard government response.

The rules governing the moment of interruption are clear and normally no exceptions are made, though in 1997 when ministers in the new government 'talked out' their business on a handful of occasions, the Chair and the House forgave their inexperience.

Not all debates last, or are intended to last, an entire parliamentary day. More frequently in the past than today, government would invite the House to debate the second readings of two or even three smaller bills in a single day, a result readily achievable if prior agreement of the Opposition had been obtained. A return to the older pattern would avoid the occasional debate where interest sags in mid-evening, causing the whips to scour the House looking for Members prepared to keep matters going till the wind-up speeches.

Some business such as secondary legislation (see pages 467–8) may by Standing Order be debated for no more than ninety minutes after the moment of interruption, and when that time has expired the rules empower the Chair to break into the ongoing debate to bring the House to decision without further need for nail-biting stage-management. Motions separately authorising expenditure in connection with a bill (see page 264) involve a more complex version of the same procedure. If the motion is made on the day on which the parent bill was read a second time, it is to be decided without debate; if on another day, a debate lasting three-quarters of an hour is permitted.

There are many instances where the government wishes to vary the normal arrangements for debate laid down in Standing Orders, either to exempt certain business from time limits which otherwise would govern it, or to bring an item to a conclusion, otherwise—usually earlier—than the rules envisage. This is achieved by the government tabling a Business Motion, a junior version of what emanates from the Rules Committee in the US House. Business Motions simply to exempt bills or motions from the moment of interruption are decided without debate when that moment arrives. Since they add to rather than diminish time for debate, Oppositions usually let them pass without a division. Nevertheless, such motions can carry significant dramatic charge. Several times in the course of the European Communities (Amendment) Bill 1992 the government declined to move a Business Motion allowing more debate which they themselves had tabled, their majority having declined so substantially earlier in the evening.

A more complex Business Motion will allow a government to ensure that a debate unravels completely at the moment of interruption. These are agreed prior to the main debate. They may order the Speaker to break into debate at the moment of interruption and put the question on the amendment under discussion, then the questions on the other selected amendments (or if the government are feeling particularly stern, only all their amendments), and finally the main question, as amended or not, as the case may be. Opposition suspicions may surface in these circumstances. Even if the front benches arrive at a satisfactory concord (and if they do not, there is apt to be a short but noisy debate on the Business Motion) there is no guarantee that dissent from the back benches will not appear. Insensitive manipulation of business in their own interest may well bring inconvenient retribution when least expected, and both front benches know it.

After the moment of interruption and any division, the Chamber empties, Members usually gossiping noisily, despite the Chair's demands for quiet so that remaining business can proceed. Unless there is business which the rules exempt from the effect of the moment of interruption, or the government has specifically moved to prolong the sitting, the business which emerges from the din is the briefest introduction by a Member of a constituent's petition to the House, and finally half an hour's debate on the motion 'That this House do now adjourn'—for the most part in a deserted House—when a backbencher may raise a matter of local interest or the problems experienced by a constituent, in order to evoke a reply on the record from a minister.

The sitting day in the Lords is slightly different. The House normally meets at 2.30pm on Mondays and Tuesdays, 3pm on Wednesdays, and 11am on Thursdays. There is no fixed time for concluding the sitting, though Monday, Tuesday and Wednesday sittings have a target time of rising of 10pm, and Thursdays 7pm. Friday sittings are not regular, but when the House meets on Friday the sitting begins at 10.00am and is expected to end about 3.00pm. After prayers, usually read by a bishop, the House previously proceeded to any judicial business to be disposed of, in the form of the reading of the decisions of the law Lords. Other Lords by firm and long-standing practice did not participate in such business and after the creation of the Supreme Court (see page 57) are not able to.

Next will come Questions for oral answer addressed to the government as a whole rather than individual ministers as in the Commons, with a limit of four questions in thirty minutes (see page 345). Questions are followed by oral ministerial statements, often arranged to be made at the same time as an identical communication to the Commons, and similarly subject to an informal time limit.

The main business of the day then follows—bills, secondary legislation and motions. In complete distinction to the Commons, government business in the Lords does not prevail over other business except where the rules specify otherwise. Fitting business, both government and non-government, into time available is a matter of negotiation between the parties and the crossbenchers. On the other hand, in both Houses standing arrangements are made for the protection of non-government initiatives.

In the Lords, motions have precedence over legislation and select committee reports every Thursday for most of the session. Motions 'for papers' are neutral in form, though the debate need not be. Amendments are not tabled to these motions and they will normally be withdrawn at the end of the debate. Motions 'to take note' of a subject also provide a platform for discussion without the prospect of a specific decision at the conclusion. Other motions will be intended to result in a resolution expressing the view of the House. Most Thursdays are divided by agreement between the parties and the cross benches, within an overall limit of debate—there are usually two such motions—of six hours. On one Thursday a month there are two time-limited debates led by a cross bench or back-bench Lord selected by ballot. These motions are by custom not combative in their terms, and simply a peg on which to hang a debate neither wide-ranging nor disputatious, and not likely to give rise to a division.

Government business in the Lords is not customarily protected by guillotines, programme motions or fierce Business Motions fixing limits on the period for debate on motions or amendments or prescribing when and how the decision is to be made. No such need arises, since there is no fixed time for the Lords to rise on any day. Time limits on individual speeches from both the front and back benches are however an important part of Lords' use of time (see pages 172–3), together with a strong attachment—even on the part of veterans bearing the scars of all-night struggles in the Commons—to arranging the affairs of the House on a consensual and informal basis, which resonates with the public and may be quietly envied by some in the Commons.

Debate in Congress

The sanctity of debate in both US Houses is recognized in Article I, section 5 of the Constitution in the provision which prevents the questioning of Speech or Debate in any other place. This privilege is based upon the comparable protection afforded to Members of the British Parliament by the Bill of Rights Act 1689. By providing that basic protection of the independence of the legislative branch and of each of its Members, the Founding Fathers acknowledged the overriding importance of debate in the decision-making process.

Debate in any parliamentary body is an essential element of the process of consideration of business, or may be part of the daily session even where no business is pending. The various elements of debate—its initiation and control, orderliness (including relevancy), duration, and recordation, each merit separate discussion. Some common factors apply to each of these characteristics in the House and Senate and between the Houses of Parliament and Congress.

Any Member seeking to engage in debate must be recognized by the Chair for that purpose. This basic tenet is part of the parliamentary principle that by rule and custom, in order to offer a motion, make an objection, or address the House, a Member must first secure recognition from the Chair. Recognition to call up or move the adoption of any matter or measure is not simultaneously recognition to begin debate on that matter. Flowing logically from the Chair's decisions as to whom to recognize to proceed to an order of business, is the next immediate step—the discussion of it. Subsequent recognition

by the Chair of a Member to gain the floor to begin debate is therefore a necessary parliamentary step, even though the two recognitions often seem to blend together. Until
the Member having the floor in debate has been recognized for that purpose, intervening
motions may be in order and the Member is not yet in a position to avoid being taken
from his feet or from the floor. As a general rule, debate on a measure is not in order
until a debatable motion has been offered and stated by the Chair or read by the Clerk.
However, debate may be initiated upon recognition of a Member reserving the right to
object to a unanimous consent request (the pending business), when a question of personal privilege is raised, and when free standing debates such as 'one-minute' and 'special order' speeches have been permitted by unanimous consent or by lists submitted by
the party leaders at the end of legislative business.

When a specific measure or matter is before the body by motion, the Chair's designation, special rule or having been called up, debate then is controlled by one or more
Members when separately recognized for that purpose. Under some standing rules, special orders or unanimous consent requests, the Chair is required to divide recognition,
such as 'general debate to be equally divided and controlled by the chairman and ranking Minority member of a committee', or by a proponent and an opponent. Normally the
Majority manager of the measure is entitled to open the debate. He has procedural
advantages enabling him to expedite its consideration and passage which derive from the
general House rule that the chairman of a reporting committee has a duty under the
rules to take steps to have the matter considered and voted upon (Rule XIII, clause
2(b)), and is entitled to prior recognition unless he surrenders or loses control of the floor
or unless a preferential motion is offered. If the measure is to be taken up in the House
under the standing rules—the most frequent example being a special order of business
reported from the Committee on Rules—the manager calling it up is entitled to one hour
of debate, which he may in his discretion yield to other Members (normally one-half to
his Minority counterpart). He may at any time during his hour move the previous question, thereby bringing the matter to a vote and terminating further debate, unless he has
yielded control of some block of his time, in which case that time must first be consumed
or yielded back.

The manager of a bill enjoys a similar advantage in the Committee of the Whole
where the bill is being considered under a unanimous consent agreement. The Majority
manager has the right to both open and close general debate, which precedes the amendment process. A Majority manager who represents the primary committee of jurisdiction
is entitled to close debate as against another manager of an additional committee of
jurisdiction.

General debates on measures in the modern House of Representatives are controlled
by managers who are entitled to that control by standing or special rule and who yield
time to other Members, rather than time being allocated by the Chair solely through the
power of recognition. To begin debate and beyond initial recognition, the Chair is relieved
of responsibility for applying long-standing priorities (such as committee seniority and
alternation between parties) and is guided instead by decisions for yielding made by the
managers at most stages of debate.

Some argue that control of general debate should be allocated based on positions for
and against the proposition, rather than on party affiliation. Nevertheless, most special
orders equally divide general debate between two committee managers, and leave it to

them to sub-allocate sufficient time to Members within their party who are opposed. In some contexts, the principle of true opposition is recognized. For example, on motions to suspend the rules, equal division of forty minutes between the party managers can be reversed where the ranking Minority member cannot qualify when challenged as being opposed to the motion, whereupon the challenging Member can control one-half the time if opposed himself. Similarly under some statutory schemes where measures of disapproval of a proposed Executive action—such as a trade agreement to be voted on without amendment—are before the House or Senate, the law will allocate time equally between Member(s) in favour of and opposed to the joint resolution of approval or disapproval.

Debates on certain matters are divided by standing rule between parties, such as motions to instruct conferees, conference reports, motions to dispose of Senate amendments in disagreement, with the caveat that should both parties' managers be in favour of the proposition, one-third of the time can be allocated to a Member opposed. Other matters, such as questions of the privileges of the House, are guaranteed equal division of debate time between parties by standing rule. Certain important motions during the pendency of a measure, such as the motion to re-commit with instructions pending final passage, are guaranteed equal division of time between a proponent and an opponent.

These expectations have been extended to debates on issues beyond pending legislation, as time for debates on one-minute speeches, five-minute and longer 'special order' speeches is allocated and alternated between the two parties based either on the Chair's recognition or on standing orders giving party leadership an allocation prerogative.

In the Senate, the allocation of time for debate, absent a unanimous consent order which usually makes an equal allocation between the two parties or the two sides of an issue, is based on recognition by the Chair. The general priority given to the Majority Leader and then to the Minority Leader for recognition at all stages of Senate proceedings somewhat mirrors priorities of recognition in the House and suggests an approximate equal allocation of debate time to the two parties. This allocation of debate time is to be distinguished from the constant priority accorded the Majority Leader for recognition to offer amendments or motions to expedite business as in cloture situations.

The right to prior recognition in the Senate to debate a measure or matter or to recommend unanimous consent orders to accomplish that priority, belongs at every stage to the Majority Leader, then to the Minority Leader, then to the committee Majority manager, and then to the Minority manager, unless and until the Senate has imposed a unanimous consent order for allocation and control of debate time on other Senators, has invoked cloture by a three-fifths vote, or is operating under a statutory rule which otherwise allocates debate time. These priorities, from which the presiding officer does not deviate, have been established despite the standing rule (similar to a House rule) that the Chair shall recognize the first Senator addressing him. When the Majority Leader seeks recognition from the presiding officer, he is per se the first Senator addressing the Chair. Beyond that right of first recognition, where there is no allocation of time, subsequent recognition remains within the discretion of the presiding officer, subject to the Majority Leader's continued right of first recognition in order, for example, to 'fill the amendment tree', discussed at page 438. No Senator may yield the floor to another, but rather must retain the floor while yielding for questions. When there is a debatable matter before the Senate and debate is not limited, a Senator who has been recognized may proceed without interruption. Under these circumstances, a Senator may keep the floor as long as he or she remains standing and continues to debate, and the Senator may decline to yield to other Senators and may speak on any subject. One seldom-enforced exception to the lack of requirement for relevance in debate is 'the Pastore Rule',[5] which requires that during the first three hours of session each legislative day, debate must be germane to the question pending before the Senate. This three-hour rule is only observed where Senators do not obtain the usual unanimous consent to proceed 'as if in morning-hour business' in order to speak to a matter not then pending. Under 'controlled' debate, where time is allocated to and yielded by Majority and Minority managers pursuant to a unanimous consent order, debate is not normally required to be germane to the pending measure, and the Pastore Rule is implicitly waived by unanimous consent.

House standing rules and special rules reported from the Rules Committee normally accommodate the Minority party in the House by equally dividing control between managers from the two parties. References 'to be equally divided and controlled by the chairman and ranking Minority Member' or 'by the Majority and Minority Leaders or their designees' reflect the acknowledgment in both standing and special rules of the two-party dynamic at both leadership and committee and subcommittee levels in the distribution of the control of debate time. Despite the emergence of a third or coalition position in anticipation of plenary session debate on an issue, the control of time is seldom divided three ways, especially for general debate on the merits of a measure which precedes specific debate on amendments. Exceptions are made by unanimous consent orders in either House as specific accommodations, but more often Members seeking an allocation of debate time while not reflecting the position of either party must obtain that recognition by being yielded time from one of the party managers. Some rules relating to debate on motions to suspend the rules or to instruct conferees permit a three-way allocation with one-third controlled by opposition where both Majority and Minority managers are on the same side of the issue. Other special arrangements may include four, six or eight-way allocation of time among the Majority and Minority party members of several committees having jurisdiction of the measure, but the allocation normally remains by party designation.

While the five-minute rule for debate on amendments does not distinguish between membership deriving from one of the two parties, but rather from a position with respect to the amendment, by precedent committee membership based on Majority or Minority party status often becomes a factor in determining a priority of recognition by the Chair. In modern practice, the five-minute rule (which has as its premise the right of all Members to engage in debate on amendments regardless of party), gives way to 'structured' rules or unanimous consent orders where control of debate is divided between the proponent of the amendment and an opponent. Members from either party then seek an allocation of time from one of those two managers, depending as much on their position on the amendment as on party affiliation. Even on motions which are the prerogative of the Minority party such as the motion to instruct conferees or the motion to re-commit a measure with instructions, time is equally divided and half goes to the Majority party if opposed. On questions of privilege initiated by the Minority party, debate, if it occurs, is equally divided between the two parties' leaderships. This was not always the case, as the general 'hour' rule gave control of time only to the Member calling up the question of privilege, but in modern practice (since 1993) standing rules or practices usually require a party division of control, in order to provide a simplistic formula to assure that at least two sides of an issue will be heard on an equal division of time.

On occasions where both the proponent and opponent of an amendment are from the same political party, there is often a sub-allocation of time by unanimous consent to accommodate management of time from both political parties on both sides of the question. The absence of an organized third party in either House makes these arrangements convenient and predictable, and Members of all political persuasions have come to expect predictability in time allocations based on party management control. In fact, control of debate time is one of few prerogatives which the Minority party shares equally with the Majority, as in most other aspects of its organization and conduct of business the partisan majoritarian nature of the contemporary US House results in diminished Minority participation.

With respect to the initiation of debate at the amendment stage in the House, the proponent of an amendment is by standing rule and tradition the first Member recognized to debate the amendment. In the Committee of the Whole, the same right to initial debate inures to the proponent of an amendment, followed by the first opponent to seek recognition under the five-minute rule (Rule XVIII clause 5). The Chair will recognize the Majority manager of the bill if opposed to the amendment, or the Minority manager if the Majority manager is the proponent or is not opposed. Subsequent recognition for debate alternates between committee Majority and Minority Members in decreasing order of seniority, and those Members offer their own pro forma amendments ('to strike the last word') to gain their own five minutes of recognition. If second-degree or substitute amendments are in order as under standing rules, similar priority of recognition for debate thereon is accorded to the proponent and an opponent under the five-minute rule.

In the House, breadth and spontaneity in debate on amendments have been greatly inhibited in recent years by Majority leadership refusal in special orders to permit the offering of many germane amendments and by advance allocations of time and control of debate on those amendments made in order, all in an effort to achieve predictability of time and issue. Members are less able to obtain their own five-minute time by pro forma amendment, and are relegated to time yielded by the two managers—often less time than otherwise available under the five-minute rule—resulting in prepared speeches in an accommodation to televised coverage, and in less yielding ('giving way') to other Members. Each Congress is presented the opportunity to restore 'regular order' by implementation of the standing five-minute rule on an ad hoc basis. As 'modified closed rules' became the norm over time, Members' institutional memories of open debate on germane amendments were diminished (see chapter on Legislation at pages 428–9).

One must further distinguish in both Houses between orders and motions which, as is usual in the House of Commons, impose limits on debates to times certain by the clock, and those where the limit is on the number of minutes or hours of debate. In the case of debate limitations to a time certain, intervening business or delaying tactics such as calling for record votes will reduce otherwise available debate time. Where debate time is limited to minutes or hours of actual debate, however, intervening record votes or other business will not constrict, but rather will prolong, prearranged periods of debate. As a general proposition, debate limitations in the House of Representatives are more frequently limited by numbers of minutes or hours, whereas in the House of

Commons and, by unanimous consent, in the Senate, debates are more frequently limited to a time certain by the clock.

In the House, standing rules have recently been amended to permit postponement and clustering at the Chair's discretion (usually upon instructions from the Majority leadership) of record votes in many situations, including sequences of amendments, motions, and measures on final passage. This practice, now commonly employed to minimize the periods of time Members must spend on the floor during actual debate and to maximize certainty for voting times and for 'whipping' opportunities (when Members are required to remain on the floor for a series of votes), continues the trend that debate no longer greatly influences votes. Not-so-distant traditions when Members would attend and participate in important debates, often on spontaneously offered amendments which would be immediately followed by votes thereon, have given way to controlled debate periods on pre-noticed amendments separated from votes on those issues. Many important votes are usually not contemporaneous with the debates but are conducted at a later time.

Distinctions both institutional and political combine to explain the relative importance of the availability of time in Parliament and in Congress. In Parliament, the available time, usually predictable well in advance, belongs to the government except to the extent it chooses to make time available to the Opposition or to individual Members. Individual Members are seeking to hold the government 'accountable' for its programme, presented as public bills, through the mechanisms of debate, and to a lesser extent, through amendments and alternative or Opposition motions.

In the US House, relatively non-controversial matters considered by unanimous consent are often debated under a reservation of objection to the unanimous consent request, where the Member reserving the objection is recognized by the Chair and may yield to others under his reservation until such time as he objects, withdraws his reservation, or is subject to a demand for 'regular order' by another Member, at which point the Chair queries for objection. If objection is heard, the matter is no longer before the House, but if there is no objection, debate may proceed either under the terms of the unanimous consent agreement or controlled by the Member making the request under the general hour rule in the House. Debate under a reservation of objection is often more spontaneous and informative than debate controlled entirely by the manager, as the Member making the request must be deferential and responsive to the Member(s) reserving the right to object, in order to accomplish the purpose of his request. (See also Legislation at page 419.) Generally debate is more structured and less spontaneous when the House proceeds under standing or special rules which limit and allocate control to managers rather than to individual Members under separate recognition.

In modern practice, forty-minute debate on motions to suspend the rules is most common on at least three days of each week. The proliferation of those unamendable motions which must be adopted by a two-thirds vote has been accelerated in recent years, and debate is often separated from record votes on those motions. Control of the time is equally divided between the manager (usually the full or subcommittee chairman of jurisdiction) and the ranking Minority committee member. Where both are in favour of the motion, a Member opposed may claim the twenty minutes in opposition. Since no amendments are in order during this period, the debate normally consists of prepared speeches usually prepared in advance with knowledge that the Member will be yielded a sufficient block of available time to complete his speech without always yielding. The willingness of Members under recognition to yield on their allotted time to opposing points of view has decreased in contemporary controlled debates, with Members preferring to suggest that the opponent obtain his own time independently so that the allocated time can be fully consumed with prepared remarks and the televised proceedings will not prove an embarrassment to the yielding Member. This combination of a disconnect between debates and votes, control of all available time by two managers rather than independently by individual Members, and televised coverage has had the negative effect of minimizing the impact of debates upon votes and on the spontaneous inclusion of varying points of view at crucial portions of the debate.

These same tendencies hold true during 'general' debate on a particular measure—a period of time made in order by the terms of a special order governing its overall consideration. Control is vested in committee managers, although it is sometimes allocated to include separate segments for all committees of relevant jurisdiction. There is no separate ability of a Member opposed to the measure to control a portion of general debate, unless he is the Minority manager of the controlling committee, and the Rules Committee does not allocate separate general debate time to opponents per se. On major and highly complex measures, several hours of general debate may be granted by the Rules Committee, but seldom do spontaneous colloquys materialize during these periods, most Members choosing instead to make their positions known by reading prepared remarks on time allocated to them by the committee managers.

While legislative history as to the meaning of a measure is often articulated during general debate, most spontaneous debate occurs during the amendment stage. The five-minute rule is the procedure in the Committee of the Whole, wherein recognition is by practice alternated between Majority and Minority committee members and then among non-committee members to debate first- and second-degree amendments and 'pro forma' amendments—to 'strike out the requisite number of words'—a term of art fashioned as an oral amendment to the pending proposition merely to obtain an additional five minutes of debate time and not as a substantive amendment to be voted upon. This traditional recognition technique, while not spelled out in the standing rules, has the tendency to invigorate spontaneous debate on pending amendments or portions of a measure. It is a mechanism by which Members, not satisfied with allocations of yielded time by managers in controlled debate situations, can be recognized for responses to other Members.

Other than with respect to Appropriation bills, the five-minute debate has gradually been replaced through special orders on virtually all other important measures by allocations of amendment debate. In lieu of pro forma amendments, all amendments under 'modified closed rules' are debatable only for specified periods equally divided and controlled by a proponent and an opponent, and are not subject to second-degree amendments or to further debate by pro forma amendments (unless on complicated bills permitted to be offered by the managers of the overall measure in order to obtain more time). Individual Members are less likely to immediately engage each other during controlled debate. They are forced to obtain separate scarce time from their party manager and do not always immediately expect to be yielded time by the Member having the floor.

The preferential motion to 'strike the enacting clause', is a technique for obtaining ten additional minutes of debate time on a measure or on an amendment, although if the motion is actually adopted it may have the effect of defeating the measure as a test vote before the House ever comes to the question of final passage. Beyond this seldom-used method to obtain additional time, unanimous consent requests to extend time are only entertained if they tend to equally divide the additional debate between the managers of the pending amendment. This constraint reflects consistent rulings that once the House has adopted a special order of business governing the consideration of a measure, such as by limiting the number of amendments and debate time thereon, the Committee of the Whole may not, even by unanimous consent, materially change the terms of that adopted special order. On the other hand, non-material changes may be permitted by unanimous consent if 'congruent' with the terms of the special order, for example an extension of time equally divided. On occasion, additional debate time sought by one of these techniques reflects the need for more voices to be heard before a vote is taken, but the disruption of a predictable time schedule desired by many Members often restricts their utilization.

In Congress the greater priority is not as much what is discussed, by whom and for how long, but rather what is voted upon and when, and the impact of those decisions on Members' voting records. Together with the fund-raising capabilities of incumbent Members, voting records are the most objective yardsticks by which Members' re-electability every two years is measured. It is to the Majority party's advantage to maximize the issues upon which Majority Members vote for their agenda and opposing Members are forced to vote against, while at the same time minimizing the Minority party's ability to force recorded votes on its own agenda. That control of presentation of issues, when combined with the scheduling of votes at convenient and predictable times, by utilization of procedures permitting postponement and clustering of votes at the Chair's discretion, tends to minimize the influence of actual debate on the outcome of votes, and to maximize leadership whipping efforts conducted before and after the debates.

Does debate in the contemporary Congress have the same propensity to influences votes as had traditionally been the case? Of course, the basic notion that a question is to be debated before rather than after it is voted upon, remains the logical sequence under the rules and practices of both Houses. If debate is more frequently conducted without many Members being collegially present, but rather prepared remarks are uttered or inserted in the Record without meaningful opportunities for contemporary rebuttal (even though observable off the floor through televised means), it is fair to conclude that such utterances will have less impact on votes than if collegial questioning and ability to offer and debate alternatives were permitted.

For the entire history of the House of Representatives until the advent of televised proceedings in the House in 1978 and even for much of the next decade, debates were conducted in the House under 'open' procedures wherein Members needed to be on the floor to become familiar with and to participate in, debates on measures which were to be voted on immediately following that debate. Particularly with respect to debate on amendments and second-degree amendments thereto, usually offered with no pre-clearance or pre-publication and debatable under the standing 'five-minute rule', with quorum calls always available to compel attendance, Members were constrained to be on the floor and thereby more inclined to engage in debate, both to establish legislative history and to take issue with political positions expressed in those debates. Any Member could separately seek recognition in such debates, without being yielded time by either the proponent or opponent of the amendment. Members who were under recognition were more inclined to yield to other Members, even opponents, during their allotted time, since it was likely that the interrupting Member could obtain his own recognition under the five-minute rule for prompt rebuttal if not yielded to. Televised coverage of proceedings tended to make Members under recognition during the amendment stage less likely to yield to opponents, so as not to be upstaged by contrary points of view during their allotted time. Along with this reluctance, the trend toward 'modified closed rules' began in the 1980s wherein the Rules Committee at the behest of Majority leaderships began to orchestrate the amendment process in special orders of business to promote certainty in time and issue by prescribing the order of amendments, a two-way division of debate thereon, and the prohibition of second-degree amendments to those permitted to be debated. As these special orders became more commonplace, especially in the last decade, the two managers of time on important amendments have tended to sub-allocate portions only to Members on their side of the issue, rather than spontaneously to Members with questions or rebuttals on the other side. Members increasingly tend to rely on legislative staff to observe, summarize and even make recommendations and prepare entire speeches in writing, unless they plan to be directly involved in the debate, while they attend to other committee, constituent and fund-raising responsibilities during the typical three days of the work week they are in the Capitol. Together with the increased likelihood that votes on important amendments will be postponed and clustered with other such votes for resumption later that day or on a subsequent day, the attention personally paid by Members to debates in progress and therefore the relative importance of the quality of those debates has diminished. Even where votes are postponed until a subsequent day, and the opportunity is enhanced for Members to read the debates in the printed Record before voting, that option may be delegated to staff, with the Members, given the frenetic nature of the time available to them, relying on representations from the whip organizations.

On the several general Appropriation bills considered annually, where the traditional 'openness' of amendment consideration under the five-minute rule is not as often impacted by the operation of special orders, spontaneity of debate and thus the impact of debate on voting have been diminished by the utilization of unanimous consent agreements—now commonplace on all such bills—which enable the House to agree on the precise number and sponsorship of amendments to be permitted. This 'universe' of amendments normally lists those Members who may offer amendments, identified either by pre-publication numbering or by a described subject matter, while limiting debate on each such amendment, prohibiting second-degree amendments and equally dividing the debate thereon between the proponent and an opponent. This contemporary process on Appropriation bills has been accepted by both parties' leaders and bill managers in the interests of certainty of time and issue, which their rank and file have come to expect. Unanimous consent is obtainable because any Member wishing to be on the 'universe' list is included, although their amendments are often withdrawn or ruled out of order as in violation of rules uniquely applicable to general Appropriation bills and discussed at page 285.

The major exception to the observation that debate, because not spontaneous, does not influence votes, occurs during standing committee and subcommittee mark-up proceedings. At the committee level in the House, debate is relatively spontaneous once a measure's mark-up gets under way. Prior to the consideration of a measure for amendment in committees under the five-minute rule, opening statements by all committee or subcommittee members are normally permitted. Committee mark-ups are not normally televised to the same extent as hearings, other than on the websites that several committees have established for the information of internet viewers. Coupled with the earlier observation that committees are not free to establish limiting special rules or motions to suspend the rules except by unanimous consent, it remains true that a large percentage of informed writing of legislation is accomplished at the committee level where all members are free to offer amendments, amendments thereto, and where Chairs often tolerate more informal give-and-take under the five-minute rule.

Members wishing to engage in televised coverage of debates when no measure or matter is pending in the House have several opportunities to do so each legislative day. With the advent of televised proceedings in 1978, special order debates soon became speeches to a television audience rather than debates among Members through the Chair. Previous rules proscribing the use of visual aids during debates were relaxed to permit charts, graphs and photographs (but not electronic pictures) without separate permission, unless of an unparliamentary nature. This is in marked contrast to debates in Parliament, where visual aids are not permitted because the Hansard reporters cannot properly record them. Special order speeches are seldom orchestrated to encourage adversarial debate and are usually allocated to permit one party to control an entire hour. Together, these tendencies have convinced Members and the viewing audience that spontaneous debate is not occurring. While the television cameras operated by House employees at the direction of the Speaker do not depict a relatively empty Chamber by wide-angle panning, and the camera focuses primarily on the Member speaking, a caption appears at the bottom of the screen to indicate that legislative business has been completed for the day.

As special order speeches were required to be televised by the standing rule governing complete and unedited coverage of all the proceedings of the House, the Speaker was not free to discontinue televised coverage once legislative business had concluded. Much like adjournment debates in the House of Commons, all Members wishing to participate were free to do so if yielded to by the Member under recognition, although the subject matter to be discussed was not selected by the Speaker and was not required to be published in advance. Even so, Members from the opposite party would not expect to participate in a party-organized special order until their own party's allocated time arrived. By 1994, it was determined that an 'experiment' with bipartisan debates on pre-announced topics should be implemented in order to present the spontaneous debate to the viewing audience lacking in the special order format. Thus the House agreed by unanimous consent to conduct, at a time designated by the Speaker, structured debate on a mutually agreeable topic announced by the Speaker, with two participants from each party in 'Oxford-style' debates. As a precursor to those structured debates, there had been in 1993 one 'Lincoln–Douglas' style debate involving five Members, with one Member acting as 'moderator' by controlling an hour of debate time under the general hour rule[6]. While this format initially provoked curiosity, it was discontinued after three Oxford-style debates for lack of sustained viewer interest.

While it is important to provide a forum for Members to engage in debates on issues of their choosing which are not on the legislative agenda, and while such debates, as adjournment debates in the Commons for back-bench Members to express constituency concerns, are for the information of Members and the public, the search goes on for a format which attracts broader Member and therefore viewer interest. It is also incumbent upon the Members who do engage in special order debates to follow proper rules of decorum, by addressing the Chair and not each other as in the second person, in order to convey the appearance of orderly debate. Finally, the demoralizing daily impact of up to four hours of staged speeches on the Official Reporters of Debates might suggest that, unless determined by party leaders to be genuine debates and unless rationed among Members more equitably, they be conducted elsewhere, as in the House Recording Studio.

Debate in Parliament

In the Commons, conduct of debate is in the hands of the Speaker, assisted by his or her three Deputies. In the absence of the Speaker, the latter occupy the 'upper' Chair in the House but the 'lower' chair—where the Clerk of the House normally sits—when the House is in Committee. (The Speaker has never presided over Committees of the whole House and no Speaker has spoken in one for about a century and a half.) While presiding, all are completely impartial. At General Elections, however, the Deputies must contest their constituencies in the interests of the parties to which they belong, and re-election to their offices if returned as Members is usual but not universal.

In debate, Members will be called alternately from the government (on the right of the Chair) and Opposition side, on the Speaker's left. Selection of Members to speak and the order in which they speak is a matter exclusively for the Speaker, whose choice is completely impartial. Some parliaments operate a system of arranged lists of speakers, perhaps basing them on party nominations. The Commons, unlike the Lords (see page 172), has never been convinced, since an arrangement of that kind was thought to be likely to be inimical to such spontaneity as remains in modern debate. Members will individually notify the Speaker in advance of or even during a debate whether they wish to speak, but the parties have no role beyond intimating in advance to the Speaker who will lead and wind up for them.

Members of Opposition parties other than the official Opposition—the largest party not in government—usually do a little better in terms of calling of Members than their numbers could justify on a strictly arithmetical basis. The same is probably true of party mavericks, wherever they sit. When an issue does not split the House on party lines, considerations of balance continue to apply, though sharing debating time between intangible arguments rather than visible parties is much harder for the Chair. The Speaker keeps records of Members' interventions, in the interests of fairness over a parliamentary session—and woe betide the Member who asked to speak for ten minutes in a debate where speeches were not time limited and meandered on for half an hour. For a while, whenever he or she rises, the Chair's eye may inexplicably alight elsewhere.

One of the more elusive buttresses of the authority of the Chair in these and other matters of debate is the 'common sense' of the House as a whole, which can sometimes override the political allegiances of individual Members. The House makes largely unspoken demands on the debating skills of its Members. A Member who repeatedly fails to meet these expectations—or bores the House—may look in vain for sympathy and support even (indeed, particularly) from his own side. Conversely, the engaging personality or the clear-minded expert, whatever his or her political views, will tend to be generally respected. In matters of conduct, including but not limited to ethical aspects, the House as a whole may be an effective reinforcement of guidance given from the Chair.

There are a number of conventions to be observed in speaking in the Commons. Though sometimes difficult for new Members to assimilate, they are (as the Modernisation Committee recently observed) intended to assist the flow of debate and facilitate an orderly exchange of views. Many are common to Parliament and Congress. Members must speak standing and address the occupant of the Chair. There are hidden pitfalls. New Members vary in the time it takes them to stop saying 'you'—which can only imply the Chair—when they mean to refer to another Member. It is in fact a solecism not always avoided by the most experienced Members. Nevertheless, use of the proper formulae in referring to other Members in debate is consistently enforced by the Chair. The more rococo versions—'the right honourable and gallant (or learned) gentleman, the Member for...'—are sadly disappearing, but the basics remain. Members on one's own side are 'my honourable Friend'—'right honourable' if the colleague is a member of the Privy Council—and those on the other are 'the (right) honourable lady', or '(right) honourable gentleman'. Much scorn has been heaped on these traditions but there is no doubt that they add simple dignity to proceedings—and getting one's tongue round one of these circumlocutions has the additional benefit of providing just enough time for self-suppression of the disorderly comment trembling on the tip of the tongue.

It is not in order to refer in debate, tabled Question or notice of motion to active proceedings, civil or criminal, before a court of law. Except when the House is legislating, it is recognized that Parliament should not intrude into areas where the decisions properly fall to the courts, and there should be no question of a widely publicized debate in either House impacting on a case at law. Individual Members sometimes understandably find the rule irksome, when a constituency problem seems to be of wider public interest than any court proceedings which may have been engaged by part of it. The House tries to be scrupulous about keeping its side of the unspoken bargain, and is never knowingly in breach of its own rule. The Speaker's power to lift the prohibition is only very rarely invoked. By contrast, there is no rule or usage in Congress similar to this 'sub judice' restriction in Parliament, and debate in either House may include references to active court proceedings.

There are some persons who can be mentioned in debate only within limits. The Sovereign must not be the object of disrespectful remarks. Political attacks on opponents inside or outside Parliament are the stuff of everyday debate, but there is a group which includes the Speaker, Members of either House, and judges incidental personal criticism of whom which puts their bona fides in doubt is forbidden. They may be subjected to such charges only in debate on a temperately worded but direct motion of censure. Tabling the kind of motion which will permit personal charges is rare. It is even less likely that the government will find time to debate them if they are tabled, except for those critical of an occupant of the Chair, which are very rare but must be disposed of quickly, to clear the air. (For criticism of a Speaker other than in debate on such a motion, see page 36.) Thirdly, some phrases used in debate are always unacceptable.[7]

Members may not be accused, for example, of deliberately misleading the House or lying. If such a remark is made, the Member who made it is at once required to withdraw it. Of course, quick-witted Members can find their way round these prohibitions. Winston Churchill was made to withdraw the word 'lie'; but he got away with 'terminological inexactitude', because it has no overtones of dishonour. Moreover, the buoys marking the channel of the acceptable have drifted closer over the generations. Nowadays, the Chair is uneasy at the use of 'invertebrate' by one Member to describe another. In the mid-nineteenth century Benjamin Disraeli, party leader and Prime Minister (who was Jewish by birth), had no protection when called 'the direct descendant of the impenitent thief'.

It is bad form for Members (other than ministers expounding policy) to read speeches, or at any rate to do so very obviously. The two Houses of Congress are much more tolerant in that regard in modern practice. The aim is that debate should not be declamatory but almost conversational, and in an ideal world all contributions would be short, spontaneous, and unscripted—as indeed the most effective ones often are. Within living memory, the Commons regularly boasted Members (not all of them on the front benches) able to draw to the Chamber political friends and foes alike whenever they rose to speak. No doubt compelling parliamentary speakers will in future illuminate debate, but for the most part, Members nowadays tend to make 'copious use' of notes, a stock phrase used by the Chair to administer a gentle rebuke to those who too slavishly follow their prepared text. At the same time, it may be true that classical parliamentary oratory was as rare in the days of Fox, Pitt, Gladstone and Churchill as it is today. Lord Byron found Parliament in 1822 short of oratorical eloquence, but 'there must be a leaven of thought and good sense sufficient to make them know what is right, though they can't express it nobly'.[8] Even the eighteenth-century phenomenon of 'single-speech Hamilton' (though it was evidently a glorious speech) has its twentieth-century parallel in a Member who in the course of a long career spoke on the floor of the House only once, and then in proceedings on a private bill.

The practice of 'intervening' in the course of a speech of another, to question or expand on the development of an argument, is an important part of the cut and thrust of debate. Members need not give way but if they do not, especially if there is no time limit on speeches in force or if they have directly referred to the colleague who wishes to break in, they may incur audible disapproval.

A Member who has spoken should not leave the Chamber until the end of the speech which follows his, and should be present for the concluding speeches of the debate, in which his points will—he expects—be answered. This is more than a matter of simple courtesy. It is very important that debate should be made up of connected contributions, rather than a series of unrelated observations. A committee recently described the kind of debate in which Members did not listen to and try to respond to each others' views as 'a sorry affair'. Members watching proceedings on television sets in their offices have been known to hurry to the Chamber to comment on what they have seen on the screen. Those lucky enough to be called would be unwise to begin by referring to what prompted their appearance in the Chamber. The Chair will not be pleased to have inadvertently called someone who has not heard preceding contributions, and is apt to say so.

Members ought not to move between the colleague addressing the House and the Chair, or to cross the lines on the carpet in front of each of the front benches. The customary explanation of the lines is that they are exactly two sword breadths apart. Swords are long gone, but the rule remains (along with ribbons on which swords are intended to be hung in the Members' Cloakroom). The ring of a mobile/cell phone will attract immediate reproof from the Chair, though silent electronic devices have been permitted. Visitors in the gallery must not be referred to, probably a legacy from days when the House sat in private and was suspicious about being reported or observed. An eighteenth-century case of a dagger being used to illustrate a point made in debate still resonates in a dislike of the production of objects for such a purpose. A recent Speaker has sharply observed that the English language ought to be vehicle enough to persuade others. Indeed, the House should not be addressed in a language other than in English, unless a translation is offered immediately afterwards in the speech. How otherwise would the Chair be able to tell whether or not the speech was in order?[9] There is no ban on learned quotations from modern or ancient languages, though these are less frequent than they once were (or so tradition insists).

Though often characterized as simply enforcers of party discipline, the whips play a significant informal role in the smooth running of business in the Commons. The caustic comment of Enoch Powell, a senior Conservative politician of the post-war era, that 'whips are essential to civilisation—like sewers', though clever, is essentially unfair. Relations between whips of all parties are very important in easing the orderly progress of business, without diminishing anyone's right to oppose. They are an important conduit of information between the Chair and Members on front and back benches in the course of a sitting, carrying information on who can expect to be called next, or who must leave to attend a committee and would be grateful to be called later than anticipated. Business from week to week is planned by the Leader of the House and the government Chief Whip, who will nevertheless listen to strongly held views on the other side of the House, even if in the end no agreed solution can be reached.

Many conventions in the Lords are similar to those in the Commons, but there are some which are not. The Lord Speaker does not regulate debate, though general procedural advice on correct procedure may be given. Speeches in the Lords are made to the House and not to the Chair. Unlike the Speaker in the Commons, the Lord Speaker presides in Committee of the whole House. When more than one Lord rises to speak at the same time, and there is no speakers' list (see below), it is not for the Lord Speaker to decide which should be heard first. Normally those concerned will courteously sort the matter out between them, but if they do not the decision rests with the House itself. Time limits are enforced by the front benches. Reading speeches is even more frowned on than in the Commons. Erskine May's *Parliamentary Practice* damns the practice as 'alien to the custom of the House and injurious to its debates'.[10] In short, as the Lords Companion to the Standing Orders puts it, 'The word "undesirable" is used in the House of Lords as the equivalent of the expression "out of order" in the House of Commons.'[11]

A list of Lords who have indicated a wish to speak in a debate is published—but by the government whips' office, after consultation with the other parties, and not by the Lord Speaker. The order is not rigid and may on occasion be varied. Those not on the list may manage to intervene, but only once all those on the list have spoken and if there is time before the winding-up speeches. In the Lords, unlike the Commons (see page 203), there is no rule limiting speaking time imposed by the Lord Speaker. In general, however, in non-time-limited debates frontbenchers opening or winding-up are expected to speak for no longer than twenty minutes and the remainder of the House for fifteen. In time-limited debates, there is a tariff of permitted speaking times for the front benches depending on the amount of time set aside for the debate, the remaining time being divided equally between the remainder of the Lords on the list of speakers.

Conventions in the Lords which are similar to those prevailing in the Commons include the calling of Lords to speak alternately from government benches and other benches. Lords must not come between the Woolsack (on which the Lord Speaker sits) and the Lord who is speaking. Appropriate formulae—in the days before the departure of most hereditaries even more elaborate in character than in the Commons—must be used when referring to other Lords in a speech and not their proper names. Interventions may be made in the speeches of a Lord who has the floor with the latter's permission; and Lords are expected to hear not only the speech before and after their own, but also the wind-up speeches at the conclusion of a debate in which they have participated. Reading of speeches is frowned on. Disrespectful remarks aimed at the same group of protected persons as in the Commons (page 173) are not to be used in debate. The sub judice rule in the same terms as in the Commons is as much part of the underpinning of Lords debates as it is in the Commons, though the discretionary role of the Speaker in the lower House is in the Lords assumed by the Leader of the House.

Decision making: motions and amendments

The basic framework of decision making in the House of Commons is simple. Prior notice of any proposal must be given unless the rules waive the requirement (for example, in the case of a motion to commit a bill to a Committee of the whole House made immediately after second reading) or if the business is of such a character that notice is impossible, such as a closure motion.

Notices of motions or amendments for business in the House of Commons will appear in print the day after they have been handed in, and will be reprinted on the Order of Business of the day on which they are to be considered (see also below). A motion is made, usually with an explanatory speech, by a Member in whose name the motion stands on the Order Paper. If a Member is not among those who have given notice, he or she may not make the motion. Any Member may move an amendment, however, and any member of the government may move any item of government business. No seconder is required either of motions or amendments. Members may speak only once to a question, unless the House unanimously gives them leave to intervene again or they are exercising a right of reply in winding up debate on a motion (not a bill or amendment). In Committee of the whole House these rules are slightly varied: any Member may make a motion even if he or she was not among those who gave written notice of it, and it is permissible to speak more than once to the same question. Unlike the rule in Washington, once a motion has been moved and the question proposed for debate, it is considered to be in the hands of the House and may be withdrawn only if there is no dissenting voice.

Amendments for consideration on the floor of the House of Commons should be tabled two sitting days in advance (the notice necessary for public bill committees is longer). An amendment handed after the limit has expired is likely to fall foul of the Speaker's power of selection (see below).

In both British Houses, amendments which are out of order fall at the first fence: those which are at all points opposed to the original proposal, those which if carried would wreck the text by rendering it unworkable or nonsense, those dependent on others previously negatived or inconsistent with amendments already made are examples. Relevance—germaneness in Congress—is of course an important qualifying characteristic in Westminster, but much less elaborated than across the Atlantic. Erskine May's *Parliamentary Practice* throws up its hands and declares it 'impracticable to attempt to classify...all the grounds on which amendments have been held to be irrelevant to a question'.[12] On much the same lines (and for reasons connected with the non-partisan character of the Chair sketched on pages 36–7) decisions on order at Westminster are more a matter of first principles than precedent.

The Speaker will not submit disorderly amendments to motions or bills for debate. They will simply be passed over, though if required the Speaker will explain the reasons for his decision. The Speaker's judgment on order is never challenged by the House.

Amendments to motions do not customarily raise issues of order. Amendments to bills do. All bills have a long title which states often at length the purposes and contents of the bill: all clauses—and ex hypothesi all amendments—should fit snugly within that. If they do not, they may be out of order. There is however sometimes an escape clause. If the House has agreed to an Instruction to a committee, amendments may be made which are within the scope of the bill—the area of life or law with which the bill deals—even though they are not strictly within the title. The title may then be amended to fit. A bill which by its long title regulated fee-charging employment agencies was amended following an Instruction to admit amendments relating to non-fee-charging agencies. Thus an amendment beyond the scope is always disorderly; an amendment beyond the title may be brought into order.

Amendments are out of order if they negate the purpose of the bill, as that will have been affirmed at second reading. They must be within the scope of the clause of the bill to which they are offered, though if they are not but are within the scope of the bill they may be moved as New Clauses. Amendments leaving out the operative words of a clause or offered at the wrong place in the bill are disorderly. Finally, amendments which are 'vague, trifling or offered in a spirit of mockery' are inadmissible.

The practice in the Lords on the orderliness of amendments is broadly similar.

The Speaker (but not the Lord Speaker) has power to select or not select for debate otherwise orderly amendments to motions and to bills. Amendments of secondary importance will not be selected: limited time ought to be devoted to the salient issues. Amendments likely to lead the debate away from the matter under discussion or which overlap with crisper, more succinct propositions, are equally unlikely to pass the Speaker's scrutiny. The power of selection is potentially a very contentious one. The Speaker never explains the reasons for his selection to the House, and he will act sternly against any attempt from the floor to challenge his decision. He may however on appropriate occasions and at his discretion privately explain to a Member the basis on which his decision was arrived at. Wise Governments and Oppositions consult before tabling potentially problematical amendments, but in principle the rules apply as much to them as to backbenchers: the Speaker has quite recently declined to select a Government amendment to an Opposition day motion. The Speaker's ability to deny the House a debate on an orderly amendment and not to say why seems to put into his hands a very powerful weapon, especially since the number of non-selected amendments may be much larger than those selected. The reality is rather different. Discussions between Members and Clerks before amendments are tabled will often flag up problems of both order and selectability, at a time when defects can (if at all possible) be cured. Sometimes Members are content to leave unselectable amendments on the paper, to show what they would have moved had it been possible. Members are always able privately to make representations to the Speaker before the critical decision is taken. Really ill-tempered disputes on the floor of the House about selection are very unusual. Without the trust underpinning the exercise of the power, Commons business would probably grind to a halt. Moreover, decisions on process, which may raise passions momentarily but have little lasting significance, are by this means not allowed to crowd out discussions on merits.

These are the kind of complex judgments which a Speaker has to make nearly every day, balancing the interest of Members in discussing matters of political significance to them with the House's need for a coherent framework of debate which allows views to be expressed not only on the floor but in the division lobbies, taking account of the interests of the frontbenchers who speak for their parties and those of individual back-benchers who otherwise might be pushed aside.

If there is only one amendment to a motion and the amendment is both in order and selected, there is usually a single debate on motion and amendment. Where there is more than one amendment, each is considered in the order in which it bears on the text of the motion. If there are a number of selected amendments on the same theme, the Speaker may group those together, in order that there should be a common debate on all the related aspects. If the lead amendment is negatived, the others in the group will normally fall without further debate or decision. If the others are consequential on a successful lead amendment, each will be put for separate decision without further debate.

For example, let us assume there is a motion to assert 'That this House believes the moon is made of green cheese'. The amendments tabled might read:

1. Leave out all the words after 'House' and insert 'has no confidence in HM Government's space policy';
2. Leave out 'is' and insert 'and planets are';
3. Leave out 'green' and insert 'blue';
4. Leave out 'green' and insert 'red Leicester'; and
5. At end add 'with holes'.

The first amendment would be likely to be ruled out of order. Space policy goes much wider than a motion about the moon, and even if that were not so the amendment if selected might lead the debate away from the central issue, moon dust.

The second raises similar problems, though the decision is harder. Is the debate only about the moon, or could the argument that it shares its make-up with other celestial bodies bring the amendment into order and make it worth selecting? It might be a ticklish decision, which the Speaker would have to resolve on the particular merits as he or she saw them. There would be no attempt to find precedents.

The third amendment (blue cheese) and the fourth (red Leicester) are certainly in order. They are obviously connected, and would probably be selected for a joint debate. If at the end of the debate on the first amendment, the House came down in favour of blue cheese, the red Leicester amendment could not be put for decision, because the House would have already decided what colour of cheese the moon was made of. If however the blue cheese amendment were defeated, the Speaker might feel able—particularly if the red Leicester possibility had featured significantly in the joint debate—to put it to the House for decision, though not for further debate.

The last amendment, to add 'with holes', is in order but would probably not be selected. The Chair might feel that it was of limited importance, and debate would simply occupy time better spent in discussing the more substantial amendments.

Finally, the House would have to decide what it thought about the motion as a whole in its original or amended form.

In the Lords, there is no authority which has the power to declare a motion or an amendment out of order. The House expects that advice given to Lords by the Clerks will be taken. Nor does the Lord Speaker have the power to select some amendments for discussion, ignoring others. Motions, which in the Commons may bear a host of names, which is sometimes useful in demonstrating the weight of political push behind an apparently innocent amendment, stand in the Lords in the name of one Lord only, and one Lord may authorize another to make the motion if he or she is absent.

In Congress, a House rule (clause 7 of Rule XVI) requires amendments to be germane to the matter under consideration, by providing that 'no motion or proposition on a subject different from that under consideration shall be admitted under colour of amendment'. This rule has been in effect in the House since the first Congress (when it applied only to substitutes and then to all amendments, beginning in 1822) and has proven indispensable to the orderly operation of a 435-Member body. The requirement for germaneness of amendments has even been applied as part of the 'general parliamentary law' applicable in the House prior to adoption of the rules at the beginning of each Congress. It serves to prevent hasty and ill-considered legislation as propositions that might not reasonably be anticipated as additions to or alternatives for those matters made in order. On one of the most important historical applications of the germaneness rule in the House—the Chair's ruling in 1998 that censure of the President was not a germane amendment to a resolution to impeach the President, the Chair quoted former Majority Leader (later Speaker) Carl Albert's observation in 1965:

> It is a rule which has been insisted on by Democrats and Republicans alike ever since the Democratic and Republican parties have been in existence. It is a rule without which this House could never complete its legislative program if there happened to be a substantial minority in opposition. One of the great things about the House of Representatives and one of the things that distinguishes it from other legislative bodies is that we do operate on the rule of germaneness. No legislative body of this size could ever operate unless it did comply with the rule of germaneness.

House Practice[13] at Chapter 26, section 1, asserts that 'no such rule existed under the practice of the early common law or under the rules of Parliament'. This is based on

Thomas Jefferson's characterization of the rule of Parliament when he wrote in his Manual in 1801 that 'amendments may be made so as totally to alter the nature of the proposition; and it is a way of getting rid of a proposition by making it bear a sense different from what it was intended by the movers, so that they vote against it themselves'.[14] *Hinds' Precedents*[15] carries a precedent in the House of Representatives from 1880 that 'in the absence of an express rule, the amendment would not be liable to a point of order upon the ground that it was inconsistent with or not germane to the subject under consideration, for, according to the common parliamentary law of this country and of England, a legislative assembly might by an amendment, in the ordinary form or in the form of a substitute, change the entire character of any bill or other proposition pending'.

Erskine May, however, describes the current requirement for relevance of amendments as follows:

> The fundamental rule that debate must be relevant to a question also means that every amendment must be relevant to the question to which it is proposed. Stated generally, no matter ought to be raised in debate on a question which would be irrelevant if moved as an amendment, and no amendment should be used for importing arguments which would be irrelevant to the main question.[16]

May cites a precedent formalized in 1883 in support of the requirement for relevance of amendments, perhaps suggesting that it had not been the basis of practice in the House of Commons prior to that time. Apparently Thomas Jefferson thought so. While the symmetry of the dual requirements for relevance in debate and of amendments to pending text is more apparent in British parliamentary jurisprudence, and while debate relevancy is consistently enforced there at the initiative of the Speaker, the US House does have a separate rule requiring relevance in debate (clause 1(b) of rule XVII requiring 'remarks in debate...shall be confined to the question under debate, avoiding personality'. Neither rule is self-enforcing in the US House, however, as a Member must raise a point of order against an amendment or against irrelevant debate to enforce either rule. Unlike the House of Commons, the Speaker does not take the initiative under either rule, rather awaiting a point of order from the floor and at times hearing argument on the point of order before ruling. Relevance in debate is discussed in this chapter at page 186.

Appeals from the selection of amendments by the Commons Speaker are not permitted, while appeals from all rulings on questions of order, including germaneness rulings, are permitted in the US House. Such appeals have traditionally been infrequent, however, as the question is only on the procedural correctness of the Chair's rulings rather than on the substantive merits of the underlying amendment. The Chair's rulings, when appealed from, are virtually always supported by bipartisan majorities or more recently at least by the Majority party, out of deference to the importance of precedent and the Speaker's acceptance of non-partisan advice in rendering his ruling. Nevertheless, the frequency of appeals by the Minority from rulings on germaneness has increased in recent Congresses, as have other appeals (discussed subsequently in this chapter at pages 209–11), if only in order to establish 'voting records' improperly represented as decisions on the merits of issues otherwise denied direct votes. Appeals from germaneness rulings became more fashionable with the historic impeachment decision in 1998. On that occasion, the Minority had no procedural alternative. Germaneness appeals have extended to ordinary legislative matters where the Minority's alternative agenda has not been made in order. As a recent example,[17] to a bill temporarily extending a Foreign Intelligence Surveillance Act for a short period, an amendment in a Minority motion to re-commit to include permanent law changes including immunity to communications companies facing lawsuits for warrantless wire taps, was correctly held non-germane citing a direct precedent in point. An appeal was taken from the Chair's decision, and was tabled by a record vote which was immediately characterized publicly as a decision on the merits of the amendment ruled out of order. A successful appeal on any such question would establish an unfortunate precedent that an instant majority of the House could overrule the Chair on appeal and could immediately determine the agenda of the House without notice or resort to the standing germaneness rule.

The House frequently waives the rule of germaneness by adoption of a special order from the Committee on Rules. Thus the distinction between the non-partisan nature of the Chair's rulings, on the one hand, and special rules recommended by the Majority party which the Chair will fairly interpret, on the other, is essential to an understanding of House practice. This dichotomy becomes blurred in the public mind when the Minority characterizes an appeal from the Chair's ruling as a vote on the merits of the proposition ruled out of order.

While the Senate is less encumbered with germaneness requirements except under cloture, it does not enjoy a comparable ability to adopt special orders of business waiving points of order by majority vote. On occasion, the Senate has voted on appeal to overrule germaneness and other decisions of the presiding officer which inhibit its ability to proceed to certain business, in order to obtain a vote on the merits of the underlying proposition. While this is not common in modern practice with respect to the germaneness of amendments, its frequency relative to the lack of any successful appeals in the House underscores the occasional temptation to depart from non-partisan rulings of the presiding officer in the Senate. This trend has been evidenced more at the final conference stage than at the amendment stage in the Senate and will be discussed in the chapter on Legislation at page 458. More commonly in the Senate, unanimous consent agreements are entered which waive procedural impediments short of invocation of cloture, in order to permit initial or subsequent consideration of a measure as well as to accommodate individual Senators who would otherwise object, while also imposing time constraints and ad hoc relevancy or germaneness requirements on unspecified amendments which may be offered.

The existence of literally hundreds of precedents in the US House over more than 200 years, compared to the paucity of recorded relevancy rulings regarding amendments in the House of Commons over several more centuries, is explained by the British Speaker's truly non-partisan position and his advance selection power over amendments, where relevance is a factor to be privately determined on the advice of non-partisan Clerks. The Commons Clerks may advise Members on the likelihood of selection based on relevance, but details are not published as precedent as in the USA. In the USA, the Speaker's actual ruling must await the offering of the amendment in the plenary session. The fact that the US Speaker or his Deputies are more partisan in their ordinary roles as Majority Members suggests strongly that the Chair's rulings, to be perceived as fair, be documented by resort to published precedent on the recommendation of a statutorily defined non-partisan parliamentary advisor. Where an amendment selection process is totally delegated—as it is to the British Speaker—without the availability of a partisan Rules Committee to recommend waivers of points of order—the disparities in the process between the two Houses for determining relevancy of amendments can be more readily understood.

In the House of Representatives, the concept of germaneness implies more than the mere relevance of one subject to another. It is frequently stated that the fact that two subjects are related does not necessarily render them germane to each other. For example, the germaneness of an amendment may depend on the relative scope of the amendment and the pending text. Thus a proposition of narrow or limited scope may not be amended by a proposition of a more general nature. One important purpose of the germaneness rule is to prevent the House from having to consider matters for which it is not fully prepared. Accordingly, one frequently cited test of germaneness is whether the subject matter of the amendment falls within the jurisdiction of the committee reporting the bill.

While numerous precedents have been chronicled with respect to the germaneness of amendments in a wide variety of contexts, it is essential to note that the Chair, in determining which of the tests of germaneness is most applicable, must first understand the nature and scope of the pending portion of the proposition being amended, and then the relationship of the offered amendment to that pending text. By initially arriving at a textual understanding, the Chair is then advised to follow the most appropriate line of precedent in rendering a ruling. It is therefore possible to avoid the misperception that an equally compelling germaneness test can be applied and precedent cited to support either side of a germaneness point of order. In evaluating an amendment, the Chair considers the pending text, as perfected by prior amendment. The Chair considers the relationship between the amendment and an existing statute that the bill seeks to amend only if the existing statute is so comprehensively amended by the pending bill as to call into question all its provisions. The Chair does not rely in any primary sense on language in accompanying reports not contained in the pending text.

An amendment that might be considered germane if offered at the end of the reading of the bill for amendment may not be germane if offered during the reading, before all the provisions of the bill are open to consideration. Thus a perfecting amendment should relate to the pending section or paragraph (or clause), and an amendment adding a new section should only come after a sufficiently broad portion of the bill has been read to render it germane to the entire portion already read.

A problematic question of germaneness is presented where the pending text is so diverse in scope and in subject-matter content as to virtually eliminate application of the germaneness rule, especially where the amendment is in the form of a new provision at the end of the bill or a motion to re-commit with instructions and is to be judged in relation to the underlying measure as a whole rather than to any particular provision in that text. The emergence of 'omnibus' bills in recent Congresses—the work product of numerous committees or inserted by leadership and woven together by special orders reported from the Committee on Rules which often 'self-execute' the adoption of additional provisions—can undermine the application of a more precise subject-matter test of germaneness. The committee jurisdiction test sometimes remains a barrier against adding other provisions not within the jurisdiction of the committees reporting the measure, but ceases to be a persuasive test when the measure has been expanded beyond the jurisdictions of several committees in order to satisfy a political expediency. A compelling argument can be made that a reinterpretation or rewrite of the germaneness rule should be undertaken in order to prevent consideration of amendments not related to at least one provision in such omnibus measures. That reinterpretation would not be within the Speaker's proper role in determining questions of order based on precedent (unless the Speaker were to take the extraordinary step to invite an appeal in order to establish new precedent). It would need to be put in place by proper amendment of the standing germaneness rule (clause 7 of Rule XVI) itself.

The test of the germaneness of a second-degree amendment[18] to—or a substitute for—a pending amendment (except for an amendment to an amendment contained in a motion to re-commit) is its relationship to the pending amendment and not to the bill to which that pending amendment has been offered. In the unlikely event of a Majority amendment to a Minority motion to re-commit, the test of its germaneness is to the bill in its perfected form and not merely to the amendment contained in the original re-committal motion. Traditionally and properly the Majority refrains from amending a Minority motion to re-commit (achievable by first voting down the motion for the previous question), preferring to honour the sanctity of the Minority motion, if otherwise in order, so that it may receive a direct vote. Similarly, amendments to motions to instruct House conferees need be germane only to some provision in the House or Senate-passed version and not necessarily to the original motion to instruct. These germaneness distinctions are based on the need to remain relevant to the pending business, either to the first-degree amendment, or more broadly on motions to instruct where the entire measure is before the House pending final passage or commitment to conference.

The germaneness of an amendment is not judged by the apparent motives of the Member offering it. The Chair does not determine the legal effect of the bill, law, or amendment in question. The Chair rules only on whether the amendment addresses a 'subject different' from that under consideration. The Chair does not rule on the consistency of amendments with those previously offered, deciding only whether the amendment seeks to amend text already amended in its entirety.

The title of a bill is not controlling in evaluating the germaneness of amendments, as the actual text and not the formal title are controlling. Thus the heading of a portion of a bill as 'Miscellaneous' will not by itself permit amendments to that portion that are not germane to its actual content unless they are so diverse as to permit an amendment to be tested by its relationship to the bill as a whole.

An amendment may relate to the subject matter of a bill but may still not be germane. For example, to a proposal authorizing a programme to be undertaken, an amendment for a study to determine the feasibility of undertaking such a programme may be germane as more limited in its result. Conversely, an amendment requiring certain action is not germane to a proposal that would merely require a study, as being more ambitious in scope.

A comparison of the fundamental purposes of the bill and amendment may be an appropriate test of germaneness. This test is particularly applicable to an amendment in the nature of a substitute. Thus if the purpose of a highway bill is to connect points A and B, an amendment specifying a different route between A and B would reflect the same fundamental purpose, while an amendment connecting A and D would have a different (non-germane) purpose. As well, an amendment must not only have the same fundamental purpose as the matter sought to be amended, but also must contemplate a method of achieving that end that is closely allied to the method encompassed in the bill. For example, if the purpose of a bill is to support the health of schoolchildren by mandating oranges in a school lunch programme, an amendment providing free vitamin C supplements in school lunches may be germane. On the other hand, to a bill establishing an independent agency within the Executive branch to accomplish a particular purpose, an amendment emphasizing committee oversight and authorizing committees to order the agency to take certain action utilizes a sufficiently different method (internal House procedures) and is not germane.

One individual proposition is not germane to another individual proposition, unless the pending individual proposition is broadened by prior amendment to become more general in scope, at which point further amendment within the newly expanded class may be germane. Then the test of germaneness changes to suggest that to a measure containing two or more diverse propositions within the same class, an amendment may add a third proposition on the same subject. Thus to a bill regulating apples, an amendment adding oranges is not germane, but to a bill regulating apples and oranges, an amendment adding another fruit (but not a vegetable) may be germane.

A specific proposition may not be amended by a proposition more general in scope. Thus an amendment applicable to fruits of all kinds would not be germane to a bill dealing only with apples. Even an amendment that merely strikes words from a bill may be ruled out if the amendment has the effect of broadening the scope of the bill. On the other hand, a general proposition may be amended by a specific proposition or one more limited in nature if within the same class. Thus, a bill regulating fruits of all kinds could be amended by language applicable specifically to oranges. To a bill conferring a broad range of authority to accomplish a particular result, an amendment granting the same entity specific authority to achieve that result is germane. Similarly, an amendment that makes a specific exception to or exemption from a general proposition is germane.

The rule of germaneness applies to committee amendments as well as to those offered by individual Members, and a committee amendment that is not germane to the bill as introduced, if it is not ruled out of order in committee, may require a waiver of points of order by a special order from the Rules Committee, or may be considered under a motion to suspend the rules and pass the bill as amended.

The germaneness rule applies to instructions in a motion to re-commit a bill to a committee. It is not in order to propose as part of a motion to re-commit any proposition that would not have been germane if proposed as an amendment to the bill on the floor. The cited example of censure not being germane to impeachment was posed in the form of a motion to re-commit. The test of germaneness is the relationship of the instructions to the bill taken as a whole as perfected, and not merely to the separate portion of the bill specifically proposed to be amended in the instructions.

A condition or qualification sought to be added by way of amendment must be germane, and cannot make the effectiveness of a bill contingent upon an unrelated event or determination, including compliance with unrelated legislation. For example, an amendment conditioning the availability to certain recipients of funds upon their compliance with Federal law not otherwise applicable to those recipients and within the jurisdiction of other House committees may be non-germane. To a bill amending a statute, an amendment prohibiting assistance under that Act or under any other Act for a particular purpose, thus affecting laws not being amended by the bill, is not germane.

To a bill conferring discretionary authority, an amendment restricting the exercise of that authority may be germane. Amendments that merely place restrictions on the use of funds that are authorized or appropriated in the bill are generally upheld as germane, so long as they are confined to the agencies, authorities and funds covered by the bill or portion thereof being read for amendment and do not range to other Acts. An amendment limiting the use of funds by a particular agency funded in a general Appropriation bill may be germane at more than one place in the bill, either when the paragraph carrying such funds is pending, or to an appropriate 'general provision' affecting that agency.

Amendments that merely postpone the effective date of the legislation to a date certain without stating a condition have been held germane. Less clear are amendments which make the effectiveness of a bill contingent upon an external event or finding. If the suggested contingency is unrelated to the bill, such as the enactment of separate unrelated legislation or fulfilment of actions not involved in the affected programme, it will be ruled out of order. An amendment may subject the operation of the bill to an external benchmark, so long as it does not constitute an unrelated condition. An abstract standard may be used as the measure of availability of funding provided by the bill, or as the measure of applicability of a fiscal or budgetary feature of the bill if, for example it serves to connect the bill's funding to a broader fiscal condition (for example, no funds in the bill to be available during periods in which public debt borrowing increases) without legislating a change in overall fiscal policy such as the public debt limit.

Unless a bill so extensively amends existing law as to open up the entire law to amendment, the germaneness of an amendment to the bill depends on its relationship only to the narrow portion of the law being amended and not to the entire law. Thus an amendment repealing a law is not germane to a bill which amends only a specific portion thereof. Where, however, the pending bill so comprehensively amends an existing law in diverse respects, the entire law may be subject to amendment or repeal. Conversely, where a bill proposes to repeal an entire law, amendments proposing instead to change that law in a manner related to the law are germane. On the other hand, to a bill repealing one narrow subsection of existing law, an amendment comprehensively changing the whole law is not germane.

Where the pending bill incorporates by reference provisions of a law from another committee and conditions the effectiveness of the bill upon actions taken pursuant to that law, an amendment to alter that section of the law may be germane if it is being effectively changed by the bill. A bill extending an existing law may open up the law being extended to germane amendment or to repeal. However, to a bill extending or changing one existing law, an amendment to another law may not be germane. For example the language 'notwithstanding any other provision of law' in an amendment may render it not germane if it has the effect of waiving a statute not amended by the bill.

The fact that so many precedents under each of the tests of germaneness have been documented and distinguished in appropriateness of application is testament both to the different role of the Speaker in the US House from that of his British counterpart, and to the higher level of importance attached to published precedent where a truly non-partisan presiding officer is not entrusted to render non-appealable rulings.

This chapter at page 175 describes the hypothetical application of a relevance principle to amendments tabled in the House of Commons by assuming the pendency of a motion asserting 'That this House believes the moon is made of green cheese'. The first hypothetical amendment: leave out all the words after 'House' and insert 'has no confidence in HM Government's space policy' would likewise be ruled non-germane under US House precedents that a specific proposition cannot be amended by one more general in scope. Under the second amendment, the Chair would have no trouble applying similar precedent that inclusion of 'and planets are' broadens the subject to the entire solar system which is not otherwise referenced in the motion. The argument that the moon shares its make-up with other celestial bodies, while compelling as an astronomical matter, is not broached by the text and cannot be insinuated by inference to be part of that text. The third amendment (blue cheese) and the fourth (red Leicester) would, as in the UK, be ruled germane as confined to the textual matter of the physical composition of the moon, and likely as substitutes for each other if offered in that form rather than as separate amendments to the main motion. Beyond the germaneness rule, however, the Chair might be constrained not to permit the offering of the fourth amendment if the third amendment has already been offered and adopted. As a substitute for a pending third amendment, however, both amendments could be pending at the same time for debate, and would both be voted on regardless of the success of the first vote. If both were adopted, the substitute, rather than the perfecting amendment, would be considered as finally adopted. This is to say that other rules and precedents beyond the germaneness rule govern the order of amendments in the first and second degree, and the effect of the adoption of one amendment on the offering of another, depending upon its form, and will be discussed at greater length in this chapter.

One might then ask whether the permissible range of amendments must be confined to a variety of cheese, or whether other non-cheese substances might be substituted as the suggested geological essence of the moon. If the fundamental purpose of the motion is to discern the true composition of the moon, then amendments suggesting other matter would be germane as confined to that purpose, but amendments suggesting that NASA not travel there because they will be disappointed by what they find would not be in order.

While the fifth amendment 'with holes' would be germane as a further limiting definition of green cheese, there would be no power of selection within the Chair that could, under standing rules and precedent, prevent its being offered and debated. No subjective judgment about its 'limited importance' would be within the purview of the Chair, although a resolution emanating from the Committee on Rules and adopted as a special order of business might make that recommendation.

In contrast to the House practice, there is no general Senate rule prohibiting non-germane amendments, except where cloture has been invoked by three-fifths of the Senate in an effort to limit debate under Senate rule XXII, clause 2, and by law pursuant to title III of the Congressional Budget Act with respect to concurrent resolutions on the budget and budget reconciliation bills. In those limited contexts the presiding officer is called upon to make rulings of germaneness, and appeals from those decisions are decided without debate. Also, questions under 'the defence of germaneness' of legislative amendments to general Appropriation bills are submitted to the Senate without debate under Senate rule XVI, and the Chair does not rule on the question so long as there exists some

House-passed legislative language in the bill being amended to which the Senate amendment might relate (see page 281). On specific occasions, pursuant to unanimous consent agreements, the Senate sometimes prohibits non-germane amendments to particular bills, or may prohibit a certain class of non-germane amendments to a bill. In other unanimous consent orders, the Senate may impose a less precise 'subject-matter' or 'relevance' standard without mentioning germaneness. In this sense, the Senate enters into a unanimous consent contract whereby it promises to bring a measure to a vote in exchange for a promise that the measure to be voted on will consist of known and foreseeable issues. Since it is difficult to know in advance the limits of what proposals might be relevant to a measure, the Senate precedents interpreting germaneness, while not as numerous as in the House, have generally imposed a more restrictive standard than simple relevancy. As in the House, the Parliamentarian's advice on germaneness is accepted as persuasive to the Chair. The Senate Parliamentarian is sometimes called upon to furnish to the leaderships advisory lists of submitted amendments which he considers germane or non-germane (or arguably so) in advance of their being offered, especially in a post-cloture situation where advance filing of amendments is required. In the House, the Parliamentarian is more reluctant to publish advisory opinions in advance of an actual point of order but will render advice to all who inquire.

By statute, under section 305 of the Budget Act, amendments offered in the Senate to concurrent resolutions on the budget must be germane, as must amendments to budget reconciliation bills under section 310 of that Act. As will be discussed at page 228, the Senate and the House have by this law agreed to be bound by expediting procedures where consideration of budgetary targets and implementing legislation in accordance with an annual prescribed timetable becomes essential.

Because the Senate seldom enforces a germaneness requirement absent invocation of cloture, there is a comparative lack of precedent upon which the presiding officer may rely. Riddick's *Senate Procedure* carries approximately ten pages of discussion of the application of a germaneness principle which generally mirror but are not based upon more formally established House precedent. Riddick posits that amendments fall into four classes for determining germaneness. Amendments in the first two classes are considered germane per se. Class one consists of amendments that strike language without inserting other language (in the House such an amendment might be non-germane if having a broadening effect); class two consists of amendments that propose to change numbers and dates; class three consists of non-binding language such as sense of the Senate or Congress provisions if within the jurisdiction of the committee that reported the measure to which offered; and class four amendments that add language to a measure other than as described in classes 2 and 3. The Chair first identifies into which of these four classes an amendment belongs. If an amendment falls within any of the first three classes it will be considered germane. Any other (class 4) amendment is examined on a case-by-case basis to determine whether it adds a new subject matter, whether it expands the powers, authorities or constraints being proposed, whether it amends existing law or another measure, as opposed to the measure before the Senate, whether it involves another class of persons not otherwise covered, or additional administrative entities, is within the jurisdiction of another committee, or is 'foreseeable'. (Senate Parliamentarians may apply tests of germaneness from House precedent, without admitting that they are so reliant.)

Consequently, these tests, together with the lack of an abundance of controlling published precedent, suggest that the Chair will take a relatively mechanical approach such that limiting or restrictive amendments will be germane while expansive or enlarging amendments may not be. On occasion, the Senate has, on appeal, been more willing than the House to overrule the presiding officer's determination of non-germane matter inserted in a conference report beyond the scope of differences, in order to permit a vote on the underlying merits of the proposition. Prior to 2007 the Senate's scope rule limiting matter inserted in conference reports, while very similar to the comparable House rule, had been construed far more broadly as in effect a standard which permitted inclusion of any matter so long as not totally unrelated to some provision in either the House or Senate version. (This standard is discussed in greater detail under conference reports at pages 456–60.) This trend was more apparent in the decades of the 1970s through 1990s than today.

In the culture of the Senate, Senators are anxious to protect their individual prerogatives to offer amendments at any time. Until recent Congresses, where certainty of time and issue has emerged in both Houses as of paramount concern in setting schedules, Senators more frequently challenged the Chair's rulings. This can also be explained by the lack of a Majority (Rules Committee) capability to recommend waivers of points of order to the Senate, all part of the general observation that the Senate is less able than the House to set agendas, absent unanimous consent, by an orderly and predictable majority process. It is commonplace in the Senate for unanimous consent to 'set aside' a pending amendment in order to permit the offering and pendency of an unrelated first degree amendment at a mutually convenient time. This accommodates individual Senator's schedules, especially if their amendments are non-controversial and can be quickly disposed of before debate resumes on the originally pending amendment. Failing that, unanimous consent orders often establish the order of voting on a series of amendments which have 'set aside' previously offered amendments, with brief concluding debates permitted between votes to summarize remaining amendments 'stacked' by such an order of the Senate.

In order to preserve its reputation as the world's 'greatest deliberative body' where every Senator is afforded the opportunity for unlimited debate and amendment, the germaneness rule and the rule of relevancy in debate have not been imposed by the standing Senate rules in ordinary circumstances but only by super-majority cloture votes, by unanimous consent, or pursuant to a statutory exercise in rule-making authority in order to expedite an issue which has a time-sensitive priority.

The lack of a germaneness rule in the Senate has repercussions in the House, as when non-germane amendments are attached to House-passed measures and therefore must be disposed of in the House in order to finalize a legislative measure for presentment to the President. Formerly, a Senate amendment was not subject to the point of order that it was not germane to the House bill, and the Senate could foist an unrelated agenda item on the House for potential disposition as part of a more comprehensive package without it having been considered separately in the House. Today, under changes in House rules adopted in 1972, points of order may be made against non-germane Senate matter in a conference report or in a motion to concur in a Senate amendment with or without amendment. The Speaker is then called upon to apply the germaneness rule by comparing the House-passed measure as a whole to the Senate provision. If sustained, separate votes may be demanded on motions to reject the non-germane portion. The purpose of the 1972 rules change was not to vitiate the Senate's action entirely, but to isolate and permit separate House votes on non-germane portions added in the Senate. Should the House reject any such non-germane portion, the more comprehensive conference report of which it was a part falls and the remaining matter is 'ping-ponged' back to the Senate as a new House amendment. In most recent Congresses, however, this aspect of the House germaneness rule is waived by a special order waiving all points of order against a conference report, and comprehensive conference reports including non-germane Senate provisions are not subjected to separate votes (see page 456.)

The rule that amendments must be germane applies to amendments to motions to re-commit to a committee or to instruct conferees in the House. While a measure being sent to conference is subject to one initial motion to instruct House conferees which must be germane to some provision in the House or Senate version in order to come within the scope of conference, and is the prerogative of the Minority, the test of germaneness of an amendment to the motion to instruct in this context is likewise the relationship of the amendment to the entire subject matter of the House and Senate versions of the bill, and not merely to the original motion to instruct. This is in order to give a Majority of the House the ultimate ability to instruct its conferees on any matter being committed to conference and not merely on the matter chosen by the Minority. Modern tradition in the House suggests, however, that the Majority will not attempt to amend a motion to instruct conferees offered by the Minority, since it is not binding on the conferees such that it must become a necessary insertion into the final measure.

Similarly, a Minority motion to re-commit a bill pending passage in the House, while subject to amendment which must be germane to the bill as a whole and not necessarily to the Minority motion itself, is normally not amended by the Majority. In modern practice, the Majority chooses not to amend the Minority motion—honouring the tradition that the Minority is entitled to one direct vote on its proposal.

Orderliness in debate: relevancy

In Congress, a Member addressing the House must confine himself 'to the question under debate, avoiding personality'. The rule is directed against irrelevant discussion, not mere redundancy. While Jefferson suggests that 'no one is to speak...tediously', the Chair does not enforce this admonition, the hour rule and other time limits being regarded as sufficiently restrictive in that regard. In early Congresses, Speakers held Members strictly to the question before the House without waiting for a point of order from the floor. Under modern practice the Chair rarely calls a Member to order on his own initiative for irrelevant debate, but applies a more liberal latitude of relevance, requiring only the maintenance of an ongoing 'nexus' between the pending measure and broader policy issues rather than an entire focus on the pending matter. On occasion, where a Member intends to speak to an issue totally unrelated to that under consideration, he will seek unanimous consent to proceed 'out of order', and that request is usually granted as a matter of comity.

While debate in the House and in Committee of the Whole under a special order must be relevant to the subject matter under consideration, the Chair does not enforce relevancy on his own initiative, but rather awaits parliamentary inquiries or points of order from the floor. This reluctance on the part of the Chair is in stark contrast to the House of Commons, where more experienced occupants of the Chair take the initiative to call to order on the slightest deviation from the immediately pending question. This tendency is particularly evident during one-hour debates on special orders reported from the Committee on Rules, which at the instigation of the Minority often deviate from their 'nexus'—the measure being made in order—to dwell on unrelated issues as a protest against the agenda-setting prerogatives of the Majority leadership.

In recent years where the Minority has insisted on debating alternative agendas during the pendency of business (especially where that Minority is otherwise prevented from offering alternatives by the Majority's restrictive special orders of business), the Chair has made its position known on relevancy in response to parliamentary inquiries, from which appeals cannot be taken. The Minority often wish to discuss an alternative agenda, sometimes a subject entirely different from that being made in order. (By precedent, when a special order from the Rules Committee is pending, debate must be confined to that special rule and to the merits of the bill made in order thereby, not to the merits of a matter not to be considered.) This irrelevant debate often takes place for up to thirty minutes without a point of order, as the Majority is either comfortable participating on that topic or is concerned about possible delay by way of challenges to the Chair's rulings. So long as the Majority Members will vote in unison to adopt the 'procedural' motion for the previous question at the end of debate on a special order, in order to prevent a non-germane amendment being made in order, the Majority leadership will tolerate superfluous debate as the price for relative certainty in the timing and outcome of the party-line vote on that 'procedural' question.

The Chair's reluctance to take the initiative in calling Members to order for irrelevant or other improper debate can also be explained by the fact that so many different Members (all Majority) serve as Speakers pro tempore. They are not all sufficiently expert at discerning proper order, and are content to rely on points of order from the floor and then on the advice of the non-partisan Parliamentarian in response. This is in marked contrast to the role of the Speaker and Deputy Speakers in the House of Commons, where their expertise and non-partisan role (having eschewed debate and voting) better qualify them to take immediate initiatives to admonish wayward Members (see pages 38–9 for further discussion).

Debate in the Committee of the Whole occurs in two segments. First, 'general debate' is normally confined to the bill (and occasionally to non-germane amendments made in order by the governing special rule). Then, debate under the 'five-minute rule' is confined to an explanation of the pending amendment, and amendments thereto, and their relationship to the underlying bill. Debate on pro forma amendments to 'strike out the requisite number of words' while a substantive amendment is pending must be relevant to the pending amendment, but relevancy is not enforced by the Chair, absent a point of order from the floor. Where a special rule permits only designated amendments to be offered and no amendments thereto, a Member may speak to another subject by unanimous consent. Debate on a preferential motion to strike the enacting clause, offered during the five-minute rule and separately debatable for ten minutes even during the pendency of an amendment, may range to the entire subject of the bill, because the motion itself, unless withdrawn, is a test vote on the viability of the bill during the amendment stage and its adoption can result in re-committal to committee or in rejection of the measure.

At Westminster, the rule that speeches should be relevant to the question before the House must be observed at all times. In the case of the reply to the Gracious Speech at the beginning of a session, when the motion before the House reveals no specific topic, on the first few days debate may range widely; on the final two days, topics are chosen by agreement between the parties and the Chair will restrict Members accordingly, though the motion has not changed!

The occupant of the Chair determines when the rule has been breached, and from his or her ruling there is no appeal. The Chair's attention may be drawn by an individual Member to an alleged breach of order in that respect, but once convinced that something disorderly has occurred, the occupant of the Chair will never wait for prompting from the floor. Scope of debate on motions or amendments to bills is normally quite easy to determine. Scope of debate on a second reading of a bill may range quite widely, to include alternative means of achieving the end of the bill. Perhaps the aspect of the rule which Members find easiest to overlook is that on third reading of a bill, only what is in the bill and not what was left out or amendments not made can be mentioned (see page 443). There as elsewhere the judgment of the Chair is final and openly queried only by the very unwise.

Debate in the Lords must be relevant, as in the Commons, to the question before the House, but the Lord Speaker does not deliver procedural rulings either on her own initiative or in response to an appeal from the floor (see page 40).

Order in debate: discipline

In Congress, the basic rule of the House on calls to order provides that:

> If a Member in speaking or otherwise, transgresses the Rules of the House, the speaker shall, or a Member may, call to order the offending Member, who shall immediately sit down unless permitted on motion to explain... The Member making the call to order shall indicate the words excepted to, which shall be taken down in writing at the Clerk's desk and read aloud to the House. The Speaker shall decide the validity of a call to order. The House, if appealed to, shall decide the question without debate. If the decision is in favour of the Member called to order, the Member shall be at liberty to proceed, but not otherwise. If the case requires it, an offending Member shall be liable to censure or such other punishment as the House may consider proper. A Member may not be held to answer a call to order, and may not be subject to the censure of the House therefore, if further debate or other business has intervened.[19]

The role of the Speaker under this rule seems unambiguous, that he 'shall' call an offending Member to order, but in practice the Chair takes the initiative only in limited circumstances, preferring to await points of order from the floor when Members engage in personalities against other Members in debate. Because the person occupying the Chair is not a full-time non-partisan presiding officer, but rather is a Member of the Majority party selected by the Speaker to perform a non-partisan role for a temporary period from a large pool of Majority Members (the only constraint being that they not be a member of the committee managing the pending measure on the floor), the occupants of the Chair are understandably more reluctant to render rulings on their own initiative. Other Members are presumably present on the floor to initiate proceedings by points of order or parliamentary inquiries. Only with respect to personal references to the President, the Vice President or to a Senator does the Chair normally take the initiative, as Thomas Jefferson suggests in his *Manual* that 'it is the duty particularly of the Speaker to interfere immediately, and not to permit expressions to go unnoticed which may give a ground of complaint to the other House, and introduce proceedings and mutual accusations between the two Houses, which can hardly be terminated without difficulty and disorder'. House standing rules explicitly incorporate Jefferson's *Manual* as part of the practice of the House to the extent not inconsistent with other standing rules and orders.

Jefferson also wrote that in Parliament it was out of order to speak 'irreverently or seditiously against the King'. No analogous constraint exists in the rules of the House, as Members in debate are permitted wide latitude in the use of language that is politically critical of the President and Vice President, so long as not personal in nature. For example, it has been ruled out of order to describe the President as 'cowardly', 'intellectually dishonest', 'a liar', 'a hypocrite' or 'a demagogue'. This standard is established entirely by precedent and has been extended to references to nominated candidates for President or Vice President whether or not incumbents (so as not to permit separate standards of reference depending on current status). Enforcement has been by initiatives by the Chair, much as with respect to Jefferson's standard incorporated as a rule regarding references to the Senate, in order to maintain comity between the two Houses and the two elected branches of government, and based on the assumption that the objects of the personal attacks are not there to defend themselves. Even personal references in debate to any appointed Executive or Judicial officer are tolerated by precedent, as less inimical to maintenance of mutual respect between elected officials. As all other Executive branch officials confirmed by the Senate and all Federal judges are subject to impeachment by the House, it is permissible to discuss their official and personal conduct in debate. With respect to the President and Vice President, during the pendency of an impeachment resolution, it is appropriate to debate the personal conduct of the official whose impeachment is sought. During a Joint Session to receive a message from the President, a personal reference to the President as a liar is a breach of decorum and was in 2009 collaterally challenged by a question of privilege in the House disapproving the improper conduct of a Member.

Senate Rule XIX is very similar to House Rule XVII, one difference being that appeals from the presiding officer's rulings on questions of order are debatable. Ironically, the Senate does not incorporate Jefferson's *Manual* by reference as part of its rules, although written when Jefferson was President of the Senate as Vice President in 1800. Thus the presiding officer is not compelled to call Senators to order when making personal references to Members of the House or to the President, absent a point of order from the floor. Some Senate precedents suggest that egregiously offensive language will be called to order as a breach of propriety, but not as a violation of Senate Rule XIX or any other rule, if a point of order is raised. Political criticisms in Senate debate of the House or its Members, or of the President, Vice President and Executive officials are commonplace and are normally not challenged, suggestive of the wide latitude of debate tolerated in that body. Until 2005, references in debate in the House to the Senate or its Members were proscribed by precedents based on Jefferson's *Manual*. In the 109th Congress, however, clause 1(b) of Rule XVII was amended to provide that 'remarks in debate (which may include references to the Senate or its Members), shall be confined to the question under debate, avoiding personality'. This rules change instantly overrode two centuries of precedent based on the standard stated in Jefferson's *Manual*, and relieved the Chair of the constant responsibility to admonish Members against political criticisms of the Senate or individual Senators. Jefferson's sense that partisan or institutional criticisms of 'the other place' in debate would jeopardize relationships between the two Houses gave way to the modern reality that partisan statements and explanations of activity or inactivity in a bicameral system are aired on or off the Senate and House floors by television in any event and that their interdiction would do little to preserve any remaining comity between the two Houses. The unstated rationale of the rules change, adopted with little fanfare, was the need to legitimize critical references in televised House debate to the Senate and to each Senator, in order to rationalize success or failure, and where critical references to the House and its Members were commonplace in the Senate. Discarded was the need to maintain a higher institutional standard in the House, especially where many House Members coveted election to the Senate and were anxious to make their case in debate to the television audience.

The Chair in both Houses enforces other standards of decorum on his own initiative, as where Members pass between the Chair and the Member under recognition, direct their remarks to the President, the press, the television audience, or refer to occupants of the galleries, or to other Members by their first names. While Members are required to address each other in the third person through the Chair as 'the gentleman or gentlewoman from a particular state', the Chair does not always take the initiative so often taken in the House of Commons to admonish against references in the second person ('you'—as then the Chair becomes the object of the debate) rather than through the Chair to the intended Member as in the third person, often resulting in less orderly debate in the Congress than in Parliament.

Rules regarding general comportment on the House floor prohibit the use of wireless telephone or personal computers (including laptop computers) by any person. That restriction was relaxed in 2003 (at the instigation of leadership staff) from a general prohibition against all electronic devices in order to permit the use of inaudible text messaging which did not constitute computer use. While that medium may be less a breach of decorum than audible and larger devices, the change in the rule opened the door to electronic communications into or out of the chamber in contravention of the tradition that the chamber be considered a 'sanctuary' for Members free of direct contact with outside interests. That loophole in the rule has permitted Members to be regularly distracted, but it reflects the modern reality of electronic communication. The Senate enforces a restriction not part of its standing rules prohibiting all electronic devices, including BlackBerries, out of respect for the sanctity of its proceedings.

Ultimate enforcement of rules of debate and decorum in both Houses is by the whole body, because appeals from the Chair's rulings are explicitly permitted, and may be followed by votes on whether the offensive remarks should remain part of the Record and whether the offending Member should be permitted to proceed in order. Where a Member has exhibited a lack of contrition upon being ruled out of order, the House has on occasion not permitted him to proceed in debate for the remainder of the day. Jefferson mentions the British practice of the Speaker 'naming' a disorderly Member, but the sanctions which include suspension from the Chamber for the remainder of the day, or by vote of the House for a longer period, are not applied beyond the proscription against further participation in debate on that day. House rules do not empower the Speaker to be the ultimate arbiter, but leave it to the House to determine appropriate sanctions. It has been suggested that a suspension from proceedings, by depriving the offending Member (and his constituents) of voting representation for even a brief period, might come up against a constitutional obstacle, although the authority given by Article I to each House to punish its Members for disorderly behaviour would seem to extend to suspensions and in any event could not be collaterally challenged. Nevertheless, the House and Senate have not considered suspension from proceedings an appropriate sanction in modern practice, relying instead on censures, reprimands and other punishments recommended by its ethics committees in addition to contemporaneous proscriptions from participation in debate, all the while protecting Members' voting rights. (See also page 520.)

In practice, the interval between a formal demand that a Member's words be 'taken down'—a sanction once but no longer employed at Westminster—and the actual transcription and reporting of those words to the House (often several minutes) permits the offending Member to request unanimous consent to withdraw the words, if he is informally advised that they will be ruled out of order, or permits the Member making the point of order to withdraw it without a ruling from the Chair if the words are not unparliamentary. That period for negotiation relieves the Chair and ultimately the House of the need to deal with the consequences of a formal ruling. Even in an increasingly partisan atmosphere Members have respected this tradition and have not been willing to deprive the offending Member of continued participation in debate on that day. The motion in the House to permit the offending Member to proceed in order, is normally decided in favour of that Member's continued participation unless he is totally defiant of the ruling of the Chair. The Chair may utilize general words of caution in response to parliamentary inquiries or on his own initiative to quell improper debate, but when the demand that words be taken down is actually pending, will not give anticipatory or hypothetical responses. During a special order speech following legislative business where no further votes (as on non-postponable appeals) are anticipated, the Chair may declare a recess under clause 12(a) of Rule I upon a demand that a Member's words be 'taken down', after denying the offending Member further recognition and forcing him to be seated as required by Rule XVII. The short recess thus declared because no business or recognition is pending at that point avoids an immediate vote on the Chair's ruling while preserving the process for a ruling and appeal upon resumption of proceedings.

In the Committee of the Whole, the Chair can respond to parliamentary inquiries or rule on points of order based on disorderly debate unless they are a specific demand that words be taken down. In that event, the Committee, which has no control over the composition of the Record, rises without motion and reports the offending words to the House, and the Speaker rules on their propriety, subject to a decision of the full House by unanimous consent or on motion to expunge them from the Record and to permit the offending Member to proceed in order.

There is a decided contrast to the House of Commons, where the credibility and traditional stature of a truly non-partisan Speaker and panel of three Deputies who eschew all political activity in the Chair allow them to take initiatives to preserve order, and those initiatives are not subject to challenge by appeal. There are many similarities respecting language which has been considered out of order. For example, an allegation that a Member, Senator or the President has 'misled' the House will be ruled unparliamentary, if intent to deceive is expressed or implied by the context and tone of the debate, whereas unintentional misleading is not grounds for complaint. Charges must be directed at a particular Member or specifically identifiable group (such as the elected Majority leadership), to be actionable. Beyond these similarities, however, a Member called to order in the House of Representatives requires unanimous consent to withdraw or modify his words in order to avoid a ruling by the Chair, while in the Commons the Member's unilateral withdrawal suffices as a display of adequate contrition.

The general rule that words cannot be challenged once there is intervening debate is not applicable regarding personal references to the Speaker. As an additional safeguard to the preservation of institutional decorum, such improper references may be collaterally challenged even if further business is conducted. Whenever any occupant of the Chair is accused of being unfair or having disregarded the rules, and those words are challenged on a point of order, the Chair is turned over to another occupant who would have no conflict of interest in ruling on them. Thus when the Speaker's conduct is a matter of debate, as pending a report from the Committee on Standards of Official Conduct, he appoints a Speaker pro tempore to preside. Another exception from the rule in 2007 permitted a question of privilege to be offered collaterally censuring a Member for prior improper debate constituting ethical misconduct bringing discredit on the House (See Privilege and Contempt, at page 482)

Though at Westminster the rules often read differently from those in Congress, the outcome is surprisingly similar. The scope of the rule governing persons against whom personal charges may not be made in debate is broader at Westminster than in Washington and charges against groups rather than individuals usually escape censure in Parliament, but the principle is the same. A Member will usually be instructed by the Chair to withdraw an improper remark, but he or she does not need general consent to do so.

More significant differences exist in terms of the sanctions usually involved. The majority of punishments nowadays are imposed for breaches of the House's rules concerning standards, and are dealt with in that chapter (page 529). So far as concerns exclusion from the Chamber and the precincts of the Palace of Westminster, the penalties are graded in accordance with the perceived seriousness of the offence. A Member who persists in disorderly conduct or behaves in a grossly disorderly manner may be ordered by the occupant of the Chair, after due warning, to withdraw from the House for the remainder of the sitting. The intervention of the House is not required: this is an authority entrusted by Standing Order to the Chair.

If however the Speaker or Deputy in the Chair[20] thinks that the preservation of the authority and dignity of the House would not be adequately assured by use of that power, he or she may 'name' the offending Member. After sufficient warnings, the occupant of the Chair rises, and pronounces the formula 'I name Mr ...' for grossly disorderly conduct (or disregarding the authority of the Chair, or wilfully obstructing the business of the House by abusing its rules). At that point, the senior minister present will rise—even if the offender sits on the government benches—and move to suspend him or her from the service of the House. The question may not be debated or amended but must be decided at once. An adverse decision by the House implies that the offender will be excluded for five sitting days for a first offence in a session, twenty days for a second, and for any subsequent offences until the end of the session or any earlier order of the House. If force has to be used to remove the Member, the longest of the suspension periods is automatically imposed. A Member suspended does not receive his or her salary, and is not permitted within the precincts of the House during the term of the suspension.

Naming, like expulsion, has its pitfalls. The authority of the occupant of the Chair is very sensitive to the outcome of any division on a motion to suspend a Member. A naming during lightly attended business or at an unexpected time—during the half-hour adjournment at the end of the sitting day when a Member was named for actions not undertaken in his place but in a heated private exchange at the Chair, for example, or when a Member attempted to address the House during prayers—may fail to deliver a large majority in support of the Chair, for reasons which have nothing whatever to do with the offence or the ruling. At the other end of the spectrum, naming during very highly charged party exchanges, which may be when the need is greatest, risks exacerbating feelings across half the House or weakening the authority of the Chair if the House in general feels that the judgment made was harsh or ill advised. There is provision for collective naming of a group of Members who have together defied the Chair, but such occasions in particular have in the past involved the use of force to remove the Members, a circumstance from which the authority of the Chair can only rarely emerge undamaged.

Since 1980-1, twenty-nine Members have been ordered by the Speaker to withdraw from the Chamber because their conduct has been grossly disorderly, and sixteen have been named and suspended for the same offence. Over the same period, twenty-four Members have been named and suspended for disregarding the authority of the Chair, or persistently and wilfully obstructing the business of the House. Force has not been used to remove a Member since 1931, and the last time the Serjeant at Arms was called on to remove a Member was in 1981. Given the sometimes tumultuous character of the Commons, these figures are relatively modest. None recently can boast the nineteenth-century record of John Redmond, later the leader of the Irish party, who took his seat, made his maiden speech and was named—all in the course of a single sitting.

If, as happens rarely nowadays, there is uproar in the House and it is impossible to continue debate, though no individual Member or Members are the obvious culprits—when relations between the parties have broken down, for example—the Chair has power to suspend or adjourn the House. In most cases, the exercise of the power permits a time-out, when tempers cool and wiser heads bear down on those with short fuses.

The Lord Speaker has no armoury of disciplinary provisions to deal with unruly behaviour. The tone is set in the Lords by a Standing Order deploring 'all personal, sharp or taxing speeches', but the only procedural recourse the House has against a speech which transgresses the usual canons of proper behaviour is a motion 'That the noble Lord be no longer heard,' which understandably is a rarity. There is no individual authority in the Lords—save the government minister who is Leader of the Lords in an advisory way, and the House itself in the last resort—which can declare a motion or amendment disorderly, far less a power of selection. The House expects that Lords ought in these matters to accept the advice of the Clerks.

Dilatory motions

The purpose of a dilatory motion is, as the term suggests, to put off a decision on a matter under discussion.

At Westminster, adjournment motions may fall into the category of dilatory motion. Even though there is already a question before the House (but, unlike closure, not when another Member has the floor) a Member may offer a motion to supersede it in the form, 'That this House do now adjourn,' 'That the debate be now adjourned,' or (when a bill is before the House) 'That further consideration of the bill [or the Lords Amendments] be now adjourned'.[21] The forms of the motion are fixed: no elaboration in the terms of the motion, for example explaining why this course of action is desirable or fixing a date for the resumption of the debate or the sitting is permitted. The occupant of the Chair must then decide whether or not to give his or her consent to the making of the motion. If the Chair considers the dilatory motion an abuse of the rules of the House, he or she may either decline to propose the question or put it forthwith without debate: the former is much the more usual of the two.

A dilatory motion which clears these hurdles will usually raise some unexpected happening of significance to the current debate or of first importance politically. For example, in 1995, when the then Prime Minister suddenly resigned not as head of government but as leader of his party and stood for re-election, the Palace of Westminster was buzzing with and puzzled by the news. It seemed strange that the one place where it could not be raised was the floor of the Commons, where the debate happened to be on the third reading of the Crown Agents Bill. The Chair however permitted a dilatory motion to be made, Members were able to enquire of the government what was going on, and after a reasonable period, the Chair accepted a closure motion. Closure being agreed to, the motion to adjourn was negatived without a division, the temperature dropped, and the House returned to the original debate.

The previous question, which figures so prominently in Congressional procedure, is a great rarity at Westminster, and has made an appearance in living memory only in the course of private Members' business or on a motion for the issue of a writ for a by-election. The previous question is moved after a debate has begun, and is put for decision in the form 'That the question be not now put'.[22] If agreed to, the original question goes off to another day appointed by the Member in charge of the business to which it relates. If the previous question is negatived, the original question must be put immediately.

Like other dilatory motions, the previous question may be moved only by a Member who has the floor. The previous question attracts a number of other restrictions. It is out of order in Committee; it cannot be moved when an amendment is before the House; and it cannot itself be amended, though it can be subject to closure.

In Congress, Speaker Thomas B. Reed in 1890 described a pending parliamentary situation 'during the last few days' wherein 'the ordinary and proper parliamentary motions were being used solely for purposes of delay and obstruction...when a gentleman steps down to the front, amid the applause of his associates on the floor, and announces that it is his intention to make opposition in every direction, it then becomes apparent to the House and to the community what the purpose is'. In that context, Speaker Reed ruled a motion to adjourn to be dilatory, declaring that 'the object of a parliamentary body is action, and not stoppage of action'. This ruling, made in the face of the rule giving the motion to adjourn the highest priority of any motion in either House, was supported on appeal by a vote of 163—0 where the opposition did not vote but a quorum was present. Thereupon the House adopted the current rule (clause 1 of Rule XVI) that 'a dilatory motion may not be entertained by the Speaker'. Thirteen years later in 1903 Speaker Joseph Cannon went even further, after ruling a series of motions to be dilatory, by declining to permit any debate on or appeal from his ruling, declaring that 'the very object of the rule would be defeated if a motion to appeal were entertained'.

While the rule against dilatory motions remains in place today, contemporary Speakers have not exercised that discretion in the face of delaying motions over the course of a legislative day, aware that other points of order and questions of privilege remain available and appealable to a Minority intent on obstruction should the Chair rule a particular motion to be dilatory. Specious points of order, for example, against words spoken in debate as being unparliamentary could intervene on a regular basis, and could provoke appeals upon being overruled, resulting in the same amount of delay as would a continuing use of dilatory motions. While Speaker Reed's landmark ruling on dilatoriness, premised on the importance of legislative action over the stoppage of action, remains symbolically important as justification for expeditious conduct of business by the Majority, contemporary Speakers have been cautioned against its utilization premised on the availability of other procedural options. This reluctance, coupled with the Chair's more recently acquired authority to declare short recesses and to utilize special orders from the Rules Committee to restrict dilatory motions, have all combined in modern practice to minimize the discretionary declaration that a motion is dilatory.

The only constraint against the use of dilatory motions in the Senate is stated in Rule XXII to the effect that once cloture is invoked by a vote of three-fifths of the Senate, dilatory motions and amendments are not then in order. The decision of the presiding officer in this post-cloture posture that a motion is dilatory is not subject to appeal, and an appeal from any other ruling in that circumstance is not debatable. The Senate has at its disposal the motion to lay on the table, often an effective tool against the proliferation of amendments.

Limitations and time limits

The fundamental parliamentary sequence of motion–amendment–decision is not always assured in the procedures of the US House, although a presumption in favour of some form of an amendment process prior to final disposition is imbedded in the standing rules and until recent Congresses has been, with few exceptions, a traditional expectation. Under some circumstances there might not be a triggering motion, but rather a declaration of the Chair, to bring a matter under consideration. Original or main motions are generally intended to set the stage for an amendment process, to enable the body to perfect the matter under consideration prior to its final disposition. To that end, the standing rules of the House assume, but do not guarantee, that an amendment stage will intervene between initial consideration and disposition. Rule XVIII, clause 3 provides that all public bills, resolutions or Senate amendments 'involving a charge on the people, raising revenue, directly or indirectly making appropriations of money or property or requiring such appropriations to be made, authorizing payments out of appropriations already made, releasing any liability to the United States for money or property, or referring a claim to the Court of Claims, shall be first considered in the Committee of the Whole House on the state of the Union'. A measure that fails to comply with this clause is subject to a point of order against its consideration. The purpose of the clause is to assure that most public measures (which directly or indirectly involve some charge on the people, expenditure of funds or disposition of property) be initially considered under a process which assures the chance for amendment by all Members. The 'five-minute rule' implementing that assumption permits germane first-degree amendments, second-degree amendments thereto, substitute amendments therefor and amendments to substitutes, to be debated with five minutes allotted to each Member recognized to amend or to speak to an amendment. The general purpose of this rule is to assure the participation of more Members on most legislation under limited debate conditions (five minutes rather than one hour as in the full House), but under procedures where the intervening motions to adjourn, to lay on the table, for the previous question, to postpone and to refer, are not applicable. Because those motions are only in order in the full House, such intervening motions to prevent amendments from being offered in the Committee of the Whole are not in order. This maximizes Member participation in the amendment process before final disposition in the full House, where those motions again become available.

In contemporary Congresses the House has restricted individual Members from full participation under the five-minute rule in the Committee of the Whole, at first selectively only on tax and tariff measures during much of the twentieth century. By the 109th and into the 110th Congress, these restrictions have extended on an ad hoc basis to virtually every important measure, through the utilization of special orders reported from the Committee on Rules. Because such special orders supersede standing rules once adopted, and may be reported from the Committee on Rules on a daily basis, they have had the pervasive effect of minimizing amendment opportunities—a reversal of tradition on virtually all major measures which had come to be expected as 'regular order' in the first 200 years of procedure in the House.

Where a measure is not considered in a Committee of the Whole, but rather is considered 'in the House' under the hour rule, (as for example, the procedure under 'general parliamentary law' prior to adoption of the rules described above) only one Member is initially recognized to manage the measure and he may move the previous question to prevent further debate and amendment. For this reason the motion for the previous question is among the most essential tools available to the Majority in the House to prevent further debate and amendment and to proceed to votes on final disposition of the underlying measure or matter. In that circumstance, the priority to amend is reversed and the House must first reject the motion for the previous question so as to permit recognition of another Member to offer an amendment to and continue debate on the pending measure. The same restriction on the right to offer an amendment exists where a typical special rule reported from the Committee on Rules and adopted by the House 'orders the previous question on the pending measure to final passage or adoption without intervening motion except one motion to re-commit with or without instructions'. In that event, ordinary amendments are precluded in the House and the Minority is left to one amendment or other procedural option in the form of a motion to re-commit. This Minority party motion cannot be denied by the Rules Committee pending initial final passage of a bill in the House, but must be germane and otherwise conform to standing House rules (for example, the motion may not constitute a change in standing rules). A sampling of standing rules and orders in Parliaments over the world suggests that this protection of a minority right to amend or to propose return to committee pending a vote on final passage is a unique parliamentary procedure not assured in most legislative bodies.

Motions to suspend the rules are in order if recognized at the Speaker's discretion at least Monday through Wednesday of every week, and normally include passage of a measure as part of the motion. No intervening motions, including amendments and motions to re-commit, are in order pending that motion other than amendments included in the motion itself ('I move to suspend the rules and pass the bill H.R....as amended'). Because such motions are not separately amendable, and have limited (forty-minute) debate, they require a two-thirds vote of the Members voting, a quorum being present, for adoption.

In standing committees, as discussed in greater detail at page 409, the process is described as 'the House as in Committee of the Whole', where the five-minute rule is utilized for debate and amendment purposes but where intervening motions, particularly the motion for the previous question, are sometimes in order to enable the Majority to cut off amendments. While committees are not free to use motions to suspend the rules or to adopt special orders which restrict the rights of individual Members to offer germane amendments, the utilization of the motion for the previous question may prevent amendments. Generally speaking, procedures utilized during mark-ups in standing committees more often honour the importance of the amendment process than do modern procedures in the contemporary plenary sessions of the House, if only because committees are not free to depart from standing rules and practices which favour the amendment process, except by unanimous consent.

In the Senate, the presumption in favour of amendment prior to final disposition is virtually guaranteed unless the Senate has by unanimous consent or by operation of law restricted the offering of amendments. The Senate prides itself as being the 'world's greatest deliberative body', theoretically permitting unlimited debate and amendment under most circumstances. Even when cloture is invoked, amendments may be offered to the underlying proposition for up to thirty hours if germane, with 100 hours of debate permitted on the entire bill. Because the Senate has no rule permitting a majority vote to curtail amendments, it must rely on the motion to table when wishing to adversely dispose of an amendment on an ad hoc basis once pending, without further debate. This distinction between the two Houses is basic to an understanding of their essential differences, as is a requirement for germaneness or relevance of amendments.

Standing rules, statutes, special orders from the Rules Committee and unanimous consent orders all contribute to the essential need to impose temporal limits on debates in the US House, usually by a number of minutes rather than to a time certain by the clock. As well, motions to end debate in the House—the motion for the previous question, or in the Committee of the Whole to limit debate on a pending portion of a bill and/or on a pending amendment and all amendments thereto—are frequently utilized to terminate debate after it has begun and no finite limit has been established in advance. Recognition for those limiting motions is normally the prerogative of the manager of the bill. Only on certain interlocutory questions, such as debates on points of order, is the duration of debate within the discretion of the Chair. In addition, the number of one-minute speeches at the beginning of a legislative day, although not the length of each speech beyond one minute (the Speaker will not entertain unanimous consent to extend beyond one-minute, one-hour, or five-minute special orders) is within the discretion of the Speaker. The Chair monitors the time of Members who participate, and his announcement is not subject to challenge. By recent tradition, time allocated in debate to the Speaker, Majority and Minority Leaders in the House is not governed by a monitor from the Chair, as 'additional latitude' for time is extended to them and, although sometimes abused, is not subject to collateral challenge.

There exist various motions to prevent any debate on matters coming before the House by preventing their consideration altogether, such as the motion to lay on the table or the question of consideration which themselves are not debatable. If a measure is under consideration and the motion for the previous question is ordered on a matter on which there has been no debate, there is permitted forty minutes of debate on the underlying proposition. This guarantee can be circumvented by allowing a brief amount of debate to proceed before the motion is made. In practical terms, the ordering of the previous question prior to the expiration of Minority or opposition debate is circumvented either because the standing rules guarantee opposition debate time or the motion is not in order until time yielded to the Minority for its control is consumed or yielded back.

On major bills, a special rule typically specifies the length of time for general debate, usually a number of hours, and identifies the Members by chair and ranking Minority status of a managing committee, to control that time. If a bill or resolution comes to the House without such a time limit, the general hour rule in the House[23] applies to limit the time for debate to one hour per Member, which debate may be terminated by adoption of the motion for the previous question.

The duration of debate under a reservation of objection to a unanimous consent request is at the sufferance of the House, as any Member may at any time 'demand the regular order' to terminate debate which has been controlled by the Member who has first been recognized to reserve the right to object to the pending request. At that point, the Chair is required to put to the House the unanimous consent request, and no further reservation of objection is permitted. Traditionally, while any Member may discontinue debate on a unanimous consent request, much tolerance toward extended debate is exhibited in the House under reservations of objection, both in order to permit the manager making a unanimous consent business request to accomplish a complete explanation of the matter to be considered, and to obviate subsequent duplicative debate on the measure itself if the unanimous consent request is granted. It is important to distinguish between unanimous consent orders which result in the disposition of the underlying measure, and those which merely permit subsequent consideration under defined debate and amendment limits.

In the House of Representatives, proceedings in a Committee of the Whole House on the state of the Union are governed by House standing rules and orders, special orders and unanimous consent orders, and additionally by unanimous consent orders or motions adopted in Committee of the Whole where not inconsistent with House rules or orders. Thus where the House has set limits on the duration of debate, the Committee of the Whole may not by motion extend or further limit that debate, but may by unanimous consent permit extensions of debate on amendments so long as congruent with allocations ordered by the House. For example, where the House has equally divided debate on amendments between proponents and opponents, unanimous consent to extend or further limit that debate in Committee of the Whole must allocate time equally to both sides. Such changes, including requests for a proponent to control time allocated to an opponent where no Member qualifies as being opposed, are viewed as de minimis variations which do not fundamentally alter the debate scheme imposed by the House and have been tolerated by precedent. In all events, managers controlling time during general debate or on amendments may yield back the balance of their time, thereby shortening debate.

Where the House has not limited debate time on amendments, precedent limits the number of times each Member can be recognized under the five-minute rule, but not the overall duration of debate. Those limits are left to be imposed by the Committee of the Whole, either by unanimous consent or by motion. The Committee can impose virtually any limit on amendment debate, either by number of minutes or by the clock, and may allocate control between or among Members. A motion to limit amendment debate is itself undebatable, may only apply to the pending portion of the measure, amendments and amendments thereto, but may not allocate time. A limitation once imposed may not be rescinded or modified except by unanimous consent. When debate on an amendment is limited by motion, but control is not allocated, the Chair has the discretion to allocate time between a proponent and an opponent for them to yield, to recognize all Members standing at the time of the limitation in order to divide the remaining time equally among them, or to proceed under the five-minute rule. In modern practice, the allocation between two managers has proven more efficient in shifting responsibility away from the Chair and on to managers in micro-managing remaining time. As a general matter, the contemporary expectation for certainty in time is pervasive throughout the membership and suggests that the House and the Committee of the Whole will normally impose time limits on amendments enough in advance of their actually being offered to accommodate individual Members' schedules.

In ordinary legislative debates in the Senate,[24] debate is limited primarily by unanimous consent orders, there being no motion such as the previous question by which a majority of the Senate can terminate debate. Under various statutory schemes, the Senate has imposed debate limitations on certain measures where it is considered necessary to expedite consideration and to avoid 'filibusters' thereon. Most notable in this joint exercise of rule making has been the Congressional Budget Act, where debates on concurrent resolutions on the budget and on budget reconciliation bills are limited to a finite number of hours, obviating the need to invoke cloture by a three-fifths vote of Senators.

Beyond unanimous consent orders and statutory limitations, however, the Senate proudly adheres to the protection of its traditions of unlimited debate. When an amendment is pending, any Senator may offer the non-debatable motion to lay that matter on the table. That motion is normally employed when the Majority wishes to end debate on a pending amendment immediately, or to avoid a direct vote on the amendment.

Otherwise, only rule XXII is available to permit a super-majority of the Senate—three-fifths of all Senators, or two-thirds if on a motion to close debate on a measure containing an amendment to Senate standing rules—to bring unlimited debate on a pending matter to an eventual close and to trigger remaining consideration (not merely debate) under prescribed time and germaneness limitations. Specifically, rule XXII requires a cloture petition (signed by at least sixteen Senators) to be presented to the Senate. Two days later, and one hour after the Senate convenes, the presiding officer is required to order a live quorum call and, after its completion, to put this question to the membership: 'Is it the sense of the Senate that debate shall be brought to a close?' If sixty Senators vote in the affirmative, cloture is invoked and the Senate is subject to post-cloture procedures that will eventually end the debate and bring the pending clotured question—a bill, amendment or motion, or a confirmation—to a vote. If a matter is not pending or unfinished business, a cloture petition cannot be filed as an anticipatory matter. Those post-cloture features include a thirty-hour time cap on further consideration of the clotured question, with time used for roll-call votes or quorum calls, reading of amendments and points of order charged against the cap. The thirty-hour period may be extended by unanimous consent or if three-fifths of all Senators agree to the increase. Under cloture, each Senator is entitled to an hour of debate on a 'first come, first served' basis, subject to the overall thirty-hour limit. Senators may yield all or portions of their one hour to a floor manager or a party leader but neither may be yielded more than two additional hours. Any Senator may yield back to the Chair some or all of his one hour but that would not reduce the total time available for consideration of the clotured matter. In practice, post-cloture procedures are often collapsed well below the thirty-hour limit and unanimous consent arrangements for distribution of remaining time and amendment are adopted, the Senate having symbolized by a super-majority vote its willingness to expedite subsequent consideration on the pending matter (as by the Majority Leader having 'filled the amendment tree') and having removed the political incentive for further delay.

Only amendments that have been filed before the cloture vote may be considered once cloture is invoked. If a large number of amendments are timely filed, they may only be offered during the thirty-hour time frame, and even though germane, may not be offered following that terminating time. This restriction on the consideration of amendments post cloture is to be distinguished from a comparable twenty-hour period of debate on budget reconciliation bills under section 310 of the Budget Act (discussed at pages 234, 239), where germane amendments may be offered following expiration of the time period but are decided without debate (the so-called 'vote-o-rama' process of potential filibuster by amendment where the amendments do not have to be filed in advance).

Under cloture, first-degree amendments must be filed by 1pm on the day after the filing of the cloture motion, and second-degree amendments may be filed until at least one hour prior to the start of the cloture vote. The presiding officer takes on authority not otherwise available during ordinary Senate proceedings, such as rulings of dilatoriness and the actual count for a quorum. All amendments and debate are to be germane to the clotured proposal, and the Chair may take the initiative in this regard. Points of order and appeals therefrom are decided without debate.

As a general matter, it is important to document the increased use of cloture petitions to bring pending matters to an up-or-down vote, not merely as originally utilized to close off actual 'filibusters' where individual Senators are refusing to relinquish the floor. The procedure is also used to test the viability of matters which are pending but upon which actual debate may not have begun or has become prolonged. Cloture procedures have not only been invoked more frequently in modern Senate practice to terminate actual debate which may have begun on a wider variety of measures, but also by the leadership to signal strength on the motion to proceed, to reduce the bargaining position—often on other matters—of those individual Senators threatening filibusters to influence other scheduling, or to impose an immediate germaneness requirement against amendments before they are offered, failing unanimous consent.

A marked increase in attempts to invoke cloture has characterized recent Congresses. For example, the decade 1961–71 saw 5.2 cloture votes per Congress, whereas during the 107th Congress (2001–3) alone, there were sixty-one cloture votes. The number of cloture petitions filed on the Majority Leader's motion to proceed to consideration of legislation or nominations increased from only two motions filed during the 96th Congress (1979–81) to thirty-five cloture petitions filed during the 102nd Congress (1991–3).

When a filibuster occurs or is threatened, a cloture motion to terminate debate on a contested matter may be filed. The vote on that motion cannot occur until two days after it is filed. Cloture could be required up to six separate times on a single bill since it cannot be invoked one time on all legislative stages if not yet pending. Those six stages may include the motion to proceed to the bill, on the committee substitute, on the bill itself, and then three times to get to conference with the House—on the motions (1) to insist on Senate amendments or disagree to House amendments; (2) to request a conference with the House; and (3) to authorize the Chair to appoint conferees. In all cases, if a three-fifths vote is not forthcoming or predictable to limit debate at any of these stages, the measure can be displaced by recognition of the Majority Leader to request unanimous consent to proceed to other matter or to proceed 'as in morning hour' on other business. The Majority Leader, being guaranteed the right of first recognition, has on occasion moved to proceed to a controversial measure's consideration, has then immediately filed a cloture petition on that motion, and then withdrawn the motion to proceed so as to go on to other business, while setting the vote on the cloture motion at a predictable time two days hence, in order to negotiate support for its consideration, even before knowing of the likelihood of a filibuster on that measure.

Another extreme use of cloture by the Majority Leader in recent Congresses (utilized in equal manner by Majority Leaders of both parties) has involved the 'filling of the amendment tree' when a controversial measure is pending. By relying on the primacy of recognition, the Majority Leader may be first recognized to offer a first-degree amendment to a pending bill. He may then ask for the ordering of the yeas and nays on that amendment, as the first step to prevent modifications by other Senators. The ordering of the yeas and nays is considered under Senate precedent to be action on the first amendment, such that he may then offer a second-degree amendment to his own

first amendment, thereby offering the final degree of amendment permitted to be pending at one time and 'filling the amendment tree'. (In contrast to the House, Senators are
permitted to amend their own amendments or to modify them without unanimous consent after the yeas and nays are ordered.) While the Majority Leader's amendments are
pending, he may then file a cloture motion—not merely on his pending amendments but
effectively on the entire pending bill if the pending first-degree amendment is in the
nature of a substitute (often a committee substitute) which would rewrite the entire bill.
This motion, if adopted two days hence by a three-fifths vote, imposes a subsequent
germaneness requirement as well as the overall thirty-hour germane amendment and
100-hour debate limitation on the entire bill (much or all of which can then be consumed
on the Majority Leader's pending first- and second-degree amendments) and has the
effect of curtailing the offering of subsequent amendments by any other Senator to any
part of the bill (including motions to re-commit with instructions to amend which would
otherwise take precedence over amendments). This combination of procedures represents
the ultimate tool at the Majority Leader's disposal to expedite consideration of a measure in the Senate. It has resulted in a marked tendency for the House and Senate to
'ping-pong' amendments between the two Houses rather than to establish conference
committees, partially to avoid multiple filibusters on the various stages required in the
Senate to send a matter to conference.[25]

In sum, the cloture rule reflects the super-majoritarian nature of the Senate, without
the invocation of which each Senator is assured greater flexibility than Representatives
in the House to offer amendments, whether or not germane, and to debate measures
without time limits unless they are imposed by unanimous consent, by statutory limitations, or by non-debatable motions to table amendments once pending. Only the combination of the invocation of cloture and the 'filling of the amendment tree' by the Majority
Leader can have the ultimate effect of permitting the Senate to accomplish the equivalent of adoption of the motion for the previous question, to shut off further debate and
amendment in order arrive at an eventual majority vote on the underlying proposition.
In recognition of the modern reality that the Senate requires sixty votes to do its business, unanimous consent requests which impose a super-majority requirement on the
adoption of amendments, not merely on closing debate thereon, have been utilized in lieu
of the full invocation of the rule in order to set predictable debate periods and voting
times while not departing from the sixty-vote threshold.

There never seems to be enough time for every Member who wishes to address the
House of Commons to do so at the length he or she would wish. A report from the
Modernisation Committee[26] recently recorded the frustration of some newer Members
at never knowing for certain whether or when their patience in sitting for hours in the
Chamber would be rewarded. Though the practice of according priority in debate to
Privy Counsellors has been abandoned, there was still believed to be a bias in favour
of senior Members. A different perspective was given by the Chairman of Ways and
Means. His experience was that occasions when too many Members wished to speak
than could be fitted into the time available were 'increasingly sparse...the opposite
was the case, as whips tried to find people to speak in debates to fill up the time available'. The Committee reconciled the two points of view by concluding that the few
occasions when debates were oversubscribed were probably those that mattered most
to Members.

Figures based on session 2005–6 were produced for the Committee indicating that back-bench Members might expect to be called in the Chamber between three and five times a session, with Opposition backbenchers doing slightly better than those on the government side. On average backbenchers spoke for about thirteen minutes (constrained no doubt by speech limits; see below).

There has been since 1988 a procedure which allows the Commons Speaker to limit the time available to individual Members when there are more requests to speak than can be fitted into the time likely to be available, thus abbreviating speeches but increasing the number of speakers. Whether or not compression of their arguments positively concentrates or renders less coherent Members' contributions, the rule has gained acceptance, balancing the natural wish of individual Members to deploy their arguments at adequate length with that of their many colleagues waiting to speak who see the minutes rushing by and the moment of interruption looming. The rule provides that the Speaker may announce a time limit on all contributors to debate or on contributions between certain times. Ministers, Opposition spokesmen, and one Member speaking for the second largest Opposition party are excepted, unless the Speaker limits them to twenty minutes. If necessary, the Chair can withdraw or vary the time limit as debate progresses. There is provision for 'injury time' if Members accept interventions.

Whether in the shadow of the moment of interruption (page 157) or any other case in which a Member considers that the House should come to a decision, he or she may move, even breaking into the speech of a colleague, 'That the Question be now put'. The effect of carrying the motion will be to bring the House at once to a decision, though the debate has not been concluded. The Chair has absolute discretion whether to put the question for closure to the House. If the motion seems to be an abuse of the rules of the House or infringes the rights of the minority, the Chair will withhold assent without further explanation and the debate must go on. For that reason government whips may sometimes be seen privately consulting the Chair in advance about the likely acceptability of a closure motion—often to jeers from Opposition Members who are well aware of what is afoot. If the Chair is prepared to put the question to the House, not only must the proposal command a majority in the lobbies in order to take effect, but at least one hundred Members must vote in the majority. The hurdles of the consent of the Chair and the enhanced majority ensure that a balance is struck between progress and delay—the government (and it is mostly the government which takes advantage of the procedure) gets its business in reasonable time, but the rights of the minority are not abused, despite the cries of horror, some real, some affected, which may greet the moving of the closure.

Though the closure procedure exists in the Lords, its use is exceptional. Before the Lord Speaker puts the motion 'That the Question be now put' she informs the House that it will not be accepted 'save in circumstances where is it felt to be the only means of ensuring the proper conduct of the business of the House'.

Points of order, parliamentary inquiries, and appeals

In the House of Commons, the occupant of the Chair is the custodian of the procedure of the House and in particular the protector of backbenchers. He or she will intervene in debate, if necessary, to remind the House of the scope of debate on the matter before it, to reprove any departure from the rules or conventions of debate. In addition, however, any Member may at any time, even during a division if the matter arises from the conduct of the division, rise on a point of order to ask for the ruling of the Chair or to urge the Speaker to take up a matter alleged to be of legitimate and important concern to the House. The Chair will normally reply substantively as soon as a point of order has been raised. If necessary, he or she will defer an answer if all the facts of the case need to be inquired into.

Sometimes points of order arise from genuine puzzlement about exactly what the House is currently doing and why it needs to do it. These receive a full answer from the occupant of the Chair. Some—it cannot be denied, though they are far fewer than once they were—are bogus, raised by Members frustrated at their inability to participate in the past or current debate. Others are the vehicle for political point-scoring across the Chamber. Quite often, the point of order is genuine enough in intention but the answer does not lie within the responsibility of the Chair, or has in regard a problem which, at the time the point of order is raised, is no more than hypothetical.

Within limits, bogus points of order are put up with. After all, they must be heard before they can be perceived to be bogus. They are understandable enough when they are outlets for frustration, and at worst they may be simply irregular contributions to debate. A particularly difficult situation arises when points of order multiply on a single topic, despite the Chair having answered the original query or having made clear that the matter at issue is not one for him. In that situation, points of order have become a weapon in inter-party hostilities, and the task of the Chair—to know how far to let them run and when to refuse to hear any more—is a very difficult one. Both action and inaction may give rise to suspicions of partisanship. For example, in 1972, when it became clear that the rules of the House would permit only limited amendment of the bill to provide for the UK's becoming a member of the (then) European Economic Community, the official Opposition kept points of order going through the night. The patience and stamina of all concerned—especially the occupants of the Chair—were severely tested, though in retrospect it is generally recognized that the tactic was not unreasonable in the circumstances. But when limited time for serious debate is eaten into by frivolous, obstructive or self-regarding points of order, the Chair's authority is robustly deployed.

In Congress, the rationale of the point of order is sometimes narrower and sometimes broader than in Parliament. The role of the Chair is established in Rule I, clause 5 which states that the Speaker decides 'all questions of order, subject to appeal by a Member, Delegate or Resident Commissioner'. Questions of order are raised by points of order or their equivalent, or are initiated by the Chair in some circumstances. Ordinarily the Chair will rule out a proposition only when a point of order is raised and only when he is required under the circumstances to respond to the point of order. It is not the duty of the Chair to decide any question that is not directly presented in the course of the proceedings of the House. In another segment on disorder in debate, the Chair's initiative (by mandate of Jefferson's *Manual* and by precedent) is discussed relating to the call to order of a Member who engages in improper references to the actions to the Senate, to Senators, or to the President or Vice President. Rule XVII, clause 4 requires the Chair to call to order any Member who transgresses the rules of decorum and debate, and also invites any other Member to make that call to order. While the rule would seem to impose a mandatory duty on the Chair at all times, in practice the Chair's initiatives are confined to improper debate references to the Senate, the President or Vice President, the gallery, or the television audience, or to infringements of decorum.

The Chair may decline to rule on a point of order until he has had time for examination, and he may in his discretion hear argument on any point of order. Such debate must be confined to the point of order and may not go to the merits of the underlying proposition. As debate is totally within the discretion of the Chair, Members may not yield to each other, may not revise their arguments for the Record, and must be separately recognized by the Chair, who may decline further recognition when ready to rule.

In contrast with the House of Commons, points of order in the US House and Senate are made during the pendency of a measure or matter, and not separately for the Chair to rule upon as an anticipatory matter, or in response to a past proceeding unless relevant to pending business. The use of the term 'point of order' in the House of Commons is extremely broad, and often is a statement relating to a minister's responsibility to Parliament, to the fairness of business motions already adopted, or to some other political sentiment, upon which the Speaker cannot rule. Yet the Speaker often tolerates the statement of a 'point of order' to enable Members to get matters on the record for the attention of Ministers.

In the Congress, a point of order must ordinarily be based on the assertion that the pending matter violates some rule of the House or Senate. As at Westminster, the Chair will not make anticipatory or hypothetical rulings, nor put procedural issues in a historical context, either in response to a point of order or a 'parliamentary inquiry'. In part, this is because those are matters better discussed in debate. The occupant of the Chair is often not a procedural expert to the extent that the British Speaker and his Deputies are. For that same reason, the Chair seldom initiates rulings on the relevancy of debate, or on personal references to other House Members, preferring to await points of order from the floor. Of course, the Chair will take the initiative as suggested in Jefferson's *Manual* to preserve order and decorum in the House where there are inappropriate references to the President or to the Senate, persons not present to defend themselves.

The Chair is barred by rule and practice from entertaining unanimous consent requests to waive or suspend certain rules, including Constitutional requirements (for example, for the yeas and nays or a majority requirement for a quorum for business) because the House, while constitutionally free to make its own (additional) rules, cannot waive provisions of the Constitution which themselves constitute the most basic rules of the body. Also, rules on admission to the floor or references to persons in the gallery may not by their terms be waived, even by unanimous consent, and are thus always enforceable on the Chair's initiative or on points of order from the floor. Otherwise the House may by proper means—by unanimous consent, by special order, by a motion to suspend the rules, or by forbearance or a lack of timeliness—waive any point of order which would otherwise inhibit the consideration of a measure or matter.

Points of order may be raised against the consideration of a measure or matter, or against a portion of a pending measure, based on a specific rule of the House or Senate which prohibits its consideration or inclusion. Examples of points of order against consideration include violations of rules requiring availability and inclusion of certain matter in accompanying reports, or provisions of law which enable points of order against consideration of certain bills, resolutions, amendments or conference reports. Generally such points of order must be raised when the measure or matter is first called up for consideration, and come too late after consideration has begun (in distinction from practice at Westminster, where if it appears after debate has begun that an amendment or a new clause offered to a bill is out of order, the chairman will withdraw it from the consideration of the committee). Examples of points of order against provisions within measures, which must be made when those offending provisions are separately being read, include legislation or unauthorized items in reported general appropriation bills, appropriations in legislative bills, and tax or tariff provisions in bills not reported from the committee on Ways and Means. Points of order against non-germane amendments must be raised or reserved when the amendment is first being considered, and come too late following some debate on the amendment. The underlying notion that points of order, while presumptively necessary to assure regular order in the House, may be waived if not made or reserved at the outset of consideration, incorporates the principle of laches. It assures that the time of the House will not be wasted on objectionable matter, by requiring that objections must be disposed of as consideration begins, while also requiring the Member raising the point of order to be on his feet seeking recognition at that moment. That requirement is embodied in the rule that objectionable debate must be challenged immediately upon utterance, before any subsequent debate intervenes. By precedent, the timeliness of points of order on most other matters is similarly confined to the moment of initial consideration. In furtherance of this principle, where by unanimous consent a portion of a general appropriation bill is, for example, considered as read and open to amendment at any point, the Chair queries for points of order against any of the pending portion before entertaining amendments, so that the text of the measure to be amended is known to the Committee of the Whole before amendments have been offered. As a protection against the need to immediately rule on points of order against amendments, or to allow the proponent of the amendment and others to temporarily debate its merits, the Chair may permit the reservation of a point of order at the outset, to be subsequently disposed of upon the insistence of the Chair while the matter remains pending.

Only two points of order in the House are stated by rule to be so sacrosanct as to be exceptions from the general requirement for timeliness of the making or reservation of a point of order immediately upon consideration of the offending matter. Points of order may be raised 'at any time' during the pendency of a portion of a reported bill or an amendment thereto which contains an appropriation or a tax or tariff, to protect the jurisdictions of the Committees on Appropriations and on Ways and Means against encroachments discovered in measures reported from other committees. Those points of order must nevertheless be raised when the offending portion of the reported bill is being read for amendment or when the offending amendment is under consideration, and come too later thereafter.

In the contemporary practice of the House there are two points of order which, while they may be made by any Member and then require a period of debate, are not ruled upon by the Chair but rather are decided by a vote of the House on whether to consider the allegedly offending measure. In 1995 Congress enacted the Unfunded Mandates Act which was intended to limit Federally imposed spending mandates on State or local governments by requiring them to spend their own funds without Federal reimbursement.

Rather than proscribe by a ruling of the Chair the consideration of a measure arguably containing a mandate on a State or local government to spend their own funds above an annual threshold level, Congress sought merely to isolate those provisions for separate consideration and vote. During the drafting of that bill it became evident that the Chair should not be made the final arbiter of what constituted an unfunded inter-governmental mandate, as the legislative language which might arguably constitute such a requirement would be beyond the ability of the Chair to discern in response to a point of order. Instead, the point of order against the provision, or against language in a special rule which waived that point of order, triggered a separate twenty minutes of debate on whether the provision constituted such a mandate, to be followed by a vote on the question of consideration, as the collective response of the House to the point of order. At this writing the effectiveness of the point of order as a fiscal constraint is debatable, as the House has not refused to consider any measure despite the obvious inclusion of unfunded mandates.

Beginning in the 109th Congress and again in the 110th Congress, the House adopted a rule to encourage the identification and reporting of 'earmarks' (special set-asides for identifiable beneficiaries) in Appropriation and revenue acts, the failure to identify or disclaim the existence of which would trigger a point of order against consideration of the measure similar to the Unfunded Mandate point of order. In the event of a waiver of that point of order in a special order reported from the Committee on Rules, a point of order against consideration of that special order is to be followed by twenty minutes of debate and a separate vote on the question of consideration as dispositive of the point of order. As with the Unfunded Mandate point of order, the Chair was properly spared the responsibility of ruling, in this case on whether particular bill or report language constituted and was adequately described and identified as an earmark, together with its Member-sponsor. Thus the rule permits either an identification or disclaimer printed in the report or in the Congressional Record by the committee chairman or a vote on consideration of the measure or of a special order of waiver to suffice to resolve the point of order. This is further discussed at page 281. These examples of points of order as triggers of separate debate and vote, rather than as matters for the Chair to rule upon, are responses to a media and public reaction against measures which impose undue spending requirements on other units of government, or which contain special-interest fiscal advantages, respectively, while avoiding the onerous responsibility of the Chair to interpret bill or report language based on fiscal or economic criteria beyond the Chair's expertise.

The burden of proof to establish or defend against a point of order upon which the Chair does rule varies, depending on the matter which is the focus of the point of order. Burdens of proof are not written in the standing rules, but are articulated in precedent where uncertainties are sufficient to enable the Chair to rule that a point has not been proven by a preponderance of the argument by the Member presumably most knowledgeable about the matter. The manager of a bill must normally defend against any point of order which would otherwise inhibit the consideration of the measure or of a provision therein, while the proponent of an amendment must convince the Chair that his proposal is germane and otherwise in compliance with House rules. For example, the chairman of a committee must produce a transcript showing a quorum actually present during the committee vote to order the measure reported, and must cite a law sufficient to indicate that a provision in a general Appropriation bill is authorized by or does not change existing law. The proponent of an amendment to such a bill, on the other hand, must show that it is authorized and does not change existing law, and that it does not increase levels of budget authority or outlays above permissible limits, as when offered en bloc with offsetting changes under rule XXI, clause 2(f).

Two points of order are conclusively decided on the basis of estimates submitted by the Budget Committees, and do not depend upon meeting a burden of proof. In both Houses, the Chair is required to rely on those estimates, which are obtained from the Congressional Budget Office and are not formally accepted by the committees, in ruling on points of order under section 312 of the Budget Act. By that statute, the Chair is properly spared the responsibility of making estimates of levels of budget authority and outlays contained in the bill or amendment in comparison with a baseline set in the Congressional concurrent resolution on the budget.

In the 110th Congress, the House adopted a rule requiring new spending or reduction of revenues in a bill or amendment which increase the Federal deficit to be offset by other language reducing a comparable amount of spending or increasing a comparable amount of revenue (the 'pay-go' rule). Enforcement of this new rule, like the Budget Act, is to be based on estimates submitted from the Committee on the Budget (which in turn receives information from the non-partisan Congressional Budget Office).

Beyond these unique rules where the Chair's rulings are either guided by extraneous entities, or where the House determines the point of order by voting on the question of consideration, the Chair relies on non-partisan advice from the House and Senate Parliamentarian. The Parliamentarians, in turn, rely upon precedent which they are required by law to publish. In the House, any advice given to Members by the Parliamentarian is held in confidence as part of an attorney–client privilege upon insistence of the Member, and anticipatory rulings are not advertised. The Chair may eventually be called to rule upon any such point of order, and the Parliamentarian must eventually discuss otherwise confidential advice with the Chair. In the Senate, the Parliamentarian observes similar confidentiality, while on occasion publishing lists of advisory opinions on the germaneness of submitted amendments in a post-cloture environment. On those occasions the lists distinguish between clear and arguable advice, and in the latter category Senators are invited to engage in further discussions with the Parliamentarian to properly discern the nature and scope of the measure being amended and the purpose of the proposed amendment.

The Senate is less precise than the House as to the timing of points of order, permitting amendments to be challenged at any time during their pendency, even when a second-degree amendment has been offered, without having to be made or reserved at the outset of consideration. Rule XX provides that a question of order may be raised at any stage of the proceedings, except when the Senate is voting or ascertaining the presence of a quorum, and unless submitted to the Senate, shall be decided by the presiding officer without debate, subject to an appeal to the Senate. In modern practice, points of order in the Senate arise most frequently under the Congressional Budget Act, and may be waived by a vote of three-fifths of the Senate pursuant to section 312 of that law. The point of order can be raised at any time, and the votes on the waivers are normally conducted before the Chair rules to sustain it. Where the Chair overrules the point of order, a three-fifths waiver is not required, although any Senator may appeal the ruling in which event a majority vote is required to sustain the ruling. Similarly, germaneness points of order against amendments offered post-cloture (which must be noticed prior to the vote) can be raised at any time, although an anticipatory list of the presiding officer's likely responses prepared by the Parliamentarian is published in both cloakrooms and has a determinative effect from the outset.

In both US Houses, parliamentary inquiries are entertained at the discretion of the Chair, but may not interrupt the Member having the floor without his permission. Where a Member having the floor yields for that purpose, time consumed is taken from that Member's time. Parliamentary inquiries entertained in the Chair's discretion are for the edification of Members generally regarding the pending business. Similarly to responses to points of order, under this principle the Chair has declined to respond to parliamentary inquiries raising hypothetical questions, to questions on matters not yet pending, and to requests to place pending proceedings in a historical context. With respect to both points of order and parliamentary inquiries, the Chair will not entertain them: to rule on the sufficiency of committee reports, beyond compliance with House rules: on the legal effect of language: on the constitutionality (see page 243) or on the merits of the pending proposition: on the consistency of amendments: to interpret a special order before it is adopted by the House: to construe politically the result of a vote: to interpret the rules of the other body: or to opine on the anticipated order of business unless within the control of the Chair through the power of recognition (the announcement of scheduling being the prerogative of the Majority Leader).

Parliamentary inquiries are sometimes the equivalent of points of order in the House of Commons in the sense that they will normally be entertained where relating to the pending business, and that there is no appeal from the opinion of the Chair. When made outside the context of the pending business, there is greater latitude in the Commons for the Speaker to set aside a portion of the day to entertain points of order not related to the pending business. Often those points of order are not within the cognizance of the Speaker, but rather relate to ministerial action or inaction, or to information best obtained through 'the usual channels'. In both parliaments, the Speaker has the discretion to defer a response until he has examined the matter.

One of the most defining procedural differences between the Parliament and Congress involves appeals from rulings of the Chair. Jefferson in his *Manual* asserts that 'in Parliament, all decisions of the Speaker may be controlled by the House', and Erskine May's *Parliamentary Practice* on page 447 of the 23rd edition recites that 'the ultimate authority on all these matters is the House itself; but the Speaker is the executive officer by whom its rules are enforced'. One must first examine the nature of the questions of order that the presiding officers are called upon to decide in both Parliaments. In the UK, the Speaker's role as non-partisan presiding officer makes him the final authority on questions of order which focus primarily on debate and decorum, while in the USA the Speaker's role extends as well to interpretations of House rules governing the scheduling, consideration and content of measures, committee jurisdiction over them and the appointment of Members to conference and select committees (and party caucus authority over nominations of Majority members of the Rules Committee). In virtually all these functions, the Speaker's role is impartial, but remains subject to the will of the House. Exceptions from the appealability of questions include the Speaker's discretionary power of recognition (but not where his recognition is mandated by rule or statute); his count of division votes and quorums, and the ordering of the yeas and nays; his rulings on dilatoriness (seldom exercised in modern practice), responses to parliamentary inquiries; counting of time consumed; appointments to select and conference committees; and declinations to rule on constitutional issues. Within all these exceptions from appeal-ability runs the need for immediate finality in order to facilitate the business of the House. In both US Houses, any ruling of the Chair, whether appealed or not, has the effect of precedent—the equivalent of common-law *stare decisis*—which that House fol-lows just as it would its rules, unless and until that House should reverse, modify or waive that precedent. Where the decision of the Chair is sustained on appeal, it may have even greater precedential effect in the Senate. One defining difference, as shown in a 1996 ruling by the Senate presiding officer correctly sustaining a point of order against extraneous matter beyond the scope of differences in a conference report, but then over-ruled on appeal, indicates the extreme effect that a successful appeal from a ruling in the Senate may have on the underlying rule itself and is discussed in detail under 'conference reports' at page 458.

Riddick's *Senate Procedure* on page 145 carries the following statement relating to the effect of the Chair being overruled as a matter of precedent: 'Unless the Chair is supported by a majority vote of the Senate, the decision of the Chair is overruled. This decision of the Senate becomes a precedent for the Senate to follow in its future proce-dure until altered or reversed by a subsequent decision of the Chair or by a vote of the Senate'.

On that occasion,[27] the Senate chose to overrule a decision of the presiding officer that a conference report containing totally unrelated matter was out of order, so as to vote on the merits of the conference report including that language. By that action, the Senate interpreted that result on appeal as tantamount to a de facto repeal, although there was no precedent for such a far-reaching interpretation, vitiating its scope rule (Rule XXVIII) entirely. There the matter stood for nearly two subsequent Congresses, before finally being overtaken by the enactment of a law[28] explicitly rein-stating the earlier state of Senate practice to the effect that matter entirely unrelated to the House or Senate version would once again be held a violation of the Senate's scope of conference rule. Thus the Senate, rendered powerless to enforce its scope rule against several subsequent conference reports containing totally unrelated matter, eventually reactivated the rule in a 'must-pass' omnibus Appropriation Act conference report, ironically at a time (it not yet having been enacted into law) when the fact that it was totally unrelated matter could not have been challenged under the then current interpretation. This distinction between House and Senate interpretations of the impact of successful appeals on points of order, coupled with the House's far greater ability to waive points of order or to change its rules prior to rulings by the Chair by majority vote through privileged reports from the Rules Committee, demonstrates the consequences of efforts in the Senate to overrule the Chair in order to get to the merits of the underlying matter. Since that ruling, there were several conference reports con-taining totally unrelated matter inserted by the conferees. Following restoration of the Senate's scope rule, and its further enhancement in Rule XXVII in 2007 of a more rigid scope rule requiring a three-fifths waiver in the event of new matters 'air-dropped' into conference reports (discussed at pages 457, 459–60) the Senate Parliamentarian has indicated that he would treat a future decision of the Senate on appeal as a precedent unless distinguishable on its facts.

Appeals from rulings of the Chair in the House have increasingly been utilized in recent years to politicize issues, especially where the Minority may have been foreclosed from a separate vote on the merits of a proposition of their choosing, or by adoption of a restrictive special order even from offering an amendment otherwise in order under standing rules and traditions. By this tactic, the Minority has required recorded votes on the matter which the Chair has correctly ruled out of order. The Minority has then improperly characterized these issues not as votes on the correctness of the Chair's ruling, but rather as votes on the merits of the underlying proposition. Examples include appeals from proper rulings on: words uttered in debate; whether a resolution constitutes a proper question of the privileges of the House; the non-germaneness of an amendment previously discussed in this chapter at page 177; violations of the pay–go rule which requires inclusion of offsets of revenue reductions to prevent deficit increases; whether an amendment constitutes legislation on an Appropriation bill; and the applicability of the super-majority (three-fifths) vote requirement for final passage of a bill containing an income tax rate increase. In all these cases, the Minority established voting records for Members which it then described as votes on the merits of the matter ruled out of order. This is an inappropriate departure from various other permissible means of expressing disagreement, and if ever successful in reversing the ruling of the Chair would establish a 'precedent' that an instant majority of the House could by appeal conduct a vote on the merits of a proposition that is clearly not in order under standing rules and has not been made in order by a special order or rule. The procedural uncertainty which would result from this departure from regular order by resort to appeals would undermine the non-partisan status of the Chair. Votes on such appeals should properly be characterized as 'procedural', commanding Majority if not bipartisan and institutional support. Until recent Congresses, bipartisan majorities sustaining rulings of the Chair on appeal usually included the Minority Leader and other Minority Members more interested in preserving the institutional tradition of fairness from the Chair and less inclined to 'spin' the vote as 'substantive'.

Taking decisions: majorities and super-majorities

All parliamentary bodies recognize the essential responsibility to come to a decision on measures or matters properly pending before them. Jefferson reflects that 'the voice of the majority decides; for the *lex majoris* parties is the law of all councils, elections, &c., where not otherwise expressly provided'. Thus it becomes the duty of the Chair in the House of Representatives as stated in Rule I, clause 6 to state and then to put the pending question to a vote at the proper time, that being when all debate and amendment opportunities are exhausted, by ordering the previous question or by any standing rule requiring a vote after a certain period of debate, as on a motion to suspend the rules following forty minutes.

Correspondingly, the standing rules of each US House provide that it is the duty of all Members and Senators to vote on every question put, unless excused or unless they have a direct personal or pecuniary interest in the event of such question (Rule III, clause 1) or a 'conflict of interest' (Senate Rule XIII, clause 3). In both Houses, the determination of whether there is a conflict of interest belongs to the individual Member and not to the Chair or to the House, although a question of privilege collaterally challenging a vote cast by a Member with an alleged conflict could allow the House to address the matter as an ethics issue. Members and Senators wishing to be excused may seek the permission of their House, which is normally granted by unanimous consent. In the Senate, there may be a vote on whether to excuse a Senator from voting, as Rule XIII, clause 2 requires the presiding officer to put the question without debate after a roll call and before the result is announced, unless unanimous consent is obtained. Members and Senators may vote 'present' prior to the announcement of the result with a brief explanation that a vote on the merits would in their opinion constitute a conflict of interest. Absent Members may also insert signed explanations into the Record explaining how they would have voted if present, and those explanations appear immediately following the vote if submitted on the same day. Proxy voting has never been permitted in either House, and becomes an ethics issue when a Member's vote is cast in his absence. (Proxy voting has been banned in all committees of the House since 1995, but is permitted in Senate committees other than in its Budget Committee.)

In both Houses of Congress, the basic duty of the Chair to put the pending question to a vote may be circumvented when the body is asked to complete action on a legislative measure or matter by unanimous consent (see also Legislation, at pages 419–20). Especially in the Senate, unanimous consent requests often extend not only to consideration but the final passage or adoption of a variety of non-controversial measures. By this procedure, the Chair is not required to put the question on final passage or adoption to a vote, but rather the lack of objection to a unanimous consent request constitutes final disposition, subject to the laying on the table of the motion to reconsider that final action also by unanimous consent. The Senate has even permitted unanimous consent requests to deem 'as passed' measures not yet messaged from the House, especially conference reports where the final text is available. Senate amendments to House-passed bills are sometimes 'deemed' adopted where the Senate has completed action on its companion measure and wishes to amend the expected House-passed version and to send it to conference. These extraordinary Senate actions are taken by unanimous consent where the convenience of Senators' schedules conflicts with waiting upon final House action. Of course, where record votes are to be demanded or the outcome of Senate action is uncertain, unanimous consent permission to deem a Senate action to have been completed is not attempted. Nevertheless, the Senate has in recent years taken final unanimous consent action on conference reports on major legislation where the outcome is a foregone conclusion, to accommodate Senators' travel or to avoid the possibility of a demand for the yeas and nays at a time, especially near the beginning of a recess periods, when the outcome is certain but many Senators may be absent.

In the House, there has been a traditional reluctance to permit unanimous consent requests which deem a conference report or a House-originated bill to be passed, the preference being to limit the scope of the request just to permit consideration of the measure, but subject to a subsequent vote on a question put by the Chair. Less reluctance has been demonstrated in entertaining unanimous consent requests to concur in Senate amendments or to amend Senate amendments, where there is no controversy, and in order to avoid the demand of an individual Member for a record vote. Another segment of this chapter portrays unanimous consent orders in both Houses as necessarily expeditious methods of achieving consideration—and often completion—of relatively non-controversial measures. In the House, custom and tradition suggest greater transparency than in the Senate, as the number of 'deeming' requests entertained by the Speaker are fewer, debate colloquys cannot merely be inserted in the Record as if spoken, and the official papers must always be in possession of the House when the request is entertained. By contrast, the Senate as a body more dependent upon the permission of individual Senators, tolerates expeditious requests in order to avoid politically unnecessary and time-consuming votes on many issues, and to accommodate the demands of individual Senators where acceptance of unanimous consent often depends on unstated trade-offs on unrelated matters.

Beyond unanimous consent, the Chair in both bodies is required to put a pending question to a vote at the appropriate time. In the House, that means that there will always be a voice vote on a matter before there can be a division (standing) vote or a record vote. Specifically, clause 6 of Rule I requires 'the Speaker shall rise to put a question but may state it sitting. The Speaker shall put a question in this form: "Those in favour of the question say 'Aye', and after the affirmative voice is expressed, "Those opposed say 'No'." After a vote by voice under this clause, the Speaker may use such voting procedures as may be invoked under rule XX'. Unless a rule already orders the yeas and nays on a matter, the Chair will not bypass the putting of a question to a voice vote. The Chair's announcement of the result of a voice vote is not subject to challenge by appeal, even where that discernment may be contradicted by a more audible vote on the other side. On occasion, a few occupants of the Chair have been tempted to indicate a partisan preference in the call of the voice vote, although in modern practice presiding officers diligently call the result as it is objectively discerned, in either case with the knowledge that subsequent procedures exist to more accurately determine the will of the House on the question.

Following a voice vote, two options for a more precise vote are available. Any Member may demand a division, or the Chair may require Members to stand 'and remain standing until counted' on his own initiative where his ascertainment of the voice vote is in doubt. The Chair requests those in favour of the question to rise and remain standing until counted. After they are seated, those opposed are asked to rise and remain standing until counted. The Chair announces his count to the House or to the Committee of the Whole, from which count there is no appeal. In modern practice, if record votes are anticipated following voice votes, they may immediately be demanded by any Member, and such demand takes precedence of a demand for a division vote if both demands are made at the same time (if a division vote is in progress, the Chair will not interrupt it to entertain a demand for a record vote). Thus the House usually proceeds immediately to a record vote following the voice vote, unless the demand or ordering of a record vote is postponed under standing rule authority now in place. Because of the ease with which a record vote may be ordered in the House and in Committee of the Whole, Members seldom demand division votes which will be superseded in all likelihood. On the few occasions when an overwhelming majority of the House does not wish to conduct a recorded vote on an issue, however, the division vote may stand as the final vote where only the totals, but not each Member's position, are recorded.

For both Houses, the Constitution provides that one-fifth of the Members present may order the yeas and nays upon any question. In the House, that Constitutional protection inuring to one-fifth of those actually on the floor when the question is put may not be diminished by House rule. Nevertheless, when the House is sitting in a Committee of the Whole, the right of one-fifth of the Members present to order the yeas and nays is not applicable, as only proceedings in the full House are covered by the provision in Article I, section 5. To compensate for that inapplicability in Committees of the Whole, the House has adopted since 1970 a standing rule permitting twenty-five Members to order recorded votes. This change in House rules must be characterized as one of the major reforms of proceedings in the last century, as prior to 1970 no recorded votes were permitted in Committee of the Whole where most amendments to bills were initially considered. Only amendments adopted in Committee of the Whole and reported to the full House were then subjected in their perfected form to record votes by a demand for the yeas and nays under the Constitution. Until 1970, amendments voted on in Committee of the Whole by division or teller vote (Members passing between appointed tellers in the centre aisle to be counted but not recorded by name) were not susceptible to record votes, and many controversial amendments which were rejected there never received record votes unless re-offered by the minority as a motion to re-commit pending final passage in the House. At that time, the House changed its rules to permit twenty Members to demand a recorded vote, and pending that demand any Member could make the point of order of no quorum. Should the Chair count fewer than one hundred Members present in Committee of the Whole, a quorum call would ensue prior to the Chair counting for a recorded vote, and that quorum call could either be 'live' where every Member recorded his presence and a five-minute vote would follow, or a 'notice' call which the Chair could abort when 100 Members responded (but the recorded vote following would be of fifteen-minute minimum duration). The Chair would then ask Members to stand to discern whether twenty (now twenty-five) Members ordered a recorded vote. That practice, still part of the standing rules for Committees of the Whole, has given way to the Chair's expected willingness to conduct a liberal count of those supporting a recorded vote, in order to avoid time-consuming preliminary quorum calls. The Chair, armed with authority to postpone demands for recorded votes and to cluster them at subsequent times with other postponed votes on amendments, is able to save the time of the Committee of the Whole by reducing the time on subsequent votes to five minutes (the first in the cluster requiring a minimum of fifteen minutes), while virtually assuring that all the clustered votes will be ordered when most Members are predictably gathered in the Chamber. This assurance of recorded votes in Committees of the Whole resulted in more transparency on many contentious issues, but beginning in the 1980s and continuing ever more frequently to this day was counterbalanced by restrictive special orders emanating from the Committee on Rules which severely limited the number of amendments which could be offered (see Legislation, at pages 428, 431).

In the full House, in addition to the Constitutional guarantee that one-fifth of the Members present can order the yeas and nays, additional rules permit one-fifth of a quorum (44 of 218) to order a recorded vote, even where one-fifth of all the Members present (88 of 435 if all Members are present) might not order the yeas and nays. In the alternative, any Member may under a rule adopted in 1896 object to a voice or division vote in the House on the ground that a quorum (218) is not present, in which event the record vote becomes 'automatic' if the Chair cannot count a quorum or unless the Chair postpones the vote for up to two legislative days as permitted by Rule XX, clause 8 adopted in 1979. None of these demands for record votes is in order until the Chair has first put the question to a voice vote and discerned the result, and once the demands are denied by a count of the Chair they may not be renewed except by unanimous consent. In the House, however, all three avenues to order a record vote are in order, despite the refusal of the House to order the vote by one of the other two methods.

In marked contrast to the timeliness requirement in the House, the demand for the yeas and nays in the Senate can be made at any time during the pendency of an amendment, and can be renewed by any Senator even if previously denied by one-fifth of those Senators present. While Article I, section 5 literally requires one-fifth of those present to support the demand, such that if five or fewer Senators are present, only one Senator is necessary to order the yeas and nays, that requirement in the Senate has been interpreted consistently to require one-fifth of a quorum of the Senate (11 of 51 Senators) to be physically present in the Chamber when the yeas and nays are ordered. In modern practice, where both the Majority and Minority Leaders or floor managers are in support of the demand for the yeas and nays, the Chair will not look further to ascertain whether at least eleven Senators are present, but where there is not such bipartisan support the Chair will count for the presence of one-fifth of a quorum. This apparent inconsistency is countered by the ability of a Senator to renew his previously unsuccessful demand for the yeas and nays at any subsequent time prior to disposition of the question, when more Senators are present.

Electronic voting was initiated in the House in 1973 and has revolutionized the manner and frequency with which votes are recorded in the House and in Committee of the Whole. While recorded votes were permitted in Committee of the Whole from 1970, they were until 1973 conducted by ballot cards handed to Member-tellers assisted by clerks using different aisles of the Chamber, and a simultaneous result was then announced by the Chair. That procedure remains an available back-up procedure in the event of the inoperability of the electronic system, but has not been utilized since 1973. No minimum or maximum time limit was placed on their duration. Upon installation of the electronic system, the standing rules provided for a minimum of fifteen minutes (or five minutes for clustered postponed votes following the first vote in the series where there is no intervening debate or business) for Members to be recorded by use of individual voter identification cards. Those cards are not transferable between Members or to any other person having floor privileges. It has always been an ethics violation for anyone but the Member to cast his or her own vote, and proxy votes are not permitted even by unanimous consent. Votes must be cast in the Chamber at one of forty voting stations located behind seats throughout. Members who do not possess their voting cards are permitted to sign ballot cards in the well of the House for processing by the clerks, or to change their votes if the electronic voting stations have been turned off near the end of a record vote and prior to the announcement of the result by the Chair. During fifteen-minute votes Members may change their votes electronically during the first ten minutes without the change being announced, as is the case at any time during a five-minute vote. Where a Member is required to change his vote by submission of a ballot card, however, that change is announced to the House and is printed in the Record. The final time period between the turning off of voting stations and the announcement of the final result may be crucial where Members are changing their votes with great frequency, in order that final vote changes be identified for the Record.

During the vote, electronic displays in the Chamber indicate each Member's vote by a green or red light next to his or her name, and simultaneously indicate a running total of the yeas and nays on panels which also show the decreasing time remaining. There are graphic displays of the yea and nay status of the vote by party, but not by individual Member, on television monitors, to enable the viewing audience to be kept aware of the running total. Party whips have additional capability inside the Chamber to examine the status of pending votes by party, state or regional breakdown. Pressures to force the display outside the Chamber of individual Members' votes during the conduct of the vote have been properly resisted, consistent with other rules preventing intrusive electronic communications into and out of the Chamber, and in order to better assure the sanctity of deliberations in a representative system where outside pressures at the final stage of voting are to be discouraged. Individual votes are published electronically within a few minutes following the final result, and are recorded in the Congressional Record and Journal the next day.

While the Chair endeavours to conclude votes within a reasonable and predictable time following expiration of the minimum, Members who enter the Chamber seeking to vote prior to the announcement of the result should not be denied that opportunity. The mere recitation of the status of the yeas and nays by numbers is not the equivalent of the final result, as the Chair must then announce that the (question) is agreed to or not. That is the moment of finality at which point the electronic voting system itself, and not merely the voting stations, is turned off. Nevertheless, Members entering the Chamber or wishing to change their votes may still be recorded so long as the electronic system remains operative at the rostrum and the tally clerk can enter those late votes electronically without use of the voting stations. On one occasion in 1995 the House was forced by unanimous consent to rescind a record vote and conduct it de novo the next day where the Chair had deliberately declined to permit two Members who had entered the Chamber prior to announcement of the final result to be recorded. Had unanimous consent not been obtained, a question of privilege in the form of a resolution alleging a deliberate violation of the rules by the Chair, if adopted, could have forced the rescission of the vote.

A recent occasion of a voting irregularity in the House highlights the importance of adherence to proper norms of conducting electronic votes. On 2 August 2007, the House was voting on a Minority motion to re-commit an Appropriation bill, with instructions to 'promptly' amend the bill. At the conclusion of the fifteen-minute voting period, the electronic tally board showed the vote at 214–214, although the clerk had not yet processed several possible vote changes submitted by ballot card. The Speaker pro tempore was audibly importuned by the Majority Leader to close the vote at that point, as a tie would defeat the motion. The Chair prematurely announced the result without the benefit of a traditional written tally slip handed up from the clerk signifying that all changes had been entered into the system. At that moment, a changed ballot card vote processed by the Clerk momentarily resulted in an affirmative majority, but several moments later additional changes again showed defeat of the motion, which the Chair finally acknowledged. At no time did the Chair announce the result based on the tally slip, but only from his perusal of the electronic board, which had not been finalized. The Minority Leader offered a resolution the next day as a question of privilege establishing a Select Committee to investigate the conduct of the vote, and the House adopted the motion upon acquiescence of the Majority Leader. At its first hearing on the matter, the Select Committee was informed that despite the absence of a standing rule requiring the Chair to rely upon the clerk's certification, the consistent traditions of the House reflected in precedent mandated that procedure, even prior to the advent of electronic voting. The sanctity of the vote must be attested by the Clerk (who under standing rules 'conducts' the electronic vote) for the Chair to announce the result. The Select Committee submitted a report recommending that the Speaker announce the proper practice requiring the Chair to base his announcement of the result solely on a certification submitted by the Clerk. That announcement was forthcoming on the opening day of the 111th Congress.

At the beginning of each Congress, the Speaker makes an announcement regarding the fifteen-minute minimum voting period as follows: 'The Chair wishes to enunciate a clear policy with respect to the conduct of electronic votes...a policy of closing electronic votes as soon as possible after the guaranteed period of fifteen minutes,' while not precluding any Member who is in the Chamber wishing to vote or to change his vote from doing so prior to the announcement of the final result. Nevertheless, in recent Congresses the Chair has on several occasions permitted the electronic vote on the final passage of a measure to remain open for periods ranging well beyond the minimum, even beyond one hour in order to affect the result of the vote, where absent Members were not on their way to the Chamber, but where Majority Members were being importuned by their leadership to change their votes in order to pass the measure.

On 22 November 2003, the House was considering a conference report on a bill to provide a prescription drug benefit to beneficiaries under the Medicare law. An electronic vote on the adoption of the conference report commenced at 3am that Saturday morning, and was held open by the Speaker pro tempore (at the insistence of the Speaker who was on the floor privately requesting Members to change their votes) for almost three hours. During most of that three hour period, all Members of the House except one who was present had recorded their votes and remained in the Chamber, and the board showed 216 yeas and 218 nays. While there were no audible objections to the length of the vote made during the entire period, and while it appeared that the Majority leadership might be preparing to enter a motion to reconsider that vote with the intent to adjourn until the next legislative day in order to gather needed support, that leadership was in fact engaged in private conversations with Members who had cast 'No' votes to convince them to change their votes. Several Members ultimately came to the well and changed their votes by ballot card handed to the clerk, and the conference report was finally adopted. A subsequent collateral challenge to the legitimacy of that vote was attempted by the Minority Leader on 8 December 2003 in the form of a question of privilege 'denouncing this action in the strongest terms possible, rejecting the practice of holding votes open beyond a reasonable period of time for the sole purpose of circumventing the will of the House, and directing the Speaker to take such steps as necessary to prevent any further abuse'. The preamble of the resolution alleged that the Majority Leader had improperly attempted to coerce a Member to change his vote based on a promise of campaign finance support to that retiring Member's son who was running for office in the next Congress. (That allegation later became a basis for an admonishment of the Majority Leader in a letter from the Standards Committee, where the alleged 'quid pro quo' was a campaign contribution to a Member's relative in return for a favourable vote by that Member.) The resolution was laid on the table following partisan debate during which it was mentioned that Speaker Wright had on 28 October 1987 permitted a vote to be held open for almost one half-hour in order to secure the change of one vote and pass a bill. On that occasion, the Minority Whip Cheney had decried the then unprecedented delay as 'the most arrogant, heavy-handed abuse of power I have ever seen in the ten years I have been here', and that it was 'the most grievous insult inflicted on the Republicans in my time in the House, and that there is no sense of comity left'. One observing the consistently more egregious relaxation of the fifteen-minute minimum vote requirement since that occasion could conclude that the partisanship of contemporary Congresses has influenced process to the point where rules and traditions, which have as their basis a respect for comity among Members, become subservient to the political determination to win votes and to minimalize Minority party options.

At the beginning of the 110th Congress, the new majority in the House, having raised the extraordinary length of that 2003 vote as a campaign issue suggesting 'a culture of corruption' in the House, adopted a rule prohibiting the use of the electronic voting system 'solely' to reverse the outcome of the vote. The Chair's discretion to hold votes open in order to accommodate Members arriving in the Chamber or to establish an accurate result rather than solely to change the outcome, could not be challenged under this rule, because it required the Chair's discernment of his own intent in prolonging the vote. To permit a point of order under this rule during the conduct of a record vote would invite a possible appeal from the Chair's ruling and a vote within a vote which the electronic system could not accommodate, and the Chair so ruled in 2008 by requiring collateral challenges as questions of privilege. The Chair on several initial challenges treated them as parliamentary inquiries which permitted him to articulate his reason for holding the vote open while not subjecting his response to a challenge on a point of order. As had happened on 8 December 2003, a collateral challenge to the action of the Chair was raised as a question of privilege by the Minority Leader on 3 August 2007, but not during the irregular vote on the previous day. The Select Committee to investigate the voting irregularity of 2 August 2007 recommended that the rule be repealed since the Chair on that occasion claimed to have been compelled by that rule to close the vote prematurely, and since the Chair on several subsequent occasions held votes open on request of the Majority Leader in apparent violation of the rule. That recommendation was adopted in the rules changes on opening day of the following Congress.

Five-minute votes in the House or in Committee of the Whole are normally confined to that minimum time frame, since Members have assembled in the Chamber on the first fifteen-minute vote and remain on notice of one or more consecutive five-minute votes to occur without intervening debate or business. While there is not the need to await the arrival of absentees, Members can be importuned to change their votes to influence the outcome. Where a long series of five-minute record votes have been clustered by the Chair or are anticipated, the House has on occasion, by unanimous consent, reduced the minimum time to two minutes on amendments in Committee of the Whole in order to accommodate Members' schedules. Beginning in 2009, the House began to obviate the need for unanimous consent for two-minute clustered votes by utilizing special orders to permit the Chair to ignore the five-minute minimum requirement in favour of two minute voting on amendments to general appropriation bills. On such occasions, the Chair will not entertain unanimous consent to further reduce the time below the minimum set in standing rules or in special orders unless assured that all Members are on notice of the change in advance of the beginning of the votes. Thus the Chair will not entertain unanimous consent to reduce the fifteen-minute time on the first vote, since absent Members will not have been notified and will be relying on that full period to reach the Chamber.

If the electronic system is inoperative, standing rules provide back-up procedures for record votes, normally by a call of the roll, although a recorded teller option is available. Whether an electronic vote which becomes inoperative during its execution is terminated and conducted de novo as a roll call, or is continued from the point of interruption by roll call, depends on the retrievability of the electronic votes already cast and the severity of the malfunction. The time taken for a roll call is not limited by rule, as each Member's name is called alphabetically and is called a second time if not responding on the first call. The reliability of the electronic voting system has increased since its installation in 1973, and its presumed infallibility prohibits unanimous consent requests after the announcement of the result to change or include votes. Members may announce for the Record how they would have voted, but may not be recorded by unanimous consent as they once could be following a roll call during which human clerical error may have caused the incorrect result. The Speaker may announce a change in the result of an electronic vote when required to correct an error in identifying a voting card submitted in writing in the well of the House.

The Senate has not instituted electronic voting, preferring the traditional roll-call system when the yeas and nays are ordered, in order to assure flexibility and accommodation to individual Senators while requiring them to come into the Senate well to be recorded. When unanimous consent or a voice vote has not determined the final result, the Senate in modern practice does not normally utilize division voting, as it is not an option under standing rules but is only a device by which the presiding officer confirms his call of a voice vote (no totals being announced). As in the House, a bell and light system alerts Senators to votes in progress. By standing order they are permitted a minimum of fifteen minutes to be recorded on an initial vote, and by unanimous consent on an ad hoc basis immediate subsequent votes can be reduced to ten minutes. Traditional practice whereby individual Senators could signal their imminent (or eventual) arrival in the Chamber, in which event the vote would be held open as an accommodation, gave way in the 110th Congress to the Majority Leader's insistence that votes be closed as near to the fifteen-minute time as possible. Of course, where the Majority Leader is intent upon encouraging Senators to change their votes, he exercises the discretion to request the presiding officer to leave the vote open. Senate Rule XIII provides that Senators may not, even by unanimous consent, vote after the announcement of the result but may, by unanimous consent, change or withdraw their votes 'for sufficient reason'. This procedure is seldom utilized in modern practice.

In both Houses, the motion to reconsider is an essential protection of the body's ability to finalize its votes. Until the motion to reconsider has been disposed of (normally by unanimous consent, or failing that, by motion to lay it on the table), a vote is not final in either House. There is no motion to reconsider in a Committee of the Whole, as it would be inconsistent with the expeditious actions which characterize those deliberations and which on adopted amendments can be reconsidered if reported back to the House in any event. By this motion in the House, any Member who has voted on the prevailing side can enter and then call up a motion to reconsider a vote just conducted.

The entry of the motion technically remains available through the following day, but is disposed of at once under most special orders so as to immediately finalize the vote. On non-recorded votes any Member may enter the motion, but absent Members may not. In the Senate, the entry of the motion extends for two additional legislative days and can be made even by a Senator who has not voted on the question. In the House, a question once reconsidered cannot be reconsidered a second time, even if the result has changed, whereas in the Senate there can be a second reconsideration in the event the first result is changed. More often than its use as a method of changing the result, the motion to reconsider is utilized as a delaying tactic in the House to prolong a measure or matter where there may be a dispute on a collateral issue. In that event the Member making the motion sometimes changes his vote to be recorded on the prevailing side of the question in order to qualify. The motion to reconsider is normally not debatable unless the question on which it is moved is debatable. The motion can only be made on one question at a time, such that if a Member wishes to reconsider an amendment and the House has proceeded through final passage, the House must seriatim vote to reconsider the votes on final passage, re-committal, engrossment and third reading, and the ordering of the previous question in order to vote on an amendment again.

The Constitution requires certain issues to be resolved by two-thirds votes, including Constitutional amendments, and votes on overriding Presidential vetoes, removal of political disabilities, expulsion of Members, and in the Senate on ratification of treaties and conviction of impeached officials. Additionally, House and Senate standing rules and statutory rules impose several super-majority voting requirements to permit expeditious action under certain procedures, including two-thirds votes for suspension of the rules motions in both Houses (a seldom used procedure in the Senate following one day's notice of the particular measure and the specific rule to be waived) and consideration of special orders from the Rules Committee on the same day reported. In the Senate, there are a number of three-fifths voting requirements in place which generally govern the waiver of points of order under the Budget Act, on the inclusion of new matter in conference reports, and most importantly the invocation of cloture to limit debate (and a two-thirds requirement to invoke cloture on proposals to amend Senate rules). The Senate has never imposed a super-majority voting requirement for final adoption of a defined type of measure beyond requirements of the Constitution.

Since 1995, the rules of the House, however, have imposed one super-majority (three-fifths) voting requirement on a specific type of legislative measure, namely bills or amendments which contain 'tax rate increases' as narrowly described in the House rule. This extraordinary use of the standing rules to impose a super-majority requirement for approval of a politically described fiscal measure (in order to make it more difficult to enact tax rate increases by directly amendingspecified subsections of the Internal Code) was adopted in 1995 by a new House majority (and retained by the subsequent new majority in 2007) and was unprecedented in the history of either House. Indeed, the rule was amended in 1997 to further narrow its applicability depending on the drafting technique utilized, while retaining the essential rule itself as a political statement. This rule runs counter to the Constitutional presumption that all ordinary legislation need be enacted in either House by a majority of those present and voting, a quorum being present, even though procedural barriers requiring some super-majority votes for preliminary consideration of measures generally are commonplace. It represents an inappropriate intrusion within House rules of an issue-specific requirement contrary to the majoritarian scheme contemplated in Article I of the Constitution, adopted to emphasize a political position on a fiscal policy, yet easily avoided in practice so as to escape the three-fifths requirement.

Though the method of taking decisions in both Houses at Westminster looks decidedly antique (and it is) it is also very straightforward. Neither Lords nor Members are obliged to vote and conversely they need not have been in the Chamber to hear the question put to qualify to vote. There are no proxies, abstentions are not recorded, and those unable to be present cannot pacify their whips by the submission of an account of the way they would have voted had they been in the House. The rules in Committee are the same as those in the House. There is no unanimous consent procedure (although the same result can be achieved when the Chair puts a question for decision and only one side calls 'Aye' or 'No' (or 'Content' or 'Not Content'), the other remaining silent). There are only two methods of voting, by voice and by recorded vote. Votes cannot be held open for latecomers or for political reasons. There are no motions for reconsideration.

When a debate in the Commons, whether in the House or in Committee of the whole House, reaches its conclusion, the occupant of the Chair will 'put' the question to the House, inviting those in favour to say 'Aye' and those against, 'No'. In a full House there will be successive roars from the two sides: otherwise only the voices of two weary whips on the front benches may successively be heard. The Chair will then make an impartial judgment 'on the voices' as to which side is in the majority, and will pronounce 'I think the Ayes [or the Noes] have it'. At this point, one side or the other may falter or fall silent, unwilling to go to the next stage of an actual division, perhaps anxious, having made their view known, not to take up time voting which could be used for debating.

If however the vote is to proceed, the division bells are rung and the exit doors from the Aye and No division lobbies, two corridors parallel to the long sides of the Chamber, are locked. Members begin to move into the lobbies, Ayes to the right of the Chair, Noes—at the opposite end of the Chamber—to the left. The Chair will wait two minutes and put the question again. If neither side then backs down by falling silent, four tellers are appointed—usually whips—two from either side, to stand at the now open exit doors. One teller from each side stands at each door. As Members leave the lobbies, their names are recorded by Clerks and they are counted by the tellers. When they pass the tellers, they give a slight nod. The explanation usually given is that this recalls days when the House sat in St Stephen's Chapel, and those with large hats had to duck to get through the gap in the rood screen, which was how divisions were then counted. However that may be, its utility today may be that it is easier to count the repeated action of nodding heads than bodies hurrying past.

Not less than eight minutes after the first putting of the question—in the case of one division immediately following another the interval may be informally shortened, the equivalent of the five-minute divisions in Congress—the Chair orders the entrance doors to the lobbies to be locked. Within that period, Members not in the Chamber when the question was put are expected to have made their way from all parts of the parliamentary estate. Once all Members in the lobbies who wish to vote have done so, the four tellers make their way to the Chamber. They line up at the bar, bow, and solemnly pace up the House to the Table (to the accompaniment of ironic comment if the tellers are not whips, and the back benches decide that their drill is not all it might be). The senior teller of the winning side announces the result, which the Chair repeats, and then orders the lobby entrance doors to be unlocked. The House goes on to next business. Division lists with full details are published the following morning.

In a full House, a division can take a quarter of an hour. It is a substantial investment of scarce parliamentary time, the more so when—as has happened on several occasions—the House of Commons spends the best part of a tetchy night doing nothing but dividing. Nevertheless, there are good arguments for the practice. It brings Members, including ministers, to the Chamber, facilitating the informal contacts and discussions without which parliamentary and political life would be diminished. The grandest minister, deprived of the barrier of his or her private office, can be waylaid and made to listen to the grievances of the newest backbencher. Constituents watching televised debates often complain of dreary unoccupied green benches, but a critical division, as the Chamber fills and the noise builds, can put theatre back into parliamentary life. Nothing can rival the buzz as the House strains to see who is the teller standing on the right of the four at the bar, because that will indicate, even before the numbers are announced, which side has won. In any case, it is not the processing through the lobbies which takes time, but rather Members' journeys to the lobbies from their offices or other facilities across the parliamentary estate. By whatever means voting is arranged in future (and electronic voting recently teetered on the brink of acceptance) that journey will still be necessary.

A means of reducing the inroads made by divisions on debating time in the Commons and also releasing Members from the necessity of attendance late in the evening for no purpose other than to go through the lobbies is the deferred division procedure, Westminster's alternative to clustering of votes in Congress. After the moment of interruption and for only some types of business—excluding for example where the outcome of a division on one question will determine whether there has to be a division on a later one—the procedure on divisions set out above is halted in mid-career. Once the Chair is satisfied that a vote is demanded, he or she will declare the division deferred. On the Wednesday afternoon of the following week, while the House is sitting, the votes will be cast in the lobbies on paper ballots.

The benefit of deferred divisions is obvious and practical—no waiting around till midnight or later to cast a vote to produce a result that could nearly always have been predicted. There are however arguments on the other side. Deferred divisions allow Members who were not present for a debate to determine the outcome, and may mean that some of those who were present for the debate are prevented by engagements from voting later. The taking of democratic decisions after debate is subordinated to the convenience of individuals. At the same time, the problem is one which vexes a number of legislatures as well as Congress and Parliament. The New Zealand House of Representatives has adopted a radical solution. Unless the Speaker in Wellington considers that the subject of a vote is a conscience issue or the decision is so close that a personal vote may make a difference to the result, one Member may cast the votes of all members of his or her party present, including proxy votes and (on certain conditions) the votes of Members absent on House business. Members who have given notice that they do not wish to vote with their party are excluded. Against that background, deferred divisions at Westminster, so deeply unattractive to procedural purists, seem quite modest.

It sometimes happens—and never when it is expected—that divisions result in a dead heat. The occupant of the Chair, who would not normally vote, must resolve the deadlock. The casting vote can be given in accordance with his or her personal views, though the last time that was done was in 1846. Since then, three abstract principles have been formulated on which the Chair in the Commons relies in giving a casting vote without putting at risk absolute impartiality. Where further discussion is possible, the Chair always votes for that. Where it is not, the final decision should not depend on the Speaker's casting vote but should have the backing of a majority. The third—which is really a special case of the second—is that a casting vote on a bill should leave the bill as it was when the last majority decision was taken.

Divisions in the Lords are conducted on basically the same lines as in the Commons. The opposing sides are not Ayes and Noes but Contents and Not Contents. The Lord Speaker may vote but does not have a casting vote. Lords do not bow to the tellers. The quorum in divisions, which in the Commons is thirty-five, is in the Lords thirty for votes on bills or subordinate legislation and for other votes three. There is only one teller in each lobby, and they may have their vote counted, which tellers cannot in the Commons. The rules which determine the outcome of a tied vote are slightly different from those in the Commons. A proposal to reject or amend a bill, reject a piece of subordinate legislation, or reject or amend a motion in relation to the stages of a bill is deemed to be negatived unless there is a majority in its favour. Otherwise, the ancient rule of *semper praesumitur pro negante* prevails—every tied vote amounts to a negative.

In the Commons, a Member may not change his or her vote: if a vote is mistakenly cast in the wrong lobby, the only recourse is for the Member to vote a second time in the opposite lobby. In the upper House, a Lord goes to the Table of the House with the tellers, declares the mistake, and the numbers are then and there corrected.

By contrast with Congress, there are no super-majority provisions affecting procedure in either House at Westminster. The nearest equivalent is the requirement in the Commons that in order for a closure motion to be effective, the question must be carried by at least 100 Members voting Aye (see page 203).

Notes

1. Paul Silk and Paul Seaward in ed Vernon Bogdanor *The British Constitution in the Twentieth Century* 2003 p 134 recall a story told by Harold Laski of a dinner in 1923 at which the host complained of the limitations on private Members' initiatives in the years after 1918. He was answered by Augustine Birrell, who recalled a dinner in the 1880s at which Gladstone bemoaned the same thing: for him the great days of the backbencher were the 1830s and early 1840s.
2. HC Deb (2007–08) 481 c458.
3. First Report 2006–07 HC 337.
4. Clause 6 of Rule XIV.
5. Senate Rule 19, paragraph 1(b).
6. Clause 2, Rule XVII.
7. The prize in these stakes must go to the Irish lower House, Dail Eireann, where, between the wars, a deputy asked if it would be in order to call a minister a sewer rat. The Chair assured him clearly and correctly that that would by no means be so. 'Thank you very much, *a Cheann Comhairle,*' said the deputy—perfectly in order—'the sewer rats will be grateful for that ruling'. Those who mourn

the absence of the list of disorderly expressions once contained in successive editions of Erskine May's *Parliamentary Practice* should consult *The Table*, the Journal of the Society of Clerks at the Table in Commonwealth Parliaments, where they will regularly find much to amuse them from across the Commonwealth.

8. *The Pimlico Companion to Parliament*, ed Christopher Silvester (1996) p 80.

9. Though the Member for West Kerry managed in 1901 to speak in Irish, without the Speaker realizing. Hansard, to their great credit, retrieved the remarks and reproduced them not only in grammatically perfect Irish, but set in half-uncial type and with a translation (Parl Deb 4th series LXXXIX cc 546–7). We are grateful to Mr P. M. Judge, formerly an officer of the *Oireachtas*, for locating this long-lost reference. It is in order in the Commons to take the oath of allegiance when a Member takes his or her seat in Scottish Gaelic or Welsh, provided the oath is then repeated in English.

10. 23rd edition 2004 (ed Sir William McKay) page 522.

11. 2007 edition page 44.

12. 23rd edition 2004 (ed Sir William McKay) page 400.

13. 2nd edition 2003 (ed W. Holmes Brown and Charles W. Johnson).

14. *Precedents of Proceedings in the House of Commons*, 1818 John Hatsell volume II pages 79; 4, 82, 84.

15. 1907 volume V, section 5825.

16. 23rd edition 2004 (ed Sir William McKay) page 400.

17. Congressional Record, 13 February 2008 at page H905-6 (daily edition).

18. The equivalent in Parliament to a second-degree amendment in Congress would be an amendment to an amendment.

19. Clause 4, Rule XVII.

20. Appropriate arrangements are made for a report to be made to the House (which alone may impose the punishment) if the offence is committed in Committee of the whole House.

21. In Committee of the whole House, dilatory motions may also be moved in the forms That the Chairman do now leave the Chair and That the Chairman do now report progress and ask leave to sit again. The first supersedes the order of the day for Committee (though that can of course be revived): the second brings proceedings in Committee on that day only to an end.

22. The form of the question was changed to the negative, in contrast to that used earlier and still used in Congress, when the closure procedure ('That the question be now put') was introduced in Parliament. The practice at Westminster is simply a relic, and ought to be suppressed.

23. Clause 2 of Rule XVII.

24. For discussion of debate in the Senate on Presidential nominations, and extraordinary 'nuclear' options under consideration to permit a majority of Senators to restrict debate and bring the question of confirmation to an up-or-down majority vote, see pages 72ff.

25. In the 110th Congress, Oleszek in his Congressional Research Service paper entitled *Whither the Role of Conference Committees: an analysis* explores the proliferation of 'ping-ponging' amendments between the two Houses, using several case studies to demonstrate leadership decisions both to avoid the repeated need to invoke cloture in the Senate and the application of the strict new Senate scope rule (akin to the Byrd rule governing Reconciliation conference reports) permitting a point of order against any newly inserted conference matter to vitiate the entire report and require the pending question to be the remainder of the conference report minus the material ruled out of order, absent a three-fifths waiver to retain it. This matter is discussed in greater detail in the segment on Legislation relating to conference reports at pages 448ff.

26. First Report 2006–07 HC 337 paragraphs 20–23, 75–76.

27. 3 October 1996, 142 Congressional Record at page S17148-50.

28. P.L. 106–553, section 801.

6

The Power of the Purse

Executives and legislatures: one source, two models

The power to authorize the raising of taxes, the limitation and appropriation to particular areas of government spending of the taxes collected, and the right to initiate spending on new purposes, is the area where Washington and Westminster are furthest apart.

The classical statement of the situation in the UK is to be found in Erskine May's *Parliamentary Practice*: 'the Crown requests money, the Commons grant it, and the Lords assent to the grant'. The Commons do not vote money unless required by the Crown, and they do not impose taxes unless necessary for the public service, as declared by ministers having the confidence of the Crown.[1]

In Britain, the initiative in matters of tax and expenditure is denied to the legislature. At the beginning of every parliamentary session, the Queen's Speech conventionally contains the phrase: 'Members of the House of Commons: Estimates for the public service will be laid before you.' This, the Crown's demand for Supply, is the mainspring of the complex mechanism of parliamentary authorization of the release of funds to the government. Erskine May describes the need for an initiative from the government before spending or taxing as 'a principle of the highest constitutional importance'.[2] The rule was part of the constitutional and political innovations ushered in by the Revolution of 1688–9. The founding fathers of the USA also held Revolution principles in high regard. Agreement on the importance of these principles is however no guarantee of parallel, let alone similar, development.

The necessity for Crown—in modern times, government—initiative casts a long shadow. The House of Commons may neither impose conditions on the grants which it makes nor alter the purposes to which the resources are to be applied except on the proposal of the government. If no demand is made, Parliament may not impose a tax nor authorize the government to spend. Even the power of delay is diminished by the timetable for the granting of resources to the government which is set out in the Standing Orders (see page 260) which in turn are of course the work of a government majority.

The transatlantic contrast goes beyond taxing and spending. Without the power of initiating appropriation, there can be no real parliamentary analogy to the Congressional appropriation process and thus no analogy to the distinction between authorizing and appropriating. Contrast the extensive and authoritative appropriation process in Washington with Commons Standing Order No. 56:

> When a motion shall have been made for the second reading of a[n] ... Appropriation Bill, the question thereon shall be put forthwith, no order shall be made for the committal of the bill, and the question for third reading shall be put forthwith...

Such aspects of financial control as the setting of central government budgetary totals or progressive reconciliation of individual commitments with overall projected spending totals, which are at the heart of Congressional decision making, are at Westminster the responsibility of government. Individual members of the Commons would find it impossible to earmark items of expenditure for their constituencies. The very idea of a refusal of royal assent to an Appropriation bill passes credibility. The powers of the House of Lords are much more limited than those of the Senate.

By comparison with Congress, then, the financial authority of the UK Parliament seems marginal. It has been said with justice that:

> Parliament often seems at its weakest in the control and scrutiny of public money. Taxes and duties are raised, and public money is spent with formal parliamentary authority. However, such authority is almost invariably granted in the form proposed by the government. While suggestions for reform have often focused on ways to give the House of Commons a greater institutional involvement in these processes, progress has been more marked in the retrospective scrutiny and audit of government decisions.[3]

Another critical observation characterizes Parliament as no more than 'an interested and acquiescent bystander' in financial scrutiny and control.[4]

But account being properly taken of the constitutional differences, there is no need to characterize parliamentary performance in matters of finance as more feeble than it really is. Even critics concede that 'overall, Parliament and its financial agencies do more financial scrutiny than ever before, and do it better'.[5] Congressional and parliamentary aims as well as methods diverge, for clear constitutional reasons, and direct comparisons are inappropriate. In contrast to Congress's direct authority over taxing and spending, the purpose of financial scrutiny at Westminster has recently been identified as

> to make government's financial decisions transparent; to give those outside Parliament the opportunity to comment; to have the opportunity to influence government's financial decisions; and to hold government to account, thereby improving official decisions, management and reforms.[6]

Control need not imply a power to reject government proposals, but a requirement to justify demands made and outcomes achieved.

'Power of the purse' in the USA is analysed in the context of privileges and prerogatives of the House of Representatives with respect to the origination of revenue and appropriations measures. In addition, the four levels of basic decision making in the Congress—the revenue process, the budget process, the authorization process, and the appropriations process are discussed in the chapter on Scrutiny and Oversight with respect to investigative responsibilities and in the chapter on Legislation with respect to procedures generally applicable at all stages of the legislative process, as well as the expedited procedures in the Congressional Budget Act for the consideration of concurrent resolutions on the budget and of reconciliation measures. This chapter will examine each of those four areas of decision making as they relate to the collection and disposition of public moneys. Also included as an adjunct to the segment on revenues will be an analysis of the process of statutory borrowing of money on the credit of the United States, that is, increases in the public debt limit, when revenue collection is insufficient to pay government bills as they become due. Together, these are basic prerogatives of Congress under separation of powers as delegated in Article I, and the emphasis will be on the exercise of rule making in both Houses to facilitate decision making in these areas.

Article I of the Constitution was conceived, drafted, and ratified in reaction to excesses of demands of the Crown for money. The framers were familiar with efforts by British kings to rely on extra-parliamentary sources of revenue for their military expeditions and other activities. Some of the payments came from foreign governments. Because of those transgressions, Britain lurched into a civil war and Charles I lost both his crown and his head.[7] The rise of democratic government is directly traceable to legislative control over all expenditures. That separation of powers and conferral on the legislative branch includes the power to lay and collect taxes, duties, imposts, and excises, and the restriction that no money shall be drawn from the Treasury but in consequence of appropriations made by law. The exclusion of the Executive branch from the grant of overall financial power basically distinguishes the American constitutional arrangements from the British. In Federalist no. 48, James Madison explained that 'the legislative department alone has access to the pockets of the people'. The power of the purse, he said in Federalist no. 58, represents the 'most complete and effectual weapon with which any constitution can arm the immediate representatives of the people, for obtaining a redress of every grievance, and for carrying into effect every just and salutary measure'.

While this constitutional delineation is textually accurate, it must be remembered that Article II of the Constitution confers on the President the authority to veto all bills and joint resolutions which either raise revenue, authorize appropriations, or actually appropriate funds. Thus while the Executive branch is not conferred any of the power of the purse role directly, it is the modern reality that the President influences, in advance of legislative enactment, levels and sources of revenue, policy decisions in law regarding spending of those revenues, and actual appropriation levels and disbursement, both through the annual triggering of the budget process and through the veto threat. This is symbolized and procedurally activated by the President's annual budget, which is required by law to be submitted near the beginning of each calendar year prior to legislative actions in any of these areas. As the calendar year progresses, Congress's response to the President's budget must always take into consideration real or implicit veto threats which often influence the original drafting of legislation in all of these areas. The Office of Management and Budget (OMB) within the Executive branch serves as liaison with the Congress on formulation of all such legislation and in effect gives the Executive an influential if not co-equal role in the exercise of the power of the purse.

In addition, the Impoundment Control Act of 1974 enables the Executive, at least temporarily, to rescind or defer the expenditure of appropriated funds in addition to the power of veto over entire Appropriation bills. These combined Executive authorities conferred by Article II and by law therefore greatly enhance the role of the Executive not merely to 'faithfully execute' laws enacted by Congress, but to influence their content and timing. The political reality of a Congress, especially where controlled by the same majority party as the Executive, being attentive if not deferential to Executive branch budget priorities from the very outset of both the annual and multi-year revenue, policy and appropriations processes, blurs the roles of the respective branches in the ultimate exercise of the power of the purse.

When a spending or revenue Act is sent to the President for his consideration, he must approve or veto the measure in its entirety. After a spending measure has become law, the President may propose to impound funds through rescission which cancels the funding, or deferral which delays the expenditure. In response, Congress exercises its responsibilities either through expedited procedures established under the Impoundment Control Act of 1974 or through the regular legislative process.

Advocates of greater budget discipline proposed the Line Item Veto Act, which became law in 1996[8] and was to remain effective until 2005. It was declared unconstitutional by the Supreme Court in *Clinton v City of New York* 524 US 417 (1998). Under that law the President could (and did twice) exercise his authority to cancel dollar amounts of discretionary budget authority, direct spending, or limited tax benefits. Those cancellations were to remain effective unless disapproved by law, and expedited procedures were provided for Congressional review within thirty days of measures disapproving the cancellations. The law was declared invalid because it violated the presentment clause of Article 1, section 7 of the Constitution which requires approval or veto of an entire Act of Congress. By imposing an ultimate two-thirds vote of each House to override a presidential veto of a bill disapproving one of his cancellations, the law improperly tipped the balance in the President's favour to disapprove portions of a bill after its enactment, and then only to need one-third of Members voting in either House to sustain his veto of a disapproval.

In the years following the Supreme Court decision, various proposals have been made in Congress (including a recommendation by President Bush in 2006 to grant line item veto authority to the President in a manner that arguably passes constitutional muster—by permitting the President to propose cancellations of budget authority or tax benefits in enacted bills and then to allow Congress under expedited procedures to approve (rather than disapprove) his cancellations by law enacted by subsequent majority vote. To date, one such proposal has passed the House but not the Senate, as concerns remain about the balance of power between the Congress and the President over budget decisions.

Congress: the budget process

There are three stages in the complex process by which Congress approaches its constitutional responsibility in exercise of the power of the purse in the allocation of the fiscal resources of the Federal government. None has a close parallel in British parliamentary procedure.

First, there is an authorization process under which Federal programmes are created in response to national needs. Second, there is an appropriations process under which funding is provided for those programmes. Both of these stages are subsequently discussed in this chapter. Third, there is a Congressional budget process that annually establishes an overall fiscal policy of spending and revenues and that institutes a complex web of procedures to enforce those budgetary decisions. The overall fiscal policy is established by the annual adoption of a concurrent resolution on the budget not requiring the President's signature.

After the Second World War, the assumption that the presidential budget, annually submitted pursuant to the 1921 Budget and Accounting Act, maintained fiscal control in Congress gave way to the view that Congress needed its own budget process. Dependence on the Executive budget had bolstered the President's fiscal powers at the expense of Congress's, although the 'power of the purse' has always been a legislative power granted in Article I, sections 8 and 9 of the Constitution. As long as Congressional financial decisions were fragmented, it was argued, Congress could not effectively control expenditures. The 1974 Act established a Congressional budget process centred around a concurrent resolution on the budget, scheduled for adoption each calendar year prior to House or Senate consideration of revenue or spending bills. The Act provided an overall legislative framework within which the many separate measures (revenue, spending, debt limit, and reconciliation) would be considered, sometimes under expedited procedures.

The advent of the Congressional budget process in 1974 was a culmination of years of fragmented Congressional decision making in revenue, policy, and appropriations areas, resulting in a loss over time of a coordinated capability to respond to Executive branch initiatives reflected in the President's annual budget, to impose timely constraints, and to consider legislative initiatives and plans in each of those areas. The size of the budget and of the surplus or deficit were not subject to effective controls. To address these problems, both Houses enacted over the President's veto the Congressional Budget and Impoundment Control Act of 1974, consisting of ten titles which established: (1) new committees on the Budget in both Houses, and a Congressional Budget Office (CBO) designed to improve Congress's informational and analytical resources with respect to budgetary process; (2) a timetable and controls for various phases of the Congressional budget process centred on a concurrent resolution on the budget to be adopted before legislative consideration of revenue or spending bills; (3) various enforcement procedures; (4) standardized budget terminology; and (5) procedures for Congressional review of presidential impoundment actions. In 1995, the Unfunded Mandates Act added new sections to the 1974 Act to permit separate challenges to legislation which imposed unfunded intergovernmental mandates on State or local governments beyond a certain threshold amount. Detailed discussion of the Balanced Budget and Emergency Deficit Control Act of 1985 (Gramm–Rudman) is omitted because its enforcement mechanism (across-the-board sequestration of discretionary budget authority found at the end of each year to have exceeded proscribed limits) was permitted to expire in 2002. The fundamental purpose of that law—one of deficit reduction, has since been replaced by pay-as-you-go (pay-go) procedures adopted in the rules of each House discussed in this chapter (pages 232, 245–50).

The House and Senate Budget Committees draft the concurrent resolution on the budget, with a focus on the budget as a whole as it reflects national economic policy. Those committees also have jurisdiction over the budget process, and can recommend procedural changes governing either or both Houses during the Congress covered by the concurrent resolution. That jurisdiction overlaps in the House with the Rules Committee, which modifies or adds procedures in the recommended budget resolution during its consideration of any special order governing consideration of the budget resolution, as well as during its consideration of each legislative measure with respect to necessary waivers of points of order.

Section 300 of the Budget Act includes a non-mandatory timetable for various stages of the Congressional budget process as follows: on or before the first Monday, the President submits his budget to Congress, after which the two Budget Committees begin hearings on the budget, the economic assumptions on which it is based, the economy in general and national budget priorities; on or before 15 February, CBO submits an annual report to the Budget Committees dealing with overall economic and fiscal policy; not later than six weeks after the President's budget submission, committees submit their views and estimates to the Budget Committees; by 15 April, Congress completes action on the concurrent resolution on the budget, normally through adoption of a conference report (the resolution may also include revisions of the previously adopted budget resolution for the current fiscal year as part of its resolution for the ensuing year); by 15 May, regular general Appropriation bills may be considered in the House despite lack of a final budget resolution (so as to encourage enactment prior to the 1 October fiscal year deadline); on or before 10 June, the House Appropriations Committee should have reported its final regular bill; and finally Congress is encouraged to complete action on recommended reconciliation legislation by restrictions on adjournments during July (often waived). Other than the 1 October beginning of a new fiscal year (on which date budget authority enacted into law for a fiscal year expires) the dates established in section 300 are targets only for each year, which failures to meet do not inhibit consideration of measures beyond those dates.

The budget resolution which is supposed to be adopted annually by 15 April, suggests total revenue and spending levels for at least five fiscal years. These totals generally are binding for the first year and the sum of all five years, through the application of points of order against fiscal legislation not complying with the levels or the timing suggested in the resolution. Because a concurrent resolution is not presented to the President for his signature or veto, the budget resolution does not have statutory effect, but the procedures which it puts in place profoundly restrict the range of fiscal options which may be presented to each House. For example, Section 311 of the Budget Act bars Congress from considering a bill or amendment thereto that would either cause total revenues to fall below the level set in the budget resolution, or would cause total new budget authority or outlays to exceed the budgeted level. Section 302 of the Act further bars both Houses from considering any measure or amendment that would cause the relevant committees' allocation contained in the final version (conference report) on the budget resolution to be exceeded. This point of order is most often enforced by sub-allocations of spending made by the Appropriations Committee to each of its twelve subcommittees. In addition the Act in section 303 contains 'timing' points of order to bar consideration of any revenue, spending, entitlement, or debt-limit measure prior to adoption of the budget resolution, with the exception that in the House, Appropriation bills may be considered after 15 May even if the budget resolution has not been finally adopted by both Houses. Especially with respect to section 302 points of order, the practical effect of this enforcement is regularly seen during consideration of annual general Appropriation bills when floor amendments are offered to increase budget authority in certain accounts. Based on estimates from the Budget Committee, and since the reported bill from the Appropriations Committee is usually at its maximum permitted level of funding, the Chair is constrained to sustain these points of order unless the increases are offset by comparable decreases in other accounts in the bill. As is further discussed in the segment of this chapter on appropriations at page 280, other procedural points of order involving the lack of authorization in law, the inclusion of legislative language changing existing law offered on a general Appropriation bill, and the requirement of germaneness of amendments all combine to erect procedural barriers to consideration of amendments to increase discretionary spending. Only the Budget Act points of order are based upon an internal discipline for both Houses to remain within a predetermined budgetary framework.

The budget resolution is Congress's fiscal response to the President's budget. In part, the budget resolution sets total new budget authority and outlay levels for each year covered by the resolution. It also distributes Federal spending among twenty functional categories (such as national defence, agriculture, and transportation) and sets levels for each function. Within each House, the total new budget authority and outlays for each fiscal year are also distributed among committees with jurisdiction over spending, thereby setting spending ceilings for each committee (usually in the joint explanatory statement accompanying the conference report on the budget resolution—the so-called section 302(a) allocations). The Appropriations Committees receive ceilings on budget authority and outlays only for the upcoming fiscal year, because appropriations measures are annual.

The budget resolution serves as an internal framework for Congress in its action on separate revenue, spending, and other budget-related measures. The contents of budget resolutions and accompanying reports are governed by section 301 of the Budget Act, and in addition to aggregate totals contemplated for revenue, debt, budget authority, and outlays for five fiscal years, may contain 'such other procedures relating to the budget, as may be appropriate to carry out the Budget Act'. This 'elastic clause' is particularly important in the Senate because it enables that body with the concurrence of the House to adopt rules and procedures—including points of order, without the need for a super-majority to permit it to come to a vote.

While budget resolutions are 'privileged' for consideration in both Houses and do not require unanimous consent or special orders of business to be called up, in the House the Rules Committee in modern practice recommends a special order which limits amendments only to those in the nature of substitutes which present alternative and mathematically consistent budget plans—for example, Minority party, the Congressional Black Caucus, moderate coalition, or even the President's plan in the form of an alternative concurrent resolution. At issue are different levels of taxation, spending, and resulting deficits as a matter of political and economic philosophy. It is instructive that the Budget Act forecloses motions to recommit budget resolutions in the House—a procedure otherwise guaranteed to the Minority to present a proper alternative on any measure, in order to remove the element of uncertainty inherent in motions to recommit and to force up-or-down votes on final adoption. In the Senate, amendments to the budget resolutions must be germane and are limited by overall time restrictions on consideration—therefore not filibusterable requiring the invocation of cloture by a super-majority. Section 303 of the Budget Act precludes consideration of certain budget-related legislation for a fiscal year until the budget resolution for that year has been adopted by both Houses. The essence of this section is timing, and reflects a judgement that legislative decisions on expenditures and revenues for the coming fiscal year should await annual adoption of the budget resolution.

Section 301(b)(2) of the Budget Act provides for the inclusion of reconciliation instructions in a budget resolution and for the reporting and consideration of legislation. Instructions are general in form, and direct spending or revenue committees of jurisdiction to recommend changes in existing law to achieve the goals (for example, deficit reduction, or merely tax reduction) contemplated in the budget resolution. The importance of this authority to instruct committees lies primarily in the Senate, where the resulting measures reported from the directed Senate committees become 'privileged' for expedited consideration under procedures precluding extended debate and non-germane amendments—restrictions not otherwise achievable in the Senate, absent unanimous consent or a change in standing rules requiring a two-thirds super-majority. The privileged status of responsive reconciliation measures is less important in the House, where the Rules Committee's special orders normally expedite consideration by restricting amendments and further reducing available debate limits. The 'Byrd rule' in section 313 of the Budget Act, while precluding extraneous matter only as a Senate rule, indirectly impacts what may have been proposed by the House as well if contained in the conference report. Taken together, these expedited procedures are intended to assure enactment in both Houses by majority votes, without the attachment of extraneous matter and the need for super-majorities in the Senate to limit debate.

Recent Congresses have seen a proliferation of 'reserve funds' in final budget resolutions, especially those directed at Senate measures. These provisions permit subsequent consideration of direct spending measures where legislative committees may within that fiscal year report measures which will be scored as direct spending. Under the most recently adopted budget resolution for fiscal 2008, there are as many as thirteen sections reserving funds to committees in the event they report legislation involving direct spending (for example, health, education, tax relief, and housing programmes) the cost of which is not built into the aggregate spending baseline in the budget resolution and therefore in excess of that spending level. In return, the legislative committee must offset those new spending initiatives, if reported, with pay-go comparable savings or revenue increases so as not to increase the deficit. Reserve funds targeted to the Appropriations Committees do not require similar offsets, since they can be implemented as 'Emergency' designations by legislative language in Appropriation bills. This reserve fund technique is therefore consistent with the precedent that pay-go offsets mandated by House and Senate rules do not apply to appropriation measures, but only to other committees with 'direct spending' jurisdiction.

To expedite its adoption of a budget concurrent resolution by 15 April, the 1974 Act contains special procedures to assure its consideration and adoption in both Houses. Thus, to avoid unlimited debate, to bypass the need for consent agreements or the invocation of cloture in the Senate, and to establish an annual timetable for the consideration of budget-related rules and legislation, the Senate and the House enacted a unique law permitting expedited consideration of budget concurrent resolutions. This is followed by comparable expedited procedures in both Houses of 'budget reconciliation' legislation to enhance Congress's ability to change current law in order to bring revenue, spending, and debt-limit policies in existing laws into conformity with the fiscal policies and levels underlying the previously adopted concurrent resolution on the budget.

As the first step in the accelerated process, the 1974 Budget Act contains several procedures which are uniquely applicable to the consideration of budget concurrent resolutions. In the Senate, amendments are required to be germane, and debate on the resolution and on amendments is limited in the Senate, subject to unanimous consent agreements imposing additional limitations, in order to facilitate consideration prior to 15 April. Nevertheless it is important to note that the limitation imposed by section 305 is on hours of debate, and not on consideration of the budget resolution itself. In the House, special orders reported from the Committee on Rules establish the terms and conditions of consideration, usually limiting the number of amendments permitted to substitutes for the entire resolution that present broad policy choices. At issue are different levels of taxation, spending, and debt as a matter of political and economic philosophy. Debate on final conference versions is limited in both Houses. Uniquely, the Budget Act prohibits motions to recommit or to reconsider budget resolutions in the House, so as to remove the element of uncertainty inherent in those motions.

Not only is the timing of budget resolutions expedited, but the contents of those resolutions further permit Congress to initiate new procedures governing levels of revenue, spending, and public debt. Reconciliation directives may be included in the annually adopted concurrent resolution on the budget effective with respect to the ensuing and multiple fiscal-year consideration of revenue, spending, and debt-limit legislation. Both Houses are enabled through the 'elastic clause' in section 301 of the 1974 Act to include in the budget resolution 'any other procedure, relating to the budget, as may be appropriate to carry out the purposes of this Act'. Thus the Budget Act contemplates a departure from House and Senate standing rules both by expediting consideration of the resolution itself and of resulting reconciliation legislation, and by erecting procedural barriers against other legislation which is inconsistent with the levels assumed in or the timing required by the resolution. The House and Senate have used authority under the elastic clause to modify reconciliation procedures over time in many significant ways, including advancement of the use of reconciliation instructions to the spring budget resolution and extending the time frame from one year to multiple years.

Some of these expedited procedures have led to extraordinary rulings and responses to parliamentary inquiries in the Senate. For example, the requirement that amendments be germane in the Senate to budget resolutions has led to a series of rulings focused on whether a proposed procedure was within the jurisdiction of the Senate Budget Committee. Under the elastic clause the Senate with House concurrence is free to adopt 'procedures' by majority votes consistent with the purposes of the budget resolution, with limits on debate and germaneness without going through a formal rules change requiring a two-thirds vote to consider. The Senate over the years has entertained many amendments suggesting procedures toward enforcement of deficit reduction, including a pay-go requirement which since 1993 creates a point of order needing a three-fifths waiver against any amendment increasing the deficit. That amendment has been a standard enforcement mechanism since that time. By contrast, amendments offered in 2008 to erect similar points of order against tax rate increases and against earmarks in other bills were ruled to be not germane as beyond the jurisdiction of the Budget Committee, since addressing matters not related to the purposes of the Budget Act. To a parliamentary inquiry against such an amendment, the Chair responded that those non-germane amendments if adopted would be 'corrosive' of the underlying resolution, as they would encumber it with provisions which could eventually destroy the privilege of the budget resolution and prevent its further consideration absent a three-fifths waiver. Moreover, the Chair responded that inclusion of such non-germane provisions in a conference report on the budget resolution, even if originally part of the Senate version sent to conference, would be 'fatal' to the conference report and would destroy its privilege under the Budget Act. These responses, while not formally binding as precedent since only occasioned by parliamentary inquiries, nevertheless demonstrate the vagaries of Senate budget processes and that body's reluctance to broadly interpret the elastic clause—especially at the conference stage—to further enhance a majoritarian disposition of issues beyond those clearly related to the Congressional budget process, insisting instead upon its traditional requirement of a super-majority to limit debate and amendments as on other measures.

The limitation imposed on debate in the Senate by section 305 is on hours of debate, and not on consideration of the budget resolution itself. Thus an anomalous budget process in the Senate, known as its 'vote-o-rama'—the disposition without debate of numerous Senate amendments to budget resolutions after the expiration of debate time, whether or not germane, is permitted. Many roll-call votes result from the offering of amendments, often in the form of 'sense of Congress' expressions, 'reserve funds', or non-germane process amendments, lasting many hours on the final day of initial consideration of the budget resolution in the Senate. For example, on 12 March 2008, forty-two amendments were offered and voted on in some way in a 'vote-o-rama' following the expiration of debate time, and only by unanimous consent were two minutes of debate permitted on each amendment prior to those votes. Several of those votes were on motions to waive points of order against germaneness requiring three-fifths majorities, while others were on the merits of the amendments. The important difference between this 'vote-o-rama' under the statute and cloture under normal Senate rules is that the former is a limit on debate and not on consideration of amendments, while cloture once invoked is a termination of consideration after thirty hours, beyond which no further amendments may be offered.

As originally framed, the 1974 Act required the adoption of two budget resolutions each year. The first budget resolution, to be adopted in the spring, set advisory budget levels for the upcoming fiscal year. The second budget resolution, to be adopted by 15 September, just prior to the start of the new fiscal year on 1 October, set binding budget levels and contained optional reconciliation instructions, on which action was to be completed by 25 September. In the early 1980s, Congress abandoned the practice of a second budget resolution, and reconciliation instructions were advanced to the single 15 April budget resolution to allow committees more time to develop their recommendations, and more time for their consideration in each House and in conference.

Budget reconciliation bills

Just as the Budget Act contemplates two stages of expedited procedures, the second step—reconciliation—is itself a two-stage process. First, reconciliation directives are included in the budget concurrent resolution reported by the respective House and Senate Budget Committees, instructing the appropriate legislative committees to develop legislation within a certain time frame (usually several months) achieving the desired budgetary outcomes regarding revenue, spending, and public debt levels. The instructed committees are not told to focus on any subject area, and are free to recommend any legislation within their jurisdictions to achieve those targets.

The original purpose of the 1974 Act was to require the implementation of reconciliation bills to achieve deficit reduction, and the reconciliation procedures focused on spending reductions and revenue increases on a net basis. In the Senate in 1981, a ruling of the Chair held that reported reconciliation bills which did not reach the prescribed deficit reduction target stated in the budget resolution would be subject to amendments (whether or not germane) which would bring the net savings in the bill up to that deficit reduction amount. That precedent remains applicable in the Senate. Beginning in the latter part of the 1990s, particularly when large surpluses emerged in the Federal budget for the first time in decades, the focus on reconciliation was shifted to reduction of revenues. This has tended to increase deficits for the years included in the scheme of the budget resolution. In a recent budget reconciliation for fiscal 2006, reconciliation directives entailed reductions in both revenues and spending. For fiscal 2008, with new majorities in both Houses, the emphasis was away from 'tax relief' (revenue reductions) and once again on deficit reduction. In 2007, only one House committee (Education and Labor) and no Senate committees were directed by the House-passed resolution to report reconciliation legislation. The Senate version had no reconciliation instructions to any of its committees. Nevertheless the conference report was expanded to include instructions to comparable Senate committees as well, since without Senate committee reconciliation authority, no expedited consideration of their work product would be possible in that body. Senate Parliamentarians advised that the conference report was not subject to a scope point of order, although Senate committees were being directed for the first time without any instruction in the original House or Senate-adopted versions, as that insertion was a 'not totally irrelevant' addition to the versions committed to conference. In 2008, several House and Senate committees were directed to report legislation on aspects of healthcare, including Medicare and Medicaid law changes. The issue arose whether the conferees could adjust the final directives to enlarge Senate committee alternatives, while remaining within the scope of conference. Citing their 2007 advice, Senate Parliamentarians advised that the budget resolution conferees had this flexibility. It is in the Senate where reconciliation instructions become binding, as privilege and expedited procedures attach to those bills, while in the House reconciliation bills can always be made in order (or not) by special orders from the Committee on Rules.

In 2009, a finally adopted budget resolution directed reconciliation legislation to be reported in both Houses by 15 October of that year on healthcare reform and education, in order to reduce deficits in each area by $1 billion per committee over a five-fiscal-year period. It was argued that a majoritarian reconciliation process had never been and should not be imposed upon the Senate on policy matters of such magnitude, although some of the same Senators making that argument supported a departure from the deficit reduction premise in 2001 and 2003 in utilizing reconciliation expedited procedures for tax reduction. As has been demonstrated by the multitude of variations in the reconciliation process in the past, future Congresses will continue to search for ways (consistent with application in the Senate of the 'Byrd' rule which constrains inclusion of 'extraneous matter' in reconciliation legislation), to expedite enactment of legislation where 60-vote party majorities may not exist in that body. This search will be made difficult by the requirements of the 'Byrd' rule itself, including parliamentary determinations whether policy provisions are 'merely incidental' to the outlay and revenue features of the legislation as suggested in exception (D) of that rule.

During periods of changing fiscal emphasis, based on differing political priorities, the Senate permitted budget resolutions which assume reconciliation instructions that increase deficits to come to the Senate floor, when reported from the Budget Committee, as privileged. This has not been without considerable debate in 1997, 2001, and 2003 over whether a departure from the stated original intent of the 1974 Act—deficit reduction—and a shift to a focus on tax reductions (scored 'dynamically' to initially increase deficits but projected to stimulate economic growth and thereby revenue flows with resulting decreases in deficits over five years) should disengage the expedited procedures applicable to budget resolutions in the Senate. There is no language in the 1974 Act which prohibits the consideration of budget resolutions which do not direct deficit reduction. Following those revenue reduction years and with new political majorities in 2007, some renewed emphasis on deficit reduction was imposed by establishment of a Senate point of order against reconciliation bills which result in a net cost increasing the deficit by more than $10 billion in a fiscal year. Such bills remain subject to a sixty-vote majority for consideration in the Senate.

Named committees are instructed to develop legislation achieving the desired budgetary outcomes, with the legislative language to be supplied by the instructed committees. If the budget resolution instructs more than one committee in either House, then the instructed committees submit their recommended legislative language to their Budget Committee by the deadline prescribed. The Budget Committees then incorporate those recommendations without substantive change into an omnibus reconciliation bill. In cases where only one committee is instructed in either House, that committee reports its legislation directly to the House or Senate.

Section 310(f) of the Budget Act is intended to enforce in the House the 15 June deadline for completing action on reconciliation legislation (the deadline stated in the timetable in section 300 but normally extended by dates in the budget resolution itself). It does so by barring the consideration in July of an adjournment concurrent resolution providing for the traditional August recess if the House has not completed action. The House normally waives that barrier to summer adjournment by a special rule from the Rules Committee. The Senate has no comparable restriction on adjournment.

In the House, four procedural steps are necessary: (1) the development of legislative recommendations by the instructed committee; (2) the preparation of an omnibus measure by the House Budget Committee; (3) the special rule providing for the consideration of the reconciliation bill; and (4) floor consideration.

With respect to committee action, the Budget Act does not include any special procedures, and House committees generally follow standing House rules and practices discussed in 'Legislation' at page 407 as they pertain to committee procedures generally, including hearings, markup of the text for amendment under the five-minute rule, and ordering the measure reported with a majority quorum present. While the germaneness rule pertaining to amendments applies in these markups, the diversity of provisions within the committee's jurisdiction contained in the measure placed before the committee determines the relevance of amendments, which might include additional recommendations not necessarily related to any particular provision in the drafted measure but related to the overall budget purpose of, and within the jurisdiction of, the recommending committee. A key decision in the markup process is selection of the text the committee will consider, which may be a bill introduced and referred to the committee. Alternatively a chairman's 'mark' or draft that has not been introduced but prepared by staff is in order, where the committee is only submitting recommendations to the Budget Committee. In the latter case, House rules regarding contents of the accompanying committee report, such as minority views, are not applied since the recommendation is only in the form of a letter to another (Budget) committee and not a formal report to the House. However, in the case of submissions to the Budget Committee, the instructed committees are urged to submit the following material: legislative text; transmittal letter signed by the committee chairman; summary of the major policy decisions; section by section description; committee oversight findings; constitutional authority statement; committee votes; 'Ramseyer' changes in existing law; performance goals; and additional and minority views—the same reporting requirements under House rules for bills reported directly to the House. All those matters must eventually be included in the Budget Committee's report filed with the House.

Each instructed committee is expected to comply with its reconciliation directives by the date specified and with legislative changes expected to produce the necessary budgetary changes. Neither the 1974 Act nor the standing rules of either House provide a point of order or any other sanction against a committee's recommendations for non-compliance with budget resolution directives. Rather the amendment process is relied upon in the two Houses to achieve compliance. In the House the Rules Committee is given a role under the 1974 Act (and can 'self-execute' adoption of amendments in the special order it reports) to achieve compliance. In the Senate the Budget Committee may recommend amendments. In the House, tardy recommendations are often included in the measure by the Budget Committee without sanction, as they are in the Senate, unless that Budget Committee chooses to bring the matter to the floor by amendment.

The Budget Committees' roles to package the submitted recommendations in an omnibus bill are more ministerial than legislative, since they must write a bill for report to the House concerned 'without substantive revision'. The House Budget Committee has, however, traditionally entertained motions to direct the Budget Committee chairman to request that the Rules Committee make in order certain amendments. While the Senate Budget Committee's role is likewise considered 'ministerial', it has assumed over time certain responsibilities toward compliance, including examination of estimates for accuracy, permitting as much as a 20 per cent 'fungible' interchange (a procedure also permitted in the House) between revenues and spending by each revenue committee directed to report both types of fiscal change in order to measure overall compliance, and permitting filing beyond the deadlines. Since the Senate has no equivalent Rules Committee to report special orders of business to enable changes in text, its Budget

Committee assumes these additional authorities to bring amendments to the floor in any area where their inclusion in reported text would otherwise be considered 'substantive revision'.

If the emerging bill contains revenue provisions, it must originate in the House under Article I, section 7 of the Constitution. Reconciliation bills do not come to the House floor for immediate privileged consideration once reported from the Budget Committee. That is because immediate consideration of those measures if considered as privileged under the general rules of the House would be under 'open rule' procedures imposing no limits on debate or on the number of germane amendments. Thus the Rules Committee recommends 'structured rules' as with most other major legislation, and places restrictions on debate time and on the offering of amendments either to achieve compliance with the budget resolution or to include other procedural or policy provisions deemed necessary by the majority leadership. In contemporary Congresses the Rules Committee recommends that any point of order which might otherwise lie against consideration of the reconciliation bill or any provision therein be waived. That same protection does not extend to amendments contained in final Minority motion to recommit with instructions following the amendment stage in Committee of the Whole, since those motions cannot be circumscribed by the Rules Committee but conversely do not enjoy waivers of points of order. Motions to recommit, unlike those Minority amendments which the Rules Committee has scrutinized and has determined to make in order during the amendment stage, are normally not published in advance of offering, and therefore must comply with the Budget Act and all standing rules, including germaneness.

To place special orders on reconciliation bills in some historical perspective, all special rules since reconciliation was first utilized in 1980 have placed restrictions on amendments in the House. In three instances, special orders have prevented any amendments but more often the amendments made in order are confined to one substitute to be offered by the Minority, or to a few perfecting amendments, none of which are subject to second-degree amendments. These restrictions are commonplace in the contemporary House on most controversial legislation, and reflect the Majority leadership's determination to limit time, issue, and Minority options.

Because it is an optional procedure, reconciliation has not been used in every year that the budget process has been in effect, and then not always to expedite both revenue and spending legislation. Following its first use in 1980, it has been used in most years, but in 1998, 2002, and 2004, the House and Senate did not agree on a budget resolution.

Under current interpretations in the Senate, only one reconciliation measure on each type of budgetary change—revenue, spending, and debt limit—is allowed each year, notwithstanding an elastic clause flexibility which would seem to permit the two Houses as an exercise in rule making to instruct their committees to undertake multi-tiered reconciliation recommendations and expedited procedures. The Senate Parliamentarian has continued to interpret the elastic clause in a limited way so as not to allow instructions in a budget resolution which would permit, for example, two reconciliation bills for spending, or two for revenues, or two for the debt limit, to both come to the Senate floor under expedited procedures. This attitude reflects Senate officials' reluctance to interpret the 1974 Act as a wholesale departure from standing Senate rules permitting unlimited debate and amendments, even though the elastic clause by its terms would seem to invite such a departure. The House permits greater latitude in the development of multiple reconciliation measures, which may mix together different categories (for example, revenue and spending) of changes in existing law, or instruct a committee to report more than one set of recommendations for inclusion in different bills, while still taking advantage of expedited procedures. For example, for fiscal 1997 the budget resolution provided for the potential consideration of three separate reconciliation measures in the House so that any of the spending or revenue changes assumed in the first bill could, if not enacted, be achieved in the third bill. Absent this flexibility under rulings in the Senate, the House and conferees are constrained from imposing expedited procedures on the Senate more than once a year.

Like other legislation, reconciliation measures must be in compliance with budget enforcement procedures, as spending levels in the measure must not cause any committee's spending allocation under the budget resolution to be exceeded or revenue levels to go below allocated numbers, unless points of order are waived by three-fifths votes. Debate on first-degree amendments is limited to two hours, and on second-degree amendments to one hour unless varied by unanimous time agreements. Amendments must be germane. Some flexibility is permitted in amendments included in motions to recommit with instructions, to allow instructed committees to report provisions not contained in their original recommendations but necessary to achieve compliance with savings directives. When the twenty-hour debate limit is reached, Senators may continue to offer amendments and motions to recommit with instructions without debate unless unanimous consent is granted. Like consideration of multiple amendments to the budget resolution itself at the conclusion of the debate period, this process has also come to be known as 'vote-o-rama' with accelerated voting procedures put in place. The Senate considered thirty-eight amendments to a reconciliation measure in 2000, fifty-nine in 2001, and sixty-five in 2003.

During the first several years' experience with reconciliation, the legislation reported in both Houses contained many provisions that were extraneous to the purpose of achieving budget resolution policies. The reconciliation recommendations from committees included provisions that had no fiscal policy effect, that increased spending or reduced revenues when the reconciliation instructions called for the opposite, or that violated another committee's jurisdiction, all to take advantage of expedited procedures in the Senate. Although reconciliation and other expedited procedures that limit debate and the offering of amendments run counter to the long-standing practices of the Senate applicable to most legislation, many Senators in the 1980s were willing to surrender these freedoms in order to expedite reconciliation legislation, but with a means of confining the scope of such legislation to its budgetary purpose. In 1985 and 1986, the Senate adopted the 'Byrd' rule (sponsored by Sen. Robert Byrd, D, W.Va.) on a temporary basis as a means of curbing such extraneous matters. In 1990 the rule was made permanent as a Senate rule as an amendment to the 1974 Act.[9] A point of order under that rule if sustained by the Chair in the Senate strikes extraneous matter already in the bill as reported, in amendments, or in conference reports notwithstanding their possible prior adoption by the House. This application to conference reports significantly impacts on the House which, while it has no comparable rule, must enter conference negotiations with the Senate cognizant that provisions already passed by the House may be subject to Senate points of order even though within the scope of conference unless waived by a three-fifths vote in the Senate. While the House can by majority vote waive points of order against new matter added in conference, if that matter is deemed extraneous in the Senate it can be stricken and the conference report rejected. The rule itself states six definitions of extraneous matter, including: (1) a provision not producing a change in spending outlays or revenues; (2) a provision producing an outlay increase or revenue decrease when the instructed committee is not in compliance with its instructions; (3) a provision outside the jurisdiction of the recommending committee; (4) a provision producing a change in outlays or revenues which is merely incidental to the non-budgetary components of the provision (a subjective test posed to the Chair and subject to inconsistent interpretation); (5) a provision increasing the deficit for a fiscal year beyond those covered by the reconciliation bill; or (6) a provision recommending changes in Social Security. The rule then states mitigating factors if agreed upon by a bipartisan determination by committee chairmen and ranking Minority members. The Byrd rule has been applied to twenty reconciliation measures considered by the Senate from 1985 to 2005. In forty-three of the fifty-five actions involving the Byrd rule, opponents were able to strike extraneous matter twenty times or bar amendments twenty-four times by points of order. Nine of forty-one motions to waive the Byrd rule, in order to retain or add extraneous matter, were successful by three-fifths votes.

The rule has been used only five times during consideration of a conference report on a reconciliation measure, but has impacted on the negotiations in conference concerning inclusion of extraneous matter, since the super-majority barrier for waiver in the Senate must be taken into account. Typically, when a point of order is successfully raised against a conference report in the House or Senate, the conference report is considered as rejected. Pursuant to the Byrd rule, however, the Senate may remove language from the conference report which, while causing the conference report to be rejected, permits the Senate to further amend the matter in disagreement with text consisting of the remaining provision of the conference report left intact, by unamendable motion with two hours of debate, so that the two Houses have a vehicle in place to resolve the remaining differences under ongoing expedited procedures in the Senate. In the 110th Congress this same procedure was made applicable in the Senate to conference reports generally where matter outside the scope of conference is inserted ('air-dropped') and cannot be protected by a three-fifths waiver, and is subsequently discussed at page 282 and in the segment on conference reports at page 458.

In the 109th Congress,[10] the presiding officer summarily sustained three points of order en bloc against provisions which the Senate Parliamentarian considered to be extraneous in a $40 billion reconciliation spending conference report. The Chair merely relied on procedural advice from the Parliamentarian without elaboration, and even indicated that he would summarily overrule a fourth point of order in response to a parliamentary inquiry while all the other points of order were pending. The provisions stricken consisted of reporting requirements which had no discernible budgetary impact, and of a hospital liability provision which had only incidental budgetary impact. Following a failed effort to waive those points of order by a three-fifths vote, the points of order were sustained and the conference report was deemed rejected. Then, the pending question was stated as a 'motion to amend the House amendment to the Senate bill with the text of the remaining portions of the conference report not stricken on points of order'. The Senate was evenly divided 50:50 on that question, and the Vice President voted in the affirmative to break the tie and return the measure to the House (which had previously adopted the now-rejected conference report) for further action on the new Senate amendment.

Generally, the amount of time and legislative energy spent on the formulation and final adoption of the annual concurrent resolution on the budget in a bicameral legislature with differing rules and political priorities detracts from time and attention once traditionally available to the authorization process in the early part of each calendar year. This third level of annual budget decision making, imposed on Congress since 1974, requires many votes in both Houses—at least in a symbolic sense—on the same programmes and priorities as in the other two stages, and sometimes leads to conflicting results. While the budget process does to a limited extent expedite a portion of the authorization process through the utilization of reconciliation instructions by requiring committees to report revenue- and spending-related policy measures by a time certain and by giving those reported measures 'privilege' especially in the Senate, that procedure is not utilized every year. It was not intended as a substitute for authorizing committees' consideration of policy adjustments and initiatives in advance of consideration of actual appropriations.

Revenues

Article I of the Constitution confers authority upon Congress to 'lay and collect taxes, duties, imposts and excises', and in the 16th Amendment to 'lay and collect taxes on income, from whatever source derived, without apportionment among the several States, and without regard to any census or enumeration'. Article I, section 7, clause 1 of the Constitution requires that 'all bills for raising revenue shall originate in the House of Representatives; but the Senate may propose or concur with amendments as on other bills'.

Revenue laws enacted pursuant to this provision typically grant long-term or permanent authority for the government to collect various taxes, or vary the rates at which taxes will be assessed for shorter terms based on political and policy constraints of revenue levels imposed by concurrent resolutions on the budget. Periodically, Congress repeals obsolete provisions, extends expiring provisions, and makes other adjustments as an integral part of the budget process. New revenue legislation, and revisions of existing revenue laws, may be considered by the House and Senate as free-standing measures, but in that context are subject in the Senate to the requirements for super-majorities to impose limitations on debate. In recent years, however, such changes have frequently been considered as part of the budget reconciliation process. In any event, revenues are expected to conform to the level established by Congress in the budget concurrent resolution, and must be considered under the procedures found in the Constitution, the Congressional Budget Act of 1974, and the rules of the House and Senate.

The origination clause is discussed in the chapter on Privilege and Contempt (see pages 478–9). This clause governs proceedings in both the House and Senate, but is not self-enforcing. The prerogative must be raised and resolved as a question of privilege in the House by disposition of a resolution generally asserting the prerogative without specifying the offending provision and purporting to return the entire Senate bill or amendment to the Senate as an infringement. Debate on the resolution then details the offending matter. 'Blue-slipping' is the term applied to the process by which the House returns an offending measure to the Senate, as the resolution if adopted is printed on blue paper. Any Member may offer such a resolution, but it normally is presented by the Chairman of the Committee on Ways and Means as the institutional guardian of the House's revenue-raising prerogative. Traditionally the House on a bipartisan vote supports the position taken by the Chairman of Ways and Means despite the political acceptability of the measure containing the offending provision. Assertion of the prerogative in the House is not confined by time to the original receipt of the measure from the Senate, but may be asserted any time the House is in possession of the official papers, even following the filing of a conference report containing the Senate provision. This gives the conferees an opportunity to remove the offending matter from their report and avoids the necessity of returning the entire measure to the Senate. Also, the House could merely ignore the offending measure and originate a bill of its own that would give the Senate a legitimate legislative vehicle for its revenue provisions. Because the Senate is constitutionally free to propose amendments to House-originated revenue measures, and does not have a standing rule restricting non-germane amendments generally, the Senate may originate tax provisions as amendments, which may not be germane to the House-passed revenue measure. For example, the Senate may take a House measure concerning minor tariff or tax adjustments and amend it to include major revenue provisions.

On one recent occasion (27 July 2000) however, the House declined by one vote to support the Ways and Means Chairman and ranking Minority member's contention that a House- and Senate-passed Appropriation bill had been encumbered with a revenue provision emerging from a House-Senate conference and should be recommitted to the conference committee, the House not having originated the provision. That omnibus Appropriation bill was considered by the House leadership to be so essential to the financing of the government that the leadership refused to support the committee's bipartisan assertion raised as a 'blue-slip' question of privilege of the constitutional prerogative. At issue in a practical sense was the Ways and Means Committee's traditional prerogative of origination, rather than by conferees on a non-revenue bill. The measure was subsequently vetoed by the President, and therefore the revenue provision, not having been enacted into law, would not have been ripe for collateral challenge in the courts. One must distinguish between an internal resolution of the constitutional prerogative to originate revenues on the one hand, and a subsequent challenge to the validity of a provision of law which may contain an offending Senate-originated revenue provision on the other. The courts will not normally look behind the origin of the bill containing the matter, if the measure has an HR original number and it appears that the Senate did not originate the revenue nature of the measure. By declining to enforce the House prerogative in this case, the House was implicitly distinguishing between the improper Senate origination of a revenue measure, and a conference committee origination inserted into a House bill on which the House was acting first. In any event minimal precedential significance should be attached to this anomalous instance, as the House in its modern history has otherwise consistently insisted upon its origination prerogative, regardless of any political expediency, when so advised by a bipartisan recommendation from the leadership of the Committee on Ways and Means and when the Senate refused to retreat from its position.

In the Senate, when a question is raised regarding the constitutionality of a measure, such as whether the measure contravenes the origination clause, it is submitted by the presiding officer directly to the Senate for its determination. Similarly an amendment proposing to raise revenues if offered to a non-revenue House bill would also be submitted directly to the Senate and would be debatable and decided by a majority vote.

Another recent trend in the origination of revenue focuses on House or Senate committee initiatives not emanating from the Committee on Ways and Means. There have been Senate originations of revenue enhancement measures which are not taxes, but rather are user fees imposing charges on users benefiting from a government service, where the proceeds from the fees are applied to offset the costs of providing those services. At issue has been the proliferation of fee legislation from committees not having jurisdiction over tax or tariff measures. In 1983 the House adopted a rule ostensibly intended to protect the jurisdiction of the Committee on Ways and Means against Senate revenue amendments to non-revenue House bills. It was quickly asserted as well against encroachments by other House committees into Ways and Means revenue jurisdiction, including amendments in the form of limitations to general Appropriation bills. The rule was patterned after a long-standing rule against appropriations in bills not reported from the Committee on Appropriations. Both rules protect the jurisdictions of those 'exclusive' committees. The Speaker in 1991 announced that:

> most of the questions of order arising under this clause (5(a) of Rule XXI) have related to provisions that clearly affected the operation of the Internal Revenue Code or the customs laws. Standing committees of the House have jurisdiction to consider user, regulatory and other fees, charges and assessments levied on a class directly availing itself of, or directly subject to, a governmental service, programme or activity, but not on the general public, as measures to be utilized solely to support, subject to annual appropriations, the service, programme, or activity for which such fees, charges, and assessments are established and collected and not to finance the costs of Government generally. The fee must be paid by a class benefiting from the service, programme or activity, or being regulated by the agency. In short, there must be a reasonable connection between the payors and the agency or function receiving the fee. The fund that receives the amounts collected is not itself determinative of the existence of a fee or a tax. The Committee on Ways and Means has jurisdiction over 'revenue measures generally' under rule X. That committee is entitled to an appropriate referral of broad-based fees and could choose to recast them as excise taxes. A provision only re-authorizing or amending an existing fee without fundamental change, or creating a new fee generating only a de minimis aggregate amount of revenues does not necessarily require a sequential referral to the Committee on Ways and Means. The Chair intends to co-ordinate these principles with the Committee on the Budget and the CBO, especially in the reconciliation process, so that budget scorekeeping does not determine, and reconciliation directives and their implementation will not be inconsistent with, committee jurisdiction. Further, it should be emphasized that the constitutional prerogative of the House to originate revenue measures will continue to be viewed broadly to include any meaningful revenue proposal that the Senate may attempt to originate.

One area of jurisdictional tension between the two exclusive House committees with primary jurisdiction over 'the purse'—Ways and Means and Appropriations—arose in the last two decades as the result of a conflict between interpretations of two rules— one permitting negative annual limitations on funds in general Appropriation bills (to be discussed subsequently in this chapter at page 284) and the other prohibiting tax or tariff measures on such bills. In the 108th Congress, the House established a new standard for determining whether, to a general Appropriation bill containing funds for all operations of the Internal Revenue Service, an amendment in the form of an annual limitation (otherwise in order as not constituting legislation) restricting the use of funds by, for example, the Internal Revenue Service, to enforce or carry out a revenue provision of the tax code, was a tax or tariff measure in disguise. Before the change in 2003, a Member raising a point of order against a limitation provision in, or an amendment to, such a general Appropriation bill affecting the use of funds therein carried the burden of showing a necessary, certain, and inevitable change in revenue collections, tax status, or liability as required by previous precedent in order for the Chair to rule it out of order. The rule changed the standard applicable to such limitation amendments to one of showing a textual relationship between the amendment and the administration of the Internal Revenue or tariff laws—an easier burden of proof than having to demonstrate the inevitable and necessary effect on collections. This change, at the insistence of the Ways and Means Committee, represented a reassertion of more complete jurisdiction over tax and tariff matters and a protection against inclusion of certain limitations in general Appropriation bills. While obviously an arcane internal rule adjusting jurisdictional prerogatives between two committees, it reflects ongoing concern about the exclusive ability of the Committee on Ways and Means to impact revenue levels and policy.

Thus the House has erected barriers against the improper origination or consideration of revenue measures either by the Senate, by non-revenue committees, or by individual Members of the House, which are enforceable by points of order and jurisdictional determinations by the Chair as well as by assertions of privilege. It should not be implied, however, that the House Committee on Ways and Means remains a free agent in recommending revenue measures. The Congressional Budget Act of 1974 was designed, in part, as a mechanism for coordinating both spending and revenue levels into an annual legislative plan. That Act requires that the budget resolution set forth appropriate levels for total Federal revenues and the amount, if any, by which the aggregate level of Federal revenues should be increased or decreased by bills to be reported by the appropriate (House Ways and Means and Senate Finance) committees. The budget resolution thus provides a guideline for the amount of Federal revenues, but not for their composition. The budget resolution may also include reconciliation instructions directing those committees to report legislation making appropriate changes in the level of revenues, but not directing specific changes in revenue laws. Those measures, when reported, enjoy procedures which, especially in the Senate, protect them from delay by filibuster and assure consideration and passage by majority votes. The reconciliation process is discussed elsewhere in this chapter.

In addition, the budget resolution is required to include suggested revenue amounts as binding levels at least for each of the four ensuing fiscal years, with 'out-year' planning targets extended to as many as ten years. Consideration of revenue legislation is also tied to the budget resolution by its timing. Congress must first consider a budget resolution for a particular fiscal year before it can consider a measure that would affect the revenue level for that year, the only exception being one which allows the House to consider measures increasing or decreasing revenues which first become effective in a fiscal year following the fiscal year to which the concurrent resolution applies. In other words, Congress can consider revenue legislation a year or more prior to its becoming effective without being tied to adoption of the budget resolution, since presumably Congress will have time to reconsider its actions during the fiscal year for which the budget resolution operates. Of course, these procedural points of order can be waived by majority vote in the House on a resolution reported from the Committee on Rules, or by a three-fifths vote of the Senate, and to that extent are only tentative internal disciplines.

While the original stated purpose of the Budget Act was to facilitate deficit reduction in the Federal budget by providing expedited procedures only for those revenue bills reported from the Senate Finance Committee which tended to accomplish deficit reduction, for example by increasing revenues, the Senate in 2001 nevertheless took the politically expedient step of deciding that revenue reduction (tax relief) bills which increased the deficit could nevertheless be considered as 'reconciliation measures' under expedited procedures (limiting debate to twenty hours 'without filibuster' and limiting content under the 'Byrd rule' which precludes extraneous provisions or amendment) if the annual budget concurrent resolution so directed. It was determined that year that a budget concurrent resolution which directed the Senate Finance Committee and the House Ways and Means Committee to report revenue reduction legislation was itself privileged for expedited consideration in the Senate, as would be the reconciliation legislation when subsequently reported. This was an accommodation to the President's budget submission which called for tax reductions to be expedited by a majority in the Senate (and House) of the same party as the President. It represented a political philosophy that tax reductions, while initially impacting revenues in the Treasury, would have the longer-term effect of stimulating the economy through private sector investment, resulting in increased tax revenues. This procedural determination in the Senate through the presiding officer was necessary because, unlike the House, the Senate does not possess the ability to waive points of order by majority vote through action on a report of the Rules Committee. The reconciliation process can now be used to prevent filibusters in the Senate against measures making changes in revenue or direct spending (or both) and even to increase deficits through tax reductions.

In 2007, as part of its pay-go reform prohibiting the consideration of measures which increase the Federal deficit, the House adopted a rule making any budget resolution which contained revenue reduction instructions resulting in deficit increases, as well as any reconciliation or other bill proposing non-offset tax reductions or spending increases (other than general Appropriation bills) subject to a point of order in the House. Thus the flexibility enjoyed in the Senate at least since 2001 to expedite revenue reduction (and deficit increasing) budget resolutions and reconciliation measures was indirectly impacted by the new pay-go philosophy of the House, suggesting that it would be less likely for the two Houses, at least in the 110th Congress, to consider and adopt a concurrent resolution on the budget and reconciliation measures which did not result in deficit reduction.

In recent years changes in revenue laws have frequently been enacted as a part of the reconciliation process rather than as free-standing legislation. In some cases, revenue legislation has been considered as part of an omnibus bill in order to better coordinate changes in both revenues and in direct spending (though not in the Social Security Act). When multiple committees receive reconciliation instructions, including those concerning changes in the level of revenues, all such committees are expected to report their recommendations in the form of legislative language to the House and Senate Budget Committees, rather than directly to their respective bodies. These recommendations are packaged without substantive change by the Budget Committees and then reported as an omnibus bill. Such an omnibus bill containing revenue must originate in the House under the Constitution.

Amendments to reconciliation bills are prohibited in both Houses if they would have the effect of reducing revenues in the bill, unless other changes in revenues or direct spending programmes offset them. Amendments in the Senate are also restricted by two additional provisions, the first of which (section 310(e) of the Budget Act) imposes a germaneness requirement just as it is imposed on the budget resolution itself. The Senate may not consider amendments to a reconciliation bill that would expand the scope of taxes already included in the measure under Senate precedents governing germaneness requirements. The Byrd Rule prohibits the Senate from including extraneous provisions in, or offering amendments to, reconciliation bills or to conference reports thereon. Extraneousness is distinct from non-germaneness because the focus of this test is primarily budgetary impact, rather than subject matter. Under this latter rule, an amendment is generally prohibited if it does not have budgetary impact, or if it has such impact beyond the period called for in reconciliation instructions. Thus revenue provisions in reconciliation bills are subject to 'sunset' provisions in the Senate under the Byrd Rule in order to limit their budgetary impact to the fiscal years covered by reconciliation instructions, and extensions of revenue reductions (tax cuts) beyond that period must be subsequently enacted to continue those lower rates. Politically, inaction on expiration of such temporary tax cuts has been described by some as advocacy of tax increases, while others contend that a reversion to pre-existing tax rates in existing law does not constitute the raising of taxes above amounts already contemplated by law. The ongoing rhetoric from both sides on this issue of 'raising taxes' can obscure the fiscal and economic soundness of the tax in question.

Under section 308 of the Congressional Budget Act, as amended, whenever a committee of either House reports a measure providing for an increase or decrease in revenues or tax expenditures for a fiscal year or years, or such a measure is reported from conference, the accompanying report shall contain a statement, or one shall be separately available if not in the report, prepared with a projection from the CBO if available by timely submission prior to the report being filed, explaining how the measure will affect the levels of revenue or tax expenditures under existing law for such fiscal year and for the ensuing four fiscal years. This is a statutory requirement imposed as a joint exercise in rule making on committees of both Houses which may restrict the consideration of revenue legislation unless a timely CBO projection of resulting revenue levels, if there is one, has been furnished, or unless the requirement is otherwise waived.

Throughout the 1990s, the Budget Enforcement Act of 1990 was a statutory pay-as-you-go requirement impacting indirectly on both House and Senate procedures. Under the statutory pay-go requirement, the net budgetary impact of revenue and direct spending legislation in current and future fiscal years was recorded on a rolling pay-go 'scorecard'. If the director of the Office of Management and Budget (OMB) determined at the end of each Congressional session that revenue and direct spending legislation enacted for the immediate fiscal year yielded a net cost (that is, an adverse impact on the existing deficit or surplus when added to any existing balance already scored) then across-the-board cuts in non-exempt direct spending programmes would occur automatically to eliminate the net cost, thereby reducing the balance to zero, under a procedure known as sequestration. This statutory requirement was extended twice, but effectively was terminated at the end of the 2002 session, when the out-year balances on the scorecard (through 2006) were set to zero. No sequester of direct spending programmes ever occurred while the statutory pay-go requirement was in effect. This was attributable in the earlier years to effective compliance, and in the later years to statutory intervention in the process using directed score-keeping provisions in subsequent spending or revenue laws to avoid end-of-the-session sequestrations, despite the increase in spending or the reduction of revenues which would otherwise have had an adverse net impact on the scorecard. In the case of decreased revenues over the course of a year, they must either have been offset by spending reductions enacted elsewhere, or the President must have issued a sequester order to reduce spending in all non-exempt direct spending accounts. This control mechanism was not based on achieving a specific level of deficit or surplus, but instead focused on the net impact of newly enacted legislation on the deficit or surplus. The procedural discipline was result-oriented, impacting on overall availability of remaining discretionary spending under the entire budget for that fiscal year. It did not serve as a direct bar to consideration of legislation scored by OMB to exacerbate the deficit. At this writing in 2009, Congress is considering legislation to reimpose pay-go as a statutory mechanism putting in place a sequestration discipline.

By contrast, the pay-go rules separately put in place for the two Houses differ from the expired statutory sequestration requirement in that they apply during the consideration of legislation, rather than after the session has ended. Both mechanisms, however, adopt a long-term approach to enforcement by virtue of their multi-year time frame for recording future-year costs on the rolling scorecard. Pursuant to 'elastic clause' authority under the Budget Act of 1974, the House and Senate, as an exercise in joint rule-making, have sometimes included special procedures in the concurrent resolution on the budget for the ensuing fiscal year or years, applicable usually only to Senate proceedings. The Senate's pay-go rule was established in 1993 under such authority, on a one-year basis, as part of the fiscal 1994 budget resolution. Subsequent budget resolutions continue to impose only on the Senate an additional free-standing point of order prohibiting consideration of any direct spending or revenue legislation that would increase or cause an on-budget deficit for up to ten fiscal years, which could only be waived by a three-fifths vote. The time periods as well as the terms of the Senate point of order have varied since that time. When it was first adopted in 1993, it served to complement the statutory pay-go sequestration discipline, by prohibiting the consideration of any revenue or direct spending legislation that would cause or increase an on-budget deficit (it excludes the budgetary transactions of the off-budget Social Security trust funds and Postal Service Fund) for any one of three applicable time periods: (1) the first fiscal year covered by the budget resolution; (2) the first five fiscal years covered by the budget resolution; and (3) the next five fiscal years after that. In its most recent form, the Senate rule does not apply to revenue reductions or direct spending increases that are assumed in the budget resolution and accommodated under a pay-go scorecard maintained by the Senate Budget Committee. The application of the Senate rule to Appropriation bills was imposed by separate Senate resolution in 2002 due to expired discretionary spending limits and the absence of a budget concurrent resolution for fiscal 2003, but was terminated in 2003 by adoption of a new budget resolution extended to the end of fiscal 2008. Because the Senate is a continuing body, rules made applicable to the Senate by concurrent resolution may carry over into a subsequent Congress if so stated by a future expiration date, which was stated in the budget resolution to be 30 September 2017.

It was not until the 110th Congress in 2007 under a new party majority that the House instituted its own form of internal pay-go discipline, one not based on a presidential sequestration order curtailing the across-the-board availability of discretionary spending, but rather on a point of order in the House prohibiting consideration of any legislation (other than Appropriations measures) which, in the case of revenue reductions, was not fully offset by comparable revenue increases or reductions in spending. The scoring of the measure or amendment is by the House Budget Committee relying on baseline estimates from the CBO, and not on OMB Executive branch scoring as under the lapsed pay-go statute. The new House rule, like the current Senate rule, was held in 2008 not to apply to Appropriation measures. pay-go applies to any other measures or amendments affecting direct spending or revenues and having the net effect of increasing the deficit in any one of three fiscal periods—the current fiscal year, the next five fiscal years, or the next ten fiscal years. To comply with the rule, each measure projected to increase direct spending or reduce revenues must also include changes to existing law that would result in a reduction in direct spending, an increase in revenues, or both, by equivalent amounts. Appropriations measures are not covered by the pay-go requirement because their scoring as new spending is already built into the baseline submitted by CBO, so as not to require estimates of further deficit increases above those levels deemed acceptable by the budget. This 'loophole' in the House rule has had profound implications in the Senate, where new direct spending measures such as a Veterans' Educational Benefit Entitlement programme not offset have been added by amendment. This exception was formally affirmed in the House by a ruling of the Chair on 15 May 2008 interpreting the definition of 'direct spending' in the House rule. The Chair reasoned that because the term was not directly defined in the new rule and

> because clause 10 of rule XXI is a budget enforcement mechanism, the Chair finds it prudent to look to other budget enforcement schemes for guidance in defining this term. In a review of relevant budget enforcement statutes, the Chair finds a definition of the term 'direct spending' in section 250 of the Balanced Budget and Emergency Deficit Control Act of 1985. The definition provides in pertinent part that 'direct spending' means budget authority provided by law other than Appropriation Acts.

The Senate rule specifically referenced the 'on-budget' deficit. The House merely references the 'deficit'. The Senate rule specifically excludes the 'off-budget' programmes of the government from its analysis. The revenues and outlays of the two Social Security trust funds (the Old-Age and Survivors Insurance Trust Fund and the Disability Insurance Trust Fund) and the transactions of the Postal Service are off-budget. The Senate rule defines 'direct spending' legislation as that term is defined in the Balanced Budget and Emergency Deficit Control Act of 1985 (Gramm–Rudman). The House does not define either direct spending or revenues. Where a point of order was raised against an Appropriation bill as direct spending not offset, the point of order was held not to lie, whereas in the Senate, provisions in Appropriation bills that constitute changes in mandatory programmes with direct cost are required to be offset unless waived by a three-fifths vote.

Another asymmetry between the two Houses involves the use of prior surplus (scorecard) to pay for increases in the on-budget deficit. The Senate rule is specific in that such an increase must occur when taken together with all direct spending and revenue legislation enacted since the beginning of the calendar year. It also excludes savings from reconciliation legislation from the scorecard. The House rule does not contemplate a scorecard. Together with application of potentially different baselines from which deficits are measured, it becomes evident that the presence of seemingly similar pay-go points of order in each House can be belied by different applications of scoring which may lead to different responses to points of order in the two bodies. In 2009, the House aligned its rule with the Senate's, so that both Houses would use the same CBO baselines.

From adoption of the rule in the 110th Congress and up to the last day of its first session, the House majority was adamant against waiving that point of order in order to expedite consideration of any legislation containing direct spending or tax reduction which was not fully 'offset'. While in the House the mechanism exists through special orders from the Rules Committee to waive points of order by majority vote, a new Majority party leadership, determined not to retreat from deficit reduction, had dictated that reluctance. In the process, it led to several procedural anomalies, including the broadening of the test of germaneness to bills containing unrelated offsets. For example, to a bill granting voting representation to the District of Columbia in the House of Representatives and estimated to require a certain amount of direct spending by virtue of establishment of that office, the inclusion of an unrelated tax increase provision so broadened the test of germaneness to the combined bill as a whole that a Minority amendment on the issue of gun control in Washington, DC, and not related to either provision separately, was arguably germane to the measure as a whole, resulting in the temporary withdrawal of the bill by the Majority leadership and in its separation into two measures merged only after each had separately passed, so as to prevent such an unrelated provision from being offered. As a general proposition, the inclusion of a pay-go offset in the form of a revenue increase is usually unrelated as a subject matter to the tax reduction or direct spending provision that it offsets, and so the resulting test of germaneness to the combined hybrid bill has led to unanticipated inclusion of subject matter in the Minority party's protected motion to recommit with instructions.

While the House had remained adamant in 2007 in enforcing its new pay-go rule, the Senate refused to enforce its own pay-go requirement in addressing the so-called Alternative Minimum Tax (AMT). Upon receipt of a House measure containing a revenue-increasing provision (a tax on 'hedge fund' managers' income but passed in the

House by less than a two-thirds veto-proof majority) as an offset to the AMT revenue reduction, the Senate struck the revenue-increasing offset by the necessary three-fifths Senate pay-go waiver vote and returned the amended measure to the House. Under a Presidential veto threat against the offset, the House concurred in the Senate amendment and for the first time waived its pay-go requirement. Bicameralism and separation of powers demonstrated the limits of fiscal disciplines imposed under one House's internal rules where an impending adjournment and threatened Presidential veto combined to overcome the House's pay-go requirement.

At the beginning of the 111th Congress in 2009, facing the likelihood of rapidly increasing deficits, the House amended its pay-go rule to provide for emergency exceptions from the offset requirement imposed two years earlier. The exception is to be written into the spending or revenue bill itself in response to essential and unforeseen circumstances leading to sustained low economic growth. Any such designation triggers an automatic vote on the consideration of the measure, so as to isolate the pay-go emergency exception for an automatic separate vote rather than necessitate waivers in special orders. The fiscal reality of the deepening economic and fiscal crisis was thus recognized in House rules by removal of the discipline which the House had struggled to maintain in the previous Congress. The procedure was first utilized on the 'stimulus' bill, HR 1 in section 5, on 27 January 2009. That same section waived the pay-go provisions imposed on the Senate by the current budget resolution. As a concession to Members insisting on retention of some deficit reduction disciplines, the House by rule required all committees to conduct regular oversight to eliminate 'fraud, waste, and abuse' (discussed in the Scrutiny and Oversight chapter at pages 314, 317). The House also further amended the pay-go rule to provide that where there was no emergency exception declared, but the revenue offset was passed as a separate bill, their combined engrossment pursuant to a special order as one bill to be messaged to the Senate would allow the bill to be scored as having been offset while not expanding the germaneness test on either bill when considered separately. See also the chapter on Legislation at page 436.

Other House rules uniquely impacting on the consideration of revenue legislation include the requirement that revenue measures must first be considered in the Committee of the Whole House on the State of the Union. (At Westminster, the requirement for such measures to originate in Committee of the whole House was abandoned only as (relatively) recently as 1966.) This is to be contrasted with the current practice in the House of Commons by which Finance Bills are divided by clauses for consideration between public bill committees and the Committee of the whole House only at the committee stage. Both procedures give presumptive importance to amendments. Nevertheless, in the House of Commons the offering of amendments to revenue measures is controllable (by the Speaker's or Chairman of Ways and Means' selection of amendments to be offered, see pages 174–5). In the Congress, the House employs special orders of business reported from the Committee on Rules to restrict the amendment process on specified measures as they are about to be considered. Consideration in a Committee of the Whole under the five-minute rule permits each Member to offer germane amendments and amendments thereto, prior to final action on the bill by the full House. Nevertheless, in the 1930s the House last considered a revenue (Smoot–Hawley) tariff bill under an 'open rule' permitting all Members to offer germane amendments and consideration extended beyond predictable limits for weeks. Since then the House has traditionally considered all tax and tariff measures under 'closed' procedures either prohibiting or severely restricting individual floor amendments. The rationale for such restrictions has been the complexity of the tax or tariff code and the relative competence of the Committee on Ways and Means to legislate in this area to the exclusion of individual Members. Thus special rules from the Rules Committee adopted by the House in modern practice often do not even permit any consideration of revenue measures in a Committee of the Whole, but rather order the previous question in the House to prevent any amendments other than perhaps one specified minority alternative for the entire measure.

Another recent restriction on consideration of revenue measures in the House is the rule adopted in the 104th Congress in 1995, upon the ascendancy of a new majority party, touting relief to taxpayers, requiring that any bill or amendment containing a Federal income tax rate increase or retroactive rate increase receive a vote of three-fifths rather than a majority of the Members voting. On 5 April 1995, the Chair overruled a point of order that a bill containing a repeal of a ceiling on total tax liability attributable to a new capital gain was in effect a tax rate increase. This ruling proved problematic, since the discernment of the rate of tax upon a repeal of another provision of tax law was difficult to measure, so as to require an amendment to the rule in 1997 to render its violation virtually impossible: (1) by requiring the provision to be an amendment to a pertinent subsection of the Internal Revenue Code; (2) to impose a new rate of tax thereunder; and (3) to comprise an increase in the amount of tax thereby imposed. Any effort to impose a new tax rate increase need now simply be drafted either to add a new and superseding subsection to the income tax rate portion of the Code, rather than directly increase the rate in the proscribed subsection, or have an impact on net income tax liability by virtue of operation of other provision in the tax code, in order to avoid application of the three-fifths requirement. In any event, the requirement has subsequently been waived by a majority vote on a special order reported from the Rules Committee. Thus the rule is only a symbolic admonition against an attempt to raise income tax rates, since it is so easily circumvented. It also stands alone as an issue-specific super-majority voting requirement, virtually unprecedented in House rules as a result-oriented barrier against the passage of a specified politically unpopular type of legislation. While the Democratic party majority objected to its adoption when in the minority in 1995—as a uniquely and unfairly targeted procedural obstacle—it declined to repeal the three-fifths requirement in 2007, perhaps realizing the political backlash which such an action might stimulate while being well aware of the ease of its avoidance. In the process, the sanctity of the standing rules of the House as predictable and generally applicable guidelines to the proceedings of the House suffered in the wake of that issue-specific super-majority 'discipline' which was only a political expediency lacking meaningful applicability and deterrent effect.

Finally, House rules have recently been amended to include three provisions relating to information to be provided in connection with reported tax legislation prior to its consideration. A 1999 addition required the inclusion of a 'tax complexity' analysis in Ways and Means Committee reports. Then a 2003 requirement of a 'macroeconomic impact analysis' of any bill amending the tax code to be included in any accompanying Ways and Means Committee report replaced a provision added in 1997 that authorized a 'dynamic estimate of revenue changes proposed in a measure designated by the Majority Leader as major tax legislation'. The dynamic estimate requirement included assumptions concerning the potential for macroeconomic feedback effects. These reporting requirements, unique to the Committee on Ways and Means, are in addition to recent House rules which have required economic related information to be included in accompanying committee reports generally, such as a (since-repealed) requirement for an 'inflation impact statement' and other current cost analyses.

Beginning in 2006 in the House and in 2007 in the Senate, 'Congressional earmarks' consisting of limited tax or tariff benefits—special revenue treatment of ten or fewer beneficiaries—must be separately identified in report or Record statements (including the names of the requesting Member or Senator) prior to consideration (in the Senate for at least forty-eight hours). This disclosure provision is waivable in the House by a separate majority vote on consideration of a special order providing for a waiver, and in the Senate by a three-fifths vote of all Senators. This earmark disclosure requirement applies also to Appropriation measures containing special spending on the request of individual Members or Senators, and is intended not to foreclose consideration of those measures altogether, but only to give timely notice to the Members of each House and to the public of their inclusion prior to consideration and to permit a separate debate and vote on any waiver of the notice requirement.

In the Senate, its standing rules are not nearly as specific in relation to revenue measures and issues as in the House. The only specific language dealing with revenue legislation in Senate rules (in addition to the Congressional earmark rule added in 2007 by Senate Rule XLIV similar to the House disclosure rule described above) pertains to the issue of jurisdiction. Rule XXV, clause 1(i) confers on the Committee on Finance jurisdiction over 'revenue measures generally, except as provided in the Congressional Budget Act of 1974' (relating to the Senate Budget Committee's packaging of reconciliation recommendations) and 'revenue measures relating to the insular possessions'. That committee's jurisdiction is protected against encroachments by other committees by a general rule (Rule XV, clause 5) providing that it shall not be in order to consider any proposed committee amendment (other than technical and conforming) which contains any significant matter not within the jurisdiction of the committee proposing such amendment. That rule applies only to amendments reported from committees and may be circumvented by floor amendments offered by individual Senators and not encumbered by a germaneness restriction.

Public debt (borrowing)

Article I of the US Constitution, section 8, clause 1 empowers Congress to lay and collect taxes, duties, imposts, and excises. Clause 2 of that section empowers Congress to 'borrow money on the credit of the United States'. Both revenue and borrowing powers of Congress are conferrals of authority to enact laws, and require the President's approval or passage over his veto. The authority to borrow money on the credit of the United States is the fiscal antithesis of the authority to impose taxes, although both statutory processes generate funds for the support of government activities. With revenues, the proceeds are the property of the government to 'pay the debts and provide for the common defence and general welfare of the United States'. With public debt borrowings, however, the funds are ultimately owned by and owed to the bond holders of the debt transactions, together with interest paid on those certificates of indebtedness. Almost all borrowing by the

Federal government is conducted by the Treasury Department, within the restrictions established by a single, statutory limit on the total amount of debt that may be outstanding at any time. Most adjustments to the debt limit have been increases.

The annual budget concurrent resolution includes recommended levels of the public debt limit for each fiscal year covered by the resolution. Because a budget resolution does not itself become law, Congress and the President must enact legislation in order to implement budget resolution policies, including debt limit increases. Such legislation adjusting the debt limit is considered in one of three ways: (1) under regular legislative procedures in both Houses, either as free-standing legislation or as part of a measure dealing with other subjects; (2) pursuant to the House's so-called 'Gephardt' rule (see below); or (3) as part of the budget reconciliation process provided for under the Budget Act of 1974. Each of these procedures merits separate attention.

For many years after it became necessary for Congress to pass legislation permitting government borrowing through the issuance of bonds in order to compensate for insufficient revenues in support of programmes, the House and Senate would consider and, with political difficulty, pass legislation pursuant to 'regular order' procedures increasing the public debt limit. The House Committee on Ways and Means and the Senate Finance Committee have traditionally had legislative jurisdiction over the 'bonded debt of the United States'. Such legislation traditionally originated in the House, although not a 'revenue' measure within the origination clause of the Constitution. The Ways and Means Committee would resist originations by the Senate and argue a House prerogative, despite borrowing authority being the constitutional and practical antithesis of revenue-raising for support of the government. In recent years, the House has not insisted on this 'prerogative' since political realities have overtaken this quaint notion and have given way to several Senate originations, where it has proved easier to pass such legislation than in the House. Also, the Ways and Means Committee jurisdictional statement also requires that committee to hold public hearings and to submit its debt-limit recommendations to the Budget Committee for inclusion in the budget resolution. The budget resolution need not originate in the House, and its final adoption of a compromise House–Senate version by the House triggers the automatic passage in the House of a joint resolution adjusting the public debt limit as hereinafter explained.

Given the difficulty of passage in the House of separate legislation adjusting the debt limit upward, where Members have been portrayed by such votes as supportive of additional future debt, the House since 1980 has adopted a standing rule (named the 'Gephardt rule' after its author Rep. Gephardt of Missouri) providing that upon final House action on a concurrent resolution on the budget in each fiscal year (usually on the conference report) a separate joint resolution adjusting the public debt limit to reflect the level in that budget resolution would be deemed to have been passed by the House by the same required record vote as that taken on the budget resolution itself. This standing rule eliminated the need for separate consideration of a measure in the House but not in the Senate, where consideration under ordinary procedures was retained. While this rule had its origins in a Democratic-controlled House, it was retained by Republican majorities in every Congress except the 107th from 2001 to 2002. It is the only standing rule in the history of the House which deemed a bill or joint resolution to have been passed upon the final House adoption of a separate legislative vehicle—a concurrent resolution—and as such it removed the need for a separate majority vote as well as the guarantee of a minority motion to recommit with instructions pending final passage. Because a vote on the budget resolution reflects the majority party's blueprint for revenues, spending, and debt borrowing, and is not confined merely to the issue of payment of debt, application of the Gephardt rule relieves Members from the political difficulties of casting votes solely on the issue of increased borrowing and the ratification of the incursion of past debt.

It is extremely difficult for Congress to effectively influence fiscal and budgetary policy through action on legislation adjusting the debt limit. The need to raise the limit at any particular time when the total level of existing borrowing authority is about to be exhausted is driven by many previous decisions regarding revenues and spending stemming from legislation enacted earlier in the Congress or in prior years. From 1990 to 2008, nineteen debt-limit measures were enacted into law, three times in omnibus budget reconciliation legislation, and three times pursuant to the Gephardt rule (most recently in 2007 as of this writing). In the remaining instances, debt-limit increases were considered under regular legislative procedures in both Chambers, either as free-standing legislation (five times) or as part of legislation involving other matters (including continuing Appropriation Acts, two dealing with timely payment of Social Security benefits, the Contract with America Advancement Act, and in 2008 a major bank recovery bill in partial response to an international financial crisis). Increasingly, the need to include debt limit increases in unrelated but 'must-pass' legislation has demonstrated the political uncertainty of separate consideration of the issue. In 2009, an additional $1 trillion in public debt borrowing authority was added to the Senate's version of the 'stimulus' bill and was included in the final version in response to new spending of that approximate amount in that bill.

Compared to regular legislative procedures, the Gephardt rule accelerates action in the House but not in the Senate, while the budget reconciliation process expedites consideration in both Houses. The Senate has nevertheless refused to permit a House-passed joint resolution triggered by the Gephardt rule to be considered as a reconciliation measure subject to expedited consideration in that body. It has through the budget resolution instructed its Finance Committee to report debt-limit recommendations as part of a broader reconciliation measure, but has not permitted separate expedited consideration of a measure which the House has not itself treated as a reconciliation measure. Where the Senate has been able to treat debt-limit measures as parts of broader reconciliation measures, it has under section 305 of the Budget Act been able to avoid extraneous nongermane matters from being offered as floor amendments. In all, the choice by both Houses as to which, if any, of the above described procedures to utilize for the consideration of debt-limit increase measures varies from year to year, depending on the immediacy of the need for enactment, on the status of the annual budget resolution itself, and ultimately on prospects for a majority for separate passage, especially in the House.

Parliament: Ways and Means

In the UK, the role of Parliament and its procedure for the raising of revenue, or Ways and Means, is less complex. Budget levels are set and reviewed, and proposals worked out for the rates of tax not in a parliamentary committee or on the floor of the legislature but in HM Treasury. Indeed, the powers of individual Members to propose the imposition of a new tax, an increase in the rate or extension of the scope of an existing tax, and the continuation of an expiring tax are very limited. Only the Crown may bring such proposals before the House, whether in the context of the Budget resolutions, the Finance Bill (see below) or indeed any other bill. Backbenchers on either side of the House may move only to relieve burdens on the people, by the reduction or limitation of the tax burden.

There are limitations too on the power of the House of Commons as a whole. The constitutional principle that a charge on the people may not be considered, far less imposed, unless it has been demanded by the Crown cannot be waived. Equally, no more money ought to be demanded in taxation than is necessary to cover the Supply required by the Crown. Any bill which has as its main purpose the imposition of a charge on the people must be preceded by a Ways and Means resolution (though the historic need for such a resolution to be considered in Committee of the whole House was abandoned in the 1960s). No Member other than a member of the government may make such a motion or introduce such a bill.

The comprehensive taxation provisions of the annual Finance Bill, itself at the heart of government's analysis of the condition of the economy in general, the public finances, and central government expenditure, are central to the business of Ways and Means. Debate on the macroeconomic aspect of government proposals is of course in no way restricted by the formal limitations on backbench tax initiatives. The process begins towards the end of a calendar year, when the Chancellor of the Exchequer makes his Pre-Budget Report (PBR) to the House of Commons, updating previous figures and forecasting likely trends and demands in the coming year in both expenditure and taxation. The PBR prefigures the contents of the budget proper, the detailed measures of which no longer emerge without warning from the purdah into which the Chancellor of the Exchequer customarily retreated in the months before his budget speech. The PBR is of considerable political and economic significance—not least the PBR of 2008, equal in significance to most Budgets—and is regularly the subject of a report by the Treasury select committee, but it does not give rise to legislation nor is there a substantive resolution before the House.

In the following March or April, the Chancellor presents his budget judgement to the Commons. The budget speech sets out the prospects for the national economy, the requirements of the public finances, and the consequences for taxation and borrowing. At its conclusion—by practice heard without interruption and presided over not by the Speaker but by the Chairman of Ways and Means—the Treasury formally lays and arranges for the immediate distribution throughout the Chamber of a series of Ways and Means resolutions. These incorporate the Chancellor's proposals for the incidence and levels of national taxation, setting the levels of income and corporation taxes, imposing new duties, and increasing or decreasing existing ones. On these resolutions the Finance Bill, which confers legislative authority on the government's demands, will subsequently be founded.

The Budget resolutions are often long, complex, and opaque. For many years a high proportion of the lines of print appearing on the Order Paper the day after the Budget concerned road tax on showmen's vehicles. Those fixing the levels of personal or corporate taxation are more immediately assimilated.

The income tax and corporation tax resolutions in March 2008 read as follows:

That income tax is charged for the tax year 2008–09; For that tax year

(a) the basic rate is 20 per cent;

(b) the higher rate is 40 per cent.

That corporation tax is charged for the financial year 2009; For that year the rate of Corporation tax is

(a) 28 per cent. of the profits of companies other than ring-fence profits; and

(b) 30 per cent. on ring-fence profits of companies.

An example of a more complex resolution increasing existing duties is that relating to alcohol, which reads:

That—

(1) The Alcohol Liquor Duties Act 1979 is hereby amended as follows.

    (1) In section 5 (rate of duty on spirits) for £19.56 substitute £21.35;

    (2) In section 36 (1AA)(a) (standard rate of duty on beer) for £13.71 substitute £14.96;

    (3) In section 62 (1A) (rates of duty on cider)

        (a) in paragraph (a) (rate of duty per hectolitre in the case of sparkling cider of a strength exceeding 5.5. per cent.) for £172.33 substitute £188.10;

        (b) in paragraph (b) (rate of duty per hectolitre in the case of sparkling cider of a strength exceeding 7.5 per cent. which is not sparkling cider) for £39.73 substitute £43.37; and

        (c) in paragraph (c) (rate of duty per hectolitre in any other case) for £26.48 substitute £28.90

The resolution goes on to specify seven separate rates of duty per hectolitre of wine, depending on the alcoholic strength of the product.

On budget day, only the first Budget resolution, known as the Amendment of the Law resolution, is moved. Its terms are very broad:

That it is expedient to amend the law with respect to the National Debt and the public revenue and to make further provision in connection with finance.

Debate on that motion lasts four or five days.

In addition, the Amendment of the Law resolution usually reinforces the general rule limiting non-ministerial initiatives in matters of taxation. It does so by prospectively debarring certain otherwise orderly amendments to the Finance Bill. Amendments to Value Added Tax (VAT) provisions in the bill which would have the effect of zero-rating any supply or varying the rate of the tax other than in respect of all goods or services are declared inadmissible. It is thus impossible for trade associations or the like to persuade the House to ease the VAT burden on their product alone. The motion for the Amendment of the Law resolution could of course itself be amended to lift these restrictions, and indeed it was in 1994–5 when a successful amendment to the resolution caused the government to abandon its proposal to increase the rate of VAT on fuel: but such backbench victories are very rare.

Taxes may be imposed or varied only by statute or under its authority. Budget resolutions, even when agreed to by the House of Commons, are not themselves sufficient. What then is to happen in the period between the announcement of a tax change in the Budget speech and its implementation by a Finance Act? The problem is solved by the Provisional Collection of Taxes Act 1968. At the end of the Chancellor's Budget speech, even before the Amendment of the Law resolution is moved, the House is presented with a motion specifying which of the Budget resolutions, still to be agreed to, should have the benefit of the 1968 Act. If the motion is agreed to—it may not be debated—the resolutions specified have statutory force, within a time limit which allows for the Finance Bill to be passed validating the resolutions, subject of course to the resolutions not being disagreed to. Only changes in existing taxes may benefit from the procedure: new taxes cannot be demanded until the bill itself has become law, though special arrangements are made for new customs and excise duties.

When after several usually consecutive sitting days the Budget debate comes to an end, the House disposes of the Amendment of the Law resolution, and then works its way through sometimes up to forty individual Budget resolutions, some agreed on a division, most passed 'on the nod'.

A few weeks thereafter, the Finance Bill is introduced, incorporating and setting in legislative form the provisions of the Budget resolutions. One of the oldest and most important rules affecting Finance Bills is that they must be restricted to national finance or its administration, in order to avoid accusations of 'tacking'—that is, attaching to bills in respect of which the powers of the Lords are restricted material not of the character to which the restriction properly applies. The line is sometimes difficult to find in modern circumstances, when (for example) reciprocal financial disclosure arrangements within the European Union present themselves as candidates for inclusion in Finance Bills, but there is a possibility of easing without abandoning the limits of the rule by means of a declaratory resolution validating the inclusion of otherwise doubtful provisions, which the Commons agree to after the Budget resolutions themselves.

The Finance Bill is now regularly much the longest piece of legislation with which Parliament is faced. Many of its clauses concern tax management or administration, or close tax loopholes of terrifying complexity by provisions even more Byzantine. Few of these provisions feature in a specific Budget resolution. Partly for that reason, partly because over the past half-century fewer Members have business experience in banking or finance, and partly because the bill is now regularly divided between committees (see page 439) the overwhelming dominance of a parliamentary session by the Finance Bill is a thing of the past. Pressure in favour of two bills, one for tax and the other for tax management, never made much progress, though the principle remains a sound one in view of the colossal size of the Finance Bill session after session, and the way large blocks of complex text inevitably obscure the underlying policy. Two bills would probably expose the management clauses to a higher degree of parliamentary attention than there is time for at present—a good outcome, but not one most governments would willingly bring on themselves.

The Commons Treasury select committee, in a usually very compressed inquiry, takes evidence from Treasury officials and the Chancellor of the Exchequer, and reports on the broad framework of the budget. The committee's report customarily directs its attention not to the particular tax proposals but the overall stance. The Committee's views are usually available to the House before the second reading of the Finance Bill. In the Lords, the Economic Affairs Committee endeavours not only to inform debate in the upper House but also to assist the Commons by reporting before the end of committee stage of the bill in that House. The Lords Committee concentrates on technical issues of tax administration, clarification, and simplification rather than individual measures such as tax rates (see page 363).

Debate on bills brought in on Ways and Means resolutions, as the Finance Bill is, may continue without limit even after the moment of interruption. After second reading the Finance Bill is regularly divided, the more significant clauses going to Committee of the whole House, the rest to a public bill committee of a larger size than usual. The details of the split are agreed by the House, once they are settled between the parties. Since the Finance Bill is not committed to a public bill committee under a programme order, oral evidence may not be taken. Thereafter report and third reading follow as for other bills, though the former is normally rather longer than in the case of most bills.

The Finance Bill is the major but not the only taxing instrument considered by Parliament. Any bill may, as a peripheral element in its provisions, impose a tax or (less usually) increase the rate or scope of a tax, or withdraw an alleviation. In such a case, where the intention is to raise revenue or otherwise benefit the public at large,[11] a separate Ways and Means resolution of the Commons will be required to authorize the charge on the people. In the usual way (see page 225) the resolution must be moved by a minister. A non-ministerial Member may seek to diminish but not increase the charge or widen its scope. The provisions of a bill which attract the need for a Ways and Means resolution are identified by being printed in italics, and the bill cannot proceed in committee until the resolution has been agreed in the House. Ways and Means resolutions where the imposition of taxation is not the main purpose of the bill are usually decided immediately after a bill has been read a second time. No debate is permitted if the resolution is taken on the same day as second reading; forty-five minutes is allowed on any other day.

The Ways and Means provisions in a few bills are so central to their effect that a special procedure, similar to that applicable to the Finance Bill, is followed. When taxation is the main object of a bill, the resolution precedes the first reading of the bill; and of course such a bill may be introduced only by a minister.

Supply

At Westminster, resources (based on Estimates) are granted to the Crown out of the receipts of taxation—a process known as Supply—and the grants (and no sum greater than that granted) are then authorized to be spent on—'appropriated to'—certain specified purposes and no others. The House of Commons' decisions on both Supply and Appropriation are implemented by legislation.

There are annually laid before the Commons between fifty and sixty separate Main Estimates[12] of future spending (which are really annual maxima not to be exceeded or—in general—carried over from one year to the next) one for each government department and a few for non-ministerial departments such as the House of Commons

Commission (see page 39). The activities of the departments are broken down into functions, and each function has an associated request for resources. Broadly speaking, every Estimate contains a figure for the net amount of resources required—that is, current (not capital) expenditure carrying revenues and costs in the year in which they are earned or incurred, when goods and services are received or assets used. An Estimate will also contain a net cash requirement, including both current and capital expenditure and provision for long-term liabilities, and limits on the retention of any income which accrues to the department as a result of its activities. Finally, it will include a more or less precise description of what activities the resources are intended to fund. In addition, the resources sought are analysed by type of expenditure—administration, grants to persons, forecast capital acquisitions, and so on—and also by a series of functional heads. Expenditure may not be reallocated from one head to another without the approval of the Treasury and even then the switch must not be of prime importance or increase the overall total.

For example, the Estimate for the Department of Education and Skills for 2007–8 began with a request for resources (RfR1) 'to help build a competitive economy and inclusive country', which was then elaborated into a longer list which included purposes such as 'loans to voluntary-aided schools, provisions relative to former grant-maintained schools...Qualification and Curriculum Authority...'. The total request for resources, including two others as well as that mentioned, came to £62,581,430 million, of which £27,882,581 million was already authorized in the Vote on Account, leaving a balance to complete of £34,698,849 million. The total net cash requirement was £64,417,254 million, less £28,846,668 million in the Vote on Account, leaving £35,570,586 million to complete. RfR1 was then broken down by type of expenditure as described above and by function. The list of functions included such activities as support for all functions, support for schools not through local education authorities, higher education, loans to students, and grants in aid of various non-public bodies.

In addition to the normal requests for resources made by the Ministry of Defence, there are three service Votes which also come before the House of Commons, one each for the Royal Navy, the Army, and the Royal Air Force. These do not contain proposed spending figures but seek annual parliamentary authority for a maximum number of personnel to be maintained in the regular and reserve forces. They are what remains of the traditional parliamentary suspicion of the retention of a standing army in time of peace.

The timing of the process is as complex as the form of the Estimates. Each successive annual cycle of events in Supply overlaps both with the preceding and with the subsequent cycle. The Main Estimates are laid in April, at the beginning of the financial year to which they relate, and the rules of the House demand that they should be disposed of and the money voted by the beginning of August. Obviously, therefore, the funds required by government for the period between April and August are unlikely to be voted before the government needs access to them, and so in the preceding November the Commons will have agreed to a Vote 'on Account', amounting to just under half the anticipated yearly total, to get the show on the road from the following April. In May or June, when the need for any adjustments to the Main Estimates for the current year has become apparent, Summer Supplementary estimates will be laid. When the new session begins in the autumn, the financial year which began in April is still running. There will usually be a need for further resources in November, resulting in the laying of the Winter

Supplementaries, and the same again in February, which gives rise to the Spring Supplementaries. In February, any Excess Votes for the previous financial year (ending the preceding April) are laid before the Commons. These set out the details of any overspend by a government department beyond what it had been authorized to spend, or for a purpose which at the time the expenditure was made did not have parliamentary authority. Before Excesses are voted by the House itself the Comptroller and Auditor General will have reported to the Committee of Public Accounts (see page 300) and the Committee will have considered whether there is any objection to granting the amounts.

Despite the elaborate care taken to present to the House of Commons a very detailed account of the Supply requested by the Crown, the House does not go through the Estimates request by request or even department by department. Debate on the Estimates is structured and limited. On no more than three days before 5 August in any year, Standing Orders direct the House to consider very large 'rolled-up' totals for the various types of Estimate—

not later than 6 February[13]	Votes on Account and Winter Supplementaries
18 March	Service Votes, Spring Supplementaries, Excess Votes
5 August	Main Estimates and Summer Supplementaries

Thus on 7 July 2008, the final roll-up day for that year, the House of Commons resolved, without debate,

That for the year ending with 31 March 2009—

(1) further resources not exceeding £233,217,966,000 be authorized for use for defence and civil services as set out in [specified House papers];

(2) a further sum not exceeding £230,753,553,000 be granted to Her Majesty out of the Consolidated Fund to meet the cost of defence and civil services [as set out in specified House papers]; and

(3) limits [as set out in specified House papers] be set on appropriations in aid.

And that a bill be brought in upon the foregoing Resolutions...

In other words, a global demand for resources, a cash requirement and the limit on retained income across the whole of government are, so far as not already authorized, all rolled up in a single resolution.

Divisions on these questions are rare and the deadlines are never missed, thanks to the government's majority in the Commons. The Commons may, of course, refuse to agree an Estimate, but the occasions on which this nuclear option is deployed are rare indeed. One occasion was in 1895, reducing the salary of a Secretary of State because of a shortage of cordite and small arms ammunition, which may have contributed to the fall of the Rosebery government, though there were evidently other causes. The strength of the response is not always commensurate with the intrinsic importance of the objectionable expenditure. In 1919 the Commons refused to vote an Estimate granting funds to pay for a second bathroom for the Lord Chancellor's residence. From a government's point of view, defeat on an individual Estimate is bad enough. Defeat on a roll-up motion would be an entirely different kettle of fish, but it is hard to imagine such a motion (which cannot be debated) as the chosen vehicle for the expression of a loss of confidence in a government as a whole.

The proceedings on 9 March 2009[14] are a good example of how an Estimates day proceeds. The spring roll-up was preceded by two debates. The first centred on a report from and evidence taken by the Business, Enterprise, and Regulatory Reform select committee on financial support for small and medium-sized enterprises and the department's role in the current crisis. The peg on which this hung was a Supplementary Estimate. The second concerned rail strategy and rail fares and franchises, also on a Supplementary (in the course of which debate it was alleged that it could be cheaper to travel from London to New York than from London to York). The two debates were opened by the respective committee chairmen, and were entirely separate. At the end of the second debate, the two Supplementaries for 2008–9 were agreed, followed by undebatable resolutions on the numbers to be maintained for the three armed services in 2009–10, the total resources and sums needed to make good excesses on the 2007–8 Estimates, and a global figure for other Supplementaries for 2008–9. A Treasury minister thereupon presented a bill to authorize the use of appropriate resources and apply sums out of the Consolidated Fund for the years ending in March 2008 and March 2009, and to appropriate the supply granted for these years. The bill was taken through all its stages the following day.

Appropriation

The procedure of appropriation is less complex than that of Supply. Supply resolutions, like Ways and Means resolutions (see above) do not themselves convey authority but must be given statutory form, by detailed appropriation of particular sums issued from the Consolidated Fund, in effect the government's bank account, to particular ends. There is a Consolidated Fund Act in December, permitting the use of resources and the issue of the global cash sum sought in the Vote on Account, without appropriation. In March, the first Appropriation Act releases money from the Consolidated Fund and appropriates to the specific purposes mentioned in these Estimates the resources and cash sought in the winter and spring Supplementaries of the closing financial year and any earlier Excess Votes. In June or July the Main Estimates and summer Supplementaries are appropriated in the same way. As mentioned earlier (page 226) none of the stages of either of these bills may be debated. They are not so much an exercise of parliamentary authority as the framework within which the National Audit Office regularity audit of the government's accounts takes place.

Supply: select committees

It is to select committees that the House of Commons has come to look for scrutiny of the details of government financial requirements and spending, but development was slow. Estimates Committees were in existence from the second decade of the twentieth century, not long after the Balfour reforms, but for a number of reasons an experienced and informed system of scrutiny did not develop (see page 360). Now however departmental select committees play the major role in the scrutiny of government financial activity on the basis of their accumulated expertise across a broad front. These committees are better able to pursue issues in detail than the Chamber as a whole, and their time, though very limited, is at less of a premium than that on the floor. On their reports hang such debates as the Commons undertakes on Supply.[15]

The choice of the reports and the related Estimates for debate is made by the Liaison Committee (see page 362) on the basis of published select committee reports. It is usual, though not necessary, for the days on which particular Estimates are debated following committee reports to be those on which the House proceeds to the roll-up procedure for voting Estimates. Two debates are often fitted into a single Estimates day. Estimates day debates are led by the select committee whose report is 'tagged'—that is, specified on the printed Order of Business under the relevant Order of the Day—as background to the debate. Although the question before the House on an Estimates Day is the approval of a specific grant of Supply, these debates are rarely if ever cost-cutting exercises. They hang on the committee report, which will concentrate on the policy choices behind the expenditure. There is neither the expectation nor the likelihood that the government stands at risk of defeat on an Estimates day: denying or reducing Supply has too much in common with an issue of confidence. The Liaison Committee has concluded that this artificiality in linking Estimates day debates and the details of the Estimates is why the former have not reached their potential.[16]

Two questions are critical to the effectiveness of this system of select committee scrutiny followed by debate on the floor of the Commons. In the first place, much turns on the wisdom of the Liaison Committee's choice of reports for debate. The range of subjects reported on is wide: the range of government expenditure many times wider. In a form adapted for legislatures, the maxim *gouverner, c'est choisir* is relevant. The Defence Committee has recently pointed to a technical difficulty faced by select committees in responding to the Liaison Committee's appeal to line committees for suggestions for matters to be discussed on Estimates days. There is too little time between the laying of the Estimates and the taking of the decision on which report should be debated to allow for a mature committee decision. This 'tends to result in already existing reports, not linked to Estimates, being chosen for debate'. The Defence Committee's argument was a traditional one: the House of Commons should not 'forget that its power to grant or to deny the government's requests for resources represents a formidable control on the executive'.[17] Such revolutionary murmurings are, one may hope, indicators of a future observably different from the past.

Secondly, the range of choice open to the Liaison Committee itself rests on the degree of interest shown by individual select committees in the financial side of the administrative areas they cover. Until fairly recently, there was general and rather despairing agreement that this side of committees' work was not pursued with the same tenacity as those topics which could offer a quicker, more political, more easily understandable return. There has been a remarkable sea change in the last few years, as a result of or at least contemporaneous with the creation of the Scrutiny Unit (see page 377). The Unit has put into committees' hands effective and interesting tools with which to tackle the complex issues of official financial targets and achievements, such as its annual reviews of departmental Annual Reports. When the Communities and Local Government Committee reviewed their department's Annual Report, they quoted with approval the

Scrutiny Unit's assessment of the document as being of comparatively reasonable length and its language reasonably accessible.[18] It is an area of the Unit's work in which the Liaison Committee has recognized there is room for further development,[19] and indeed the build-up of expertise by the Unit in general will surely help to redress some of the balance between Legislature and Executive in favour of the former.

All departmental select committees now take oral or written evidence on departmental Annual Reports, and around half publish a report on their expenditure findings. The Foreign Affairs Committee has commented that the Foreign and Commonwealth Office Annual Report was 'at the heart of our work...Policy work may always be seen as the more exciting area...but scrutiny of expenditure and administration is as important as scrutiny of policy...'.[20] Memoranda on the Main Estimates and Supplementaries are routinely submitted to committees by government departments (and their quality is by general consent improving). Government financial dispositions also seem to find a more extensive part in topical reports than previously. The Defence Committee (which in its report on the Main Estimates in 2006–7 was much more complimentary than the Communities and Local Government Committee about departmental documentation[21]) undertakes an annual inquiry into the Ministry of Defence Resource Accounts in the departmental Annual Report, monitors expenditure plans, holds an annual Defence Procurement inquiry, and includes particular procurement programmes in its regular reports. At the same time, the committee is much disturbed by the practice of including military operational expenditure in supplementary and not main Estimates, which results in the incurring of costs without parliamentary approval and without even providing Parliament with even an outline indication of what level of cost may be expected.[22] The Committee shadowing the Department of the Environment, Food and Rural Affairs made very trenchant comments about the department's £200 million deficit at the end of 2006–7. The departmental reply defended the official corner, but was obliged to concede that 'lessons have been learnt and changes put in place'.[23]

Progress is not of course without its difficulties. The Foreign Affairs Committee was annoyed to find out that there had been two departmental reports on Foreign and Commonwealth administration of which they had not been told.[24] The Public Administration Committee has 'not always found the financial information provided by the Cabinet Office to be timely, helpful or complete'[25] though the committee also had words of commendation for the department.

Some important areas of government financial activity are difficult for select committees to capture. One much discussed is the Private Finance Initiative in which public and private sectors cooperate in the planning, financing, and development of major capital investment such as a hospital or a prison, the latter bearing the risk but also hoping to reap the financial benefit. Value for money in these enterprises is something in which Parliament has a proper interest, but the concept is politically contested and the accounting background complex. One much-respected former Chairman of a select committee commented in that context that 'the number of occasions on which we were informed that the figures we were seeking were unavailable due to commercial confidentiality became more than a joke'.[26] In theory, commercial sensitivity cannot justify anyone denying to Parliament or its committees information properly sought. Of course, demands ought to be made after much consideration for both the instant case and the wider issue of parliamentary powers. Nevertheless, the authority to demand information exists, as well as practical means to safeguard the dissemination and use of information received. To date, most work in this area has been done by the Public Accounts Committee, on the basis of reports made to it by the National Audit Office. Proposed expansion of the Scrutiny Unit might enable committees to tackle the issues of complexity.

Despite such problems, discharge of their responsibility with regard to the expenditure element of the core tasks (see page 374) features in nearly every select committee annual report, suggesting that a common culture of financial work is emerging. The Liaison Committee has reported that for its part it is 'impressed by the rigour that many committees are bringing to their financial scrutiny work'.[27] The proposal to create separate Finance and Audit subcommittees[28] would probably do no more than return expenditure work to the ghetto from which it has only recently emerged.

Parliamentary scrutiny of government requests for resources—Estimates—is complex. Even allowing for the constitutional restraints on the initiative of the Commons and recent improvements in committee work, it is capable of improvement. Certainly, the House will need to keep up with changes in general and governmental accounting practice and move away from the traditional estimating framework if it is to retain a hold on public finance. There is every sign that the need is appreciated, however hard its realization may turn out to be.

New expenditure

Government proposals for expenditure come before Parliament other than as annual demands for Supply. Most bills introduced into either House have financial consequences. Where these consequences extend to new expenditure or include the writing-off of sums due to the Crown, agreement by the Commons to a resolution sanctioning the spending of 'money provided by Parliament' must form part of the bill's progress. Though the resolution sets out the purposes for which the money may be laid out, it does not normally specify the amount involved. Later, when the expenditure is included in an Estimate, a specific figure will of course be given. As might be expected, a Money Resolution requires what is called the Queen's Recommendation, which only the government may signify. The Resolution may not be amended in any way which will involve increases in scope (and therefore amount) of expenditure, though attempts to reduce these are in order.

The Money Resolution for the Apprenticeships, Skills, Children and Learning Bill agreed by the House of Commons on 23 February 2009 is in a very common form. It reads:

> That for the purposes of any Act resulting from the Apprenticeships, Skills, Children and Learning Bill it is expedient to authorize the payment out of money provided by Parliament of—
>
> (a) any expenditure incurred by virtue of the Act by the Secretary of State;
>
> (b) any expenditure incurred by virtue of the Act by the Office of Qualifications and Examinations; and
>
> (c) any increase attributable to the Act in the sums payable by virtue of any other Act out of money provided by Parliament.

The limits which such a broadly drawn resolution imposes on non-ministerial amendments to the bill are hardly oppressive. It is not easy to imagine amendments otherwise within the scope and purpose of the bill which would fall foul of the terms of such a broad resolution. At the same time, the initiative of the government in proposing expenditure is preserved.

The provisions of a bill which involve expenditure covered by the resolution are identified by being printed in italics (unless—curiously—the bill originates in the Lords—see page 266). Money Resolutions are usually considered immediately after the second reading of a government bill. In the case of private Members' bills, if the government is prepared to bring forward a Money Resolution—which it will normally but is not obliged to do—the Resolution is put before the House for decision on a day later than second reading. In the first case, the motion for the resolution is disposed of without debate, on the tacit understanding that the financial consequences of the bill will have formed part of the second reading debate, and in the second a forty-five-minute limit is placed on debate. Unless a Money Resolution has been agreed to, the italicized provisions in a bill may not be considered by the committee to which the bill may be sent and the career of the bill comes to an untimely end, an unusual but not unheard of eventuality.

The financial initiative of the Crown is further buttressed by the rule that a bill the main (not incidental) object of which is a public charge, whether originating in the Commons or the Lords, may be proceeded with only if introduced or taken up by a minister.

Supply, Ways and Means, and the Lords

The financial pre-eminence of the House of Commons rests on the need for the consent of the representatives of the tax-paying governed to expenditure proposed by the government. That is as true of the fitting out of a fleet to fight the French in the eighteenth century as it is of transfers to the European Union which may fund Anglo-French cooperation in the twenty-first. In spending and taxing, the Lords have by long-standing constitutional practice only very limited rights. These are described below, though it should be remembered that the upper House is not debarred from possessing and expressing views on these matters, as is clear from the work of the Economic Affairs Committee (see page 363).

The Commons resolved as long ago as 1678

> That all aids and supplies and aids to His Majesty in Parliament are the sole gift of the Commons, and all bills for the granting of any such aids ought to begin with the Commons; and that it is the undoubted and sole right of the Commons to direct, limit and appoint in such bills the ends, purposes, considerations, conditions, limitations and qualifications of such grants, which ought not to be changed or altered by the House of Lords.

The Lords may thus concur in the grant of Supply for the service of the Crown (see page 225) or the levying of a charge on the people by taxation when these are contained in bills originating in the Commons: they may not initiate such legislation. This is always true of what might be called heartland financial bills, known as 'bills of aids and supplies' (in practice the annual Finance Bill for taxation and the Consolidated Fund Bill for expenditure) which can never originate in the Lords. Rejection by the Lords of such a bill sent to them by the Commons would involve a constitutional crisis of the very first order, as the latest instance (a century ago) amply demonstrated (see page 64). It would be an unacceptable affront to the Commons were the Lords as much as to seek to amend a bill of aids and supplies. The upper House usually does not even go into committee on these bills. The Lords long ago declared however that any attempt by the Commons to steal a march on them by adding to bills of aids and supplies matter irrelevant to the bill's purpose would be 'un-parliamentary and tend to the destruction of constitutional government'. Though suspicions of such 'tacking' give rise to occasional grumbling, the matter has not been a serious *casus belli* between the Houses for a very long time.

If rigidly applied, however, the exclusive right of the lower House to initiate financial legislation would limit the role of the Lords to an unreasonable extent. Most modern legislation has financial clauses which are clearly subsidiary to the main thrust of the bill, and in such cases the Commons has long since ceased to insist on every scintilla of its financial privileges. An expedient has been found which preserves the principle while modifying the practice. Bills with financial clauses, whether increasing or reducing a charge—assuming they are not bills of aids and supplies—may originate in the Lords provided that they arrive in the Commons containing a clause, printed in bold type and inserted in the Lords at the latest possible stage in the bill's career there, to the—obviously fictional—effect that nothing in the Act is to impose any charge on the people or public funds, or vary the amount or incidence of or otherwise alter any charge in any manner. The Commons then authorizes the charge involved by agreeing to a Money or Ways and Means Resolution (see page 264) and then strikes out the misleading but convenient disclaimer from the bill.

If the Lords should amend a Commons bill (other than a bill of aids and supplies) in ways which infringe Commons financial privileges, the lower House has a choice of courses of action. The Speaker draws attention to the fact that the House's financial privileges are affected by a Lords Amendment or Amendments. The Commons will usually waive its privileges and agree to the Lords Amendment, especially in the case of Amendments made on a government motion in the upper House. In such cases they will previously come to a Money Resolution (see page 264) to 'cover' the expenditure.

The Commons need not however take this cooperative line. If the Commons is faced with a Lords Amendment affecting privilege which is within the original Money or Ways and Means Resolution but not acceptable to the government majority, the proposal is likely to be disagreed to. In such a case, the Reason returned to the Lords by the Commons (see page 462) is more than usually terse, not explaining even in shorthand the background to the disagreement but simply announcing in what way the House's financial privileges have been engaged, and not offering any further Reason, 'trusting that the Reason given may be deemed sufficient'. Finally, if a Lords Amendment requires the cover of a Money or Ways and Means Resolution and none is likely to be forthcoming, the Speaker has powers to declare the Amendment disagreed to, without any debate, as was done for example on 15 July 2008 in connection with Lords Amendments to the National Insurance Contributions Bill.

A second bulwark of Commons financial privileges, in addition to ancient constitutional rights, is to be found in the Parliament Acts 1911 and 1949, the origin and status of which is described above (pages 63–4). The principal purpose of these statutes is to remove from the Lords the right which they would normally possess to reject even if they cannot amend bills which engage the Commons financial privileges. It has been estimated that of the Finance Bills sent to the Lords since 1911, all of which were bills of aids and supplies, only about half qualified for the specially protected status conferred by the Parliament Acts.[29] For the purposes of the Parliament Acts, the definition of 'financial privileges' is not that of ancient practice. The Speaker will certify as a Money Bill within the definition of the Parliament Acts a bill which contains only certain provisions respecting taxation, the imposition or variation of charges on the Consolidated Fund or money provided by Parliament, and supplementary matters connected with public money. Disqualifying provisions are usually easy to spot and there is normally little disagreement over whether a particular bill fits the frame or not. Any extraneous matter unless subordinate or incidental to the main thrust of the bill will take it beyond the statutory definition. At the same time, the provision in the 1911 Act that the Speaker's certificate is conclusive and may not be challenged in a court of law might nowadays prove a less reliable defence against judicial interference than was originally intended.

The normal practice of the Lords is not to go into committee on such bills. A Money Bill within the meaning of the Parliament Acts sent by the Commons to the Lords at least a month before the end of the session of Parliament and not passed without amendment within a month after it has been sent up, is presented for the royal assent without the consent of the upper House.

Congress: authorization for appropriations

A primary avenue for exercising Congress's power of the purse is the authorization and appropriation of Federal spending to carry out government activities. While the power over appropriations is granted to Congress by the US Constitution, the authorization process as a prerequisite to the consideration of appropriations is derived only from House and Senate rules. The formal process consists of two sequential steps: (1) the enactment of an authorization law that may create or continue an agency or programme as well as authorize the subsequent enactment of appropriations; and (2) enactment of appropriations law to provide funds for the authorized agency or programme. Since 1974, both these processes have become intertwined with the Congressional budget process through enactment of the Congressional Budget Act, which may place spending ceilings on budget authority and outlays for a fiscal year and which otherwise provides a mechanism for allocating Federal resources among competing government programmes. Those three levels of decision making thus form the annual fiscal year procedural basis for the determination of levels and conditions of spending of funds from the Treasury.

The authorizing committees in each House are sometimes called 'legislative' committees, as they have no jurisdiction over appropriations but do have jurisdiction over policy and programme initiatives, revisions, and repeals or renewals. Most committees in each

House fit that definition, and only a few committees have no jurisdiction whatsoever over measures providing for the enactment of authorization of appropriations. Every standing committee of the House, other than the Committee on Standards of Official Conduct, as well as the Permanent Select Committee on Intelligence, possesses a statement of legislative jurisdiction in Rule X. With a few notable exceptions, authorizing committee jurisdictions are delineated in Rule X on the basis of subject matter (for example, immigration policy and non-border enforcement in the Judiciary Committee) rather than—as in the House of Commons—on the basis of Executive branch organization (for example, the Immigration and Naturalization Service) and authorization measures are referred by the Speaker on the basis of non-partisan Parliamentarian's Office guidelines to one or more committees, which in turn report measures authorizing appropriations for an Executive branch entity to carry out programmes and activities in those subject-matter areas. These jurisdictional issues are further discussed in the chapter on Legislation. An authorization Act frequently sets spending ceilings for the programmes and activities which may be permanent, annual, or multi-year in duration. In the latter two examples, re-authorizations are required when those laws expire, in order that Congress may re-examine both levels of spending and policy and programme initiatives to be enacted, modified, or repealed during those subsequent years. Thus an authorizing measure can establish, continue, or modify funding parameters for an agency or programme for a fixed or indefinite period of time. The language of authorization is normally stated as follows: 'There is hereby authorized to be appropriated for the fiscal year ending 30 September 2008, not to exceed $—— to carry out program x; there is hereby authorized to be appropriated for the fiscal years ending 2008, 2009, and 2010 respectively the following sums...$——;' or 'there is hereby authorized to be appropriated such sums as may be necessary for the fiscal years...'. Sometimes those authorized sums are also permitted to 'remain available until expended', that is, beyond the fiscal year in question, so as to enable subsequent Appropriation Acts to continue the actual availability of those funds beyond 30 September without being subject to a point of order in the House or Senate. The authorization law may also set forth the duties and functions of an agency or programme, its organizational structure (as in an 'organic statute' originally establishing the entity) and the responsibilities of programme officials.

This is not to say that Congress may not end up spending Federal funds through the appropriation process for projects and programmes not previously specifically authorized by law. The authorization prerequisite is not self-enforcing, as increasingly in both Houses appropriations are considered and even enacted in regular general Appropriation bills, in supplemental appropriations measures, and in continuing appropriations joint resolutions, to continue funding for government entities despite the lack of an authorization law being previously or sometimes ever enacted for the period of the appropriation. The authorization–appropriation process in both Houses imposes a series of rules establishing points of order which require a sequence of enactments and which prohibit a crossover of provisions between the two types of measures. The rules prohibit appropriations for unauthorized agencies or programmes, and an appropriation in excess of an authorized amount is considered an unauthorized appropriation. House rules prohibit the inclusion of legislative or authorization language (that is, changes in existing law) in general Appropriation bills, and conversely prohibit appropriations from being carried in authorizing legislation. These respective protections of the separation of the process are nevertheless often ignored, waived, or blurred, based on the statutory need under the Anti-deficiency Act of 1921 and the Congressional Budget Act of 1974 to enact actual spending (Appropriation bills) prior to the beginning of a new fiscal year (or else face a lapse in spending authority). Many authorizing committees confront timing and political uncertainty in consideration of their policy and authorization measures, as they normally face no comparable statutory deadline for enactment into law. While the rules presume the integrity of the process, a point of order must be raised to enforce them. Such rules are often waived by unanimous consent, by a motion for suspension of the rules, or by a special order of business reported from the Committee on Rules. If unauthorized appropriations are enacted into law through circumvention of House and Senate rules, in most cases the agency may spend the entire amount. Only in isolated examples have authorizing laws required that subsequent appropriations must first be specifically authorized by separate law before the funds may be spent (such as military and intelligence funding) but those laws may be waived to permit immediate spending upon enactment of an appropriation.[30]

As a procedural matter, whenever there is a question of order in the House regarding sufficient authorization in law, the burden of proof is upon the proponent of the appropriation—the committee with respect to the reported bill or the offeror of the amendment containing the funds, to convince the Chair by a preponderance of the evidence that there exists either in the organic law establishing the agency or programme, or more frequently in subsequent specific enactments, statutory authority for the consideration of the appropriation for the fiscal year in question. The trend toward periodic authorizations is reflected in the rule adopted in 1970 that requires each standing committee to ensure that appropriations for continuing programmes will be made annually 'to the maximum extent feasible'. Programmes for which appropriations are not made annually may have 'sunset' provisions that require their review periodically to determine whether they can be modified to permit annual appropriations. A general grant of authority to an agency may be found sufficiently broad to authorize items or projects that are incidental to carrying out the purpose of the basic law. On the other hand, where the authorizing law permits a lump-sum appropriation and confers broad discretion on an Executive in allotting funds, an appropriation for a specific purpose may be ruled out as inconsistent with the basic law. Executive orders do not constitute sufficient authorization in the absence of proof of derivation from a statute which itself is the necessary basis. The inclusion of unauthorized appropriations in previous Appropriation Acts which escaped points of order and have become law for one fiscal year is not sufficient authority for subsequent fiscal years' appropriation, unless the language has permanent effect by its terms or forms the basis of a 'work in progress'.

In the House, where multiple referral of legislation has been in place since 1974, the overlaps of authorizing committees' jurisdictions have resulted in a slow-down in the expeditious reporting of authorizing legislation. In the Senate, while there are seldom multiple referrals of authorizing measures, the fact that many Senators serve on both authorizing and appropriation committees, together with the ease with which authorizing and policy provisions can be placed on general Appropriation bills having time deadlines for enactment, has led to an even greater delay in the enactment of timely authorization measures in recent years. Indeed, in contemporary Congresses where the availability of time and expeditious political will is at a premium, where the Congressional budget process has introduced an additional annual decision-making requirement siphoning much time and energy, and where legislative policy issues can be easily injected into the annual appropriations process despite varying degrees of procedural separation in each House, the traditional relevance of authorizing committees to overall decision making has been called into question with increasing frequency.

In the Senate, unauthorized appropriations and legislation in Appropriation bills are treated separately. The Senate rule regarding such language applies only to amendments to general Appropriation bills, such as those offered on the Senate floor, reported by the Senate Appropriations Committee to the House-passed measure, or proposed as a substitute for the House-passed text. The rule does not apply to provisions in Senate bills or conference reports, and is less restrictive than the House rule on unauthorized appropriations. For example, the Senate Appropriations Committee may report committee amendments containing unauthorized appropriations and an appropriation is considered authorized in the Senate if the Senate previously passes the authorization bill during the same session of Congress. In contrast, in the House, the authorization must be in law. Although the Senate rule generally prohibits unauthorized appropriations in non-committee amendments, Senators rarely raise this point of order because of exceptions to the rule.

The Senate rule prohibits legislation in both Senate Appropriations Committee amendments and in individual Senators' amendments. However, under Senate precedents, an amendment containing legislation may be considered if it is germane to language in the House-passed Appropriation bill. That is, if the House 'opens the door' by including a legislative provision in a House-passed Appropriation bill, the Senate has an 'inherent right' to amend it. However, if the Senate considers an original Senate Appropriation bill, rather than the House-passed bill, for amendment, there is no House language to which the legislative provision could be germane. Therefore, the defence of germaneness is not available. As a general proposition, Senate rules in this area are not as strictly enforced as in the House, due to the comity and deference traditionally shown among individual Senators to permit each of them separate votes on the merits of their amendments.

When from time to time select committees are created, they are given legislative jurisdiction over authorization measures or not, depending on the enabling statute or resolution. For example, the Select Committee on Homeland Security in the 108th Congress was given jurisdiction over amendments to the Department of Homeland Security Act of 2002, and by implication jurisdiction over authorizations for certain activities of that department during that Congress. Subsequently the creation of the Standing Committee on Homeland Security in the 109th Congress formalized jurisdiction over authorization of appropriations and over many of the policy functions of that department in one Standing Committee. By contrast, the Select Committee on Climate Change created in the 110th Congress was given no legislative jurisdiction to report authorization measures to the House. As a general proposition, only the Permanent Select Committee on Intelligence of all current select committees reports annual authorization legislation to the House, although the levels of authorization for intelligence-related programmes and activities throughout the Executive branch are classified and are attached by reference in the measure to a secret annex which can be seen by Members only in the rooms of the Intelligence Committees of either House (see page 404).

Agencies and programmes funded through the annual appropriations process by discretionary spending generally are overseen, authorized, and funded through this two-step process. Not all Federal programmes, however, are funded through this process, as in some cases of 'entitlement' or mandatory spending, funds are either provided by the authorizing legislation itself or are required to be appropriated by virtue of entitlement payments to individuals meeting certain qualifications defined in those laws. Such direct spending constitutes about two-thirds of all Federal spending, and derives either from permanent appropriations in the authorizing law (such as social security payments) or from Appropriation Acts where the amount annually appropriated is controlled by the authorizing legislation (as Medicaid payments). The 'mandatory' or 'entitlement' nature of those payments is premised on the legal certainty that recipients qualifying for those payments will receive them directly by operation of law, failing which they can sue the government which has become liable for payments of claims to those recipients. In between mandatory and discretionary spending programmes has emerged a quasi-mandatory form of legislated spending based on advance contract authority in transportation laws, where the source of funding is in part a special trust fund containing revenues collected from users and where procedural firewalls exist in the rules of the two Houses by imposition of a floor or minimal amount of spending which cannot be limited in the aggregate by the appropriations process.

It can be generally stated that the House standing rules are more stringent than are Senate rules in requiring the prior enactment of specific authorization law prior to the consideration of general Appropriation bills. Senate standing rules permit that body's Appropriations Committee to report unauthorized appropriations as amendments to funding bills received from the House, and the defence of germaneness permits that body by majority vote to consider legislative provisions to such bills. The House, unlike the Senate, however, empowers its Rules Committee to report special orders of business which waive its stricter standing rules. As a practical matter, therefore, the House on an ad hoc basis adopts resolutions waiving the application of the two-step process, while relaxation of that requirement in the Senate is more collegial, often based on forbearance of individual Senators to make points of order. This is yet another example of the uniqueness of the House of Representatives among parliamentary bodies over the world in its ability on an ad hoc basis, by majority vote literally overnight from the time of recommendation by the Rules Committee, to depart from standing rules or orders in order to expedite consideration of appropriations business which its majority leadership considers important on its daily and weekly agenda.

Whether authorizing committees are in danger of becoming marginalized in the two Houses is debatable. The ease of waiving the requirement for initial enactment of authorizing measures into law, the legal requirements for timely enactment of appropriation measures prior to a fiscal year, and even the occasional incorporation of authorizing legislation and policy provisions into regular and 'omnibus' appropriation laws, all combine directly to assure their status as law and to avoid separate time-consuming consideration near the end of session. The constraints of available time, together with super-majority requirements to overcome filibusters in the Senate, and with the political realities of often divided government between the two branches, render less likely the separate and preliminary consideration of many authorization measures. Conferences on authorization bills are often made more cumbersome by the appointment in the House of conferees from all committees having jurisdictional claims over portions of the House or Senate version of the measure, while conferee appointments on Appropriation bills are generally confined to the members of the Appropriations subcommittee which has handled the bill in each House, despite the inclusion of extraneous legislative provisions by one or both Houses during their plenary debates. Policy provisions which traditionally have been contained in authorization bills are included instead by waivers of points of order at various stages of the appropriation process with the tacit acquiescence of authorizing committees, in order that they may become attached to vehicles with more timely chances of enactment. Add to this blending of the two processes, the time-consuming nature of the Congressional budget process during the first several months of each calendar year, and the occasional utilization of budget reconciliation instructions to authorizing committees which expedite consideration of budget-related policy, and the result is the diminution of time for separate scheduling of authorization measures, especially in the Senate.

As available time and political will enabling hearings by authorizing committees to scrutinize the Executive branch, a traditional precondition to the reporting of authorization bills, has decreased, especially during periods of one-party control of either or both Houses and the Executive, members of those committees are more inclined to be away from the seat of government during the beginning and ending of legislative weeks, preferring instead to be in their districts raising campaign funds or performing constituent services. Votes are scheduled in the House primarily from Monday evenings until Thursday evenings. Thus motivation and available time (Mondays and Fridays) for hearings to enhance the authorization process throughout the year is minimized. Only continued efforts on the part of authorizing committees such as Armed Services to report and consider annual measures, or multi-year enactments by transportation authorization committees to erect 'firewalls' in order to mandate at least minimal amounts of funding obligations, have enabled those committees to regularly assert policy prerogatives, and in the latter case overall funding levels, in relation to the Appropriations committees. All of this is in competition for available time with the Congressional budget process.

Appropriations

Congress annually considers several appropriations measures, which provide funding for numerous activities, such as national defence, education, homeland security, crime, and general government operations. These measures are considered by Congress under certain unique rules and practices, the most important of which involve the annual appropriations cycle, differentiation among various types of appropriations measures, spending ceilings for appropriations associated with the annual budget resolution, and the relationship between authorization and appropriation measures.

When considering appropriation measures, Congress is exercising the power granted to it under the Constitution, which states that 'No money shall be drawn from the Treasury, but in Consequence of Appropriations made by Law.' This legislative prerogative is enforced in part by laws which set limits on US government officials, who may not, for example, commit the government to spend more than the amount appropriated by law and may not make such government funding obligations before an appropriation funding those activities becomes law, unless preliminary action is itself statutorily authorized. This prohibition, in the Anti-deficiency Act of 1921, originated from a statute enacted in 1870. An appropriation may be used only for the programmes and activities for which Congress made the appropriation, except as otherwise provided by law (such as 'reprogramming authority' conferred by law). This requirement was originally enacted in 1809. The Supreme Court has recognized that Congress has a wide discretion with regard to the details of expenditures for which it appropriates funds and has approved the frequent practice of making general appropriations of large amounts to be allotted and expended as directed by designated government agencies (*Cincinnati Soap Co. v United States* 301 US 308 (1937)).

The President has an important role in the appropriation process by virtue of his constitutional power to approve or veto entire measures, unless Congress overrides a veto. He also has influence based on various duties imposed by statute, such as submission of an annual budget to Congress, which formally begins the annual appropriations cycle under House and Senate joint rules in the Budget Act (see pages 230, 273). Beyond that formality, his influence is pervasive on levels and conditions of spending, ultimately in order to avoid the temporal, political, and fiscal difficulties occasioned by actual vetoes. The President's former statutory Line Item veto authority was declared invalid by the Supreme Court in 1998 (see page 228).

The House and Senate Committees on Appropriations at the time of this writing in the 110th Congress have reorganized their subcommittees following informal bicameral discussions, in order that they may have parallel jurisdictions over respective portions of the Federal budget. Each committee has twelve subcommittees organized generally (alphabetically) as follows:

1 Agriculture, Rural Development, Food and Drug Administration and related agencies;

2 Commerce, Justice, Science and related agencies;

3 Defence;

4 Energy and Water Development, and related agencies;

5 Financial Services and General Government;

6 Department of Homeland Security;

7 Interior, Environment, and related agencies;

8 Departments of Labor, Health and Human Services, Education, and related agencies;

9 Legislative Branch;

10 Military Construction, Veterans' Affairs, and related agencies;

11 Department of State, Foreign Operations, and related programmes; and

12 Departments of Transportation, and Housing and Urban Development, and related agencies.

These parallel divisions of responsibility, reflected formally in the rules adopted by each committee, facilitate predictable conference appointments and negotiations between the two Houses, assuming separate consideration of each of the twelve general

Appropriation bills in conference, or separate sub-conferences or more informal negotiations if conducted in the context of combined 'omnibus' appropriation measures. In several recent Congresses this parallel alignment was not always the case, as the House committee realigned several of its subcommittees for political advantage (for example, separating NASA from the subcommittee traditionally providing veterans' and housing funds, so as to enhance an allocation of funds for the space agency located in the district of the Majority Leader).

In 2007 the House, for the first time since the creation of the Appropriations Committee in 1865, merged the authorization and appropriations committees' investigative and oversight (but not legislative) process in a formal way. This was accomplished by creation in a separate resolution (reported from the Rules Committee) of a Select Intelligence Oversight Panel of the Appropriations Committee, consisting of three members of the authorizing Permanent Select Committee on Intelligence and ten members of Appropriations. This select panel does not participate in actual funding decisions for intelligence activities, that responsibility being confined to the appropriations subcommittee's members, but rather makes oversight and funding recommendations to the Defence subcommittee as a liaison from the authorization committee. It is an acknowledgement of the need for greater Congressional oversight over intelligence activities of the Executive branch, through a combination of authorization and appropriation committee members having joint access to classified information.

Requirements of the Budget Act

The President initiates the appropriations process by submitting his annual budget for the upcoming fiscal year (beginning 1 October of that calendar year) on or before the first Monday in February. The President recommends spending levels for various programmes and agencies of the Federal government in the form of budget authority because Congress provides budget authority (not cash outlays) to agencies. Budget authority is provided by Federal law to Executive entities to incur financial obligations that will result in immediate or future expenditure. Examples of financial obligations include contracts to build a ship or purchase supplies. The resulting outlays are payments from the Treasury, usually in the form of checks or electronic funds transfers. When the President submits his budget to Congress, each agency generally provides detailed justification materials to the House and Senate Appropriations subcommittees with jurisdiction over its funding.

An appropriation not only provides the authority to make obligations, but also gives the agency legal authority to make the subsequent payments from the Treasury, and must be obligated in the fiscal year(s) for which they are provided. Appropriation measures normally provide new budget authority (as opposed to previously enacted budget authority) although under House rules they also may reappropriate unexpended balances of previously enacted appropriations if not already spent, which would otherwise lapse.

Not all new budget authority is expended in the fiscal year for which provided, as outlays may occur over several years as various stages of the project are completed. In other cases, such as Federal employee salaries, the outlays may occur in the same fiscal year for which the appropriations are provided, because the salaries are entitlements to cash for services performed during that fiscal year. As Congress considers appropriation measures providing new budget authority for a particular fiscal year, discussions on the resulting outlays only involve estimates. Data on the actual outlays for a fiscal year are not available until the fiscal year has ended.

Once the House and Senate Appropriations Committees receive their allocations from an adopted budget resolution, they separately distribute the funding among their respective subcommittees (the result of full committee meetings to report so-called section 302(b) allocations). This full Appropriations Committee meeting is crucial to the committee, the only time when the full committee formally determines priorities of discretionary funding among its subcommittees, forming the basis for enforceable points of order against consideration of bills or amendments exceeding those ceilings. The allocations fall into two categories; discretionary spending and mandatory spending (including net interest). Discretionary spending is controlled by the annual Appropriation Acts, while mandatory spending is controlled by authorization or legislative committees through laws requiring payments to recipients meeting defined qualifications. Of total outlays for fiscal 2006, only 38 per cent was discretionary spending; the remaining 62 per cent was mandated by law, including 9 per cent net interest. In that same fiscal year, discretionary spending outlays were distributed 51 per cent for defence activities, 45 per cent for domestic activities, and 4 per cent for international activities.

The mandatory spending provided in appropriations measures is predominantly for entitlement programmes funded through a two-step process. First, authorizing legislation becomes law that sets programme parameters through eligibility requirements and benefit levels; then the Appropriations Committee must provide the budget authority needed to meet the commitment. Should it fail to do so, unpaid eligible recipients would be able to bring claims against the government in court, and the amounts would eventually be paid as judgements against the United States. Thus Congress does not control mandatory spending by setting specific spending levels. Rather it controls mandatory spending by establishing parameters for government commitments in permanent law, such as Social Security benefit levels and eligibility requirements.

With respect to discretionary spending, Congress does set levels of new budget authority for specific programmes, activities and agencies in annual appropriations measures, but first Congress gives itself direction through the budget resolution. Section 302(a) of the Budget Act provides for an allocation to each committee of 'appropriate levels' of new budget authority and outlays, which are published in the joint statement of managers accompanying a conference report on the budget resolution. Each committee is allocated an overall level for discretionary spending that is consistent with the Congressional budget plan. If the budget resolution is significantly delayed or is never completed (as has been the case in three fiscal years since the Budget Act's enactment in 1974) there are no total spending ceilings, budget resolution (302(a)) allocations or responsive Appropriations Committee (302(b)) allocations to enforce. In that event the House and Senate separately adopt 'deeming' resolutions, providing temporary 302(a) allocations based either on prior year allocations (initially continued in place in the House by adoption of a rules package containing an appropriate standing order on the opening day of a new Congress) or subsequently by adoption of special 'deeming' orders imposing levels provided in the initial budget resolution adopted by the respective House prior to final agreement on a conference report on the budget. While there is no penalty if the budget resolution is not completed by 15 April, there may be significant difficulties in addition to the lack of enforceable spending ceilings. Under the Budget Act, the Senate cannot consider appropriations measures for the upcoming fiscal year until completion of the budget process, absent a three-fifths waiver by sixty Senators. In the House, even if the budget resolution is not completed it may consider appropriations measures after 15 May for the ensuing fiscal year to begin on 1 October. In the last analysis, the Budget Act contemplates a start of the appropriations process, especially in the House, despite lack of completion of the budget process, since appropriation measures must be enacted for budget authority to be available by 1 October as a matter of law, despite internal Congressional inability to agree on a blueprint for the distribution of budget authority.

Two Congressional Budget Act points of order under sections 302(f) and section 311(a) are meant to enforce spending ceilings. The section 302(b) point of order prohibits floor consideration of Appropriation bills, amendments, and conference reports thereon that provide budget authority exceeding allocations to the Appropriations subcommittees. Any Member may raise a point of order under that section against a bill, amendment, or conference report that would exceed the relevant committee allocation. Examples of amendments which have been ruled out of order under this section include an amendment to a general Appropriation bill proposing to strike a provision scored as 'negative' budget authority, thus providing new budget authority in excess of the relevant allocation, and a motion to recommit a bill with instructions proposing to provide new budget authority in excess of the relevant section 302(a) allocation. Again, in the House this restriction can be waived by a special order reported from the Committee on Rules and adopted in the House by majority vote, and in the Senate by three-fifths (sixty) of all Senators. When the Chair decides questions of order under title III of the Budget Act in either House, section 312 requires him to rely on estimates provided by the Committee on the Budget in determining levels of new budget authority, outlays, direct spending, new entitlement authority and revenues. In turn, the Budget Committees receive those estimates from the non-partisan CBO and to that extent are free from political manipulation.

The section 311(a) point of order prohibits floor consideration of any such measure that would exceed the total new budget authority or outlay ceilings in the budget resolution. As Congress acts on various spending bills for a fiscal year, the amount of total new budget authority and resulting outlays accumulate and the budget resolution ceilings are eventually reached. Status reports of completed spending measures are published from time by the Budget Committees of each House, and points of order against provisions in excess of those ceilings are ruled upon by the presiding officers based upon estimates submitted by those committees, which estimates are, in turn, based upon CBO analysis. In this context, the Chair is not called upon to interpret a rule, but rather to judge levels of spending from a predetermined baseline. The Chair is therefore not exercising separate judgement and is not a free agent in ruling upon these enforcement points of order, but rather must rely on estimates furnished to him. This is as it should be, since the Chair is not an economist. If the estimates are not available, the Chair cannot rule and the measure could be held in abeyance until the estimates are furnished. As a practical matter, Budget Committee estimates are handed to the Chair just as consideration of the measure begins, in order to be up to date. One exception from the section 311 total ceiling point of order in the House (but not in the Senate) is the so-called 'Fazio' exception which exempts a subcommittee-reported bill from the point of order if it has remained within its sub-allocation, despite a Budget Committee estimate that total spending on previously enacted bills may, by lack of prior enforcement, have caused an overall breach in total levels.

Beginning in the 110th Congress in 2007, a new rule in the House extends enforcement of section 302(b) subcommittee allocations to Appropriation bills after they have been amended in the Committee of the Whole at the point where the Committee is by motion about to rise and report the bill back to the House for final action. If the Chairman of the Committee of the Whole sustains this last-minute point of order based on a Budget Committee 'snapshot' estimate that the bill has accumulated additional excessive spending through the amendment process, the Committee of the Whole then by voting on the motion to rise and report, decides whether to allow the bill to remain in this condition of excessive spending. If the decision is in the negative, one amendment may be considered reducing funds in the bill to bring it into compliance with the allocation.

The most important difference between House and Senate enforcement of these points of order against excessive levels of spending is the relative ease of waiver, as in the House waivers may be secured by majority vote if contained in a special order reported from the Committee on Rules, while in the Senate all such points of order require three-fifths of all Senators (sixty) to achieve a waiver.

Since 1990, both Houses have developed procedures to exempt from the above-mentioned spending ceilings funding for emergencies, which in the House have been extended to 'contingency operations directly related to the global war on terrorism, and other unanticipated defense-related operations'. In practice, House emergency and contingency operation designations may be included in the committee-reported bills and conference reports, but not in floor amendments. Even so, such designations are drafted as legislative language which is otherwise prohibited in reported general Appropriation bills. Utilizing the Rules Committee, the House nevertheless waives that point of order by majority vote, to permit emergency spending in reported measures notwithstanding a point of order under a separate rule prohibiting legislative language.

By contrast, under Senate precedents such designations of emergency are not considered legislation on an Appropriation bill, and may also be included in Senate floor amendments as well as in reported measures. Yet in the Senate, emergency designations for non-defence spending are subject to a separate point of order imposed by recent budget resolutions which can only be waived by a three-fifths vote of all Senators. In the most recent completed fiscal year as of this writing (fiscal 2008) both Houses established in the annual budget concurrent resolution for that year different ceilings on designated funding exemptions. Under House procedures, there was for fiscal 2007 a $5.450 billion limit on non-defence discretionary spending, any additional such designated funds only being exemptible if approved by the House Committee on the Budget. There was no House ceiling on defence spending 'contingency operations'. The Senate, by contrast, set a total limit of $86.3 billion on all funds designated as an emergency, whether defence or non-defence related. These recent disciplines are meant to impose caps on unlimited designations of emergencies during the course of a fiscal year, which had tended to proliferate to avoid three-fifths waiver requirements.

Requirements of House and Senate rules

Beyond rules and procedures contained in the Congressional Budget Act and in annual budget resolutions, intended to achieve fiscal discipline, are House and Senate standing rules uniquely applicable to general Appropriation bills. Their purpose is to separate the respective functions of the authorizing (legislative) and appropriations committees and to confine their responsibilities to measures within their jurisdictions. In the House, for example, restrictions against the inclusion of appropriations in legislative bills and amendments thereto are provided by clause 4 of Rule XXI. A bill carrying appropriations may not be reported by a House committee not having jurisdiction to report appropriations, although the rule has been determined inapplicable to unreported bills which are before the House. The prohibition is applicable to Senate amendments to House-reported bills. A common violation of this rule of separation is language in an authorizing bill directing that funds previously appropriated be available or be used for a new purpose or beyond the time specified in the original appropriation (not merely 'authorized' to be used if so provided in subsequent Appropriation Acts). To highlight the importance of this protection against such jurisdictional encroachments, the point of order is uniquely permitted to be made 'at any time' during the pendency of the offending provision, and not merely at the outset of consideration of the offending provision, as is the case with points of order against legislation on general Appropriation bills. While there is no comparable rule in the Senate, there has not been a proliferation of Senate appropriations in legislative measures, since the point of order exists in the House to strike those provisions if they are messaged to the House and are called up in reported bills there.

To understand this division of responsibility, it is necessary to examine in detail the work of the Appropriations Committees, the amendment processes on the floor of each House on various reported measures from those committees, and the conference or 'ping-pong' amendment procedures uniquely applicable to resolutions of differences between the two Houses on those measures.

After the President submits his budget, each subcommittee holds hearings on the segments of the budget under its jurisdiction. They focus on the details of the agencies' justifications, primarily obtaining testimony from agency officials as well as from recipients of payments from those agencies. After the hearings have been completed and the subcommittees have received their spending section 302(b) allocations of budget authority made by their respective full committees, the subcommittees begin to mark up the regular bills under their jurisdiction and report them to their respective full committees. The subcommittee chair usually proposes a draft bill (the chairman's mark). The chair and other subcommittee members may offer amendments to the draft. In the House committee, these markup procedures are uniquely informal, as House rules of germaneness, restrictions against unauthorized appropriations and legislation in Appropriation bills, and Budget Act violations are traditionally not enforced in appropriations subcommittees, either with respect to the chairman's mark itself or to subcommittee amendments. The 'unwritten practices' of the House Appropriations Committee suggest that maximum flexibility for all subcommittee members is the norm, and as a matter of comity among members those points of order are not even raised. Clause 1 of Rule XI provides that 'the Rules of the House are the rules of its committees and subcommittees so far as applicable'. While each committee is not totally free to determine the applicability of House rules to its own proceedings, there are unwritten traditions which govern the Appropriations Committee's deliberations, to the extent that the publication of those 'practices' in the Congressional Record at the beginning of each Congress symbolically consists of a blank space. All other committees (with the additional exception of the Committee on Rules) must eventually act on measures introduced through the hopper and referred to them by the Speaker, and so the formality of applicability of House rules relating to the amendment process in those committees is to be expected. The germaneness rule is applicable in most committees to prevent unrelated amendments from being offered. Nevertheless in Appropriations Committee markups of chairmen's marks or subcommittee prints—unreferred documents originated by their chairmen—the germaneness rule is traditionally not enforced and is under committee practice considered inapplicable.

The other points of order mentioned above are also not enforced at the committee level—those rules are enforceable only in the full House, as committee chairs would lack the parliamentary expertise to respond to points of order. They are either prohibitions against provisions reported to the House or in the case of the Budget Act against consideration in the full House, as not susceptible to estimates from the Budget Committee to be enforced at the committee markup stage. The same tradition exists at the full committee level, with the expectation that offending provisions which are reported to the House in a bill originated in Appropriations Committee are subject to points of order in the full House or in Committee of the Whole unless waived by House adoption of a special order reported from the Rules Committee or by unanimous consent.

Traditionally the House initiates consideration of appropriation measures and the Senate subsequently amends the House-passed bill. For fiscal years 1998 to 2005 the Senate Appropriations subcommittees and committee did not always wait for the House bill. Instead they reported original Senate bills and even considered some of them simultaneously or prior to House consideration. In no event, however, did the Senate originate and send to the House a Senate-numbered bill, preferring instead to await receipt of the companion House measures and then to amend them with substitute language so as not to offend House sensibilities to the origination prerogative of the House, deriving from its traditional interpretation of Article I, section 7 of the Constitution. In three recent fiscal years, the Senate has awaited House passage prior to floor consideration.

In 2008, unique veto threats based on excessive spending concerns, and separate strategies in each House led the Senate Appropriations Committee to report separate bills, while the House delayed those actions (following a particularly acrimonious full committee markup where the lack of a germaneness requirement permitted the substitution of one politically popular measure (offshore oil drilling) for an entire general Appropriation bill). The House then originated one continuing appropriations measure funding most departments and agencies (except Defence and Homeland Security) at existing levels only through the first two months of the next calendar year, assuming that a newly elected President might be more inclined to cooperate with the majority party in the next Congress.

The House Committee on Appropriations may report the twelve regular general Appropriation bills which it has originated separately to the full House, at which time they are numbered and placed on the Union Calendar (the receptacle for reported measures requiring consideration in the Committee of the Whole House on the State of the Union). The Speaker does not make sequential referrals of reported Appropriation bills to legislative committees despite inclusion of legislative provisions because of the time sensitivity requiring their enactment prior to the start of the new fiscal year on 1 October, preferring instead to allow the House to determine whether waivers of points of order against those offending provisions should be permitted if the relevant authorizing committee does not support inclusion of legislative matter.

The House and Senate Committees on Appropriations have comparable jurisdiction over all appropriations including the twelve regular general Appropriation bills, general or special supplemental Appropriation bills which may be reported from time to time, and over continuing appropriations reported to provide ongoing budget authority into a new fiscal year pending adoption of the regular bills. The committees also have jurisdiction over rescissions of appropriations, whether recommended by the President under the Impoundment Control Act or originated by the committee, over transfers of unexpended balances of prior appropriations, and over new entitlement spending authority in bills reported from other committees at levels in excess of amounts allocated to those committees.

In the House, most of the regular bills are reported in June or July, although the Budget Act gives added flexibility to the consideration of general Appropriation bills after 15 May each year in the event the Congressional budget resolution is not finalized. This reflects the realization that Appropriation bills must be enacted into law by the beginning of the fiscal year on 1 October, in order for government programmes to continue, despite the possible lack of a Congressional blueprint being in place for allocation of budget authority.

There are a variety of reporting requirements, restrictions, and prohibitions uniquely governing the consideration of Appropriation bills, or the inclusion of provisions therein, which do not apply to reports from other committees. They are intended to separate the authorization (policy) and appropriation processes and to require separate disclosure of and where necessary votes on waivers of provisions which may violate that separation. The Appropriations Committee is given some flexibility in the use or reduction of previously appropriated funds, and some leverage over spending reported from other committees. For example, the reports on Appropriation bills must contain a concise statement describing the effect of any provision that directly or indirectly changes the application of existing law, and a list of appropriations in the bill for expenditures not previously authorized by law. Provisions in general Appropriation bills and amendments thereto may not contain funds unauthorized by law, or reappropriations of unexpended balances, except for general funds from the Treasury for 'public works and objects already in progress'. Similarly, such bills and amendments may not change existing law. That includes actual changes in the text of existing law, the enactment of law where none exists, the repeal of existing law, or the waiver of a provision of existing law.

Other examples of 'legislation' in general Appropriation bills include the imposition of conditions precedent to or commensurate with spending, such as future events, reports, Congressional action, and the execution of affirmative new duties not otherwise required by law by officials responsible for the expenditure of funds. Also, language construing or incorporating by reference existing law not otherwise applicable to the funds in question, mandating expenditures to change statutory directions for distributions, changing allocation formulas, affecting funds appropriated in other Acts (past and future enactments) are all impermissible approaches to conditions on funding in general Appropriation bills, absent waivers or failure to assert timely points of order.

Exceptions from this restriction on the Appropriations Committee include germane legislative reductions (retrenchments) of amounts covered by the bill, rescissions of prior appropriations, and 'limitations' or negative restrictions on the availability or use of funds during the fiscal year. All of these exceptions to the separation of the authorization and appropriations processes enhance the ability of the Appropriations Committee to influence policy by addressing the availability of funds to carry out programmes. In the Senate, which does not have the ability to waive points of order by majority vote, additional flexibility is given to the Senate Appropriations Committee to include legislative provisions to House-passed Appropriation bills if the House has 'opened the door' by having already legislated in a related way. Once the House has implicitly invited the Senate to address policy issues on Appropriation bills, the Senate is free under the 'defence of germaneness' to add additional policy or legislative changes by amendment which, if that point of order is raised, a majority of Senators may find are related to issues in the House-passed measure.

Beginning near the end of the 109th Congress in 2006, reports from all House committees, but primarily Appropriations, were required to also identify 'earmarks' contained in those bills or reports—which are defined in House and Senate rules to mean language included primarily at the request of a Member providing, authorizing, or recommending a specific amount of discretionary budget, credit, or other spending authority for a contract, loan, loan guarantee, grant, or other expenditure with or to an entity, or targeted to a specific geographic entity, other than through a statutory or administrative formula-driven or competitive award process. This disclosure requirement is satisfied if an accompanying committee statement asserts that the measure contains no such earmarks. The essential disclosure feature of earmark reform is a bar against the consideration of legislation that does not identify individual earmarks and the Members who sponsored them, the distribution of such information in a way that makes it readily available before the legislation is considered, and certification by earmark sponsors that neither they nor their spouses have a financial interest in the earmark. The requirement may be waived by special order reported from the Rules Committee and separately voted upon by the House on the question of consideration of the special order, and is not applicable to an unreported measure under consideration where the chairman of the committee of initial referral has printed in the Record a statement that the measure contains no Congressional earmarks.

Adopting a similar procedure made applicable in the House in 1995 to unfunded intergovernmental mandates in authorization bills, the 'earmark disclosure' point of order is not intended to stop consideration of the underlying measure upon a ruling of the Chair or a direct appeal therefrom. Rather the rule allows disposition of the point of order by a separate vote on initial consideration of the allegedly offending measure following focused debate on that question of separate prioritized treatment and identification of the sponsoring Member or Senator. This approach to rule enforcement relieves the Chair of being the final arbiter on disclosure compliance about which (like estimated levels of unfunded mandates in authorization bills) he possesses no particular expertise. As discussed previously at page 000, the same Congressional earmark disclosure requirement is also applied by House and Senate standing rules to measures containing limited tax or tariff benefits for ten or fewer beneficiaries, in order to force the public disclosure of Member-initiated special provisions in revenue bills, prior to final disposition of those measures.

Concern about existing earmarking practices arose because some of them were inserted into legislation or accompanying reports without any identification of the sponsor. It was argued many earmarks were not subject to proper scrutiny and diverted resources to lower priority items without sufficient justification, thereby contributing to wasteful spending or revenue loss. Earmarks may be proposed by the President or may be originated by Congress. The leverage from an earmark derives from Congress's ongoing oversight over the account from which those funds derive. Failure of an agency to abide by report language can significantly impact on the agency's budget in the next cycle or even elevate the language into the measure itself. In 2007, an enhanced earmark disclosure requirement covering all legislation was incorporated into House rules and was subsequently expanded to cover conference reports on regular Appropriation bills containing earmarks that were not submitted to conference by either House. This standing order was intended to curtail or at least illuminate the practice of 'air-dropping' earmark provisions, not first passed by either House, at the conference stage.

A similarly worded earmark disclosure requirement was imposed upon the Senate in a comprehensive 'Honest Leadership and Open Government' Act of 2007,[31] having originated in the Senate-passed version of that law as an exercise in rule making. While appearing to apply to all measures under consideration in the Senate, including authorization bills, the new Senate Rule XLIV has been interpreted there to apply only to Appropriation bills containing 'Congressionally directed spending' and to special tax or tariff provisions in revenue bills. The standing order of the House applied the earmark disclosure rule only to conference reports and not to amendments between the Houses. Both Houses have nevertheless applied the spirit of the rule to major Appropriation bills which have been disposed of by 'ping-ponging' amendments between the two Houses rather than by joint statements of managers accompanying conference reports. In such a case as the omnibus Appropriations Act for fiscal 2008, the chairmen of the Appropriations Committee in each House inserted identical explanatory statements of earmarks into the Congressional Record.

The Senate earmark rule also prohibits the inclusion of 'new Congressionally directed spending' ('air-dropped' earmarks inserted into a conference report or accompanying joint statement on an Appropriation bill but not contained in either House or Senate version committed to conference). In this respect, the Senate rule specifically relating to earmarks is more onerous than the House earmark rule merely requiring disclosure, in that a violation of the Senate rule subjects the entire report to a point of order which may be waived only by a three-fifths vote of all Senators. Failing such a waiver, the conference report is rejected and the pending question is on a new Senate version consisting of the remainder of the report. In the House, it was not considered necessary to adopt a separate 'air-drop' rule on new Congressionally directed spending, the existing scope rule in the House (Rule XXII) being sufficient to preclude inclusion of such new items but also being waivable by a majority vote on a special order reported from the Rules Committee. This has resulted in avoidance of the Senate rule by 'ping-pong' amendments between the Houses rather than by conference reports (for example, a final Senate amendment to the House amendment to the Senate amendment to a House Appropriation bill) so as not to trigger the 'air-drop' earmark point of order in the Senate requiring a super-majority for waiver.

In both Houses, the disclosure requirements have been received by Members and Senators with mixed feelings, some anxious to have made public their sponsorship of special spending requirements benefiting their constituents, while others, having obtained earmarks on behalf of political contributors or other special interests, not quite so anxious. The most salient feature of the new rules in both Houses is that it is only a disclosure requirement and not a barrier to consideration of legislation containing earmarks. The proliferation of earmarks, especially in Appropriation bills, both in absolute dollar terms and as an increasingly large percentage of the domestic discretionary budget in the past decade, has been rapid. With closely divided party alignments in both Houses, and with newly elected Members importuning their leaderships to give them political credit for providing assistance to their constituencies and other supporters, the notion that the Executive branch can more objectively allocate available discretionary budget authority by applying competitive bidding and favourable cost–benefit requirements has receded under the mantra that Members of Congress best know the needs of their districts.

Procedures for consideration

The House Appropriations Committee is unique among House committees in having the 'privilege' to bring reported measures directly to the floor for consideration (all other committees must first obtain a special order of business from the Rules Committee to permit consideration of reported bills and joint resolutions). Nevertheless as a practical matter all general Appropriation bills first receive special orders from the Rules Committee in order to remove procedural obstacles (including the three-day availability of the committee report, potential Budget Act points of order, legislative provisions and unauthorized items in the bill itself and, on occasion, either self-executing the adoption or limiting the offering of specified amendments during the five-minute rule). The House considers all regular Appropriation bills in the Committee of the Whole House on the State of the Union. Following general debate controlled by the chairman and ranking Minority member of the relevant subcommittee, the bill is read for amendment by paragraphs unless by unanimous consent larger portions of the bill are opened to amendment at any point. While amendments are normally confined to the pending portion of the bill, a special rule (clause 2(f) of Rule XXI) permits en bloc consideration of amendments reaching forward solely to transfer equal amounts of budget authority and outlays between accounts. Because Appropriation bills as reported usually contain aggregate levels of new budget authority at the limits set in the budget resolution and in the 302(b) allocations, any floor amendment adding new budget authority, even if authorized by law, is subject to a Budget Act point of order unless offset by a comparable reduction elsewhere in the bill. Thus the en bloc authority permits individual Members to suggest reprioritization of funding among accounts in the bill.

Another special procedure for offsetting amendments—the so-called 'reach-back' amendment (offered at the end of the bill as a new paragraph in order to be germane to the entirety of the bill although coming beyond the paragraph containing those funds)—has evolved by practice and precedent. It permits indirect changes in authorized amounts previously considered in the bill, and may permit across-the-board spending reductions as offsets, but may not be accompanied by legislation, or increase prior unauthorized amounts permitted to remain in the bill.

In addition to the requirement that amendments containing funds must be authorized by law and within budget resolution levels, amendments must also be germane to the portion of the bill to which offered, and may not legislate by 'changing existing law'. There exist several tests which have emerged in the precedents of the House (and many fewer but consistent precedents in the Senate) for determining whether language in a general Appropriation bill or in an amendment thereto which limits the availability of funds is in reality a change in existing law, rather than a permissible negative limitation on those funds. Again, the burden of proof that language is a 'limitation', and not 'legislation', is on the proponent of the language, and must be established to the satisfaction of the Chair by a preponderance of the evidence. Indeed, throughout the modern history of the House, general Appropriation bills are viewed as an important avenue for affecting policy by way of annual funding restrictions on the administering agency without the need for a waiver of points of order, by utilization of language which falls within the 'limitation' exception under the precedents to the proscription against changes in existing law. The proliferation of limitation amendments at any time during the reading of a general Appropriation bill for amendment led the House in 1983 to amend clause 2 of Rule XXI by providing a new procedure for consideration of limitation amendments only when the reading of a general Appropriation bill has been completed and only if the Committee of the Whole does not adopt a motion to rise and report the bill back to the House. At that time a standing rule defining permissible limitations which might be offered but only at the end of reading for amendment and not during the reading in Committee of the Whole was adopted as follows: 'amendments proposing limitations not specifically contained or authorized in existing law for the period of the limitation'. This definition incorporated the hundreds of rulings by presiding officers over many years by reference through the use of the term 'limitation' but left open the offering of amendments at any time during the reading if existing law specifically permitted Appropriation Acts to address negative restrictions on the availability of funds. By narrowing the opportunity to offer limitation amendments to one procedural moment, the unpredictability of the timing of their consideration under a traditional 'open rule' process was minimized and made subject to preferential leadership motions to cut off their consideration altogether.

At the same time, the consideration of general Appropriation bills in the Committee of the Whole continued until the 111th Congress to follow the traditional application of the five-minute rule by permitting at the outset of the amendment process the timely offering of any and all other proper amendments and amendments thereto—those which are germane, are within budget resolution levels, and do not change existing law. Because of the proliferation of amendments throughout the 1970s and early 1980s which impacted public policy by limiting the use of funds in a pending paragraph of a general Appropriation bill for an agency or programme for the fiscal year in question, the standing rule adopted in 1983 postponed but did not totally prohibit consideration of limitation amendments while continuing to permit other amendments, for example, to amounts in those paragraphs, as well as pro forma amendments—motions to 'strike the last word'—which enable each individual Member to debate the bill or pending amendment for five minutes. Thus although consideration of regular Appropriation bills under an 'open' process provides a forum that maximizes deliberation, it also means that the time spent considering such measures is uncertain and open to wide variation.

In recent years, until the 111th Congress, unanimous consent agreements were negotiated by committee and party leaders and interested Members and then entered into in the House, which restricted the 'universe' of subsequent permissible amendments in the Committee of the Whole. These orders reflected bipartisan acknowledgment that the House should impose a measure of predictability to an appropriation amendment process which has traditionally been open and unpredictable at the outset, once it becomes evident to the leadership on both sides that a finite number of amendments remain to be offered. Such unanimous consent agreements supplant the open rule, limit the amendments that may be offered, restrict and equally divide control of debate thereon, and bar certain time-consuming procedures otherwise in order. The practice of bringing up a regular Appropriation bill under an open rule in order to waive necessary points of order which would otherwise prohibit their consideration and jeopardize provisions, and shortly thereafter replacing the open procedure with a comprehensive unanimous consent agreement structuring further debate and amendment, was largely unseen prior to the 104th Congress (1995–6) but was commonplace until 2009. In 2007, eight regular Appropriation bills that came to the House floor under an open rule were subsequently regulated by such a unanimous consent agreement. Such agreements act in a manner similar to a 'structured' or 'modified closed' rule from the Rules Committee with one important difference, every Member can have a say in the content of the agreement and dictate its terms by threatening to object, whereas special rules are reported from the leadership's Rules Committee and are adopted by a majority. Such agreements were increasingly accepted because all parties get something they want. Party leaders got increased certainty about the floor schedule while being able to claim a remnant of an 'open rule' process on the most important business, the Appropriations Committee was able to move its bills forward more readily, and Members were permitted to offer the amendments of their choice, albeit without any waiver of points of order. If the amendment permitted to be offered was subject to a point of order as unauthorized, as legislation, or as a budget violation, it remained susceptible to that challenge upon reservation of the point of order, and such amendments were ordinarily withdrawn by unanimous consent before being ruled out of order.

Unanimous consent agreements must be entered into in the House and not in Committee of the Whole, since they change special rules previously adopted by the House. They routinely limit the amendments that can be offered to those listed by sponsor and subject, or by printed amendment number. The amendments then may only be offered by the named Member or his designee, and their readings are waived. Such 'universe' amendments are not normally subject to second degree amendments, and debate thereon is limited to a specified time (varying from ten minutes to longer periods) equally divided between the proponent and an opponent (usually the committee chairman) with only the managers of the bill able to gain additional debate time by the use of pro forma amendments. These agreements do not provide complete certainty as to how long floor consideration of a given bill will last, because they do not regulate time spent on every procedural step that may occur, including voting on the amendments themselves, quorum calls, and points of order. Nevertheless, in contemporary Congresses featuring one bipartisan interest on which both parties agree—the need for predictability in time and issue—

the 'universe' of amendments unanimous consent agreement in the House has gained favour. The fact that second degree amendments are not normally permitted by such orders has the tendency to prevent compromise and to present a direct choice between the amendment made in order and the Appropriations Committee's reported position.

In the 111th Congress this tradition of 'open' consideration of appropriation bills in the Committee of the Whole gave way to adoption at the outset of 'modified closed' special orders on each general appropriation bill which limited amendments to those selected in the Rules Committee report. Several of those 'structured' rules even gave one Member the option to offer an arbitrary number of the several amendments (striking 'earmarks') he had submitted, all in the interests of certainty of reduced time and issue and all greatly decried by the minority.

Two contemporary examples of the use of limitations in general Appropriation bills demonstrate the importance of that procedural technique in the House. As has been explained, negative limitations on the use of funds may not contain legislative exceptions or conditions. Since the 1980s Federal funding for Medicaid abortions has been a volatile and polarizing issue in American politics, as part of the philosophical debate among 'pro-life' and 'pro-choice' forces in society. The issue of the extent to which taxpayers should subsidize abortion services for poor women has consistently captured the country's attention and has been addressed in legislation in a variety of contexts. Most frequently, the annual general Appropriation bill containing funds for the Department of Health and Human Services for Medicaid abortion services has been the lightning rod for language attempting to restrict that funding. Language in the reported bill, or as an amendment, which provides that 'no funds in this bill shall be available for abortion services' has under House precedent been consistently held in order as a negative limitation which did not impose any additional duties on Federal officials in the administration of funds. It was a blanket prohibition. However, when coupled with exceptions such as 'in the case of rape or incest' or 'where the life of the mother might be endangered if the foetus were carried to term'—exceptions which were more politically palatable between the extremes of no funding whatsoever and funding for abortion on demand—the limitation became impermissible 'legislation'. In that form the language required Federal officials to make ad hoc determinations of the cause of the pregnancy or the welfare of the mother—determinations not otherwise required by existing law as conditions to the receipt of Medicaid funds. Attempts to include those exceptions with the limitation on Medicaid funding were consistently ruled out of order as legislation in a general Appropriation bill in violation of clause 2 of Rule XXI. In the early 1990s, a proponent of the pro-life restriction against such funding discovered a House precedent which supported such a permissible exception if stated as follows: 'No funds in this bill for Medicaid abortion services unless it is "made known" to the Federal official that the pregnancy is the result of rape or incest or the life of the mother would be endangered if the foetus were carried to term.' This so-called 'made-known' exception had both recent and almost century-old legitimacy, and served as sufficient precedent to justify the Chair holding the amendment in order despite the general expectation that the inclusion of such exceptions would, as had been the case without the 'made-known' language, render the amendment out of order. The premise for the precedent was that the administering Federal official was being described as the mere passive recipient of information only if it came to his attention, and who was not being required to make new affirmative determinations. The 'made-known' line of precedent not only permitted pro-life abortion restrictions on Medicaid funding to survive points of order in the House and to be enacted into law for several years, it also served as a procedural invitation for other limitations on annual funding bills which could have unforeseen policy consequences.

Clause 2 of Rule XXI was amended in the 105th Congress in 1997 to render impermissible per se provisions that condition the availability of funds on certain information not required to be furnished by existing law being 'made known' to an Executive official. The special significance of this rules change was that it demonstrated an unusual reinterpretation of the rule by a definitional change at the beginning of a new Congress in the text of the rule itself, in order to prevent a proliferation of amendments in that narrow area. This approach permitted the Majority leadership, rather than an ad hoc majority potentially utilizing an appeal from the Chair's previous rulings which had relied on precedent, to control the process going forward in a more orderly way. The Chair would no longer be required by application of precedent to conclude that the limitation language did not, due to its passive nature, affirmatively impose new duties to examine the cause or life-threatening effects of the pregnancy. Rather, henceforth the language if contained in a general Appropriation bill or amendment was to be deemed out of order and could not be employed to raise volatile policy issues in the guise of a limitation, absent a waiver of points of order.

Other tests of whether language constitutes a change in existing law by imposing new duties, authority, contingencies, conditions, or interpretations where none exists in law, continue to be persuasive guidelines for the Chair. Those published rulings of the Chair constitute the equivalent of the common law for the House in this area and are applied in a non-partisan manner by any occupant of the Chair. They serve to maintain the traditional separation between the authorization (legislative) and appropriation processes while permitting within the latter some flexibility for annual examination and impact on policy to the extent that a negative restriction on the use of funds for all or a portion of an authorized purpose or programme may have that effect.

In 1972 Bradshaw and Pring[32] in describing the relationship between authorization committees and the Appropriations Committee wrote:

> the scope of the Appropriations Committee's operations has been shrinking since World War II. A feature of this period has been an increased tendency to write into authorizing legislation a variety of 'permanent' devices by which legislative programmes are to be financed. The effect of these devices—the institution of permanent contracts and the creation of trust funds are examples—take these programmes beyond the reach of the annual appropriation process and leave Congress nothing to do except pay the bill according to prescribed arrangements. This kind of legislation is written by the relevant standing committee. But it is apt to be supported by mayors of cities, governors of states and the departments and agencies of the Executive branch, who like to be able to count on a regular flow of funds without annual checks, and perhaps cuts, by Congress. Between 1945 and 1970 the percentage of total budgetary expenditure falling under these special financial arrangements— officially termed 'relatively uncontrollable' expenditure—rose from about 25% to 69%. The trend has already weakened the power of the appropriation processes. There is no sign of its being halted.

This observation, to the extent of the growing percentage of 'entitlement' spending versus 'discretionary' spending, remains generally accurate, with the exponential growth of social security, Medicare and other entitlement programmes One must also consider whether multi-year 'contract authority' spending out of special trust funds such as the highway trust fund, is more appropriately described as 'mandatory spending' rather than discretionary spending. Current law establishes 'firewalls' around highway and mass transportation spending as a 'transportation discretionary spending guarantee'.

The funding guarantees are set up in a way that provides spending at a level dictated by revenue accruing to the Highway Trust Fund and makes it difficult for overall funding levels to be altered as part of the annual budget/appropriations process.

It is not, however, correct to say that the scope of the Appropriations Committee's operations has been 'shrinking' in absolute dollar terms or in importance with respect to domestic, foreign and military discretionary spending. In fiscal 2007, the overall percentage of mandatory 'entitlement' spending in the Federal budget was roughly 62 per cent, with total discretionary spending at 38 per cent. Within discretionary spending controlled by the appropriation process, military expenditures assumed an increasingly larger portion of the discretionary budget than domestic and foreign spending, especially since 9/11.

Other committees

It is accurate to describe some other committees, particularly the Committee on Transportation and Infrastructure, as 'spending' committees competing with the Appropriations Committees for allocations of new spending authority in specified jurisdictional areas. This contrast can be illustrated by an examination of spending for Federal highway and urban mass transit programmes out of the 'highway trust funds' financed both by a variety of transportation (for example, gasoline) taxes assessed on users, and also in part by general revenues from the Treasury. Over time, the House Transportation and Infrastructure Committee has enhanced its jurisdiction over transportation spending by House and Senate rules changes and by enactment of requirements for advance contract authority which involve binding decisions on budgeting, leaving the Appropriations Committee to appropriate 'liquidating cash' to pay contractual obligations already incurred under laws enacted by the authorizing committee. The Appropriations Committee nevertheless has continued to regard its historical ability to impose 'limitations', for example on the salaries and expenses of transportation officials administering those programmes, as an effective annual constraint on objects if not on overall levels of transportation spending. In 1995, Congress enacted the Transportation Equity Act for the twenty-first century which, with the blessing of the House Rules Committee, added clause 3 of Rule XXI to House rules, precluding consideration of (Appropriation) bills and amendments that 'would cause obligation limitations for the highway category or the mass transit category to be below the level for any fiscal year set forth in section 8103 of that law'. The rule was intended to restrict the ability of the appropriation process, by an annual control of liquidating and administrative funds, to reduce overall obligational levels and to limit 'High Priority Projects' specifically described in the authorizing law. The Appropriations Committee countered this mandate for a floor on aggregate spending in 1999 by inclusion of statutory language of its own directing that 'any obligation limitation relating to surface transportation projects under that law shall be assumed to be administered on the basis of sound programme management practices that are consistent with past practices of the administering agencies permitting States to decide High Priority Project funding priorities within State program allocations'. This interpretation was later incorporated into clause 3 of Rule XXI as a 'truce' between these competing jurisdictional assertions, and is now intended to allow annual Appropriation bills to include limitations denying funding for specified High Priority Projects so long as the receiving State can reallocate those funds to other projects using management practices in such a way as not to diminish the overall obligational commitment for priority projects in each State. In a subsequently enacted authorizing law (sect 8003 of a 2005 enacted highway law) new obligational floors were established for all projects in each State. Thus the appropriation process can theoretically continue to limit annual funds for specific transportation projects it deems unworthy, so long as the overall spending for a State's authorized priority transportation projects is honoured. There is no comparable point of order in the Senate, where the jurisdictional prerogatives of the authorization and appropriation committees are not so zealously guarded.

A similar authorization law written by the Transportation Committee for aviation programmes sets overall obligational floors on total budget resources, both from the Airport and Airway Trust Fund and from general revenues in the Treasury, below which any provision in an Appropriation bill or amendment limiting overall spending would be subject to a point of order in both the House and Senate. This law reflects the same attitude on the part of the authorizing committee with respect to highway and mass transit spending, that it be able to set binding spending levels unencumbered by the appropriation process in both Houses. At this writing, the Congress has extended aviation spending statutory points of order through fiscal year 2011 by enactment of new levels of total budget resources for airports, facilities and equipment, research and development, below which 'floors' appropriation levels may not descend.[33]

In all, the distinction between mandatory and discretionary spending programmes generally defines the extent of the influence of the appropriation process in annual policy making, and is reflected annually in separate allocations of spending authority between authorizing and appropriation committees in the concurrent resolution on the budget. Some unique quasi-mandatory programmes have emerged in law, such as those transportation trust-fund-financed programmes based on advance contract authority and protected procedurally against encroachments by the annual appropriation process. Whatever the category of spending, it is accurate to assert that the American public has become increasingly reliant on appropriations of funds from the Treasury or from special trust funds to satisfy entitlement expectations written into law, or public service expectations which State and local governments and the private sector are not financially capable of providing. From the discretionary portion of the Federal budget, funds for domestic programmes either provided directly to recipients by Federal agencies or through grants to the States are annually anticipated. When budget authority is not enacted in a timely fashion, advance planning by recipient agencies may be delayed and impacted. When a regular or a continuing appropriation resolution funding portions of government operations is not enacted, entire segments of the Executive branch may be forced to curtail operations. Such was the situation at the end of calendar year 1995 when Congress and the President (of opposing political parties) failed for months to agree on various levels and objects of domestic spending contained in several annual Appropriation bills, resulting in actual or threatened vetoes and in a partial government shutdown. While political explanations differed as to the cause of that stalemate between a Congress of one political party and a President of the other, it represented in the appropriation process envisioned by the Congressional Budget Act a breakdown by lack of availability of budget authority of such a scale as to be subsequently avoided at all procedural costs. This has led to a combination of continuing appropriation resolutions (CRs) and to measures combining more than one general Appropriation bill when reconciled between the two Houses in order to bridge funding gaps.

House–Senate relations

In twenty-eight of the past thirty-three fiscal years (1977–2008, 2010) Congress and the President did not complete action on a majority of the regular bills by the start of the fiscal year on 1 October. They completed action on all the bills on schedule only four times: fiscal 1977, 1989, 1995, and 1997. Before the 1 October deadline, Congress and the President generally complete action on an initial CR that temporarily funds the outstanding Appropriation bills. In contrast to funding practices in regular bills (that is, providing discrete appropriations for each account) temporary CRs generally provide funding by a rate or formula, most typically the lower of previous levels or those passed by the House or Senate in the unfinished bills, and only to a date certain or until enactment of the regular bills, if earlier. Once the initial CR becomes law, additional interim CRs are frequently utilized (averaging four each year) to sequentially extend the expiration date. Unlike general (regular or supplemental) Appropriation bills, CRs are not subject to rules against legislation and unauthorized items, and often contain Appropriations Committee-originated legislative riders in addition to continued funding. They are not considered under 'open' procedures in the Committee of the Whole, but rather in the House under 'closed rules' from the Rules Committee prohibiting amendments under the five-minute rule. In a recent ruling by the Chair a Minority motion to recommit a CR with instructions to amend by inclusion of permanent legislative language was ruled non-germane, as the underlying measure only applied to the current fiscal year.

As several fiscal years subsequent to 1996 began without the enactment of many individual Appropriation bills into law, new comprehensive alternatives called 'omnibus' or 'minibus' measures emerged either from a House–Senate conference or by amendments between the Houses which contained variations of some or all of those bills previously passed by one or the other House, together with measures not yet processed. By the end of several recent calendar years, Congress was forced either to enact omnibus bills in order to begin the next calendar year with annual budget authority in place (so as to concentrate on a new budget cycle) or to enact CRs into the new calendar year and, on two occasions (2006 and 2008) into a new Congress. When in 2007 a new political majority in Congress faced the previous Congress's failure to enact the entire budget, and instead left most government funding on a short term CR into February, it was forced to spend the first two months packaging budget authority (with many new Members not familiar with the previous Congress's issues) and for a fiscal year already half over, for the remaining six months of the present fiscal year, before it could begin the upcoming fiscal year budget cycle. Special orders have even been utilized to make in order 'omnibus' general Appropriation bills (in February 2009 a bill not even marked up or reported from the Appropriations Committee and containing staff-negotiated compromises) covering a major portion of the Federal budget for the fiscal year already underway. The fact that by the end of February 2009 the full Appropriations Committee had not even met to mark up and report most of that bill, caused in part by the pressing need to first consider an emergency supplemental 'stimulus' bill, speaks to the unprecedented breakdown of the regular annual appropriation process and the utilization of procedural expedients in order to provide appropriations for government programmes and avoid government shutdowns.

Several unique procedural obstacles face the two Houses when they attempt to package 'omnibus' appropriation measures. In the House, utilization of special orders from the Rules Committee may initially expedite consideration to prevent a duplication of an open amendment process already had on the regular bill previously passed, or to permit consideration of amendments from the Senate. In the Senate, however, the three-fifths vote obstacle can prevent consideration of combined measures in a conference report not supported by a super-majority of that body, as was demonstrated in 2007 when the House–Senate conference effort to combine a Labor-Health and Human Services passed bill with a Veterans-Military Construction measure was rejected in the Senate under a new rule (Senate Rule XXVIII) prohibiting the inclusion of new 'directed spending' provisions beyond the scope of the measure as committed to conference. The rule governing Senate conference proceedings was made part of a law on lobbying reform as the result of previous additions for the first time in 'must-pass' appropriations conference reports, including earmarks, of unrelated matter which had not been formally committed to conference by one or the other House on that particular measure. Since conference reports are unamendable, the Senate was left to accept or reject the entire package, usually under pressure to enact new budget authority near the end of a session, but beginning in 2007 a point of order against conferees' inclusion of new directed spending matter was sustainable unless waived by three-fifths of the Senate. Failure of a three-fifths waiver now results in automatic rejection of the report and in a vote on the remainder of the report in the form of a new Senate amendment which the House must once again consider despite its prior adoption of the conference report. Further discussion of House–Senate conference procedure generally, and the interaction in the Senate between the general scope rule and the new directed spending rule will be undertaken at pages 292–3, 459.

Bicameralism in the form of two co-equal Houses with vastly different rules of order, together with separation of powers from the Executive, presents enormous procedural challenges to the enactment of law, especially in a timely manner as is required for Appropriations Acts. With closely divided party control in the Senate making invocation of cloture or waivers of Budget Act and scope of conference points of order problematic, and with the absence of a germaneness requirement thereby permitting the encumbrance on House-originated Appropriation bills with unrelated legislative 'riders', the timely passage by the Senate and commitment to conference have lagged in recent Congresses. And so, what annually begins as an 'open' and deliberative amendment process in both Houses on initial consideration of Appropriation bills may become at the end stage of the process a truncation, due to coalescing disputes among the two

Houses and the Executive, the pressures of a fiscal year timetable, and individual Members' demands for special new earmarks at the end of a session. Combined with the ease of waivers of points of order in the House against conference reports and amendments between the two Houses, the end of session processes on Appropriation bills resemble 'take it or leave it' approaches to combined measures, often with precious little time for Members to scrutinize the final version.

Until the late 1980s, Senate amendments to House-passed general Appropriation bills were always in the form of 'numbered' perfecting changes in the House measure, rather than an amendment in the nature of a substitute for the entire text incorporating all Senate changes as one amendment. The Senate's recent use of one amendment to each House Appropriation bill, replacing what had typically been a large number perfecting amendments to specific pages and lines, has had a profound impact on the resolution of differences between the Houses, permitting just one up-or-down vote in each Chamber on the version reported from conference containing all compromises in one report. House standing rules have since 1920 required that any conferees' agreement or amendment to a Senate amendment containing unauthorized appropriations or changes in existing law (legislation) be separately identified by number and reported from conference in 'technical' disagreement, so as to permit separate subsequent votes in both Houses on prearranged motions to dispose of those Senate provisions where there was actual but not technical agreement inside the conference report. This requirement complemented what had been the traditional practice of conferees' isolating and reporting true disagreements for separate votes on motions to recede and concur in the Senate amendment, with or without further House amendment, or to insist on disagreement (in an order of precedence discussed at page 447). House conferees are not permitted to agree to such Senate amendments within a conference report (absent special authority procured in advance by adoption of instruction motions) as House rules contemplate separate motions in that regard. Since the Senate began to experiment with the one amendment incorporation of all disagreements approach, House conferees were forced (not necessarily against their will) to deal with all issues in disagreement within one conference report which would be subject to a point of order in the House, and then to seek waivers of points of order from the Rules Committee when they have exceeded their authority, to protect their work product. Both parties in the House have come to expect such waivers of points of order, and those waivers have routinely been forthcoming so that the procedures in both Houses are expedited and do not leave separate issues unresolved for disposition by subsequent motions. Of course, all Senate amendments must be disposed of before an appropriation (or any other) measure is finally passed. Until the last decade, the disposition of Senate amendments outside of a conference report remained necessary, often permitting either House, but especially the Senate, to add additional legislation or even non-germane provisions so as to prolong the process. The subsequent chapter on House–Senate amendments and conferences will describe in further detail the variety of processes for resolution of appropriation matters. With appropriation disagreements between the two Houses now confined to one up-or-down vote on the conference report disposition of the one amendment in disagreement, both Houses are spared the need to separate issues of spending and policy.

However, the new Senate rule (XXII) on provisions 'air-dropped' into conference reports, that is, directed spending provisions not contained in either version as committed to conference, enables separate Senate disposition of new spending provisions (either entitlement or discretionary budget authority) in a conference report, provoked by a minority of the Senate, when the presiding officer sustains a point of order that the matter is indeed newly injected into the conference report and the Senate is then unable to waive the point of order by a three-fifths vote. To that extent, a minority (forty-one) of Senators can force both bodies to reconsider the terms of a conference report on which a majority of each body might otherwise agree. This new Senate rule has had an immediate impact on Senate and House proceedings, as newly injected directed spending matters once considered in order in the Senate (as being merely germane specific modifications of general funding matters committed to conference by one or both Houses and therefore within the liberally construed Senate scope Rule XXII) can now be isolated and made the subject of a three-fifths vote on waiver of the new prohibition. The presiding officer of the Senate is now required to rule, for example, that a conference addition inserting specific spending for a project which is not mentioned in either House's version but which falls within the general funding of an agency covered thereby—which would have previously withstood a point of order in the Senate as being a germane modification not totally unrelated to one or the other House's version—is subject to a point of order requiring a super-majority waiver. Failing that waiver, the conference report is considered rejected and the pending question is the remainder of the conference report, in the form of a new Senate amendment to the original House version on which the House must act again despite its earlier waiver of scope points of order and adoption of the conference report. On an important appropriation measure in the Congress since the enactment of the new Senate rule, the two Houses sought to avoid implementation of that conference report restriction during consideration of the Omnibus Appropriation Act for fiscal 2008. To accomplish the end result of actual agreement on all issues while avoiding a conference document following informal negotiations to resolve the actual text of the matters in disagreement, the House began by amending the Senate amendment in the nature of a substitute to a general Appropriation bill on foreign operations, through utilization of a special order amending the Senate amendment to substitute two House amendments—one on military spending for Afghanistan and Iraq, and the second on all other spending for the entire government. The Senate in a 'ping-pong' series of two votes then adopted the House (negotiated) compromise amendment on general spending, and then further amended the House-amended military spending amendment to add some funds (half of the $70 billion requested by the President) for operations in Iraq. Finally, the House adopted that final Senate amendment to the House amendment no. 2 to the Senate amendment to the House bill, without ever going to conference and without subjecting the many new directed spending provisions included in the compromise to the need for a three-fifths waiver in the Senate. To be sure, the final Senate amendment once pending might have been subjected to an actual filibuster requiring a three-fifths vote to invoke cloture, but its initial consideration was expedited by a Senate rule (XIV) permitting the Majority Leader to offer a motion which would not be subject to the question of whether to proceed. The Senate found it politically expedient to avoid a super-majority requirement it had imposed on itself as a 'reform' intended to discourage conferences from inserting new directed spending not originally considered by either House. The Senate utilized amendments between the Houses, rather than the traditional conference report, to finalize the budget for virtually the entire operation of the Federal government almost three months after the beginning of the fiscal year in question.

Supplemental appropriations by definition are additional sums of new budgetary authority to those contained in the twelve (or combined mini or 'omni') regular general Appropriation bills for each fiscal year or in continuing appropriations already made. Unforeseen or purposefully delayed expenditures are continually identified by both Congress and by the Executive (in the form of supplemental budget requests submitted by the President) as the fiscal year progresses. Bills to accommodate those needs and requests are often reported from the Appropriations Committees as general Appropriation bills subject to the same restrictions with respect to the need for authorization, to remain within Congressional budget resolution levels or to be declared 'emergency' spending and, when reported, to be free of legislative provisions changing existing law. As a practical matter, special orders from the Rules Committee waive points of order in the House against those restrictions and often limit individual Members' amendments so as to permit supplemental Appropriation bills to be expeditiously considered. As a further departure from regular order in 2009, a special order brought to the full House an unreported $800 billion 'stimulus' supplemental Appropriation bill in response to an economic crisis, stitched the bill together with other spending and revenue legislation which had been separately marked up in several committees (Appropriations, Ways and Means, and Energy and Commerce) and presented it to the House for expedited disposition, limiting the procedural rights of individual Members (the Minority was permitted one substitute amendment). The Senate added a public debt limit extension (to $12.140 trillion) to the House-passed package.

Several weeks later the necessary annual ('omni') bill providing appropriations for nine of the twelve subcommittees' jurisdictions (which had been 'continued' in the prior Congress only until 5 March) for the fiscal year already in progress was made in order with only three of those subcommittee's portions having been considered by the full Appropriations Committee, and then only in the prior Congress. These wholesale departures from regular order in the House (although 'regular order' was resorted to when the two Houses avoided 'ping-ponging' by sending the bill to conference and adopting a conference report) symbolize the contemporary recurring need to depart from regular order as emergencies or statutory deadlines arise.

Having originated in the House they are then considered and amended by the Senate and either sent to conference for resolution or through amendments between the Houses in the same manner as are the regular bills. The timing of their enactments varies depending on political and economic urgency.

Executive review of appropriations

The Executive branch has no inherent power to impound appropriated funds. In the absence of express Congressional authorization to withhold funds appropriated for implementation of a legislative programme, the Legislative branch must expend all of the funds. The impoundment of appropriated funds may be proposed by the President pursuant to the Impoundment Control Act of 1974 (title X of the Budget Act). Two types of impoundments are referred to in this statute: (1) rescissions, which are the permanent cancellation of spending; and (2) deferrals, which impose a temporary delay in spending. To propose a rescission, the President must send a special message to Congress, detailing the amount and its reasons, and a summary of the effects the rescission would have on the programmes involved. Under the Act, the Congress then has forty-five days within which to approve the proposed rescission. If the rescission bill is not approved, the President must allow the full amount appropriated to be spent (absent statutory authority to 'reprogramme' or otherwise delay spending). While the Act sets forth detailed procedures expediting rescission bills in both Houses (including privileged motions in both Houses to discharge rescission bills after twenty-five calendar days of continuous session if seconded by one-fifth of the House involved) they are rarely invoked in modern practice, since the Appropriations Committee takes the initiative to include rescissions informally agreed upon with the Executive as separate provisions in general Appropriation bills under special procedures which exempt rescissions from the general prohibition against inclusion of legislation. Deferral authority of the President also contained in the Impoundment Control Act of 1974 has been restricted by the courts in the wake of the Chadha decision in 1983, since the one-House disapproval mechanism of deferrals has been declared invalid. In 1987, Congress abolished the single-House disapproval mechanism by law, and limitations were placed on the purposes for which deferrals could be made—that is, 'to provide for contingencies', 'to achieve savings made possible by or through changes in requirements or greater efficiency of operations', or 'as specifically provided by law', so as to prevent the President from invoking deferral authority to implement 'policy' impoundments, while preserving authority to implement routine 'programmatic' impoundments. Today, Congress may disapprove a presidentially proposed 'programmatic' deferral only by enactment of law (usually in an Appropriation Act).

While the Act sets forth detailed procedures expediting rescission bills in both Houses (including privileged motions in both Houses to discharge rescission bills after twenty-five calendar days of continuous session if seconded by one-fifth of the House involved) they are rarely invoked in the modern practice, since the Appropriations Committee takes the initiative to include rescissions informally agreed upon with the Executive as separate provisions in general Appropriation bills under special procedures which exempt rescissions from the general prohibition against inclusion of legislation.

In the modern context of the proliferation of 'earmarks' in appropriation measures, a President determined to reduce their number and fiscal impact has several incomplete weapons at his disposal. They include a veto of the entire bill, resulting in delay in enactment of the measure. A rescission recommended by the President under the Impoundment Control Act of 1974 faces an uncertain chance of success, as under that law the funds proposed to be rescinded must be made available for obligation after forty-five days of continuous session if Congress has not enacted a law approving the rescissions. While the motion to discharge an introduced rescission bill is in order during that period in each House upon initial support of one-fifth of that House, the chance for timely enactment into law is minimal, as the forty-five day period runs quickly and politically agreed-upon rescissions are usually included in annual and supplemental Appropriation bills by the committee and are protected against points of order. The propriety of a recent effort by the President, in a 'signing statement' accompanying the enactment into law of the 'omnibus' Appropriation Act for fiscal 2008—suggesting that he might issue an Executive

Order directing the OMB Director to unilaterally withhold earmarked funds—has been called into question. It should be remembered that most Congressional 'earmarks' are 'provisions of report language included primarily at the request of a Member of Senator authorizing or recommending a specific amount of discretionary budget authority, credit authority, or other spending authority...with or to an entity, or targeted to a specific State, locality or Congressional district, other than through a statutory or administrative formula-driven or competitive award process'. While most earmarks are contained in accompanying report language, or in a joint statement of conferees accompanying a conference report and are not textually stated in the enacted bill, they nevertheless represent subsets of amounts of budget authority which are contained in those laws, the entire expenditure of which the recipient agencies are not free to ignore. In some cases, agencies which are told by the Congress in report language to spend for a particular earmarked project may have authority to reprogramme or require competitive bidding for those funds. For the most part, Congress fully expects those earmarked funds to be spent by the Executive as suggested in those reports. Failure of an agency to abide by Congressional report directives might well impact on that agency's budget the next fiscal year.

President Bush announced in his final State of the Union address on 28 January 2008 that to cut the amount and number of earmarks in half he would issue an Executive Order the next day directing Federal agencies to ignore any future earmark that was not voted on and included in a law approved by Congress. The announcement suggested that 'this will effectively end the common practice of concealing earmarks in so-called report language instead of placing them in the actual text of the bill'. This means earmarks will be subject to votes, which will better expose them to the light of day and help constrain excessive and unjustified spending. The Executive Order will provide that with regard to all future appropriations laws and other legislation enacted into law, Executive agencies will not commit, obligate, or expend funds on the basis of earmarks from any non-statutory source, including requests in Congressional committee reports or other Congressional documents, or communications from or on behalf of Members of Congress, or any other non-statutory source, except when required by law, or when an agency itself decides that a project or other transaction has merit under statutory criteria or other merit-based decision making. The Executive Order cites a 1993 Supreme Court decision that committee reports and other legislative history materials do not bind Executive agencies. 'A fundamental principle of appropriations law is that where Congress merely appropriates lump-sum amounts without statutorily restricting what can be done with those funds, a clear inference arises that it does not intend to impose legally binding restrictions, and indicia in committee reports and other legislative history as to how the funds should or are expected to be spent do not establish any legal requirements on the agency,' citing *Lincoln v Vigil* 508 US 182, 192 (1993) and *Cherokee Nation v Leavitt* 543 US 631 (2005) to reiterate that 'language contained in Committee reports is not legally binding'. In some Appropriation bills, earmark language contained in committee reports is incorporated by reference into statutory law, without the statute containing the full text of the earmark. This is often done at the request of the spending agency which feels it does not have the authority to spend on certain specific earmarks, absent the statutory incorporation by reference. Implementation of this policy by the President, who also recommends numerous earmarks in his annual Budget, could result in a proliferation of amendments in each House, striking statutory earmarks or negatively limiting the use of funds in the pending bill for one or more earmarks whether they were originally recommended by Members or by the President. Even if earmarks remain as report language only, limitation amendments are in order in each House to prevent funding in the bill for that express project or activity.

Enforcement of this Executive Order was problematic, as the total amount of budget authority of which the earmark may be a suggested subset would remain enacted in law. Nevertheless the President threatened to veto any bill (at least for fiscal 2009, the final year of his Presidency) containing earmarks in accompanying reports. Thus it might appear that only by informal negotiations with the President can restraints be placed on the proliferation of the number and dollar amount of Congressional or Executive-originated earmarks. Even newly elected Members' expectations of success in recent years have, with leadership support and despite new requirements for public disclosure, caused the dramatic increase in the number and cost of earmarks and in a corresponding decrease in time and inclination of the Appropriations Committees to properly scrutinize their cost–benefit characteristics.

Audit and value for money

Following early experimentation in examining reports of Executive officers of accounts, the US House in 1814 set up a standing committee for Public Expenditures. In 1816 six more committees on the expenditures of particular departments were established, and later corresponding committees were set up in the Senate. This network remained in existence until the 1920s, during which time audits were conducted by Treasury Department auditors who were responsible to the Comptroller of the Treasury established in 1894, an Executive branch official whose interpretations of appropriations laws were binding on departments. The 1921 Act replaced the Treasury auditors and Comptroller with the General Accounting Office headed by a presidentially nominated and Senate-confirmed Comptroller General for a fifteen-year, non-renewable term. A unique recommendation process begins the selection process with a special bicameral commission of legislators from both parties presenting names to the President. The Office is declared to be independent of the Executive Departments. In the same 1921 law, Congress established the Bureau of the Budget, the forerunner to the OMB, and established presidential authority over the budget formulation process. In sum, the 1921 Act was a comprehensive effort to modernize and consolidate both Executive and Legislative branch responsibilities reflective of Congress's need to conduct effective scrutiny of Executive branch activities.

In 1985, a constitutional conflict arose over powers delegated to the Comptroller General (CG)—a Legislative branch office—when Congress gave him specific budget-reduction authority under the Balanced Budget and Deficit Control Act (discussed in an earlier segment under pay-go). The CG was to review recommendations about such reductions and report his findings to the President, who in turn was to issue a sequestration order mandating across-the-board spending reductions specified by the CG when overall spending above prescribed amounts was reached at the end of a fiscal year. The

Supreme Court held in *Bowsher v Synar* 478 US 714 (1986) however, that the delegation of authority to the CG was unconstitutional, as 'the powers vested in the CG by section 251 of the law violate the command of the Constitution that the Congress play no direct role in the execution of the laws'. There followed a law in 1996 (the General Accounting Office Act) transferring to the OMB in the Executive branch certain specific 'executive' powers of the CG relating to determinations about executive assistance and services, disputes over certain purchases made by Executive agencies, and conduct of identified audits of Executive accounts or prescribing regulations for specified Executive operations.

Congress followed suit by combining its various committees on expenditure into one committee in each House to review audits. Beginning in 1947 the Committee on Government Operations (now the Committee on Oversight and Government Reform) and the Committee on Governmental Affairs in the Senate were given the function under standing rules to 'receive and examine reports of the Comptroller General of the United States and submit to the House such recommendations as it considers necessary or desirable in connection with the subject matter of the reports'. Reports from the CG to Congress can be responses to requests from any committee or Member, or can be self-initiated.

The focus of those committees in evaluating audits and overall performance by the Government Accountability Office has recently been demonstrated, as a subcommittee of the House Committee on Oversight and Government Reform has held oversight hearings in 2007 for the first time in a number of years. Until the 110th Congress, neither committee prioritized that responsibility. This is not to say that other committees are lacking responsibility and jurisdiction in the area of audit review. The House Appropriations Committee, for example, is empowered to 'conduct such studies and examinations of Executive departments and other Executive agencies as it considers necessary to assist it in the determination of matters within its jurisdiction'. The Appropriations Committees, with annual hearings and ongoing review of all Executive branch budgets, conduct closer scrutiny of Executive and Legislative agencies, including the Government Accountability Office (GAO), than do the committees charged with reviewing their audits and accounts.

The CG, while independent of the Executive branch, is required by law to approve the accounting and auditing standards of every department and agency. In addition, his office audits the financial transactions of all Executive agencies, and is authorized to settle all accounts of the government and supervise the recovery of all debts due the government. While the office was originally intended to be 'independent of the Executive departments' as 'Congress's watchdog' and its 'investigative arm', GAO now is required by law to provide a variety of services to Congress that extend beyond its original functions, including oversight, investigations, review, and evaluation of Executive operations. The GAO is mandated to investigate the receipt, disbursement, and use of public moneys by all Executive entities upon proper Congressional request or on its own initiative. In order to fulfil its mission, the office has been given broad powers including administrative subpoena authority to gain access to information and materials of government entities.[34] While full and direct access to Executive branch records is provided in most cases, there exists an auxiliary authority, seldom used, to compel recalcitrant offices and even private persons to release information. This power to sue a non-complying agency for the production of records permits the CG to make a written request for information from the agency head, who has twenty days to explain why the records are not being made available. Then after notice to the President, the Director of OMB, and Congress, the CG may file suit to require production of the requested records. The Comptroller may also issue subpoenas to private persons when the record sought is not produced through the requested agency.

For the same basic reasons discussed in the chapter on Scrutiny and Oversight regarding Congressional access to intelligence information beyond special arrangements with the Intelligence Committees, the GAO's authority to investigate foreign intelligence agencies and activities upon objection of the President has been limited by statute for national security reasons. Practices within the House and Senate select committees on Intelligence which, while encouraging audit, investigation, and review activities at the request and under the auspices of those committees, do not permit independent audit and scrutiny by GAO of Executive branch intelligence activities. Indeed, informal GAO initiatives toward information sharing between Congress and the Executive in intelligence and related homeland security areas have met with resistance by the latter branch, including Justice Department legal opinions on the limited extent of GAO access.

Additional GAO functions include special investigations of alleged violations of Federal criminal law, particularly conflict of interest or procurement and contract fraud, and resolution of bid protests that challenge government contract awards. The GAO is now Congress's largest support agency with a budget of more than $488 million and a staff of 3,159 in 2007. Congress's two smaller support agencies established by law and responsible for information and advice on fiscal (although not on accountability) matters are the CBO and the Congressional Research Service (an Office of Technology Assessment established in 1970 having remained unfunded since 1995).

In the UK, the National Audit Office (NAO) was created in 1983 (though its predecessor body began work under a statute of 1866) with the duty of auditing and laying before Parliament the accounts of central government departments, their agencies, and other public bodies. It is in effect the external auditor of the activities of government, reporting to the legislature. The NAO's 850 staff are wholly impartial and independent in the discharge of their official responsibilities, not concerned with the merits of the policies behind the accounts. To emphasize that fact its head, the Comptroller and Auditor General (C & AG) is not a civil servant but an officer of the House of Commons, appointed by the Crown on a motion in the Commons in the name of the Prime Minister, with the agreement of the Chairman of the Public Accounts Committee. He may be removed only if both Houses agree. The NAO's budget is settled not by ministers but by a statutory Commission of backbench Members of the Commons.

Each government department may expect from three to five examinations annually, and the larger departments slightly more. The NAO gives its opinion, like any other auditor, on whether the resource accounts under consideration present a true and fair view of the transactions they represent. In addition the audit report will comment on whether the accounts have been drawn up in accordance with Treasury guidelines and whether the transactions they record comply with the underlying statutory—Appropriation Act—authority. These audit examinations, of which there were 462 in 2007-8 covering some £450 billion in income and expenditure, ranged from large sums involved in the Ministry of Defence major projects to BBC procurement, by way of Coastal and

Flood Defences and the Budget for the 2012 Olympics. The NAO expects to qualify about ten to fifteen audit opinions a year. There were eleven qualified resource accounts in 2006–7, though in 2005–6 such opinions were issued on 22 sets of accounts. In 2004–5 the accounts of a major department of State attracted the even more unfavourable outcome of a 'disclaimer of audit opinion' and another department had its accounts qualified for eighteen successive years, by reason of loss arising from fraud and error in benefit payments.

If these reports are akin to snapshots of proceedings, the NAO makes value for money reports comparable with moving pictures. It is claimed that the NAO saved £656 million in 2006–7, representing £9 for £1 of departmental costs. Currently, about sixty major value-for-money reports are made each year, and are laid before the Public Accounts Committee. In these the NAO is concerned with economy—were the costs kept down; efficiency—did the balance of output and input turn out as it should; and effectiveness—did the expenditure do the job? Some value-for-money studies are follow-ups of previous reports. Some are based on the activities of a single department; some are cross-governmental, including sustainable construction on the government estate and government's use of the internet. The NAO particularly assists Parliament by reporting on the Budget Assumptions and on the Pre-Budget report. It supports the Public Accounts Committee, and in the most recent year assisted seventeen other select committees.

The Public Accounts Committee is charged with the examination of the appropriation accounts and such other accounts as the Committee thinks fit. The work of the Committee centres on the reports of the NAO, and the C & AG attends all their hearings. The witnesses are normally the principal officials of the department under scrutiny, who bear personal responsibility for the effectiveness of the systems intended to deliver financial probity. A Committee hearing will usually be the last scene in a long drama of NAO investigation into some aspect of the financial affairs of the department, so that by the time of the hearing the ground will be clear, allowing Members to concentrate on the salient (or from the departmental point of view, sensitive) issues. The number of Committee reports is greater by some number than those made by any other committee, and their recommendations more likely to be accepted in full than is the case for other committees.

The Public Accounts Committee has the particular responsibility of reporting whether there is any objection to the grant of Excess Votes to cover departmental overspends (see page 260). The House of Commons will not assent to the grant of resources to make good overspends unless the Committee has reported. In 2006–7, the cash excess was nil, as opposed to a figure of £5.1 million in the previous year. There were only two underestimates of resource requirements, and the Committee commented that departments and other bodies funded by Parliament were able to manage their expenditure in cash and resource terms. For 2007–8, the Committee reported a cash excess which had risen again to £5.8 million, but three resource excesses totalling £4.9 million, down from £102.7 million.[35]

The Public Accounts Committee is the House of Commons' major weapon in ensuring that taxpayers' money is spent to best effect, but the financial work of departmental committees referred to on pages 261ff. often impinges also on this concern. The NAO for its part assisted thirteen Commons select committees in 2006–7. It briefed the Treasury Committee on tax credits, examined data on cost escalation in road building for the

Transport Committee and gave sustained advice to the Environment Audit Committee on UK progress towards climate change targets. Briefings on departmental performance are planned to assist select committees across the board in their oversight function. NAO staff are attached directly to a number of committees. The next stage might be for select committees to build NAO reports, with those of the Scrutiny Unit, more systematically into their programmes of work.[36]

Outcomes

How successful are the two systems of control of the economy and the public finances?

If the proliferation of annual budget deficits and increases in the outstanding Federal debt levels are any indication, Congress has failed since 2000 to impose effective fiscal discipline in its exercise of the power of the purse. At the macro level, despite the adoption of internal rules and procedures in both Houses intended to enhance deficit reduction, recent Congresses have taken separate steps to reduce revenues flowing to the Treasury, while at the same time increasing expenditures beyond planned or anticipated levels, resulting in increases in the public debt limit and in borrowings by the Treasury to finance those deficits. In turn, the issuance and resultant costs of interest on Treasury bonds has greatly increased interest payments to those bond holders (often foreign investors) and that amount has represented an ever greater percentage of discretionary budget authority which would otherwise be available to finance government spending programmes. This increase in interest payments has been described as a 'hidden tax' on all taxpayers, reducing otherwise available funds in the Treasury. At this writing, the demise of an automatic sequestration mechanism (where total annual discretionary spending exceeds prescribed levels requiring across-the-board reductions at the end of each calendar year) has not been replaced by effective internal House and Senate disciplines, such as pay-go rules and Budget Act points of order, as those rules are often waived by either House, often at the end of a Congressional session, for political and time expediency. Defence-related expenditures and Legislative and Executive earmarks have increased discretionary spending. A proliferation of entitlement programmes has likewise increased 'mandatory' spending to programmes and beneficiaries. Emergency supplemental spending as a response to an economic and fiscal crisis has been greatly increased. Together, these spending pressures and revenue reductions have combined to impose debt obligations on all taxpayers and on future generations. A vast array of specific decisions which run counter to procedural constraints, including veto forbearance, have been taken with some political justification as accommodations to Congressional timetables and majorities. Despite the existence of internal mechanisms designed to control public finances and to encourage economic growth, and jurisdictional allocations intended to assure proper Congressional scrutiny, both the micro- and the macro-manipulation of public expenditures and revenue receipts (for example, through waivers of points of order and special earmarks) have contributed to the temporary demise of the political majorities in Congress which permitted them to proliferate.

An extraordinary example of the exercise of the power of the purse in the US Congress came in 2008 with the enactment of the Emergency Economic Stabilization Act of

2008.[37] Section 118 of that law, enacted in response to the global financial crisis, provides the following:

> For the purpose of the authorities granted in this Act, and for the costs of admin-
> istering those authorities, the Secretary may use the proceeds of the sale of any
> securities issued under chapter 31 of title 31, United States Code, and the purposes
> for which securities may be issued under chapter 31 of title 31, United States Code,
> are extended to include actions authorized by this Act, including the payment of
> administrative expenses. Any funds expended or obligated by the Secretary for
> actions authorized by this Act, including the payment of administrative expenses,
> shall be deemed appropriated at the time of such expenditure or obligation.

In addition, section 122 of that law provides that 'Subsection (b) of section 3101 of title 31, United States Code, is amended by striking out the dollar limitation contained in such subsection and inserting "$11,315,000,000,000".' Separate consideration of this increase of borrowing authority would have been procedurally complicated, as described in this chapter at page 253.

By virtue of the 'deeming' of this open-ended funding enactment, Congress permitted the immediate funding from the Treasury of at least one-half of obligations incurred under that Act, as well as extensive new borrowing through issuance of bonds, in circum-vention of the regular borrowing authority, budget, and appropriations processes, while complying with the constitutional requirement that money can only be taken from the Treasury if appropriated by law or borrowed to the credit of the United States by law. For the remaining half ($350 billion) of the TARP (Troubled Assets Relief Program) Congress reserved to itself through expedited procedures the ability to quickly disap-prove Presidential requests for that emergency spending by the Executive, again without following 'regular order', but failed in 2009 to exercise that constraint. To date this is the most vivid (and costly) single example of the expeditious exercise of the power of the purse in the history of the United States.

At this writing in 2009, the new Congress and Executive are confronted with ever greater urgency to address the world economic and financial crisis. The standards of transparency and protection of individual Members' rights, and the deliberative capacity traditionally fostered by committee consideration, which have long characterized House proceedings, have been significantly set aside. The extent of Senate complicity in that effort depends upon cloture votes where three-fifth majorities remain necessary.

At Westminster, two bills were introduced, the first to enable the government to take into public ownership UK-incorporated banks. This was passed—through all stages in both Houses—in two days. The government declared that it had no intention of using the broad powers in the bill in any case other than that which triggered the crisis. A second more general bill establishing a permanent regime under which the authorities can deal with banks in financial difficulties followed. On the financial side, after a three-hour debate a Supplementary Estimate was agreed in order to replenish the Contingencies Fund (which is set at up to 2 per cent of the cash released from the Consolidated Fund in the previous year) after the making of certain specific payments in connection with the crisis, and to provide resources for the banks' recapitalization. It was agreed to grant £42 billion out of the Consolidated Fund, the appropriation of which passed without amendment or debate—though of course the crisis and the need for resources was the subject of debate and informal questioning of ministers after statements on twelve occasions between the beginning of October and mid-November.[38]

In Congress, a streamlined process containing a complex response to the banking crises took several procedural forms, and ultimately waived the standing rules of both Houses to accomplish an expeditious result with only one day consideration in each House. The informally negotiated measure combined matter within the jurisdictions of several committees as a political expedient to facilitate its ultimate passage. The Emergency Economic Stabilization Act of 2008 (finally enacted as PL 110-343) was patched together by informal House and Senate leadership and committee negotiations utilizing special orders from the Committee on Rules in the House and a unanimous consent order in the Senate to make in order votes on amendments between the Houses. The arrangement avoided formal committee referral and report of introduced measures, and amendments in the House pending final action. The jurisdictions of the Committee on Financial Services (with respect to comprehensive authorities relating to financial institutions); the Committee on Ways and Means (with respect to tax treatment and increase in the public debt limit); the Budget Committee (with respect to budget procedures); and the Appropriations Committee (with respect to one summary appropriation covering all spending incurred by the bill) were all of all matters as one amendment to a previously passed unrelated revenue measure. In the House limited debate on the special order and on the motion made in order thereby were the only debates permitted, with no floor amendments. The House initially rejected a comprehensive compromise amendment on 29 September 2008. The Senate obtained unanimous consent to consider another previously passed House revenue bill by one compromise amendment with a sixty affirmative vote requirement for adoption, reflecting that super-majority voting requirement while otherwise avoiding the need for cloture, subject only to one amendment which it made in order to obtain unanimous consent and then rejected, bypassing all other Senate rules otherwise permitting unlimited debate and amendment. The Senate amendment contained some changes in the previously rejected House amendment, including a temporary increase in the limit on Federal Deposit Insurance Corporation provided depository insurance as well as extensive tax provisions that had previously been separately considered by one or both Houses. Two days later, the House reversed its previous rejection and adopted the Senate-initiated compromise on 3 October 2008, again utilizing a special order from the Rules Committee and disallowing any amendments

It becomes apparent that the multiple levels of decision making in the Legislative branch in the United States regarding revenues, authorizations, debt, budget, and appropriations, together with the leverage exercised by the Executive through limited impoundment authority or the threat or reality of Presidential veto, involve the Executive as a virtual co-equal player from the outset. It bears little similarity to the ministerial prerogatives and adhered-to timetables in all these areas in the UK Parliament, and renders comparisons between the two systems difficult. Predictability in both the timing and content of revenue and appropriation measures is greater in the UK, given the relative absence of effective opposing forces to the government's exercise of the power of the purse. By contrast, the exercise of these constitutionally separated powers in the United States has become so politically and institutionally unpredictable between the two Houses and the two branches and within each House, as those layers of decision making unfold annually, as to suggest that whatever standing rules and norms may exist toward their resolution they will either be changed or waived or else will remain insurmountable obstacles toward the timely enactment of a budget for the Federal government. No two fiscal years in modern history end up having followed the same timetables, combinations of measures, and procedural accommodations within each House, between the two Houses, and with the Executive. While the prerogatives of individual Members are not always procedurally protected if they involve changes in existing law or increases above pre-established budget resolution levels, they are enhanced under standing rules which encourage limitation and reduction amendments, and transfers of funding priorities reflected in the pending bill. It may be suggested that the House and the Senate have retained for the most part their traditional protections of individual Members' ability to offer amendments to Appropriation bills in full committee and in plenary session, but that tradition has been constrained and even discarded when emergencies or deadlines arise. The interactions of these four levels of decision making, with practices which sometimes encourage but do not guarantee individual Members' participation in the appropriation process, thus render the overall Congressional exercise of its power of the purse an unpredictable and confusing labyrinth, especially in comparison with a more expeditious system in the United Kingdom.

That there are advantages of regularity and (relative) simplicity in the British system of parliamentary control of finance is undeniable, even if they do not permit an answer to be given to the question posed at the beginning of this section. On the other hand, there is much in the observation that 'the government decides the value of the cheque, to whom it should be paid and when, and Parliament simply signs it'.[39] The parliamentary weapon of sustained debate intended to influence policy may never be as satisfying as the smack of direct Congressional authority, but it is well worth developing, particularly in the direction of more support for select committees, so as to enable them to participate with more authority and at an earlier stage than at present.

Secondly, the general rule that public expenditure may not be increased except on the initiative of the government means that only amendments to reduce the figures before the House are in order (and not always then—see page 256). Pressure in debate on the Estimates and their associated select committee reports is therefore more often for more spending than for economy and retrenchment, which may run against the logic of scrutiny. There have been ingenious suggestions of how the general prohibition on proposing increased spending might be bypassed, by allowing increases to be proposed provided that offsetting decreases are part of the package. This proposal has foundered partly on the difficulty of ensuring that the decreases will in the event balance the increases and that there will be no unexpected outcomes in both affected areas. It may now however be worth revisiting the approach, given the leading role in the scrutiny of Estimates now played by select committees, who have the experience and the expertise to make judgements on the finer details of transfers and could have the assistance of an enlarged Scrutiny Unit, not as large as but working on the same basis as the CBO. Opposition to the suggestion has rested on the suspicion that surrendering to Parliament any part of the age-old financial initiative of the Crown is apt to engage the law of unintended consequences in a big way. Yet it is hard to see that much would be lost by allowing the Commons to express its opinion, in an abstract motion based on an informed select committee report, about future transfers between major elements of expenditure. However when the Liaison Committee returned to just such a proposal in 2007–8, the government's reply was uncompromisingly negative. The grounds for refusal were not however very compelling—that the House needs to take clear decisions with precise legal effect in authorizing expenditure, and motions of the kind suggested would not have this advantage.[40] Since the committee were proposing motions which bore on their face a clear statement that they were the abstract opinion of the House and not part of authorization of expenditure properly understood, it is hard to see the government's position withstanding determined assault.

Next, unlike many other areas, Commons financial procedure has not yet been subject to really thorough overhaul. The Liaison Committee has described a series of fundamental flaws. The Estimates, to which scrutiny procedures are in form directed, are the least comprehensible of reporting documents. They reflect decisions already taken, and are hard to reconcile with Accounts. The Committee found that even government departments struggled to understand the Estimates. The Estimates time frame, a single year, is too short, Estimates do not cover the whole of departmental expenditure, and they are debated too late in the sequence of events for the House's decision to be effective. The quality of the information given to the Commons and its committees needs to be improved and refined, and directed more clearly to standards of performance and objectives, both across government and on a department-by-department basis. The Treasury are engaged in an Alignment Project, intended to make it easier to reconcile Estimates, Spending Plans, and Accounts, which if achieved will go far to enhance the ease with which the Commons can scrutinize government finances. In the context of consideration of the Comprehensive Spending Review, the Treasury Committee has recently suggested that the present arrangements should be replaced by others more clearly linked with public expenditure planning and control, allowing the House of Commons to consider and, if it chose to do so, authorize departmental spending limits. Greater relevance could then be given to consideration of expenditure in excess of these limits and requiring subsequent approval.[41]

Finally, one of the most testing issues confronting any reform will be how it balances some reinvigorated version of traditional concern for actual resources granted or withheld with the persistent tendency for finance to become the vehicle for a much broader party debate. Accountability will inevitably be diminished if the House of Commons again takes the tempting path towards party political debate with few resource implications and not the strait and stony way to efficient financial scrutiny. Fortunately, there are signs that that lesson has been learnt.

Notes

1. Erskine May's *Parliamentary Practice*, ed Sir William McKay (23rd edn, 2004), 848.
2. Ibid 853.
3. John McEldowney and Colin Lee, 'Parliament and Public Money', in P. Giddings (ed), *The Future of Parliament, Change or Decay* (2005), 78. The analysis is borne out by an International Monetary Fund comparison of national legislatures in respect of their budgetary processes. The UK scores one (ahead only of New Zealand) and the USA the maximum of ten (quoted in Alex Brazier and Vidya Ram, *The Fiscal Maze: Parliament, Government and Public Money* (2006), 34).
4. Brazier and Ram, *The Fiscal Maze*, 9.
5. McEldowney and Lee, 'Parliament and Public Money', 85.
6. Liaison Committee, Second Report 2007–8, HC 426.

7. Paul Einzig, *The Control of the Purse* (1959), 57.
8. PL 104-130.
9. Congressional Budget Act, sect 313.
10. 21 December 2005, 151 Congressional Record pp S14204–5 daily edition.
11. Local taxation, reasonable fees paid for services to organs of government, or levies on an industry strictly for its own benefit are not included (see page 243 for the parallel considerations in Congress).
12. The Estimates laid before the Commons are not the same as total public expenditure. Supply procedure does not cover a significant proportion of Total Managed Expenditure within departmental spending limits, and some monies voted by Parliament are not part of Total Managed Expenditure. For further explanation of these *arcana*, see Erskine May's *Parliamentary Practice*, op. cit., 858–9.
13. In all these cases, the roll-up is usually taken well before the deadline.
14. HC Deb (2008–9) 489 cc 46 and 269.
15. In addition, the debates in Westminster Hall (see pages 55, 379) on select committee reports—most with at least some financial content—take up the equivalent of eight days' debate in the Chamber every full session.
16. Second Report 2007–8 HC 426.
17. Fifth Report 2006–7 HC 233 para 21. The Committee thought that the system required review but the Liaison Committee was not convinced.
18. This did not prevent the Committee from concluding that the text of the report showed inadequate care and was 'bluntly sub-standard' (Third Report, HC106 (2006–7), paras 16 to 18). The Committee also condemned a departmental submission on the 2006–7 Winter Supplementaries as 'still largely an unhelpful turgid document that did little to elucidate the Estimate', an icy blast which evidently brought about some improvement (First Report 2006–7 HC 198 para 4).
19. First Report 2004–5 HC 419 Appendix 4 para 33. The Liaison Committee's manifesto for change (see page 374) makes reference to the critical need for the enlargement of the Unit to accompany the kind of procedural development which it calls for.
20. First Report 2006–7 HC 206 para 30.
21. Twelfth Report 2006–7 HC 835 para 4.
22. Ibid and para 18.
23. Second Special Report 2006–7 HC 522.
24. First Report 2006–7 HC 206 paras 51–2.
25. First Report 2006–7 HC 258 para 31.
26. Brazier and Ram, *The Fiscal Maze*, 51.
27. First Report 2006–7 HC 406 para 32.
28. Brazier and Ram, *The Fiscal Maze*, 32.
29. Erskine May's *Parliamentary Practice*, 23rd edition (2004), ed Sir William McKay, 930.
30. 10 USC 114 and 50 USC 414.
31. PL 110-81.
32. *Parliament and Congress*, K. A. Bradshaw and D. A. M. Pring 327.
33. PL 110-190.
34. 31 USC sect 716.
35. Seventh Report 2007–8 HC 299; Seventh Report 2008–9 HC 248.
36. The Foreign Affairs Committee (Third Report 2005–6 HC 903 paras 79 and 83) commented on an NAO investigation of the British Council, and recommended that a further value for money study should be carried out by the NAO.
37. PL 110-343.
38. HC Deb (2007–8) 482 c 952.
39. Brazier and Ram, *The Fiscal Maze*, 10.
40. Third Special Report 2007–8 HC 1108.
41. Sixth Report 2006–7 HC 279 para 110.

7

Scrutiny and Oversight

Introduction

Scrutiny of the actions of the executive is a primary responsibility of any legislature. It is also one of the most difficult to discharge. The oversight function of the US House and Senate arises from their duties to exercise continuous vigilance over the administration and execution of the laws by departments and agencies of the Federal government. This function has statutory and internal rule foundation but gains basic if not explicit legitimacy from the Constitution itself. Congress controls appropriations from the Treasury, and is empowered to tax and coin money, regulate foreign and interstate commerce, declare war, provide for the creation and maintenance of armed forces, establish post offices, and confirm and impeach Federal officers. Congress is empowered by the 'elastic clause' in Article I to 'make all Laws which shall be necessary and proper for carrying into execution the foregoing powers and all other powers vested by this Constitution in the Government of the United States, or in any Department of Officer thereof'.

While this empowerment is 'to make all laws...', there is no express empowerment of Congress to conduct oversight in the Constitution itself. The founding fathers believed the review function did not require specific mention in the Constitution. 'It was not considered necessary to make an explicit grant of such authority, as the power to make laws implied the power to see whether they were faithfully executed,' argues historian Arthur M. Schlesinger Jr.[1]

Some notable thoughts on legislative oversight emanate, for example, from James Wilson, an architect of the Constitution and Associate Justice on the first Supreme Court, who said, 'the House of Representatives (and the Senate) form the grand inquest of the state. They will diligently inquire into grievances, arising both from men and things.' Woodrow Wilson, perhaps the first scholar to use the term 'oversight' as a review of the Executive branch, said, 'quite as important as legislation is vigilant oversight of administration'. 'It is the proper duty of a representative body to look diligently into every affair of government and to talk much about what it sees. It is meant to be the eyes and voice, and to embody the wisdom and will of its constituents.' 'The informing function of Congress should be preferred even to its legislative function.'[2] John Stuart Mill, British utilitarian philosopher, suggested that 'the proper office of a representative assembly is to watch and control the government; to throw the light of publicity on its acts; to compel a full exposition and justification of all of them which any one considers questionable'.

Traditionally, the UK Parliament's duties in respect of scrutiny were closely bound to the granting of supply to the Crown. The medieval principle which insists on redress of grievances before the grant of supply remained (and remains) an axiom to which universal respect is paid. Supply and scrutiny were opposite sides of a single coin, and as late as 1900 a third of the Commons sessions were taken up with discussion of the government's tax and spending proposals.[3] Yet by that era government domination of the House's rules and time had rendered the possibility of refusal of supply a very unlikely circumstance. The financial pre-eminence of government over the Commons began not long after the Revolution of 1688–9. Parliament was far from supine in these decades, and parliamentary grievances were pressed, but it was as early thereafter as 1713 that the House of Commons resolved that it would proceed on no motion for a charge on the public revenue or for a grant of money voted by Parliament 'unless recommended from the Crown', a reminder which stands today in Standing Order No. 48, with the tacit understanding that by 'Crown' should now be understood 'government'.

To the traditional financial aspect of scrutiny there was added, from about the first third of the nineteenth century, use of the weapons of scrutiny in the interests of party advantage. The shifting alliances of aristocratic groupings of the later eighteenth century were succeeded, certainly by the time of the first great electoral reform in 1832, by parties which were more coherent in terms of policy and more disciplined in the House. It was a development not fully in place till much later in the century—and not consummated till after the Liberal party split in 1886—but with it came the use of the weapons of scrutiny in the interests of the party in the House and not in those of the House as an institution.

Finally, the representative function of individual Members has assumed greater significance the more the works of the state have impinged on the lives of their constituents and the more the latter have come to expect of their elected representative by way of advice or action when the activities of central or local government need to be challenged.

As a result, the same proceeding on the floor of the House of Commons can accommodate traditional, party and individual elements of scrutiny: any oral Question session (see pages 337ff.) can illustrate that fact.

How the oversight function is discharged

Even before 1900, it was beginning to be realized in the House of Commons that government was too complex, debate too blunt an instrument, and party politics too intrusive for the floor of the House of Commons to be a satisfactory forum for exercise of the scrutiny function in its traditional form, holding government to account. Despite occasional nostalgic sighs since for 'traditional' methods of scrutiny—and there have undoubtedly been recent occasions on which scrutiny on the floor has lived up to all classical expectations[4]—detailed and persistent oversight of a modern executive by 646 temporarily non-partisan Members, within the limits of a session which must accommodate far more business than a century ago, is simply not realistic. Even when procedures are specifically devised in the Commons as a vehicle for scrutiny of government—principally Opposition days (see below)—the topics are perfectly properly selected with party advantage in mind, and the purpose of the debate is to make political points, bankable for the next general election or opinion poll. There is no attempt to range at large or systematically over the doings of the executive. Indeed it is difficult to see how that could be attempted or accommodated within the procedure.

It was plain to informed observers as long ago as the late nineteenth century that the House of Commons preferred debating political issues to picking over the financial implications of government activity. The expectation that every penny voted—or at least every million pounds—should be justified at the dispatch box before being grudgingly conceded to what the House believed was by definition a spendthrift government was a pipe dream even in the late Victorian House. A. J. Balfour, when a senior minister in the Conservative government in 1896, described the suggestion that the discussion in the House on the business of Supply could act to diminish expenditure as 'flattering unction to our souls'.[5] Opposition days (originally called—as indeed they still are by the older inhabitants of the Palace of Westminster—Supply days) were then devised to balance the government's right to secure Supply in normal circumstances with the House's right to debate outstanding issues in Supply on a specified number of days.

Currently, twenty days on the floor of the House of Commons are devoted to motions tabled by Opposition parties. The lion's share, seventeen days, is of course taken by the official Opposition, but provision is made for the remaining three days to be at the disposal of the smaller parties. The government will select the day but the Opposition party will select the topic (or topics: Opposition days may informally accommodate two debates) which is or might be made a matter of current public interest. The text is therefore normally critical of government policy. The government will table an amendment, leaving out all the effective words of the Opposition motion and affirming the desirability of its own approach. When the time comes to vote, the Standing Orders instruct the Chair to put the first question not, as would be normal, on whether the amendment should be made but on whether the original words should stand part of the question. The purpose of this unusual procedure is to preserve the place of the Opposition at the centre of the decision making. They vote 'Aye' on the first division. When, presumably, the Noes have it and the Opposition words are not to stand part of the question, the next decision is whether the government words should be added—as they normally will be. The Chair then declares the main question as amended to be agreed to, without any further decision of the House.

Normally the purpose of the procedure is realized by simply scheduling the debate, giving non-government Members an opportunity to scrutinize government actions: Opposition victories in the lobbies are unusual. Recently, however, the third largest party attracted sufficient support in other parts of the House to defeat the government on Gurkha settlement rights. Though there was strictly no necessity to do so, the government immediately respected the will of the House and changed their policy, a remarkable if unusual tribute to the scrutiny process.

Balfour was right about the inability of the Commons as a whole to direct its attention to the details of government spending. Supply/Opposition days have over the decades become, quite properly, opportunities for the Opposition to select battlefields across which to direct general political fire at the government. All the same, though the details are often complex, the issues sometimes difficult to convey to the electorate at large, and the need for preliminary ground clearing most acute, it would hardly be sensible to allow financial arguments never to surface in the Chamber. The House of Commons has therefore begun to use the expertise of select committee reports as foundations for Estimates days, as a parallel method of scrutiny (see pages 261ff.).[6] One of the most testing issues confronting any reform of Supply procedure will be how it balances some reinvigorated version of traditional concern for actual resources granted or withheld with the persistent tendency for finance to become the vehicle for a much broader party debate.

There is one demand connected with scrutiny made on the floor of the House of Commons which regularly surfaces in points of order. The House—and the new Speaker—insist that major government announcements and decisions should be made first to the House—not of course necessarily in the Chamber. Governments of all parties accept the obligation in principle, but there are repeated disputes over whether some awkward revelation has been 'hidden away' as a written ministerial statement or in response to a Question for written answer, prearranged between the questioner and the government department—what is colloquially known as a 'plant'. Of course Opposition Members demand more oral statements than the parliamentary day can often accommodate. There may be some statements which a department thinks not important enough to fall within the practice at all, on which the constituency Member takes an entirely different view. There is no single means of resolving such disputes. The House tries daily to be as far upstream as possible of the doings and decisions of government, because without such an advantage, scrutiny is much harder.

The most articulated means of parliamentary oversight at Westminster is thus in the hands of select committees, particularly those whose remit is the activities, policy, and finance of government departments. Since it is difficult if not impossible to separate out those oversight activities from committees' other functions, details are not given here but at pages 372ff.

In addition, the resources of the Parliamentary Office of Science and Technology (POST) is at the disposal of individual Lords and Members and of select committees. POST is a small independent unit which is active in four main areas—biological science and health; physical science, IT and communications; environment and energy; and science policy. It is responsible for publications, analysing science policy, and advising the Houses and their committees by means of short briefing notes and longer reports.

In the United States, a number of laws directly augment Congress's authority, mandate, and resources to conduct oversight and are discussed at other places in this chapter. Various statutes include protections to persons providing information to Congress, the creation of independent Congressional agents of oversight such as the Government Accountability Office (GAO) through the Comptroller General and the Congressional Budget Office, House and Senate committee reorganization and empowerments enacted into law as exercises in rule making, and mechanisms within the Executive branch such as Inspectors General to monitor their own activities.

In chronological sequence, legislative oversight as a continuing statutory function was initially given to all standing committees by the Legislative Reorganization Act of 1946, which provided that each standing committee 'shall exercise continuous watchfulness' over administrative agencies. That law implicitly subdivided oversight responsibility in both Houses among (1) authorizing committees (to review Federal programmes under their jurisdiction and propose legislation to remedy deficiencies); (2) Appropriations Committees (to conduct fiscal oversight to scrutinize agency spending); and (3) the Government Operations and Government Affairs Committees (to investigate inefficiency, waste, and corruption). The Legislative Reorganization Act of 1970 subsequently required periodic reports by committees on their oversight activities. Since 1995 at the beginning of each Congress standing committees of the House have been required to adopt oversight plans, in a public meeting with a quorum present, by 15 February, and to submit them to the Committee on Oversight and Government Reform, which in turn is given forty-five days to submit a consolidated report on coordination of plans to the House. These plans are simultaneously submitted to the Committee on House Administration for formulation of a biennial budget for committees, which emerges in the form of a privileged resolution presented to the House providing funds for each committee's investigative activities for the two-year period of that Congress. At the end of each Congress all committees are required to submit activities reports which summarize and evaluate oversight activities actually undertaken in that Congress. These separate final reports represent the extent of review of oversight already undertaken and are not subsequently consolidated or evaluated by any committee except as the next Congress might continue or re-prioritize past oversight activities.

In 1995 the House amended its rules to grant explicit authority to the Speaker with the approval of the House to appoint 'special ad hoc oversight committees to review specific matters within the jurisdiction of two or more standing committees'. This authority given to the Speaker has not been directly utilized to date. The first attempt at the creation of a House select oversight committee since the 1995 rule came in 2005, when the House, utilizing the Rules Committee rather than the Speaker's establishment authority, created a 'Select Bi-partisan Committee to Investigate the Preparation for and Response to Hurricane Katrina'. That select committee was never fully appointed, as the Minority leader (subsequently to become Speaker in the next Congress) refused to recommend Members' names to the Speaker on the premise that the committee's composition was not truly 'bipartisan' in terms of equal numbers. Nevertheless the select committee held hearings attended only by Majority party Members. By unanimous consent the committee permitted participation by a few Minority non-committee Members of the House from the geographic areas affected by the hurricane, although they could not vote on the report ultimately filed with the House. The Minority leader's perception of the need for equal numbers was misplaced despite the title of the select committee as 'bipartisan', as no investigative or legislative committee in contemporary Congresses, other than the Committee on Standards of Official Conduct, has been truly bipartisan in terms of equal numbers. Oversight is ultimately driven by political decisions, often partisan ones, and the Minority party's refusal to participate displayed the extent to which partisanship can overtake a demonstrated need for fact finding into the performance of the Executive branch. The Minority non-committee Members who were permitted to participate in the hearings had no standing to represent their leadership's concerns about the performance of the Executive agencies controlled by the opposite political party. That opportunity was left to Minority members of the standing committees on Homeland Security, Transportation and Infrastructure, and Appropriations which retained ongoing oversight jurisdiction over those aspects of the Federal Emergency Management Agency—the entity which the new select committee had been called upon to investigate.

In 2007, an ad hoc select committee on Global Climate Change was created, despite the standing committees on Energy and Commerce and on Science and Technology having overlapping jurisdiction over energy, public health, and over environmental research and development respectively. The new select committee was created by adoption of a special order reported from the Committee on Rules coupled with the 'self-executed' biennial funding resolution for all standing House committees for the 110th Congress. The Speaker's ultimate influence was again evident through utilization of the Rules Committee—a super-majority of which Members she had appointed. The select committee on Global Climate Change was not given legislative jurisdiction but was given subpoena authority to compel information on global climate change—particularly the impact of auto carbon dioxide emissions—an authority motivated by the Speaker's judgement that the relevant standing committees might not be sufficiently attentive to that issue.

In 1999 the House further amended its rules to permit committees to have a sixth subcommittee (beyond the general limit of five) if it were an oversight subcommittee. In 2007, eleven standing committees established oversight subcommittees in addition to (or in two cases comprising a function of one of) their legislative subcommittees.

There is no comparable specific subdivision of oversight subcommittee responsibility for legislative committees under Senate rules and practices, beyond the ongoing establishment since 1948 of the Permanent Subcommittee on Investigations of the standing committee on Homeland Security and Governmental Affairs. The authority given to all Senate committees, express and implied, under Senate rules to conduct investigations and inquiries is considered sufficient authority to enable all of its subcommittees to conduct appropriate oversight.

House rules impose general oversight responsibilities on all its standing committees, commensurate with their respective legislative jurisdictions, to assure proper administration of enacted laws. Special committees such as the select committee on Global Climate Change are empowered in resolutions providing for their establishment, normally as investigative entities to examine specific events or issues without legislative jurisdiction, only to report results of their investigations to the House.

Many laws passed by Congress contain general guidelines and sometimes their wording is deliberately vague or convoluted. Implementation of these laws commonly requires the Executive agencies to draft administrative regulations and agency officials to undertake day-to-day programme management. A key goal of general legislative oversight is to hold Executive officials accountable for their implementation of delegated authority. The Supreme Court held that the investigative power that is exercised by the House and Senate through their committees is inherent in the power to make laws (*Watkins v United States* 354 US 178 (1957)), and encompasses inquiries concerning the administration of existing laws and the need for proposed legislation. The courts will not look to the motives which may have prompted a Congressional investigation, nor to the wisdom of the investigation or its methodology (*Doe v McMillan* 412 US 306 (1973)) if in conformity with committee rules requiring approval by a majority of the parent committee (*Gojack v United States* 384 US 702 (1966)). Also, oversight authority extends to studies of social, economic, or political problems, and probes departmental corruption, inefficiency, or waste at the Federal level. Although broad, this power of investigation is not unlimited. It may be exercised only in aid of the 'legislative function' (*Kilbourn v Thompson* 103 US 168 (1881)). The Supreme Court has said that Congress has no general power to inquire into private affairs and that the subject of inquiry must be one 'on which legislation could be had or would be materially aided by the information which the investigation was calculated to elicit...the power of inquiry—with the process to enforce it—is an essential and appropriate auxiliary to the legislative function' (*McGrain v Daugherty* 273 US 135 (1927)). In *Eastland v United States Servicemen's Fund* 421 US 491 (1975), the Supreme Court in expanding on *McGrain* declared that 'to be a valid legislative inquiry there need be no predictable end result'.

In the context of the 10th Amendment to the Constitution, which 'reserves to the States respectively, or to the people, the powers not delegated to the United States by the Constitution nor prohibited by it to the States', there is an ongoing debate in the United States about the proper relationship between the Federal government, the States, and the people and specifically the respective roles to be played by Congress, State legislatures, local governmental units, and by the private sector in scrutinizing matters within their respective spheres. From a committee investigative perspective, the proper role of Congress in determining whether an activity is inherently governmental or commercial, for example, and thus more suitable to being contracted out to the private sector, is debatable. A popular subject of debate in Federal agencies relates to jobs which can be shifted from the civil service to the private sector, for example, a matter which suggests that Congressional committees have a stake as they oversee the implementation of Federal law to arrive at a proper balance of Federal involvement and delegation to other units of government or to private contracting entities through legislation or the annual appropriations process. Much depends on the political majority in control of the oversight agenda in each House as to whether following hearings legislation should emerge which increases or lessens government regulatory authority over the activity in question. Whatever the political balance achieved at any point in time, the jurisdictional ability of Congress to investigate activities of State or local governments and the private sector remains in place under House and Senate rules. In the House, the Committee on Oversight and Government Reform is directed to 'study intergovernmental relationships between the United States and the States and municipalities' and to 'review and study on a continuing basis the operation of government activities at all levels with a view to determining their economy and efficiency'.

The Congressional Review Act of 1996 (CRA) is one of several statutes enacted in the last half-century which ostensibly enables Congress to review and disapprove major agency rules and regulations once finally promulgated. Other such statutes are discussed more specifically in the segment on Legislation, with the emphasis there placed on the procedural mechanics for expedited consideration of measures of approval or disapproval in each House. The CRA provides for expedited procedures of an introduced joint resolution of disapproval. Under the Act, Congress has sixty legislative days to exercise a regulatory veto power under expedited procedures, after which the proposed regulation will go into effect. The law has been seldom utilized, as between 1996 and 1999 only seven joint resolutions of disapproval were introduced in Congress, pertaining to five of 186 major regulations (those having at least a $100 million annual impact) promulgated during that time. On one occasion (2001) the House adopted a joint resolution of disapproval, but no such joint resolutions have become law. Nevertheless the law remains an example of joint exercise of rule making primarily to enable the Senate to expeditiously consider joint resolutions disapproving specific agency regulations—by permitting thirty-five Senators to sign a discharge motion to bring it to the Senate floor for an up-or-down vote following ten hours of debate and without amendment. From 2001 to 2003, the Senate passed two such joint resolutions of disapproval but they were not considered by the House. The statute contains no comparable procedures for expedited House action, preferring to retain flexibility for the leadership through utilization of the Rules Committee to make in order a disapproval resolution reported from committee or to discharge a committee of jurisdiction if necessary.

While the law was enacted to symbolize the ability of Congress to respond to major agency rule-making regimes without micro-managing their formulation, its lack of utilization shows that it is not a panacea in addressing regulatory excesses or inadequacies. The assumption is that the President would veto any joint resolution disapproving a regulation emanating from an agency whose membership and policy direction he controls, and that a two-thirds vote of each House would be required to enact the disapproval over his veto. Nevertheless, Congress and the Executive branch have, as suggested by Oleszek, 'adapted to the post-Chadha era largely through informal accommodations and statutory adjustments. On the one hand, Executive agencies want discretion and flexibility in running their programmes; on the other hand, Congress is generally unwilling to grant open-ended authority to Executive entities.'[7]

This assumption is buttressed in the context of other laws (discussed in the chapter on Legislation at page 473) which contain various forms of 'legislative veto', where the impact of *Immigration and Naturalization Service v Chadha* 462 US 919 (1983) has required the conversion of a variety of simple and concurrent resolutions of disapproval or approval mechanisms into joint resolutions in order to satisfy the presentment clause of the Constitution.

General oversight by each House of Congress (that is, ongoing responsibility to review all aspects of Executive branch activity) is conducted in one of three ways: (1) authorizing committees which review Federal programmes and agencies under their jurisdictions; (2) fiscal oversight by the House Ways and Means or Senate Finance Committees examining revenues and spending programmes within their jurisdictions, and Appropriations and Budget Committees scrutinizing Executive spending; and (3) ongoing investigative oversight into any aspect of government activities at all levels, a responsibility assigned to the Oversight and Government Reform Committee of the House and to the Senate Homeland Security and Governmental Affairs Committee. Each of the three overlapping jurisdictional categories of oversight is intended to evaluate programme administration, ongoing usefulness, and to eliminate waste, fraud, and abuse. They are grouped in the standing rules into the category of 'general oversight responsibilities', and are supplemented by 'special oversight functions' and 'additional functions' assigned to specified standing committees.

This involves areas of overlap with other standing committees' general responsibilities or particularized duties and even contemplates in one area joint hearings between the House and Senate Appropriations Committees. Taken together, House and Senate rules mandate ongoing oversight in all areas of Congressional concern. Coupled with subpoena power conferred upon all committees, additional compulsory interrogatory and deposition authority conferred on committee staff in some circumstances, and the biennial adoption of committee budgets presumably responsive to planned oversight, the rules provide all the procedural tools necessary to accomplish meaningful fact finding in preparation for possible legislation. The underlying challenge is always to find the time and determination to conduct oversight, in recognition of the primacy of the Congressional responsibility under separation of powers, despite counter-pressures where the same party affiliation of the Congress and Executive and other political influences may detract from that responsibility. Ultimately, the decision whether to conduct oversight is a political and collegial one requiring the approval of a majority of the committee or sub-committee concerned, although chairmen normally take the lead in announcing and scheduling committee inquiries and their decisions are not often subjected to formal committee votes. The fact that committee staff are all partisan and that Minority committee staff have no independent capability of compelling the production of information reinforces the conclusion that effective committee scrutiny over the Executive branch flows from the Majority party chairman and his staff (sometimes having been stimulated by the Majority leadership's overall agenda), and from the partisan decision made by the entire House or Senate on a biennial basis on the extent of funding for the hiring of investigative committee staff.

Requests from committee chairmen for biennial funding are usually bipartisan in nature, and reflect decisions at the organizational meetings of each standing committee of the contemplated size of committee investigative staff for the next two years, two-thirds to be controlled by the Majority through the chairman and one-third by the Minority through the ranking member. These amounts are referred to the House and Senate administrative committees with jurisdiction over committee budgets, which regularly report resolutions reducing from the requested levels the overall size of the committees' investigative budgets based on constraints on total Legislative branch spending in the annual Congressional budget resolution.

In the 110th Congress, for example, standing committee chairmen submitted committee budget increase requests ranging from 5 per cent to 40 per cent over the previous Congress. In the House, the Committee on House Administration and then the full House pared those increases to 2 per cent, while in the Senate the Rules and Administration Committee recommended a 5.4 per cent increase. The ultimate ability of committee staffs to perform oversight is dependent upon their size and quality, which in turn is influenced by competing salary levels in the private sector where the most capable staff might otherwise seek employment. Despite the 2 per cent increase in committee investigative budgets in the 110th Congress, chairmen in the new Majority have been able to hire a sizeable number of additional Majority staff to conduct aggressive oversight since they are no longer in the minority and are not constrained by access to only one-third of the committee budget.

Only the Committees on Appropriations in the House and Senate have their own capability to establish funding levels for its investigative staff, as under House and Senate rules all other standing and select committees have their budgets biennially set by the committees on Administration and by their respective House. The annual

Legislative Branch Appropriation Bill establishes the investigative budget for the House and Senate Committees on Appropriations by separate line item, based on the premise that the bipartisan history of those committees and their jurisdictions over discretionary spending for the entire government justify recommendation of their own level of investigative activity directly to their respective Houses rather than to the filtering Administration committees.

Since the mid-1940s, the House Appropriations Committee has provided under its rules the unique ability to conduct 'studies and examinations' at the joint request of a subcommittee chair and ranking Minority member acting together, and ratified by the full committee chairman and ranking Minority member also acting jointly. This committee rule allows the employment of investigative staff, normally professional former FBI or GAO investigators, to be retained on a contract basis, in addition to fifteen permanent investigative committee staff, to conduct the requested investigations and to report back to the requesting Members. The results of such study and examination are not made public unless so determined by the subcommittee. This technique permits immediate and focused response to a perceived problem based on bipartisan cooperation, conducted by professional investigators. This committee rule represents an investigative tool in addition to ordinary annual subcommittee hearings and markups enabling the Appropriations Committee to oversee a targeted aspect of the Executive branch with a degree of confidentiality. Despite readoption of such a committee rule each Congress, its implementation can break down where leadership pressures are brought to bear to inhibit certain inquiries. For example, the Appropriations Committee in the 110th Congress has re-instituted the employment of contract investigators which had been discontinued by the predecessor committee chairman despite the existence of the committee rule. The Senate Appropriations Committee has no comparable staffing arrangement in its rules.

Of the three levels of oversight capability described above, the authorization process in the House and Senate has in modern Congresses been the least productive in terms of time spent conducting investigative hearings. While under the rules of both Houses annual appropriations must be first authorized by laws enacted prior to their consideration in general Appropriation bills, in modern practice those authorization laws often are not enacted or even considered prior to consideration of annual general Appropriation bills. This dichotomy (discussed more extensively in the chapter on the power of the purse at page 268) results from the need to enact actual budget authority (appropriations) on an annual basis prior to the beginning of a new fiscal year on 1 October, in order for the Executive entity being funded to operate at all. Conversely, authorizations for those appropriations, while often expiring at the end of a fiscal year, are merely conditions precedent to the consideration of appropriations in the House and Senate rather than legal preconditions for agency operation. In this regard it is important to distinguish between authorizing statutes which empower a department or agency to operate as a matter of law and those which primarily serve as policy guidelines for eventual funding. Most authorization laws establish parameters for spending as conditions precedent under internal House and Senate rules for consideration of the appropriation items, but do not normally serve as conditions precedent to actual spending. If, as regularly happens by waiver of points of order, the relevant appropriations are considered and then enacted into law despite the lack of or in excess of a statutory guideline internally operable in each House, the incentives within many authorizing committees to conduct preliminary oversight on an ongoing basis may not be as compelling as would be the case if the rules requiring prior enactment of authorizing law were being strictly enforced. Even in the two notable areas (national defence and intelligence) where the authorization laws are annually enacted and where their enactment is stated as a condition precedent to actual spending, those precondition laws[8] are routinely waived by language in the annual defence Appropriation bill providing that 'notwithstanding any other provision of law, funds are hereby appropriated'.

The impact of these annual appropriation bill waivers on authorizing committee oversight is difficult to measure. The firewalls between the authorization and appropriation processes, enacted into law to preserve the supremacy of the authorization law as the primary policy vehicle in the defence and intelligence areas have not necessarily served to assure increased oversight by the Armed Services and Intelligence Committees. The enactment of those annual authorization laws is often delayed for political reasons during a calendar year, while the need for enactment of new budget authority (or the 'continuation' of budget authority from the preceding fiscal year) by 1 October is an annually occurring reality. Appropriated funds become unavailable to the recipient agency by operation of the Anti-Deficiency Act of 1921 and may force the closure of the affected government entity.

Since multiple referrals of measures have been permitted in the House, beginning in 1974, secondary or 'sequential' authorizing committees have increased demands on Executive officials for testimony. Seen from the perspective of the Executive branch, these demands on the time of the Executive in delivering testimony and documents to a large number of committees can be counterproductive. Some have advocated joint hearings where a number of authorizing committees can simultaneously gather information, although that procedure requires unanimous cooperation by all the committees involved under special rules to coordinate member participation. The establishment of Homeland Security Committees in both Houses following the creation of the Department of Homeland Security in 2002 resulted in part from that department's assertion that it was required to report to as many as eighty-seven committee and subcommittee units of the two Houses. The establishment of those overarching authorizing committees has relieved some demands for Executive time and testimony by a number of relatively marginal panels, although any committee intent upon asserting its legislative and oversight jurisdiction over an aspect of 'homeland security' may, while admonished to coordinate its plans with other committees, exercise that oversight separately.

In 2009, the House Committee on Homeland Security was given added oversight responsibility over aspects of that subject commensurate with its primary legislative jurisdiction, so as to require Executive branch reports to that committee as well as to other standing committees. Also at the beginning of the 111th Congress all committees were given added responsibility to hold mandatory public hearings on 'fraud, waste and abuse in the Executive branch' as a response to projected increasing deficits and relaxation of pay-go (see page 250) spending offset disciplines.[9]

Many Senators serve on both authorizing and appropriations committees, and with limited available time are often better able to influence the enactment of policy into law by attachment to an annual Appropriation bill (which must be enacted for spending to occur) rather than to the separate, sometimes legally unnecessary, and not always annually recurring authorization measure. Many authorization laws contain multi-year levels of suggested funding, and thus do not need to be re-enacted each year. Coupled with other distractions which may occupy authorizing committee members' available time, including fund-raising priorities, weekly schedules resulting in Members' attendance at the seat of government only from late Tuesdays through Thursdays, and political disincentives which discourage Majority party scrutiny of an Executive of the same political party, it is understandable that authorizing committees may be less motivated to conduct the general and specific oversight they are required by House and Senate rules to perform. In the 110th Congress, where in 2007 the majorities of both Houses were of the party opposing the Executive for the first time since 2000, increased levels of oversight activities on the part of authorizing committees were undertaken. Generally, though, it has been left to the greatly expanded oversight capability and inclination of the Committee on Oversight and Government Reform (to be subsequently discussed in this chapter) to conduct televised oversight in order to increase public awareness of Executive branch activities and policies.

Although the Budget Committees of each House are required by internal rules to conduct hearings in advance of the annual Congressional budget resolution and in response to the President's budget submission in February, those hearings are often perfunctory and do not involve in-depth examination of specific agencies' operations. After all, the ultimate work product of the Budget Committees is only an internal political document containing 'macroeconomic' totals rather than specific sub-allocations below the functional category level—a concurrent resolution on the budget, which is required to be produced by April of each year. The Budget Committees' work product does not have the force and effect of law, and, like most authorization laws, only serves as an avoidable or waivable guideline for actual annual spending. Thus the Budget Committees' oversight activities, while required by rule to be 'ongoing', tend to diminish once the Congressional budget resolution is reported each year. It is not an 'exclusive committee'—that is, their Members also serve on authorization or appropriations panels where their legislative attention for the remainder of the year is required. The Budget Committees' jurisdiction being confined to the preparation of the budget resolution and to Congressional budget process, rather than extending to statutory legislation and to specified line-item amounts of budget authority, their corresponding oversight efforts are less significant than those of the Appropriations Committees.

The subcommittees of the House and Senate Appropriations Committees, therefore, conduct much of the meaningful oversight of the Executive branch as an annual precondition to the enactment of funding within the timetable of the fiscal year (by 1 October) set out in the Congressional Budget Act of 1974. Those committees define the precise purpose for which money may be spent, adjust funding levels, and often attach provisos prohibiting expenditures for certain purposes. The appropriations process as an oversight technique has been described as comparable to 'a Janus-like weapon: the stick of spending reductions in case agencies cannot satisfactorily defend their budget requests and past performance, and the carrot of more money if agencies produce convincing success stories or the promise of future results'.[10] While subcommittee hearings serve as the formal forum for agencies to justify their continued existence, the informal relationship between those agencies and staff of the subcommittees, together with the 'surveys and investigations' staff retained for targeted studies and examinations on the House side, constitute effective tools in bringing concerns to the attention of subcommittee members.

Printed hearings and reports often enunciate guidelines which are the result of ongoing oversight and some unpublished staff reports from House Appropriations Committee 'studies and examinations' (commonly known as surveys and investigations (S & I) investigators, the degree of cooperation often stemming from the realization that the same agency must again justify its requested budget in the next years to the annual satisfaction of a panel which traditionally operates in a relatively bipartisan manner. Informal communications between agency and appropriations subcommittee staff on an ongoing basis 'are probably the most prevalent technique of oversight'.[11] Language in hearings, reports, floor debates, and joint statements accompanying conference reports often include the verbs 'expect, urge, recommend, desire, feel' to convey varying degrees of urgency in attempts to influence agency behaviour, and are the outward manifestations of even more informal communications often not reduced to writing.

There are nevertheless some unique (now commonplace) distractions from Appropriations Committees as they undertake oversight responsibilities, including the emergence of 'earmarks'—set-asides in either bill or report language for specific programmes requested for constituents and other special interests by individual Members and by the President in his annual budget. (The specific definition of an 'earmark' in House rules beginning in the 110th Congress, for purposes of a new rule requiring their disclosure prior to consideration of a measure and permitting a separate vote on any attempt to waive the disclosure requirement, is as follows: 'a provision or report language included primarily at the request of a Member or Senator providing, authorizing or recommending a specific amount of discretionary budget authority, credit authority, or other spending authority for a contract, loan, loan guarantee, grant, loan authority, or other expenditure with or to an entity, or targeted to a specific State, locality or Congressional district, other than through a statutory or administrative formula-driven or competitive award process'. As earmarks have multiplied in recent Congresses, the available time for oversight, including evaluations of the legitimacy of earmark requests, has correspondingly diminished. With the successful enactment of earmarks, special-interest lobbying organizations have correspondingly increased their efforts, and with Members' names now publicly attached to those successful earmarks, campaign contributions to many more Members have accordingly increased.)

Also, continuing requests from the Executive for 'emergency supplemental appropriations' for both military and domestic emergencies, unbudgeted in the President's annual message but arising during a current fiscal year, are a further distraction from Appropriations subcommittees' ability to conduct oversight in preparation for more predictable annual fiscal year activity. Nevertheless, House and Senate Appropriations Committee members from both parties have successfully opposed the concept of biennial budgeting, preferring annual review of the President's budget and the attendant hearings, markups, and enactment of general Appropriation bills. 'Biennial budgeting' assumes actual funding by law once every two years, coupled with an increased number of supplemental bills in the second year. While the premise of biennial budgeting is to enhance oversight opportunities in the second calendar year of a Congress during a session when general Appropriation bills are not being reported, appropriators argue that it is the requirement for annual funding which forces them to conduct, and agencies to respond to, preliminary oversight each fiscal year, at least in the hearings which form the basis for the annual bills.

The third level of oversight contemplated in the rules of both Houses (an area greatly enhanced in the 110th Congress) involves those standing committees created for the express purpose of conducting investigations of any matter at any time without regard to standing rules conferring jurisdiction over the matter on another standing committee. As mandated in the standing rules, 'the findings and recommendations of the Oversight and Government Reform Committee of the House in such an investigation shall be made available to any other standing committee having jurisdiction over the matter involved'. It is difficult to imagine a broader conferral of oversight jurisdiction.

In the Senate, the 'Permanent' Subcommittee on Investigations was first established in 1948 by Senate resolution as a sub-unit of the Government Affairs Committee to conduct ongoing investigations into all aspects of government activity. It was an outgrowth of the 1941 Truman Committee (named after then Senator Harry Truman) which investigated fraud and mismanagement of the nation's war programme. This 'Permanent' Senate subcommittee is given extraordinary authority in the biennial funding resolution which finances all Senate Committees, in addition to subpoena authority conferred by standing rule, to conduct staff depositions and interrogatories of witnesses under oath without Members present. The leverage this authority gives staff to coax or compel information from the Executive branch cannot be overstated. It eventually became a model for the comparable House committee.

In the 110th Congress, the House for the first time in its standing rules (clause 4(c) of Rule X) conferred similar authority on staff of the House Committee on Oversight and Government Reform to conduct interrogatories and depositions for information required to be furnished under oath without the need for Members to be present in a formal hearing. Minority committee members are to be given adequate notice to attend and participate, and at least one Minority staff person may participate in the deposition or interrogatory. Until 2007, that authority had only been conferred on House staff in the context of specific investigations (ethics or impeachment inquiries) by separate resolutions reported from the Committee on Rules. This conferral in 2007 was in contemplation of wide-ranging oversight by a committee with a new political majority opposite from the Executive branch, and mirrored a long-standing Senate delegation to staff. After one year of implementation, this empowerment proved generally successful in coaxing, if not coercing, the cooperation of potential witnesses, both governmental and private, before the Committee on Oversight and Government Reform, without the need for the formal issuance of subpoenas. In summary, in the first session of the 110th Congress, the Committee on Oversight and Government reform held forty hearings, issued twenty-six subpoenas, took nineteen depositions, and conducted ninety-one witness interviews.

Transcribed witness interviews of that Committee pursuant to its internal Rule 22 are unsworn proceedings and are generally less formal than committee depositions. Witnesses are permitted to be represented by counsel. The Committee permits agency counsel to be present in transcribed interviews with employees of that agency in circumstances where such presence does not involve a substantial conflict or otherwise pose the potential of impeding the Committee's ability to conduct an efficient, effective, and fair interview proceeding. Questions during transcribed interviews are alternately asked by the Majority and Minority staff. There are no fixed rules that govern how the questioning proceeds. This is usually worked out informally in a manner that ensures each side an equal opportunity to question the witness. Witnesses are not placed under oath, but are required by law to answer questions from Congress truthfully, subject to prosecution for perjury. A witness or his counsel may raise objections to questions, and if they cannot be resolved in the interview, the witness can be required to return for a deposition or hearing. The Committee has discretion whether to recognize non-constitutional privileges, such as the attorney–client privilege. The Committee does not generally recognize objections that are not based on a privilege, such as hearsay or speculation. Witnesses will be given an opportunity to review the interview transcript at the Committee's offices. They may submit suggested changes to the transcript for the record. Substantive changes are timely submitted in letter format. Copies of the transcripts are not given to witnesses, but are only for the official use of Members of the Committee. They are investigative tools and are not routinely released publicly, but there is no prohibition in the Committee rules on their use in hearings, reports, or correspondence.

The potential for committee retaliation based on refusal of witnesses to respond to such staff inquiries under oath could result in unfavourable publicity and ultimately in the certification of contempt reported to the House or Senate, but only after the witness has been afforded the opportunity to appear before a formal hearing with Members present, under procedures guaranteeing the witness right to counsel and to have Members determine any claim of constitutional rights, irrelevancy of questions, or whether testimony which might tend to defame, degrade, or incriminate be taken in closed session. In fact, the new rule assures equitable Minority party participation in any such discovery proceeding and provides that 'information secured pursuant to this authority shall retain the character of discovery until offered for admission in evidence before the committee, at which time any proper objection shall be timely'.

A procedure unique to the House of Representatives and not available in the Senate is a resolution of inquiry—a method to request factual information from the Executive branch. While it lacks the element of compulsion necessary to punish failure to respond by a contempt certification, the resolution of inquiry has the advantage of assuming or encouraging Executive branch compliance pursuant to principles of comity between the branches of government, with an underlying threat of compulsory process (committee subpoena) or other indirect retribution, for example by funding cut-off or other subsequent Congressional response. House rules contain no specific provision for enforcing resolutions of inquiry, and in cases of refusal or declination the House may renew its request or demand a further or more complete answer.

The important feature of the rule is the conferral of privileged status on such an introduced resolution if reported from the committee(s) of referral, or after fourteen legislative days of session if not reported by those committees. Any Member may introduce a resolution of inquiry and call it up after fourteen legislative days if the committee has not filed its report, by utilizing a privileged non-debatable motion to discharge the committee of referral. If the motion to discharge is successful, the motion to proceed to consideration of the resolution itself is then in order. If all the committee(s) of referral have filed reports on the resolution, whether favourable, adverse, or without recommendation, only the chairman or other authorized committee member can call up the resolution, and the motion to discharge the committee is no longer available. If one committee of joint referral has not reported, but others have, the motion to discharge is applicable to the non-reporting committee, but even if successful only the reporting committees may then proceed to call up the resolution subject to the three-day layover requirement for the report. To qualify as privileged the resolution must be addressed to the President or to a Cabinet Secretary, and must request the production of factual information (usually documents within the official's possession) rather than an expression of opinion or the request for an Executive investigation. The unique importance of the resolution of inquiry as a procedural tool rests in the enhanced ability of an individual Member or a reporting committee to obtain a vote in the House, symbolizing House interest in the factual information requested and most often resulting in informal accommodations for access to the relevant committee. In the event of voluntary Executive department compliance during the pendency of the resolution in committee, that committee usually then files an adverse report on the resolution so as to forestall unnecessary votes on a motion to discharge. At the same time all Members have access to the supplied information once it becomes a file of the committee.

Bipartisanship in Congress

Bipartisanship at Westminster is discussed in the chapter on Committees at page 360. There is no standing or select committee of either US House which is truly bipartisan with equal numbers of Republicans and Democrats, other than the House and Senate Ethics Committees. In every other committee, a majority with a quorum present is ultimately required to undertake any committee activity. No House or committee rules authorize either ranking Minority Members or individual Members to institute official committee investigations, hold hearings, or issue subpoenas. Individual Members may seek the voluntary cooperation of agency officials or private persons, but no judicial precedent has directly recognized a right in an individual Member, other than the chair of a committee, to exercise the authority of a committee in the context of oversight without the permission of a majority of the committee.

One anomaly in statute runs counter to this majoritarian model, namely the provision in title 5 of the US Code (section 2954) which permits any seven members of the Committee on Oversight and Government Reform of the House or any five members of the Senate Homeland Security and Government Affairs Committee to demand information from an Executive agency. This has been interpreted by at least one Federal Court in a case (later vacated on appeal) to be the equivalent of compulsory process, allowing fewer than a majority of members of either committee (not even a majority of the minority) to compel information. While it may be persuasively argued that Congress did not intend to confer the equivalent of subpoena authority upon a minority of members of those panels when that law was enacted in 1928 as part of a paperwork reduction reform on reports to Congress, the use of the term 'shall submit any information requested of it' conveys a sense of compulsion to agencies from which information is sought. Nevertheless, dismissal of that initial District Court ruling on appeal, coupled with a more recent Federal district court opinion that Congressional plaintiffs lack standing to sue under that statute for lack of personal injury, citing the Supreme Court opinion in *Raines v Byrd* 521 US 811 (1997), cast doubt on its enforceability by a court.

The rules of the Senate provide substantially more effective means for individual minority-party Members to engage in 'self-help' to support their own oversight objectives than afforded their House counterparts. Senate rules emphasize the rights and prerogatives of individual Senators in enabling or disabling the conduct of business requiring unanimous consent. The basis for this leverage is the guarantee of unlimited debate and the absence of a germaneness requirement unless an extraordinary majority votes to invoke cloture. Objections to or 'holds' against (discussed at page 73) Senate floor proceedings may be based on an individual Senator's insistence upon committee activity such as oversight in another (unrelated) area. The Senate cloture rule may not be invoked in committee, thus further enabling wide leverage to enhance individual or minority investigatory oversight interests. At least two Senate Committees (Judiciary and Finance), however, have adopted rules (not considered inconsistent with Senate rules) enabling debate to be limited by majority vote (e.g. in Judiciary, there must be ten affirmative record votes, at least one by a minority Senator).

Evidence, witnesses, and subpoenas

In the USA, the basic tool enabling the effective conduct of Congressional oversight is the subpoena power conferred on all committees of the House and Senate by standing rule to 'require, by subpoena or otherwise, the attendance and testimony of such witnesses and the production of such...papers as it considers necessary'. In modern practice the full House does not issue subpoenas, but instead delegates that authority to all standing committees and their subcommittees and, when permitted by full committee vote, to the chairman of that full committee. Until 1975, only a few standing committees possessed subpoena authority under standing rules, and specific authority was conferred on all others by resolutions reported from the Committee on Rules each Congress. The authority to compel information by 'subpoena or otherwise' has not been interpreted to permit committees on their own initiative to confer interrogatory or deposition authority on any single member or on staff, absent initial conferral by the House. Such staff empowerment has happened only in the context of a few investigations involving ethics or impeachment, and has been generally conferred on only one investigative committee of each House covering all oversight in an entire Congress, beginning in 1948 in the Senate and in 2007 in the House. With those exceptions, collegial action is contemplated by all committees and subcommittees in the issuance of subpoenas, even requiring a full majority quorum to be present in open session to vote on their authorization. This authority does not extend to other sub-units of a committee such as 'task forces', absent House conferral. Full-committee chairmen may authorize subpoenas when that authority is delegated by the full committee, either on an ad hoc basis or by committee rule. The delegation of that authority is subject to abuse, as evidenced by the action of the chairman of the Committee on Government Reform in 1998—later challenged (unsuccessfully) by the Minority in the House as a question of privilege alleging deliberate violation of rules. Having been delegated unilateral subpoena authority, he proceeded to issue hundreds of subpoenas *duces tecum* and then to unilaterally release sensitive materials received in response, in violation of a committee rule requiring collegial determination of the public status of those materials. The standard requirement for collegial action with a full quorum present to determine whether to issue specific subpoenas remains a safeguard against unilateral action by one Member, and full committees can countermand the delegation of unilateral authority, if abused. This requirement of majority quorum presence in the House (one-third is the minimum quorum requirement in the Senate for the issuance of subpoenas) is significant, as is the majority quorum requirement in both Houses to report contemptuous conduct to either House, dependent upon more collegial involvement than on other interlocutory matters.

Failure to comply with compulsory process can result in House votes to certify the recalcitrant witness for prosecution for criminal contempt (a process discussed in the chapter on Privilege and Contempt). More often with respect to Executive branch agency witnesses, however, it is the threat of budget constraints or policy changes imposed by Congress in law which encourage compliance with requests for information, short of the actual issuance and enforcement of subpoenas. In fact, there is often a hiatus between the authorization and actual issuance of subpoenas of witnesses, in order to encourage voluntary appearance and/or production of documents prior to service of process.

On rare occasions of subpoenas issued to assistants to the President, a claim of Executive privilege (discussed in greater detail at page 329) can prevent compliance. In the 110th Congress, failure of Executive branch officials (Presidential assistants) to comply with subpoenas by the House and Senate Judiciary Committees in an oversight investigation of the Justice Department relating to the firing of US Attorneys led the House committee to recommend a contempt resolution to the House. As explained in greater detail in the chapter on Privilege and Contempt, the House on 14 February 2008 adopted a resolution which had two purposes: (1) to direct the appropriate US Attorney to initiate criminal contempt proceedings pursuant to law; and (2) to authorize a civil action for the first time in the history of the House, because the Attorney General had indicated that the US Attorney would not assume their prosecutorial responsibility out of respect to the Executive branch assertion of 'Executive privilege' in the matter. This confrontation between the two branches in the scheme of the separation of powers—the House and Senate exercising proper oversight over the Department, and the President claiming an overriding Constitutional Executive privilege over confidential communications involving him and that Department, presents a situation which at this writing has been resolved by the committee and subpoenaed witnesses in a manner supportive of the legitimate powers of Congress (see Privilege and Contempt at page 497).

For any hearing, House and Senate rules contain several protections to witnesses. Committee investigations must be conducted in accordance with the Constitution. Witnesses cannot be compelled to give evidence or testimony against themselves, cannot be subjected to unreasonable search and seizure, and cannot have their 1st Amendment freedoms of speech, press, religion, or political belief and association abridged (*Watkins v United States* 354 US 178 (1957)). Although the 1st Amendment, by its terms, is expressly applicable only to legislation (laws) which abridges those freedoms, the court has applied those protections to Congressional investigations. In *Barenblatt v United States* 360 US 162 (1959) the court held that where 1st Amendment rights are asserted to bar government interrogation, resolution of the issue always involves a balancing by the courts of the competing private and public interests at stake in the particular circumstances shown. Thus, unlike the 5th Amendment privilege against self-incrimination, the 1st Amendment does not give a witness an absolute right to refuse to respond to Congressional demands for information. The court has indicated that the 4th Amendment's prohibition against unreasonable searches and seizures is applicable to Congressional committees in the context of protections to witnesses against a subpoena that is unreasonably broad or burdensome.

The privilege against self-incrimination may be invoked by a person subpoenaed or requested to testify or to produce materials notwithstanding the fact that a Congressional investigation is not a 'criminal case' in the conventional sense. The assertion of the privilege against self-incrimination need take no particular form, provided the committee can reasonably be expected to understand it as an attempt to invoke the privilege (*Quinn v United States* 349 US 155 Z (1955)). At the same time, a witness may waive the privilege by failing to assert it, expressly disclaiming it, or testifying on the same matters concerning which he later claims the privilege (*Rogers v United States* 340 US 367 (1951)). The assertion of a self-incrimination defence may later come in the context of a criminal trial for contempt of Congress after the subpoenaed witness has had his assertion overruled by a vote of the investigating committee and has been certified by a vote of the full House or Senate for prosecution.

A witness who refuses to testify before a Congressional committee on the basis of his privilege against self-incrimination may be granted 'use' (not 'transactional') immunity by court order under a statute permitting two-thirds of the entire membership of the full committee to recommend such a court order. This statute[12] is unique in that it requires a two-thirds vote of an entire full committee for approval, and thus can serve as a means by which a minority of a committee can influence compulsion of testimony. During a recent attempt at utilization of this extraordinary procedure in the House Government Reform Committee in 1997, Minority committee members successfully blocked conferral of immunity on several witnesses during an investigation of political fund-raising irregularities by Executive officials. Protests that the ranking Minority committee member's opposition was somehow censurable—representing an 'obstruction' of a valid investigation—were unfounded, as otherwise a question of privilege seeking to punish an obstructive Member could be based merely on a Member's 'no' vote and not on any unethical conduct on his part.

Court cases involving assertion of a common law (judicially imposed) deliberative process privilege in committee hearings would apply as well to assertions of an attorney–client privilege as a defence during a committee hearing. Courts have employed a balancing test between the need of the committee for information and danger to the witness if this privileged relationship is breached. *In re Sealed Case 'Espy'* 121 F 3d 729 (DC Cir 1997) at 738 made it clear that the common law deliberative process privilege disappears altogether when there is reason to believe that government misconduct has occurred. For the same reason, a reviewing court might apply that rationale with respect to overcoming the deliberative process privilege in the face of a Congressional investigation of misconduct, the same balancing test applies as well to a claim of attorney–client privilege, and will not be honoured where the committee investigation involves government misconduct.

Both the House and the Senate have adopted rules permitting a reduced quorum for taking testimony and receiving evidence. House hearings may be conducted if at least two Members are present; most Senate committees permit hearings with only one committee member in attendance. For statutory perjury prosecution purposes, the quorum requirement must be met at the time the allegedly perjured testimony is given, not at the beginning of the session. These reduced quorum requirements facilitate the receipt of evidence and testimony, while retaining larger quorum requirements for collegial determinations of assertions by witnesses and of the consequences of failure to produce that information.

House and Senate rules require committees and subcommittees to afford any person who may have been defamed, degraded, or incriminated by testimony or evidence the opportunity to appear voluntarily as a witness. The threshold question of whether a person may be defamed, degraded, or incriminated if he responds to a certain line of questioning in a hearing can itself be debated in closed session if a majority of the Members present (at least two in the House and a minimum of one in the Senate) agree that there be executive (closed) session discussion, but if there is disagreement, a majority quorum of the committee must vote to conduct those discussions in open session. Thus there is an initial presumption in favour of protection of the witness to shield those discussions from the public, which presumption can be overcome by a majority vote with a full quorum present.

The rules also require committees and subcommittees to dispose of requests from such persons or from committee members during hearings to subpoena additional witnesses and papers. Where evidence or testimony is initially received in executive session for any reason, the receiving committee may subsequently vote to release or make public that matter, utilizing the majority quorum requirement. As long as the material remains executive session files of the committee, Members may have access to the material but may not disclose it or make copies. With the exception of the Intelligence committees, all Members have access to all committee files but may not share that information with others until the committee votes to release that material.

There is no doubt that with respect to much Congressional oversight activity, a primary objective of information gathering is to permit its selective or public release in order to influence public opinion. With respect to intelligence or intelligence-related information, that essential objective must give way to national security concerns. In this regard, House and Senate rules reserve a primary oversight responsibility under special conditions of access to the Permanent Select Committees on Intelligence, while reserving to all other committees oversight directly affecting their jurisdictions. The recommendation of the 9/11 Commission that the Congress establish either a Joint Committee or separate House and Senate standing committees on Intelligence, with both authorization and appropriations jurisdiction, was not followed. Instead, the House has created a hybrid panel of the Subcommittee on Defense Appropriations, adding three members of the House Committee on Intelligence to combine the expertise of the authorizing committee members, while retaining control in the ten-Member Defense Appropriations Subcommittee, which has jurisdiction over the bulk of the classified Intelligence budget. The hybrid panel can only submit recommendations to the relevant Appropriations subcommittees. In the Senate, while the Appropriations Committee was directed in 2004 to create its own Intelligence Subcommittee, that committee has not taken such an action. The Senate has retained its Intelligence authorization committee.

The Select Committees on Intelligence (called 'Permanent' in the House) are permitted by House and Senate rules to adopt their own rules and procedures which may restrict access to non-committee members, thereby enabling them to weigh Executive department classifications of their files against the need for non-committee Members to examine them. Beginning in 1995 the Code of Official Conduct was amended in the House to require all Members, officers, and employees to sign an oath of secrecy before having access to any classified information, whether in committee files or possessed by the Executive branch. That rule now also requires the names of Members to be inserted in the Record when they sign the oath of secrecy. Several Members who refused to sign the oath were denied access to classified briefings for the House conducted by the Executive branch. By this rule (and by a similar code of conduct provision in the Senate although only requiring an oath of secrecy for employees), a breach of which would constitute an ethics violation, the two Houses initially defer to classifications of information as determined by the Executive branch. Ultimately, the House and Senate permit committees to release or make public all executive session files in their custody, including those having security classifications, in which event the committee effectively declassifies the file and relieves Members of the restriction against disclosure contained in the oath of secrecy. With respect to information within the possession of the Intelligence Committees, however, additional safeguards exist to permit separate secret debate and votes in the Committee and in the House or Senate on release of matter where there is a disagreement between the Committee and the President concerning the continued classification of the material.

By House rule (clause 11(a)(2) of Rule X) the Speaker and Minority Member are ex officio members of the House Intelligence Committee. Existing law[13] permits the President to provide classified information on certain covert activities to 'a group of eight' (the Speaker, Minority Leader, Senate Majority and Minority Leaders, and chairmen and ranking minority members of the two Intelligence Committees) without informing the other members of the committees. This special briefing arrangement led to a controversy in 2009 concerning an alleged briefing received by the Speaker (when formerly Minority Leader in a previous Congress) regarding means of interrogation in the 'war on terror', a matter upon which she may not comment under the oath of secrecy rule. At this writing, the controversy escalated on 21 May 2009 to a Minority party attempt to question the 'accuracy' of the Speaker's public remarks in her capacity as recipient of classified information, by offering an alleged 'question of privilege' resolution sending the matter to a special subcommittee for investigation. The resolution was properly held not to constitute a question of privilege because it did not allege unethical conduct and necessarily called for an investigation of the CIA—a matter which destroyed the privilege of the resolution, as not confined to the conduct of a Member. Not satisfied with the Chair's ruling, the Minority appealed the ruling of the Speaker pro tempore and that appeal was laid on the table by a record vote, not coincidentally taken on the day of an expected recess. For further discussion of the inappropriate technique of appeals from rulings of the Chair in order to create voting records for political purposes, see the chapter on Procedural Basics at page 211.

While the Senate does not impose a specific oath of secrecy requirement on its Members, it does have a standing rule (Rule XXXVI, clause 5) which prohibits Senators and staff from disclosing the secret or confidential business of the Senate or of its committees, subject to expulsion or to punishment for contempt. Like the House committee, the Senate Select Committee on Intelligence may under a standing order of the Senate (79.13) impose additional restrictions on non-Intelligence Committee members' access to committee files. In addition, the Senate panel is authorized to disclose classified information publicly on its own, following elaborate procedures in which the President and the full Senate have an opportunity to act. If the President objects to Senate committee release, the full committee can (1) approve the disclosure; (2) disapprove the disclosure; or (3) refer all or any portion of the matter back to the committee to make the final determination.

Informal arrangements may be made for classified briefings of Members by the Executive branch using the House Chamber or other facility during recesses or adjournments, even to the extent of permitting questions and responses which are not otherwise formally contemplated in a plenary setting, and are not recorded or reported. Members must have subscribed to the oath of secrecy to have access to such briefings.

Under House rules, questioning of a witness appearing before a committee in an oversight or investigative hearing, whether subpoenaed or voluntarily present, proceeds under the five-minute rule. Each committee or subcommittee member (usually in the order of committee seniority alternating between the parties) must be given an opportunity to question each witness for five minutes, even where several witnesses comprise a 'panel'. Committees may permit extended examinations of witnesses for thirty additional minutes by designated Members, or by staff, of each party.

Whenever a hearing is conducted, the Minority members have the right to call witnesses of their own choosing to testify on that measure or matter for one day. Such a request must be supported by a majority of the Minority members and submitted to the chairman before completion of the hearing, at which point the chairman may set the day under a reasonable schedule. This does not permit the chairman to limit the number of Minority party witnesses, but does allow Majority and Minority members to question each witness under the five-minute rule.

At the beginning of any hearing, the Chair usually makes an opening statement which defines the subject matter of the hearing and thereby establishes the pertinence of questions asked the witnesses. Not all committees administer an oath to their witnesses, but leave that question to the discretion of the Chair, subject to ultimate control by the committee or subcommittee. If a committee wishes the potential sanction of perjury to apply as a criminal offence under 18 USC 1621, it should administer an oath to its witnesses, although false statements not under oath are also subject to criminal sanctions.[14] Under those felony statutes the witnesses' perjury or false statement must be 'wilful', must be made before a competent tribunal (a quorum present), and involve a material matter. A witness does not have a right to make a statement before being questioned but that opportunity is usually accorded. Committee rules may prescribe the length of such statements and also require written statements to be submitted in advance of the hearing.

The right of a witness to be accompanied by counsel is recognized by House rule and the rules of Senate committees for the purpose of advising them concerning their constitutional rights. The Senate Permanent Subcommittee on Investigations has a rule which prohibits counsel 'coaching' witnesses during their testimony. Committee chairmen have complete authority to control the conduct of counsel to the extent of exclusion from the hearing and censure, and the committee can cite the offender for contempt. There is no right of cross-examination of adverse witnesses during an investigative hearing based upon court rules of evidence, beyond each Member's rights under the five-minute rule to interrogate any witness.

In the 'informal transcribed interview' procedures of the Committee on Oversight and Government Reform in the House, the right to counsel during depositions of an Executive agency witness using his own agency's counsel to advise him rather than being required to use and compensate personal counsel, can be circumscribed in the event the committee wants counsel to confine his activities to advising the witness, and not to report back to the employing agency which is under investigation. The Committee on Oversight and Government Reform, for example, has adopted a committee rule (Rule 22, 110th Congress) placing restrictions on the witnesses' choice of counsel to allow only personal and not agency counsel, absent a special arrangement for confidentiality.

Congress has also enacted laws that indirectly strengthen its oversight capacities. These laws establish mechanisms within the Executive branch that provide Congress with information and assessments, such as mandatory reports on paperwork reduction, regular financial statements, and on cost-effective procurement. Those Executive communications, when received, are referred to all the committees of jurisdiction. Congress has created statutory offices of Inspectors General (IG) in nearly sixty major Federal agencies and departments. Granted wide latitude and independence by the Inspectors General Act of 1978, these officials conduct investigations and audits of their agencies and regularly report to all relevant Congressional committees. Since the creation of those IG offices, committees have investigated allegations of attempts within some departments or agencies to compromise their independence.

Congress has further strengthened its oversight capabilities indirectly by establishing study commissions to review and evaluate programmes, policies, and operations of the government. By laws enacted in the latter part of the twentieth century, Congress has imposed various procedures within the Executive that improve the Executive's ability to monitor and control its own operations, while at the same time, providing additional information and oversight-related analysis to Congress.

A description of scrutiny by British parliamentary select committees is found at pages 372 and 378.

Committees of the Legislature and the Executive

An analysis of the legal and historical claims of Executive privilege upon demands from Congress for information is necessary toward a comprehensive treatment of the accountability of the Executive to the Legislative branch. The Supreme Court has not ruled directly on the extent to which the President can withhold information from Congress on the ground of Executive privilege—the need to protect the confidentiality of information shared by the President and his aides from compulsory process served by Congress or by the courts. The Supreme Court's only sustained consideration of the scope of the privilege, in the 1974 decision that ordered President Nixon to turn over the Watergate tapes to a special prosecutor, is of only limited help in understanding assertions of Executive privilege in the legislative setting. In *United States v Nixon* 418 US at 705 (1974), the court was addressing a claim of Executive privilege in response to a court subpoena issued during a criminal trial to the President, at the request of the Watergate Special Prosecutor. The court said that it 'was not concerned here with the balance between the President's generalized interest in confidentiality and Congressional demands for information' (because it was a prosecutor and not the Congress seeking the information), while it also made clear that the claim of Executive privilege in any context was not absolute. The court stated that the case for Executive privilege was strongest where there was a need to protect military, diplomatic, or national security secrets, while not denying its application in personnel matters. Also, partial disclosure to Congress may constitute a waiver of the privilege when further information is sought.

The Nixon case established the contours of the presidential communications privilege. The President may invoke the privilege in response to judicial or Congressional requests for information 'when asked to produce documents or other materials which reflect presidential decision making and deliberations that the President believes should remain confidential'. In the case *In re Sealed Case 'Espy'* (121 F 3d 729 DC Cir 1997) the Court of Appeals for the District of Columbia examined the scope of the privilege—whether and to what extent the privilege extended to presidential advisers, whether the President must have seen or had knowledge of the material at issue, and the standard of need necessary to overcome the presumption of privilege. The court held that the presidential communications privilege extended to communications authored by or solicited and received by presidential advisers that involved information regarding governmental operations that ultimately call for direct decision making by the President, and he need not have actually seen the documents for which he claims privilege. The court confined the privilege to White House staff, but not staff in agencies, and then only to staff having 'operational proximity' to direct presidential decision making.

There is no case law applying the standards of the *Espy* and *Judicial Watch v Department of Energy* (412 F 3d 125 (2005)) cases (the latter involving a suit against the Vice President to compel production of documents from an informal energy policy advisory group) to Congressional requests for allegedly privileged Executive information. To date the closest case is *Walker v Cheney* 230 F Supp 2d 51 (DDC 2002), where the Comptroller General (CG) was denied information he sought from an energy task force headed by the Vice President pertaining to the scope and composition of meetings that were to provide the basis for the subsequent formulation of recommendations and advice to be presented to the President regarding the development of a national energy policy. At issue was whether the GAO sought information regarding the direct deliberations of individuals in 'operational proximity' to the President in formulating policy advice—the standard imposed in the *Espy* case to allow a claim of Executive privilege where the President himself was not privy to the information being sought. The case was dismissed by the trial court on the grounds of lack of standing by the CG, whom the court found had suffered insufficient institutional injury to merit judicial resolution of issues affecting the balance of power. There was no appeal from this dismissal. It is relevant to ask whether Congressional delegation of access enforcement authority to its agent, the GAO, is less likely to involve the compelling Legislative branch need for information necessary to overcome a presumption of Executive privilege where presidential advisers, and not the President himself, are the targets of the requested information.

In addition to lawsuits brought by Congressional investigative agents such as GAO, when Executive privilege is invoked Congress has several tools at its disposal, including negative publicity, utilization of the power of the purse, the possibility of withholding Senate confirmation for some Executive officials, and the possibility of holding potential witnesses in contempt. Just as Congress's investigative power is not explicitly granted in Article I of the Constitution, neither is a presidential claim of Executive privilege specifically guaranteed in Article II or elsewhere in the Constitution. Thus the question is always a balancing one, the importance of information being furnished to Congress compared with the need for confidentiality within the Executive—a recipe for constitutional confrontation.

In 2007, a Senate committee subpoenaed the White House, the Office of Vice President, and the Justice Department for information regarding the Executive's constitutional assertion that the President's authority as Commander-in-Chief extended to pre-emptive unilateral actions including domestic electronic surveillance, despite laws permitting interceptions of domestic communications only with court-approved warrants—by permission of the Foreign Intelligence Surveillance Act (FISA) courts especially created for that purpose. This subpoena was the culmination of investigations by both House and Senate committees questioning the apparent disregard of that 1979 statute. The position of non-compliance asserted by the Executive extends the notion of the supremacy of the Executive as Commander-in-Chief beyond any argument theretofore made, as the warrantless wire taps were undertaken in direct disregard of statutory law requiring (FISA) court sanction.

At the same time as the issuance in the FISA wire tap case of subpoenas in June 2007, both House and Senate Judiciary Committees subpoenaed the President's political advisers at the White House for documents relating to political influence in the dismissal of US Attorneys by the Attorney General. In another potential court challenge to the ability of Congress to scrutinize the Executive, the President and some of his former staff claimed 'Executive privilege'—the right to refuse to comply based on confidential communications potentially involving the President. At this writing, a Federal appellate court has stayed a lower court order directing compliance with the subpoena, based upon assumed mootness of the case by the end of the 110th Congress. In the subsequent Congress in 2009, those witnesses were re-subpoenaed as the House determined to litigate the expanded claim of Executive privilege in the context of witnesses' declining to appear to testify. An agreement with the House Judiciary Committee was reached in March 2009 requiring their appearance but permitting ad hoc assertions of Executive privilege during hearings, to be evaluated by the committee at that time. (For further discussion see Privilege and Contempt at page 497.)

The assertion of Executive privilege in the case of the Justice Department's dismissal of US Attorneys—who serve at the pleasure of the President—presents an interesting contrast of the constitutional underpinnings of these two recent refusals to comply with legislative demands for information. The Justice Department's claim of Executive privilege in the US Attorney inquiry might well have a stronger constitutional basis, as the Congressional position that US Attorney offices are 'inferior offices' created by Congress suggests that the legislature has a legitimate need to investigate the operation of those offices.

The assertion, in resisting committee subpoenas, of supremacy of the President as Commander-in-Chief over any interest that Congress might have in examining a statute prescribing an exclusive means of obtaining court approved wire taps presents the issue of legislative scrutiny in yet another context. In either case, it was by no means assured that the issue would be fully litigated in the courts before the term of President

Bush had expired. Nor is it certain that the new Administration will continue to assert the privilege on behalf of the former President. The strategy of the Executive branch in 'running out the clock' until the end of term was given credence by the stay of a Federal court order issued by an appellate court. As in most cases where Congressional subpoenas have been issued to the Executive branch, the likelihood of final court interpretation of the constitutional prerogatives of the two branches is minimized, either through eventual cooperation or by extended delay in the courts until the end of a Congress. Historically, the resolution of this balance is most often struck, following confrontation, by accommodation rather than by litigation. For example, of ten cabinet officers cited by House or Senate committees for contempt since 1975, only one case, in 1983, was endorsed by the full House and was then settled, as the cabinet officer—the Administrator of the Environmental Protection Agency—complied with the subpoena prior to the contempt trial. In all the other cases, the subpoenaed cabinet official and the requesting Congressional committee reached a negotiated accommodation for access to documents and testimony prior to a vote in either House on a contempt certification.

More common than Executive privilege or Commander-in-Chief assertions are claims by departments and agencies and by private persons that common law testimonial privileges, such as the attorney–client, work product, and deliberative process privileges, afford a shield against Congressional investigative inquiries. Although there has never been a definitive Supreme Court ruling on the question, the strong constitutional underpinnings of the legislative investigatory power, long-standing Congressional practice, and recent appellate court rulings casting doubt on the viability of common law privilege claims by Executive officials in the face of grand jury investigations, support the position that committees may determine on a case-by-case basis whether in the total discretion of the committee to accept a claim of privilege. Such common law privileges cannot be claimed as a matter of right by a witness, and a committee can deny them simply because it believes it needs the information sought to be protected in order to accomplish its legislative functions. In actual practice, all committees that have denied claims of privilege have engaged in a process of weighing considerations of legislative need, public policy, and the rules and statutory duties of Congressional committees to engage in continuous oversight over the laws that fall within its jurisdiction against any possible injury to the witness.

By establishing a public record of the policy views of nominees, Senate confirmation hearings allow lawmakers in both Houses to call appointed officials to account at a later time through subsequent oversight hearings and committee investigations to explore whether commitments have been kept by the office holder. While the Constitution permits the President to fill up all vacancies that may happen during the Recess of the Senate, by granting Commissions which expire at the end of the next Senate session, the avoidance of the confirmation process by this tactic has its limits and often exposes the nominee and his policy positions to even greater Congressional scrutiny during and following that recess period (see 'The Four Houses' at page 76).

Similarly, the Senate's constitutional duty to advise and consent to the ratification of treaties affords that body another unique responsibility for oversight, both during the treaty negotiation process, and then during the open-ended period for Senate ratification with or without reservations or amendments. This role of the Senate is discussed in greater detail in the chapter on The Four Houses. Of course, once a treaty is ratified and assumes the status of law, both Houses have ongoing oversight responsibilities over administration of those laws and over the need for implementing legislation requiring the approval of both Houses. In addition, the proliferation of international executive agreements negotiated between the Executive branch and foreign governments, the authority for which derives from statutory law, necessitates ongoing Congressional oversight over their implementation. As a matter of special oversight, for example, the Committee on Foreign Affairs in the House is specifically directed to conduct ongoing oversight over international fishing agreements. More generally all House and Senate committees of legislative jurisdiction have oversight responsibility for the formulation and implementation of international agreements, especially if they have been negotiated as an alternative to treaties which require Senate ratification.

Though there is no distinct executive privilege to protect UK ministers as there is in Washington, only a House may order a Secretary of State (and all Cabinet ministers are now of that rank) to attend a parliamentary committee or to lay documents before it. That power is denied to select committees acting on their own authority: they must rely on persuasion. No minister can be made to produce papers not of an official or public nature. While there have been difficulties in that area (see below), in practice ministers are prepared to attend select committees, the better to highlight their point of view or their achievements. It was not always so. However central ministerial thinking may now be to select committee inquiries, not so many years ago governments hesitated before permitting even junior ministers to appear before committees, lest they should be seduced into discussing matters of policy. Today, ministerial appearances at Commons select committees, joint committees, and subcommittees stand at 111 even in the short session 2004–5, a figure which includes 27 appearances by Members of the Cabinet and the Prime Minister. Parallel figures for the long session 2005–6 are 161 and 78, for 2006–7, 121 and 71, and for 2007–8, 167 and 68. If therefore the agreement of senior ministers to attend is any measure, select committees have established themselves as important forums in which to explain and justify government policy, and—from Parliament's point of view—represent an effective organ of scrutiny.

A code of Rules governs the appearance of government officials (as opposed to ministers) before select committees.[15] It stipulates, perfectly accurately, that as a matter of constitutional principle, it is ministers who are accountable to Parliament and not their officials: the latter give evidence on behalf of the former. As a matter of practice, officials are usually invited by the committee to give evidence and are not compelled. The choice of individual is generally left to the department, but if the committee expresses a view, the minister will very often agree. Nevertheless, who should represent him or her remains a matter for the minister. If agreement cannot be reached on which official should attend or whether an answer should be given to a particular question, the Rules stipulate that the minister will appear. In the last resort, if the committee remains dissatisfied, it is provided that the matter will be brought to the floor for resolution. Neither House nor any select committee has given agreement to these Rules, perhaps sensing that too much will rest on the interpretation put on them by even the most benevolent government. The Rules remain an indication of how far the bureaucracy will go in making officials available to committees. They have not always worked in a way the Commons was prepared to accept.

For the most part, governments are sympathetic to committee aspirations, and help-ful in principle; yet individual cases may blossom into *causes célèbres*. Any attempt to deny a committee access to the official of its choice is bound to be open to accusations of obstruction, leading the committee to flourish its traditional and notionally unquali-fied power to send for 'persons, papers and records'. Official reluctance to offer what is considered to be the wrong hostage to fortune is understandable, but more will usually be lost by government exposing itself to allegations of 'cover up' than will be gained by successful public fisticuffs with a select committee. If the committee manages after a struggle to confront a witness and he or she then turns out to have been a bad choice and their evidence irrelevant, the loss is the committee's in time and energy. On the other hand, this is evidently not a point of view always shared by all ministers. The Science and Technology Committee in 2002–3 complained that a senior minister had taken steps to prevent the committee from hearing certain witnesses from his depart-ment and sought to instil this uncooperative attitude in other departments. The com-mittee charged that ministers 'seemed to think they had a role in determining the remit of select committee inquiries. They do not.'[16]

The appropriate minister or official having appeared before the committee, the qual-ity of their testimony is of course crucial to effective scrutiny. Ministers are expected by the House of Commons Resolution on Ministerial Responsibility and by the Ministerial Code to give accurate and truthful information to Parliament, and to require their civil servants to provide 'accurate, truthful and full information' in accordance with the Civil Service Code. Of course, in any particular case, there may be differences of opinion about whether these tests have been met. The Foreign Affairs Committee concluded following an inquiry into the alleged use of the island of Diego Garcia for the extraordinary rendi-tion of terrorist suspects that ministerial responses were unclear and failed properly to address the issues.[17]

There are particular areas of official activity which ministers or officials may always be reluctant to expose to select committee hearings. National security is the most obvious example. Even there, closed hearings may be held, and elaborate arrangements have some-times been made to permit committees (but no one else) to see extremely sensitive mate-rial under agreed conditions, such as inspection of papers in private on official premises without notes being taken. Nevertheless, some committees have had occasion to complain of undue reticence or unnecessary confidentiality. In 2007–8, the Defence Committee, hav-ing heard evidence about the Iran hostages perforce in private, expressed their reservations about conducting scrutiny of the government on the government's terms.[18]

A second area of understandable reluctance is where a committee insists on having access to the very earliest stages of the formulation of policy advice to ministers by offi-cials. Thirdly, where disciplinary proceedings are in prospect against an official, it will usually be sensible for a committee to hold its hand.

All these issues may, given the appropriate degree of trust on both sides, be adjusted by negotiation. Trust is the key. Wide—but in the last resort unenforceable—committee powers, matched by an equally wide variation in the degree of official cooperation is never likely to produce concord. If a common authoritative interpretation of the scope of committee power to send for 'persons, papers and records' cannot be devised, perhaps a reasoned if ex parte statement of the parliamentary view, codifying the many precedents and expedients to which experience has given rise, might be a useful and practical means of ensuring that governments can be held to their own best practice and cannot retreat from it, however tight the corner.

Much ground nevertheless remains to be cleared. Two examples in the Commons will illustrate how much.

In the autumn of 2004, the Commons Liaison Committee welcomed the assurance of the then Leader of the House that evidence could be given to committees by special advisers to ministers (who are not career civil servants and generally have either a political advisory role or undertake strategic thinking). Requests for such evidence would, the Leader said, be dealt with on a case-by-case basis, but within a general presumption of advisers' availability. A brief two months later, however, the Public Administration Committee reported that it had been told that a special adviser to the Prime Minister would not appear before them. To aggravate the offence, the same committee in late 2005 wished to hear the evidence of another Prime Ministerial special adviser, who this time happened to be a member of the House of Lords. He declined to come (it was in fact his second refusal) to discuss what the committee characterized as 'relatively technical and non-contentious process issues'. In the first case, the committee might have insisted on the appearance of the witness, though the prospect of success was not encouraging and failure would have only exposed the gap between the committee's powers on paper and the reality of their exercise. In the second, they were without remedy at all: it is a very old convention that Members of one House may not be compelled to appear by the other, though they may consent to do so.

The practice governing the evidence of special advisers ought logically to be precisely that of civil servants: a ministerial refusal to allow them to appear ought in the last resort to generate ministerial public oral evidence in explanation. The special case of Lords who are invited to give evidence before Commons committees and vice versa, whether or not special advisers, ought to be taken up as part of the realignment of the relationship between the Houses arising from reform of the upper House. This would give effect to the expectations of the Commons Liaison Committee that Lords who are ministers would be likely to attend, in line with the convention that ministers will normally attend select committees when requested to do so and that of the Modernisation Committee that limitations on the power of committees to require witnesses—including in particular Members of either House—to give evidence should be reviewed.

The second problem arose from the work of the Foreign Affairs Committee. In the summer of 2003, the committee embarked on an inquiry into *The decision to go to war in Iraq*. When it came to report, the committee complained that it was 'entitled to a greater degree of co-operation from the government on access to witnesses and to intelligence material'. The government would not allow certain very senior members of the intelligence community to appear before the committee, and access to official papers considered by the committee to be important to its work was restricted to having material read to them or reading extracts in private session. What was worse, a number of witnesses whose appearance was denied to the select committee appeared before the Intelligence and Security Committee. The latter, though composed of Members of the Commons recommended to the Prime Minister by the Committee of Selection, is not a House organ but a statutory committee[19] which in this case the government considered a more appropriate forum for the inquiry. Matters deteriorated yet further when some of the missing witnesses and papers turned up before an official inquiry into the tragic death of a government adviser who had given evidence to the select committee. Nothing could have demonstrated more clearly the disadvantage select committees can find themselves at. Neither of the other bodies involved had the power to compel the attendance of witnesses, yet it was before them that the witnesses appeared. The official inquiry received original correspondence: the select committee saw only government statements of the facts. Now, some of this undoubtedly arose because of the perennial suspicion of select committees in the context of quasi-judicial inquiries (see page 360): but it remains a profoundly unsatisfactory situation.

It was not difficult for the Foreign Affairs Committee to contrast all this with the cooperation its predecessors enjoyed in inquiries into the Falklands War in 1984 and the intervention in Sierra Leone in 1997–8. Nor was the committee extravagant in its demands. It recommended that it should see intelligence material only when it could demonstrate that what it wanted was 'of key importance to a specific inquiry' and raised no 'genuine concerns for national security'. Even when the government found these modest suggestions unpalatable, the committee did no more than set out the nub of the problem—what should happen when a minister refuses to appear, when he or she will not allow an official to appear, and when papers and records are refused.

Individual legislators and oversight

In the US Congress, oversight is generally considered a committee activity. However, both casework and other project work conducted in a Member's personal office can result in findings about bureaucratic behaviour and policy implementation, which in turn can lead to the adjustment of agency policy and procedure. Sometimes individual Members or Senators will conduct their own investigations or ad hoc hearings, or direct their staffs to conduct oversight studies, although individual Members have no authority to issue compulsory process or conduct official hearings. The Government Accountability Office or other Legislative branch agency such as the Congressional Budget Office or Congressional Research Service, a specially created task force, or a private research group, might be requested to conduct an investigation for a Member or informal group of Members. The function of the GAO, headed by the Comptroller General, is discussed in greater detail in the chapter on the power of the purse at page 298.

In Parliament, Questions, participation in debate, and membership of select committees are the means by which Members of both Houses contribute to Parliament's scrutiny function. Individually, in particular interventions, their impact may be limited. Only a small proportion of Questions can pass through the eye of the needle to receive an answer on the floor of the Commons (see pages 338–9). Pressure on time for debate in the Commons frequently reduces the length of time a Member may address the House, and in any case the number of interventions most Members can make in the Chamber per session is not large. The short debates which end the day in the Chamber or are held in Westminster Hall, for example (see pages 55, 158) certainly hold ministers to account, but they are almost exclusively snapshots of matters of limited or constituency interest, neither general nor systematic. The impact of scrutiny is naturally enhanced if it is bipartisan, but this demands an approach from government and sometimes Opposition backbenchers in the Commons which may compete with their proper personal ambitions, not to mention their broader political loyalties. The special case of the substantial exclusion of partisanship from select committees is an advantage to which the Commons fell heir almost by the historical accident that when modern parties were forming select committees were in the doldrums (see page 360).

There are also a substantial number of relatively informal groups of Members drawn from both sides of the House who share a common interest in a particular topic—association football, for example. Such parliamentary groups may undertake inquiries and publish conclusions concerning matters within their area, but they do not receive the assistance of any official organ of either House or of the government.

The House of Commons is not nearly as powerful as either House of Congress, but the reasons for that are more constitutional than institutional. The Commons Chamber is a place where governments are always at risk, and more so than was the case a generation ago. The days of cast-iron whipping are gone. Topics such as genetic research, some aspects of education, or detention without charge for terrorist suspects can threaten majorities against the government, despite the efforts of the whips. Governments may not stand or fall on one division—though even in days of strong whipping by today's standards the Callaghan government did so in 1979. But if and when the electorate begins to turn against an incumbent government, its collective performance in the Chamber of the House of Commons, perceived shortcomings in its mastery of its brief, and apparent inadequacy of its response to scrutiny by individual Members on the floor of the House will be the snowball that starts the avalanche.

Questions

Though in the UK the first parliamentary Question is always said to have been asked in 1721 (in the Lords and in a form which would nowadays be out of order in the lower House) oral Question Time in the Commons has developed from an informal—even slightly irregular—procedure in the last third of the nineteenth century into one of the most significant opportunities for backbenchers on both sides to scrutinize everything for which a government minister is responsible. Questions (which may be for oral or written answer, at the discretion of the Member asking them) have increased very substantially over the past forty years or so.

A study of Questions in the Commons published in 1962[20] estimated that there was then time to answer orally only a half to two-thirds of those tabled. The situation has deteriorated more steeply since then than might appear. Some orderly Questions tabled for oral answer are now discarded before they reach the Order Paper, so that if the Table 7.1 in the Annex, which sets out the percentage of Questions which receive an oral answer on the floor of the House, were on the same basis as the 1960s, showing all Questions tabled for oral answer, the percentage answered in the Chamber would be substantially smaller.

Questions for oral answer in the Commons may be put to ministers for roughly the first hour of a day's sitting on Mondays to Thursdays.[21] No Questions are asked on Fridays. The Member putting the Question calls out the number of his or her Question on the Order Paper. The initial ministerial reply is frequently bland, and the exchanges gather pace only when the questioner is called to ask a supplementary. The supplementary must be relevant to the original Question. For example, details of hospital waiting-times in Cornwall cannot be asked for (or not without considerable ingenuity shading into *chutzpah* and with a weather eye open for the reaction of the Chair) as a supplementary to a Question about waiting times in Northumberland, at the other end of England. A questioner cannot be prevented from airing such a disorderly inquiry, but the Speaker will probably intervene to instruct the minister that he or she need not answer.

The Speaker tries to make progress through the list of Questions, in the interest of those backbenchers who are waiting their turn to intervene with a greater or lesser degree of patience. In pursuit of this aim, the Chair frequently demands shorter supplementaries and shorter ministerial replies. Indeed, if a questioner or a respondent is too prolix, the occupant of the Chair will say so and may require the offender to resume his or her seat. The really effective parliamentary performers know the value of brevity, realizing that a succinct supplementary does not give a minister as much time to gather his or her thoughts as a rambling enquiry. A Member whose supplementaries were sometimes a pithy 'Why?' was particularly successful in inducing ministerial fluster from which unintended candour might emerge. The Speaker's dilemma is as constant as it is insoluble: how to balance the speed of progress through the list with his responsibility to the House and to individual questioners not to cut short a particularly productive exchange. Different Speakers have come to different solutions.

A century ago, it was not unusual for a Member to be perfectly content with the ministerial answer to his Question, and no supplementary followed. Even in the 1960s there were calculated to be no more than three supplementaries for every two original Questions. These leisurely days are gone, and one of the consequences has been the introduction of complexity in the practice of the House regarding oral Question Time. The widening imbalance between the number of Questions tabled for oral answer and the limited time for answering them has made it essential to find ways of compressing the quart to fill the pint pot. Over a much longer period, a separate set of rules has grown up to govern the form and contents of Questions. Vague Questions or Questions not engaging ministers' official responsibilities, for example, are not allowed to be tabled; time taken on the floor answering such as these would simply crowd out more meritorious business.

The primary Commons rule in bringing the number of Questions likely to receive an oral answer into rough alignment with the time available for answer is that an individual Member may table only one Question for oral answer by a particular minister for a particular day, with an overall limit to all ministers of two on that day.[22]

A further limitation is that the department which is the target of a particular Member's Question answers on the floor of the House only at intervals. On each sitting day usually only one but on some Thursdays six smaller departments answer oral Questions. An example based on departments answering in the first week after the Christmas adjournment in 2008–9 is found in Table 7.2 in the Annex.

The departments answering in mid-January were not in the firing line again until six weeks later, the week beginning Monday 23 February. The same interval is observed for all departments. Scotland, for instance, answered on Wednesday 4 February, but not again until 18 March. On days when a number of smaller departments reply in succession, a time is fixed not later than which each is to begin. As usual, a balance has to be struck between extensive and intensive questioning. Shorter intervals between appearances of a particular departmental minister at the dispatch box will imply that that department will have to share the more frequent days with others.

Questions for oral answer on the floor of the House of Commons (including topical Questions) may be tabled as soon as oral Question Time to a particular minister ends and not later than three days (excluding Fridays and weekends) before the Question is to be answered.[23] The great advantage of this relatively new arrangement is that Questions tend to be tabled at the latest possible moment, so that when they are asked the matter they raise is still relatively fresh.

Since 2002 there has been a quota of Questions for each department which varies with the length of the time allocated to that particular Question Time. Since the number tabled is normally well in excess of the quota, it is necessary to establish which are to go forward and which are to fall by the wayside. This is done by a computer programme which selects notices of Questions and electronically arranges them into a random sequence. Those notices of Questions not selected simply disappear.

Finally, a would-be questioner must take into account that pressure on Question Time is so great that there is no guarantee that even all the Questions which surmounted all the obstacles and appeared on the Order Paper for any day will receive an oral answer (see Table 7.3 in the Annex). They may not be reached, and if they are not deferred they are answered in written form. No opportunity arises for the Member who tabled the Question to fire off the supplementary which was the point of the exercise.

The pressure of Questions on the limited resource of Question Time imposes certain conventions about participation. It is regarded as a high crime and misdemeanour not to be present in the Chamber to ask a Question of which one has given notice, though there is nothing objectionable in withdrawing or deferring it before the time comes for it to be answered. In the same way, leaving the Chamber once one has received a reply, without waiting at least for the end of the connected exchanges, is very likely to attract public reproof from the Chair. Reading a supplementary Question is too obvious a betrayal of the spontaneity which ought to characterize Question Time, and is also frowned on.

The second code of Commons rules governing Questions concerns their form and content. All Questions must be addressed to a specific minister, and must concern matters within his or her official responsibilities. The limitation is a real one. A Question tabled to one department which ought properly to be asked of another will be transferred (by the government, who need not and do not seek any kind of parliamentary sanction) to the more appropriate quarter. If the misjudgement has been made in relation to a Question for oral answer, and that Question has been randomly selected for answer, the disaster is the greater. Such a Question will receive only a written answer. No opportunity for the damaging supplementary will arise, and the Member must suppress his or her impatience until the next occasion on which the minister aimed at is top and a redrafted Question can be tabled—without any guarantee of a repeat of earlier good fortune as respects priority in the list. That happy day may be a month away, so that there is also a high risk that the chosen issue will by then lose topicality.

Questions must seek information or call for action. Of course, party politics is at the heart of many Questions, but a Question too obviously intended only as point scoring is out of order. A Question must not argue, convey its own point of view, or communicate rather than attempt to elicit information. This last rule—like a surprisingly high proportion of the rules for Questions—is nineteenth century in origin. In days when Questions were read out in the House as a preliminary to the answer—nowadays the questioner simply calls out its number—an Irish Member wished to know why the Royal Irish Constabulary had removed from a wall in the west of Ireland a particularly inflammatory slogan chalked there. This gave him the opportunity to read out the offending wording in the Chamber. That of course was the point of the exercise: the ministerial answer presumably came as an irrelevance. The Speaker then ruled that such shenanigans were not to be allowed in future, and that remains the case.

A Question which covers the same ground as one already answered earlier in the same session is out of order, though the House has authorized the Speaker not to be too restrictive in the application of the rule. If a minister declines to give information or take the action requested, the Question may be repeated after three months or earlier if some significant intervening event may be thought to have altered the situation.

The limitation to public responsibilities means also that ministers cannot be asked for their speculative opinions on matters of current interest, nor should a Question be based on rumour or press gossip (which sometimes blocks off the most interesting topics!). Questions seeking interpretation of the law—which is a matter for the courts and not the government—are not admissible. Questions may not arise on the activities of elected devolved or local government or any other public body for the doings of which ministers have no responsibility. A limitation of which ministers—sometimes even the most senior—are occasionally reminded from the Chair is that Question Time is exclusively an opportunity to ask the government, not the Opposition, to explain and justify its policy. Ministerial pots calling Opposition kettles black will be brought to order.

In general, the restrictions on the contents of Questions have eased appreciably over the past decades. For example, the rule which demands that Questions should engage with ministerial public responsibilities was always hard to enforce in the foreign policy area. It was not admissible to ask Questions about the internal affairs of other countries: these were matters not for Her Majesty's government but for the governments of the states concerned. In late twentieth- and twenty-first-century conditions, this was a serious limitation, and the boundary of admissibility now is whether, in the light of foreign policy and international obligations, an official dispatch might reasonably be expected to reach Whitehall from a British diplomat stationed in the country in question. A similar restriction on Questions designed to find out what minister A wrote to minister B in some apparent interdepartmental wrangle—'the internal workings of government'—has now been eased, especially if the discussions relate to an announcement already made. Some Questions, though they may be orderly, by convention do not receive an answer. A Question about the tax affairs of an individual, for instance, would be met with the response that it was not the practice to divulge such details. 'Matters of their nature secret', that is, national security matters, are treated similarly. While refusals of this type remain, the number of blocked-off areas has much diminished over the past decade, perhaps because so much material can be extracted from departments by the alternative means of the Freedom of Information Act. Other obstacles in the way of Members nevertheless remain. The government sets a financial limit to the cost of answering Questions, and if the cost of the work involved in answering exceeds £750 or eight times the marginal cost of answering a single Question, no substantive reply will be forthcoming on the ground of 'disproportionate cost'.

Oversight of compliance with these rules of order is initially the responsibility of the clerks in the Table Office to whom Members bring or send the texts of Questions. They will advise Members on the applicability of the rules and may suggest changes not affecting the substance of the Question which, if accepted, will bring a disorderly Question into order and qualify it to go on the Order of Business. A Member who cannot accept advice so given may not insist on tabling his version, but may ask the Speaker privately for an authoritative ruling. It is a tribute to the skill and persuasive ability of the Table Office that appeals are relatively few. Once Question Time is under way, of course, the Speaker in the Chair will intervene to police the boundaries of order. What he will not do is to rule on the quality or accuracy of the answers to Questions. If a Member complains that he or she has for some reason not received a satisfactory or comprehensible answer, the Speaker will usually direct the aggrieved Member to the Table Office to see if they can help to devise another version of the original Question, in the hope that a change in the angle of attack will enjoy greater success.

Topicality is an important element in Question Time. Questions (especially those for oral answer) on stale or long-past events will usually represent a poor use of the House's time. Even the now-reduced notice period for oral Questions can sometimes rob a good idea of its shine. At the prompting of the Modernisation Committee in 2007, the government agreed to tackle the need to improve the degree of topicality at oral Question Time (and also in debate, see page 156). On Mondays, Tuesdays, and Thursdays—not Wednesdays when of course the topicality of Prime Minister's Questions fills the gap, nor Fridays when there are no oral Questions—the last fifteen minutes[24] of departmental Question Time are devoted to Questions of which notice is not given. The minister is asked to make a statement on his or her departmental responsibilities. He or she will do so briefly, perhaps by touching on the matters of recent significance, and there follows a series of short Questions—ideally in what the late Speaker on several occasions called a 'punchy' manner—which any minister in the department may rise to answer and which may range at large over everything within their official concerns. Members enter a ballot for the right to ask a topical Question, and others are brought in by the Speaker to ask supplementaries as matters progress. Opposition front-bench spokesmen may participate but are not permitted to dominate. Both the Questioner and the minister responding are expected to be succinct, and the number of Members called in the course of any one subject raised is usually quite small. Numbers of topical Questions answered in a typical week and the number of Members intervening are detailed in Table 7.4 in the Annex.

The aim of topical Questions is 'to maximise the opportunities for the House to consider the pressing issues of the moment'.[25] That this should be an aim of procedures such as Question Time is unarguable. It was never sensible that some very recent significant event could not be touched on at Question Time, the elephant in the room which no one was allowed to mention, simply because when Questions were being tabled no one could have foreseen the matter. At the same time, the period of notice for oral Questions has been drastically reduced, and such a situation is much less likely now than a decade ago. It would be a pity if the press headlines of the day crowded out Questions of a less political, more humdrum sort, which are also part of scrutiny.

Topicality, reinforced by importance, is the rationale of the Urgent Question. Such Questions must relate to 'matters of public importance'. They are so topical as not to require notice even on the preceding day. On the other hand, to prevent abuse or overloading of the system, such Questions may be asked only with the agreement of the Speaker, whose decision on applications, taken privately, is final. Only one such Question may be asked by any Member on one day, and it is rare for more than one application to succeed on any day, understandably in view of the effect which such a concession would have on the timing of regularly scheduled business. Indeed, the overall number of Urgent Questions asked in any session is a very small proportion of the applications, as is clear from Table 7.5 in the Annex.

Questions may normally be answered only on sitting days, but in the interests of topicality a procedure has been devised which enables Members to receive answers to Questions for written answer on three days in September, though the House is then adjourned for the summer. The opportunity is valued. In 2008, over 800 Questions were tabled in the three days[26] and a similar procedure was operated in 2009.

Oral Questions are asked of the Prime Minister for half an hour on every Wednesday on which the House of Commons sits. Nearly all Questions to the Prime Minister adhere to a strange formula: they ask for details of his engagements on the day on which the Question is to be answered. This is a consequence of the rule about ministerial responsibility. Since Questions on most matters of policy or administration, however important, will lie within the responsibility of a departmental minister, they would be transferred from the Prime Minister to his ministerial colleague primarily concerned. A Question about what the Prime Minister himself is doing in his official capacity can hardly be transferred. Problems however remain. The supplementary cannot be tied to the matter raised in the original notice of the Question, for there is none. The Prime Minister is left to defend every aspect of government and administration without any prior indication even of the broad area of the likely supplementary (though advance official briefings about the interests of the Member asking the Question can, it seems, usually improve anticipation). Given the tireless ingenuity of Members, this defect is probably incurable and certainly adds flavour to the exchanges. There is a story, perhaps apocryphal, of the Member who tabled a Question asking the Prime Minister if he would pay an official visit to Damascus, a once popular formula intended—like engagements Questions today—to render Questions proof against transfer. After no doubt hours of briefing on Middle Eastern policy, the Prime Minister must have been surprised to hear the supplementary, which began: 'And on the road to Damascus, will the Prime Minister reverse his government's policy on…?'

Prime Minister's Question Time is often used as a stick with which to beat the contemporary House of Commons. It is alleged to be noisy, rude, and unconstructive, Members' behaviour approaching a bear garden. Such views are beside the point. Prime Minister's Questions can be tumultuous, but who could ever expect a contest between the major political figures of the day, anxious to display their relative abilities in formulating and communicating policy, to be otherwise? Are the respective political supporters to preserve an ecclesiastical calm while the contest is playing out in their presence? It is after all their seats which are at stake. Important public perceptions are formed from impressions of Prime Minister's Question Time. The House of Commons is—among many other things—political theatre and party battleground. What it is not is a seminar.

As a general rule, if a Question is not immediately urgent or perhaps has a purely informational aim it will be tabled for written answer, though the Member's purpose may well be to accumulate data for a later party political shaft delivered as a supplementary to an oral Question. Some Questions for written answer do not specify a day for answer: others, the priority written Questions, require a response on a named day. That day may not be earlier than three days (excluding weekends) after that on which notice was given. Questions in this category are limited in number to five per Member per day. There is no limit to the number of Questions in the first group, which on occasions has given rise to concern as individual Members (through their research assistants) laboriously accumulate information in relation to some aspect of administration.

The expansion in the number of Questions tabled for written answer is both recent and substantial. In the 1960s, an average of forty-six Questions were tabled for written answer each sitting day. In the 1980s, the figure had risen to 139. In 1997–8 there was an average of 252 Questions for written answer every sitting day. Since then the figures have advanced even further, as the Table 7.6 in the Annex demonstrates. Replies to Questions for written answer are published in the daily Hansard report of debates.

It is hard to arrive at clear conclusions on the contribution of Question Time to the effectiveness of parliamentary scrutiny. Underlying all the complex procedural arrangements there is a fundamental cleavage. Some Questions—mostly those tabled for written answer—are (or may be answered as if they were) purely informational, whatever use is subsequently made of the information. When the Procedure Committee asked their colleagues in 2001–2 what they thought of the effectiveness of Question Time,[27] the informational aspect of Questions seemed very important to the respondents. They felt that it was one of the few areas where a backbencher could make a direct impact; that ministers could be pressured into justifying or explaining policy (or the lack of it); and that by Questions statistics otherwise unavailable could be teased out and local persons or campaigns assisted.

On other occasions, perhaps the same Members who asked informational Questions are concerned to advance the party struggle in Parliament. Opposition Members will relentlessly press for answers to what they hope are awkward Questions in order to maximize their advantage from a favourable issue. Members on the government side may lob easy balls to the minister which he or she can effortlessly dispatch to the boundary. Both modes are not only in order but perfectly sensible approaches to the opportunities offered. Scrutiny need not always take the cool classical form of the extraction of neutral facts and statistics.

Question Time in the Commons is a kaleidoscope. The atmosphere in the Chamber may often depend on the personal standing of the minister and his or her relationships with colleagues on both sides. Scottish Questions when the late Donald Dewar answered were usually calmer and much wittier, the whole temperature lower, than was the case when some of his more combative ministerial colleagues appeared at the dispatch box. The increased pressure of numbers however remains the underlying problem. It cannot be satisfactory—though it seems inevitable—that Questions tabled for oral answer must be discarded. Issues of quality as well as quantity arise. A committee has commented that until relatively recently 'the government's approach to answering Questions [was] characterized as minimising the opportunity for scrutiny of its actions through careful and skilful crafting of answers'.[28] Since the early 1990s, however, the situation has been improved by the issue of a series of government codes and guidance culminating in the Freedom of Information Act 2000. The number of areas where replies will not be given has been diminished (see page 340) and the government's Guidance for Officials in drafting answers to Parliamentary Questions[29] comes down heavily in favour of candour: 'approach every Question predisposed to give relevant information in full, as concisely as possible, in accordance with guidance on disproportionate cost...Do not omit information sought merely because disclosure could lead to political embarrassment or administrative inconvenience.'

This is of course far from saying that everything is exactly as Members would wish it to be. At an increasing pace over the past two decades or so, some departments under governments of both main parties have failed—sometimes very substantially indeed—to meet the deadline for answer to priority, named-day written Questions. Interim, purely formal, replies are given on the day, with the substantive reply coming later, sometimes very much later. Criticism from the Chair and the efforts of successive Leaders of the House have not solved the problem. An informal survey in 2003–4 revealed that departmental performance in giving substantive answers within the allowed period varied from an excellent 96 per cent to an unsatisfactory 22 per cent. In March 2008, a Member drew attention to the fact that one department's record of answering within the allotted time had fallen from 79 to 51 per cent and that of another from 87 to 49 per cent while a third simply refused to reveal the figure for the number of replies made within or after the due time on the grounds of disproportionate cost![30] Some months later, a Member complained that of the eighty-five Questions for written answer on a named day which he had tabled, fifty-five were substantively unanswered on the day, and on average replies to the eighty-five were nineteen days late.[31] Of the 800 Questions tabled for reply on a named day in September 2008, only 57 per cent were answered on the appropriate day and at the end of the month nearly 20 per cent were still unanswered.[32] A recent study by the Procedure Committee has concluded that setting a deadline would risk more delayed answers than occur at present, and proposed that the committee itself should monitor the situation, assisted by an end-of-session list which would identify the greatest departmental offenders.

On the one hand, the inexorable upward movement in the sessional totals of Questions for written answer, bringing with it a greater burden on departments, can be advanced as an explanation for the failures. On the other is the suspicion that the priority given to parliamentary business in some parts of the government machine is not as great as it was in immediately post-War years. Named-day Questions were an attempt to improve the situation without restricting the number of written Questions Members might table. Though the Procedure Committee and the government are in agreement against limitation, if the latest attempts to bring delays in answering written Questions under control are not successful, it may then be necessary to consider whether a further adjustment needs to be made by imposing on Members a generous but finite weekly ration of Questions for written answer, both the named-day and the others, and on government a cast-iron obligation to give substantial answers to them all within the appropriate period.

Questions, both oral and written, are asked in the Lords as well as the Commons. As is frequently apparent in these pages, the balance between business and time in the upper House is different from that in the Commons. In general, decisions about the conduct (as distinct from the merits) of business tend to be more consensual and therefore in less need of direction by rules or rulings. Consequently, Question Time in the Lords operates rather differently from Question Time in the Commons. Questions are not addressed to particular ministers but to 'Her Majesty's Government'. Rules on admissibility, while they echo those of the Commons in demanding (for example) that only matters for which ministers are responsible should be covered, are far fewer, and in disputed cases are enforced by the House and not the Lord Speaker.

As in the Commons, Question Time takes place in the Lords on Mondays to Thursdays. Only four Questions for oral answer may be asked each day, within an overall time limit of half an hour. No Lord may have more than one oral Question on the Order Paper at any time for any day. The last Question for oral answer on Tuesdays, Wednesdays, and Thursdays is a 'topical' Question chosen by ballot, but a Lord may not enter the ballot for any day if he or she already has a Question for oral answer on the Order paper for that day. Questions for oral answer in the Lords 'are asked for information only, and not with a view to stating an opinion, making a speech or raising a debate'.[33] Supplementaries may be asked, but there are conventions prohibiting them from being long, complex, or argumentative. There is also a convention limiting the length of ministerial replies, a limitation which in the Commons is at the discretion of the Speaker.

By contrast, some Questions are expected to give rise to short debates. They may be tabled for any sitting day, and are taken either just before the lunch or dinner adjournment (when they may last for an hour) or as the final business of the day, when debate may continue for ninety minutes. There is a limit on individual contributions of ten minutes for the questioner and twelve for the minister replying: other Lords intervening divide the remaining time available. Questions for short debate may also be taken in Grand Committee (see page 443), normally for ninety minutes.

Private Notice Questions are the parallel in the Lords to Urgent Questions in the Commons. The preliminary decision whether to allow an application rests with the Lord Speaker after consultation, though as in analogous cases the final word, if the preliminary view is challenged, rests with the House itself. Private Notice Questions are taken at the end of Questions for oral answer, and the same conventions about supplementaries apply. 'Comment should be avoided'[34] and Private Notice Questions are not expected to take longer than ten minutes, a shorter time than in the Commons.

As in the Commons, Lords are permitted to table Questions for written answer in the summer months when the House is not sitting. In 2007, 313 Questions were answered and fifteen written statements made.

Lords may not table more than six Questions for written answer on any one day, and they are expected to be answered within a fortnight. The Lords, like the Commons (see above), have struggled against official dilatoriness in observing the limit. They had a practice of reprinting Questions for written answer not replied to within the time limit, in an effort to shame departments into compliance. Unfortunately, it did not work and has been replaced by the printing of a list showing the Questions for written answer outstanding, arranged by Lord asking the Question, the date on which a reply was due, and the department responsible. In mid-January 2008, there were thirty-two Questions for written answer which had not been answered within the appropriate period, the oldest having been tabled on 6 November 2007. Not too long ago, these statistics would have been regarded as completely unacceptable: any occasion on which a department appeared to have made no attempt to answer a Question within the time allowed would have given rise to complaint. The Lords might contemplate a system similar to that suggested above for the lower House.

The framers of the US Constitution sought to require accountability of the Executive to the Legislative in great part by conferring the power of the purse on the Congress. Article I, section 8 enumerates powers conferred on Congress, and at the end of that clause empowers Congress 'to make all laws which shall be necessary and proper for carrying into execution the foregoing powers, and all other powers vested by this Constitution in the Government of the United States, or in any Department or Officer thereof'. Yet by imposing a strict separation of powers by denial of the simultaneous holding of incompatible offices within both branches, it was apparent that it would be more difficult for the Legislative branch to question the actions of the Executive directly in a collegial or debate format. The Constitution thereby abandoned a provision of the Articles of Confederation which had contemplated floor privileges and periodic debate participation by Executive branch officials in response to Questions, a remnant of ministerial membership and participation in the debates of the House of Commons.

Jefferson in his *Manual* contemplated persons being 'examined before a committee or at the bar of the House', and by law the Speaker or Chairman of the Committee of the Whole are authorized to administer oaths to witnesses. But those persons to be examined at the bar have never been representatives of the Executive branch. In the modern practice virtually all questioning is done by standing and select committees of the House and Senate.

Bradshaw and Pring[35] devote a meaningful chapter of their work to the similarities and differences between the two systems of scrutiny culminating in a discussion of the centrality of 'Questions' from individual Members to ministers. Their analysis begins with constitutional distinctions as a matter of separation of powers, and suggests that

> the relationship between government and legislature is so different that oversight of the one by the other has different purposes in each country and takes different forms. The British constitutional system is designed to ensure that government and Parliament are working along the same lines; in the United States, the Constitution operates so that President and Congress can usefully coexist without accord between them.

The need to retain the 'confidence' of the legislature triggers the need for ministers to be accountable under the parliamentary system—as a vote of no confidence can effectively remove a minister or even the government itself, while the lack of confidence in an Executive official in the United States need not be a disabling reality (short of impeachment for high crimes and misdemeanours). Bradshaw and Pring go on to suggest that 'if a President loses the confidence of Congress on a political issue, there is no question of his resignation from office. The oversight, while it stems from the need to carry out the duties which the Constitution imposes on Congress, has become an expression of the rivalry between two powerful bodies.' There is no dissolution of Congress or possibility of elections resulting from any lack of confidence which may result from scrutiny and a failure to be properly accountable. Additionally, two Houses of the legislature conduct oversight in the United States, while it is only the House of Commons which conducts meaningful scrutiny of ministers which may result in a vote of no confidence or in the dissolution of Parliament. The government's primacy as the initiator of legislation, the fact that only the government can take any financial initiative, that Members cannot propose new expenditure or taxation unless the government sanctions it, and cannot increase expenditure or taxation beyond the limits which the government sets, all serve as disincentives for Parliament to conduct oversight in order to directly enhance a legislative position or agenda separate from the Executive.

There are discernible differences in the character of the cabinet and of the public service in the two countries. Cabinet ministers are themselves Members of one or other House of Parliament and are in constant contact with other Members, often having been backbenchers themselves and perhaps to be again. This proximity and collegial relationship brings an awareness that they are accountable to their colleagues, and that the consequences of failure leading toward removal are more extreme. Bradshaw and Pring's assertion that 'the formal standing of the cabinet in the United States is less high than in Britain; the President may convene them only infrequently and may not share his major decisions with them'[36] is accurate to a point, although a Departmental Secretary's standing in the United States can be statutorily or personally enhanced to belie that stereotype. Congress often delegates enormous authority to Executive officials while retaining an ultimate power of review through the power of the purse and through statutory mechanisms of approval or disapproval. One may speculate about the structural and personal variables which factor into ultimate Executive accountability to the Legislature, ranging from constitutional considerations to statutory or Executive instruments required to create and define the duties of departments or ministries, to the annual exercise of the power of the purse, and even to the familiarity of the Executive official with the Legislative branch based on the likelihood of prior membership. In the final analysis, however, both systems insist upon some measure of accountability.

In the 102nd Congress in 1992 a Member introduced a resolution calling for periodic question periods in the House, whereby departmental secretaries would be entitled to debate time to respond to Questions posed to them by individual Members or their parties. The resolution (H Res 155) called for two hours on the first Tuesday of each month to be devoted to a Question period in the House Chamber during which an invited cabinet member could respond to pre-printed questions from Members and one relevant, unprinted follow-up question. Questions would be printed in the Record and submitted to the invited Cabinet Secretary on the Thursday prior to the Tuesday question period. On the day of the Question period the majority and minority leaders would designate the order of the questions from their party members, and questioning would alternate between the parties. Answers to the initial Questions would be limited to five minutes, and follow-up Questions to two minutes. The resolution was referred to the Committee on Rules which on 18 March 1992 held a hearing on the proposition but did not report back to the House. So the notion of Question periods during a plenary session of the House was never implemented. While this proposal was made at a time of divided government, when the House majority represented a different political party from the Executive, the Rules Committee declined to suggest any departure from the primary means of oral responses to Questions, that is, in standing or select committees. That is not to say that individual Members of Congress are denied the opportunity to rhetorically pose oral questions to the Executive during plenary debates. In fact, Members in both Houses, by addressing the Chair, often pose questions to the President or other Executive branch official. Of course there is no immediate oral response, unless another Member chooses to engage in debate 'on behalf of' the Executive. While the President and all cabinet secretaries are granted the privileges of the House and Senate floors, only informal conversations but not debates are possible with Members.

An exception from this general separation in direct questioning may occur at classified 'briefings' held at times when the House is not in session, where the Speaker permits the Chamber or another space to be used for direct questioning of Cabinet, military, or security officers, which only sitting Members may attend. These briefings have sometimes been described as joint party briefings, chaired by party caucus chairmen but not open to the public.

On the annual occasion when the President delivers his state of the Union Message in person, both Houses are technically in session (jointly) and the President is free if he wishes to entertain questions from Members. Speaker Champ Clark on 13 January 1915, in response to a parliamentary inquiry as to whether a Member or Senator could interrogate the President, indicated that

> the Chair investigated that once, and nothing of the sort has happened in Congress since Thomas Jefferson was sworn in as President the first time, because no President since that time has read a speech before Congress except President Wilson. But before that it does seem that they interrogated the President—not very frequently, but it was done. The opinion of the present occupant of the Chair is that the President would have the right to refuse to be interrogated. In the opinion of the Chair, the Speaker has nothing to do with it and a Member or Senator should address the President directly. It might be in order, but it would be exercising wretched taste.

Presidents seldom appear before House or Senate committees to respond to questions, preferring instead to send Cabinet or White House officials for that purpose. One notable exception was the voluntary appearance of President Gerald R. Ford before the House Judiciary Committee in 1974 to answer questions in open session concerning his pardon of former President Richard M. Nixon. That occasion reflected an overwhelming need for the public to be informed and for the Legislative branch to be voluntarily involved, absent compulsory subpoena, notwithstanding its constitutional lack of any prerogative in the pardoning process.

Primary among statutory enactments intended to enhance Congressional oversight was the creation of the General Accounting Office (now the Government Accountability Office) in 1921 by the Budget and Accounting Act, discussed in greater detail in the chapter on the power of the purse at page 298. GAO's primary function is to conduct financial and management audits and reviews of Executive agencies and programmes at the request of committees and Members of Congress to ensure that public funds are properly spent. GAO also conducts field investigations of administrative activities, prescribes accounting standards for the Executive branch, prepares policy analyses, and provides legal opinions on government activities. The head of GAO, the Comptroller General, is appointed for a single fifteen-year term by the President subject to Senate confirmation. The GAO works only for the Legislative branch, and its staff of over 3,000 submits hundreds of reports to Congress annually (see page 299).

In 1970 Congress established the legislative Office of Technology Assessment (OTA) in the Legislative Reorganization Act. The Office was created to provide Congress with a separate non-partisan source of scientific and technological information separate from the Executive branch, and initially focused upon nuclear technology and the space race. The Office was overseen by a Technology Assessment Board consisting of six Senators and six Representatives who appointed the Director for a six-year term. It produced long-range reports which often took up to two years to complete and which overlapped to some extent with reports from GAO and Congressional Research Service. Its funding, although not its statutory existence, was discontinued under a new Congressional political majority in 1995, and its renewal (not widely anticipated) has been weighed against the Comptroller General's recommendation that GAO can fulfil the same role through its quarterly study of the Executive's technology operations. The resurrection of the OTA may depend upon the size and priorities within the Legislative branch budget under a new Congressional majority.

Reporting requirements tend to proliferate in law, and may be enacted either to further Congressional oversight capability or as conditions to the enactment of legislation or the availability of funds. Several thousand reports are submitted to Congress by departments and agencies each year, and periodically efforts are made in the name of efficiency to eliminate duplicative or unnecessary reporting requirements by 'paperwork reduction' laws.

A case study: war powers

The common feature of the roles of Parliament and Congress in holding the Executive accountable for the conduct of war or other commitment of military force is the ability to inquire into government intentions, preparedness, and performance. The explicit authority under Article I of the US Constitution for Congress to declare war by statutory instrument contrasts so vividly with the absence of a comparable role exercised by the UK Parliament that the war powers of the legislature are perhaps better discussed in this chapter on Scrutiny and Oversight than in the chapters on Legislation or Power of the Purse.

Congress has chosen to enact laws pursuant to its explicit constitutional authority, to authorize the use of military force in the same area of hostility (Iraq) that the House of Commons has endorsed by motion (see pages 353–4). In the other major theatre of hostilities—Afghanistan—the Commons has not voted to support the use of force by motion, relying instead on the UK's treaty obligation with the United States to respond to military attacks against its treaty partner. Congress has from time to time attempted to exercise its power of the purse to place limits on the use of military force, sometimes with success, other times being unable to surmount super-majority vote requirements in the Senate to consider the matter, or ultimately to have its Appropriation bill vetoed by the President and the veto sustained. By contrast, it is hard to imagine circumstances in which a majority of the House of Commons might similarly impose their will on the government, and if they succeeded the consequence would be not simply to restrict the use of force but to bring down the government.

Not only has Congress exercised its declaration of war authority by statutory instrument in response to specific hostilities, as in the First and Second World Wars and respecting the use of force in Afghanistan and Iraq, it enacted a statute authorizing the Congress to restrict or countermand at any time the President's unilateral commitment of military force pursuant to his power as Commander-in-Chief. Today Congress is confronted with additional assertions of pre-emptive Executive authority in the name of national security, such as domestic wire-tap surveillance, where the constitutional rationale for unilateral action asserted by the Executive is the role of the President as Commander-in-Chief in a national emergency created by attack upon the United States, even in the face of statutory law requiring judicial approval of domestic wire taps in all circumstances. This extension of the President's authority as Commander-in-Chief is beginning to be scrutinized by Congress as it conducts oversight over implementation of the Foreign Intelligence Surveillance Act of 1978. An amendment to that law to authorize warrantless wire taps of certain foreign-based electronic conversations was sped through Congress in 2007 without committee oversight conducted in public session (but with classified briefings), as a condition imposed by the President to the 2007 summer recess for Congress. At this writing, a further extension of the warrantless wire-tap authority into 2008 is being debated and has been tied to the issue of retroactive immunity from litigation for telecommunications companies which facilitated the wire taps and would otherwise face privacy violation lawsuits.

The 'Necessary and Proper Clause' in Article I, section 8 of the US Constitution has been cited in this work as the implicit basis for Congressional oversight 'for carrying into execution not only its own powers but also all other powers vested by the Constitution in the Government of the United States'. Article I, section 8 confers upon Congress exclusive authority to 'declare war', meaning the ultimate decision whether or not to enter a war. The President as Commander-in-Chief under Article II has constitutional power to command the US forces once the decision to wage war has been made, and to defend the nation against an attack. Whether this authority extends to the power to commit armed forces to 'hostilities' has resulted in initiatives taken by Congress in the process of exercising oversight and its power of the purse to respond to Executive assertions of authority. By the early 1970s, following the Korean and Vietnam wars—both waged without a Congressional declaration of war or other statutory authority—the Congressional majority view was that the constitutional balance of war powers had swung too far toward the President and needed to be corrected. Opponents argued that Congress always held the power to forbid or terminate US military action by statute (signed by the President or passed over his veto) or by refusal of appropriations through the power of the purse. In 1973 Congress enacted over President Nixon's veto the 'War Powers Resolution'[37] based on a reassertion of Legislative branch power regarding the initial and continued use of military force in hostilities.

The primary purpose stated in section 2 of the law was to 'insure that the collective judgment of both the Congress and the President will apply to the introduction of United States armed forces into hostilities, or into situations where imminent involvement in hostilities is clearly indicated by the circumstances, and to the continued use of such forces in such situations'. Section 2 recites that the powers of the President as Commander-in-Chief are exercised only pursuant to (1) a declaration of war: (2) specific statutory authorization; or (3) a national emergency created by attack on the United States, its territories or possessions, or on its armed forces. The President is required in section 3 'in every possible instance to consult with Congress before introducing forces into hostilities and imminent hostilities', and to continue consultations as long as they remain. This role of consultation was considered in the House report to extend beyond the mere provision of information to the active participation of Members of Congress in preparation of and response to information furnished by the President to leadership and appropriate committees. Section 4 requires the President to report to Congress whenever he introduces US armed forces into hostilities or imminent hostilities abroad within forty-eight hours and mandates periodic reports thereafter.

Section 5 and 6 extend the law beyond an expression of the need for Congressional scrutiny to the establishment of expedited procedures for the consideration of legislative approval or disapproval vehicles in both Houses. Section 5(b) provides that after a report is submitted pursuant to section 4, the President shall terminate the use of US armed forces after sixty days unless Congress (1) has declared war or authorized the action; (2) has extended the period by law; or (3) is physically unable to meet as a result of an armed attack on the USA. The sixty days can be extended for thirty additional days by the President if he certifies that 'unavoidable military necessity respecting the safety of US forces requires their continued use in the course of bringing about their removal'. Section 5(c) requires the President to remove the forces at any time absent specific statutory authorization if Congress so directs by concurrent resolution. The Supreme Court *Chadha* decision requiring presentment to the President for approval or veto effectively nullifies this subsection. Section 6 and 7 provide expedited procedures for Congressional consideration of either a joint resolution authorizing the use of armed forces under sections 5(b) or of a concurrent resolution to withdraw forces. Similar procedures in both Houses require committee reports within twenty-five days of referral of those measures and permit votes on motions to discharge committees which have not filed reports. The reported or discharged measure becomes the pending business of the relevant House and must be voted upon in both Houses in final conference form within sixty days. These expedited procedures take the War Powers Resolution beyond a blueprint for future exercises in Congressional oversight and become an exercise in joint rule making intended to assure not only a prescribed time for legislative review of the required reports but also a time certain for required House and Senate action which legitimizes or delegitimizes the Executive's use of force as Commander-in-Chief.

President Nixon in his veto message challenged the constitutionality of the War Powers Resolution, particularly two provisions: (1) that the legislative veto provision, permitting Congress to direct the withdrawal of troops by concurrent resolution (section 5(c)), was unconstitutional, as not requiring presentment of the disapproval measure to the President; and (2) that the requirement for withdrawal of troops after sixty to ninety days unless Congress passed legislation authorizing such use was unconstitutional because it checked Presidential power without affirmative Congressional action. Every President since the enactment of the War Powers Resolution has taken the position that it is an unconstitutional infringement on the President's authority as Commander-in-Chief. With respect to the procedure for withdrawal of forces by concurrent resolution, the subsequent decision by the Supreme Court in 1983 in the Chadha case supports the argument against its constitutionality, as a concurrent resolution requiring the concurrence of both Houses is not presented to the President for his signature or veto as required by Article I, section 7 of the Constitution. Nevertheless

Congress has utilized the expedited procedures which have remained in the law to permit expedited consideration of concurrent resolutions requiring the withdrawal of troops, despite acknowledged misgivings about the validity of those statutory rules, if only to express a collective opinion as an exercise of scrutiny over Executive conduct of involvement in hostilities. On three occasions the House Committee on Foreign Affairs reported concurrent resolutions under expedited procedures directing the President to remove forces he had committed to hostilities (for example, from Somalia by 31 March 1994, from Bosnia and Herzegovina by 12 March 1998, and from Yugoslavia by 28 April 1999). Congress has also enacted a law[38] permitting the Senate to utilize joint resolutions for the removal of forces under expedited procedures applicable only to that body, leaving it to the House to determine its own procedures for expedited consideration of such joint resolutions.

Section 8 states that authority to introduce armed forces is not to be inferred from any provision of law or treaty unless it specifically authorizes such introduction into hostilities. The specific authorization for use of force in both Iraq wars and in Afghanistan was contained in joint resolutions enacted 'consistent with', but not pursuant to, the War Powers Resolution, prior to the actual commitment of armed forces by the President. Nevertheless, Congress was properly exercising its constitutional role in legislating the equivalent of a declaration of war prior to the commitment of armed forces in those recent areas of hostilities.

The importance of the impeachment power of Congress as a unique oversight tool of last resort when conventional forms of oversight fail should not be underestimated. The mere threat of impeachment presents a constitutionally mandated method for obtaining information which might otherwise not be made available by the Executive. Also, Congressional oversight over the Federal Judiciary is uniquely enhanced by the impeachment authority given the House with respect to all Federal judges. In the last two House impeachment inquiries involving Presidents Nixon and Clinton, the House armed its Judiciary Committee with extraordinary interrogatory and deposition authority in addition to subpoena authority already possessed, to gather information by compulsion if necessary.

With respect to Congressional oversight of the Federal Judiciary, Congress has a clear constitutional basis in addition to an examination of the conduct of judges in the context of possible impeachment. In the areas of court jurisdiction and the compensation of Federal judges, both Houses exert annual scrutiny in response to the Annual State of the Judiciary report from the Chief Justice, through their Committees on the Judiciary and Appropriations subcommittees on the Judiciary.

After the Revolution of 1689 in Britain, ministers inherited the undefined but wide authority of the royal prerogative. The prerogative is no colourful but ineffectual relic. Its scope is remarkable. Under the prerogative forces may be deployed into combat overseas, treaties made or ratified (see page 71), diplomatic relations conducted, ministers appointed and removed, dissolutions recommended, passports issued or withdrawn, and advice given on the appointment of bishops of the Church of England and the granting of most honours.

As things stand, ministers are answerable to parliamentary scrutiny after the event for the use made of prerogative powers, but the effectiveness and degree of scrutiny depends on how far governments are prepared to concede more than a deliberative role to the Houses. In 2007, very substantial changes were proposed in this area (as in others, see page 354) which would rebalance the respective roles of government, Parliament, and the people.

Before considering the changes contemplated in one of these areas, it may be worth looking more broadly at present arrangements.

Giving the Houses more initiative in use of the prerogative will undoubtedly present a challenge to Parliament. How far are the Members of the majority party in the Commons in particular prepared publicly to voice (and support with their votes) the kind of demand for change which effective scrutiny can generate? They may thereby put at risk the administration they were elected to support, their personal political futures at Westminster and in the constituency, even their party's long-term expectations. Opposition parties, hoping for future power, will naturally try to find a way to strike at the government in office without wounding their own prospective authority.

There are perfectly respectable arguments—arguments which until recently prevailed—in favour of the current position. Possession of prerogative powers allows governments to respond quickly to unprecedented and threatening situations. The prerogative can be restricted by Parliament, and has often been superseded by statute or even without it; and statutes such as the Human Rights Act constructively modify the operation of the prerogative on a broad front. Politically, the more important the area within which prerogative powers are being exercised, the less likely it is that ministers would embark on a course of action they knew or suspected Parliament would disown. Finally, the courts as well as Parliament can review the exercise of the prerogative, and will not allow new prerogative powers to be created.

There are also powerful arguments for change. Ministers do not routinely report actions taken in exercise of the prerogative nor is there an exhaustive definition of exactly what may be done in exercise of it, which is at least an oddity in modern times. In issues of the highest importance—embarking on hostilities, for example—it must be more satisfactory for any government to have behind it the positive agreement of those who represent the people at large. Above all is the consideration of principle which persuaded the government to propose change: the executive should draw its power from the people, through Parliament, and should not be able to act in the name of the Monarch, without the people and their representatives being consulted.

The prerogative power to go to war has been in the foreground of the argument about the prerogative. It is hard to say when and why a head of steam began to build up behind the enhancement of parliamentary authority in this area. It may be (as Aristotle said of revolutions) that the cause must be distinguished from the occasion. The occasion may be parliamentary dissatisfaction at Members' limited role in authorizing a sequence of deployments to the Falklands, Iraq, the Balkans, Sierra Leone, and Afghanistan. These were debated on neutral motions for the adjournment of the House; none ended in positive resolutions of support, however united the sentiments of the House, until specific parliamentary authorization was given to the deployment of troops to Iraq, before fighting began, in March 2003.[39] Growing parliamentary assertiveness is surely the cause.

In the Commons the Public Administration select committee reported in 2004 in favour of more parliamentary control over the executive area of the prerogative, especially as regards deploying armed forces into action, and making and ratifying treaties.[40]

The government at that stage were not convinced that the statutory framework recommended by the committee would be much of an improvement. They preferred to proceed case by case. In 2005–6, the Lords Committee on the Constitution came to a conclusion similar to that arrived at in the Commons, though recommending progress by means of convention rather than legislation. The Committee argued that the major problems might be overcome by the tabling in both Houses of a resolution specifying the objectives of the deployment, its legal basis, and the likely size and duration of hostilities.[41] The government reply was both late and (in the Committee's view) inadequate. It looked like a complete refusal to contemplate change, asserting that vital decisions on peace and war must lie with the elected government. In February 2007, this drew the acerbic response from the Committee that Parliament too was an elected organ of the state.[42]

Only months later, the government changed its mind. In May 2007, a successful government amendment to an Opposition motion in the Commons proclaimed that 'the time has come for Parliament's role to be made more explicit in approving or otherwise of the decisions of government relating to the major or substantial deployment of British forces overseas into actual or potential armed conflicts'.[43] In July, a consultation paper entitled *The Governance of Britain*[44] intended to rebalance power between government and the citizen and between government and Parliament. The government agreed to surrender or limit certain executive prerogative powers which it felt should no longer be exercised exclusively by the executive. These included 'significant non-routine deployment of the armed forces into armed conflict' to the greatest extent possible.

Many problems remain. How can parliamentary debates avoid damaging forces' morale or telegraphing their punch; where is the balance between fully informing Parliament and denying intelligence to a potential enemy; what conflicts would be within the definition and what would not; how would mission creep be tackled without shackling commanders in the field; and in days when declarations of war are a rarity[45] how are actions taken in haste at times of unforeseen emergency to be coped with?[46] What should be the role of the non-elected House? Finally, the UK's international treaty obligations involving cooperative action will have to fit into whatever structure is devised.

The government discussion paper *War Powers and Treaties* which followed *The Governance of Britain* made some official suggestions towards solution.[47] The government favours limiting the requirement to inform Parliament of proposed deployment to a statement of location and objectives, together with comment on legal issues. It would be for the Prime Minister to determine the timing of any such statement, and the level of information it contained. Neither statute nor convention alone should be the basis for the procedure, but a combination of the two. Reports of progress after first deployment would be made, but there would be no requirement for further expressions of Parliamentary approval. Similarly, in cases of emergency, Parliament would be informed after the event, but would not be asked to approve what had been done.

However these details settle down, two general observations may be made. Sustained pressure by and on behalf of Parliament has shifted an important balance: the ancient and powerful legacy of the right to use the prerogative, not only in connection with hostilities but in other areas, will now be shared between the original legatee, government, and Parliament. Parliamentary scrutiny of the executive will enter a new forum. Secondly, the process illustrates clearly how changes are made in a polity where constitutional arrangements are fluid rather than enshrined once and for all.

Self-scrutiny

'Scrutiny' in a complete sense must include the ability of a legislature to examine itself. This is treated in part under the chapter on Ethics and Standards, with respect to the official conduct of Members, officers, and employees. Beyond investigations of covered individuals, the Committee on Standards of Official Conduct in the House of Representatives and the Select Committee on Ethics in the Senate have investigative and oversight jurisdiction over the Code of Official Conduct and to recommend administrative actions as it may consider appropriate to establish standards of official conduct for Members, officers, and employees.

In the House, the Committee on Rules serves as the committee of oversight over procedures of the House, and has two subcommittees to conduct its oversight. Its subcommittee on Legislative and Budget Process has 'general responsibility for measures or matters related to relations between the Congress and the Executive Branch', and its subcommittee on Rules and Organization of the House has 'general responsibility for measures or matters related to relations between the two Houses, relations between Congress and the Judiciary, and internal operations of the House'. Many of the responsibilities of the Legislative and Budget Process subcommittee fall at Westminster to the Leader of the House, a government minister who is concerned with the House's relationship with government—ideally the House's man or woman in Cabinet and not vice versa.

The Congressional Committee on House Administration has legislative and oversight jurisdiction over accounts of the House and their auditing, and, while retaining authority of the chair to establish oversight 'task forces', created for the first time in 2007 Subcommittees on Capitol Security and on Elections, both with legislative and oversight jurisdiction.

In 1992, in the wake of internal scandals involving the House Bank and Post Office, the House created its own non-partisan office of Inspector General, jointly appointed by the Speaker and Majority and Minority Leaders, to conduct audits of financial and administrative functions of the House and of joint entities. The House periodically contracts with a major accounting firm to conduct comprehensive auditing review of its spending practices. The House Office of Inspector General is subject to the policy direction and control of the Committee on House Administration. The Senate, not having experienced similar scandal, has no formal counterpart, but utilizes its Committees on Rules and Administration, and on Homeland Security and Government Affairs, to scrutinize its own operations, jurisdiction over funding for the Senate, and review of Senate rules and procedures, while the latter committee has jurisdiction over 'organization' of each House, and of the two Houses acting together, to examine itself. This is treated in part under the chapter on Ethics and Standards, with respect to the official conduct of Members, officers, and employees. The Committee on Standards of Official Conduct in the House and the Select Committee on Ethics in the Senate, have investigative and oversight jurisdiction over the Code of Official Conduct and to recommend administrative actions as it may consider appropriate to establish standards of official conduct for Members, officers, and employees.

It is the Legislative Appropriation subcommittees of the House and Senate Appropriations Committee which exercise the most continuous oversight of the internal operations of their respective bodies, since their work product is presented annually, rather than biennially, to the Congress and is the result of hearings held to review the operation of all offices of each House and of joint entities such as the Architect of the Capitol and the Capitol Police force. While the House Legislative Branch subcommittee was temporarily abolished in the 109th Congress and its functions retained at the full committee level, the 110th Congress re-established that subcommittee to match its counterpart on the Senate side.

There are unusual circumstances where the need for joint Congressional entities to oversee an aspect of its operations transcends the jurisdictional parameters of all the above-mentioned housekeeping committees and the elected leadership. An example is the statutory establishment of the United States Capitol Preservation Commission, recently given responsibility over the planning, engineering, design, and construction of the Capitol Visitors' Centre. The commission consists of the Speaker and President pro tempore of the Senate, the chairman and vice chairman of the Joint Committee on the Library, the chairman and ranking minority members of the two Committees on Administration, the Majority and Minority Leaders of each House, and three additional Members from each House (who represent the Appropriations Committee). By this mechanism the two Houses can oversee a particular project having equal interest to both Houses, although the Appropriations Committee remains ultimately responsible for funding the project and its considerable cost overruns.

On several occasions in the latter half of the twentieth century the two Houses created Joint Committees on Congressional Operations and Organization—in 1965, 1970, and in 1993, to conduct oversight on matters of joint House–Senate relations and to report recommendations to each House, but without legislative jurisdiction. There also exist Joint Committees established by law—on Printing and on the Library, which respectively oversee and regulate the format of the Congressional Record, and the Library of Congress, Botanic Garden, and statues and other works of art in the Capitol. There are currently no joint legislative committees in Congress.[48]

In the Commons, some of the functions above are the responsibility of the House of Commons Commission (page 39), which lays the Estimate for all House services and oversees staff appointments. Audit, security, and the upkeep of the fabric of the Commons portion of the Palace of Westminster together with funding and overseeing new works also fall to staff responsible, through the Clerk and Chief Executive, to the Commission. The Administration Committee (page 362), an organ of the House unlike the Commission which was created by statute, makes recommendations on services to the Commission and in particular is charged with considering proposed additional expenditure. The Procedure and Modernisation Committees (page 361) are concerned with the never-ending task of *aggiornamento*, updating and refining House procedures. Proposals to set aside standing rules or to impose time limits on particular debates do not however emanate from these committees but depend on motions put before the Commons by the government, frequently under Standing Orders. For the most part, these motions may not be debated or are open to debate for only short periods. When the proposals are particularly stern, one may perhaps be forgiven for drawing the conclusion that the two systems are closer than might otherwise appear. The Lords arrangements are broadly similar (see page 364), and there have been movements recently in the direction of joint operations, so far achieved only in the area of IT.

For a discussion of recent unprecedented creations in both legislatures of outside 'offices' comprising non-Members to investigate, examine, and report on various aspects of Members' conduct in Congress, and on Members' allowances in Parliament, see the chapter on Ethics and Standards at pages 542–3, and the chapter on Representatives, Members, Lords, and Senators at page 143, respectively.

Notes

1. *Congress Investigates: A Documented History 1782–1974* (1975), p xix.
2. *Congressional Government* (1885), 297.
3. Vernon Bogdanor (ed), *The British Constitution in the Twentieth Century* (2003), 165.
4. HC Deb (1995–6) 271 cc 1144 ff, the debate on the report of the Scott Inquiry into the supply of arms to Iraq.
5. Parl Deb (4th series) vol 37 cc 723–36. I am indebted for this quotation to my former colleague Colin Lee.
6. Very much the present system of select committee reports preceding debates in the Chamber was however put to a select committee in 1888.
7. Walter Oleszek, *Workshop on Congressional Oversight and Investigations* (1978), 199.
8. 10 USC 114, and 50 USC 414.
9. H Res 40, 17 January 2009.
10. Walter Oleszek, *Congressional Procedures and the Policy Process*, 6th edn (2004), 296.
11. Ibid 299.
12. 18 USC 6002.
13. 50 USC 413 (c)(2).
14. 18 USC 1001.
15. Known as the Osmotherley Rules. The Rules were last updated in 2004: see evidence given to the Liaison Committee on 19 October 2004, 2003–04 HC 1180-I.
16. Science and Technology Committee Eighth Report, 2002–3 HC 415-I paras 226–8.
17. First Report 2008–9 HC 113 para 51. See also the Second Report from the Innovation, Universities, Science and Schools Committee 2007–8 HC 49 paras 46–8: 'there have been occasions when the government has been less than fully co-operative'.
18. Fourth Report 2007–8 HC 181 para 5.
19. The government agreed that Commons members of the Committee should be proposed to him by the Committee of Selection, and undertook to increase the number of public sessions and provide additional investigative support. Lords members will be appointed by the House, on a motion the terms of which will have been agreed by the usual channels. Existing—if antique—methods of reinforcing the confidentiality of select committees do not seem to have been explored, which is a pity. But Parliament is not Congress, and on balance the solution is probably right in present circumstances.
20. D. N. Chester and N. Bowring, *Questions in Parliament* (1962), 114.
21. Business in Westminster Hall (see page 56) may include Questions for oral answer particularly where the subject matter of the Questions crosses departmental boundaries, but the procedure has not been used since 2003–4, when 64 Questions were reached on six days.
22. The progression by which the daily allowance has declined is instructive—eight in 1909, four in 1919, three in 1920, and two in 1959.
23. In the case of Scotland, Wales, and Northern Ireland the limit is five days.
24. Ten minutes in the case of the smaller departments.
25. HC Deb (2006–7) 465 c 447.
26. HC Deb (2007–8) 480 c 403.
27. Third Report HC 622, para 22.
28. Public Administration Committee Third Report 2003–4 HC 355 para 2.

29. Quoted in Public Administration Committee Fifth Report 2004–5 HC 449-I Appendix 1.
30. HC Deb (2007–8) 472 c 1918.
31. Ibid 480 c 403.
32. Ibid 480 c 19 WS.
33. House of Lords Companion to the Standing Orders (2007), 70.
34. Ibid 73.
35. K. A. Bradshaw and D. A. M. Pring, *Parliament and Congress* (1973), 355.
36. Ibid 356.
37. PL 93-148.
38. PL 98-164, 22 November 1983.
39. A similar vote at the time of the Korean War may be the only and partial parallel.
40. Fourth Report 2003–4 HC 422 paras 18 ff.
41. Fifteenth Report 2005–6 HL 236-I para 110.
42. Third Report 2006–7 HL 51. The Committee also suspected that the government was in two minds on the issue.
43. HC Deb (2006–7) 460 c 582.
44. Cm 7170. See also the later discussion paper 'War Powers and Treaties' Cm 7239.
45. According to the Lords Committee on the Constitution (Fifteenth Report 2005–6 HL 236 para 10) the last time the UK declared war was against Thailand in 1942.
46. Some of these issues were addressed by the Lords Committee which proposed that in cases of emergency, Parliament should be informed *ex post* within seven days, and should in any case be kept informed of developments. If the nature or objectives of the deployment change significantly, further parliamentary consent should be sought (ibid, para 110).
47. As did a debate in the Lords, HL Deb (2007–8) 698 c 747.
48. The last joint committee with authority to report legislation in Congress was the Joint Committee on Atomic Energy, abolished in 1977. Joint committees are normally utilized for ceremonial, investigative (with authority to report to the two Houses but not on legislation), and administrative purposes. For a list of contemporary select and joint committees in Congress, see *House Practice* 2nd edition 2003 Chapter 11 (ed W. Holmes Brown and Charles W. Johnson).

8

Committees

Introduction

Most discussion of the role of committees in the two legislatures is to be found elsewhere than in this chapter. This is because committees of all kinds are so intimately connected with the power of the purse, legislation, privilege, ethics and standards, and scrutiny and oversight that no text on these subjects is practicable without extensive reference to the relevant committees. This chapter is therefore principally about UK select committees in general, and the organization and staffing of Congressional Committees.

In Parliament, unlike Congress, investigative or scrutiny committees have long been distinct from legislative committees, though a functional overlap is beginning to appear. A parliamentary select committee consists of a relatively small group of members of either House and sometimes both Houses. It inquires into and reports on a prescribed subject or department of State. Congressional select committees resemble their parliamentary counterparts in some ways but not others. They are a less permanent variety of Standing Committee, a body without parallel at Westminster: on the other—like those in the UK—they are 'created primarily to investigate conditions or events',[1] and sometimes do not possess legislative jurisdiction.

The *modus operandi* of select committees is much the same on both sides of the Atlantic but while such committees at Westminster are steadily becoming more influential, there will never be—short of breaking through the limits of what may be understood as the British Constitution—any question of their achieving the independent power of Standing Committees in Washington. Nor, for constitutional reasons, do British select committees originate effective proposals for taxation or government expenditure. Once the absence of independent legislative or financial authority is taken into account, however, the steady growth in authority and expertise in the British select committee system makes comparison between the two more interesting than it was a generation ago.

Bipartisanship in Parliament

The practice of nominating a limited group of Members to gather facts and report their opinions to the House of Commons is four centuries old and more. In the nineteenth century, with the exception of the Public Accounts Committee first nominated in 1862, development was hesitant,[2] and came to almost a complete halt around the turn of the twentieth century, when two select committees were dispatched into minefields of alleged personal and political guilt on the part of ministers, and succeeded only in descending into bitter party dispute. One was asked to decide whether the Colonial Secretary had forced war on the South African republics, and the other, a few years later, had to consider whether the Chancellor of the Exchequer, the government Chief Whip, and others had made money out of insider dealings in a public contract.

The lesson which should have been learnt from these disasters (and others) was that select committees are neither courts nor a cut-down version of impeachment. Though such a limitation on the capacity of Commons select committees has been generally recognized[3] it is not universally accepted, as is evident by the recent proposal for a select committee to review government actions in the lead-up to war in Iraq.[4] It was however a different (if equally mistaken) conclusion that was in fact derived from the two early twentieth-century failures—that select committees were, at best, of their nature inept and at worst politically suspect.

Throughout the first half of the twentieth century, therefore, while select committees were reluctantly appointed in the Commons to scrutinize the government's estimates of expenditure (and there were repeated proposals for the invigoration of the system), committees' remits were deliberately limited, adequate staff and budgetary resources were denied. Exclusion from policy was fatal to their growth. On the other hand, from today's perspective, a long fallow period served to distance modern select committees from the political storms surrounding their predecessors, and allowed their non-partisan character to recover. The two world wars saw brief increases in tempo, and from the 1950s and 1960s more life flowed gradually into the system. The exclusive and arid concentration on detailed financial scrutiny waned, as brighter policy horizons came into view. Some new committees were set up—the Nationalised Industries Committee is the best example—and oral evidence began routinely to be taken in public. The new Expenditure Committee developed a higher profile than the earlier Estimates Committee. Committees asserted their right to travel abroad, much against the will of the government of the day. It was not however until a 1978 Procedure Committee report gave rise the following year to the present generation of Commons select committees related to government departments that a systematic degree of authoritative scrutiny could even be glimpsed.

In the Commons, then, bipartisanship is an accident of history. However important it may now be to the effectiveness of Parliament, no rule of either House demands that select committees should conduct their business without primary regard to party politics, or that their members should—by and large—be free from external party discipline in respect of their actions as committee members. Yet that this is the way select committees in fact operate is in part borne out by the fact that in the preparation of nearly 390 reports in 2007–8, select committees divided on some 230 occasions, three-quarters of which were in five committees. The number of divisions has nearly doubled from the previous session, but the figures may not reveal increased politicization since seventy-five are accounted for by the European Scrutiny Committee, which is something of a special case. The convention is reinforced by the realization that, as the conclusions of select committees become more central to public discussion of matters of concern, outcomes indistinguishable from the presuppositions of party policy are easy to ignore. There is equally no specific rule against political attempts to influence or hinder select committees, and such attempts are sometimes made, subtly or otherwise.

Success in designing an independent method of selecting members of committees may (or more probably may not) have been attained (see pages 365–6), but even if it has not the fact that the issue is regularly aired probably closes it off as a reliable means of directly applying improper pressure. In any case, committees once under sail tend to develop a group loyalty which often transcends party in the context of committee work. Trying to dissuade a committee from undertaking a particular inquiry or publishing unpalatable conclusions, unless very indirect or well camouflaged, is apt to find its way into public knowledge and be justly condemned as an outrageous breach of convention. Suspicion has sometimes been voiced that a committee report had been leaked just before publication by a member of the committee, to enable the government department concerned to get its retaliation in first, but such a practice is so frowned on that, while it may occur in future, it may be hoped that it will be very rare—though it is unlikely to be any easier to find the culprit in the future than it has been in the past.

Commons select committees

The increase in the number of individual select committees in the Commons over the past twenty-five years or so has not been very marked, but the rise in the total of Members involved is significant. This fact is borne out in Table 8.1 in the Annex.

In the Commons, select committees (including joint committees) currently fall into five groups. The first are the nineteen appointed 'to examine the expenditure, administration and policy' of government departments and associated public bodies. Each covers a major department of State, such as the Treasury or the Ministry of Defence. To their number should be added two others with similar purpose, though their area of inquiry is not defined by a single government department. The Environmental Audit Committee considers whether government policies and programmes 'contribute to environmental protection and sustainable development', and audits performance against targets. The Public Administration Committee reviews 'matters related to the quality and standards of administration provided by civil service departments and other matters relating to the civil service'. It also receives reports from certain statutory commissioners or ombudsmen, who inquire into complaints of maladministration.

In the second group are eight committees concerned with the business or facilities of the House. The Modernisation Committee takes a long-term view of the changes needed in the way the House operates. Unusually, it has since its inception been chaired by a minister, the Leader of the House, who is responsible for relations between the government and the House and in part for the planning of the government's business in the House. In recent sessions, the committee has not been as active as previously. The Procedure Committee, a body of longer standing, reports on more detailed aspects of the House's practice and procedure. Between them (and adding to their contribution those of other committees since about 1990) they have energized a transformation of the way the House does its business more far-reaching than any for a century. Most recently, a committee on the Reform of the House has been added to their number. The work of the Standards and Privileges Committee is mentioned at pages 528–9. The Administration Committee, subsuming from 2005 a number of separate committees, keeps under review the services provided for and by the House to its Members and the public. The related Finance and Services Committee (now reinforced by the presence of the Chairman of Ways and Means) has in charge the expenditure and administration of these services. Finally, the Committee of Selection (see page 365) nominates Members to all general and most select committees.

Leaving aside the recent trend towards setting up specially constituted joint committees, select committees, or their subcommittees to consider particular draft bills (of which there were three in 2005–6 and 2006–7 and six in 2007–8, three of which were the subject of inquiries by more than one committee), a number of joint and select committees report on specific types of primary or secondary legislation. These include the joint committees on Consolidation Bills, Tax Law Rewrite Bills and Statutory Instruments, and the Commons Select Committee on Statutory Instruments. The European Scrutiny Committee, the Regulatory Reform Committee, and the Human Rights Committee (the last a joint committee) also belong in this group.

Two committees stand out from the general framework. The Public Accounts Committee reviews the Appropriation Accounts detailing all government spending, with economy, efficiency, and effectiveness in mind (see page 300). The Liaison Committee began life as an informal gathering of the chairmen of the newly appointed committees in the late 1970s, managing budgets and discouraging turf wars. Since then, it has become an essential element in the growth and coherence of the select committee system. The chairmen of no fewer than thirty-two committees who sit on the Liaison Committee take a broad view of the system as a whole and may advise individual committees in cases of difficulty. The allocation of parts of the committee budget is discussed and agreed in the Liaison Committee. There is a National Policy Statements Subcommittee which may consider statements laid before the House under the Planning Act 2008. As the capstone of the scrutiny work of individual committees, the Liaison Committee now takes evidence twice a year from the Prime Minister on the broadest of fronts, 'matters of public policy', thus overturning a long-standing convention (dearer to government than acceptable to Parliament) that Prime Ministers simply did not give evidence to committees.

The last group comprises the nine regional select committees, each covering one of the planning regions of England and London with the responsibility of 'examin[ing] regional strategies and the work of regional bodies' for the region with which it is connected. It is provided that these committees should have nine members each, but with the power to invite Members of the House who represent constituencies in the relevant region but are not members of the committee, to 'participate in its proceedings at specified meetings' but who are not to make motions, vote, or be counted in the quorum. Regional select committees have met in the appropriate parts of England, have taken questions, and conducted general debates. The arrangement is temporary until the end of the present Parliament, but its beginnings have not been auspicious. Only the government has so far nominated members to the committees, and the Liaison Committee, concerned at the demand they make on already stretched numbers of Members active in select committee work, feared that regional committees would lead to unfortunate overlaps of work and exacerbate membership problems (see page 365). They were not alone. The Children, Schools and Families Committee observed: 'the supply of time—and indeed of eligible and willing Members—is finite, and care needs to be taken that standards of scrutiny are not put at risk'.[5]

Lords select committees

In the Lords, as in the Commons, there are a number of select committees in existence for an entire Parliament, some explicitly constituted in that way, others so in practice. Yet others are set up to perform a specific task, on the completion of which they cease to exist.

The Lords does not have a set of committees covering every department of government as the lower House does. Nevertheless, there is a small group of select committees in the Lords, most of fairly recent creation, which do not always find a parallel in the Commons. This includes the Economic Affairs Committee, which must of course take prudent regard for the sensitivities about Lords involvement with finance so keenly felt at the other end of the Palace of Westminster. Nevertheless, the Committee found ample scope for comment on the annual Finance Bill, and most recently concentrated on capital gains tax, residence and domicile, and enterprise. A subcommittee examines every Finance Bill, and in 2008 considered issues such as clarification or administration, and not rates or new impositions. Broad matters engaging the attention of the full Committee include the economics of renewable energy, apprenticeships, and the impact of immigration. The Science and Technology Committee was first appointed in 1979 following the elimination of a similar committee in the Commons. (The Commons Committee reappeared, then became defunct, its responsibility assumed by a departmental select committee and has recently been resurrected once more.) Recent topics of inquiry have included waste management and follow-ups of inquiries into air travel and health, and personal internet security. The European Union Committee is the equivalent of the Commons European Scrutiny Committee, though the Lords Committee makes extensive use of subject-related subcommittees which include Lords specially co-opted to each, as the Commons body does not (see pages 27–8). In an inquiry into the impact of the Lisbon treaty, however, the Committee combined all its forces, a total of eighty Lords. The Constitution Committee, set up on the recommendation of the Royal Commission on the House of Lords in 2001, reviews the constitutional implications of all bills coming before the Lords—looking for what it calls matters of principle affecting principal parts of the constitution—and will normally report before second reading. In 2007–8 there were five such reports. In addition, the Committee has before it Welsh Legislative Competence Orders (see page 21). It mounts subject inquiries into such matters of constitutional significance as Reform of the office of Attorney General and Relations between the Executive, the Judiciary, and Parliament.

Since 1993 the Lords has regularly appointed every session an ad hoc committee on a subject of particular general interest. One such has been on the work of the major UK economic regulators, succeeded by another on the formula which determines the funding for devolved administrations. The choice of topic is made by the Lords Liaison Committee.

A further group comprises committees which undertake functions in connection with legislation, and to some of these the Commons has no counterpart. This category includes the Delegated Powers and Regulatory Reform Committee, first appointed in 1992. Part of its remit is similar to that of the Commons Regulatory Reform Committee, but it must also report whether any bill inappropriately delegates legislative power or subjects the exercise of power under the bill to an inappropriate degree of parliamentary scrutiny. To that end, the Committee reviews all public bills after introduction seeking explanations from officials on why delegated powers are proposed to be taken, and why a particular level of control has been chosen, reporting to the House in time (usually) for the committee stage. The government usually tries to accept the committee's view. The Statutory Instruments Merits Committee has a duty broader than the Joint Committee on Statutory Instruments, which is discussed at page 471.

Some select committees in the Lords perform functions similar to or in conjunction with Commons committees. The Lords has appointed a committee on Communications, intended to continue until the end of the present Parliament, which considers topics in the same field as the Commons Culture, Media and Sport Committee, including the ownership of the media and government communications.

There are domestic committees on Administration and Works, Refreshment, and Information. There is of course a Committee for Privileges, which as well as considering matters of privilege, has a subcommittee on Lords Interests, which though not hitherto in the public eye has currently disposed of some high-profile cases (see page 127). The Procedure Committee performs the duties undertaken in the Commons by the Modernisation Committee and the Procedure Committee. The House Committee takes on many of the responsibilities which in the lower House fall by statute to the House of Commons Commission.

The Lords Liaison Committee has a broader remit than that in the Commons. It advises the House on the resources needed for committee work, and their allocation between committees, considers requests for ad hoc committees, seeks to ensure that there is no unnecessary duplication of committee activity between the Houses, and considers the availability of Lords to sit on select committees. The Committee has indicated that at the beginning of future parliaments it will review the work of policy select committees before their reappointment.

Joint Committees, when a committee from one House sits with a committee from the other, both with the same objective and for the most part the same powers, include those on Tax Law Rewrite, Consolidation Bills, Statutory Instruments, and Human Rights.

Parliamentary select committee membership and activities

In neither House at Westminster is there a standard size for select committees. In the Commons they range from nine to thirty-two—the larger figure being the unusually constituted Liaison Committee. Membership of the departmentally related committees ranges from eleven to fourteen. In general, experience seems to show that, to keep a committee together and allow every Member an opportunity for connected questioning, smaller is on the whole better. As a select committee chairman remarked recently in the course of a debate, 'a committee of fourteen is just too big'[6] both to sustain lines of questioning and to engage every member. There is a further consideration leading to a preference for less over more. The appearance of regional committees, has increased the number of permanent select committee places to 515 in 2008–9, double that of 1978–9. Once account is taken of ministerial office, 'shadow' portfolios and other factors, the House of Commons must be perilously near the limit of willing participants in select committee work. As the Liaison Committee pointed out, the proof of this lies in the fact that only four select committees had an attendance record of over 70 per cent and a similar number achieved an attendance of under 60 per cent: the obvious conclusion drawn by the Liaison Committee was that the size of committees should be reduced.

In the Lords, a committee may be given power to co-opt to its membership Lords not originally nominated to it.

However large or small a committee, it is important that those nominated to it should serve for long enough to build up sufficient knowledge to enable them to sustain an informed dialogue with official and non-official experts, and that their attendance should be regular. In the Lords, there is a rule of rotation under which, with regard to most select committees, Lords must retire from service on a committee after (usually) three sessions' service and are not eligible for reappointment until a further session has elapsed. A different view is taken in the Commons where there is no general rule of rotation, except for chairmen (see below).

Irrespective of the arrangements made for the balance between the parties, at Westminster members of select committees ought in principle to be backbenchers. The Modernisation Committee and domestic committees apart, no government ministers (including whips) are conventionally nominated to most select committees, and especially not to committees related to government departments. The very possibility has been damned by the Liaison Committee. Feelings in the Commons are divided on whether front-bench Opposition spokesmen should sit on committees. When an Opposition is relatively small in numbers or in cases where a spokesman sits on a committee not connected with the responsibility on which he or she speaks for the party, it is felt in some quarters that the practice can be acceptable. But again the Liaison Committee was not happy.

Whatever the pool from which select committee members are chosen, the actual choice should of course be as impartial as possible. The choice of Members to sit on those select committees regularly appointed under Standing Orders is made by the House on the proposal of the Committee of Selection. There are some exceptions—Selection itself, Standards and Privileges, Liaison (see pages 362), the Members' Estimate Committee (see page 141), and a committee to look into the search of offices on the parliamentary estate set up in December 2008, the members of which were initially to be nominated by the Speaker (though the order was discharged and the committee was subsequently nominated by the House). Committees not in Standing Orders are nominated on motions moved by the government. Any Member may however seek to amend a list of nominees to a select committee. The Committee of Selection has a government majority, but by convention its choice of Members to sit on other committees reflects, so far as it arithmetically can, the balance of parties in the House. The system is not perfect—the smaller parties sometimes complain bitterly that it disadvantages them—but none better has emerged since 1979.

When at that time the new generation of select committees came into being, the Committee of Selection was seen as the means of locating the power of nomination in the back benches, rather than in the party hierarchies. But the Selection Committee had long understood its role in respect of select committees as similar to that relating to standing (now public bill) committees. It nearly always confirmed the individual nominations put forward by the party whips, while respecting the rule or convention governing overall party balance. Since government whips were sometimes accused of trying to see that the awkward squad on their own side were denied seats on committees where their activities might be thought 'unhelpful', the Committee of Selection—through no particular fault of its own—was not perceived as the completely independent arbiter which had been hoped for.

Discontent with this arrangement rumbled through the 1990s, and over the next few years other ways of insulating choice of select committee members from party pressure were brought forward. One was to replace the Committee by three very senior Members, specially nominated, or by the Chairmen's Panel sitting as a Committee of Nominations and considering proposals made by the parties after internal consultations. A third was direct election by the House at large. When there seemed no majority for any variant, the temperature began to drop.

When the committees were being renominated across the board in the summer of 2005, the then Leader of the House said that 'an inordinate time [was] spent on transparently and fairly selecting the Labour party's representation' on select committees, at a meeting of the full parliamentary party. One of his back-bench colleagues evidently described what had happened as 'a seismic shift' in the direction of democratic choice in the selection of Labour Members for seats on select committees. In the Conservative party in 2005, Members seeking places on select committees were invited to submit their names to the whips, with supporting representations, and the whips then made the choices. Subsequently, however, things seem to have gone backward. Discontent at the role played by the whips in the selection of committees reappeared and became part of the demand for change which followed the expenses crisis in summer 2009, and the appointment of chairmen and members of select committees is one of the principal subjects likely to be before the recently appointed select committee on Reform of the Commons.

In the Lords, the Committee of Selection proposes to the House the membership of nearly all select committees.

The chairmanship of a select committee is a prize more desirable even than simple membership. The convention in the Commons is that the range of chairmanships is divided between the parties in rough proportion to the political balance of the House. The rule is thus quite different from that in the House of Representatives, where the majority claims every chair. As the Modernisation Committee observed in 2002, there is at Westminster no possibility of the situation where, when a US Senator moved from one party to another in a neatly balanced Chamber, every single committee chairmanship changed hands. Normally the convention apportioning chairmanships by agreement between the parties is not in practice difficult to reconcile with the Commons rule that it is for the committees themselves to choose their own chairmen. Most Chairmen, once appointed, soon settle into the independent role demanded of them. The Leader of the

House grumbled recently that as soon as government members become chairmen of select committees, 'they go native'. Problems have however surfaced when, in a new Parliament, parties appeared to try to jettison sitting chairmen, in both recent cases of their own rather than another party. An irritated House of Commons refused in the summer of 2001 to agree any of the nominations to two committees until the whips reinstated in the lists the names of the two former chairmen. Since a decade earlier the whips had got away with exactly what was then complained of, progress had undoubtedly been made. A Standing Order now provides that no select committee may elect as its chairman a Member who had served in that capacity for two previous Parliaments. Waiting for time to do the job for them may act as a further disincentive to whips anxious to remove incumbent chairmen.

Certain select committee chairmen in the Commons are paid an allowance in addition to their salaries and allowances as Members. This is partly in recognition of the increase in workload and partly a move in the direction of a purely House of Commons career ladder, distinct from that climbed by ministers. With the benefits however go certain restrictions, intended to reinforce the independence of the post.

Indeed, all members of select committees are required to declare their interests, pecuniary or non-pecuniary, when the committee first meets, and the declaration is then published. Members who find that they have an interest directly affected by any aspect of the work of the committee should withdraw from participation in that matter. In some circumstances, even questions to witnesses need to be prefaced by an oral declaration of interest.

Witnesses before parliamentary committees

It is essential for the satisfactory working of committees in legislatures that they should be able to call on evidence or testimony from those individuals, whoever they may be, who are in the best position to assist them. The Commons devolves on its select committees its own unwritten but extensive power to send for 'persons, papers and records'. (The Lords does not, though their Procedure Committee has recommended that it should.[7]) It is a formula (in one form or another) many centuries old. There have been recent occasions however when Henry Hotspur's reply to Glendower—who boasted an equally broad authority (in his case to call spirits from the vasty deep)—has seemed only too apposite: 'but will they come when you do call for them?'[8] The legal basis of the power to compel witnesses is, in the UK, unhelpfully open to interpretation. By comparison, the United States has established a clear and relatively modern rationale linking good law with the quality of information available to a legislature.[9] It is an argument which ought to hold good on both sides of the Atlantic. However, in reviewing problems at Westminster, it is worth recalling that they would never have arisen had not the select committees of the House of Commons marched in the direction of the guns of government.

Witnesses before a select committee are not usually under oath but all, whether ministers, officials, or others, have an obligation by the law of Parliament (not statute law) to give truthful and complete answers to the questions put to them. If they fail in that duty, they may be proceeded against for the parliamentary offence of contempt. The general law and the courts are not involved. There are no limitations, other than those which may be imposed informally by agreement of the committee, on the time during which any committee member may question a witness or the arrangement or direction of questioning. Nor are there specific rules about the character of the questions which may be put to any witness. There are of course no US-style constitutional protections and the practice of the courts is not necessarily followed. If a member of a committee believes a question is unfair, he or she may ask to have the room cleared and the appropriateness of the question settled by the committee. Such a proceeding is rare—as indeed are substantiated grievances by witnesses. There is no practice which confers on persons criticized before a committee the right to appear to clear their name, though in such cases those who feel themselves aggrieved will almost invariably be successful if they have a genuine ground of objection. Witnesses may sometimes be allowed to be advised by counsel in the committee, but are not—except in very unusual instances indeed—represented by them.

On the other hand, while a recalcitrant non-official witness is nowadays something of a rarity, when a problem does arise there is no really satisfactory way of successfully deploying the committee's authority. When a journalist declined to disclose the source of certain information given to a committee, on the grounds that 'free journalism' would be impossible if he did so, the Committee had little real choice in their response other than to invite the House to consider the matter. A House of Lords committee which recently encountered a reluctant witness felt it had no recourse other than to refer the matter to the Lords Procedure of the House Committee.[10] In a modern plural society, the traditional weapon of committal for contempt in such cases is not practical. It is more than likely that, failing a witness's refusal to testify in full at a critical point in a high-profile inquiry, matters will be left to the ingenuity of committees in securing most of the information they need without provoking crises which may not have satisfactory endings. There are usually ways round the problem.

There is further discussion of the problems which arise from the reluctance of ministerial or official witnesses to appear before select committees or to answer as fully as Members might like, in the context of Scrutiny at pages 333–5.

Committees in Congress: organization

Other discussion of committee investigations and oversight in Congress is contained in the chapter on Scrutiny and Oversight, at pages 311ff. Discussion of committee jurisdiction and of committee legislative procedures is contained in the chapter on Legislation at page 407.

Chairmen of most standing committees are not selected by their committees, but rather by the Majority party Leadership steering committee, the Majority party caucus, and then ultimately elected by the House. This has not always been the case, since in the earliest Congress the rules permitted the first named (most senior) Member to be chairman unless the committee by majority vote elected someone else. Beginning in the 1970s the rules were amended to require chairmen to be nominated by the Majority party caucus,[11] rather than by a committee on committees which to that time had consisted of the Majority members of the Committee on Ways and Means. Until then full committee chairmen were chosen strictly on the objective basis of consecutive seniority on that committee. They became by virtue of seniority alone the central figures in the legislative process. The full committee chairs' power, and the further decentralization of power away from elected Majority Leadership to more junior subcommittee chairmen was for a time, beginning in the 1970s, accelerated under pressure from newly elected Members and from some senior Members who sought to distribute power more equitably. The most significant change came when both parties in their caucuses modified the seniority system. Seniority meant that chairmen normally came from safe Congressional districts, were repeatedly re-elected, and served until their retirement or death. Because many such safe districts in the 1950s and 1960s were in the conservative Democratic south, chairmen were often politically at odds with Democratic Presidents, Congressional leaders, and the Majority caucus. Nevertheless, they could not in a practical sense be removed by the caucus utilizing secret balloting or by a decision of the steering committee based on political considerations. Beginning in the 1970s, under pressure from the large number of new Members elected to the House, Republican and Democratic caucuses in both Houses changed their rules to permit their respective steering committees to nominate candidates other than the incumbents, and to permit secret ballots on committee chairmen and ranking Minority members, making them more accountable to at least a majority of their respective caucus or conference, and resulting in the replacement of several senior chairmen during that period. Further, bidding procedures were put in place which enabled re-elected Members to retain at least one, but not all, previous subcommittee assignments before newer Members were permitted to bid, all in an effort to redistribute and broaden power and influence among the membership.

While the overall size of standing committees is no longer prescribed by rule but rather is the composite result of elections of Majority and Minority Members pursuant to ratios informally negotiated between the two leaderships, all Members including the chairmen must be elected to standing committees by the House. This ratification is normally a pro forma matter through separate Majority and Minority resolutions from the respective caucuses. Disputes over ratios are usually unavailing to the Minority, since the Majority has the ability to adopt its own committee rosters while rejecting the Minority rosters if not reflective of these ratios. These elections also establish the seniority of each committee member by the order in which they are listed in the resolution. On occasion, newly elected committee members are specifically ranked ahead of others in order to accommodate leaves of absence granted by the party caucus or switches of party affiliation where past service is taken into account. Traditionally, deference to strict party loyalty is expected to prevent any influence by the other party in the selection of chairmen or ranking Minority members, and the privileged resolutions emerging from the respective caucuses ratifying those choices by the full House are adopted by voice vote without debate, absent issues of the ethics of the Member being elected.

House rules restrict the number of committees and subcommittees on which each Member can serve unless waivers are granted. This limit was the result of a reform imposed by the Republican majority in 1995 and has been retained by the switch in majority parties in 2007, to distribute more widely committee and subcommittee responsibility. On occasion it has been tacitly waived when no issue was raised in the House, in order that each party might populate all of its subcommittees with sufficient Members while retaining the proper Majority–Minority ratios. Members cease to serve on committees when they no longer belong to the conference or caucus which nominated them, but they cannot be removed by the House, once elected, unless the caucus or conference brings a privileged resolution to the floor directly removing them or changing the composition of a committee or unless the matter is raised as an ethics issue alleging misfeasance on the committee.

Beyond the diminution of the strict seniority system in the 1970s, a significant reform in committee membership rules came in 1995 with the advent of the Republican majority for the first time in forty years in the House. All committee and subcommittee chairmen were limited by House rule to three consecutive terms without mention of waiver. While that restriction could have been imposed merely by changing party conference rules, it was elevated to a House rule in order to make its waiver more difficult by requiring actual amendment to the House rule by the full House. In the 109th Congress in 2005 that rule was amended to provide an exception for the Chairman of the Committee on Rules, in order to continue the service of a chairman who had proved himself particularly effective in furthering the Majority leadership's agenda over six years. The rule was intended to restrict the accumulation of power by entrenched chairmen beyond six years. Senate Republicans emulated this House rule two years later in 1997 as a party policy (not a Senate rule) to likewise impose six consecutive year term limits on chairmen. When the Senate switched majorities in 2007, the new Democratic majority did not impose such a restriction on its chairmen.

At the beginning of the 110th Congress, when Democrats regained the majorities in both Houses, the rules were not changed in this respect. Several senior Democrats regained chairmanships which they had held prior to losing majority status in 1994, but with new six-year term limits imposed upon them (prior chairmanships or ranking Minority memberships not being counted against them). The new Republican Minority even sought to strictly impose the six-year limit on several former chairmen who had just served their three-term limit but who sought to gain ranking Minority member status under their conference rule. They were denied that status by a vote of their conference, which in effect held the six-year conference limit on chairmanships or on ranking Minority memberships to be cumulative, rather than a separate restriction on consecutive service in each position. This action represented an extreme view of term limits by combining the two senior positions into one for purposes of calculating the limit, so that for example a ranking Minority member serving four years in that capacity could under conference rules (although not House rule) only serve two years as chairman if his party regained the majority. That House rules should impose these arbitrary limits on service, rather than caucus or conference rules alone, symbolized the 'reform' steps which House leaders, together with their more junior rank-and-file Members, have taken to minimize the accumulation of political power at the committee level over lengthy periods of time, and to centralize that power within the elected party leadership. Thus when the Majority party leadership desires to give a 'waiver' to a chairman to serve more than six years, it first needs to amend House rules, rather than merely grant the waiver within the caucus or conference to permit the longer consecutive committee service. Some would argue that elected chairmen become 'lame ducks' as early as their second term, as their long-term power and influence was perceived to be diminished, at least in the eyes of special interests intent upon influencing public policy and particularly capable of financial contributions to political action committees of their potential successors. The term-limit requirement was repealed in the House in the 111th Congress following defeat by secret ballot in the Majority caucus of an incumbent chairman's bid to be renominated upon being challenged by a junior member of his committee. That caucus action demonstrated the fundamentally political nature of the choice of chairman and the lack of need to impose arbitrary service limits. The Senate retained its term-limit rule on chairmen.

A major difference between Democratic and Republican caucus rules with respect to selection of chairmen involves the weighting of votes in the steering committees which submit nominations to the caucus or conference. In the Democratic Steering Committee each member has one vote, including the top elected leadership. In the Republican Steering Committee, by contrast, the Speaker has five votes and the Majority Leader three, while all other regional and whip members have only one, a weighting in favour of the elected party leadership. In return, Members vying to become chairmen to replace their term-limited or retiring predecessors must make presentations to the Steering Committee, based not only upon plans for committee organization and accomplishment of party strategies, but also upon financial contributions to leadership and Member Political Action Committees (PACs) from their own political funds. The new political party majority leadership in the House in the 110th Congress, while retaining the six-year term limit on chairmen for one Congress, also retained the secret ballot process permitting nomination of other candidates in the caucus. It resulted in the defeat of the most senior incumbent chairman in the 111th Congress.

In the Senate, organization of its committees in each Congress is undertaken to establish memberships and rules of procedure, despite the Senate being a 'continuing body' for purposes of the establishment of its standing committees and conferral of legislative and oversight jurisdiction. In its standing rules, all Senators are re-elected to committees at the beginning of each Congress, with new Senators included in an intended order of seniority. Whenever a vacancy occurs on a Senate committee, the party leader submits a resolution re-establishing the seniority of all Senators, not merely that of the Senator filling the vacancy. All committees are required to organize by 1 March of each first session by adoption of committee rules for printing in the Record, although roll-call votes in committees are not required. Under Senate Rule XXV, Chairmen of full committees may not also serve as subcommittee chairmen of any committee. Unlike the House, where the Majority controls committee ratios by virtue of voting power in the House although negotiations are undertaken, in the Senate committee ratios must be actively negotiated between the Majority and Minority Leader, since absent an accommodation each resolution electing Senators to committees is filibusterable. The roles of the Majority and Minority party Conferences are to follow the recommendations of their respective 'Steering Committees' regarding committee memberships. Any rules which govern those conferences, including secret ballot voting, are not publicly available.

The importance of campaign money in politics is discussed in a number of contexts, including ethics (page 523), elections (page 128), and campaign financing at page 132. The assignment of committee chairmanships influenced by the trend toward Member-to-Member financial political contributions in exchange for enhanced status for the contributor was just beginning to be perceived by the press and public as an area needful of 'reform', based on ethical and criminal allegations in 2006. Those ongoing investigations attempt to trace contributions from lobbyists to senior Members' campaign accounts. Contributions to leadership PACs from those aspiring chairmen out of their own PACs have followed. Upon assuming chairmanships some have influenced enactment of special-interest legislation from their committees supported by those contributing lobbyists.

The new House Democratic majority in 2007 reverted to a seniority basis in its first selection of standing committee chairmen, thereby initially avoiding the financial contribution expectations which characterized chairmanship replacements of their term-limited predecessors. The fact remains that both party leaderships assess their Members for contribution to PACs to support their vulnerable colleagues and candidates regardless of a quid pro quo based upon promised chairmanships. This runs counter to the reforms that motivated the elimination of the seniority system—namely a determination to more broadly distribute power based on legislative competence as well as on accountability to party leadership political agendas. That accountability is increasingly measured in dollar terms. The burgeoning practice of Members' contributions to political funds of colleagues of their own choosing, or under pressure from leadership, minimizes the expectation that Members' ascent to power and influence will be based only on legislative competence. The practice may have had its modern roots in the Democratic Caucus in 1978 when a junior committee member contributed his own unused campaign funds to other colleagues on his own committee who in turn supported (on a secret ballot) his candidacy for a subcommittee chairmanship over more senior committee member. Recent debates in Congress over improprieties in campaign financing have not focused on Member-to-Member contributions and their impact on the legislative process. While each House under its separate rule-making authority is free to consider internal ethics restrictions limiting contributions among Members, the importance of fund-raising advantages, from whatever source, to and between incumbents in both Houses, cannot be overstated and must at a minimum be made transparent enough to enable the public to discern the impact on the legislative process.

The work of select committees in Parliament

The approach adopted by the investigative select committees in the Commons is more or less uniform, not varying much according to particular inquiries, though of late imaginative new methods of collecting information have been tried out by individual committees (see pages 375–6). The modus operandi of Lords Committees is very similar to that in the Commons.

Evidence in written or oral form relevant to the topic the committee has selected comes from ministers, officials, statutory boards and agencies, experts from industry, commerce and academic life, and private individuals. Some will have been invited to contribute personally, others respond to a general call for evidence. Oral testimony is overwhelmingly heard in public: written evidence is also received. Committees deliberate in private, as in Washington. The scale of the operation is substantial. In 2007–8, a total of over 2,800 witnesses, official and non-official, gave evidence to Commons select committees, subcommittees, and joint committees.

The remarkable growth in importance of Commons select committee work over the past three decades is perhaps best illustrated by the growth in the frequency of meeting of select and joint committees including their subcommittees, as set out in Table 8.2 in the Annex.

In addition, all committees related to government departments and a number of others are authorized to appoint subcommittees drawn from the membership of the main committee, to take evidence and report to the main committee on specific aspects of the topic of concern to it. Use of the power varies. In 2007–8, for instance, only five of the departmentally related committees (see page 361) appointed subcommittees, though one appointed six subcommittees and another two.

There are no substantive rules about the choice of sitting days or the notice necessary to be given for select committee meetings in Westminster, which reflects the relaxed, usually non-partisan approach of British select committees by comparison with Washington. A minority of a committee has no power to call a meeting and no collective right to a proportion of the committee's time with witnesses. In the UK there are no set time limits on or control of the number of interventions. Everything is left to the good sense of the chairman.

Although some of the most successful select committee initiatives have involved hearing evidence without making a report, it is more usual for a report to be made to the House and published, detailing the committee's conclusions along with most of the oral and written evidence on which the committee relied. Minority reports are not strictly permitted, though alternative drafts or particular amendments voted down in committee are easily enough found in the committee's formal record of its proceedings. There are no mandatory requirements as to the contents of reports, as there are in Washington.

It is normal for the relevant government department to reply with its views on a Commons committee's conclusions within two months of the publication of the report, either by publishing a document themselves or by communicating with the committee, which will annex the reply to a Special Report of its own. In the Lords, six months is allowed, except for the European Union Committee and joint committees.

Some departments appear to be better than others in keeping to the Commons timetable. The Liaison Committee's review of the 2007–8 session accepted in general that the two-month limit was not always attainable, though they thought it should not be for committees to have to chase up tardy departments. Some committees however reported that there had been a distinct decline in the arrival of prompt responses to reports (Culture, Media and Sport); one spoke of 'government lethargy' (Communities and Local Government); another found departmental performance variable (Justice), while the Public Administration Committee received only one reply within the permitted time scale in 2007–8 and another eighteen months late, without any explanation. These skirmishes apart, complete if not fully satisfactory replies are important, for without timely responses the impetus generated by a committee report can easily be dissipated. More frequently than in past years, however, committees make a point of returning to subjects previously considered in order to assess progress. The greater number of opportunities now provided for debating select committee reports in the Commons (see pages 55, 379) also provides a means of ensuring that the appropriate tempo is kept up.

Parliamentary select committees: patterns of work

To be fully effective, select committee work must be systematic. Departmentally related committees of the Commons should cover their wide areas of responsibility methodically, setting their own priorities, chasing developments and monitoring outcomes, responsive to public concerns but not cherry picking topics solely on the basis of their capacity to generate national or constituency headlines. Progress has sometimes been patchy. Growing amounts of financial information, admittedly sometimes hard to interpret, and fact-filled departmental Annual Reports only slowly found a response in select committee work (see pages 262–3). The Commons Liaison Committee admitted (while conceding that there never was a golden age from which standards had fallen away) that the problem was not the House's powers but the ability and willingness of the House and Members to scrutinize such matters in the degree of detail required to hold the government to account. Nor did the increase in the number and influence of regulatory and other statutory agencies always command the attention that it might have. Nevertheless, progress is being made—2007–8 was the first year every departmental select committee took oral evidence on the relevant departmental Annual Report—assisted by the development of a list of common or core objectives.

When the prospect of such a list first surfaced, there were concerns that such a coordinated approach would encroach on the independence of individual committees, but the Liaison Committee declared that committees 'belong to the House. The House has the right to spell out what they expect of them.' In particular, committees were reminded of the desirability of following up earlier reports, something scarcely ever attempted in earlier sessions. Finally, in May 2002, the House agreed to a list of common objectives—some of them the subject of stout resistance only a few sessions earlier—which the Liaison Committee was invited to elaborate.

What was produced was to be guidance or a central agenda rather than a mechanical checklist. Select committees should cover all areas of government activity, not limiting themselves to a governmental agenda. With a view to producing reports which are capable of being debated, government department-related committees are to:

Examine policy proposals from the UK government and the European Commission, in Green Papers, White Papers, draft guidance &c., and to inquire further where the committee thinks it appropriate;

Identify and examine areas of emerging policy, or where existing policy is deficient and make proposals;

Conduct scrutiny of any draft bill within the committee's responsibilities;

Examine specific output from the department, expressed in documents or other decisions;

Examine the expenditure plans and out-turn of the department, its agencies and principal non-departmental public bodies;

Examine the department's Public Service Agreements, the associate targets and the statistical measurements employed;

Monitor the work of the department's executive agencies, non-departmental public bodies, regulators and associated public bodies;

Scrutinize major appointments made by the department; and

Examine the implementation of legislation and major policy initiatives.

The latest general report from the Liaison Committee reveals how the core tasks have become the framework of methodical scrutiny.[12] An analysis of committees' impact on policy ranges from the closure of Post Offices to the reform of postgraduate medical training. As part of its review of public service agreements and targets, the Defence Committee found that for seven of the last eight years and every year since 2002, the Armed Services had been operating at or above the level they were resourced to deliver. In monitoring the work of agencies, committees looked into bodies as various as Network Rail, the National Institute for Health and Clinical Excellence, the Copyright Tribunal, and the Ordnance Survey.

Notwithstanding the need to concentrate and systematize, select committee reports (excluding evidence from which a report did not flow) still manage to cover a large area of interesting ground in the course of a session. In 2007–8, reports covered matters as various as Energy prices, the 2012 Olympics, Domestic Violence, and—particularly topically—Banking Reform and 'The run on the Rock' (Northern Rock, a troubled bank in which the government was obliged to take a large stake). Subject reports of this kind are the staple fare of committees, but in 2007–8, three bills then before the House were the subject of reports by select committees, other than the Joint Committee on Human Rights, which considers every bill. A fourth committee kept a watching brief on four bills, though no intervention was thought necessary.

European policy initiatives also interested committees other than European Scrutiny. Among the topics covered in 2007–8 were the Galileo Project (a global navigation satellite system being built by the European Union and the European Space Agency) and the foreign affairs aspects of the EU Lisbon treaty.

It is now more than a decade since the Modernisation Committee, as part of the drive to improve parliamentary scrutiny of legislation, suggested that the government should refer more bills to committees in draft. Government of course retains the initiative in such an arrangement. The subsequent development of the proposal is discussed at pages 463–5.

The scope of select committee work is therefore very wide, and continues to widen. Apart from their role as the eyes and ears of Parliament they have, as the Commons Public Administration Committee observed in its comparison of select committees with official inquiries, become adept at filling gaps in cases where the government has not been prepared to hold any other type of investigation.[13]

The working methods of select committees in both Houses have become much more imaginative. There are pre-inquiry and post-inquiry seminars. Witness feedback may be sought. Both European Scrutiny Committees, for example, participate in COSAC, a regular meeting of all similar committees in the member States of the EU and in a meeting of chairmen of the European Committees of Parliament and the devolved assemblies. The Committee visited several candidate countries before the latest enlargement, and makes a practice of visiting the Parliament of the country about to assume the six-monthly presidency of the European Council. The Commons Foreign Affairs Committee regularly meets its counterpart in the European Parliament. The Business and Enterprise Committee makes regular visits to Brussels in order to keep abreast of

EU policy and regulations. The Culture, Media and Sport Committee held an inquiry in 2007–8 into an EU policy paper. All select committees are authorized to share their papers with committees in the devolved jurisdictions. The Welsh Affairs Committee meets committees of the National Assembly for Wales to consider legislation proposed for Wales which will come before the Houses at Westminster.[14] Committees have power to meet concurrently with others, of which the most striking example is the Quadripartite Committee on Arms Export Controls comprising Defence, Foreign Affairs, International Development, and Business, Enterprise and Regulatory Reform.

The information gathered by committees traditionally arrived, by request or spontaneously, from witnesses who appeared before them for questioning and from written papers. Now however, evidence has been gathered by video link from (for example) children in Uganda. Going beyond the traditional constituency of ministers, officials, and academic and other experts, committees have heard in confidence from serving soldiers in the course of inquiries into the duty of care as it affects military recruits and (by web forum) into army medical services. A thousand inmates of HM Prisons were consulted on their daily activities, and the outcome was, as the Liaison Committee commented, 'a picture significantly bleaker than that provided by Home Office statistics'. Online consultation was held with those who believed they could assist an inquiry into human reproductive technology, but were not identified as would have been the case had they submitted written evidence. On more than one occasion, national radio programmes drew attention to impending inquiries and actively facilitated the participation of any listener who thought they could assist.

Committees employ a much wider range of informal methods of keeping in touch with their stakeholder communities than in earlier years. These have included preparatory seminars and conferences which in turn deepen Members' understanding of the field of their concern. Some have arranged regular 'question times' in committee for ministers who sit in the Lords and would otherwise not be subjected to Commons Questions.

Congressional committee staffs

The size of House committee staffs is governed by Rule X, clause 9, which limits to thirty the number of professional staff each committee (other than Appropriations, which is not limited in number) may appoint, with not more than one-third of that number being appointed by the minority. Those numbers may be supplemented by investigative staff (including consultants and contract employees) pursuant to biennial committee budget resolutions adopted by the House. Thus the total number of employees above thirty per House committee becomes a function of the amount of funding available every two years in the committee funding resolution. Committees are also permitted to employ 'shared' or 'associate' staff whose salaries are partially paid by Members' office allowances, subject to overall availability of funds. Committee members and staff are under the same restrictions pertaining to authorization of the full committee chairman for committee-related travel and the use of committee or 'counterpart' funds therefor, including reimbursement for per diem expenses at rates established by Federal law. All such expenses must be publicly disclosed in the Record. In the Senate under Rule XXVII there are no limits on the number of committee staff stated in the standing rules, nor is there a guarantee of a certain ratio to the Minority. Rather, staff allocation 'should reflect' the overall ratio of Senators from each party and such employees shall be accorded 'equitable treatment'.

Assistance to parliamentary select committees

Though the days when each Commons committee was served by one Clerk and a secretary, and chairmen drafted reports themselves, are not quite out of living memory, the degree of support given to select committees has grown steadily to a level more nearly satisfactory than was the case in 1979. At the same time, the level of staffing—typically six to eight persons—is modest by comparison with Congress, and it is exclusively non-partisan.

Many select committees in both Houses have power to appoint advisers 'to supply information which is readily available or to elucidate matters of complexity'. In 2007–8, the great majority of Commons committees had fewer than ten advisers, though a handful of committees had more, up to eighteen. The choice of individuals and the number employed (though committees do not have assigned budgets) is wholly a matter for the members of the committee. Some advisers will contribute over the entire range of the committee's interest, and may continue in post Parliament after Parliament. Others are appointed for shorter duration, as their expertise is valuable for perhaps only one inquiry. For the most part, the appointments are uncontroversial (though there has quite recently been a division in a committee over an appointment). Unsullied political non-alignment is not of course insisted on in the engagement of these advisers, but in general appointment of high-profile party warriors is tacitly avoided.

The staff of the Committee proper is headed by the Committee Clerk, with perhaps a second Clerk, and support and administrative staff. In addition, on the inside of the tent in distinction to the specialist advisers outside it, are a group of 'committee specialists', with up-to-date skills of direct use and immediately available to the committee and its Clerks. In the Lords, the number of staff in the Committee Office alone rose from twenty-nine in 1999–2000 to fifty-seven in 2007–8.

The modest level of staffing has long been a constraint on the scope and depth of Commons select committee work, given the breadth of interest of each committee. The problem was tackled by the creation, in 2002, of the Scrutiny Unit, a specialized group of about eighteen, comprising parliamentary staff and others seconded from—for example—the National Audit Office. In addition, experts in various subjects are employed on short-term contracts. The Unit assists and may brief any select committee in its investigations, on request, particularly though not exclusively in the fields of analysis of Estimates, departmental annual reports, regulatory impact assessments, and resource accounts. The Unit compiles examples of best practice in financial scrutiny, and backs up select committee pressure towards the improvement of the financial information provided to Parliament. Training workshops are run for Members, to assist them in understanding resource accounting for example, and a guide is prepared for the use of members of committees on financial management and parliamentary scrutiny. Support is also given to select and joint committees on the legal background to draft bills. The Scrutiny Unit coordinates the evidence-taking sessions of public bill committees (see pages 441–2).

Select committees have made varying use of its resources, but even in the relatively short period of its existence, the Unit has proved particularly helpful in cross-departmental aspects of inquiries, and committees have frequently expressed their appreciation.

Parliamentary select committees: outcomes

Select committees at Westminster exist to scrutinize and not to substitute for government, and in that context what is striking about their progress over the past two decades is the quantity of information which they have brought into the public domain, and the steady growth in their—and therefore Parliament's—authority. If, as an early twentieth-century British statesman remarked, democracy is government by explanation, then committees have been transformed from a rather dull low-level interchange between politics and government to a forum for real democratic engagement. Parliament, however, ought to be more than a forum: it must also be a contributor, and so the quality of select committee outcomes needs to be considered as well as the quantity.

Two measures of the growth of select committee authority are worth noticing. The first is the increasingly confident assertion of committee views on government performance, not to the exclusion of commendation where praise was deserved (as it often was) but as part of a critical dialogue between legislature and executive. In much the same vein was the conclusion of the Foreign Affairs Committee that the Foreign and Commonwealth Office displayed 'a disturbing aversion...to proper scrutiny of its activities', that the department had 'failed seriously in its duty to the Committee' in withholding information about fraud and shown a 'woeful lack of performance skills and a disturbing series of failures in senior...management'.[15] The Ministry of Defence was denounced for giving 'the strong impression that, in its view, the important factor is providing information to and satisfying the requirements of the Treasury: parliamentary approval is to be regarded as a rubber stamp...Telling Parliament that the costs of deployment to Afghanistan is "around a billion" is just not good enough.'[16]

Secondly, an assessment of the number of committee recommendations adopted by government may stand as a rough indication of the 'success' or otherwise of select committee policy prescriptions. In general, the major influence of a committee report on government policy is sometimes freely admitted. Some detailed proposals are accepted outright, others as clearly turned down. In many cases, a guarded and polite response amounting to disagreement is quietly reversed, with or without acknowledgement, in subsequent months or years.

Many others have a concern for the outcome of select committee inquiries beyond government, and their independent judgements point to the growth in the status of committee reports. The Lords Science and Technology Committee's report on travel and health was applauded by the British Medical Association as 'generally agreed to be the most authoritative and detailed study of aviation health issues yet written'.[17] The same committee's findings on the application of science to heritage preservation evoked 'particular interest in the USA, where the committee's findings resonate well with conservation scientists who find themselves operating in a similar policy vacuum to that revealed in England'.[18]

While all a committee's conclusions may be taken forward over time by a many-sided dialogue involving the committees, government departments, agencies, academic and other experts, and private interests or pressure groups, there can be no substitute for parliamentary debate in maintaining effective pressure on government to justify their response to a report. Committees therefore have an interest in turning the spotlight on to most of their reports, and doing so with the maximum degree of topicality. Given the constraints of parliamentary time, this is very much a zero-sum game as between committees, and governments are naturally reluctant to surrender much prime time for business other than their own. Consequently, by no means all committee reports are debated in the Commons, but the proportion discussed has increased very substantially since 1978–9.

It is the practice in the Lords to debate all reports of investigative committees, unless they are made simply for information. Regular opportunities for debate in the Commons are much more limited and fall into two categories. On three days in every session, Estimates chosen by the Liaison Committee are before the House for discussion, which in practice means that debate concentrates on one or more committee reports selected for their topicality and interest. The formal peg on which debate hangs is the granting of Supply to the Crown, and amendments to reduce the sums may be moved and divided on: but such occasions are not frequent. More frequent are those where relatively few Members except those who served on the Committee speak in the debate, an outcome actually secured by the rules in Washington, but a matter of regret in Westminster. In some sense, the purpose of the debate may be achieved: government is obliged in public to defend the decision it has taken on the committee's recommendations. On the other hand, the Estimates are almost certainly not the best peg on which to hang these important debates—the Liaison Committee called them the least comprehensible of government spending documents,[19] and concluded that because of their artificiality there were too many general debates which presented less of a challenge to the government than might have been (see page 305).

In 2005–6, the time spent on the floor of the House in debates on select committee reports was just over fifteen and a half hours; in 2006–7, the figure was not quite sixteen and a half; in 2007–8, nineteen and a half. Against a sessional total of respectively 1,570, 1,120, and 1,427 hours of business on the floor, the claim of select committees is indeed modest.

Westminster Hall has to some extent come to the rescue. Standing Orders prescribe that on six Thursdays in a session, debate in Westminster Hall should focus on committee reports selected by the Liaison Committee. In practice, two-thirds of the Thursday debates are given over to committee reports. The total number of hours in Westminster Hall devoted to select committee reports was 66 out of a total of 532 in 2005–6, 57 out of 355 in 2006–7, and 62 out of 429 in 2007–8. Proportionately, select committees fare better in Westminster Hall than in the Chamber, but the figures still fall far short of what committees might expect, given the significance of their contribution to the effectiveness of Parliament. There has been pressure for a topical half-hour once a week in the Chamber in which views might be briefly exchanged on recent select committee reports. The Modernisation Committee in 2007 preferred a weekly slot of half an hour in Westminster Hall. Such a reform would roughly double the time given over to select committee in Westminster Hall, though of course there would be a corresponding diminution of time available for private Members to raise issues of their choice.

The Liaison Committee has observed, with justification, that greater focus and point would be given to these debates if they were held on a substantive motion, rather than an anodyne motion that the report has been considered. The Modernisation Committee agreed. It is hard to see what grounds for objection or delay may be. Admittedly, debate on a substantive motion critical of the government might put government members of the—bipartisan—committee in a difficult position. But since no divisions may arise in Westminster Hall—a point not addressed by the Leader of the House when this matter was debated[20]—the possibility is of limited significance. A more cogent objection would be that such a change would risk importing party controversy into select committee work. It is a difficult judgement, but on balance a risk worth taking.

Notes

1. *House Practice*, ed W. Holmes Brown and Charles W. Johnson (2003), 235, 253.
2. Gladstone remarked in 1855 that though 'a committee is extremely well-fitted to investigate truth in its more general forms, by bringing every possible form of thought to bear on the points before it...it is also well-fitted for overloading every question with ten or fifteen times the quantity of matter necessary for its consideration...'; quoted in Public Administration Committee First Report 2004–5 HC 51-I para 15.
3. A number of occasions, from the First World War to the 1990s, on which select committees were considered not to be appropriate in such cases is to be found ibid, paras 208 ff.
4. HC Deb (2005–6) 451 c 163 ff.
5. Liaison Committee, First Report 2008–9 HC 291 paras 78–81; and Children, Schools and Families Committee, Second Report 2008–9 HC 47 para 30.
6. Mr Peter Luff on 28 October 2008 (HC Deb (2007–8) 481 c 852).
7. Lords Procedure Committee First Report 2008–9 HL 39 paras 13–15.
8. *Henry IV, Part I*, Act III, scene i.
9. In *McGrain v Daugherty*, the US Supreme Court ruled that 'a legislative body cannot legislate wisely or effectively in the absence of information respecting the conditions which the legislation is intended to affect, or to change; and where the legislative body does not itself possess the requisite information...recourse must be had to others who do possess it. Experience has taught that mere requests for information often are unavailing...so some means of compulsion are essential to obtain what is needed' (273 US 135 at 174–5 (1927)).
10. Communications Committee, First Report HL 122-I (2007–8) paras 366–73, and HL Deb (2007–8) 705 c 278.
11. Clause 5(c)(1) of Rule X.
12. First Report 2008–9 HC 291.
13. First Report, HC 51-I (2004–5), para 197. Examples given are the inquiries into arms for Iraq in the mid-1990s and more recently the duty of care in army barracks.
14. Typically, when this remarkable arrangement was first agreed, in which Members of the Commons take part formally in the proceedings of another legislative body and vice versa, the House seems to have drawn comfort from a precedent of the 1930s, when Indian princes sat with the Joint Committee on Indian Constitutional Reform (Procedure Committee, Third Report Joint Activities with the National Assembly for Wales, 2003–4 HC 582 para 6).
15. Foreign Affairs Committee Second Report 2005–6 HC 522, paras 23, 48, and 69.
16. Defence Committee Fourth Report 2005–6 HC 980, paras 14 and 18.
17. Fifth Report 1999–2000 HL 121.
18. Eighth Report 2006–7 HL 168 para 9.
19. Second Report 2007–8 HC 426.
20. HC Deb (2006–7) 465 c 449.

9

Legislation

The general background

For obvious historical reasons, many of the technical terms used in the passage of legislation are common to Parliament and Congress. What now lies behind these terms, however, may often vary. At Westminster, the government in theory depends on but in practice dominates the majority in the lower House: because of constitutional separation of powers that is not true of Congress. Secondly, for reasons which are historical rather than constitutional, the Chambers remain the engine room of legislative work at Westminster, while law making in Washington has, almost from the beginning, been dominated by standing committees.

Article I, section 1 of the US Constitution begins by providing that 'all legislative powers herein granted shall be vested in a Congress of the United States, which shall consist of a Senate and House of Representatives'. Further, Article I, section 5 provides that 'each House may determine the Rules of its Proceedings'. Upon this elegant yet simple grant of legislative powers and rule-making authority has grown an exceedingly complex and evolving legislative process, much of it unique to each House of Congress, and defined not merely by changes in law and in rules but documented or understood by practice, precedent, custom, and tradition.

Jefferson asserts that one of the most practical safeguards of the British and American democratic way of life is this legislative process under established rules, emphasizing the protection of the minority, allowing ample opportunity to all sides to be heard.[1] Commitment to a deliberative, fair, and transparent process is in jeopardy in contemporary Congresses, especially in the House of Representatives, where utilization of party discipline and the unique ability to change rules on an ad hoc basis virtually overnight by majority vote allows the Majority to impose its will at the plenary stage. This is accomplished by minimizing consideration of amendments otherwise permissible under standing rules and under earlier practice, by expediting consideration prior to sufficient availability of measures to Members, by marginalizing Minority participation during negotiations between the Houses, and by maximizing the Majority leadership's own agenda, often even without formal standing committee endorsement. It will be a focus of this work to examine this dichotomy. To a certain extent, this trend in the US House is balanced by the fact that a proposal cannot become a law without consideration and approval by both Houses of Congress. As the Senate guarantees its Minority and each individual Senator an inordinate amount of leverage over its agenda by insistence on its tradition of unlimited debate and amendment (whether or not germane) and by preventing the consideration of many measures by refusals to invoke cloture by a three-fifths vote at a preliminary stage, an eventual balance is arguably struck if one measures overall Minority rights in a bicameral system, although the minorities are not always of the same political party in each House. An overall imbalance remains if one assumes a majoritarian process suggested in both Houses by the Constitution itself (super-majority procedure in the Senate is nowhere mentioned) in contrast with rapidly increasing use in the Senate of the cloture rule requiring three-fifths votes to permit consideration. By an examination of the complexities of the legislative process in each House, especially comparing wholesale departures from tradition in the House with insistence upon very different traditions in the Senate, it is hoped that the reader will be led to a more complete understanding of the anomalies of process in Congress and their impact on the formulation of public policy. To this end, the discussion of House and Senate procedure is contrasted and commingled throughout, rather than portrayed in entirely separate formats, in hopes that the reader will gain a sense of the complexity of the Congress, taken together.

In Parliament as in Congress, democratically elected majorities must and do prevail. The duke of Wellington's maxim that the Queen's government must go on is as valid today as ever it was. Government interests are predominant in striking the ever-necessary balance between business and time in the Commons, whether in terms of motions limiting the time for debate, programme motions with the effect of bypassing debate on a large number of otherwise orderly amendments to bills, or in any other way. What the Rules Committee proposes to the House of Representatives by way of altering normal procedures so as to expedite business in the interests of the Majority may sometimes be remarkably similar to one of the sterner government business motions in the House of Commons. That said, however, Jefferson's concern for the minority and their right to be heard suffers less hurt at Westminster than in the land of his birth. The rules of the House may be regularly modified but they are not normally 'changed on an ad hoc basis virtually overnight'.

A non-partisan Speakership, even-handedly overseeing the application of rules and orders restricting debate—calling Members to speak, selecting amendments or deciding on when debate is to be brought to an untimely end, for example—is able to moderate the power of the majority before it gets its way—as it must in the end. What is more, the office of Speaker represents the House over against the government when their interests collide. He or she will for example rebuke the government in public if important information on a matter of public interest is released to the press before being made available to Members.

A few Members manage not only to represent their electorates and their parties but to be 'House of Commons men'—they are usually men—who learn the intricacies of the House's practice. Never many, they were present in the Parliaments of Tudor England and are still in evidence today. Other Members, however loyal in principle to their political interest, will when they believe injustice is being done or commonsense abandoned openly agree with the opposite benches.

Finally, though the relationships between the party whips—the 'usual channels'—are confidential and it is impossible to say how far a government has in any particular case listened to Opposition protests at what they intend, the scratchy state of the House when contact breaks down seems to indicate that normally a working relationship exists. Indeed, well within living memory, a Conservative and a Labour Deputy Chief Whip shared a personal friendship, despite their differing political allegiances and responsibilities.

Where the initiative lies in proposing and amending legislation

In contemporary Congresses, the potential of the Presidential veto of legislation which derives from Article I, section 7 of the Constitution suggests that the Executive branch take certain initiatives in triggering the legislative process. While Congress remains institutionally capable of starting the legislative ball rolling on any issue at any time during its two-year existence, the expectation that Congress will not immediately embark on a measure or matter which, requiring eventual enactment into law by the President, does not have the advance blessing of the Executive, suggests that Congress will often defer to or collaborate with the Executive in the initial formulation of policy and of budgetary measures so as to minimize failure of enactment at the end of the process. Congressional initiatives often originate with House or Senate committees or with individual leaders or Members, as well as with party organizations and outside interest groups, but advance accommodations with the Executive on matters requiring Presidential signature are preferable from a time-saving perspective to confrontations ultimately requiring two-thirds votes in each House to overcome. This trend is especially evident in an era in which Members of Congress and their leaderships prefer not to be in actual session for prolonged periods of time dealing with unpredictable responses from the Executive, and to rely on a sense of certainty of time and issue when finally approving measures with the advance acquiescence of the President. The political majorities represented in both Houses and in the White House heavily influence the willingness of Congress to defer to Executive initiatives in proposing and amending legislation. Agenda-setting leaderships are more likely to schedule Executive recommendations at committee and plenary levels where they have conceptually emerged from the same political party's platform.

The distinction between law which establishes national public policy and law which provides budgetary authority is discussed in greater detail in the chapter on the power of the purse at page 267. The enactment of revenue and policy legislation is not as dependent on an annual fiscal timetable as is the enactment of budget authority, but the two obviously overlap when one acknowledges that public policy enacted into law is often reflected in the level and duration of fiscal support for that policy. There has emerged a complex body of statutory law which 'sunsets' policy, revenue, and Appropriations enactments and which, when read together with the rules of each House, tend to assure that subsequent Congresses and Executive administrations will be required as a matter of law and rule making to periodically review and re-enact expiring provisions over the course of a Congress. One might assume, based on a review of constitutional provisions which vest in Congress many itemized legislative authorities (to appropriate funds from the Treasury, borrow money, and raise and collect taxes (Article I, section 8, 9)) that all such initiatives would be conceived by the Legislative branch. In reality, it is often the Executive branch which, particularly mindful of the need to perpetuate its Administration, takes the initiative in important policy and funding formulations.

The Budget and Accounting Act of 1921 established a new budget system that permitted all items relating to a department to be brought together in the same bill, required the President to submit an annual national budget to Congress in place of the previous uncoordinated agency submissions, and created the Office of Management and Budget to assist him in this respect. This annual budget submission is required by the first Monday in February of each Calendar year, and symbolizes the acknowledgement that Congress defers to the President in the initiation of the annual budget for which Congress is primarily responsible. The 'blueprint' of the President's budget serves as the basis for subdivision of its components to the various House and Senate Appropriations subcommittees, as well as a list of recommendations for changes in existing law within the jurisdiction of various authorizing committees.

In addition, the Congressional budget process in law discussed at page 228 also assumes initiation of the annual budget and appropriations processes by the submission of the President's annual budget blueprint in February of each year. Pursuant to section 300 of the Congressional Budget Act of 1974, the Congressional timetable begins with the President's submission of his budget by the first Monday in February each year. Then, the Congressional Budget Office has less than two weeks to submit its report on the President's budget to the House and Senate Budget Committees, and within six weeks all committees submit their views and estimates to the Budget Committees.

Fundamental to an understanding of the initiation of the Congressional budget process, and the ability to initiate policy changes, is the distinction between authorizations and appropriations (further developed in the chapter on Power of the Purse). This two-step, presumably sequential, process is created by House and Senate rules and is reinforced by statute. Authorization laws once enacted establish, continue, or modify programmes or policies and give an agency or programme legal authority to operate. Until the 1950s most Federal programmes were permanently authorized, in that the basic law establishing the agency or programme was not 'sunsetted' and was intended to provide authorizations for appropriations on an annual basis for an indefinite period. Permanent authorizations remain in effect until changed by law and potentially relieve Congress of periodic responsibility of initiating extensions of lapsing authorities. In the 1960s and 1970s, authorizing committees won enactment of laws that converted many permanent authorizations into temporary authorizations. This change was precipitated by authorizing committees' determination for greater oversight over and control of Executive and Presidential activities, especially in view of the split in political majorities between the two branches and inter-branch tensions that stemmed from the Vietnam War and the Watergate scandal of the Nixon administration. Also, short-term authorizations put pressure on the appropriating committees to fund programmes at levels recommended by the authorizing panels. In contemporary Congresses, however, the legislative initiatives taken by authorizing committees have become minimized by a variety of factors, including the reluctance of committees comprised of the same political majority as the Executive to scrutinize and change departmental or agency authority. Also, the imposition in 1974 of the Congressional budget process has imposed a third level of decision making on Congress—the setting of functional category spending levels for Executive agencies and programmes for internal Congressional budgeting purposes, which has shifted the focus away from authorizing committees in setting spending levels for appropriations.

To the extent that authorization bills are enacted into law, they often are not enacted in a timely enough manner or sufficiently enforced to set binding limits on amounts and purposes of annual appropriations. Authorizations may be for one or more years, and such legislation typically recommends funding levels for programmes and agencies which serve as limits enforceable by points of order in both Houses. In practice, however, those authorization laws may not be enacted soon enough to establish the requisite statutory level of spending, and whether or not enacted are often waived in the House by special orders from the Rules Committee permitting unauthorized appropriations to be considered before the onset of the next fiscal year.

The affected department or agency often initiates the recommendation for continuation of its authority by means of an Executive Communication proposing draft legislation to that end. Those Executive branch recommendations are normally submitted in time to permit the authorizing committees to consider them and to report legislation before the onset of the fiscal year, but the ability of Congress to enact those recommendations into law in a timely manner is increasingly inhibited by the lack of urgency perceived by Members in finalizing an authorization into law prior to consideration of an annual appropriation. While House and Senate rules suggest such urgency, it is in practice replaced by a combined annual focus on the budget process and a realization that such procedural precondition can easily be waived in order to permit consideration of the appropriation bills actually carrying the budget authority and needful of enactment as a matter of law, before the fiscal year begins on 1 October.

The establishment of the authorization process is not mandated by the Constitution but rather is the result of adoption of rules in each House which attempt to require that annual appropriations should not be in order for consideration in either House until there has been enacted into law (not merely reported to or passed by one House) a law permitting the appropriation to be considered. Congress has employed this division of labour since the beginning of the Republic, as did the British Parliament in 1789 and the colonial legislatures. As Senator William Plumer of New Hampshire noted in 1806: 'Tis a good provision in the Constitution of Maryland that prohibits their legislature from adding anything to an appropriation law.' Generally called supply bills in the early Congresses, Appropriations bills had narrow purposes: to provide specific sums of money for fixed periods and stated objectives. Such bills were not to contain matters of policy.

The practice of adding 'riders' or extraneous policy provisions to Appropriations bills mushroomed in the 1830s, and delayed the enactment of supply bills. In 1837, the House adopted a rule requiring authorization bills to precede appropriations and to first be enacted into law. The Senate adopted a comparable rule shortly thereafter. In contemporary Congresses, however, the process has come almost full circle, with Appropriations bills once again containing numerous riders added by amendment in either Chamber's Appropriations Committees, on the floor of either House through waivers of points of order, and in final conference reports finalizing the two versions.

Initiatives for these efforts in the form of recommendations come from several directions, including the Executive branch, authorizing committees unable to finally process their separate legislation in a timely fashion, individual Members, and outside interest groups.

The role of the individual legislator in this three-step annual budget decision-making process and in the formulation of other legislation outside that cycle is as varied as the resulting legislative product itself. As explained in greater detail at page 387, any Member can introduce (with certain narrow exceptions) a measure on any subject at any time either House is in actual session. Executive branch-initiated business, while often recommended as a message or communication, must be formalized by a Member's introduction of a numbered bill. Individual Members, often the chairman of the relevant committee or subcommittee of jurisdiction in the case of Executive branch recommendations, become the official sponsors of the measure if only 'by request' (often meaning that the bill mirrors an Executive branch draft). The distinction between government bills and private Member's bills does not formally apply in the Congress under separation of powers, as the government is not 'in' the legislature, but in practice it becomes known upon introduction of legislation whether it has had its conceptual origin in the Executive branch or is rather the initiative of a Member of Congress.

Chairmen of committees often introduce legislation as a 'clean' bill which is the result of a committee or subcommittee 'markup' of an earlier bill or draft, in order for that committee to formally report a newly numbered bill to the House or Senate reflecting committee amendments. In that capacity, their initiative is more by direction of the committee, but the sponsorship and responsibility for its language remains that of the Member. Sponsorship can be by an unlimited number of Members, but the first named sponsor assumes the responsibility for listing all co-sponsors.

If in the House of Commons all time other than that which it chooses to surrender is the government's, it is hardly surprising that, though backbenchers introduce more bills than Her Majesty's Government, the great majority of public bills passed into law are government bills, and bills sponsored by private Members which have reached the statute book have often originated in pigeonholes in Whitehall. Details are to be found in Table 9.1 in the Annex.

By comparison, the fate of legislative proposals made by backbenchers is variable but never numerically significant, as is plain from Table 9.2 in the Annex.

A century ago, the picture was quite different. In 1900 for example, there were sixty-six government bills, but only just under half reached the statute book. There were 172 private Members' bills, of which a respectable 15 per cent became law.

In the more recent past, backbenchers' success rate has been volatile, and heavily dependent on how controversial their choice of subject matter turned out to be. In 1991–2, it reached 22 per cent and in 1996–7, 26.2 per cent. In the years immediately following those, however, the percentages plummeted to 10.5 per cent (1992–3) and 6.7 per cent (1997–8).[2] These poor figures may indicate a systemic but recent problem with backbenchers' access to time on the floor, or else that willingness to accept government 'hand-out' bills is diminishing. It has been argued that even when their bill is unsuccessful, Members will feel relatively satisfied with having raised an issue for public debate and crystallized their solution in print. If that is so, it is a pity; there are many forums in which public discourse can be carried on: only Parliament can make law.

Introduction and referral of bills: House of Representatives and Senate

Representatives and Senators sponsor public or private bills on any subject of interest to them whether or not at the request of the Executive branch or any other source, and in the House often with an unlimited number of co-sponsors, which under contemporary practice eliminates the need for separate introduction of the same bill by each Member. There is no particular ceremony or formality at the stage of introduction in the House, where the Member, Delegate, or Resident Commissioner from Puerto Rico (holding elective office and permitted by rules to introduce measures, once sworn in) signs the bill and places it in the hopper, which is the receptacle on the rostrum when the House is in session for receipt by the Clerk and referral by the Parliamentarian as the agent for the Speaker. Measures may only be introduced when the House is in session, and unanimous consent requests to permit introduction during any period of adjournment will not be entertained. Any number of bills or resolutions may be introduced by any Member who has taken the oath of office, and he need not seek recognition or permission of the House for that purpose. Once introduced, the measure becomes the property of the House. As such, the House may consider it notwithstanding the death, resignation, or replacement of its sponsor. Petitions (from private citizens or groups) or Memorials (from State legislatures) addressed to the House are delivered to the Clerk and may also be presented by the Speaker as well as by any Member for referral by the Parliamentarian. Again, the 'leave of the House' to present a petition is no longer required, and, unlike the House of Commons, no formal announcement is made other than a designation of number and referral in the Congressional Record and in the Journal.

Because the government is not the Majority Leadership in either House, but rather is a constitutionally separate Executive which can only recommend draft legislation, the actual bill or resolution must be formally introduced by a Member. Thus the role of individual Members in the context of bill introduction has an enhanced status. Only formally introduced measures, 'privileged general Appropriation bills' initiated by the Appropriations Committee, or measures which may come into existence upon the adoption of a special order of business become the numbered vehicles for possible enactment into law. All Members may propose 'public' bills, sponsored individually or jointly for the accomplishment of any general purpose, whether or not at the request of the government or any other group, but with the prime sponsor always assuming ultimate responsibility for their content. Committee and subcommittee chairmen or ranking Minority members will ordinarily be the prime sponsors of public bills whose introduction is recommended by an agency of the Executive branch, a draft of which may have been separately submitted and formally referred to the standing committee and numbered as an Executive communication.

A single Member may introduce a 'private' bill (they may not be co-sponsored), to enact law impacting specific persons or groups to change a status, respond to a claim, or provide a benefit. In practice, most private bills granting relief to individuals fall under one of five major categories: (1) bills involving claims against the United States, waiving claims by the Federal Government against specific individuals, or adjusting a status under Federal law such as patents, copyrights, or civil service; (2) bills excepting named individuals from certain requirements of the immigration or naturalization laws in hardship cases where the law would otherwise prohibit entry into or require deportation from the United States; (3) conveyances of real property rights; (4) tax or tariff treatment for private entities; and (5) vessel documentation. Private bills lack the generality of application that is normally found in public laws, and are utilized because public law cannot cover every situation that might arise. Congress may, as part of its general lawmaking function, create 'equitable law' to grant relief for a claim. This authority derives from the 1st Amendment, which sets forth the right to petition the government for the redress of grievances, and from Article I, which allocates to Congress the legislative authority to respond to a specific circumstance. Action on such a measure is regarded as a proper legislative function not constituting a Congressional intrusion into the judicial function.[3] The constitutional basis for private bills derives from the Congressional power to pay the debts of the United States.[4]

The practice of Congress in passing private bills for the benefit of specific persons or entities was taken from the British Parliament and began with the First Congress. The use of private bills steadily increased thereafter, to the extent that in some years Congress enacted more private bills than it did public bills. The 59th Congress, for example, enacted more than 6,000 private bills, while it enacted fewer than 700 public bills. In recent years, the number of private bills enacted into law has been steadily declining (as Congress has expanded administrative discretion to deal with many of the situations that theretofore gave rise to private bills) to the point where in the 105th Congress, only ten private bills were enacted into law. The introduction of private immigration relief bills was sharply curtailed when a particularly insidious administrative practice of the Immigration and Naturalization Service was ended in the 1970s. That agency had determined that the mere introduction, or reintroduction in subsequent Congresses, of a private bill preventing the deportation of a particular individual should stay the deportation of that individual for the duration of that Congress, by assuming the possibility that the bill might be enacted into law. While statistically very few such bills were enacted, the proliferation of their introduction by individual Members had become a corrupting influence which, not merely by coincidence, came to an end with the ascendancy of an ethics process in each House.

A House rule requires all private claims bills to be referred to the Committee on the Judiciary or to the Committee on Foreign Affairs if a foreign claim. Committee procedures for hearings, amendment, and reporting to the full Houses generally mirror subcommittee and full committee consideration of public bills. The Committee on the Judiciary refers private immigration and claims bills to its Subcommittee on Immigration, Border Security, and Claims, which generally takes no action unless its sponsor submits specified documentation and requests a hearing. The sponsor is generally the only witness at this hearing. The subcommittee makes available to Members' offices information on what documentation it requires, and the kinds of bills on which it is likely to take favourable action. It usually declines to report a bill if its records show few precedents for favourable House action in similar cases. Panels that handle other kinds of private bills have no similarly institutionalized procedures. Once a private bill is reported from committee, it is referred to the Private Calendar which is only called twice a month in the House. Private bills called on the Private Calendar are reviewed by an informal committee of 'official objectors' consisting of six Members—three from each party, appointed by their respective leaderships—to review reported private bills for consistency with announced policies. As a matter of policy, a reported bill must be on the Private Calendar for seven days before being called up. If two or more Members object to consideration of a bill when called in the order it appears on the Calendar, it is recommitted to the reporting committee, but more often a unanimous consent agreement to 'pass the bill over without prejudice' assures its being called on the next call of the Calendar. If a bill is called and there is no objection, it is considered 'in the House as in the Committee of the Whole', meaning that there is no period of general debate, but debate and germane amendment may occur under the five-minute rule. Usually little debate occurs and measures are disposed of by voice vote. Generally, the House and Senate devote little time to plenary consideration of private bills, as indicated by their scheduling in the House only two days each month, rather relying upon committee and objector screening to assure the propriety of such measures prior to their summary disposition on the call of the Calendar or by unanimous consent in the Senate. By tradition, private bills have not been scheduled by the Speaker for consideration under suspension of the rules discussed at page 197, as that procedure is confined to public bills, in order to avoid a proliferation of requests by individual Members. A noted example in the 109th Congress of a bill artificially drafted as a public bill and therefore eligible to be scheduled under suspension of the rules was the bill for the relief of Terri Schiavo discussed at page 7. On that occasion, language of general applicability was included in a separate section as a sense of Congress provision relating generally to the right to life issue, to permit its introduction as a public bill and its subsequent scheduling under suspension of the rules without a committee report or setting a precedent for what was essentially a private matter.

The distinction between private bills in the Congress (and in Parliament) and private Members' bills in Parliament must be made to avoid confusion. The description of a private bill in Congress goes to its nature as a measure addressing a specific person or entity, while in Parliament the term private Members' bill is used to describe an individual Member's sponsorship, rather than a ministerial or government sponsorship.

The number of public bills introduced in the last thirty-two years has declined because of rule changes permitting co-sponsorship, and because not all contemporary Congresses have generally comprised memberships envisioning, as during Democratic party majorities in the House and with a President of the same persuasion, an activist Federal legislative role. Commensurately, the political philosophy of the Republican Majority party in both Houses tended to reduce the number of days of legislative sessions, and the number of bills introduced and considered. When the Majority does not present as many contentious issues demanding a Federal response for consideration, Minority Members in the House are not in a position to place their own bills on the agenda beyond initial referral to standing committee (absent extraordinary bipartisan use of the 'discharge' rule discussed at page 426). There are no allotted 'Opposition days' as in the Commons for consideration of Opposition motions.

Coupled with a steady decline in the exercise of Member-attended oversight of the Executive branch (discussed in the chapter on Scrutiny and Oversight at page 315) the time of the Congress is freed up to permit Members to return to their districts for constituent service or fund-raising activities. Indeed, Majority Leaders of both parties in the last decade have ingratiated themselves to their rank and file by arranging legislative schedules on a weekly basis which permit the Members to be in their Congressional districts on most Fridays and Mondays, to return to the Congress by Tuesday evening for the first recorded votes of the week (a major incentive toward Members' attendance at that time being enhancement of their voting records).

This is not to say that individual Members' parochial legislative interests go unattended. An examination elsewhere in this work of the proliferation of 'earmarks' (special Congressionally initiated set-asides in spending or revenue bills for a small identifiable group of beneficiaries at page 281) reveals that Members have responded to requests from their constituents and other special interests for inclusion (often in conference reports for the first time) of such provisions in bills of more general applicability. In the 109th and 110th Congresses, the House adopted rule changes which, while not making earmarks illegal, partially required the identification of Members who had sponsored inclusion of earmarks, together with a disclaimer that the sponsoring Member did not stand to benefit from that inclusion. This proliferation has reduced the need for the separate introduction of public or private bills having as their primary purpose a financial benefit for a special interest. Because they are attached to 'must-pass' legislation, many earmarks have avoided separate committee and full House and Senate scrutiny. The 2007 enactment of a Senate-initiated lobbying reform bill contained a similar disclosure requirement applicable to that body as a standing rule.[5] That new Senate rule also proscribed the inclusion of 'Congressionally directed spending' 'air-dropped' into conference reports, absent a three-fifths waiver of points of order—a practice which had reduced the number of separately introduced special-interest bills in that body.

A Senator similarly signs the introduced measure and delivers it to the Parliamentarian as an agent of the presiding officer for referral. Often, Senators and Representatives submit statements for the Record or give floor speeches announcing introduction, but in the modern practice those steps are entirely incidental and ceremonial, as 'leave to introduce' such a measure by a vote of either House is not required. Regardless of the source of drafting and conceptual underpinning behind each measure (and those sources may include the Executive branch or any other interested individual or group) it is the elected Member who assumes the responsibility of introduction by affixing his signature to the written document. Unauthorized or fraudulent introduction has been considered an ethics violation in the House, and the primary sponsor's original signature directly affixed to the measure is an indispensable requirement for introduction. Additional sponsors may be added at any time up to final reporting merely by placing the list signed by the original sponsor in the hopper, but co-sponsors may be removed until that time only by unanimous consent in the House propounded by that co-sponsor or the original sponsor.

The circulation and public discussion of draft language prior to formal introduction is always an option to the sponsoring Member, and may include a formal communication if emanating from the Executive branch. Those communications, if Presidential messages, are delivered under seal and read to each House, and if communications not under Presidential seal or from other Executive officials, are letters delivered to the Offices of the Speaker and Secretary of the Senate and referred to committees by the Parliamentarians under the same jurisdictional rules and precedents as govern the referral of the bill or resolution when introduced. As a matter of constitutional separation of powers, there is no Minister of the executive who introduces the bill or resolution, since the constitutional restriction in Article I against holding incompatible offices prevents Executive branch officials from simultaneously being Members of either House. In practice, a draft submitted as an Executive communication may be introduced as a numbered bill by the chairman of the appropriate committee (sometimes with 'by request' indicated on the bill), or by that committee's ranking Minority member if the Executive is of a different political majority.

House rules preclude the introduction of certain public and private bills, including those of an obscene nature, those designating certain periods of time for holidays or celebrations, and (the Senate having a similar rule) private bills legislating claims against the government which are cognizable under the Federal Tort Claims Act, providing private pensions, constructing bridges across navigable streams and correcting military records. These restrictions against introduction were imposed over time to prevent proliferation of legislative responses to matters which are either considered too time consuming or separately addressable under administrative or judicial provisions in existing law. Additional restrictions in the rules added in 2001 prevent the consideration but not the introduction of measures designating a public work in honour of a sitting Member of Congress—a step designed to minimize that sort of self-serving legislation while Members are in office. A notable and sole exception from that general prohibition occurred in the 107th Congress, when a measure naming a Federal building after a beloved terminally ill sitting Member (Rep. Moakley, Mass.) was granted consideration by a special rule from the Rules Committee waiving that point of order.

From first reading to committee: Commons and Lords

The rationale of each of the several stages through which public bills must pass in Parliament is straightforward, but the unspoken assumptions underlying them are more complex. Legislative procedure has traditionally emphasized political argument rather than the consensus which takes account of the views of experts or electors. As a result, the credibility of the government, the party, and the individual minister has been closely bound up with bills more or less in the form in which they were introduced. Acceptance of amendments, however well argued or strongly supported outside the House, has sometimes tended to be regarded as political weakness. Those likely to be most affected by a proposed law must go early and privately to the department responsible and press the government to amend its own draft, since a later frontal approach in Parliament by the agency of a friendly Member is less likely to bring results. These understandings are however now under serious challenge. This part of the chapter will describe the basic procedure: changes under discussion are considered at pages 463ff.

Public bills take up just under two-fifths of the time of the Commons. In order to implement its legislative programme, a government must manage the use—by itself and others—of the critical scarce resource, time. The difficulty is to find an equitable balance between ever-growing demand—business, principally legislation—and the finite supply of time. Though the number of public bills has declined, their size and complexity have vastly increased. Through last century, the total number of pages in enacted bills per calendar year has moved steadily upwards. It began at 250 and reached nearly 1,500 in the years before 1939, and even within that period there were a few years where the total was almost 2,000 pages. After 1945, the upward march resumed. Total numbers of pages of legislation more than doubled between 1965 and 2003.[6] Length has accommodated (and been driven by) more complex prescription of detail in wider areas of life. As a result, the demands on parliamentary time, on government drafting resources, and on Members' expertise have expanded far beyond what earlier decades could have imagined. The days when a statute as important as the Official Secrets Act 1911 could be passed without recorded debate on key elements have long gone.

Private bills, in small numbers more or less comparable with those in contemporary Congresses (see above) have a career very similar in both Houses, which at first sight resembles that of public bills but on closer inspection is rather different. The distinction between the two categories is succinctly made by Erskine May's *Parliamentary Practice*. Private legislation confers 'particular powers or benefits on any person or body of persons—including individuals, local authorities, companies or corporations—in excess of or in conflict with the general law'.[7] In practice, none of the categories of private bill recognized in Congress (pages 387–8) is found in Parliament. In session 2008–9, for example, twelve bills were before Parliament, only one of them presented in that session, the rest having been or being in the process of being carried over from previous sessions. A number, promoted by local authorities, were concerned with street trading and consumer protection—private bills are often the vehicle for piloting locally potential changes in the general law; and several updated statutory authorities' miscellaneous powers. One private bill recalled the great days of such bills by extending to daughters of Freemen of Beverley, a borough in Yorkshire, the possibility of inheriting their fathers' status and adjusted the procedure for appointing the Beverley Pasture Master.

Such bills are introduced not by a Lord or Member but by the parties seeking the powers in question, who must prove the need for the bill: elaborate care is taken to see that all those likely to be affected by the bill are notified and given an opportunity to petition against it: representations in support of such petitions made directly by individuals or through counsel, together with evidence, are heard by a small committee of Lords or Members, acting in a quasi-judicial capacity: the government will report on the bill and the clauses are also scrutinized by the Lord Chairman and the Chairman of Ways and Means with the public interest in mind. As well as committee stage, private bills go through the normal process of second and third readings, when of course they may be debated on the floor like any other bill.

The government's legislative programme of public bills for the forthcoming session— usually a year long, though the session before a General Election will typically be shorter and that after an Election longer than the norm—is formally announced by the Queen in her speech at the State Opening of Parliament. A recent development has been the announcement of the government's intention to inform Parliament in the course of the preceding session what the proposed legislative programme is to contain, seeking parliamentary and public reaction (see page 50). The government's legislation nearly always comes successfully through the legislative process, defended by a constant majority against significant change.

Government bills, whether they are to go first before the Commons or are brought from the Lords, are introduced on whatever sitting day the government chooses. All public bills are sponsored by up to twelve Members. In the case of government bills, the list is headed by a senior minister, followed by junior departmental colleagues. Apart from recent developments referred to below, there is no parliamentary consideration of the bill before it is brought to the floor of the House. First reading is formal: there is no debate, and this stage is no more than the firing of the starting gun for printing the bill and permitting the minister in charge to publicize its details. A day for second reading is named in the House by a whip, usually roughly ten days after first reading. Government bills are accompanied by a detailed (but not argumentative) Explanatory Memorandum and a Regulatory Impact Assessment (though the latter have been criticized by the Commons Scrutiny Unit (see page 377) as 'rarely comprehensive or accurate').[8]

Backbenchers on the other hand may introduce bills in a number of ways. The first option open to them is to enter a ballot from which twenty names are drawn. Success in the ballot confers precedence in debate on a number of Fridays set aside for private Members, but there are no more than seven such Fridays on which second readings top the Order of Business. In consequence, all but a fortunate few backbenchers must seek to legislate on such relatively uncontroversial topics as can be disposed of in the time—if any—left after the leading bill on any Friday has been dealt with. Nowadays, even the first seven—if they wish to progress beyond a death-or-glory ride towards a failed second reading of a controversial proposal—will have to avoid highly charged topics such as homosexual law reform, abortion, or human genetics, some of which were the subject of successful back-bench bills in the past. These high-profile bills apart, it is unusual for private Members' bills to be defeated on a division on second reading. Limited time for debate loads the dice heavily in favour of opponents of changes in the law who, simply by continuing the debate in an orderly way until the moment of interruption is reached, 'talk the bill out'. A bill on which debate does not reach a conclusion on any Friday, as well as those so far down the list that there is no time at all for debate, may be deferred but must then take their places behind others already set down for the future day. Prospects of success are thus even further diminished.

There is currently no remedy, however strong the feeling inside the House or in the country. It is rare (though not unheard of) for a government to make available to a backbencher extra time from its own resources.

A second means of introduction is simple presentation of a bill with minimum formality, in the same way as government bills are presented. Such bills however have to take priority behind the balloted bills. Finally, backbenchers have an opportunity in prime time—immediately before the commencement of the main business on two days a week—to make a ten-minute speech seeking leave to introduce a bill. These motions are often not an attempt to legislate, but a means of drawing attention to a topic, perhaps with an eye to legislating in a future session. If nevertheless a bill is successfully introduced in this way, it too will come behind the balloted bills in the queue.

There are a number of practical as well as procedural discouragements to backbenchers anxious to legislate. Many Members may be reluctant to spend time on promoting a bill, given such slender chances of success. Steering a controversial bill through the House may attract broad public notice, but it will rarely if ever bring local political advantage. The government has agreed to make available financial assistance to Members whose bills have been read a second time and are 'likely to pass', but they have never increased the sum originally provided. Drafting the original text and considering proposed amendments is a laborious and complex business. The result is that many—it is impossible to say how many—back-bench Members whose bills reach the statute book are in truth acting for the government, fostering bills for which there was no time in the official legislative programme but to which individual departments attach interest.

Proposals to rebalance these procedures in the interest of the backbencher have not been scarce. One aim of the reformers is the ending of the 'procedural subterfuge' by which a single anonymous call of 'object' at the end of a private Members' Friday more or less seals the fate of bills—however well supported—for which no time for debate has been available. At least, party whips should (it is argued) be debarred from interfering in private Members' time. There should be a more consensual way of deciding which bills are sufficiently meritorious to proceed to later stages and the upper House. Such a procedure exists in the Canadian House of Commons, though it has—perhaps not unexpectedly—led to disputes.

There are also arguments against making the path too easy for would-be legislators. Like matrimony, legislation is a serious undertaking, not to be entered upon lightly or (in this context) at the behest of excited special-interest groups, in or out of the House. It would be wrong to skew procedure on private Members' bills in their favour. Moreover, government whips by definition act on behalf of the majority in the House, even when objecting to private Members' bills. Recording the name of the Member who shouted 'object' to a much-cherished proposal would certainly remove one of the persistent griev-ances, but even a single Member taking orderly steps to prevent a decision being taken in a thinly attended and un-whipped House is surely well within his or her rights.

For most government bills introduced into the Commons, second reading means a day's debate on the floor of the House, beginning after any ministerial statement and going on till the moment of interruption (for which see page 157). The minister respon-sible explains the need for and provisions of the bill, the Opposition put their case, fol-lowed by contributions from backbenchers on both sides throughout the parliamentary day. Front-bench winding-up speeches are made as the moment of interruption approaches. The Modernisation Committee has observed that a more flexible approach to scheduling second reading debates, and willingness to identify some bills which, by agreement, might be debated for less than a full day on second reading would save an appreciable number of hours, and might do away with the need for limiting the time of Members' speeches on other occasions.[9] Some decades ago second reading debates lasting less than a day were much more common than they have been recently. The disappear-ance of such arrangements was perhaps a consequence of intensification of party hostili-ties. If so, whether that particular clock can be turned back, however much sense there may be in the suggestion, is at best problematical.

The loss of a bill at second reading, were the bill a major part of the government's policy platform, would probably be a resignation matter. But such occasions are not common.

As a matter of tactics and political judgement, most government bills which are likely to be controversial are introduced into the Commons (except when a government expects trouble in the Lords and wants to take its medicine as early as possible). The legislative procedures of the Lords are broadly similar to those of the Commons, though the absence in the Lords of all-encompassing government control of the time of the House or of the Chair's power of selection are crucial differences. There is, for example, no Lords equivalent of Private Members' Fridays, because there is no formal division between government time and that on which non-government business has priority. In addition, there are rules in the Lords which either have no analogue in the Commons or are no more than conventions which governments may override at will if they are prepared for the recriminations which may follow. For example, there should be two weekends between the first and second readings of a bill in the Lords, fourteen days between second reading and committee stage, the same between the end of committee and report stage in the case of complex bills, and three sitting days between the end of report stage and third reading.

In the Lords, all bills are introduced without notice, the Lord in charge of the bill simply reading out the long title. Unlike the Commons, a question is put on first reading. The question may be opposed, though that has not happened for forty years. The first reading of bills brought from the Commons is similarly moved as soon as the message informing their Lordships of the arrival of the bill has been read. The bill is then printed.

In 2007–8, twenty-five bills were brought from the Commons to the Lords, all but three of them government bills; and twenty-three were introduced into the Lords, eight by the government and fifteen by non-government members of the Lords. All the government bills were enacted irrespective of the House of introduction, but none of the fifteen non-government bills surfacing first in the Lords became law.

It is unusual for a bill in the Lords to be rejected at second reading, though it happened twice in 2006–7.

Committees in Congress

Jurisdiction

Beyond the stage of introduction the fate of an individual Member's public or private bill in Congress is initially in the hands of the standing committee(s) to which the measure must immediately be referred (although in the Senate referral can be blocked by a single objection as will be discussed subsequently). The initial or sequential referral of legislation to committee must be distinguished from motions to refer, commit, or recommit, utilized as a procedural tactic in either House during consideration of the measure (see page 151). Referrals are based upon interpretations of often imprecise standing rules which delineate standing committee jurisdictions. In turn, Speakers have delegated to non-partisan Parliamentarians the responsibility for determining proper committees of jurisdiction. This role of the Parliamentarian and the practice of referrals based on precedent delegated to a non-partisan official have a long-established history in both Houses, and are based on the need to relieve the Speaker of partisan attempts to influence that decision. This role of the Speaker and its delegation remain one of the centrepieces in distinguishing the non-partisan role of the Speaker as presiding officer from her equally traditional but more partisan role as elected leader of the Majority party. Perceptions that the Speaker and influential chairmen exert political influence over referrals are misplaced. When a Member disagrees with the Parliamentarian's advice on referral of a measure to a committee other than that desired, that Member is free to redraft and then reintroduce the measure in a form sufficiently different to influence its referral elsewhere. The challenge to that Member is to remain true to his original legislative purpose while presenting an alternative draft which accomplishes that purpose in a manner appropriately within the jurisdiction of the desired committee under the standing rule and the precedents. Such discussion is constantly undertaken between Members, committees, their staffs, and the Parliamentarian, often prior to the date of actual introduction and referral so as not to set an undesired precedent of referral. In all cases, the Speaker is not successfully importuned to base the referral decision on any personal or partisan consideration.

While mechanisms exist under the rules of both US Houses to correct erroneous referrals by motion, these procedures are not utilized in modern practice because other means are used to accomplish that end. In both Houses, unanimous consent requests are the means by which re-referrals are made. In the House, sequential referrals to a committee which may have been omitted from an initial referral sometimes serve to correct the initial exclusion. Similarly in the Senate, a motion to change the presiding officer's referral of a measure is not used in modern practice. This reality further reinforces the tradition in both Houses that referrals are not politicized, notwithstanding rules which permit a majority of each House to be the ultimate arbiter of jurisdictional disputes.

Committee jurisdiction is determined by a variety of factors. Paramount is House Rule X, which designates the subject matter within the purview of each standing committee. That rule, however, is imprecise and is the product of an era in which governmental activity was not so extensive and relations among policies not so intertwined as now. Most of Rule X was drawn from nineteenth- and twentieth-century precedents and codified in the Legislative Reorganization Act of 1946. Although the rule underwent modest revisions in 1974 and 1980, as well as in 1995 and 2005, subject-matter omissions, a lack of clarity, and overlaps among committees in areas of jurisdiction still exist. For example, the Committee on Agriculture has jurisdiction over 'forestry in general and forest reserves other than those created from the public domain', while the Committee on Natural Resources has jurisdiction over 'forest reserves created from the public domain'. The current jurisdiction in the House over forest reserves is therefore dependent on a century-old distinction between the origin of the land as public domain or as a purchased area.

Another of many examples of jurisdictional vagueness emanating from the rule is in the area of foreign economic policy, where Rule X confers on the Committee on Energy and Commerce jurisdiction over 'foreign commerce generally', on the Committee on Financial Services jurisdiction over 'international finances', on the Committee on Foreign Affairs jurisdiction over 'international economic policy', and on the Committee on Ways and Means jurisdiction over 'reciprocal trade agreements'. Such vagaries abound and are too numerous for recitation in this work, but they reflect the importance of precedent in past referrals, depending primarily on bill language, the existing law, if any, being amended, and on the assumption that a more specific conferral of jurisdiction can supersede a more general or residual conferral, at least to the extent of selecting a primary committee. Oleszek comments that 'committees guard their jurisdictional turfs closely, and the Parliamentarians know and follow the precedents. Only instances of genuine jurisdictional ambiguity provide opportunities for the legislative draftsman and referral options for the Speaker and the presiding officer of the Senate to bypass one committee in favor of another'[10] where an accommodation cannot be made by a multiple referral. A multiple referral once made to resolve an ambiguity itself becomes precedent for subsequent referrals and in subsequent Congresses, unless the rules are rewritten to adjust to them. Such a significant change occurred in the 109th Congress, when the Committee on Energy and Commerce, which had been stripped of its jurisdiction over 'securities and exchanges' (transferred to the Committee on Financial Services in the 107th Congress in an effort to consolidate all jurisdiction over financial institutions—banks, investment and securities entities, and insurance—in one committee) nevertheless had retained jurisdiction over measures involving 'accounting standards', based on a 'Memorandum of Understanding' between their respective chairmen in that earlier Congress.[11] Four years later, the Speaker declared on the opening day of the 109th Congress that the last two sentences of that Memorandum of Understanding were no longer operative—that is, that the Energy and Commerce Committee could no longer claim referrals over accounting standards measures based on that earlier understanding and that henceforth the Committee on Financial Services was to be considered the sole committee of jurisdiction over this important range of economic activity. This consolidation implied that all the attendant lobbying and campaign finance support would be focused on members of the retaining committee. The Speaker's initiative in disclaiming the further efficacy of a Memorandum of Understanding into a new Congress was itself a precedent in the House, as the first example of the removal of tacit support by the Speaker and his reversion to the provisions of Rule X.

While some jurisdictional delineations mirror Executive branch organization (for example, the Committee on Armed Services has jurisdiction over the Department of Defense generally, the Committee on Energy and Commerce has jurisdiction over general management of the Department of Energy, and the Committee on Homeland Security has jurisdiction over that Department) there are many more conferrals of jurisdiction based on generic subject-matter description rather than on Executive branch organization.

Thus the formal provisions of the rule are supplemented by an intricate series of precedents and informal agreements governing the referral of legislation in the House. Based on precedent, once a measure has been referred to a given committee, jurisdiction is established into subsequent Congresses for that committee (assuming no rules change), especially where that committee has reported the measure to the House. The act of reporting creates a stronger claim for subsequent jurisdiction than does the initial referral of the Speaker, standing alone. If the measure is enacted into law, bills amending that law are presumed to be within the originating committee's jurisdiction. Subject-matter jurisdiction accretes to the committees in an increasing order of influence where it has (1) received an initial referral; (2) reported that matter to the House; and (3) been successful at gaining enactment of that measure into law.

Informal agreements, drafted among committees to stipulate their understanding of jurisdictional boundaries, have been used in recent years. These agreements, called 'Memoranda of Understanding' have been considered influential even in subsequent Congresses when they are supported by all the committees concerned, signed by their chairmen and inserted into the Record, although they are not formally ratified by the House. Six committee chairmen signed a Memorandum of Understanding over energy jurisdiction inserted in the Record,[12] and two committees (Budget and Rules) inserted an agreement on budget process jurisdiction[13] and generally to House Practice.[14] Committee reports or matters inserted in the Record often contain an exchange of letters between committee chairmen waiving a committee's claim to review a portion of a particular bill, with the understanding that this surrender of jurisdiction over the matter is not permanent. Typical in this area is a situation where a primary committee reports a measure and seeks to bring it to the floor expeditiously. Often a committee seeking a sequential referral will forgo a meaningful time limit imposed by the Speaker in favour of a symbolic one-day referral to signal a proper jurisdictional claim for future referrals, accompanied by an exchange of letters. Beyond these token referrals, the Speaker's discretionary authority under Rule XII to impose time limits on any committee of referral potentially injects a political calculation into the referral process. While his jurisdictional decision is non-partisan, as delegated to the Parliamentarian, his time allowance can enhance or detract from a secondary committee's ability to hold hearings and mark up the referred measure, depending on the length of time granted. The implications of the Speaker's authority to impose time limits on the referral of bills are discussed at page 399.

On 8 October 1974, the House adopted a resolution[15] which directed the Speaker to refer measures to more than one committee, either additionally upon initial introduction, sequentially upon report of the primary committee, or split for referral if they contained subject matter properly within the jurisdiction of more than one committee under Rule X and under the precedents. Prior to that date, Speakers had always referred measures to only one standing committee—the one panel with the preponderance of jurisdiction as determined by the Speaker based on prior referrals (in a manner akin to the requirement of Rule XVII that the presiding officer of the Senate refer measures to the predominant committee discussed at page 406). Over the course of 185 years of single referrals a large array of precedent had been established as to committees of predominant jurisdiction, but given the complexities of contemporary issues and the perceived need to modernize standing committee jurisdictions, the House in 1973 had established a Select Committee on Committees to recommend jurisdictional realignments and consolidations. That select committee's bipartisan recommendations were rejected by the House in favour of retention to the present day of most of the traditional fragmentation which existed even after enactment of the Legislative Reorganization Act of 1946. For example, the select committee recommended the establishment of a new standing committee on Energy and Environment, which would have assumed various jurisdictions of five or six committees, including energy policy, agricultural environment, energy and environmental research and development, military aspects of those matters, public lands and resources, and air and water pollution matters. A coalition of Members (primarily within the Democratic Caucus) were convinced that they stood to lose rather than gain power and influence in those and other major subject areas as a result of the proposed realignments, as they could not all gain assignment to the newly consolidated committee. They rejected the consolidation proposal in favour of retention of existing fragmentation. Contained in a separate section of the select committee's consolidation proposal—but only as a safeguard in the perceived unlikely event that jurisdictional overlaps might continue to occur—was a requirement for multiple referrals in the event of such overlap. A review of the debate on that occasion fails to disclose that the House consciously adopted a new requirement for multiple referral while retaining more overlapping and fragmented jurisdictions than envisioned by the select committee. If it was the policy of the prevailing coalition to multiply Members' jurisdictional involvement at the committee level by insisting on a proliferation of referrals, it was not articulated. In fact, the 'coalition' amendment was successful on the crucial vote because more Members stood to gain power and influence by guaranteeing the jurisdictional involvement of more committees and therefore of more Members, than did the select committee's consolidation alternative. Combined with the empowerment of the Speaker to place time limits on referrals in order to bypass entrenched committee chairmen who had gained their positions by seniority and were often not answerable to the leadership, this multiple jurisdictional commitment contributed immensely and immediately to profound institutional change in the House.[16]

Three changes subsequent to that date were: (1) in 1977, two years after the initial empowerment for multiple referrals, at which time the Speaker was permitted to place time limits on committees of initial as well as subsequent referral; (2) in 1995, when the Speaker's authority to refer matters jointly was changed to require the designation of a primary committee; and (3) in 2003 when the Speaker was authorized to make joint referrals to more than one initial committee without designation of a primary committee under 'exceptional circumstances'.

Prior to 1975, the Speaker could not formally impose time limits on the committee of referral. Only a formal discharge petition (discussed at page 425) or the infrequent utilization of a special order of business from the Rules Committee to effectively discharge a committee from an unreported bill could accomplish the purpose of the House to take a measure away from a standing committee as though a time limit had been imposed. The infrequency with which the Rules Committee was utilized until recent Congresses to report special orders of business which 'discharged' standing committees from unreported legislation was demonstrated on 9 February 1972. On that occasion the Committee on Education and Labor had not reported a measure ending a west coast dock strike, and the Rules Committee was utilized to bring that matter directly to the floor. The debate reflected the 'unprecedented' use of a special order to discharge a standing committee from an unreported measure[17] and a review of examples of such special orders from the 1930s until that time indicates only three similar occasions. Two years later, on 17 October 1974, the Speaker responded to a parliamentary inquiry[18] that the Committee on Rules had the authority to report a special order which discharged the Committee on Appropriations from consideration of an unreported measure, but it remained clear that the practice of the House was not to so utilize the Rules Committee. Rather, the practice remained deferential to standing committees at a time of decentralization of authority away from the elected Majority Leadership in favour of the independence of committee chairmen and formal reports from their committees.

In the 94th Congress—the first year the Speaker could impose time limits—only committees receiving secondary referral could be time limited. This restriction was quickly removed at the beginning of the 95th Congress in 1977 to permit time limits to be imposed on all referrals. While this authority has not often been exercised by Speakers, its mere conferral signalled that from the standpoint of available 'time' for committee consideration, formal limits were possible from the outset. It symbolized new leadership ability to circumscribe committees from the day of introduction, not merely following a primary committee's report, whenever that might be, in order to expedite plenary consideration. It represented the need for imposition of a degree of institutional certainty of available time at the committee stage, an enhancement of centralization of Majority party leadership, a corresponding reduction of committee and subcommittee independence, and the re-emergence of Majority Leadership dominance now commonplace in contemporary Congresses but not seen following the Speakership of Joseph Cannon at the beginning of the 20th century (1903–11) (also utilizing the Rules Committee).

From 1975 to 1995, joint referrals without the designation of one primary committee had proliferated where measures contained substantive provisions which were separately or concurrently within the jurisdiction of more than one committee, and which were not merely incidental to more predominant provisions. In 1995 the Speaker's designation of a primary committee of referral was required. In 2003, a return to the joint referral policy was permitted based on the 'exceptional circumstance' of overlapping and conflicting jurisdiction, prompted by ongoing disputes over national healthcare measures between the Committee on Energy and Commerce and the Committee on Ways and Means. The jurisdictional conflict in this area emanated from the 1974 fragmentation of the issue of healthcare financed by general revenues—conferred upon the Commerce Committee—and healthcare financed by payroll deductions, conferred upon the Ways and Means Committee. The premise that jurisdiction over healthcare should depend on the source of Federal funding—payroll tax as opposed to general revenues—ignored a third form of financing, namely premiums which were not collected as payroll taxes, and which were the primary source of healthcare funding under part B Medicare (first enacted in 1965, when the only committee of jurisdiction was Ways and Means). Both committees have continuously claimed co-equal jurisdiction in this important part B area (and currently in the part D prescription drug area enacted in 2003), since Rule X language has not been changed to clarify this omission. Combining this ambiguity in the rule with the perception in the lobbying community and among Members that the primary committee enjoys an added prestige (with attendant campaign fund raising that such a designation entails), ongoing disputes remained, despite the requirement that the Speaker select a primary committee and despite the reality that an additional committee of original referral has every bit as much opportunity to hold hearings and report such a bill within its jurisdiction from the outset as does the primary committee. Thus the 'exceptional circumstance' exception re-emerged where the rule and precedents did not enable the Speaker to easily make the determination of primary referral.

The Speaker's endorsement of the referral on each multiply referred bill reads as follows: 'the bill is referred to the Committee on (a) and additionally to the Committees on (b), (c), and (d), for consideration of such provisions of the bill as fall within the respective jurisdictions of those committees pursuant to clause 1 of rule X'. The language 'of such provisions' is of special significance as it tells each committee that upon consideration of that measure in subcommittee and in full committee, it may only permit amendment of those portions of the bill which the Parliamentarian has advised fall within their jurisdiction. Thus the committee may not permit amendments, if points of order are raised by the chair or any member which range beyond those provisions, even though arguably germane to the bill as a whole. There has been constructed by precedent in all the standing committees of the House a separate jurisdictional point of order based on rulings of committee chairmen which prevent their members from amending portions of the multiply referred bill beyond their respective jurisdictions. If a bill has only been referred to one committee initially, the same endorsement does not appear on the initial referral, because the Speaker at that stage has not made a decision upon subsequent referrals, if any. Should that initial committee report a singly referred bill containing provisions, whether or not amended, within another committee's jurisdiction, then the Speaker is required by Rule XII to sequentially refer the bill to an additional committee or committees for a time certain for 'consideration of such provisions of the original bill and amendment that fall within the jurisdictions of those (sequential) committees respectively'. This jurisdictional point of order is not spelled out in House rules and is only enforceable in committees based on the language of the Speaker's referral printed on the bill. If the committee amending the bill ignores or improperly overrules this point of order or it is not raised in committee, there is no collateral point of order that survives in the House other than one of germaneness against a committee amendment. However, if the reported bill as amended does encroach on another committee's jurisdiction, the likelihood of a sequential referral and the possibility of the matter being later addressed by the Rules Committee can militate against the jurisdictional overreach by the initial committee. The germaneness rule and its application at both the committee and House stages is discussed at page 176.

When the Republican majority was elected to the House in 1995, the rules adopted on opening day on the recommendation of that party's Conference eliminated three standing committees of the House (District of Columbia, Merchant Marine and Fisheries, and Post Office and Civil Service), and transferred those jurisdictions among several remaining standing committees. This consolidation represented the most extensive jurisdictional realignment since the 1946 Reorganization Act and was adopted as a part of a larger package of partisan procedural reforms rather than as a bipartisan effort utilizing the Rules Committee or a select or joint committee. A Joint Committee on Congressional Operations, while recommending a series of reforms in the procedures of both Houses in 1994, had in fact declined to recommend House or Senate committee jurisdictional realignments during its existence in the previous Congress, acknowledging the political difficulty encountered in the House in 1974 of accomplishing 'reform' in that area.

The creation in 2005 of a standing committee on Homeland Security was the culmination of activity in three consecutive Congresses that ended a temporary procedural anomaly in the Speaker's role in making referrals and an extensive dispute over the extent to which existing standing committee jurisdictions would either be transferred to or shared with a new entity. In the 107th Congress[19] the House established an ad hoc select committee on Homeland Security, pursuant to a resolution reported from the Committee on Rules, which was tasked to receive recommendations from twelve standing committees to which the Speaker had referred a bill establishing a new Department of Homeland Security (DHS) in the Executive branch, and to report a bill based on an evaluation of those recommendations. That select committee went out of existence upon final Congressional approval on 25 November 2002 of the bill which created the Department. Then the House at the beginning of the 108th Congress created a new select committee on Homeland Security to

> develop recommendations on such matters that relate to the Homeland Security Act of 2002[20] as may be referred to it by the Speaker; to conduct oversight of laws, programmes, and Government activities relating to homeland security; to conduct a study of the operation and implementation of the rules of the House, including

rule X, with respect to homeland security, to report its recommendations to the House on matters referred to it by the Speaker, and to report its recommendations on changes to House rules to the Committee on Rules by 30 September 2004.

The legislative jurisdiction conferred on that select committee was unusual in that it referred only to the 2002 Act which created the DHS and matters relating thereto as determined by the Speaker. Even before that matter was debated in the House on 7 January 2003, Speaker-elect Hastert, in his acceptance speech prior to taking the oath of office, pledged to the House that upon becoming Speaker and upon adoption of the rules creating the new select committee, his referrals would not be prejudicial to the jurisdictions of those standing committees that had contributed to the 2002 Act. He was promising a very restricted set of referrals of measures to the select committee so as not to diminish the jurisdictional claims of the standing committee chairmen who would reluctantly support its creation. Over the course of the 108th Congress, only a handful of measures were referred to the select committee, and only two or three to that committee as primary, although they directly amended the 2002 Act in some reorganizational or substantive respect. The Speaker personally examined each measure on the date of introduction, and did not conclusively seek the advice of the Parliamentarian. For example, if the bill proposed to expand or transfer new authority to the new department, it was likely referred to one or more of the existing standing committees because the proposed reorganization was not contained in the 2002 Act and therefore not 'related thereto'. The Speaker had taken an extraordinary step of announcing that he would protect the standing committees of the House, and further appointed virtually all standing committee chairman who had contributed recommendations to the 2002 law and who had overlapping jurisdictions, as members of the new select committee. The legislative activities of the select committee during its two year existence in 2003–4 were therefore very limited, because the Speaker would not confer an expansive jurisdictional role on it through his referrals.

When the 109th Congress convened in January 2005, the House on recommendation of the Majority Conference created a standing committee on Homeland Security with jurisdiction over both the organizational aspects of the new Department and over subject-matter aspects on a wide variety of matters relating in whole or in part to homeland security. Shared jurisdiction was made explicit in several areas, with the new committee having jurisdiction over customs except customs revenue (retained by Ways and Means), border and port security except immigration policy and non-border enforcement (retained by Judiciary), transportation security (with the Committee on Transportation and Infrastructure retaining jurisdiction over transportation except transportation security functions of the new DHS), and integration, analysis, and dissemination of homeland security information (overlapping the intelligence jurisdiction of the select committee on Intelligence). On that day, the Speaker announced that his referrals in the previous Congress to the former select committee would not be considered precedent for referrals to the new standing committee, in effect announcing that the traditional non-partisan role of the Parliamentarian in relying upon precedent would be resumed in all subsequent referrals). The calamitous and historic events of 11 September 2001 were to be reflected in the first major legislative jurisdictional realignment of standing committees of the House since the 1995 elimination of three standing committees, but only after three years of examination and trial through utilization of a select committee with very limited jurisdictional authority. After three years of Executive branch reorganization, the House could no longer resist a permanent internal reorganization reflecting a comparable prioritization in the complex area of homeland security, itself reflecting a demand from the Executive and the public that a more expeditious oversight be put in place.

The Senate also responded to the recommendations of the bipartisan 'National Commission on Terrorist Attacks upon the United States' (the 9/11 Commission) which recommended in its report in July 2004 that each House reorganize itself to consolidate committee jurisdiction over homeland security issues. On 9 October 2004, following four days of debate and amendment, the Senate renamed its standing committee on Governmental Affairs as the Committee on Homeland Security and Governmental Affairs. The bipartisan task force which had drafted this recommendation for the Senate gave the committee jurisdiction over all legislation and matters relating to the DHS, but by a series of floor amendments exceptions and exemptions emerged, such as matters pertaining to the Coast Guard, the Transportation Security Administration, the Secret Service, the Citizenship and Immigration Service, the Custom and Border Protection Agency's immigration functions, the Custom Service's revenue functions, and the Federal Emergency Management Agency's functions relating to the Floor Insurance Act of 1968. After those floor amendments, intended to preserve other standing committees' jurisdictions, especially in areas not primarily related to issues of homeland security, it was estimated that the newly named committee was given jurisdiction over only 38 per cent of the DHS budget and 8 per cent of employees.

Like the Senate action, the House exempted from its Homeland Security Committee jurisdiction over DHS's functions with respect to immigration policy (retained by Judiciary) and customs revenue (retained by Ways and Means). In contrast to the Senate, however, the House included for its new committee jurisdiction over the Transportation Security Administration and all transportation security functions of the DHS, transferring them from the Committee on Transportation and Infrastructure.

The eventual reorganization actions in both Houses in response to the events of 11 September 2001 demonstrate the difficulties inherent in accomplishing committee jurisdictional changes where other standing committees oppose total transfers and where, as in the Senate, multiple referral mechanisms are not used except for joint leadership agreement and unanimous consent. Further complicating the delineation of the new committees' jurisdictions was the realization that some of the entities reorganized under the new department had dual functions, such as the Coast Guard. This summary demonstrates the intensity of parochial desires prevalent in both Houses to delay or minimize jurisdictional realignments, especially in comparison to the relative ease with which the Congress in the immediate aftermath of 9/11 enacted a law accomplishing a massive reorganization within the Executive branch by creation of the DHS.

When the 110th Congress convened on 4 January 2007, the new Majority did not attempt to change any jurisdictional assignments. Beyond renaming some of the committees as they were when last in the majority (the Committee on Education and Workforce returned to the Committee on Education and Labor, the Committee on Resources became again the Committee on Natural Resources, and the Committee on International Relations reverted to the Committee on Foreign Affairs), the only jurisdictional restatement of any significance was a Memorandum of Understanding between the

Committees on Transportation and Infrastructure and on Homeland Security inserted in the Record clarifying the former committee's primary jurisdiction over non-terrorism-related functions of the Federal Emergency Management Agency and over port security and Coast Guard issues.

The 9/11 Commission's recommendation that each House create an Intelligence Committee with jurisdiction over both policy and funding, or a joint committee to that effect, was not implemented by either House of Congress. While a recurring Democratic party theme in the Congressional elections of 2006 was the 'full implementation of the 9/11 Commission's recommendations', the new Democratic House in the 110th Congress did not adopt the consolidation recommendation of the Commission. Rather, it created a hybrid select panel as an entity of the Committee on Appropriations, to consist of three members of the Permanent Select Committee on Intelligence and ten members of the Appropriations Committee as appointed by the Speaker (8:5 Majority membership), to oversee the intelligence budget and to report its recommendations to the Defense subcommittee of the Committee on Appropriations. This panel reflected a partial joinder of the authorization and appropriation processes for legislative oversight purposes, but its weight in favour of appropriation indicated the ultimate jurisdictional responsibility of the Appropriations Committee alone to recommend funding of all intelligence operations on an annual basis. The establishment of this entity as a standing House rule was new precedent, for it combined authorization and Appropriations Committee members in a unique way as a 'select panel' to conduct oversight without separate subpoena authority and to report annual recommendations to a subcommittee, while reserving annual funding decisions to that specified subcommittee where the three authorizing committee members did not participate. The House had never before delineated the functions of a hybrid subcommittee entity in such detail, traditionally leaving to each full committee establishment its subcommittees' responsibilities and their sub-entity identity as a panel or task force.

Select committees are further discussed in the segment on Scrutiny and Oversight at page 311, for it is the investigative or oversight role of such committees, in addition to occasional housekeeping functions, that characterize most contemporary select committees. In contrast with the British predominance of non-partisan select committees, there is now only one permanent select committee in the House of Representatives (Intelligence) and there are three in the Senate (Intelligence, Ethics, and the Special Committee on Aging). In the modern era, select committees are created primarily to investigate conditions or events in furtherance of a constitutionally assigned function of Congress. A few have been created to study and report on matters with a view toward legislative action, but without the authority to report legislation. The most recent example of a new select committee empowered to report legislation to the House was the select committee on Homeland Security in the 107th Congress and its successor in the 108th Congress. Currently only the Permanent Select Committees on Intelligence in the House and Senate have legislative jurisdiction. Those select committees are the equivalent of standing committees since they are created by the standing rules with legislative jurisdiction, and only bear the name 'select' because their Members are appointed by the leadership, rather than elected by each House through nominations from the respective party caucuses.

Select committees were used extensively by the House during the early Congresses, as they were created to draft the appropriate legislative language for the measure being introduced. By the Third Congress, 350 select committees had been named. By the 23rd Congress, the number of select committees had been reduced to thirty-five, and by the end of the 106th Congress in 2002, only the Permanent Select Committee on Intelligence remained, labelled 'permanent' because its continuation into a new Congress would be assured by readoption of the rules, avoiding the need to separately reconstitute the select committee. The comparable Select Intelligence Committee in the Senate is not labelled 'permanent' because its rules have ongoing application and the select committee remains in existence into new Congresses.

In the 107th and 108th Congresses, select committees on Homeland Security in the House were established but gave way to the standing committee in 2005. In the 109th Congress, a select committee on Hurricane Katrina was established to report to the House within a six-month period, at which time it went out of existence. In the 110th Congress, a select committee on Energy Independence and Global Warming was established to report its findings to the House by October 2008. Also in that Congress a select committee to investigate voting irregularities which occurred on a specific vote in the House was spontaneously established by resolution offered by the Minority Leader as a question of privilege. Its membership was equally divided between Majority and Minority (3:3), more akin to a special ethics panel, to investigate the conduct of involved Members and staff.

The trend toward proliferation of select committees has abated in modern Congresses, nowhere better symbolized than the House's summary vote in 1992 to reject the continuation of three select committees (on Hunger, on Children, Youth, and Families, and on Narcotics). The most recent four Congresses have nevertheless established a few temporary select investigative committees where standing committees' jurisdictions overlap and there is a need for information gathering and dissemination in a short time frame by one coordinating public forum whose membership is controlled by the Speaker, rather than by several standing committee sub-entities.

Special ad hoc committees in the House may be established pursuant to Rule XII, clause 2(c), the same rule empowering multiple referrals. It has been utilized three times, wherein the Speaker has exercised authority to refer a matter, including a legislative measure, to a special ad hoc committee appointed by him. The appointment must be made with the approval of the House and include members of the committees having legislative jurisdiction over the particular measure to be referred. A resolution authorizing the Speaker to take such action is privileged when offered from the floor at the Speaker's request. The most notable ad hoc select committee was on Energy, established in the 95th Congress, and it reported a major energy policy bill to the House. Twice, an ad hoc select committee on the Outer Continental Shelf was established by the House, in the 94th and again in the 96th Congresses, and the latter reported a measure to the House. This alternative referral authority, while utilized early in the existence of the multiple referral rule as an enhancement of the Speaker's direct referral authority, has been superseded in subsequent Congresses by more informal task forces named by the Speaker but not formally established by the House and involving a number of standing committees. In those cases, the Rules Committee was utilized to discharge standing committees and to make in order or self-execute the adoption of compromise amendments to measures reflecting the work product of those informal panels. The Senate has no comparable formal rule for the creation of ad hoc select committees by party leaders. Like the House, however, its leaders have informally created partisan or bipartisan task forces or other ad hoc devices for consideration of legislative proposals.

Oleszek makes the following observations with respect to multiple referrals in the House:

> because contemporary problems tend to have repercussions in many areas, more and more of the major bills coming before Congress, particularly those in new problem areas, will be candidates for multiple referral; to the extent that multiple referral is chosen as an option, the decentralized nature of Congressional decision making is reinforced; every time another committee is added to the legislative process, additional opportunities arise for delay, negotiation, compromise and bargaining; multiple referrals may promote effective problem-solving because more expertise is brought to bear; when the Speaker designates a primary committee, he knows where to stimulate legislative action by the threat of time-limits on other committees, but he is also required to mediate and resolve jurisdictional disputes which delay expedited consideration; the proliferation of full committee referrals results in a further proliferation of subcommittee review within each full committee; and more complex debate and amendment arrangements are needed on the floor and in the selection of conferees to resolve differences with the Senate.[21]

These observations, while accurate, are mitigated in modern practice by the Speaker's utilization of the Rules Committee to 're-centralize' power in the Majority leadership by a combination of techniques which accelerate or even bypass committee action and which minimize separate amendment and voting possibilities in the full House, all to the advantage of the Majority party leadership.

The legislative jurisdictions of the Senate's standing committees are established in Senate Rule XXV. The committees vary in terms of jurisdictional breadth, with some responsible for a diverse array of issues and others focused more narrowly on related policies. Under Rule XXV each standing committee has assigned to it a dozen or more subject areas, which, like the House, are not specified by organizational components of the Executive branch or specific statutorily enacted programmes, but rather by more generic subject-matter statements. Beyond the exact language of the standing rule, Senate referrals are based upon precedent of prior referral of similar measures. Formal agreements by unanimous consent orders of the Senate can set precedent for multiple referral, while ad hoc informal agreements that govern the referral of particular measures are not binding on future referrals. Under Senate Rule XVII each measure is normally referred to a single committee based 'on the subject matter which predominates' therein. Predominance can be a relatively simplistic or subjective standard and is usually determined by the extent to which a measure deals with a subject, as compared with the extent of an approach within another committee's jurisdiction. Exceptions by tradition include measures containing revenue provisions which are likely to be referred to the Committee on Finance, even though the subject does not appear to predominate. Prior to the requirement for multiple referral in the House in 1974, a similar guideline influenced the referral of measures to the House Committee on Ways and Means, regardless of the preponderance of other provisions in the bill, but since that date multiple referrals to accommodate all committees are required. While in the Senate a motion for a joint or sequential referral is in order if jointly sponsored by the Majority and Minority Leaders or their designees, this motion is not used in modern practice and multiple referrals are accomplished only by unanimous consent. Whether they have the status of precedent once entered depends upon the scope of the request and whether it is stated as an order of the Senate (the Senate Parliamentarian currently has a list of seven or eight unanimous consent orders for multiple referral which by their terms constituted precedent for subsequent referrals). The central difference from the House is that there are fewer precedents of prior referral upon which to rely, and the Parliamentarian is an informal consultant in previously negotiated bipartisan agreements involving committee and party leaders. The Senate's limited use of multiple referrals can be attributed to the variety of other formal and informal opportunities which Senators have to influence measures, regardless of the committee to which referred, including inter-committee consultation or report of original bills. (Under Senate rules all committees can originate the text of a bill without its having been referred and can report those measures to the Senate, where they are sometimes sequentially referred to another committee regardless of the 'predominance' test.) A recent example involved the sequential referral of a Senate Select Intelligence Committee-originated bill to the Committee on Homeland Security and Governmental Affairs, where the latter committee had not been evaluated as a possible committee of original jurisdiction because the bill had not been referred but had originated in the select committee.

While Rule XVII contains procedures to challenge referral decisions of the presiding officer in the Senate, they are seldom utilized because of a variety of other means of influencing legislation beyond initial referral. Those other variables include merger of bills reported from separate committees on the floor by amendment or unanimous consent, and floor amendments whether or not germane. It is this latter ability to offer non-germane amendments to any bill, either in committee or on the Senate floor, which particularly lessens the demand in that body for multiple referrals. In the Senate under Rule XV, a bill reported by a committee with an amendment containing matter within the jurisdiction of another committee renders that committee amendment subject to a jurisdictional point of order. However, sustaining that point of order on the Senate floor is of little avail since the same amendment can be re-offered as a floor amendment and need not be germane under ordinary procedures.

By contrast, the House and its committees are constrained by a rule of germaneness which normally requires the subject of any amendment to be within the jurisdiction of the committee to which the bill (or a particular portion thereof) was referred. Combining the jurisdictional point of order earlier mentioned with the germaneness point of order, and assuming the committee chairs' enforcement thereof, it is understandable why matters of jurisdictional referral and separation are of greater institutional concern in the House than in the Senate, and why the non-partisan institutional role of the Speaker regarding referrals continues to be preferred despite the changes in party majorities.

Legislative procedures

There exists no formal equivalent to ballots by which at Westminster individual Members are given random chances for plenary consideration of their introduced private Members' measures. In contrast with the Commons' scheduling of a bill for a plenary debate on second reading to be followed by committee examination (in public bill committees, sometimes in select committee and on major issues in Committee of the whole House), in Congress all measures are immediately referred to standing committees upon introduction, and then under committee rules are normally referred to subcommittees within a short time following introduction, unless the committee determines that consideration is to be by the full committee. The referral to subcommittee begins the stage of committee consideration which normally follows the initial responsibility of oversight or hearings in preparation for the legislative or markup stage. The actual introduction and referral may take place either before, during, or after hearings are conducted on the subject matter of the measure. This segment of the chapter will examine legislative action on the measure itself in committee and subcommittee, while the oversight or investigative hearing function are discussed at pages 310 and 328. In this way the subject of 'committees' will be subdivided among those chapters.

House committees are required to follow the procedures prescribed by the rules of the House so far as applicable. They are also bound by those provisions of Jefferson's *Manual* that are not superseded by the standing rules of the House. Committees are powerless to adopt additional rules that may mirror but are not 'consistent with House rules', because some House rules and practices are uniquely applicable to plenary proceedings by their terms. Specifically, committees may not adopt suspension of the rules procedures in order to report measures out of committee by two-thirds votes but in avoidance of the amendment process. Nor may committees establish rules empowering subcommittee entities to report special rule variations to the full committee at any time. The contention that such an empowerment would be consistent with House rules and should be permitted is misplaced because it would permit committees to establish special orders of business which might be inconsistent with House rules which otherwise prescribe the amendment process in all committees and which have been interpreted to guarantee markups of measures for amendment under the five-minute rule.

Jefferson describes parliamentary law governing consideration of measures in committees of the House as follows:

> the paper before a committee...may be a bill, resolution, draft ... and it may either originate with them or be referred to them...In every case the whole paper is read first by the Clerk, and then by...paragraphs, pausing at the end of each paragraph, and putting questions for amending, if proposed...but no question on agreeing to the paragraphs separately...[22]

This language describes the modern amendment process in committees of the US House, from which committees are not free to depart by motion or committee rule. The first reading, in full merely for the information of Members, is usually dispensed with by unanimous consent or by a non-debatable motion included in 1970 under a House standing rule to prevent dilatory demands for such readings. The important (second) reading in standing committee and subcommittee must be by paragraphs (or sections) and must be in full unless dispensed with by unanimous consent (not by motion). At this point, House rules assure a deliberative process in committee and subcommittee to which committees must adhere. Jefferson's *Manual* must be read together with standing Rule XVI, clause which provides:

> when an amendable proposition is under consideration, a motion to amend and a motion to amend that amendment shall be in order, and it shall also be in order to offer a further amendment by way of substitute for the original motion to amend, to which one amendment may be offered but which may not be voted on until the original amendment is perfected.

These two provisions assure that during committee and subcommittee markups germane amendments may be offered to the pending portion and that second-degree amendments thereto, substitute amendments for the initial amendment, and amendments to substitutes may then be offered and debated and voted upon in a prescribed order under the five-minute rule (clause 5(a) of Rule XVII) governing Committee of the Whole proceedings. This committee process is described as comparable to being in 'the House as in Committee of the Whole', where, while the measure is read by sections, the motion for the previous question may cut off further debate on an amendment to the pending amendment but not on portions of the bill not yet read for amendment. Thus only when the measure has been completely read or has already been amended in its entirety, can the motion for the previous question—to end debate and amendment—be utilized to stop the amendment process entirely. This restriction on a committee majority intent upon halting the amendment process gives some assurance of a deliberative consideration of germane alternatives in committees, at least up to a point. That point can be quickly reached where the chair recognizes a member to offer an amendment in the nature of a substitute, which is essentially a full-text alternative to the pending measure, either at the beginning or the end of the amendment process. The amendment in the nature of a substitute is then open to amendment at any point, but is also subject to the motion for the previous question, which if adopted cuts off all further debate and amendments to the measure being marked up. Recognition of committee members to offer amendments is usually guided by the same practices as in the House, with the chair generally alternating between members of the two parties and in the order of their seniority on the committee. Amendments can be withdrawn by their sponsors at any time prior to action thereon, and (unlike Westminster) unanimous consent is not required.

Jefferson also states the most basic rule governing committees as follows:

> a committee meet when and where they please, if the House has not ordered time and place for them, but they can only act when together, and not by separate consultation and consent—nothing being the report of the committee but what has been agreed to in committee actually assembled.

This essential statement, when combined with one of the most important procedural reforms to emerge from the Republican majority in 1995 and retained by the Democratic majority in 2007—the elimination of proxy voting in House committees—requires committee members to be physically present and collegial action to be taken at all committee and subcommittee meetings. In fact, the abolition of proxy voting led to the procedure whereby committees were empowered by House rules to postpone and cluster votes in committee under certain conditions, in order to accommodate conflicting demands on Members' time, often the need to be physically present in more than one committee on which they serve.

Smaller than majority quorum requirements are permitted—in the House a minimum of two for hearings and one in the Senate—and one-third of committee members for interlocutory actions, but majority quorums are required to be present during any vote when measures are ordered reported, when hearings or meetings are to be closed to the public, when subpoenas are authorized (one-third in the Senate), and when committee rules are adopted.

Committees remain forums where the traditions of 'openness' and deliberativeness through an amendment process, once commonplace in the full House, cannot be circumvented by a Majority intent upon restricting Minority and individual alternatives from being offered and voted upon. The full House, through the Majority Leadership's utilization of special orders of business and motions to suspend the rules, can severely restrict a deliberative and spontaneous amendment process. Such ad hoc actions by the full House can impact standing committees to the extent that measures may be discharged and brought up in the full House without being reported or even considered. While measures remain in committees, by contrast, the standing rules of the House as they relate to amendments under the five-minute rule must be followed, except where limits are placed by unanimous consent.

The Committee on Appropriations has traditionally symbolized an 'open' amendment process, where under (unwritten) practices long observed by that committee the House rules (germaneness and restrictions against adding language changing existing law or unauthorized appropriations) are not applied, so as to permit individual Members to propose amendments to a pending 'committee print' or text being originated by the committee. As indicated at page 286, however, the adoption of a special order of business from the Rules Committee can totally circumvent committee and plenary procedures otherwise applicable to general Appropriation bills. Even assuming 'regular order' in committee, its reported bill may once under consideration in the House enjoy protection of some provisions otherwise subject to points of order, while reported provisions not so favoured (for example, legislative provisions to which a relevant authorizing committee expresses its objection to the Rules Committee) will not be granted the waiver of points of order necessary to protect them from being stricken on points of order at the plenary stage.

Committees, while not free to deviate from standing House rules, may follow some practices and traditions that vary from other committees, so long as they are not inconsistent with but rather supplementary to House rules. The Committee on Rules website provides a model form for committee rules as they organize at the beginning of each Congress. House rules require all committees to incorporate certain applicable provisions of House rules into committee rules verbatim. Committees are free if they choose to adopt additional rules, sometimes because House rules specifically enable it, or because they reflect proper practices favoured by certain committees. For example, beginning in the 108th Congress committees were permitted by a House rule to adopt committee rules allowing the chairman to postpone and cluster record votes on amendments and on reporting measures (to accommodate the abolition of proxy voting in committees and the inability of members to be physically present in two committees at the same time) in a manner comparable to authority conferred by standing rule since the 107th Congress on the Chairman of the Committee of the Whole during plenary sessions.[23] Until that specific conferral of authority, however, committees were not free to do so on their own initiative other than by unanimous consent. As with the inability of committees to establish suspension of the rules and amendment processes by special order or motion, it is important to distinguish procedures which are uniquely applicable at the plenary stage and not of general parliamentary applicability to sub-entities, absent a specific enabling by the full House.

Discussion of the hearing stage is contained in the chapter on Scrutiny and Oversight at page 324, where four basic types of hearings—legislative, oversight, investigative, and confirmation—are the focus, as they are governed by the same rules and practices. To the extent that hearings relate uniquely and directly to specific legislation, they will be discussed at this juncture as well.

Committee and subcommittee hearings can be scheduled for any or all of the reasons just suggested, but when they are called specifically for the purpose of considering a measure or series of measures, the relevant subcommittee usually schedules public hearings on the measure, inviting testimony from interested witnesses in both the public and private sectors for both fact-finding and educative reasons. Witnesses from the Executive branch, concerned Members of Congress, interest group spokespersons, academic experts, and knowledgeable citizens may ask or be summoned to appear to give their opinions on a particular piece of proposed legislation. Private sector witnesses are required to submit resumes in advance of their testimony together with disclosures of amounts of Federal grants or contracts received over two years.

Much information is available to committees long before the hearings take place, as major bills have usually been the subject of public debate and media coverage, and the positions of the Executive branch and special-interest groups already well known. Because Members' positions are often established in advance of hearings, their attendance is not as frequent as during markups when votes are taken. Only two Members are required to constitute a quorum to conduct hearings (one in the Senate), because the Members' responsibility at that point is less collegial—that is, to passively receive evidence, pose questions, and make incidental determinations on the relevance of testimony and on privacy issues, and hearing transcripts are available to absent Members. On the other hand a majority must vote to order a measure reported, authorize subpoenas (one-third in the Senate) or close hearings or meetings, and at least one-third of the panel must be present to vote on other matters. One-third quorums are necessary for other interlocutory actions if the committee adopts a rule to that effect, such as votes on amendments and procedural motions. Those votes are not final and may be superseded or ratified by votes on ordering the measure reported. These varying quorum requirements reflect the importance of full quorums to accomplish final actions as committees can only act when together.

By contrast, markups in Senate committees are not as formal or as standardized as in the House, since Senate rules do not require parallelism between Senate and committee rules, only that committee rules should not be inconsistent (clause 2 of Rule XXVI). For example, rules for the Committee on Foreign Relations stipulate that insofar as practicable, 'proceedings of the Committee will be conducted without resort to the formalities of parliamentary procedure', while other committees follow formal rules. A super-majority of sixty Senators is required to invoke cloture (limit debate) in the Senate while in its Judiciary Committee a majority of its members may invoke cloture provided that at least one Minority member supports this non-debatable motion.

Senate rules do impose certain limited requirements and prohibitions on committees during the markup stage. A committee (other than Appropriations and Budget) may not meet on any day (1) after the Senate has been in session for two hours, or (2) after 2 pm when the Senate is in session, but this restriction may be waived by unanimous consent or by joint agreement of the Majority and Minority Leaders or their designees. As in the House, quorums must consist of at least one-third of the Members for interlocutory decisions and a majority of Members must be actually present to order a measure reported. In the Senate, any committee may adopt rules permitting proxy voting, except that no affirmative vote of any member of any committee to report a measure may be cast by proxy. Thus if a physically present committee majority votes 'yes' on reporting a matter, proxies could be cast to change that decision to 'no', but not conversely. Senators giving proxies must do so with knowledge of the matter on which they are being recorded and must so stipulate. Proxies may not be utilized to establish a quorum.

Based on reforms in the Legislative Reorganization Act of 1970 made applicable to both Houses, Senate committee and subcommittee meetings are open to the public unless the committee decides in open session by record majority vote to close a meeting or series of meetings. The Senate permits two additional reasons for closing meetings beyond those in House rules, namely matters of internal staff management and the release of trade secrets. Otherwise, the purpose for closing must be for national security, law enforcement, privacy of an individual, or where a violation of law or House or Senate rules would occur by remaining open.

The most frequently conducted type of Congressional hearing gathers information about the subject matter of one or more measures in anticipation that the committee will eventually mark up and report legislation. By deciding to hold a legislative hearing, a committee takes one or more measures bearing on the same issue from the many that are referred to the committee and indicates that it involves a subject upon which the panel must act (for example, an expiring law) or is otherwise worthy of consideration. A bill need not be introduced and referred for the panel to hold a legislative hearing, as information may be gathered which the committee might use in shaping legislation to be subsequently introduced. There is no requirement that legislation be drafted based on hearing testimony, or that if hearings are held a committee must mark up and report a measure. Conversely, in only a few procedural circumstances are there any requirements in House or Senate rules that a committee hold a hearing on a measure in order to take action on it, the only requirement being that 'every reasonable effort' be made to assure the availability of printed hearings to Members prior to consideration of the measure in the House or Senate. In fact, only general Appropriation bills, when reported, must be accompanied by printed hearings, if there have been any, three days prior to consideration of the measure. While most appropriation hearings occur at the subcommittee level, their availability in printed form is not always possible prior to House consideration, and that point of order is waived by a special order from the Rules Committee. A rule[24] requiring hearings by the Budget Committee 'which it considers desirable' in developing annual concurrent resolutions on the budget is, as the language implies, not a condition precedent to a report.

One unique House rule relating to legislative hearings[25] protects the ability of a committee member to pursue a point of order to the House floor if legislative hearings on the reported measure were not conducted in accordance with all the provisions of that clause (relating to openness, scheduling, calling of witnesses, and other procedures) but only if that point of order was timely raised in committee or subcommittee and 'improperly' disposed of at that time. This represents an exception from the general proposition that points of order in committees are only cognizable in those forums and do not survive to the full House except where specifically preserved by House rules. The act of reporting with a quorum present cures all other interlocutory points of order regarding committee procedure which might have been available earlier in the committee hearing or markup process. Since the inclusion of this exception in the 1970 Reorganization Act, no point of order based on an invalid hearing procedure has been made in the full House, indicating that committees dispose of such matters at the committee or subcommittee level. Points of order intended to survive at the plenary stage, including the majority quorum requirement for reporting, report content requirements, and the inclusion of matters in the measure or in amendments violative of House rules, continue to be justiciable at the plenary stage unless waived, because such rules extend beyond the mere internal operations of committees and go to the content of matter pending in the full House.

Once a measure has been referred, and following legislative hearings if any at the subcommittee or full committee, the committee has several options. It may consider and report (approve) the measure, with or without amendments or recommendation, and send it to the full House or Senate. It may rewrite the measure entirely, reject it, or simply refuse to consider it. Failure to act is usually equivalent to killing the measure, unless the House or Senate employ extraordinary means to discharge the committee or the content of a measure, while not reported, is somehow included by a special rule from the Rules Committee, by floor amendment or in a final House–Senate version. The Members of both Houses defer to committees' decisions for several reasons. Committee members and their staffs have a relatively high degree of expertise over the subjects within their jurisdiction, and the greatest attention to detail is paid at the committee stage. Thus a bill that has survived examination by the experts will likely be given serious consideration in the plenary session. When a committee decides to take up a major bill, the full committee may consider it immediately. More often the chairman assigns the measure to one or more subcommittees for hearings and study, and then for an amendment markup process under the five-minute procedure, permitting germane amendments and amendments thereto as the measure is read by section. Most legislative hearings occur at the subcommittee level, are scheduled by the subcommittee chairman with the approval of the full committee chair and sometimes the Majority party Leadership, are required to be open to the public unless closed by a record vote of the panel, and involve testimony and documentary submissions from witnesses from both the public and private sectors. The subcommittee may approve the measure unaltered, amend it, or block it altogether. If not blocked, the subcommittee will report its recommendations to the full committee. When the full committee receives the report, it may repeat the subcommittee's procedures in whole or in part, or may simply ratify the subcommittee actions. Any full committee may retrieve a measure referred to subcommittee, by motion if necessary, as empowered by a House rule which provides that each subcommittee is subject to the direction and control of the full committee.[26] If a committee reports the measure to the House or Senate, it justifies its actions in a written report which must accompany the measure but which is not separately voted on, apart from the vote on ordering the measure reported. While the language of the accompanying report may be available to the committee members at the time the measure is ordered reported, more often committee staff prepare the report, accounting for all procedural actions taken at the full committee and commenting on issues of legislative intent, after the full committee has ordered the measure reported.

House and Senate rules contain several requirements for inclusion of matter in committee reports for the information of the House or Senate (some similar in both Houses and others unique to one House), including cost estimates, record votes on amendments and on motions to report, all supplemental, additional, and minority views filed by any committee member in timely manner (within two days in the House and three in the Senate), oversight findings and recommendations, general performance goals and objectives (House), the specific constitutional basis empowering Congress to enact the measure (House), regulatory impact statements (Senate), specific changes proposed to be made in existing law ('Ramseyer Rule'), together with additional reporting requirements imposed on specific committees. Because the House and Senate themselves do not vote upon these accompanying reports, but only upon the measures they accompany, draft report language is not always available at the time of ordering reported. Committee chairmen may entertain separate motions requiring inclusion of specified instructive language in the accompanying report, but recognitions for these motions are discretionary with the chair.

To a large extent, the options available to a committee in dealing with a measure are exercised by the chairman, who has wide but not unlimited discretion in establishing the committee's legislative and oversight priorities. The chairman's sources of authority emanate from both the standing rules of the House or Senate, traditions and practices in each House, and from each committee's rules and practices. The chair has primary control of the committee's legislative agenda through the power of recognition and pursuant to committee rules which confer limited agenda-setting power. Referrals to subcommittees may be discretionary or mandated by committee rules, and management of committee funds, employment of staff (subject to ratification by committee vote), use of committee facilities, and recommendations of conferees to the presiding officers are other areas of authority conferred on chairmen. Oleszek comments that 'the chair usually has had a long period of service on the committee and is likely to be better informed than most other members on the many issues coming before the committee. Moreover, the chair is often privy to the leadership's plans and policies, especially the Speaker's or the Senate Majority Leader's legislative objectives. Chairs can use these and other resources to delay, expedite, or modify legislation.'[27]

As discussed in greater detail at pages 315 and 323 the notion that the chair can refuse to hold hearings or can limit the witnesses appearing before a panel is accurate to a point, subject to the ultimate authority of the panel by majority vote to undertake hearings, to summon witnesses, and subject to a majority of the Minority members' ability to summon witnesses for at least one day of hearings. Delays can be instigated by the chairman, or staff at his direction, to the point that the two-year term of a Congress may expire, at which time measures must be reintroduced in the new Congress, although hearings, if any, conducted in prior Congresses may remain relevant. The Chair's control over staff is particularly empowering, as House rules[28] provide that each professional staff member appointed by vote of the committee shall 'be assigned to the chairman and the ranking Minority member of the committee, as the committee considers advisable'. Throughout the rules of the House which empower chairmen, the ultimate authority of the committee or subcommittee to control his actions is clear, but is often delegated in practice to the point where unilateral decisions by the chairman control both daily and long-range committee activity. While House rules require committees to establish regular meeting dates (at least one per month), and permit a majority of all committees and subcommittees to petition for special meetings, in fact most committee meetings are called by committee chairmen on their own initiatives, with the agendas for those meetings as announced by the chairmen and subject to additional committee rules establishing notice requirements. Committees, once convened, can always refuse to consider a measure, can table (adversely dispose of) it or postpone it, and can recess or adjourn by majority vote. Thus there is a constant balance to be measured between on the one hand the majoritarian basis of the rules of the House and Senate to the extent that committees may only act when together, and the unilateral discretion of the chair to make both interlocutory and long range decisions, on the other.

Legislative scheduling

Time in the House and Senate

The standing rules of both US Houses contain provisions, largely obsolete but nevertheless available as alternative mechanisms to permit possible consideration of reported measures, which involve the calls of Calendars and limited debate and amendment opportunities on the called measures. These standby procedures, which in the House include 'Calendar Wednesday', motions to resolve into the Committee of the Whole, and 'Morning Hour' and discharge petitions, and the 'Call of the Calendar of Business Under the Rule' in the Senate do not bear further scrutiny for the purpose of this work, as they are seldom utilized in practice and are consistently supervened by more expeditious procedures. The focus is on those more often-used procedures which include unanimous consent in both Houses, motions to proceed to consideration made by the Majority Leader or other Senators recognized by the Chair in the Senate, motions in the House to suspend the rules and pass the measure, and particularly on special orders of business called up by the Committee on Rules. Also included is an analysis of special statutory procedures in laws in defined subject areas, enacted as joint exercises in rule making, which expedite either or both House's consideration of measures.

The availability of 'time' in the United States Congress is not as much directly influenced by a long-range agenda initiated and managed by the Government (as symbolized by the priorities outlined at Westminster in the Queen's Speech) and then implemented systematically with relatively precise date and debate limitations imposed by a legislature controlled by ministers. Rather, allocation of time is more the result of ad hoc determinations by the agenda-setting Majority party-elected Leaderships in each House, partially depending on party majorities in both branches, partially in furtherance of or in reaction to recommendations from the President delivered annually in a 'State of the Union Message' (and in writing and in committee testimony by the Executive from time to time thereafter), and partially to accommodate individual or party political priorities. While both systems eventually allocate time for consideration of specific legislation taking into account an annual and fiscal year Calendar, the status of existing law, and Executive branch priorities, much Congressional scheduling in addition to long range (often bicameral) leadership planning done behind closed doors in furtherance of party ideology is done on a more ad hoc basis, usually following reports of standing committees and only shortly in advance of full House consideration. This is both to maximize political advantage after party 'whipping' of Members to discern support, and sometimes to minimize Minority or other opposition opportunities in response. Resort to the element of surprise by the Majority through overnight use of the Rules Committee for previously unannounced business is commonplace. In response, the Minority's element of surprise derives primarily from motions to recommit pending measures with provocative instructions.

There are not in the House of Representatives predetermined and predictable stages of consideration, with gaps for example between second reading, committee stage, and then third reading, scheduled and known to the membership well in advance. Rather, there is usually one stage of uninterrupted plenary consideration in each House, more often continuous in the House than in the Senate, following standing committee consideration, and including consecutive stages of general debate, second reading for amendment, third reading and passage. Such scheduling, when it does take place, is normally not announced to the membership until the end of the previous week. There are few tentative announcements of business more than a week in advance on the floor, except for the recess schedule for the year, announced at the beginning of each calendar year at the start of the regular Congressional session in the context of days on which votes are anticipated, to permit Members planning flexibility while not being agenda specific. In the House of Commons, weekly announcements of the programme towards the end of each week include scheduling for the next two weeks, and are often formalized by programme motions well in advance of the various stages of consideration. The pattern of sitting days is also made known, subject to contingencies, for a session.

A discussion of the availability of time in a bicameral sense must contrast what can be debated and accomplished day-to-day and for a longer term by a partisan Majority using special orders of business in one House, with a co-equal branch where unlimited debate and individual agendas proliferate and are reflected in unanimous consent agreements. Such a discussion must focus on the planning of an agenda within each House and between the two Houses, statutory deadlines by which legislative decisions must be finalized, taking into account 'recess' periods during the calendar year, and the cooperation between two Houses and two branches of government in fulfilment of that agenda.

Some mention of the 'availability of time' in the human context of Members' ability to interact with colleagues and others is necessary to more fully evaluate the deliberative capabilities and realities of the institution and the processes by which it reaches decisions. As Members' daily personal agendas are increasingly focused on gaining partisan party advantage, especially by political fund raising, and on time spent in Congressional districts rather than on performance of a legislative role, less time remains available for personal interactions and collegiality among Members, and between Members 'across the centre aisle'. The notion that Members must be in their districts and free to 'hear from their constituents' in order to better represent their interests and to merit re-election, had become so compelling, and so encouraged by party leaders, at least through the 109th Congress, that precious little time remained in an average week for Members to conduct legislative oversight or scrutiny at the committee level. That dynamic shifted with the onset of a new 110th Congress where new political majorities in both Houses were determined to scrutinize past and present activities of the Executive representing the other party, but was partially offset by the threat of Presidential vetoes which discouraged some legislative activity even from the outset.

The reluctance of Members to establish residences at the seat of government (given the ease of subsidized travel and cost of maintenance of two residences) impacts on available legislative time and on their ability to socially interact with colleagues, and to develop friendships and levels of trust potentially enabling 'compromise' positions to emerge between the parties. Because both parties have experienced the advantages of Majority status and the disadvantages of Minority status in contemporary Congresses, their leaders are fully aware of the considerable benefits of party status in a majoritarian institution, where party affiliation is controlling not only in terms of votes but also in terms of committee chairmanships, staff capacity, and the allocation of time and agenda-setting at every level of activity. The retention of Majority party status has become the perpetual focus of both leaderships, to the detriment of individual Members' ability to utilize time through bipartisan interactions to better legislate in the public interest. This reality results in available time being spent in a less collegial manner. Members are not as inclined to participate in meaningful debate when the precise issue to be voted on is whipped in advance of the debate and only made in order when a political advantage is predicted from the result of the whip count. A renewed openness to spontaneous debate and amendments, although promised, did not materialize in the 110th Congress under a new Majority, certainly not to the norm which had been traditional in the House until the 1990s. In any event, the desire to protect vulnerable Members' voting records against difficult Minority amendment proposals, and to enable Members to raise necessary funds for the next election cycle, suggest that time and issue certainty will continue to weigh heavily on the Majority leadership as it organizes the agenda. Countering these trends was a new political activism, motivated in the 110th Congress by enhanced oversight of the opposition party Executive or in response to Executive policy failures. Legislative activism also can increase under an Executive of the same party majority where not inhibited by veto threats. Whether such increased time will translate into additional 'openness' at the plenary stage—insisted upon by the past and present Minority—remains in doubt, as politically difficult issues will continue to be rushed to the floor without complete committee consideration and then debated under special rules which restrict a full range of proper alternatives at the plenary stage.

At the beginning of the 110th Congress under a new Majority, an initial '100-hour agenda' was facilitated by a special order embedded in the resolution adopting the standing rules whereby Minority amendment options on six bills to be reintroduced and immediately considered were greatly curtailed. These restrictions on amendments were rationalized by the new Majority which had been so critical of 'closed rules' leading up to the previous election by a characterization that the six measures received some level of consideration in the prior Congress. They were described as appropriate for immediate enactment (at least in the House) prior to the President's customary initiation of the legislative process by his State of the Union Address and budget submission within the first month of the new session. This was the first signal that a return to once-traditional openness and spontaneity in debate and amendment in the House could not be realistically anticipated, despite campaign pledges to that end by the new Majority leadership. The pressures toward certainty of time and issue, as they bear on quality-of-life demands, on political protection of voting records of vulnerable Majority incumbents, and on the incessant quest for campaign funds all served as constraints against a full return to traditional process. The Majority leadership's pervasive fear of losing votes on issues in the House which had so greatly impacted another Majority's agenda-setting strategy in the three prior Congresses remained an influence on agenda setting.

In the 110th Congress a new but non-veto proof Majority was more focused on debating alternatives to the Executive's opposing agenda. A belief that those alternatives stood a lesser chance of being considered or passed in the Senate or of becoming law, however, militated against full implementation of an agenda likely to be vetoed. Concern over votes on issues which impacted upon its new rank and file also influenced decisions on whether to bring matters to final votes in the House. At the outset, an increased level of oversight of the Executive in the form of committee hearings in both Houses predominated, where the primary incentive was to inform public opinion of the failings of the Executive and to set the stage for remedial legislation. Lacking institutional memory and leadership appreciation of once-traditional openness and spontaneity, partisan political advantage in agenda setting and allocation of time continued to dominate proceedings in a House reflecting a narrow political and wide ideological divide in the nation.

The economic and fiscal crisis escalating into 2009, and the inauguration of a new President of a different political party at this writing have changed the priorities of the legislative agenda dramatically at the beginning of the 111th Congress. Some of the procedural and institutional implications demonstrated in both Houses are treated separately in this work. The urgency of enactment of 'stimulus' legislation articulated by the Executive branch resulted in many procedural departures from 'regular order'.

Much relatively non-controversial legislation sponsored by individual Members, often parochial in nature and frequently not even reported from committee, is scheduled on a weekly basis at the Majority leadership's discretion. Such measures take the form of proclamations or other 'sense of Congress' expressions introduced to benefit individual Members' political fortunes. Despite often unanimous support for these measures, they are sometimes scheduled to draw recorded votes to enhance Members' overall voting percentages and attendance records and to assemble them in the Chamber for an extended period, rather than in furtherance of public policy. These recorded votes are often conducted at pre-announced times on Monday or Tuesday evenings of legislative weeks in order to facilitate party 'whip' activity in one place—the House floor. Members are often preoccupied with their voting records, especially hoping to achieve percentages in the 90 per cent range, regardless of the importance of the issues voted upon. Given that focus, the Majority Leadership often schedules votes on non-controversial legislation to begin at 6.30 pm to accommodate all Members travelling to the capital, including many from the west coast, on that day. This scheduling, coupled with the completion of legislative business on Thursdays, enables Members to be in their congressional districts for constituent or fund-raising activities for four to five days during many weeks. The compression of the legislative work week into two or three days (at least within the 106th through the 110th Congresses) reflects both the importance of Member fund raising, constituent 'ombudsman' activities in the districts, the availability of reimbursement for official travel, and the lack of a legislative and oversight agenda commanding Members' presence at the seat of government for the entire week. The issues presented for beginning-of-the-week record votes to encourage Members to be present are often inconsequential, do not require advance whipping and are of little public policy consequence. Whether clustered votes is something into which the Commons practice of deferred divisions (page 222) will in time and under pressure develop remains to be seen: the danger has however been amply signposted.

A new party majority in the House in 1995 adopted a rule prohibiting the introduction or consideration of commemorative measures which 'designated a particular period of time in remembrance, celebration or recognition for any purpose'. This was an effort to end the proliferation of joint resolutions proclaiming as statutory law specific days, weeks, and months in commemoration of persons, entities, or events past or present, the introduction and passage of which Members were under increasing political pressure to sponsor. Drafting techniques rapidly developed which avoided the strict proscriptions of the rule, while still commemorating or acknowledging the importance of a matter in a more general time-unspecific sense. These and other measures, such as naming of Federal facilities, designs of postage stamps, congratulatory resolutions of various sorts, and foreign policy expressions—the kind of topics corralled in the Commons within the harmless confines of Early Day Motions—have become the staple of legislative vehicles considered under motions to suspend the rules, most often not reported from committee, upon which recorded votes are conducted in order to assure Members' attendance. This trend has been coupled with the Chair's discretionary authority to postpone and cluster recorded votes for up to two legislative days to announced times within that period. This agenda setting, utilizing the Chair's discretionary recognition and vote-scheduling powers to enhance certainty of time and issue, further demonstrates the ever more frequent utilization of strategies in a partisan majoritarian institution.

Time also becomes scarce when it is necessary to comply with statutorily imposed requirements for enactment into law of certain legislation (such as an annual budget for each fiscal year beginning 1 October), or other statutory expiration dates requiring renewal, and when the remaining time left to enact such legislation within a session of Congress is influenced by predetermined recess periods within a Calendar year. Much more than time being the critically scarce resource merely because there is not enough of it in an ordinary work week, it is the daily or weekly political variable of ad hoc procedural constraints on the membership in order to maximize certainty of time and issue that results in restrictions on available time.

Unanimous consent in the House of Representatives

The establishment of orders of either House by unanimous consent is an essential mechanism in both Houses of Congress, while not, with rare exceptions, in the House of Commons where 'formal agreement of the broadest possible consensus' is required for the progress of business. In both Houses of Congress, unanimous consent orders often have the effect of imposing restrictions on time and in the House are utilized to avoid the necessity of voting on resolutions from the Rules Committee or on secondary motions. It is employed to initially enable the consideration of measures not otherwise eligible for immediate disposition, or to impose time and amendment limits on any measure once under consideration. In the House, unanimous consent orders are utilized when all Members agree that more time-consuming procedures are unnecessary in achieving the dual purpose of immediate debate and expedited final action without intervening questions. In both Houses, unanimous consent when granted becomes an order governing consideration of pending or subsequent legislation constituting an instant and permissible exercise in constitutional rule-making authority which alters the application of standing rules.

In the House, the practice of allowing some action to be taken by unanimous consent began in the 1830s when the House, responding to the increased pressure of legislative activity, unanimously agreed to a special order permitting it to consider a bill which was not in the regular order of business. This use has now become commonplace and many items of business are considered as a result of unanimous consent requests. The device is also used to facilitate consideration of measures, once begun, by waiving readings or limiting or extending the time for debate. Recognition of Members to offer unanimous consent requests is in the discretion of the Chair, and must first be for some stated purpose, in response to the Chair's query: 'for what purpose does the gentleman rise?' Beginning in the 1980s, Speakers have announced and enforced a policy of conferring recognition for unanimous consent requests for the consideration of legislation only when assured that both Majority and Minority floor and committee Leaderships have no objection. Thus the Chair takes the institutional responsibility through his discretionary power of recognition, without indicating a political preference regarding the request, to minimize attempts to force Members for the purpose of political embarrassment to otherwise go on record as objecting to a variety of unanimous consent requests.

The Speaker's discretionary recognition authority for unanimous consent requests is augmented by her discretionary recognition authority (recently expanded from two to three days each week and often further by special orders) for motions to suspend the rules and pass by two-thirds votes unamendable measures. Together, these two procedures are most frequently utilized to accomplish the bulk of non-controversial business.

Most parliamentary bodies adopt standing rules which prescribe a daily order of business, and the House of Representatives is no exception. But as clause 1 of Rule XIV itself provides, 'the daily order of business (unless varied by the application of other rules and except for the disposition of matters of higher precedence) shall be as follows: first, Prayer by the Chaplain. Second, Reading and approval of the Journal, unless postponed... Third, the pledge of Allegiance to the Flag.' Beyond these first three steps, however, are seldom-used steps such as Correction of Referral of bills, Disposition of Privileged Business on the Speaker's table, Unfinished Business, the morning hour, motions to resolve into a Committee of the Whole, and 'orders of the day'. All these subsequent steps describe procedures technically available on a daily basis to conduct business, but which are in fact superseded by unanimous consent requests, by suspension of the rules motions, and by special orders of business reported from the Committee on Rules. The parenthetical language in the clause itself acknowledges that priority or 'privilege' accorded in other House standing rules, most notably the authority of the Rules Committee to call up reports under clause 5 of Rule XIII, can completely displace 'orders of the day', morning hour, or motions to resolve into Committee of the Whole to consider reported measures. In addition, 'Unfinished Business' consists of postponed and clustered votes previously ordered by the Speaker to a subsequent time and place as determined by her within two legislative days, and this specific conferral of authority supersedes the general statement that 'Unfinished Business' must be the sixth order of business every day. It is the ability of the House, unique among parliaments in the world, to depart from its standing rules and set its agenda on a daily basis, which renders unnecessary a more detailed discussion in this work of alternative unused procedures.

Unanimous consent and consent agreements in the Senate

Especially in the Senate, where time for debate and amendment is normally unlimited, except where limitations have been imposed by a super-majority by cloture motion or pursuant to a statutorily imposed scheme, unanimous consent is a necessary and common practice and tradition. Since rules do not exist which permit the Senate to impose limitations by majority motion (the motion for the previous question having gone out of use in the earliest years of the Senate) agreements by unanimous consent are often utilized to indicate a procedural accommodation for the concerns of all Senators. In theory, time is not normally considered a scarce commodity in the Senate—the 'greatest deliberative body in the world'. But in fact, time becomes a relevant factor when considering the diverse demands on Senators' individual schedules (increasingly including fund-raising activities) the complexity of legislative issues, and the scarcity of standing rules which would allow a majority by motion to set and limit time.

As essential as unanimous consent agreements are to the daily conduct of Senate business, it must be noted that by tradition and precedent, the Majority Leader is the first Senator recognized by the Chair at any stage of a legislative proceeding and especially at the initial stage of consideration. Thus the Majority Leader's control of the agenda is initially enhanced and is coupled with priority of recognition when sought to offer secondary motions such as the motion to table, to keep alternative agendas off the floor, or to 'fill the amendment tree' in cloture and some pre-cloture situations. While non-controversial measures may reach the Senate floor on a motion by any Senator if recognized, the Majority Leader normally tries to reach advance agreements on the floor schedule and is likely to oppose action that will bring measures to the floor without prior clearance from him and the Minority Leader. The Majority Leader's prerogative to receive preferential recognition from the presiding officer at all times, enables him to control the agenda of activities on the floor. A Senator who attempts to bring a measure to the floor without the consent of the Majority Leader may find the proposal subject to an immediate tabling motion made by the Majority Leader and decided without debate. To quote a Senate Majority Leader, 'I want to see the votes, and I want to see an outline of what the parliamentary situation will be, because time is a consideration around here.'[29] Unanimous consent agreements reflect the political ability of the Members of the body in unison, as negotiated by their respective party leaderships, to impose time and amendment constraints not otherwise achievable.

As was noted at page 73, Senate 'holds' have been utilized as an informal courtesy among Senators, there having been until 2007 no formal rule or order restricting the making of unanimous consent requests at the behest of an unnamed Senator not present on the floor to personally object. Beginning with the enactment of PL 110-81,[30] the Senate adopted by law a standing order requiring requests for 'holds' by absent Senators to be published by party leaders in the Record so as to identify the objector. Prior to that time, holds were anonymous and were mutually honoured by party leaders as a courtesy to Senators from their party who objected to consideration of an item of business either on its merits or to gain leverage toward the consideration of other measures or matters. This new disclosure requirement, while not prohibiting Senators from effectively objecting to proposed unanimous consent requests although absent from the floor, no longer permits the names of those objecting Senators to be kept secret if a required letter requesting and explaining the hold has been sent to the party leader for six days of session and no other Senator has extended the hold by submitting a similar letter.

In the Senate, unanimous consent for the immediate or subsequent consideration of a bill, or sometimes of a group of bills en bloc, may be stated to include adoption of amendments and final passage as well, even going so far as to permit Senators' statements to be inserted in the Record as if uttered without actually being spoken on the floor.

(This is the most extreme example of expedited consideration in the Senate, and is confined to non-controversial bills which normally are reported from committee where no Senator wishes to separately debate or amend the bill on the floor and where the 'clean-up' of multiple measures in one unanimous action is desired.) The credibility of such inserted 'debate' as 'legislative history' is questionable, and the appearance in the Record of such remarks not printed in a distinctive type style (a requirement under House rules for remarks not actually uttered) is a deceptive technique which denigrates the Senate's proceedings. Often there is no accurate indication of Senate legislative intent until the Record is printed the next day, and this lack of transparency leads to confusion and uncertainty, especially at times when the two Houses are attempting to reconcile differences between them in an expeditious way and wish to be publicly aware on the same day of what the other House has done.

A less expeditious form of unanimous consent in the Senate might initially only include permission for immediate consideration, with individual Senators then free to debate and amend the bill but with no predetermined time limits. With increasing frequency, however, the modern Senate utilizes unanimous consent requests which include time agreements (so-called 'consent agreements'). A consent agreement typically regulates one or more of the following: (1) initiating consideration; (2) limiting time for debate; (3) offering amendment and amendments thereto; (4) the use of motions; (5) concluding consideration; and (6) subsequent proceedings. The Senate uses consent agreements because its standing rules place few limits on the consideration of measures. Nor is there any motion to impose such limits for a particular measure short of cloture, which requires a super-majority vote and imposes a single prescribed set of constraints (discussed at page 437). In earlier decades, consent agreements often were entered into before the Senate began consideration of a measure, covered all phases of consideration, and followed a model standardized as the 'usual form' and roughly the equivalent of an 'open rule' reported from the Committee on Rules in the House (see prior discussion). Today's consent agreements are more often reached only after consideration begins (usually by initial unanimous consent) and address only selected aspects of the overall process. Consent agreements are not to be confused with unanimous consent requests for a single immediate purpose in the Senate, such as to dispense with the reading of an amendment or with further proceedings under a quorum call.

Most measures reach the Senate floor through unanimous consent requests that the Senate proceed to consider those measures. Such requests are usually considered consent agreements only when they also include further provisions regulating subsequent consideration. When a consent agreement is made in advance of initial consideration, however, it can include provisions for taking up the measure. Typical provisions are that the measure come before the Senate: (a) at a date (and time) certain; (b) at a time determined by the Majority Leader (often after consultation with the Minority Leader or occasionally with his concurrence); (c) only after (or perhaps only before) a date certain; or (d) upon disposition of some other measure. A consent agreement also may provide that consideration of a measure that was previously considered and laid aside resume, under one of the conditions listed. A consent agreement may include waivers of any points of order (such as two-day report availability) to which a measure might otherwise be subject.

Consent agreements that include limitations on time available for debate are also called 'time agreements'. A time agreement may establish an overall limit on debate of a measure, or may regulate only a certain day or portion of consideration. Usually, it specifies a length of time for debate on a measure, 'equally divided and controlled' by the Majority and Minority bill managers. Occasionally other Senators may also control blocks of this 'bill time' or it may be divided unequally among Senators. When time is controlled, a Senator can be recognized to speak on that question only when a colleague who controls time first yields a portion of it to the Senator. Also, until all time is used or yielded back, no vote can occur on the question, nor can an amendment or motion to table be offered.

Consent agreements often provide that amendments may be offered only (if relevant or separately 'germane') to the measure or to the amendment to which offered; or as identified by the sponsor, subject, or number in the consent agreement itself. The test of relevancy or germaneness of amendments in the Senate, if either of those standards is imposed by a consent agreement, is more subjective than in the House, since the Chair does not have a large body of Senate precedent upon which to rely—there having been no general germaneness rule in place during the Senate's existence. The Chair often makes a finding of relevance if the amendment 'is not entirely unrelated' to the text which is either a first-degree amendment or the entire text of the pending measure to which offered. The text of those amendments is available in both cloakrooms and in the Record if submitted and numbered on a prior day. Absent a restriction in the consent agreement on second-degree amendments, they are in order if relevant. Time agreements may provide separate blocks of controlled time for each amendment.

The usual form of time agreement specifies an amount of time for any 'debatable motion, appeal, or point of order' that may arise. Consent agreements may also prohibit or restrict the use of quorum calls or of various motions, such as motions to table or reconsider amendments, or to recommit the bill. As will be discussed, some consent agreements adjust the time stipulated by Senate rules for filing cloture motions, for voting on them, or for filing germane amendments to be considered under cloture. A few regulate the use of cloture in other ways, such as by providing that a cloture motion be deemed to have been filed (perhaps in advance of consideration); that the Senate take up some other measure in the middle of considering one under cloture; or even that cloture be deemed to have been invoked. See also the chapter on Procedural Basics at page 200.

A consent agreement may provide that votes on amendments be postponed until a specified time, then 'stacked' to occur in immediate sequence. It may also provide for an automatic vote on final passage at a specified time or stage, such as when all available time is exhausted, or upon disposition of all listed amendments, or at a date and time certain. Alternatively, a consent agreement may stipulate that when a specified time or stage is reached, the measure being considered will be laid aside, or returned to the Calendar, pending specified action on another measure or until a date certain, or until the Majority Leader so determines.

Consent agreements often provide that, if the Senate passes the measure in question, it should then take a House-passed companion bill, substitute the Senate text, and pass the House bill in that form. Some stipulate instead that the Senate bill be held at the desk until such a House bill is received, and that similar action then be deemed to have occurred. Both of these steps may be taken, for example, where the Senate has acted first on its own version of a revenue or Appropriation bill (which by the Constitution and tradition must originate in the House but which for scheduling purposes the Senate has first considered). Other provisions also appear for regulating the 'hook-up' of a Senate and House measure in order to begin to resolve differences between the two Houses. A consent agreement in the Senate can affect consideration of more than one measure and the legislative steps accommodated by such multiple considerations and 'deemings' can be uninformative to the outside observer, especially at the time entered and until the Record is available the following day.

By definition these unanimous consent time agreements if ordered reflect consensus between the Majority and Minority Leaders on behalf of all Senators. They are propounded by the Majority Leader through his prerogative of priority of recognition, or by his Majority party designee, and represent in their preparation a considerable degree of collegiality among all Senators. Essentially, this tradition of consent in the Senate distinguishes its proceedings from the majoritarian determinations accomplished in the House by votes on special orders of business and on secondary 'procedural' motions such as the previous question.

An illustration of the form of a relatively straightforward unanimous consent order of the Senate permitting only one substitute amendment follows:

> *Ordered*, That at a time determined by the Majority Leader, following consultation with the Minority Leader, but no later than…2009, the Committee on…be discharged from consideration of the bill S…and that the Senate then proceed to its consideration; that the measure be considered under the following limitations; that there be a total of…hours of debate on the bill and substitute amendment, with the time equally divided and controlled between proponents and opponents; provided further that the only amendment in order to be a substitute to be offered by the Senator from…and the Senator from…, that upon the use or yielding back of all time, the Senate vote on the amendment; that upon the disposition of the amendment, the bill as amended, if amended, be read a third time, and without further action or debate, the Senate proceed to vote on passage of the bill.

The unanimous consent orders of both Houses are listed in the respective Calendars and are reported in the Record, while the text of any amendments made in order are posted on the Senate Calendar of business.

Referral of a measure to committee can prolong the process necessary to bring that measure immediately before each body, especially in the Senate where the motion to proceed to consideration is not in order if the bill has been referred. In that case, the first motion must be to discharge the committee which may not be coupled with immediate consideration, and the motion itself is subject to extended debate. To avoid that additional step toward consideration where immediate consideration of a newly introduced measure 'which is at the desk' is deemed necessary, any Senator may object to its referral to committee and force its being placed on a Calendar.[31] From that point, the Majority Leader may be first recognized to move to proceed to consideration of such an unreferred bill in order to avoid the preliminary step of a successful (though seldom used) motion to discharge. In most cases, failure to obtain unanimous consent of a measure normally forces the Majority Leader or his designee to move consideration of the measure under conditions where the motion faces potentially unlimited debate.

Discharges

The most important available procedure to bypass a leadership agenda is the 'Discharge Petition'. Varying forms of Rule XV, clause 2 have been in place since 1910 in the House. A Member may file with the Clerk a motion to discharge a committee from consideration of a public bill or resolution that was referred to committee at least thirty legislative days prior thereto. More frequently, the motion will be filed against a special order of business providing for the consideration of such an unreported public bill which has concurrently been referred to the Committee on Rules for seven legislative days without a report thereon. The motion in the form of a petition is available at the rostrum for Members to sign while the House is in session. Once the petition has been filed, the Clerk makes the signatures a matter of public record on the last day of each week (a requirement ironically imposed by a successful discharge petition to adopt a rules change in 1993 which theretofore had required that the signatures remain secret). When a majority of the total membership (218 Members not including Delegates) of the House has signed the petition, it is placed on the 'Discharge Calendar', noted in the Journal and Record, and then becomes available for privileged consideration on the second and fourth Mondays of each month following its placement on that Calendar for seven legislative days. Because the petition if filed against the underlying unreported bill, if successful, would require consideration of the discharged measure under the general rules of the House—that is, with unlimited germane amendments and amendments thereto if considered in Committee of the Whole—the petitions are normally filed against special orders introduced by a Member supporting that public measure but providing expedited procedures which limit the amendment and debate process if that resolution is adopted by the House. To be eligible for a discharge motion, such a special order may make in order only one underlying reported or unreported measure and may not waive germaneness points of order against any amendments. Until 1997, the rule had been utilized to permit the filing of discharge petitions against special order resolutions which made in order totally unrelated and even unspecified 'A to Z'. This was accomplished by waiving germaneness points of order or self-executing unrelated language in the base text. This change eliminated an avoidance of the thirty-legislative-day layover requirement by preventing its application to a vehicle, allowing one or more unrelated propositions that had not been referred to committee for thirty days to be added to a 'shell' bill which had met that requirement. When the discharge motion is called up from the Calendar, it is debatable for twenty minutes equally divided, and is then voted on without intervening motion except one motion to adjourn. Its adoption by the House then permits consideration of the underlying measure pursuant to the terms of the adopted special order, for example the 'immediate consideration' thereof. In the interim between the signing of the discharge petition and its consideration in the House, the Committee on Rules may report an alternative special order which, if adopted after a one-day layover, may lay on the table the resolution to be discharged and may provide other procedures for the underlying measure. This happened twice in contemporary Congresses, both on Constitutional Amendments providing for a balanced Federal budget. As important as the actual implementation of the rule is, the realization that a petition has or is about to have sufficient signatures (usually a coalition of Minority and some Majority members) merits the consideration of the measure under terms more favourable to the Majority leadership. The publication of Members' signatures since 1993 has from time to time impacted politically on the success of the petition and has caused the Majority leadership to take into consideration the possibility of success under this otherwise cumbersome procedure.

Certain matters arising under the Constitution are privileged for consideration at any time and may therefore be discharged irrespective of the requirements for petition under the discharge rule, subject only to a two-day notice and scheduling requirement under Rule IX. Examples include propositions to discipline a Member and impeachment resolutions, a vetoed bill which has been returned to the House and referred back to committee, and a resolution involving the right of a Member to his seat.

The House Rules Committee and special orders

The House of Representatives seldom establishes 'orders of the day' which are advance dates for the consideration of certain business. Rather, such orders result from the adoption of resolutions from the Rules Committee, which normally have immediate effect and remain in effect until final disposition, even on a subsequent day. By resolving that the Speaker may 'at any time' declare a certain measure under consideration in Committee of the Whole or may recognize a Member to call up a measure at any time in the House, and by providing that the Speaker may postpone further consideration at any time notwithstanding the ordering of the previous question, this scheduling flexibility is assured.

Lacking the prospect of a two-thirds majority, special orders of business, reported as privileged matters from the Committee on Rules and having priority for consideration after only one legislative day (meaning that an adjournment and reconvening even on the same calendar day must intervene) become the procedural vehicle of choice. Thus the political composition of that committee is a crucial factor in the House. It cannot be overemphasized that a disproportionate number—nine of thirteen of that committee's members—are directly appointed by and are accountable to the Speaker to further the Majority party agenda. These expediting procedures circumvent the application of other standing rules, as there are no other viable procedures for 'privileged' or assured consideration in the House of measures reported from standing committees. The act of reporting a measure from committee does not, with only a few exceptions, result in consideration of that measure in the House, absent a Leadership initiative to arrange its scheduling. Conversely the failure to report does not necessarily prevent consideration if the Rules Committee is utilized by the leadership as an instrument to 'discharge' the standing committee from further consideration and bring the measure directly to the floor under a special procedure. Reported bills remain on Calendars which are mere receptacles and are not 'called' in modern practice.[32] Thus in the House, standing rules necessitate a special way to permit consideration of most important bills, if constraints are to be placed on debate and amendments in order to manage time and issue, which avenue is the utilization of the reporting power of the Committee on Rules. Until 2009 the House normally dispensed with the call of Calendar Wednesday at the end of the preceding week by unanimous consent, otherwise by motion requiring a two-thirds vote. Thus while the rule is intended to protect reports from standing committees against total opposition by the leadership, in practice the Speaker controls the flow of all business through suspension of the rules or through the Rules Committee. If Calendar Wednesday is utilized, only the chairman of the reporting committee can call up the measure on the Calendar unless the committee has specifically authorized another member to manage the bill under that procedure.[33]

The following excerpts from Rule XIII establish and reflect the essence of the importance of the Committee on Rules, upon which all important agenda setting depends:

Clause 5(a); The following committees shall have leave to report at any time on the following matters, respectively:...

(4) the Committee on Rules, on rules, joint rules and the order of business...

Clause 6(a); A report by the Committee on Rules on any rule, joint rule or order of business may not be called up for consideration on the same (legislative) day it is presented to the House except—

(1) when so determined by a vote of two thirds of the Members voting, a quorum being present...

    (b) Pending the consideration of a report from the Committee on Rules on a rule, joint rule or order of business, the Speaker may entertain one motion that the House adjourn. After the result of such motion is announced, the Speaker may not entertain any other dilatory motion until the report shall have been fully disposed of...

    (c) The Committee on Rules may not report...

(2) a rule or order that would prevent the motion to recommit a bill or joint resolution from being made as provided in Rule XIX, including a motion to recommit with instructions to report back an amendment otherwise in order, if offered by the Minority Leader or a designee...

It is instructive to compare the form of a traditional 'open' rule with the increasingly frequent use of a more 'closed' or 'modified closed' rule, in order to understand how the application of standing rules has given way to supervening special rules with respect to most major bills.

Open:

Resolved, That upon the adoption of this resolution it shall be in order to move that the House resolve itself into the Committee of the Whole House on the State of the Union for the consideration of the bill (H.R....) and the first reading of the bill is dispensed with. After general debate, which shall be confined to the bill and shall continue not to exceed...hour(s) to be equally divided and controlled by the chairman and ranking minority member of the Committee(s) on..., the bill shall be read for amendment under the five-minute rule. At the conclusion of the consideration of the bill for amendment, the Committee shall rise and report the bill to the House with such amendments as may have been adopted, and the previous question shall be considered as ordered on the bill and amendments thereto to final passage without intervening motion except one motion to recommit (with instructions).

Most essentially, this form of an 'open rule' requires the application of the general five-minute rule for amendments and amendments thereto, in no prescribed order except as the bill is read section by section, and without prejudice as to decisions to be made by the Chair on germaneness points of order, with each offered amendment being entitled to five minutes of debate by each Member, subject to priorities of recognition and the possible intervention of motions to limit debate, but not susceptible to the cutting off of proper amendments.

The above 'open rule' form is in contrast with the more contemporary form of special 'modified closed' rule as follows:

Modified closed:

> *Resolved,* That upon the adoption of this resolution the Speaker may declare the House resolved into the Committee of the Whole House on the State of the Union for the consideration of the bill H.R.... After general debate, which shall be confined to the bill and shall continue not to exceed... hour(s), the bill shall be considered as having been read for amendment, (and the amendments contained in part A of the report accompanying this resolution shall be considered as adopted). No further amendment shall be in order (except those contained in part B of the accompanying report, and only in the order listed and for the time allocated, and shall not be subject to amendment, and all points of order against said amendments are hereby waived). At the conclusion of consideration of the bill for amendment, the Committee shall rise and report the bill to the House with such amendments as may have been adopted, and the previous question shall be considered as ordered on the bill and amendments thereto to final passage without intervening motion except one motion to recommit with or without instructions.

These comparative forms demonstrate that once consideration is assured by ad hoc votes of the House on each special order, standing rules (that is, the 'five-minute rule' which would then otherwise permit a broader and potentially less manageable range of debate and amendments) are set aside in favour of a predictable and unamendable sequence of amendments, if any are to be permitted at all. Coupled with this ordered sequence is often the 'self-execution' of amendments contained in the Rules Committee report (for example, those referenced in Part A of the report), considered to have been adopted upon the House's adoption of the resolution. This technique has taken hold more frequently in contemporary Congresses as measures emerging from committees are sometimes extensively rewritten, often with additional and non-germane matter, merely by a vote on the special order of business resolution and not by the traditional presentation and vote on separate amendments following the standing committee stage. It has the effect of reducing the number of substantive issues susceptible to separate consideration into one 'procedural' vote on the resolution and permits the Majority leadership to negotiate 'modifications' apart from and subsequent to standing committee deliberations. This technique is often justified as a time-saving step, and may be coupled with the ability of the bill manager to 'en bloc' consideration of amendments screened by the Rules Committee into one or more 'managers' amendments' which are not amendable or divisible into separate substantive parts. Recent special orders have even combined provisions for disposition of separate bills, resolutions and conference reports, and being non-divisible for voting, can become an order of the House governing a variety of business. The profound policy implications of these expediting procedures cannot be overstated, as a variety of substantive issues are rolled into one 'procedural vote' on the adoption of the resolution in a manner which saves considerable time and political energy, and shields vulnerable Members from being forced to cast separate votes on some particular issues.

It cannot be too strongly emphasized that, increasingly in the contemporary US House of Representatives in the last decade, and in contrast to parliamentary bodies over the world, there has been a political majority intent upon restricting debate and minimizing undesirable votes, rather than following established general rules or practices. In fact, this circumvention of other standing rules and practices in furtherance of time and issue certainty has itself become the established practice, regardless of the political majority. Traditional norms which in other parliaments permit the amendment selection process to reside in a non-partisan Chair or which in Congress have been guided by institutionally established precedents based on non-partisan application of germaneness precedent, have given way to processes, depending on Majority party methods of achieving consensus, to minimize spontaneous debate and Minority opportunities, and to maximize Majority party voting majorities. In the House of Commons the right of backbenchers to intervene in debate has been diminished by standing orders or occasional business motions adopted by the House, behind which lies a broader time–business balance designed—as it must, within reason—to deliver the government's business,[34] in the US House those forces, together with party discipline, have combined to greatly circumvent the ability of the individual Member to fully participate in the plenary sessions in debate and in the amendment process. Indeed, party discipline is brought to bear on particularly difficult political issues not merely as the result of informal 'whip counts' often conducted in the days or hours leading up to a crucial vote or its scheduling, but also as the result of formally convened Majority party 'conferences' or 'caucuses' where, as a contemporary Speaker of the House has asserted, the 'majority of the Majority' must first be discerned and its position then rendered achievable by utilization of special orders of business.

For further discussion of the Speaker's role as party leader utilizing the Rules Committee, see page 426. It has become routine practice for a Majority member of the Rules Committee to announce to the House several days in advance of meeting (usually when the schedule for the following week is announced by the Majority Leader at the end of business for a week) that a 'restrictive' rule may be granted and that all Members should submit properly drafted copies of proposed amendments to the committee by a specified time on the day prior to meeting and should seek advice from the House Parliamentarian regarding compliance with House rules (primarily germaneness). The House is thereby notified of a likely screening process sufficiently in advance of floor consideration to enable party whips to interact with Rules Committee members to control the permissible range of amendments. Indeed, in the 110th Congress the Chairman of the Rules Committee has not permitted even the consideration of many requested amendments when submitted only minutes beyond the announced deadline.

When utilization of the most important standing rule and practice of the House (that which allows the Speaker to appoint a super-majority (nine of thirteen members) to the Rules Committee and empowers that committee with jurisdiction to bring ad hoc rules variations and waivers almost immediately to the House for disposition by majority vote) is combined with an unwritten standard of Majority party discipline which constrains Majority Members to invariably cast 'procedural votes' for their leadership, in order to prevent amendment and assure adoption of those special rules, the result is the circumvention of the remaining standing rules for the duration of initial consideration of the underlying matter in the House. What is forgone or sacrificed is a more spontaneous and unpredictable consideration, often in a Committee of the Whole, of amendments and the ability to isolate some issues for second-degree amendments and separate votes.

Committee of the Whole in Congress

Having analysed various procedures available in the House by which a degree of certainty in availability of time and advance notice of issue can be assured under contemporary practices and expectations, it is necessary to examine the basic counterpoint to those procedures, namely the requirement under standing rules that a Committee of the Whole first consider a scheduled measure referred to it by the House, under procedures which maximize individual Member involvement and minimize instant Majority procedural control.

A centrepiece of House rules derived from the British House of Commons from the first Congress is the rule requiring consideration, prior to final House action, of most measures (those involving 'any charge on the People') in a Committee of the Whole 'where the sense of the whole is better taken in committee, because in all committees everyone speaks as often as he pleases'.[35]

Committees of the whole House emerged in England at the beginning of the seventeenth century, in the context of the struggle between the monarch and Parliament over the right to levy taxes, sparked off by what the Houses saw as royal profligacy. The specific reason for the creation of this new parliamentary organ is unclear. It may be that the Commons feared that the Speaker might reveal details of their debates to the King. Alternatively, the House may simply have been seeking a forum in which debate was attended by less formality. Lastly, when royal intimidation became intolerable, retreat from the Palace of Westminster to the safety of the more sympathetic City perhaps made a great deal of sense. That was not something the House itself could readily do—or not without substantially raising the political temperature—but a Committee, even one comprising all Members, might and did. Whatever their origin, Committees of the whole House were subsequently seen to be so useful that they survived the Restoration of the Monarchy in 1660.

In the House of Representatives, the Speaker has since 1794 appointed the Chairman from among Majority party Members but not including those serving on standing committees which have considered the pending measure. (For the Chairman of Ways and Means at Westminster, see page 39.) Since the 103rd Congress, standing rules have permitted the Speaker to resolve the House into the Committee of the Whole without motion when no other matter is pending, if a special order has been adopted by the House permitting that designation, in order to expedite the start of business and avoid a separate vote on the question of consideration.

The standing rules governing a Committee of the Whole are uniquely designed to speed up floor action (by applying the 'five-minute' rule rather than the hour rule to amendment debate, by applying a smaller quorum requirement—100 as opposed to 218 Members—and by not permitting motions to lay on the table, motions for the previous question, or to recommit or reconsider). Conversely, some House procedures are not applicable in Committee, which may have the reverse tendency to slow down floor action (for example, by not permitting non-debatable motions to lay on the table or for the previous question).

The most essential procedure in a Committee of the Whole under standing rules requires an amendment process under the 'five-minute rule' wherein any germane amendment, amendment thereto, substitute therefor, and amendment to the substitute may be offered severally and may be pending simultaneously without advance notice and without being pre-empted by a motion to cut off amendment. The motion 'to order the previous question' is not in order in Committee of the Whole.[36] The Committee of the Whole consideration process, traditional throughout the first 200 years of the Republic with respect to most major legislation following standing committee consideration and report, has been historically applied in the House both because it has always been the standing rule and, except for complicated tax and tariff bills, because its circumvention had seldom been considered politically necessary or prudent by use of the Rules Committee for restrictive purposes. This intermediate stage of plenary House consideration remained the tradition until the mid-1980s when greater complexity of bills and proliferation of amendments caused Majority leaderships to search for ways of minimizing amendment delays and uncertainties, in order to reduce the unpredictable rewriting of the bill on the House floor, to restore manageable control of time, and to shield some Members from politically difficult votes.

Under current practice endorsed by both party majorities, the amendment process in the Committee of the Whole is now 'structured' to some degree. These variations range from a requirement for pre-printing of first-degree amendments in the Congressional Record at least one day prior to consideration in order to provide advance notice of primary amendments, with second-degree amendments and substitutes not required to be pre-printed—a 'modified open' rule—to the more commonplace 'modified closed' rule, permitting only specified first-degree amendments referenced in the Rules Committee report accompanying the governing special order, in a prescribed order and precluding second-degree amendments thereto. Under modern practice dictated by the Rules Committee, bills which normally require consideration in the Committee of the Whole because they involve the expenditure of money or raising of revenue are nevertheless considered immediately in the House without Committee of the Whole consideration if no amendments (a 'closed' rule) or only one amendment (a 'modified closed' rule) are permitted under the terms of the special order. In such cases there is not as great a procedural need for Committee of the Whole consideration since the length of and control of debate can be the same and there are no competing or conflicting amendments to reconcile under the five-minute rule. Special rules retaining consideration in the House extend to the ordering of the previous question following general debate or disposition of the one amendment made in order following general debate, as the case may be. Since amendments adopted in Committee of the Whole are automatically reported back to the House for final disposition, the potential for separate reconsideration of amendments has been minimized by special orders which require such reported amendments to be voted on en bloc.

As at Westminster (see note 21 on page 224), some motions are unique to the Committee of the Whole and are not applicable in the House. The most preferential motion is the motion that the Committee 'rise', a non-debatable motion equivalent to the motion to adjourn in the House which, though it may not be offered while another Member has the floor, may be repeated following any intervening business during the amendment process unless dilatory or restricted by a special order. By this motion the Committee tests its willingness to proceed on the measure at that time, and like the motion to adjourn in the House does not require a quorum for its adoption.

Another motion unique to the Committee of the Whole is the motion that 'the Committee of the Whole rise and report the measure to the House with the recommendation that the enacting (or resolving) clause be stricken out'. This motion is preferential to an amendment under the five-minute rule and serves as a test vote in Committee of the Whole for support for the measure. Ten minutes of debate equally divided are permitted on the motion, which may be repeated if the bill has been modified by amendment or the earlier motion has been withdrawn by unanimous consent. If the motion prevails in Committee, the full House must readopt the motion for the measure to be rejected. Pending that vote in the full House, a motion to recommit the bill with or without instructions back to a standing committee may be interposed. The motion 'to strike the enacting clause' is normally utilized not with the intention of defeating the measure but to obtain additional debate time where the House has otherwise imposed limitations on amendment debate.

Once the full House has imposed special procedures on the operation of a Committee of the Whole through adoption of a unanimous consent request or special order of business, the Committee of the Whole may not depart from those procedures where to do so would be materially inconsistent with the adopted procedure. Thus the Chairman will not entertain unanimous consent requests to permit non-amendable amendments to be amended, to be offered out of a prescribed order, or to preclude allowable amendments from being offered. Where such material unanimous consent requests are found necessary, the Committee of the Whole may rise on motion to permit the request to be propounded in the full House. This procedure is most often utilized during the consideration of general Appropriation bills where a 'universe of amendments' to be allowed is ultimately agreed upon by unanimous consent, and is described in greater detail in the chapter on Power of the Purse.

Minor modifications may be permitted by unanimous consent, such as the extension of debate time on amendments so long as congruent with the order of the House in balancing control of the debate. Also, a Committee of the Whole may by unanimous consent permit the modification of an amendment once pending if requested by the amendment's sponsor, as a modification is not a second-degree amendment offered by another Member which would otherwise be precluded by the special order.

Clearly, this special rule authority to limit the amendment process is susceptible (unlike the impartial selection of amendments by the Chair in the House of Commons, for which see pages 174–5) to use as a partisan instrument and in the contemporary House has been consistently so utilized. It is augmented by the Speaker's appointment (in his capacity as party leader rather than as presiding officer) of nine of the thirteen members of the Committee on Rules. This extraordinary empowerment of the exclusive appointment of a disproportionate majority of the agenda-setting entity derives from the Majority party's caucus rules and practices and is to be differentiated from party endorsement of other committees' majority slates, as not being subject to ratification by a vote of the full party caucus prior to formal election by the House. It virtually assures a Majority party Leadership's ability to control time and issue in the plenary body. It represents a departure from traditions of a more 'open' amendment process which characterized the House until the 1990s. Newly elected Majority Members, lacking institutional memory of those traditions of openness, are importuned repeatedly to cast 'procedural votes' for their Leadership's agenda with assurances that party public relations efforts will not portray those votes as substantive votes on the underlying measures. There are near exceptions, as on 12 March 2008 when a 'procedural' vote on the previous question on a resolution creating an Office of Congressional Ethics was held open at the direction of the Speaker to permit Whips to importune enough Majority Members to change their votes in order to preclude the Minority from offering an amendment. This occurred despite a newly adopted rule prohibiting votes from being held open beyond the fifteen-minute minimum 'solely to change the result'. In that case, party discipline trumped a clear violation of the rule. The Minority Leader offered a question of privilege to vitiate the vote and that resolution was laid on the table.

This 'closing' of the amendment process (which the current Majority decried when in the minority as described at page 548) may foreclose Majority as well as Minority individual Members from offering amendments in the plenary session (although Majority committee members will often have had their amendments adopted during the committee markups, self-executed into the reported text, or included in a non-amendable 'managers amendment'). More often than not, however, an advantage inures to Majority Members, either to offer floor amendments or to be protected from casting politically difficult votes on another Member's amendment.

Minority options: motions to recommit and other 'procedural' votes

An extraordinary example of a failure of party discipline to control the amendment process on an important bill occurred on 25 June 1981 during Ronald Reagan's first year as President, when a special rule reported from the Democratic-controlled Rules Committee provided for consideration of an omnibus budget spending reconciliation bill compiled by Democratic-controlled committees and targeted to achieve reductions in Federal spending suggested in a recently adopted Congressional budget resolution. In order to minimize the House Minority party's ability to offer one alternative 'substitute' which had been drafted to achieve more substantial savings, the reported special order only permitted an amendment process which divided up that substitute and permitted six separate amendments to be offered by the Minority. Following debate on the resolution, a coalition consisting of all Republicans and some conservative Democrats defeated by several votes the 'ordering of the previous question' (the motion to cut off debate and amendment to that resolution), and then amended the resolution to permit the Reagan-supported substitute to be offered as one amendment to the underlying measure 'without the intervention of any point of order'. That amendment was subsequently adopted as a substitute for the bill by a similar narrow coalition majority. Thus the motion for the previous question has not always been viewed as a purely 'procedural motion' which commanded Majority party loyalty and which could be explained as a 'non-substantive' vote. Majority party discipline in the wake of this type of vote, especially since the change in 1994 in political majorities in the House and continuing following the next party majority change in 2007, the narrowing of that majority, and the emergence of a more active Whip organization have combined with a more rapid turnover in a membership lacking institutional memory to result in the 'closing down' of the amendment process by straight party line majorities.

The term 'procedural vote' derives from custom and usage and not from a party caucus or House rule, and technically describes not only direct votes on procedural resolutions reported from the Committee on Rules but also the use of secondary motions to adversely dispose of or prevent amendment of primary questions on bills or resolutions. The notion that 'procedural votes' must command party loyalty has been extended beyond votes on ordering the previous question on special orders from the Rules Committee (where the rationale is the protection of the Majority leadership's agenda). Procedural votes also include motions to lay on the table various appeals from rulings of the Chair. Appeals are often taken to demonstrate political frustration with the inability of the Minority to be permitted to offer an alternative agenda although bipartisan support of non-partisan rulings of the Chair has long been the norm. Further, motions to lay certain Minority questions of privilege on the table have been characterized as procedural, commanding Majority party support, despite their effect of adverse disposition, often without debate, on the merits of privileged resolutions or on motions to which they are applied (for example, resolutions raising ethics or non-binding motions to instruct House conferees).

Virtually consistent Majority opposition to Minority motions to recommit with instructions as a matter of party discipline is not unprecedented in the House, but its rationale as a 'procedural' vote was recently inculcated by the Majority (Republican) leadership from 1995 to 2006 into the collective psyche of its rank and file, most of whom had only been Members since their party won the majority in 1995 and had little institutional memory of past substantive impacts of adoption of such motions. This party leadership discipline was pervasive until 2007, when a new Majority's rank and file began to view some Minority motions to recommit as more substantive. That once-traditional attitude was, for example, demonstrated by a vote on 25 September 1984, when the House adopted a Minority motion to recommit a continuing Appropriation measure (which had been previously amended to include unrelated policy provisions) with instructions to report back to the House forthwith (immediately, without a formal committee meeting) a substantive amendment on criminal justice. That amendment in the form of recommittal was thereupon presented to the House, adopted by an instant coalition of Minority and some Majority Members, and became part of the bill on passage. Even though the rules of the House guarantee to the Minority one final chance through 'forthwith re-committal' to properly amend a bill pending the vote on final passage, and despite occasional examples into the 1990s and again in 2007 where successful Minority motions have altered the substance of the bill, the rationale that such motions are merely 'procedural' and can be dismissed on party loyalty grounds had taken hold.

That perception changed at the onset of the 110th Congress when several of the new Minority party's motions to recommit bills began to be routinely accepted by some Majority Members and adopted by the House as substantive improvements. These Minority recommittal motions, offered without advance notice pending votes on final passage, have not changed the basic purpose of the underlying bill, but have represented politically attractive additions which Majority Members are willing to support without compromising basic party philosophy. These motions have often come at a time when the Minority was otherwise foreclosed from separately offering those amendments under the same 'closed' rules which the new leadership had so disparaged when in the minority.

On other occasions, the Minority's use of recommittal with instructions to report the bill back 'promptly' rather than 'forthwith', had the combined purpose of indefinitely delaying the measure (as subsequent committee consideration would not be assured) and of placing politically vulnerable Majority Members in the position of voting on controversial issues, including gun control, illegal immigration, and abortion. The Speaker has responded by exercising new authorities to remove some bills from consideration prior to the vote on politically provocative recommittal motions. The Majority, frustrated by the political posturing of 'promptly' motions, has responded with a rules change in the 111th Congress to force the Minority to offer either germane 'forthwith' or 'straight' (without instructions) motions to recommit, so that the vote constitutes either an immediate amendment or a referral back to committee, without the combined effect of both. Debate is now permitted on the 'straight' motion so as to permit the minority to explain its reason for an indefinite recommittal to committee.

The cited 1984 example when the current Minority party in the House was once before in the minority and successfully offered a 'motion to recommit with instructions' to report back forthwith an amendment which added a substantive new (criminal law) provision is, to the extent remembered at all, considered an anomaly which can now be averted by postponement. By objective standards, where the motion directs immediate adoption of an amendment it has 'substantive' effect, and is logically more than a 'procedural' vote on a motion to send the measure back to committee for 'prompt' or other uncertain review. That distinction had been obscured by that (Republican) Majority party caucus and by press accounts also lacking institutional memory. Until the 110th Congress, the only recent successful adoption of motions to recommit with instructions had involved a few examples where there was eleventh-hour bipartisan managers' agreement that the motion improved the substance of the bill. On one such occurrence, Majority Leadership was privately critical of a chairman who had agreed to accept a motion to recommit with a non-controversial amendment offered by a Minority Member from his committee, fearing that rank-and-file Majority Members would begin to view motions to recommit as having substantive import and would be inclined to support them if brought to a vote.

Any motion to recommit must be germane to the bill in its modified form pending final passage. The issue of germaneness can be problematic, since the motion offered by the Minority need not be shown to the Majority until its moment of offer. As a result, the element of surprise sometimes prevents the Majority from fully understanding the impact of the motion, although several tools are at their disposal to prolong the time for examination. In addition to the reservation of a point of order pending its reading and debate for ten minutes, the Majority manager can extend that debate to one hour equally divided. If the Majority does not wish to vote directly on the motion, it may as currently authorized in the typical underlying special order of business postpone the vote on the motion, thereby forestalling final passage. On one occasion,[37] a single-purpose bill was broadened by the Rules Committee to include an unrelated provision to offset the cost of the bill,

thereby expanding the fundamental purpose of the bill to one which became also a revenue enhancement measure as well as one requiring some spending. The revenue offset was
included to comply with a new House pay-go rule requiring bills which incur new spending to be offset by other spending reductions or revenue increases. Thus the test of germaneness to this newly hybridized bill was sufficiently broadened to avoid a germaneness
challenge against a motion to recommit not specifically related to either of the two dispa-
rate matters already contained in the bill. Not only did this provocative motion result in
indefinite postponement of the bill, it initiated an ultimate rules change in the 111th
Congress, requiring any motion to recommit to require either 'forthwith' reporting or
straight recommittal back to committee. This was in response to language in the motion
which required the committee which would receive the recommitted bill to 'promptly'
(not forthwith) report the bill back to the House with the suggested amendment, requiring the committee to actually meet again to consider the bill anew and by precedent
stripped of the previously adopted pay-go amendment. For 111th Congress discussion of
separate consideration of pay-go offset legislation see the chapter on Power of the Purse
at page 250. The bill if reported would not have been eligible for further privileged consideration in the House, absent a subsequent special order reported from the Committee
on Rules. All these possibilities pointed to the inherent unpredictability of the motion to
recommit with instructions to report 'promptly'. Until the 111th Congress, the rule protecting the motion (by not permitting the Rules Committee to restrict it) remained the
one assurance to the Minority party that a germane amendment might be considered,
even if it might also by directing 'prompt' reporting potentially postpone consideration of
the bill indefinitely.

While the motion to recommit is properly characterized as a 'Minority motion' to be
voted on directly pending final passage, there have been occasions where a Majority has
voted down the ordering of the previous question on the motion to recommit in order to
amend the motion prior to its adoption with language more to the liking of the Majority.
This procedure has been characterized as extremely provocative in denying the Minority
a direct vote on a motion to recommit of its own choosing, and has fallen out of use in
modern practice. Despite precedents permitting Majority intervention by way of amendment and despite the politicization of a closely divided House in so many other respects,
Majority leaderships have respected the traditional prerogative of the Minority to offer
and obtain a direct vote on a proper motion to recommit of its own choosing, unencumbered by intervening motions. Just as the germaneness of a motion to recommit is measured against the underlying bill as a whole, so an amendment to a motion to recommit
a bill is tested by the relationship of the amendment to the entire underlying bill and not
merely to the amendatory language in the original motion to recommit.

If the Majority conspired to amend the Minority motion, a Minority Member who
was his leader's designee could never be assured a direct vote on his motion. In 1995,
House rules were amended to guarantee the initial offering of a motion to recommit with
instructions by the Minority Leader or his designee, who might have been someone other
than the senior Minority member of the reporting committee traditionally recognized by
Speakers until that time. This reform, written to assure the Minority party leadership of
an opportunity to present a proper alternative for a vote pending final passage on the
Majority's measure, can only be carried out in practice if the Majority party continues
to respect this prerogative and does not attempt to amend or replace the motion to

recommit before a vote thereon. In 2002,[38] protestations that the Majority had 'hijacked' a Minority motion to recommit were misplaced, where the House voted down the previous question on a Minority Member's motion to recommit, no Minority member of the reporting committees sought recognition to amend the motion, and a Majority Member who had led the argument against ordering the previous question was then recognized to offer the amendment.

This discussion, while necessarily arcane, is essential toward a better understanding of a unique Minority protection perhaps not conferred upon other parliamentary minorities in legislatures worldwide. At least in comparison to House of Commons procedure, where no standing order or rule guarantees the Opposition a vote on any of their amendments at any stage of a bill, it is noteworthy that the protection in the standing rules of the House of Representatives reflects the existence there of only one Minority party, rather than numerous Opposition or minority third parties. The protection is also limited to the inability of the partisan Rules Committee to report special orders which restrict the right of the Minority to offer 'instructions' to amend pending initial final passage. Nothing in the Standing Orders of the House of Commons prevents consideration of a programme motion limiting Opposition amendment rights from being imposed by a majority. The protection is in the Speaker's non-partisan power of selection, which is traditionally exercised to assure Opposition input. In the US House, the rules do not extend to the absolute protection of that motion, once offered, against change by the House or postponement by the Speaker prior to a direct vote thereon.

In the United States, there is an increasing perception on both sides that it is procedurally advantageous to obtain a direct and first vote on an issue whenever possible, rather than first require rejection of an opposing motion. Other than the protection accorded the Minority party's motion to recommit described above, the convenience and even political necessity of utilization of the Rules Committee to minimize direct votes on Minority or individual Members' propositions has taken hold and is now thought of as traditional. A once-customary Minority protection, and the spontaneity and the quality of House debates, are its victims.

Cloture in the Senate

After decades of determined resistance in the Senate, Rule XXII was adopted in 1917 which gave the Senate the formal means (cloture) to end extended debate. Until that time, debate could be terminated only by unanimous consent, an impossibility in the face of a filibuster, or by exhaustion. What finally prompted the Senate to adopt the cloture rule was a filibuster that killed a bill to arm US merchant ships against attacks by German submarines. President Woodrow Wilson strongly criticized the filibuster and called a special session of the Senate, which adopted the rule on 8 March 1917 five weeks before the USA entered the First World War.

Under Senate Rule XXII a cloture petition signed by sixteen Senators first must be filed with the presiding officer. The petition must be presented when the bill or amendment to which it is directed is pending before the Senate. Two days later, and one hour after the Senate convenes, the presiding officer must ascertain (unless waived by unanimous consent) whether a quorum is present. That having been established, the presiding officer is obliged to ask: 'Is it the sense of the Senate that the debate shall be brought to a close?' A yea and nay vote is held immediately. If three-fifths of the entire Senate membership (60 of the 100 current Senators) vote in favour, cloture is invoked. Thereafter there may be not exceeding an additional thirty hours of debate with Senators permitted to speak on a first-come, first-served basis. First-degree amendments must be filed by 1 pm on the day following the filing of the petition; second-degree amendments also may be filed until one hour prior to the cloture vote. Before 1975, when the current three-fifths rule was adopted, a two-thirds majority of those Senators present and voting was required to invoke cloture. The two-thirds requirement still applies to proposals to directly amend the Senate's rules.

Absent a special statutory procedure, cloture is the only means by which the Senate can vote to limit debate on a matter, and thereby overcome a possible filibuster. It would be erroneous, however, to assume that cases in which cloture is sought are the same as those in which a filibuster actually occurs. Cloture may be sought when no filibuster is taking place, and filibusters may occur without cloture being sought. The modern expectation in the Senate of the threat of unlimited debate and delay at virtually every stage of proceedings already underway or yet to be undertaken, with only a three-fifths majority able to overcome those threats, has resulted in more unsuccessful invocations of cloture at the start of proceedings on a bill, in order to test the will of the Senate at the beginning and to allow it to go on to other business if the super-majority is not willing to begin consideration.

A separate discussion of the application of cloture, and contemporary informal agreements to invoke cloture only in 'extraordinary circumstances' with respect to debate on judicial nominations appears at page 74. As a general proposition with respect to legislative business, the uncertainty of the Senate Majority Leader's agenda-setting capabilities, including his ability to forge unanimous consent agreements or to cross party lines to find enough votes to invoke cloture, impacts on a regular basis on the ability of the two Houses to coordinate their agendas to facilitate final action on legislation. The chapter on Procedural Basics at page 202 contains a further analysis of the use of cloture in the modern Senate, including a proliferation of 'filling the amendment tree' by the Majority Leader under his priority of recognition, in order to permit the Senate by one three-fifths vote to avoid additional and non-germane amendments to a pending measure and to limit remaining debate time.

Often the House, procedurally capable of immediate Majority action, passes legislation with its leadership tentatively assuming more or less contemporaneous Senate action, only to be temporarily or indefinitely stymied by prolonged inaction there. This can be the result even where (as was the case from 2001 to 2009 when the party majority in the Senate reached 60) the Majorities of both Houses are marginally controlled by the same party, due to the traditional leverage enjoyed by individual Senators and by the Minority party in that body. Beyond the common reality of increasing partisanship, the cultures of the two Houses remain very different, and the rules, practices, and traditions of the other House are not always understood, much less appreciated and respected by the corresponding leaderships or rank-and-file membership of 'the other body'. The most obvious commonality between both Houses is limited to party solidarity, where committee chairmanships, ratios, and agenda-setting prerogatives depend upon Majority status, however narrow.

Beyond these organizational realities, however, lies the daily application of very different rules and practices in each House—the House increasingly adopting restrictive special rules and then abruptly legislating with partisan majorities, and the Senate, if unanimous consent agreements are not possible, often reaching stalemate heavily impacted by individual and Minority Senators' assertions of prerogatives through objections to unanimous consent requests or the inability of a sixty-vote super-majority to invoke cloture.

Committee stage and after: Commons and Lords

After a bill has been read a second time in the Commons, it is committed. Some bills, nearly always government legislation, are sent to a Committee of the whole House. These fall into one of three categories. The first is made up of bills whose parliamentary career it is generally agreed need not be prolonged. The Parliament (Joint Departments) Bill [*Lords*] 2007 is a good example. Secondly, there are bills which have to be enacted at great speed in response to external events. The Banking (Special Provisions) Bill, containing seventeen clauses and two schedules, took into temporary public ownership a crisis-hit bank. The bill was taken through all stages except Lords Amendments in ten hours in one day in February 2008. Lords Amendments were disposed of in an hour two days later. Bills relating to Northern Ireland at the time of the troubles were disposed of even more speedily. The last group are bills of major, often constitutional, significance. Prominent examples are the bills to devolve legislative powers to Scotland and to Wales and the more important clauses of the annual Finance Bill, putting into legal effect provisions of the Chancellor of the Exchequer's budget. The European Communities (Amendment) Bill 1992 was twenty-three days in Committee of the whole House which spent over 204 hours in the consideration of more than 600 amendments. Details of the use of Committee of the whole House are set out in Table 9.3 in the Annex.

Committees of the whole House, presided over by the Chairman of Ways and Means or one of his deputies, go through the bill committed to them (or part of the bill in cases where the 'high policy' clauses are taken in Committee of the whole House and the remainder sent to another committee, as was the case in four of the eight bills in 2005–6 and one in 2006–7 and 2007–8). The Committee considers proposed amendments, usually but not necessarily in the order of the printed clauses. Separate questions are put on whether each of the clauses and schedules, with or without amendment according to circumstances, should stand in the bill. Unlike proceedings in the House, Members may speak more than once to the same question in Committee. Oppositions will try to persuade governments to send more bills to Committees of the whole House than governments wish to. It is an understandable tactic when parliamentary time is at a premium, and there is no fully agreed definition of the type of bill which should be treated in this way. As in other instances, the matter is normally settled by political will, modified by the realization that governments will inevitably become Oppositions in due course.

The standard procedure for the committee stage of bills is not however Committee of the whole House. Most bills are sent 'upstairs' to public bill committees—previously if confusingly in this context known as standing committees—sitting for the most part at times before the House meets. Each bill so committed is considered by a public bill committee specially nominated for the task, presided over by a member of the Chairman's Panel (see page 39). In practice, the membership of such a committee is something under twenty, though committees on part of the Finance Bill typically have around thirty members. In 2007–8, the number of sittings of public bill committees to take oral evidence ranged from nil to five, and there were between one and twenty-four sittings on the bill.

A recent reform which has transformed the committee stages of most bills in the Commons is the programme motion. Traditionally, there were two ways in which the government could seek to ensure the completion of its legislative programme within a session. One was negotiation between the 'usual channels'—the whips—from whose discussions would emerge an informal, unenforceable, and unpublished timetable for a bill's Commons career. Barring a few contests with the Lords, the government's majority would then smooth the bill's way to enactment. The other was the brutal expedient of the guillotine, used principally when progress in committee was seriously falling behind what the government expected. A specific time was allocated by order of the House to defined portions of the bill. If, at the expiry of the time limit, debate on the relevant portion were not concluded, the Chair would be obliged to bring the House to the necessary decisions, however little discussion there had been—or none at all. The process would be repeated for the next portion of the bill. The interests of Opposition might be taken into account behind the scenes, as the drafting of guillotine orders might give relative preference in terms of debating time to areas of a bill the Opposition thought specially important. No one believed guillotines were a good idea, however, except perhaps government whips gripped by the need to push a bill forward in the face of what sometimes was noisy opposition without much justification—and sometimes was not. Guillotines are now rare: over the four sessions to 2007–8 there were no more than six.

For at least twenty years, in parliamentary and other studies of the issue, a different approach has been gaining ground, intended to be more robust than informal timetables, less confrontational—sometimes—than guillotines. From 1997, programme motions, the gentlemanly version of guillotines, have governed the progress of the vast majority of government bills, a sea change of quite remarkable proportions, as Table 9.4 in the Annex shows.

The decision on programming a bill and on what kind of committee the bill is to go to is taken by the House immediately after second reading, on a proposal tabled by the government. The motion may also contain detailed provision for the programming of the bill. Such motions are not usually amendable and where debate is permitted, it may last no longer than forty-five minutes. Once the motion is agreed to and unless the programme motion itself contains the necessary provisions, a Programming Committee, presided over by a Deputy Speaker, with party spokesmen and whips as members, will meet and report to the House proposals for allocating the time allowed for debate on portions of a bill sent to Committee of the whole House. It may also propose when decisions on report should be taken on each portion, and how long should be allowed for third reading. A parallel exercise is carried out by Programming Subcommittees in respect of a bill's career in public bill committee, reporting to the committee to which it has been sent. The subcommittee's resolution sets out the number of sittings the committee is to have on the bill, a detailed schedule for the completion of consideration of the clauses and schedules, and (unless the details have already been settled) when the committee is to report and what should be the programme for consideration and third reading. The public bill committee is allowed half an hour to dispose of the subcommittee's suggestions.

When, in Committee of the whole House, public bill committee, or on consideration, the time for consideration of a part of a bill specified in a programme order comes to an end, the Chair puts for decision the question on the amendment under discussion, then the question on any amendment judged by the Chair to be worthy of separate decision though without debate, anything moved by the government, and any consequential decisions.

It was inevitable that a change of such a sensitive nature should not immediately meet with wholehearted approval. At the same time, progress has undoubtedly been made. In 2001–2 every proposed programme motion at second reading was divided against. In 2006–7, the figure was just over a third.[39] The number of divisions in public bill committee on reports from programming subcommittees fell from 44 per cent in 2001–2 to 8 per cent in 2005–6, though it rose to 28 per cent in 2006–7 because of the introduction of oral evidence sessions (see page 442). The number of public bill committees finishing earlier than contemplated in programme motions has gone up from 10 per cent in 2001–2 to seven times that figure in 2006–7. Where adjustment seemed necessary, it has been made. Too many internal 'knives'—that is, times at which decisions fell to be taken on separate compartments of the bill—in programme motions governing proceedings in Committee of the whole House hindered debate. The number was reduced from 69 per cent in 2001–2 to nil in 2006–7.

Areas of difficulty remain. It is of little use parcelling out time consensually or otherwise if the outcome is less satisfactory scrutiny of the programmed bill. In public bill committees the number of debates brought to an early conclusion in 2004–5 under programme orders was relatively few, and in only two cases were a significant number of amendments or parts of the bill left undiscussed by the operation of the order. This was a striking contrast with 2001–2 when on the Proceeds of Crime Bill, twenty-two groups of amendments and 134 (out of 453) clause- (or schedule-) stand-part debates were overtaken by the fall of a knife, and were thus disposed of without debate in public bill committee. Statistics may of course be misleading. It is not clear how far a good fit between amendments and time arises not because the whips on both sides have accurately judged the balance of supply and demand but because Members are discouraged from tabling amendments which they have good reason to suspect will never be debated. On the other hand, the Deputy Leader of the House of Commons observed recently, with justice, that programming is an art and not a science, and that in response to the perceived difficulties the government have tried not to introduce wholly new matter at report stage and if that is unavoidable consideration will be given to providing more time.[40]

Unlike their predecessors the standing committees, public bill committees to which a bill or part of a bill is committed by a programme order are given power to hear witnesses, on the lines of a select committee. Public bill committees on bills committed without such an order may be given the power by an undebatable motion. It was a reform a long time in the making. Standing committees were for many years by common consent the least satisfactory part of the legislative process. The process was exclusively party political in nature. The government's political resolve and understanding of their own legislation could be vigorously tested, but serious change to the bill was rare. Such a combative format risked maximum effort for minimal outcomes. Despite an earlier and very modest experiment, it was not until 2006 when an initiative of the Modernisation Committee[41] persuaded the House to make the change, as part of 'a more collaborative, evidence-based approach to the legislative process', supplementing the traditional politically based debates. The Modernisation Committee envisaged that a public bill committee would hold at least one oral evidence session with the relevant minister and his or her officials, but a decision on the total number would depend on the recommendation of the Programming Subcommittee (see page 440). In any case, what is envisaged is not an exhaustive rerun of any previous inquiry into the background to the legislation but something which begins where a previous, perhaps pre-legislative, inquiry ended.

Once oral evidence has been taken, a public bill committee goes through the bill committed to it, considering both the clauses and schedules of the existing text and amendments offered by members of the Committee. The appropriate Secretary of State or one of his junior colleagues leads for the government. For the most part, all amendments are debated, provided they are not out of order because beyond the scope of—not germane to—the bill or the clause under discussion, or otherwise irregular. The chairman of the committee has the Speaker's power to select some amendments for debate and pass over others, however orderly the latter may be (see pages 174–6), but the exercise of that authority is usually much more sparing than on the floor of the House. In the past, government backbenchers have taken relatively little part in proceedings other than to assure the government of success in the divisions, and though Opposition Members predominated in discussion, they rarely extracted from the government much more than undertakings to consider their suggestions at a later stage. Change in these areas in the longer term will be an indicator of the success or failure of the experiment in grafting consensus and evidence-based decision-making on to what has long been a highly political process.

At the end of a bill's career in committee, a version incorporating any amendments made by the committee is reported formally to the House and reprinted, and a day is appointed for the report or consideration stage, usually a fortnight or so later. When that point is reached, the House will typically spend a day—for larger bills two days, rarely more—on the amended bill. It is the whole bill which is again open to consideration, not simply any change made by the public bill committee. No decision is taken on report—as was the case in committee—on agreeing to the individual clauses or schedules of the bill, with or without amendment. Naturally, it is at the relatively brief report stage that the greatest difficulty arises in terms of finding time to debate all amendments tabled. The Speaker, in the exercise of his power of selection of amendments offered on report, will give priority to previously unexplored issues, to at least some of those to which the official Opposition have attached special importance notwithstanding that they were dealt with in committee, and to amendments raising points which the government undertook in committee to look at again. It would be very unusual for a government amendment not to be selected, but it is not unknown.

Report stage creates the greatest problem for programme motions. On report stage of the Proceeds of Crime Bill 2001–2 mentioned above, eight out of eighteen groups of amendments were not reached for debate. That experience turned out to be atypical. The number of groups of amendments not reached in report stage debates was an overall average of three per bill in 2003–4, two in 2005–6, and one in 2006–7. When problems arise, however, they may be serious. In 2007–8, a Member indicated[42] that at the report stage of the Housing and Regeneration Bill, the House of Commons disposed of only one out of six groups of amendments. Twenty-nine out of 109 government amendments were debated but no more than four out of ninety-eight Opposition amendments. There was full debate on only three out of twenty government new clauses and five out of eighteen Opposition new clauses. In November 2008, on the Employment Bill, it was said that a majority of new clauses and amendments tabled by backbenchers were not debated because of the programme motion: five new clauses and four amendments were discussed but eight of each were not.[43] In 2007–8 as a whole, twenty-four government bills had report stages: in only seven of these cases were all groups of selected amendments debated. Even allowing for the fact that not all portions of a bill are of equal political or practical significance, these hard cases must test the degree of acceptance of programme motions. As the Deputy Speaker told the Modernisation Committee, the principle of programming bills is not necessarily objectionable, but it needs to be applied more sensitively and flexibly. If that could be done, he foresaw that something approaching a consensus on its use might be achievable.

Then—usually immediately following the end of report stage—comes third reading. Further amendment is in practice impossible. Debate may range over the text of the bill but Members must not refer to anything not in the bill, a distinction which the Chair often struggles to enforce. In 2007–8 third readings occupied nearly sixteen hours of the House's time, as opposed to 117 hours on report. Third reading is in truth usually a brief postscript to the House's work, in which Members review past debates and congratulate each other on the civilized way they have been conducted (even if they have not). That this should be so is something of a pity, especially if a bill's text has been substantially altered since its introduction. On the other hand, pressure on time is intense and arguments for prolonged third readings are correspondingly less persuasive.

The bill is then sent (or returned), by a Clerk walking between the two Chambers, to the Lords. The text of a Commons bill when first sent to the Lords will be endorsed, in Norman French, *Soit baillé aux Seigneurs*, let it be taken to the Lords.

In the Lords, after second reading, bills may be committed to a Committee of the whole House as in the Commons, and (allowing for the absence of the power of selection in the Lords) the procedure in Committee is broadly similar in the two Houses. Committees of the whole House are chaired by the Lord Speaker. Otherwise bills are generally committed to a Grand Committee. These may be attended by any Lord, and the procedure and formalities are much the same as in Committee of the whole House, except that no votes may take place and a committee room is used rather than the Chamber. Opposition to an amendment should lead to its withdrawal, and reintroduction in the House on report. If when a decision is to be taken on an amendment there is any voice against it, the amendment is recorded as disagreed to, though it may be brought forward again on report. Grand Committees are a decade old, but were not particularly intensively used until 2002–3. Thereafter the time spent in Grand Committee per session more than doubled, and though it has declined a little since, is still 60 per cent up on 2002–3.

On report in the Lords, amendments may be proposed to any part of the bill, as in the Commons. Amendments significantly different from those rejected in committee may be debated on report, but those rejected on a division in committee may not be retabled.

In the Lords, third reading is formal, but there is a subsequent stage which now has no Commons equivalent, That the Bill do pass. Immediately before that motion is made, amendments are admissible but only if they improve the drafting, clarify the meaning, or implement undertakings. The Bill is then sent or returned to the Commons (endorsed *Soit baillé aux Communes*) again in the hands of a Clerk.

Budget Act procedures in Congress

Procedures under the Budget Act governing Senate floor action on budget resolutions (and on reconciliation bills flowing therefrom) impose both time limitations on debate and a germaneness requirement on amendments that would not apply to such a bill under normal Senate rules. Three-fifths majorities in the Senate are not required for consideration at any stage of these budget measures, as consideration with mere majority approval is assured by the terms of the law.

The Congressional budget process is examined in Power of the Purse at page 228. That chapter analyses the expedited procedures contained in the Congressional Budget Act of 1974 as a unique exercise in joint rule making. Congress has by enactment of that law imposed a sequence of majoritarian procedures on the Senate, which depart from that body's standing rules and which, because of the fiscal and policy significance of the resultant laws and the extensive utilization of points of order put in place governing revenues, public debt, and appropriations, deserve special attention.

Resolving differences

Between the Houses in Congress

The US Constitution requires that the House and Senate approve the same bill or joint resolution in precisely the same form before it is presented to the President for his approval or veto. To this end, both Houses must pass the same numbered measure and then attempt to reach agreement on all its provisions. It is not enough for both Houses to pass versions of the same measure that are comparable in purpose but that differ in technical details, or have different numbers.

The two Houses must first select the same measure for ultimate consideration, and they may not each indefinitely insist on their own number. With revenue and Appropriation bills requiring origination in the House, while the Senate might act first on its own numbered bill, it will not message that measure to the House pending subsequent arrival of the similar House measure. Otherwise, as a matter of comity, the House which has acted first may suggest but not insist that its numbered bill become the vehicle. Sometimes pride of authorship, political advantage or disadvantage gained by acting first, or the inability of one of the Houses to act expeditiously on the measure of the other stands in the way of this expectation. For example, a bill's supporters may first press for floor action in the House where they think the measure enjoys greater support, with the hope that success may generate political momentum in the second Chamber. Alternatively, one House may defer floor action on a bill unless and until it is passed by the other, where the measure is expected to encounter more opposition. The House leadership may decide that it is pointless for the House to invest considerable time and for Representatives to cast difficult votes on a controversial bill until after an expected Senate filibuster on a comparable Senate bill has been avoided or overcome.

Major legislative proposals are often introduced in both Houses contemporaneously. The appropriate subcommittees and committees may consider and report their own measures on the same subject at roughly the same time. When one House sends its bill to the other, the second Chamber may have its own bill reported from its own committee and available for floor consideration. The second Chamber often acts initially on its own bill for legislative history and pride of authorship reasons. This is likely when the committee of the second House reports a bill that differs significantly from the measure passed by the other Chamber. The text selected for floor consideration generally sets the frame of reference within which debate occurs and amendments are proposed. It is usually advantageous, therefore, for a committee to press for floor consideration of its approach, rather than that of the other House. The two Houses often act on their own bills even though they have already received the other House's bill on the same subject. While it is not always avoided, it makes little sense for the House to pass its bill and send it to the Senate, while in possession of the companion Senate bill previously passed. Where each House has in its possession a bill originated by the other, they have not yet acted on the same measure and are procedurally unable to begin to resolve differences. Thus, for example, the House customarily debates, amends, and passes the House bill and then immediately takes up the counterpart Senate bill pursuant to unanimous consent or a special order of business. The bill manager then moves to 'strike out all after the enacting clause of the Senate bill and replace the stricken text with the full text of the House-passed bill' as one amendment in the nature of a substitute.

The Senate may select a House bill on one subject as a convenient 'vehicle' and amend it to include provisions on other, unrelated subjects. Sometimes the use of unrelated legislative vehicles is accepted by both Houses as a useful device to cope with different political and parliamentary conditions prevailing in the two Chambers. For example, in the 95th Congress President Carter submitted a massive proposal for major new national energy legislation. The House chose to consider the President's entire programme in a single bill. In the Senate, the Majority Leadership of the same political party concluded that an omnibus bill would inspire a filibuster that could not be broken, and so that body debated and amended five separate bills that collectively dealt with the same subjects as the House bill. To avoid separate House consideration of five Senate bills, or combined Senate consideration of one House bill, the Senate selected four neutral vehicles—minor unrelated House bills that had been awaiting Senate action. To each, the Senate added the texts of one or more of its passed energy bills as well as the text of the omnibus House bill and went to conference on each of them. This procedure was extraordinary, as normally both Houses determine to resolve their differences on one vehicle which is at least in part related to the measure the other House has acted upon.

Once the House and Senate have passed different versions of the same measure, there are basically two methods they can use to resolve the differences between their versions.

One method involves a conference committee—a panel of Members appointed by the presiding officers of each House that attempts to negotiate a version acceptable to both Chambers. Until very recent Congresses, most major bills were sent to conference committees, as their reports help define legislative history in an accompanying joint statement of the managers signed by a majority from each House, and as the reports cannot be directly amended in either House while pending. The other method makes a conference committee unnecessary by relying instead on amendments between the Houses.

Eschewing formal conferences, final agreements have been increasingly reached by an exchange of amendments between the Houses (the metaphor 'ping-pong', when employed, should not suggest that the amendments necessarily bounce back and forth with the same speed and spin, as if the two Houses were merely volleying). Under standing rules, each House has (as at Westminster) one opportunity to amend the amendments from the other House, so there can be, for example, Senate amendments to House amendments to Senate amendments to a House bill, or conversely, House amendments to Senate amendments to House amendments to Senate bills. This is not to say that amendments in the third degree are never considered in the House, as increasingly the House has permitted such a procedure under suspension of the rules or pursuant to a special order of business. While the Senate is constrained by precedent not to consider third-degree amendments except by unanimous consent, it does not consider itself similarly prohibited from considering fourth-degree amendments should a third-degree amendment be messaged from the House. In 2008 alone, the Senate amended major authorization and appropriation bills into the fourth and fifth degrees.[44] Such extreme exchange ('ping-pong') of amendments between the two Houses is the exception, as matters in difference are normally resolved by remaining within the permissible degree of amendment. If the Houses remain in disagreement—by one House insisting on its position and the other House refusing to recede, the measure cannot be sent to the President for enactment into law.

Senate amendments to House-passed bills usually remain 'at the Speaker's table' when returned to the House. They may be referred to a House committee at the discretion of the Speaker, but that seldom occurs even where the Senate amendment contains non-germane matter within the jurisdiction of another committee. At this stage, the bill and the Senate amendments are normally not privileged for floor consideration by motion in the House. The only motion that can be made at this stage prior to disagreement requiring a majority vote is to insist on the House position and go to conference with the Senate. The motion is entertained at the Speaker's discretion and must be made only at the direction of the committee(s) with initial jurisdiction over the House-passed measure. That result is achieved more often by unanimous consent following a reservation of objection in order to obtain an explanation of the need to go to conference. If there is objection, the Speaker may entertain unamendable motions to suspend the rules and concur in the Senate amendments with or without further House amendment. Second, the Rules Committee may report a special rule either making in order a motion to concur with or without amendment to the Senate amendment without other intervening motion, or 'hereby' adopting such an amendment (a 'self-executing' rule which is sometimes utilized as a time- and vote-saving device where the vote on the rule becomes the vote on the Senate amendment itself). It is within the authority of the Rules Committee to report such self-executing rules or rules permitting a non-amendable motion without permitting a motion to recommit by the Minority, as the restriction against the denial of a motion to recommit in a report from the Rules Committee is confined to consideration of a bill or joint resolution pending initial final passage and not to the subsequent disposition of amendments between the Houses. The Rules Committee is not only utilized in contemporary practice to restrict the ability of the Minority to offer an alternative amendment, but also to include the Majority party's text even in the form of new possibly non-germane matter not subject to further amendment. Under those circumstances, the only way for the Minority to amend the Majority's text is to first vote down the motion for the previous question on the special order itself—the likelihood of which is minimal, given the portrayal of a vote on the previous question as a 'procedural matter' demanding Majority party loyalty.

Assuming the use of available motions rather than special orders from the Rules Committee, 'reaching the stage of disagreement' has more significance in the House than in the Senate (where motions to dispose of House amendments are always privileged), as it marks the procedural stage following which Senate amendments to House measures can be disposed of by privileged motion without the necessity of unanimous consent, suspension of the rules, or special orders reported from the Committee on Rules. To reach that stage in the House, however, requires either a House 'insistence' on its own amendment or its disagreement to a Senate amendment with formal notice to the Senate, as the initial amendatory actions are not of themselves privileged for disposition by Majority motion. Before this threshold is reached, the two Chambers presumably are still in the process of reaching agreement. Thus amendments between the Houses, as an alternative to conference, are couched in terms of one Chamber concurring in the other's amendments, without or without further amendment. While the House by concurring with a further amendment may in fact be disagreeing to the Senate position, the House does not state its disagreement explicitly and formally at this stage because crossing the threshold of disagreement has significant procedural consequences in the House. At the stage prior to formal disagreement, the order of precedence among motions in both Chambers favours motions that tend to amend the measure further. After the stage of disagreement, Jefferson suggests that the order of precedence is reversed, with precedence being given to motions that tend to promote agreement between the Chambers.[45] After disagreement, priority is given to motions most quickly leading to agreement. However, the motion to recede and concur being divisible in the House on demand of any Member and the House having receded by a separate vote, the priority again shifts back to further amendment over concurrence, as if once again prior to the stage of disagreement.

House amendments to Senate bills or amendments are privileged for consideration on the Senate floor, meaning that unanimous consent is not required to proceed to their consideration. When the Senate receives a bill with House amendments, it normally is held at the desk. Under Senate Rule VII, paragraph 3, consideration in the Senate of House amendments suspends, but does not displace, the pending or unfinished business. The motion to proceed to consideration of the amendments is not debatable. Once the Senate agrees to consider the House amendment, motions to dispose of those amendments are fully amendable and debatable (for example, to concur with an amendment, to refer the House amendment to a committee, to agree to the House amendment, or to disagree and request a conference—in that order of preference) and once pending can continue indefinitely, absent a unanimous consent time agreement or the invocation of cloture. As a practical matter, the Senate may act on House amendments at virtually any time, even if a major bill is under consideration, both because the House amendments are privileged business and because they normally are disposed of quickly by unanimous consent, which is made easier to obtain by knowledge of the availability of the non-debatable motion to proceed to consideration. The complexities that these options can create arise infrequently because House amendments normally are not called up on the Senate floor until after a process of negotiation between the two party managers. If concurrence cannot be reached, the Senators involved normally decide to resolve the disagreements among themselves as well as with the House, in conference rather than through a complicated series of motions and amendments offered on the Senate floor. Nevertheless, in the contemporary Senate threats of filibusters have proliferated and the sequence of sending a bill to conference potentially requires a longer series of cloture petitions (for example, to disagree, to request a conference, to authorize the presiding officer to appoint conferees, and then an unlimited number of debatable motions to instruct conferees) more cumbersome than a 'ping-pong' arrangement between the two Houses.

The emergence of alternative amendment strategies in lieu of going to conference have combined to greatly impact on the traditions of the two Houses in the resolution of differences. A number of procedural obstacles in both Houses have prompted Majority leaders to avoid conferences in favour of amendments between the Houses. In the House, utilization of special orders from the Rules Committee making in order non-amendable amendments to Senate amendments, or concurrence in Senate amendments, either before or after the stage of disagreement, has avoided intervening motions such as motions to instruct conferees (initially the prerogative of the Minority) and to recommit. At this stage the Rules Committee is not disabled from denying recommittal opportunities. Informal leadership meetings (often excluding the Minority) can informally negotiate a compromise text, in order to avoid open conference meetings. A new Senate rule[46] requiring a three-fifths vote to waive points of order against conference reports containing new matter beyond the scope of conference can likewise be avoided where the Senate chooses instead to amend a House measure, and if the Majority Leader successfully 'fills the amendment tree' and thereby potentially faces only one cloture vote rather than the several which might otherwise delay a conference (discussed at page 438).

In the House, expeditious steps are more frequently taken through utilization of special orders from the Rules Committee to either combine or separate matters for politically advantageous votes in the form of amendments to or as divided questions on portions of Senate measures. All these options are in order to short-circuit formal conferences or to waive standing rules otherwise governing the consideration and content of conference reports. The House leadership, in determining which of these procedures to employ, is constantly required to understand procedural options in the Senate, as the Minority party advantage in that body has made more difficult the traditional procedures and expectations for resolving differences in conference.

Conferences

If the differences between the House and Senate cannot be resolved through the exchange of amendments, the measure can either die at the end of the Congress if both Chambers remain adamant, or the two Houses can agree to create a conference committee to seek a mutually satisfactory resolution. The formal process of arranging for a conference can begin as soon as the second House passes the bill at issue, either with numbered amendments to parts of the measure or more often with a single amendment in the nature of a substitute that replaces the entire text approved by the first Chamber. Informally however, negotiations begin at the staff and Member level prior to establishment of a conference committee, often involving only Majority party participants if both Houses have the same party majority, in order to minimize Minority party participation. The second House may pass the bill as amended and immediately insist on its amendment and request a conference with the first Chamber. The first House is not obliged to disagree to the second Chamber's amendments and agree to the requested conference, as it could refuse to act, accept, or further amend the received amendments. Another option is for the second House to amend without requesting a conference, and for the first House either to further amend, or to disagree, and to request a conference. It is important that by tradition the Chamber which asks for the conference normally acts last on the conference report.

In general, the House or Senate cannot take any action by either method unless it is in formal possession of the 'original papers'. On extraordinary occasions, one House might prospectively by unanimous consent 'deem' itself to have adopted, amended, or disagreed to a proposal from the other House or to a conference report upon receipt of the official papers and even in advance of action by the other House. This unusual procedure is normally confined in the Senate to conference reports where the text is known, the outcome is predictable and the yeas and nays need not be ordered, the Senate not being content to await an actual receipt of the message of House action. Several contemporary examples of Senate 'deemings' have involved a scheduling convenience and are an inappropriate deviation from the requirement that each body be in possession of the papers and be in session before acting. On other extraordinary occasions, the House has 'deemed' itself to have disagreed to all prospective Senate amendments and to have sent the measure to conference even in advance of Senate action, where that outcome is unanimously agreed upon or, as for the first time pursuant to a special order[47] while preserving the initial motion to instruct House conferees at a subsequent time. To its credit, the House has never, however, deemed a measure to have been finally adopted if received in a precise form from the Senate. The Senate's use of unanimous consent is virtually limitless if it is utilized for the convenience of Senators following negotiation, while in the House the formalities of action only when in actual possession of the papers have been the norm.

After either House requests or agrees to a conference, its presiding officer usually appoints conferees immediately, preceded only by one debatable non-binding motion to instruct in the House, and by an indefinite number of motions to instruct in the Senate. The Speaker's appointment of managers is not subject to challenge either with respect to number or name, although standing rules provide guidelines that the Speaker shall appoint at least a majority 'who generally supported the House position as determined by the Speaker' and shall name Members primarily responsible for the legislation and to the maximum feasible, the principal proponents of the major provisions in the House-passed measure.[48] Since 1993, the Speaker has been given unilateral removal or additional appointment authority, which is seldom exercised, at any time during the life of the conference. Only once to date[49] has a conferee been removed by the Speaker and a replacement appointed based on willingness to represent the House position.

Before the formal announcement of conferees in each Chamber, a process of consultation takes place that vests great influence in the chairman and the ranking Minority member of the committee(s) and subcommittees that had considered the measure. They themselves usually serve as conferees, and play a major role in recommending the number and naming of conferees, and the party ratio which by caucus rules is to be no less favourable than the overall ratio in the House. In the House, the Speaker is deferential to those recommendations, and in the Senate the presiding officer always follows the committee chairman's suggestions. If the bill at issue has been considered by more than one committee in either House (more often the case in the House) all the involved chairmen and ranking Minority members normally participate in determining its roster of conferees. Depending on the extent of jurisdiction, the primary committee in the House will normally receive the largest if not controlling number of conferees, to confer on all matters committed to conference, with additional initial or sequential committees appointed solely to consider the range of differences on specified provisions within their respective jurisdictions. In contemporary Congresses, some conferee appointments in the House have become so complex (with Members expecting to be named even as substitutes for others if they have sponsored specific provisions) that Speakers have publicly announced their intention to simplify appointments without prejudice to subsequent jurisdictional claims by committees. Nevertheless the advent of multiple committee referrals since 1974 has greatly complicated pressures on the Speaker to name more than a small group of senior Members—another symbol of the demise of the strict seniority system in the House. The Speaker has delegated to the Parliamentarian the same nonpartisan role in delineating House conferee participation by secondary committees as in determining committee jurisdictions on initial referral.

Often House conferees are named only to consider Senate provisions (sometimes non-germane) where there are no comparable House provisions, if only to indicate that the Senate's lack of a germaneness rule will not permit 'end runs' of relevant House committees (which may not have acted on a comparable measure) in the conference process. With respect to the number of signatures required to constitute a valid conference report on all issues, the participation of those additional conferees is specifically limited. While their withholding of signatures may impact on the majority of signatures otherwise required on each provision, they are usually fewer in number so as not to prevent a majority of the primary committees' conferees from finalizing the matter. Where conferees from one committee such as Ways and Means are exclusive conferees (for example, on a revenue portion of the measure), a withholding of a majority of their signatures prevents filing of the conference report.

One initial motion to instruct House conferees is in order after the House agrees to go to conference and prior to the Speaker's appointment, and by tradition that motion is the prerogative of the most senior Minority member of the managing committee, who unlike a motion to recommit a bill pending final passage need not qualify as being opposed to the measure to offer the motion. That is because the motion to instruct in the House is non-binding (the House cannot instruct Senate conferees). Also, the motion can only suggest that House conferees take a position on one or more issues which are within the 'scope' of differences committed to conference—that is, either the House or

Senate position or a middle-ground modification which does not range beyond the position taken by one or the other House or propose to delete matter accepted by both Houses. Debate is evenly divided between Majority and Minority parties, unless both favour the motion, in which event an opponent can claim one-third of the time. At the conclusion of debate, the motion to instruct can be amended only if the House rejects the motion for the previous question, and the Speaker may recognize a Majority or another Minority Member to offer additional or alternative instructions. That amendment must likewise be within the scope of conference, although not necessarily germane to the original instructions to which offered.

In the Senate, initial motions to instruct are similar to procedures in the House, as they are not binding (as not directed at House conferees) and must be offered prior to the appointment of conferees. They are different in that they are not limited in number and are not the prerogative of the Minority, recognition being in the discretion of the presiding officer. Senate motions to instruct are fully amendable but are subject to non-debatable motions to table. They follow a more liberal 'scope' rule which has permitted inclusion of provisions so long as 'not entirely irrelevant' to the House or Senate matter committed to conference—in effect a liberalized germaneness rather than a strict scope test.

After a bill has been sent to conference by both Houses and has remained there for twenty calendar (and concurrently ten legislative) days, any Member can offer a proper motion to instruct conferees following one day's notice to the House, again without qualifying as being opposed, because such motions are not binding and have the purpose of advancing the conference deliberations by clarifying a House position over time. Those motions can proliferate, as any Member can offer one or more properly noticed motion at any time until the conference report is filed in the House. No comparable motion to instruct following the appointment of conferees exists in the Senate. Alternative motions in the House at this twenty-day stage include motions to discharge and appoint new conferees, again with one day's notice, in the unlikely event that the House desires to change the composition of a conference committee. Such motions are not attempted in modern practice since the Speaker can unilaterally change a conference appointment. The motion cannot be used merely to discharge the measure from conference in order to force its immediate consideration. Only a special order from the Rules Committee can discharge a conference committee for that purpose, and then only if the House is in possession of the official papers. While such motions to instruct can be tabled by motion without debate, and while an opponent can claim one-third of debate time if both parties' managers favour the motion, they are most often utilized to dramatize a political position in order to influence subsequent conference decisions.

There are only a few procedural restrictions in House and Senate rules and practices governing the conduct of conference meetings, and they are not necessarily enforceable by points of order during the conference proceedings. The members of each conference committee can select their own chairman. For example, as between the House Ways and Means Committee and the Senate Finance Committee, the tradition has developed that the conference chairmanship alternates on each bill sent to conference. The conferees can also decide whether they wish to adopt any formal rules governing such matters as debate, quorums, proxy voting, or amendments, but usually they defer to each House's managers to determine for themselves how they will establish their position on all issues presented in the conference. Both Houses' conferees often permit their chairmen to utilize proxies—signed permissions by absent conferees on all or on specific issues to be discussed. The House rule adopted in 1995 prohibiting the use of proxies in its own committees is not applicable to joint conference committees, as neither House can bind the conferees of the other House by internal rules. All votes take place within the House delegation and the Senate delegation, with each delegation having one vote, and for that reason there is no requirement for each House to appoint the same number of conferees. Moreover, despite the presence or absence of rules governing interlocutory questions in a conference, all decisions are ultimately either ratified or negated by the original signatures of a majority of all conferees from each House being affixed to the conference papers for formal filing.

Until the mid-1970s, conference meetings were almost always closed to the public. Now at least one such meeting must be open unless a specific decision is taken to close part or all of a meeting. Under Senate standing rule[50] the conferees themselves determine by roll-call vote of a majority of those managers present, that all or part of the remainder of the meeting on the day of the vote shall be closed to the public. The comparable House rule[51] requires a roll-call vote of the full House to permit House conferees to vote to close a conference committee meeting. This difference between House and Senate rules has not been a source of public contention because efforts to close conferences normally are made only when they must deal with national security matters. Essentially, when conferees wish to discuss matters behind closed doors, they do so in an informal format that does not constitute a conference meeting. This recent tendency to revert to informal negotiations has provoked criticism that Minority party conferees were being excluded from conference meetings. Nevertheless bicameral negotiators commonly hold informal discussions in small or large groups, as a flexible negotiation process is necessary to reach a compromise. As a result, in the 110th Congress a new Majority adopted rules in the House that 'managers should endeavour to ensure' that meetings only occur if every House manager has been given notice and an opportunity to attend, and that all matters in disagreement are open to discussion at a conference meeting. If a point of order is made and sustained in the House that conferees met in violation of this rule, or never met at all, the conference report is rejected and the House is considered to have requested a further conference with the Senate. The Senate has adopted a similar 'sense of the Senate' statement contained in law.[52]

As a practical matter, the House by adoption of a special order of business reported from the Rules Committee waives all points of order which would otherwise inhibit the consideration of the report. Such waivers have become 'customary' or 'standard' in contemporary Congresses, and while they are not granted anticipatorily before final conference reports are filed, they often are recommended by the Rules Committee meeting only a brief time following filing so as to expedite consideration and often to minimize time available to scrutinize the reports' contents. At the same time, the expectation of general waivers in the House permit House and Senate managers to be less concerned with procedural obstacles there and to deal more freely with substantive issues. At least this was so until the 110th Congress in 2007 changed the Senate scope rule discussed at page 459 to render more difficult the inclusion of new matters not formally committed to conference by requiring a three-fifths vote for a waiver.

In some cases, conference deliberations are rather formal. One delegation puts a proposal on the table; the other responds with a counter-proposal. In other cases, conferences resemble free-form discussions in which the issues and the matters in disagreement are discussed without any apparent agenda or direction until the outlines of a compromise begin to emerge. (This is exactly the pattern of conferences at Westminster before 1836—'free' conferences, at which discussions took place and ordinary conferences which exchanged papers.) In recent years, conferences on massive omnibus Appropriation bills have created 'sub-conferences' consisting of the relevant subcommittees' managers to seek agreements on definable portions which can then be combined into a single conference report. Conference bargaining is facilitated by preliminary staff work, as by preparation of side-by-side comparisons or informal discussions with or without conferees present.

In recent Congresses, there has been a reluctance to formally establish conference committees in advance of informal negotiations, partly because an unlimited number of motions to instruct House conferees become privileged after twenty calendar days (including ten concurrent legislative days) which may politically impair the flexibility otherwise possessed by the managers. In the House, twenty-day motions to instruct conferees remain in order until the conference report is actually filed, but any pending motion to instruct becomes moot at that time unless the conference report is subsequently recommitted by the House, if acting first. There the conferees have not at that stage been discharged and the same conference committee still exists.

Instructions may not direct conferees to do that which they might not otherwise do, as to change a part of a bill not in disagreement or to include matter not committed to conference or beyond the scope of differences. One variation is that House conferees on general Appropriation bills may be instructed to agree to Senate amendments containing legislative provisions or unauthorized items (or modifications within the scope of conference but not if adding further legislation), as House appropriations conferees are only prohibited from including such provisions in their report in the absence of such specific House permission. Like motions to recommit bills, motions to instruct conferees may not include argument which becomes a matter for debate rather than part of the language of the motion to be voted upon. For example, the motion may merely instruct conferees to conduct conferences under 'just and fair conditions', but may not contend that deliberations to that point have not been so conducted. Because any number of twenty-day motions can be noticed and then offered, they may be repeated and are subject to a division of the question if containing separate propositions.

When the conferees reach full agreement, staff prepare a conference report which indicates how each amendment in disagreement has been resolved. For example, until recent Congresses the report (especially on Appropriations bills with numbered Senate amendments) proposed that the Senate recede from certain of its amendments to the House bill, that the House recede from its disagreement to certain other Senate amendments, and that the House recede from its disagreement to the remaining Senate amendments and concur in each with a House amendment (the text of which is made part of the report. When, as is almost always the case in contemporary Congresses, the conferees have considered a single amendment in the nature of a substitute by one House to a bill of the other, the report proposes that the House which originated the bill recede from its disagreement to the other House's substitute, and concur in that substitute with an amendment that is the new version of the bill on which the conference committee has agreed.

Two copies of the conference report must be signed by a majority of House conferees and a majority of Senate conferees without qualification, exception, or argument. No minority or additional views are permitted to be attached. Those copies become the original papers in each House and are sent to the Government Printing Office for printing as a House report (the Senate avoids duplicate printing). In calculating whether a majority have signed where there are multiple committees' conferees on certain provisions, the House practice is to assure that a majority of signatures, including general and additional conferees, be separately obtained on each provision of the bill and amendment. Under a simplistic Senate practice only the total number of signatures are counted per capita. A point of order may lie in the House that a conference report did not receive a majority of signatures on each issue, whereas in the Senate the practice is merely to count the total number of conferees' signatures, without a delineation that a majority have come to agreement on each issue. Conferees have been permitted to sign with qualification or exception (not argument), but in the House they are not counted toward the required majority, as they have not signed the entire agreement as a contract to be presented to both Houses. In the Senate they may be counted, as the Chair does not look beyond the number of signatures for exceptions. New House rules require that House conferees be given an opportunity to sign the conference agreement at a set time and place with the language of the report to be available.

The conference report bill text itself is not always the most informative document, because it does not describe the nature of the disagreements that confronted the conferees. Therefore, the rules of both Houses require that a conference report be accompanied by a joint explanatory statement 'sufficiently detailed and explicit to inform' the Members of its contents. The joint statement also must receive the same requisite number of signatures, and no additional or minority views are permitted except to the extent that the agreed-upon joint statement may describe those differences. The Chair does not rule on the sufficiency of the joint statement, as long as there is one which contains some explanation.

The House that agreed to the request for a conference normally acts first on the conference report, as suggested in section XLVI of Jefferson's *Manual*. This is facilitated by the asking House, having received the agreement message, then turning over the official papers to the agreeing House at the completion of a successful conference. For that reason, it can be orchestrated in advance as to which House shall request the conference so as to enable the other House to act first if and when there is a conference report filed. For example, the House may wish to delay action on a report until after the Senate has voted on it because the report may be filibustered in the Senate or conferees may agree that the House where the report might enjoy greater support should act first. On major revenue and Appropriation bills, however, the House always acts first, in furtherance of the origination clause in Article I, section 7 of the Constitution.

Only in the House acting first is a motion to recommit to conference with or without (non-binding) instructions in order. When the House requesting a conference retains the official papers rather than turning them over to the second (agreeing) House upon completion of the conference, the requesting House is technically capable of acting first, sometimes in order to remove the motion to recommit from the other House. This procedure, however, is exceptional. The House by tradition fully expects to act first and thus to enable the Minority to move to recommit on the most important conference reports—those on general Appropriation and revenue bills. Thus by tradition the Senate is always the body to ask for a conference and therefore to act second on those measures. Conversely, any attempt in the Senate to hand over the official papers to enable the House to act first, where the Senate is scheduled to so act, requires unanimous consent and is not permitted to be done informally by staff 'signing out' the papers.

The first House to consider a conference report has the option of voting to recommit the report to the same conference from which it emerged. In the House, that motion is the prerogative of the Minority, is not debatable, and the offering Member (as on bills pending initial passage, the designee of the Minority Leader) must qualify as being opposed to the conference report. In the Senate there may be multiple debatable motions to recommit to conference with or without instructions and they are not the prerogative of the Minority. Once the first House adopts or rejects the report, the conferees are discharged and there is no conference to which the second House may recommit the report. The second House can either adopt it, or reject it and insist on its disagreement and request a further conference, and then potentially instruct its conferees to that new conference. If conferees cannot agree on any of the amendments before them, or on all matters encompassed by one House's bill and the other's substitute, they may report back in total disagreement. The two Houses can then seek a resolution of the differences either through a second conference or through an exchange of amendments and motions between them. In modern practice, the conferees may submit their report to the House and Senate even though it violates their authority in one or more respects. Then in the House the Rules Committee invariably proposes a special order protecting the report against points of order involving its availability and content. In the Senate, violations of scope or budgetary constraints can be waived by a three-fifths vote of the Senate, not by a majority as in the House as discussed at page 452.

A conference report may be presented or filed at almost any time the House or Senate is in session, even pending a motion to adjourn in the House. Filing is not permitted in the Senate when in executive session or in the House when in Committee of the Whole. A conference report traditionally is unlikely to be considered immediately, because both the House and Senate have applicable availability requirements. In the House, conference reports are subject to a three-day layover requirement (not counting weekends) for printing in the Congressional Record. Since the 1980s in the House, the Rules Committee routinely has recommended waivers of points of order against availability, and waives the reading of those reports by the Clerk. Following three-day availability or adoption of a special order waiving that requirement, conference reports become highly privileged in the House and may be called up at almost any time another matter is not pending. When called up, the report is considered in the House under the one-hour rule, equally divided between the Majority and Minority parties or divided three ways if the Minority manager is not opposed to the report. The Majority manager then moves the previous question, which cuts off further debate and brings the House to an immediate vote on the conference report, subject to a motion to recommit if the House is acting first, as previously described.

In 2007, the rules were amended to require open formal conference meetings to which all conferees were invited. This stricture has encouraged informal partisan negotiations in advance of conference meetings—the very practice the new rule was intended to minimize. Conference reports are filed in the two Houses for printing in the House portion of the Record and for final votes under expedited procedures limiting debate and preventing amendment. In the House, this is accomplished by preliminary adoption of a special rule called up as privileged from the Committee on Rules, often on the same calendar day as the final complex version of the conference report first becomes available.

In the Senate, greater flexibility was until the 110th Congress accomplished by the application by Senate Parliamentarians of very expansive notions of 'scope of conference' which, in part because of that body's inability to waive points of order by majority vote, permitted conferees to include additional matters in conference versions so long as not totally unrelated to the subject of some provision in the original House or Senate provision. Even in the Senate prior to 2007, however, the insertion of new matter into a conference report had its limits. In December 2005, a provision to permit oil exploration and production in the Alaska National Wildlife Reserve was inserted by conferees in an annual appropriation conference report for the Department of Defense. That provision had not been contained in either bill but had originally been included in another Senate bill—a reconciliation spending measure—in order to avoid filibuster in the Senate, but had been rejected on that measure in the House. As explained at page 459 in this segment, the point of order was sustained in the Senate.

Points of order in the House against the contents of the conference report itself must be made immediately upon consideration, but are normally waived by a special order of business from the Rules Committee. The rule of both Houses that matter cannot be included in a conference report if beyond the scope of the House and Senate versions, was not waived in the House prior to the 1980s, and House conferees were constrained to confine their efforts to true and technical compromises between those versions.

Successful points of order (for example, against matter beyond scope of conference or non-germane Senate provisions) result in the rejection of the conference report. In the case of non-germane Senate matter, the point of order can be directed merely at that portion and not against the entire report, but if sustained has the effect of rejecting the report and placing before the House a pending motion to agree to the remainder of the conference report as a new House amendment minus the non-germane provision. In this fashion, the House can surgically remove such a provision if rejected on its merits while sending the rest of the agreed-upon language back to the Senate as a further amendment.

Conference reports may not be amended on the floor of either House, as the report represents a package settlement of all differences committed to conference. This rule in both Houses presents the greatest advantage toward resolution of differences and until recent Congresses has been preferred to the 'ping-ponging' of amendments. A new Senate rule (see page 452) has complicated consideration of some conference reports, especially those containing matter outside the scope of differences and new direct spending provisions 'air-dropped' into the conference, not having been in either the original House or Senate-passed versions, which can only be waived by three-fifths votes. The first such waiver in the Senate occurred on 18 June 2009. As discussed at page 448, these complications have forced the two Houses to consider 'ping-pong' approaches to the resolution of differences, and can be facilitated in the House by special orders reported from the Committee on Rules which dictate motions to amend Senate provisions (sometimes with numbered House amendments) in such a way as to present a series of choices to the Senate, while avoiding intervening motions, such as the motion to instruct or to recommit, in the House.

Senate Rule XXVIII requires that a conference report must be 'available on each Senator's desk' before the Senate may consider it, and prohibits a vote on the adoption of the report unless it has been available to Senators and the general public for at least forty-eight hours. This availability requirement can be waived by three-fifths vote, by unanimous consent, or by joint agreement of the Majority and Minority Leader. Under the rule, a report is considered to be available to the general public if it is posted on a government website. This is the only reference in the rules of either House to electronic rather than printed availability of reports, but may reflect a trend in the electronic age. Conference reports are privileged in the Senate, as the motion to proceed to consideration is not debatable. The Senate's usual practice is to take up conference reports by unanimous consent at times arranged in advance among the floor and committee leaders. Under a standing order adopted by the Senate in 2000 the reading of a conference report, once utilized to filibuster its consideration, is no longer required if the report 'is available in the Senate'.

When considered on the Senate floor, a conference report is debatable under normal Senate procedures, meaning extended debate unless the time is limited by unanimous consent or cloture, or if the Senate is considering the report under an expedited procedure established by law (such as budget resolutions and reconciliation measures under the Budget Act discussed at page 235). If time is limited, it is equally divided between the parties, not necessarily between proponents and opponents of the report. The Senate does not have a rule comparable to the House rule permitting an opponent to control one-third of the time. Consideration of a conference report by the Senate suspends, but does not displace, any pending or unfinished business.

As is generally true in the Senate unlike the House, a point of order may be made against a conference report (or any other pending matter) at any time that it is pending on the Senate floor. The presiding officer first entertains motions to waive the point of order if he is prepared to sustain it, and failing a three-fifths vote then summarily sustains the point of order without elaborating on his ruling. If sustained on the basis of new matter beyond the scope of differences or 'new directed spending provisions', there is then a special procedure established in the 110th Congress to strike out the offending portions of the conference report and continue consideration of the rest of the proposed compromise as an amendment to send back to the House. Amendments to this motion are not in order, and the motion is debatable under the same terms as the conference report it has replaced. This process places a defined provision before the Senate, replicating the 'Byrd rule' which strikes extraneous (non-deficit reduction) matter from a budget reconciliation conference report on a point of order (discussed in Budget Act procedures at page 239), and then retains the remaining portions of the conference report as a proposed Senate amendment to be returned to the House.

Senate rules also create a mechanism for waiving these restrictions on conference reports. Senators can move to waive points of order against one or several provisions, or they can make one motion to waive all possible points of order under the scope rule. A motion to waive all points of order is not amendable, but a motion to waive points of order against specific provisions is. Both are debatable for one hour divided between leaderships. As with virtually all three-fifths waiver requirements that have proliferated in the Senate, whether in the Budget Act or under new Senate rules, the Senate is effectively agreeing to keep the matter that is potentially in violation of the rules under consideration. The distinguishing difference from the House is that a super-majority is required for all such waivers, while in the House only a majority vote is required on a special order reported from the Committee on Rules. Again, these contrasting procedures signal a fundamental difference between the two Houses—one underwritten by a majoritarian philosophy and the other empowering at least a forty-vote minority to control the consideration of matters in violation of what are otherwise essentially similar rules of each House.

A discussion of reconciliation procedures with respect to conference reports, in particular the 'Byrd Rule' as it applies to the inclusion of extraneous matter, would not be complete without a corollary discussion of the scope of conference rule of both Houses as those rules (recently amended in the Senate in 2007) apply to conference reports generally, and as those rules interact with the Budget Act on reconciliation conference reports. 'Scope of conference' is an exceedingly technical term when applied to insertions in conference reports of matter not in either House or Senate version of the measure being conferenced. Both Houses have very similar rules restricting the authority of their respective conferees to include new matter. Senate Rule XXVIII states that Senate conferees 'shall not insert in their report matter not committed to them by either House, nor shall they strike from the bill matter agreed to by both Houses'. House Rule XXII, clause 9 is somewhat more precise, stating that while House conferees may include matter which is 'a germane modification of matter in disagreement', they may not include 'any language presenting specific additional matter not committed to the conference committee, nor may they include a modification of specific matter committed to the conference committee by either or both Houses if that modification is beyond the scope of that specific matter' as so committed. At least until 2007, precedents in the Senate interpreting this rule were very broad, to the extent that the conference report did not exceed scope so long as not including new matter which was entirely irrelevant to the subject matter of either measure. This reflected that the Senate was without the benefit of a Rules Committee as in the House which could recommend waivers of such points of order for adoption on an ad hoc basis by majority vote.

By overruling the Chair in 1996 and allowing the provision to remain in the conference report to be considered on its merits, the Senate established a new precedent, not merely that the particular provision—a labour law treatment for FedEx Corporation—was not outside the scope of conference on that occasion but that the subsequent enforcement of Senate Rule XXVIII would be suspended indefinitely. See Procedural Basics at page 210 for further discussion of the effect of the successful appeal. The Senate then operated for four years without enforcing Rule XXVIII, and new provisions were allowed to be added by the Senate conferees in many conference reports, needing only waivers of points of order in the House which were readily forthcoming. During that period, scores of extraneous matters were added to conference reports which, while sometimes assisting leadership in moving their agenda, at other times created problems for party leaders. As related by Oleszek:[53]

> On many occasions the Senate leadership had to field requests from colleagues or allies asking that an item get slipped into a conference report. Often these requests were controversial and granting the favor created a firestorm of opposition. In the end, relying on the rule was a courteous way of saying 'no' to last minute Senatorial requests.

Then in December 2000 the Senate scope rule again became effective when that conference report was signed into law, subsequently permitting points of order to be raised in the Senate against conference reports containing unrelated provisions. That explicit restoration was deemed necessary to overcome the 'precedent' that a rule becomes unenforceable in the Senate once the Chair is overruled on appeal. At this writing, the Senate has, in the event that a three-fifths waiver is not obtained under new Rule XXVIII imposed in 2007, given up some of the flexibility Senate conferees had enjoyed in the implementation of the Senate scope rule.

The 2000 restoration of the scope rule became particularly relevant in the Senate in December 2005, when an attempt was made as previously described at page 456 to add a new provision (Oil exploration in the Alaska National Wildlife Reserve) to a Department of Defense Appropriation Act. When the Senate Parliamentarian advised that the provision would be ruled beyond the scope of conference under restored Rule XXVIII, its sponsor attempted to include within the provision itself restorative language to the effect that if the chair were again overruled on appeal, the precedential effect of that Senate action would be nullified by the very same language restoring the scope rule to its enforceable condition upon enactment into law. The bootstrapping implications of such language, taking into account the 1996 interpretation of the non-enforceability of the rule upon a successful appeal, was too much for the Senate to tolerate. When it became apparent that the Senate was being asked to establish further 'precedent' to the effect that rules can be ignored by an appeal but then immediately restored by statutory language in the offending provision itself, the Senate declined to allow that conference report to proceed, thereby resulting in the inability to come to a final vote on a vital Appropriation bill. Rather than allow that scenario to play out in the closing days of the session, the Senate by unanimous consent considered a concurrent resolution stripping that extraneous provision from the conference report, in order to subsequently end the filibuster and to pass the remainder of the conference report. The House then followed suit by adopting the concurrent resolution removing the offending provision and enabling the conference report it had already adopted to go to the President in an amended form.

All the while, other extraneous provisions were allowed to remain in that defence appropriation conference report, including one added at the private insistence of the Senate Majority Leader and the Speaker (indemnification against liability for the development of an avian flu vaccine) after the conferees had signed the report but prior to its filing, and without the ability of conferees to resign or withdraw signatures. While going unchallenged by the conferees and later knowingly given a waiver of points of order by the Rules Committee in the House, this action was subjected to a collateral challenge in the House as a question of privilege, alleging the episode to have been a deliberate violation of House and Senate rules. On that question of privilege, which challenged the ethical conduct of those leaders, the House tabled the resolution without debate, unwilling to come to terms with the severity of the breach of order on that occasion.

In modern-day conference reports, at least until the Senate tightened its scope rule in 2007, scope violations by the conferees were common (although leadership insertions of language without the authority of conferees thankfully are not), and are virtually always waived in the House by special orders from the Committee on Rules. In fact, House conferees have come to expect waivers protecting their work product from points of order, and often proceed with impunity to include new matter without regard to once traditional constraints which guided their actions. If the Majority Leadership in the House approves of the new provision as a matter of policy and a majority of conferees vote for its inclusion, that acceptance will be reflected in the willingness of the Rules Committee, once it has cursorily examined the conference report (sometimes in the space of an hour), to recommend the necessary waiver, and for a majority of the House to adopt that waiver on a 'procedural vote' demanding party loyalty. Since 1995, there has only been one conference report left vulnerable to a point of order of the scores of conference reports filed, and on that occasion (14 November 2002), a bankruptcy conference report containing matter admittedly not in either House or Senate version was ruled out of order where the Majority Leadership had determined that the measure should not be finally enacted in that Congress. Only the 2007 super-majority waiver requirements imposed by new Senate Rule XXVIII have served to limit conferees' willingness to routinely violate scope rules, and instead to adopt alternative 'ping-pong' procedures which avoid conferences.

The complexity of legislation has, as in the UK, steadily increased commensurate with the enormous size of the issues being addressed. There has tacitly evolved in the Congress the concept of an 'inverse ratio' between the size and scope of a final version of a bill, on the one hand, and the time available to scrutinize and debate those measures, on the other (see page 548). With increasing frequency, bills which must be passed to meet statutory or adjournment deadlines or high priority policy objectives of the Majority party are combined with extraneous special-interest or individual provisions such as 'earmarks'—often the subjects of separately introduced bills—by being added in conference committees or in leadership-negotiated 'ping-pong' motions. At this writing, the strict scope 'air-drop' rule adopted for conference reports in the Senate in 2007 has already resulted in utilization of alternative procedures to avoid its application.

In 2009, on perhaps the most significant combined revenue, spending, and debt ('stimulus') bill in history, the two Houses chose a return to a truncated conference procedure which lasted only one day. The conference language was negotiated in advance by the Majority Leaderships without Minority participation, and a formal conference meeting was held only to ratify that agreement. The Conference report was signed only by Majority House and Senate managers and was then available to Members electronically for less than one day, despite adoption of a non-binding Minority motion to instruct House conferees, calling for forty-eight-hour availability of text to all conferees. When filed, the report was first considered in the House under a special order waiving all points of order, although it was subjected to unsuccessful Minority motion to recommit to conference. In the Senate, the report was considered and adopted pursuant to a unanimous consent agreement expediting the process by requiring one combined three-fifths vote which both waived the pay-go rule, and adopted the conference report. The urgency of the enactment in response to the international economic and fiscal crisis was decried by the Minority as an indication of the uncertainty of the measure's contents, but the President's advocacy of the overriding need to enact the legislation promptly publicly overcame institutional concerns about process. Only a week after was it discovered that a controversial provision had been inserted into the conference report without the knowledge of most of the conferees of either House—a protection of contract bonuses to be paid to employees of financial institutions being subsidized by the Federal 'bail-out'. The public outcry against that Congressional complicity and imprecision was demonstrable.

There exist in both Houses procedures permitting correction of conference reports following adoption and enrolment for presentment to the President. Concurrent resolutions authorizing the Clerk of the originating House to make specified changes in the final version require unanimous consent for consideration in the Senate and can be made in order in the House by unanimous consent, suspension of the rules, or a special order reported from the Committee on Rules. Where the measure has been presented to the President, the concurrent resolution may include a request for return of the bill and vacating of signatures. Under no circumstances is the enrolling clerk of either House authorized to make corrections, absent such specific permission. A contention in 2008, during debate on a measure directing the Justice Department to investigate an improper change of an enrolment following adoption of a conference report, revealed a misconception that such changes were permissible when there was informal bipartisan agreement. This matter is further discussed at page 538.

As demonstrated on 21 May 2008, when an erroneously printed enrolled bill had been presented and vetoed and the error was then discovered after the veto message has been read to the originating House, it is too late for the President to ask for return of his veto message, and the bill in its vetoed form becomes public law upon override, leaving it up to Congress to enact a subsequent law to correct the error. While the erroneous enrolment of that bill in 2008 was an anomaly in a number of respects—the two Houses were unable to retrieve the vetoed bill and the President did not notice the error (omission of a title) in the short time he took to veto it—the error again demonstrated that the greater the haste to finalize a measure, the more likely the possibility of error.

Further compounding this emphasis on political expediency and the resulting loss of procedural institutional integrity (as with the three-hour vote on the Medicare Prescription Drug conference report[54] have been the increased collateral challenges by Minority Leaders as questions of privilege in a partisan and non-collegial atmosphere alleging deliberate leadership mismanagement of the matter and calling for ethics investigations. Taken together, the Majority's political advantage to be gained from often uninformed and expedited consideration of complex legislative measures, especially near adjournment periods or during economic crises where the pressures of time are more acute, has encouraged a departure from 'regular order' to the detriment of Congress as an institution and to the reputations of Majority Leaderships as managers of the business of Congress.

Between the Houses in Parliament

When the second UK House to consider a bill has completed its work, it returns the bill to the first House in a form containing any amendments it has made. The originating House, when this message is received, prints and considers the amendments. Conferences, such a critical part of US law making, were practically abandoned in the eighteenth century and formally expired in the middle of the nineteenth (though their revival was briefly aired recently in evidence to a Joint Committee). The first House may agree with what has been done, and the bill then proceeds to Royal Assent. Governments often find it convenient to implement undertakings given in the first House by amendments made in the second, and these are of course likely to be accepted when the bill returns to the House of origin.

In many instances, therefore, Lords Amendments arriving in the Commons are relatively uncontested, and it is often convenient to schedule discussion in what will probably be a thin House, after the moment of interruption. Lords Amendments take up far more time after the moment of interruption than any other stage of legislation.

Lords Amendments may however prove unacceptable to the lower House (as well as Commons Amendments to the Lords), and the two views must be adjusted by a procedure euphemistically referred to, as in Congress, as 'ping-pong'. A sequence of messages shuttles between the Houses, as one agrees, maintains disagreement, or tries to reach a compromise with the judgement of the other.

Even when compromise is the expected outcome, the procedure remains difficult to handle. Governments are naturally reluctant to surrender a contested position completely at the first challenge, so that successive complicated exchanges in search of a solution requiring the government to surrender as little as possible are inevitable. On a bill with some disputed amendments, some open to compromise, and some where one House has given way, the sequence of events can become ferociously complex. As the bill moves back and forth between the Houses, cold towels are in great demand. The following is a message—the second that day on the Prevention of Terrorism Bill[55]—brought from the Lords after midnight on Friday 11 March 2005:

> The Lords insist on certain of their Amendments to the Bill, to which this House has insisted on its disagreement, for which insistence they assign their Reasons; they insist on certain of their Amendments to which this House has disagreed, for which insistence they assign their Reasons; they disagree to the Amendments proposed by this House in lieu of the Lords Amendments, for which disagreement they assign their Reason; they do not insist on their remaining Amendments to which this House has disagreed; and they agree to the remaining Amendments made by this House on which this House had insisted.

Agreement was reached in the end, but only after the Commons had sat for twenty and a half hours, interrupted by suspensions of the sitting while the Lords debated the contents of the messages sent to them.

There are certain limitations on the consideration of amendments received from the other House. An amendment proposed in one House to vary an amendment made by the other must be relevant to the subject matter of the original amendment and neither introduce new matter nor amend text on which the Houses have already agreed. That practice is quite distinct from the rule in Congress. Other practices are common to both legislatures. For example, as Erskine May's *Parliamentary Practice* puts it: 'each House has one opportunity of drawing back from the position it has taken up, unless it offers alternative proposals',[56] and if agreement or compromise cannot be reached, the bill is lost. One of the advantages of the 'double insistence' rule is that, since neither House probably wishes to lose an entire bill, the procedure predisposes them to keep on trying to narrow the gap of disagreement.

Much scorn has been heaped on these 'ping-pong' exchanges. There are certainly improvements which can be made, most notably by following the suggestion of the Joint Committee on Conventions[57] that reasonable notice should be given to either House of each new proposal when it is received. Late-night consideration of complex formulae hammered out in the other House often no more than half an hour previously—in a debate which has not of course yet been printed—can only be bad practice, though it is hard to see what is the realistic alternative if the intended end of a session is only hours away. The truth is that the gentle phrase 'ping-pong' conceals a trial of political will between government and those who do not agree with it in either House. Particularly when the session is about to end, the Opposition is in a position to force the government to choose between compromising and losing its legislation. A complete solution to the problem which will not involve the surrender by either House—and especially the Opposition—of a cherished weapon has not so far been found.

New mechanisms and changing balances at Westminster

Over the past thirty years, a series of procedural expedients have been attempted in the Commons with a view to bringing legislative time and business into better balance by shifting debate from the floor to committees. Second Reading Committees, Report committees, even (a reform not implemented) committees on Lords Amendments. Other reforms tried to solve within a purely parliamentary context the problem subsequently tackled more radically by devolution to legislative bodies in Scotland, Wales, and Northern Ireland (see pages 20–2). An elaborate but now semi-derelict structure of Grand Committees has been left behind, not much used except in some areas. Finally, a number of miscellaneous (and largely uncontroversial) changes in legislative practice have been made which severely abbreviate debate on certain types of bill—those which consolidate the law, give effect to proposals of one of the Law Commissions for improving the effect of existing law, or rewrite the law in the specialized and complex area of taxation.

The first area of change is draft bills. In the past, it was rare for either House to have any input into the drafting of a bill. Without an opportunity to express its views at that critical stage, however, Parliament is continually behind the game. White Papers foreshadowing government policy or Green Papers flying kites may be debated, and the government may listen to parliamentary views then expressed, but when the bill eventually appears, it is drafted in terms acceptable to the government alone. There is thereafter a reluctance to accept amendment of an instrument seen as fully and accurately delivering government policy in a considered way.

There are benefits for Parliament, for government, and for the law in the production of draft bills or pre-legislative scrutiny. Organized interests, large and small, can pass on their practical experience to those who draft and those who make the law. There is a general consensus that legislation which follows this route is better in quality than that which does not. From the parliamentary point of view, pre-legislation offers an opportunity to regain some lost initiative in law making by reinvigorating the link with the public. Dividends in terms of acceptance by government of amendments suggested by parliamentary (often joint) committees to which draft bills were sent have already begun to flow. Indeed, criticism of the draft Corruption Bill in 2005 was so fierce that the government abandoned the original text and started again. A second draft bill was published in March 2009.

Effective change depends on the government enthusiasm to involve Parliament in the scrutiny of draft bills. Pre-legislative scrutiny may in some cases reduce the time taken to consider a bill proper because the ground has already been cleared. In other cases, however, differences of opinion may be sharpened and the battle prolonged. Parliamentary readiness is evident. The Lords Committee on the Constitution recommended in 2003–4 and reaffirmed in 2007–8 that publication of bills in draft should be the norm, a view which the Committee reinforced by expressing its intention to publish a report on pre-legislative activity every session.[58] The Commons Modernisation Committee in 2005–6 only slightly modified the prescription by referring to such scrutiny as 'the usual course for major government bills'.[59] In fact, the number of draft bills in the past decade is set out in Table 9.5 in the Annex.

The Liaison Committee expressed its regret that the numbers should have dropped back[60] and the Lords Constitution Committee concluded that the government ought once more to achieve the 2003–4 level,[61] which evoked an official reply that no such undertaking could be given because governments needed the freedom to bring forward many bills on timetables which did not permit draft versions.

It had initially been feared select committees might be reluctant to disturb a settled programme in a long inquiry already begun in the interests of shorter legislation-related work. The apprehension was without foundation. Indeed, in 2004–5, the Public Administration Committee, impatient at government delay, even produced its own version of a bill on the civil service ahead of the version promised by the government.

In 2006–7, two draft bills were considered by select committees and there were two Joint Committees on drafts, one of which was also before a select committee. The following session, six draft bills were considered by one or more departmentally related select committees or combinations of a joint committee and one or two select committees. One select committee considered two of the drafts. In 2008–9 seven draft bills were promised, though fewer were in the event published. Two draft bills were in the Queen's Speech in 2009.

Despite this progress, some difficulties of process remain. Bills have been published so late as severely to truncate committee inquiries: one arrived the day before the inquiry was scheduled to begin. The Joint Committee on the draft Gambling Bill in 2003–4 did not see the whole bill until after the date by which it was obliged to report. Four sessions later, in 2007–8, the Transport Committee was still complaining that the timetable for the draft bill which it scrutinized was 'very challenging', and the Lords Constitution Committee commented that bills were not published in good time and not spread evenly throughout the year. The Culture, Media and Sport Committee complained that certain key clauses of the draft under its consideration did not arrive until the day before that on which the evidence on the clauses was to be taken, a concern echoed by the Innovation, Universities, Science and Skills Committee, which also examined the draft. The most trenchant criticism of this part of scrutiny came from the Environment, Food and Rural Affairs Committee: 'given the amount of time and effort that goes into the drafting of bills, we were surprised at the vague and uncommunicative way in which the government deals with the House in preparing for such scrutiny'.[62]

The government aims to allow committees three to four months but is aware that this is not always achieved, and has emphasized the advantages of liaison between department and committee to identify a mutually convenient timetable. In the last resort, the government argue that priority must be given to work on bills actually in the legislative programme.

Delay is not the only concern, however. In 2007–8 the Commons Liaison Committee took justified umbrage at a government motion which sent a draft bill to a Joint Committee, contrary to the understanding that select committees which were ready and willing to take on the work would have priority, at the House's choice. The result is duplication—the same questions addressed to the same witnesses by two committees. The Liaison Committee put its faith in a more transparent and better-organized process in future. Certainly, it would seem a pity if this potentially very fruitful initiative should falter as a result of avoidable problems.

No doubt committee pressure will be kept up. In the meantime, there is work which Parliament might do. Both Houses might devise machinery which allows them (and not the government) to determine speedily whether a particular draft bill should be committed to an existing committee of one or both Houses, or to a specially constituted group. There will be problems in handling draft bills, notably the need to preserve the bipartisan character of select committees (see page 360) in the face of contentious legislation, but if identified in advance these are surmountable and the prize—reviving parliamentary scrutiny without crossing constitutional wires by assuming the dominant share in the initiation of policy—is well worth the risk.

Secondly, there has been much recent discussion[63] of how Parliament might continue to express concern for the quality and effectiveness of legislation after enactment. The advantages of systematic—rather than occasional—post-legislative review are many. Lessons might be learned which would feed back into future law making. The need for amending legislation would be reduced, and regulation made more effective. Ministers and backbenchers alike would be obliged to take into account the practicality of what was being proposed to a greater degree than at present. Best practice could be identified and disseminated. If the system could be brought to bear also on the secondary legislation derived from the statute under review, the working of the Act could be fine-tuned to Parliament's intentions. The government has concluded that departmentally related select committees should have a 'key and leading role' in post-legislative work, undertaken three to five years after the enactment or commencement of most but not by any means all statutes. Command Papers issued some three to five years after enactment of appropriate bills would permit select committees to decide whether to undertake a specific inquiry, build the topic into an existing inquiry, or take no action. If committees did institute an inquiry, the approach would be specific, avoiding a repetition of earlier policy debates. The kind of questions which would arise would be: is the Act working as intended, is it delivering the policy aims, can anything be learned from the experience? There is an obvious drawback in that such a system would impose a further heavy demand on a machine already struggling with more familiar aspects of select committee work. On the other hand, some committees have already had experience in the field, notably the Northern Ireland Committee in its study of the effects of the Electoral Fraud (Northern Ireland) Act 2002. The scarce resource is not only skilled staff, but also the time and enthusiasm of already hard-pressed Members. Success in post-legislative scrutiny would be most welcome, but it cannot be assumed.

Next there is the carrying over of bills from one annual session to the next. When every procedural wheeze, past and present, has been tried, experience suggests that time to consider legislation will remain in short supply. It is for that reason that the barriers separating one session from another have inched open, and from 2002, bills have been able to be 'carried over' from one session to the next, being picked up in the second session where they were left at the end of the first. Opposition apprehensions that this might lead to the loss of the important weapon of delay have meant that the rule is hung about with qualifications. Carry-over motions may not apply to more than one bill; only government bills may benefit; a bill drops if it is still before the House a calendar year after its introduction unless on a government motion that period is extended; and a bill may not be subject to a carry-over motion twice. Even allowing for these restrictions, it is a little disappointing that only a trickle of bills has made its way across the sessional gap, as illustrated by Table 9.6 in the Annex.

The strictness of the sessional principle has thus been modified: but not by much, which is a pity. The benefits of carry-over in terms of avoiding congestion of business and improving the quality of scrutiny are considerable. How pre-legislative scrutiny should relate to carry-over is as yet undecided. The Modernisation Committee recently observed that 'if a Bill is to undergo an additional parliamentary stage'—that is, pre-legislative scrutiny—'without any guarantee that this will expedite the subsequent stages, then the one-session time limit arguably becomes more of a burden than a safeguard'.[64] In brief, the innovation is a bold and interesting one, but like most other procedural changes only time will show whether the Houses or the government will be the principal beneficiary.

Presidential vetoes and Royal Assent

Alexander Hamilton in Federalist no. 69 describes the President's qualified power of disapproval of legislation as follows:

> the President of the United States is to have power to return a bill, which shall have passed the two Houses of the Legislature, for reconsideration; but the bill so returned is to become a law, if upon that reconsideration it be approved by two-thirds of both Houses. The King of Great Britain, on his part, has an absolute negative upon the acts of the two Houses of Parliament. The disuse of the power for a considerable time past does not affect the reality of its existence, and is to be ascribed wholly to the crown's having found the means of substituting influence to authority, or the art of gaining a majority in one or the other of the two Houses, to the necessity of exerting a prerogative which could seldom be exerted without hazarding some degree of national agitation. The qualified negative of the President differs widely from the absolute negative of the British sovereign...

This quoted expression by a Framer of the Constitution underlies the rationale for Article I, section 7 of the Constitution—the authority for the President to disapprove or veto a bill, and the process by which the Congress can override a veto and enact a measure into law. The President has a ten-calendar day period, the day of presentment and Sundays excluded, in which to approve or disapprove a bill. He can sign the bill into law or he can return it to its House of origination with a veto message detailing why he chooses not to sign. If he fails to give his approval by affixing his signature during that period, the bill will become law automatically, without his signature, unless in very limited circumstances the Congress by its final adjournment prevents the return of the bill, in which event the bill is 'pocket-vetoed'. Various Presidents have misinterpreted their authority to pocket-veto bills during interim adjournments of the Congress, although there is a paucity of Supreme Court case law beyond the *Pocket-Veto Case* 279 US 655 (1929). In that case, the court held that the President's return of a bill to the originating House was prevented when the Congress adjourned its first session sine die fewer than ten days after presenting the bill to the President. A constitutional debate still lingers with respect to the conditions under which the President may exercise his pocket-veto authority during periods other than final adjournments of a Congress. A more recent appellate court decision held that the return of a bill during an adjournment between sessions was not prevented where the originating House had appointed an agent for the receipt of Presidential veto messages, reasoning that the validity of a pocket-veto is governed not by the type or length of adjournment but by whether the conditions of the adjournment impede the actual return of the bill (*Barnes v Kline* 750 F 2d 21 (DC Cir 1985), vacated as moot, *Burke v Barnes* 479 US 361 (1987)). As part of the concurrent resolution providing for the sine die adjournment of a first session, the Congress has affirmed its position that an inter-session adjournment does not prevent the return of the bill where agents are authorized to receive messages and where that same Congress will return in another session to reconsider the vetoed bill.

An adjournment of Congress during a session does not prevent the President from returning a bill he disapproves, where the originating House has authorized its agent to receive messages—as has the House by rule since 1981 (*Kennedy v Sampson* 511 F 2d 430 (DC Cir 1974)). The Supreme Court has held that the adjournment of the House of origin for a period not exceeding three days while the other House remained in session does not prevent the return of a vetoed bill to the House of origin (*Wright v United States* 302 US 583 (1938)). Speakers and Minority Leaders have joined on several occasions in letters to the President decrying the assertion of the pocket-veto during an intra-session adjournment, although Presidents continue to rhetorically assert the right of pocket-veto while still returning the parchment to the House of origin during intra-session adjournments. So long as the vetoed bill is physically returned to the House of origin, despite such Presidential assertions the Congress is able to reconsider the measure unless it has finally adjourned. Should the President not return a vetoed bill during a period when Congress will return into session, the courts will eventually and properly determine that such a bill becomes law without his signature.

The unconstitutional Line Item Veto Act of 1997 is discussed at page 228 and, while involving a statutory veto authority, is more relevant there as having been applicable only to revenue and Appropriation bills.

Beyond the threat or reality of Presidential vetoes, Presidential signing statements are official pronouncements issued by the President contemporaneously to the signing of a bill into law that, in addition to commenting on the law generally, have been used to forward the President's interpretation of the statutory language; to assert constitutional objections to the provisions contained therein; and to announce that the provisions of the law will be administered in a manner that comports with the Executive's conception of the President's constitutional prerogatives. While the history of Presidential issuance of signing statements dates to the early nineteenth century, the practice has become the source of significant controversy in the modern era as Presidents have increasingly employed signing statements to assert constitutional and legal objections to Congressional enactments. President Reagan issued 250 signing statements, 86 of which contained provisions objecting to one or more of the statutory provisions signed into law. President George H. W. Bush continued this practice, issuing 228 signing statements, 107 of which raised objections. President Clinton issued 381 statements, 70 of which raised constitutional or legal objections. President George W. Bush issued 152 signing statements, 118 of which contained some type of challenge. The rise in the proportion of constitutional objections made by President Bush is compounded by the fact that these statements contain multiple objections, resulting in more than 1,000 challenges to distinct provisions of law. The national debate which has ensued by this trend has led the American Bar Association to report that signing statements 'are contrary to the rule of law and our Constitutional separation of powers' when they 'claim the authority or state the intention to disregard or decline to enforce all or part of a law, or to interpret such a law in a manner inconsistent with the clear intent of Congress'.[65] No constitutional or legal deficiencies adhere to the issuance of such statements in and of themselves. Rather, the focus must be on the assertions of Presidential authority contained therein, coupled with an examination of substantive Executive action taken or forborne with regard to the provisions of law objected to by the President. At this writing, measures have been introduced in Congress to regulate the issuance and use of signing statements, but the issue has not been litigated in the courts.

At Westminster, the last stage in the enacting of legislation is Royal Assent. Most bills receive the Royal Assent by a straightforward process laid down in statute about forty years ago. Once Her Majesty has formally signified her Assent, the Lord Speaker and the Speaker of the Commons read out in each Chamber at a convenient point in ongoing proceedings the list of Acts agreed to. At the end of a session, however, the Assent is usually given in a stately process in the Lords Chamber by Commissioners sitting on the woolsack in their Parliament robes, with much doffing and replacing of cocked hats. The Commons, summoned to be present at the bar of the Lords, witness proceedings at which, as the title of each bill is read, the Clerk of the Parliaments pronounces (in Norman French) *La Reyne le veult*,[66] and the bill passes into law. Unlike the position in the United States, the consent of the head of State is never refused. The last time that happened was in 1706, though it was evidently contemplated in 1910. A Sovereign is most unlikely to refuse again, other than in circumstances beyond present imagination.

Delegated legislation: parliamentary approval and disapproval

For at least a century and a half, powers have been statutorily delegated by Parliament to the government, permitting ministers and even some other public bodies to make orders or regulations which amplify or elaborate—even, by use of what is known as a

Henry VIII clause, directly amend—primary legislation.[67] Such instruments may not themselves be amended. What began as the merest trickle has turned into a powerful stream. In 2007–8, 1,319 instruments were laid before Parliament, though many more, the effect of which is local or transitory, were not. The parliamentary procedure involved—if any—will depend on the terms of the statute under which the order-making power is exercised. As a guiding thread through the maze of detail in instruments, attempts have been recently been made to improve the background information to the delegated legislation coming before Parliament. Ministers are expected to indicate their views on whether the more important instruments are compliant with the demands of the Human Rights Act (see pages 19–20): such a declaration is also made where any delegated legislation amends statute; and explanatory memoranda and regulatory impact assessments accompany all important instruments.

Where parliamentary procedures are prescribed by each parent statute, they are more or less standard and the great majority of instruments are subject to one of two procedures. (A third, more modern in origin, is explained below.) Instruments may be made by the government or another rule-making authority and come into force, though they may afterwards be disapproved of by motion in either House within a standard period. Alternatively, the instrument will not enter into or remain in force unless positively approved. In 2007–8, 1,049 instruments subject to the first, the negative procedure, were laid before Parliament, but only nineteen were debated. There were 224 instruments subject to the affirmative procedure, laid before the House and not withdrawn, all of which had to be debated. The system seems logically watertight, allowing Parliament at the time it enacts the parent legislation to choose the appropriate procedure by reference to the intrinsic importance of the decisions entrusted to the government. Instruments of greatest significance will all be considered: the others are open to debate if debate is felt necessary.

Over time, a number of factors have emerged to fault the logic. As successive governments have legislated in greater depth in wider areas, the scope for subordinate legislation to fill in the details has expanded. At the same time, the subject matter of secondary legislation has widened. Instruments are no longer limited to ancillary or machinery provisions. Some may affect the citizen as immediately as the parent Act. Parliament was in the past slow to adapt its procedures to the new conditions, though to be fair much of the problem is a specially difficult version of the central time/business balance and more recently a number of useful procedural changes have been made.

The greater the number and reach of instruments of secondary legislation, the greater the need to sift the innocent wheat from the potentially objectionable chaff. There are two areas of concern, form and substance. Whatever an instrument's provisions, Parliament needs to be reassured that it does not impose taxes or sub-delegate without proper authority, that none of its provisions are beyond the authority conferred by the parent Act, or that its effect is clear. Review of these aspects is currently entrusted to two scrutiny committees. The first is the Joint Committee on Statutory Instruments, the order of reference of which directs it to consider and report on just such defects. In 2007–8 the Joint Committee reviewed 1,441 instruments and (having heard what the government department which made the instrument had to say) made critical reports on seventy-nine, in two-thirds of cases for defective drafting. A parallel Commons-only select committee, with a similar order of reference to the Joint Committee, considers instruments—mostly dealing with taxation—which the parent statute orders to be laid before and considered by the Commons only. That committee looked at 141 such instruments in 2007–8 and reported on only five.

There, in midstream, the process effectively stops. The situation is particularly unsatisfactory in the Commons, where there is no requirement that either committee's conclusions should act to suspend or delay the instrument's further progress until matters are put right. Departments which make instruments found to be faulty may withdraw them but they are not obliged to do so. Debate (if there is a debate) may touch on the committee's view, but there is nothing to prevent a minister from politely sweeping any doubts aside. It is even possible (and occasionally happens) that an instrument is debated on the floor before the scrutiny committee has completed its consideration. They order these things better in the Lords, where it is not possible to move to approve an instrument until the report of the relevant committee has been made.

Turning to defects of substance, the first area of concern in debating the parent bill is whether delegation of powers is acceptable at all, and what degree of scrutiny an instrument is to attract. There are no hard and fast rules to keep greater intrinsic importance in line with more searching procedure. Such rules would not be easy to draft. Some delegated legislation comes to assume far greater importance than could reasonably have been foreseen when the original bill was being drafted. While governments are not usually cavalier when proposing scrutiny procedures in bills, they can hardly be expected to impose on themselves a degree of scrutiny which they (but not the Opposition) consider unreasonable. Sometimes the final choice of procedure to be applied to an instrument depends on deals struck in committee, in contexts remote from decisions on the degree of scrutiny required.

The Lords have addressed the problem by means of a committee, the Delegated Powers and Regulatory Reform Committee, part of whose task (see also page 472) is to come to a view on 'whether the provisions of any bill inappropriately delegate legislative power or whether they subject the exercise of legislative power to an inappropriate degree of public scrutiny'. Evidence is heard on every relevant bill, and the Committee draws attention to these issues of appropriateness and especially to the inclusion of Henry VIII clauses. When, for example, in the government's Serious Crime Bill 2006–7 a clause enabled public authorities to share otherwise protected information with an anti-fraud organization, and the instrument which allowed a minister to define that information was proposed to be subject to the negative procedure, the Committee observed that such definition was central to the operation of the scheme and thus should be subject to affirmative procedure.[68]

Despite frequent discussion of the need for such a 'sifting' function, the Commons has no parallel committee. Proposals to that effect were made by the Procedure Committee in 1996 and again in 2000. When the Committee returned to the charge in 2003, the government preferred to wait to see the result of the sifting experiment in the Lords, pleading concern at the likely increase in the demands made on parliamentary and civil service time. The Committee in turn rebutted these propositions. The argument about increased time is a sound one: but that which seeks significant improvement in parliamentary scrutiny of changes to the general law is surely sounder. Moreover, though burden sharing of this kind between the Houses in technical areas may be one way forward, it is hard to see how one House will always be ready to sign up to what are in effect the political judgements of the other. The Joint Committee option of course remains available—provided the resources in terms of Members' time can be found.

The merits of delegated legislation are debated on the floor of both Houses as well as in the Merits of Statutory Instruments Committee in the Lords (see below) and Delegated Legislation Committees in the Commons. For many years, despite the logic of their role as a revising Chamber, the Lords did not consider it appropriate to vote substantively against delegated legislation, though in 1968 they had voted down a controversial Order concerning what was then Southern Rhodesia, and 'non-fatal' motions criticizing subordinate instruments were carried, though not in great numbers. The climate began to change in the 1990s. In 1993–4 a Resolution was passed claiming 'unfettered freedom' to vote for or against any subordinate legislation submitted for the House's consideration. In 2000 and 2007 instruments were rejected in the Lords. In short, as the Joint Committee on Conventions concluded,[69] the Lords retain a right to vote substantively against statutory instruments but are not expected to do so other than in exceptional circumstances.

Following a recommendation of a Royal Commission on the reform of the Lords (see page 58), the House established a Statutory Instruments Merits Committee which complements the Delegated Powers and Deregulatory Reform Committee (which looks at primary legislation) by concentrating on the acceptability of secondary legislation. The Merits Committee sifts out for the consideration of the House those instruments of political or legal importance, those which raise issues of public policy likely to be of interest to the House, those which changed circumstances since the passing of the parent Act have made inappropriate, those which inappropriately implement European Union legislation and those which imperfectly achieve their policy objectives. In 2006–7, the Committee reported on 1,139 instruments and drew to the special attention of the House the surprisingly large figure of 15 per cent of those subject to the affirmative procedure but only 4 per cent subject to the negative. For example, in March 2009, the Committee made a report encouraging the Department for Children, Schools and Families to minimize the burden placed on schools by secondary legislation, acting as gatekeeper on the activities of other departments with respect to schools, ensuring an adequate lead-in time before implementation, and directing the emphasis away from regulation of process to accountability for the delivery of outcomes.[70]

In the Commons, debates take place on the floor on instruments subject to the affirmative procedure only if the government has moved and the House has agreed to disengage the provision in Standing Orders which otherwise sends them to a Delegated Legislation Committee. When instruments are debated on the floor, the Speaker is directed to put the question for the approval of the instrument one and a half hours after its commencement. In 2007–8 fifteen affirmative-procedure instruments were debated on the floor of the Commons. Most affirmative instruments however—188 in session 2007–8—are debated by a Delegated Legislation Committee specially appointed for each instrument or group of instruments. In addition to the Members appointed to the Committee, any other Member of the House may attend and participate, but not vote or move an amendment. No evidence is taken as it would be in a public bill committee on a programmed bill. Debate is adversarial, as it is in the House, but the question before the committee is simply that it has considered the instrument, and debate is brought to an end after—again—one and a half hours (two and a half in the case of Northern Ireland instruments which sometimes resemble primary legislation). The House subsequently gives its approval (or not) to the instrument without further debate, and curiously will do so even if the Committee has voted against the motion that it has considered the instrument.

The procedure on affirmative instruments gives rise to few problems, except where the judgement as to whether to retain an instrument for the floor of the House and not send it to Committee is contentious, as it was in the Sexual Orientation Regulations 2007. It is in the negative procedure that more problems arise, and that of course is the category where the parent Act may prescribe a level of scrutiny which is later seen to be too modest. Of the 1,049 negative-procedure instruments laid in 2007–8, only two were debated on the floor. Delegated Legislation Committees may consider motions to disapprove negative-procedure instruments, but only if a minister of the Crown is prepared to make the appropriate motion. It is therefore not surprising that in 2007–8 only twenty-four were debated in committee.

This figure is lower than the number of motions tabled against negative-procedure instruments, and much lower than the number which would be tabled if there were an opportunity for debate on a realistic proportion of motions. Given the increasing importance of secondary legislation, this is an undesirable situation. The simplest solution would be to expand the compass of the Westminster Hall debates (see page 55) to negative-procedure statutory instruments, deferring—in the usual way—any consequent divisions to the House.

A third option has relatively recently been added to the affirmative and negative procedures. The super-affirmative procedure is intended to afford Parliament an enhanced degree of supervision over orders which amend primary legislation so as to lift or simplify regulatory burdens on bodies and individuals and reduce unnecessary bureaucracy. Such orders may not however remove any necessary protection nor prevent anyone from exercising reasonable rights and freedoms. New regulatory burdens may be imposed, provided certain tests of proportionality, fair balance and desirability are met. Some regulatory reform orders have been of significance, notably those on fire safety (amending fifty-seven separate Acts), patents and civil registration. Savings on a licensing order amounted to £9 million.

Proposals for regulatory reform orders are laid before both Houses and are referred to committees (but not the scrutiny committees) for examination. In the Commons, the relevant committee is normally a select committee, the Regulatory Reform Committee, with the unusual power to invite any Member of the House to attend their meetings and ask questions of witnesses but not otherwise to take part in proceedings. The Committee considers draft orders made under the Legislative and Regulatory Reform Act 2006, reporting on whether (for example) the draft is proportionate to the policy objective, balances the public and any private interest involved, and does not hinder anyone from exercising a right he or she reasonably expected to retain. Super-affirmative orders also come within the Committee's remit.

In the Lords, where the procedure is very similar to but not identical with that in the Commons, the Committee concerned is the Delegated Powers and Regulatory Reform Committee.

A similar procedure is prescribed by the Human Rights Act to deal with remedial orders needed to remove incompatibility identified by domestic courts or the European Court of Human Rights as arising between UK legislation and the European Convention on Human Rights, now incorporated into UK law. In this case, the select committee reviewing the Proposal and then the draft Order is the Joint Committee on Human Rights. There is an accelerated procedure by which in urgent cases a remedial order is made and is then subject to review by the Joint Committee and possible replacement.

Statutory legislative procedures in Congress

While the Constitution provides that each US House shall adopt its own rules, there is nothing which prohibits both Houses in an exercise of joint rule making by concurrent resolution or by statute from imposing additional standing rules or orders on either body in order to expedite business. The chapter on Scrutiny and Oversight at page 313 discusses the need perceived by Congress in the last half-century to oversee the increasingly complex activities of the Executive branch resulting from the delegation of regulatory authority to departments and agencies. This immediate segment addresses the coupling of that Executive empowerment with the reservation by law of an ultimate Congressional prerogative of approval or disapproval of the regulations once promulgated. Those laws, while not often formally utilized, represent an acknowledgement that Congress, while it prefers not to micro-manage the Executive by statutory language alone, can nevertheless reserve periods of review of delegated Executive authorities, in order to permit agencies to promulgate regulations. In turn, Congress is then permitted to expeditiously respond to specific regulations as it scrutinizes their workability. This development has taken various forms during the last half-century. In a variety of statutes, Congress has passed laws reserving to itself or to a committee thereof an absolute or limited right of review by approval or disapproval of certain actions of the Executive branch or of independent agencies. These statutes, known as 'Congressional disapproval' or 'legislative procedures' laws, usually envision some form of Congressional delegation of authority to be reviewed by subsequent legislative action falling into one of three general categories: (1) action by both Houses of Congress on a measure of approval or disapproval requiring Presidential signature; (2) action by one or both Houses on a simple or concurrent resolution; or (3) action by a Congressional committee. Although provisions in the first category remain viable under the Constitution, provisions in the latter two categories should be read in light of *Immigration and Naturalization Service v Chadha* 462 US 919 (1983). In that case the Supreme Court held unconstitutional as in violation of the presentment clause of Article I, section 7, and the doctrine of separation of powers, the provisions of a law contemplating single House disapproval by simple resolution of a decision of the Attorney General to allow an otherwise deportable alien to remain in the United States. That same year, the Supreme Court summarily invalidated provisions contemplating disapproval of Executive actions described in (2) and (3) above. Since then, Congress has amended several Congressional disapproval statutes to convert provisions requiring simple or concurrent resolutions to provisions requiring joint resolutions presented to the President for his approval or veto. This inclusion of a Presidential role renders the statutory scheme consistent with the presentment clause of Article I of the Constitution which requires any measure needing House and Senate approval and having the force and effect of law to be considered by the President for his approval or veto within ten Calendar days of presentation, Sundays excepted.

In order to allow either or both Houses a definite time frame for review, some of these laws contemplate a procedure of non-amendability and a bypass of other House or Senate rules which would otherwise restrict that House's ability to come to a vote on the legislative vehicle expressing approval or disapproval in a timely manner. The purpose of expedited procedures is not to guarantee that one or more bills will become law, but to help make it possible for the House and Senate to vote on whether they should become law. The House possesses the ability to permit votes on such approvals or disapprovals in an ad hoc but expeditious way through utilization of special orders of business reported from the Rules Committee. Of course, Congress through its constitutionally derived legislative authority can always utilize 'regular order' to enact new law in these subject areas.

The Senate, self-perceived as 'the world's greatest deliberative body', however, being essentially unable without unanimous consent or super-majority cloture to impose time and amendment limitations upon its proceedings, has from time to time participated in the enactment of laws which constitute temporary or permanent variations in Senate rules with respect to legislative review of specific areas of Executive branch decision-making. To the extent that those laws, as joint exercises in rule making, contain expedited procedures for review in either or both Houses, they have been compiled and updated in the House Rules and Manual published in each Congress.[71]

This eclectic variety of statutes enacted in the last half-century either (a) permit expedited Congressional review of Executive branch decisions; or (b) enable 'fast-track' enactment of new law in prescribed substantive areas where the substance of that bill has been informally negotiated between the branches prior to introduction. To this end, Congress has enacted expedited procedures into law when (1) the same law imposes a deadline for Congressional action on a measure in one or both Houses, and (2) Congress wants to ensure, or at least increase the likelihood, that the House and Senate have an opportunity to vote on the measure before the deadline is reached. Most often, these procedures have applied to action on joint resolutions by which Congress can approve or disapprove some action that the President or an Executive branch official (or the District of Columbia City Council) proposes to take. In other areas, Congress has enacted fast-track procedures to expedite House and Senate action on a bill that is a 'package proposal' recommended by the President, such as trade agreements in lieu of treaties, to address a complex issue. To achieve their purpose, fast-track procedures may do any or all of the following: (1) set a time limit for the committee of jurisdiction to report the measure; (2) prevent committees from killing the measure by failing to act on it; (3) make the measure privileged for floor consideration either immediately or after a brief layover period, whether the measure was reported from committee or the committee was discharged; (4) prohibit floor amendments, including committee amendments, and impose time limits on debate during floor consideration of the measure; (5) require votes on final passage within a certain number of days; and (6) provide for prompt floor consideration of any identical companion measure received from the other House. Current laws each containing variations of expediting procedures include the War Powers Act, Executive Branch Reorganizations Act, National Emergencies Act, Impoundment Control Act, Pension Reform Act, District of Columbia Home Rule Act, Trade Act, Energy Policy and Conservation Act, Arms Export Control Act, the Defense Base Closure and Realignment Act, the Congressional Accountability Act, and the Congressional Review of Agency Rule-Making Act.

The proliferation of these statutes began in the early 1970s when divided government—a Democratic-controlled Congress and a Republican President—prompted Congress to address but ultimately to delay its own final decision making. The perceived need to delegate and then to expeditiously review Executive decisions has inspired this trend whether or not there is divided government, so that both Houses can potentially disapprove decisions under specially applicable review procedures, in order not to permit amendment or other procedural uncertainties inherent in the application of standing rules, while still preserving Congress's ultimate authority in the delegated area concerned. Underlying each of these enactments has been the realization that the more traditional and time-consuming steps of conducting oversight and then enacting new law was inadequate to the task of determining in a short time frame whether to overturn or limit such Executive actions.

The House to which expedited procedures apply is free to enforce, amend, waive, suspend, ignore, or even repeal them as it sees fit, just as if they were standing rules. The House can do this through the Rules Committee's ad hoc authority to report special orders of business. In the Senate, the same procedures can be waived or superseded by a unanimous consent agreement or by prescribed super-majority waivers. Congress usually decides to enact such provisions into law, rather than adopting them separately as standing rules, because they are inextricably related politically or procedurally, to other provisions of the same law that establish public policy and affect the actions of the Executive. Because effective fast-track procedures limit floor debate and preclude amendments, whether germane or not, these procedures have greater consequences for the Senate than for the House, given the otherwise historic and strategic importance to Senators of the right of unlimited debate and ability to offer an unpredictable number of amendments.[72] The consequences for the House are less dramatic. The unique capacity of the Rules Committee to bring special orders of business to the floor, the increasing use of such special orders to bypass standing committees or modify their work product if necessary to meet agenda deadlines, and the underlying political control that the Majority Leadership has over the composition of that committee, all assure the Majority's ability to address the issue. Congress is most likely to enact fast-track procedures (sometimes applicable only to the Senate) when it places more value on making certain timely decisions on the floor (decisions often deferred by initial Congressional reluctance) than on adherence to its normal procedures and to the principles of prerequisite committee action underlying them.

Notes

1. Jefferson's *Manual*, section I.
2. Alex Brazier (ed), *Parliament, Politics and Law-Making* (2004), 47.
3. *Paramino Lumber Company v Marshall* 309 US 370 (1940).
4. *Pope v United States* 323 US 1 (1944).
5. Clause 6 of Senate Rule XLIII.
6. Law Commission, *Post-Legislative Scrutiny* (Cm 6945, October 2006).
7. Ed Sir William McKay (23rd edn, 2004), 965.
8. Scrutiny Unit briefing on Post-Legislative Scrutiny, p 3.

9. First Report HC 1097 (2005–6), para 45.

10. W. J. Oleszek, *Congressional Procedure and the Policy Process* (6th edn, 2004), 83.

11. 30 January 2001, 152 Congressional Record at 995–6.

12. 25 March 1980, 126 Congressional Record at 6405–10.

13. 4 January 1995, 141 Congressional Record at E617–8.

14. W. Holmes Brown and Charles W. Johnson (eds), *House Practice* (2003), chapter 11, sect 8 at p 245.

15. H Res 988, 93rd Congress.

16. House Rule XII, clause 2.

17. 118 Congressional Record at 3434.

18. 120 Congressional Record at 36020.

19. H Res 449, 19 June 2002, 148 Congressional Record at 10722.

20. PL 107–296.

21. Oleszek, *Congressional Procedure and the Policy Process*, 86–7.

22. *Manual*, sect XXVI.

23. Clause 2(h)(4) of House Rule XI and clause 6(g) of Rule XVIII.

24. Clause 4(b) (2) of House Rule X.

25. Clause 2(g)(5) of House Rule XI.

26. Clause 1(a)(2) of House Rule XI.

27. Oleszek, *Congressional Procedure and the Policy Process*, 89.

28. Clause 9 of House Rule X.

29. Sen. Lott at Congressional Quarterly Daily Monitor, 10 June 1996, at p 5.

30. Section 512.

31. Senate Rule XIV.

32. Holmes Brown and Johnson, *House Practice*, 223.

33. Under the 'Calendar Wednesday' rule, as amended in the 111th Congress, bills reported by standing committees and on the Calendar may be called up without a special order or the need for suspension of the rules upon one day's notice to the House by the committee manager, rather than in an alphabetical call of the standing committees on each Wednesday. This rule, put in place in the early nineteenth century to circumvent the Rules Committee dominated by the Speaker, is not utilized in modern practice because the measure called up must be considered under the standing rules—normally in Committee of the Whole under the five-minute rule, and points of order against the bill or its consideration are not waived.

34. A further protection comes on Opposition days in the Commons, where the motion is made by the Opposition and the unique form of the question on that motion allows them to vote for their text before the government vote for their amendment. There is no pre-emption—the Opposition motion is put ahead of the government amendment. The first question, on the Opposition motion, is 'That the original words stand part of the question'. The Opposition are guaranteed a vote on their text and—presumably—having lost the government vote for their amendment 'That the proposed words be there inserted'. The main question as amended is then declared to be agreed to without further debate or division.

35. Jefferson's *Manual*, sect XII.

36. Ibid.

37. 22 March 2007, 153 Congressional Record at 2860–3.

38. 27 February 2002 at 2080–5.

39. The statistics in this section are drawn from the report of and evidence submitted to the Modernisation Committee in its First Report 2006–7 HC 337 paras 121–3 and Ev 128.

40. HC Deb (2008–9) 486 c 892.

41. First Report HC 1097 (2005–6) para 71.

42. HC Deb (2007–8) 474 c 924.

43. HC Deb (2007–8) 482 c 218.

44. W. J. Oleszek, *Whither the Role of Conference Committees: An Analysis*, Congressional Research Service report dated 12 August 2008.

45. Jefferson's *Manual*, section XLV.

46. Senate Rule XXVIII as amended by PL 110-81, sect 511.

47. 7 October 2004, 150 Congressional Record at 8658 (daily edn).
48. House Rule I, clause 11.
49. 10 March 1998, Congressional Record at 3049.
50. Senate Rule XXVIII, para 8.
51. House Rule XXII, clause 12.
52. Section 515 of PL 110-81.
53. Oleszek, *Congressional Procedure and the Policy Process*, 275.
54. Congressional Record 30 April 2008; 154 Congressional Record at 2883, daily edn.
55. The bill went between the Houses eight times in thirty hours (Modernisation Committee, First Report 2005–6 HC 1097 page Ev 75). Despite the complexity of that message, one category of proposal is not included—amendment of words restored to the bill following disagreement to an Amendment which proposed to omit them.
56. Ed Sir William McKay (23rd edn, 2004), 639.
57. 2005–6, HC 265 HL 1212 para 189.
58. Fourteenth Report 2003–4 HL 173-I para 72: Eighth Report 2007–8 HL 129.
59. First Report 2005–6 HC 1097 para 30.
60. First Special Report 2006–7 HC 920, Third Report 2007–8 HC 427. Over the decade to 2007, the government published fifty-eight draft bills.
61. Eighth Report 2007–8 HL 129.
62. Second Report 2008–9 HC 95 para 18.
63. The Lords Committee on the Constitution Fourteenth Report (HL 173 (2003–4) para 180) recommended that most Acts should be subject to post-legislative scrutiny, and the Law Commission has studied the subject in detail in *Post-Legislative Scrutiny* (Cm 6945, October 2006). The government responded to the Commission's report in March 2008, Cm 7320.
64. First Report 2005–6 HC 1097 para 26.
65. ABA Report of Task Force on Presidential Signing Statements and the Separation of Powers Doctrine (August 2006).
66. Or in the case of bills of aids and supplies, the even more sonorous formula: *La Reyne remercie ses bons sujets, accepte leur benevolence et ainsi le veult.* Even in days before 1706, when Royal Assent could be refused, the formula was gracious: *Le Roi s'avisera*—The King will think about it.
67. In a particularly English (not British) procedure, Parliament also considers legislation for the Church of England. Such measures are proceeded with in very much the same way as statutory instruments.
68. Fifth Report 2006–7 HL 44 para 11.
69. 2006–7 HC 265 HL 1212 para 227.
70. Ninth Report 2008–9 HL 45.
71. House Rules and Manual sect 1130, a compilation of thirty-two laws.
72. In 2009, a memorandum was inserted at pages 513312–3 of the Congressional Record for the 111th Congress outlining the various procedures discussed in this chapter which are at the disposal of the Senate Minority under normal unlimited debate procedures, entitled 'Foundation for the Minority Party's Rights in the Senate (Fall 2009)'.

10

Privilege and Contempt

Privilege: scope and significance

The term 'privilege' arises more frequently in the rules and practices governing the procedures of the House of Representatives than it does in the Senate. The term may refer to questions of the privileges of the House, to questions of personal privilege, to the constitutional privilege of Members from some arrest or from being questioned for their speech or debate, or separately to the privilege of certain legislative business and motions. In both Parliament and Congress, the tradition of Anglo-American parliamentary procedure recognizes the enhancement of questions of the prerogatives, honour, and security (indeed of 'sovereignty' in the UK where there is no constitutional separation of legislative and executive powers) of a deliberative legislative body and of its Members.

In Congress, questions of privilege are to be distinguished from privileged questions. The latter relate merely to the order of priority of business under the rules of the House or Senate and are discussed at page 150. The House has accorded preferential status to certain institutional issues by Rule IX, adopted in 1880 but defining what the House by precedent had long established as matters of paramount importance. Under Rule IX, clause 1, questions of the privileges of the House are 'first, those affecting the rights of the House collectively, its safety, dignity, and the integrity of its proceedings; second the rights, reputation and conduct of Members, individually, in their representative capacity only...'. Some of these matters derive directly from the Constitution, as prerogatives and responsibilities delegated to each House separately under Article I. For example, questions relating to the seating of Members and the organization of the House (judging Members' qualifications, elections and returns, and their oath taking, adoption of the rules at the beginning of each Congress, election of the Speaker and other officers, and declaration of vacancy in the office of Speaker), punishment of Members for disorderly behaviour and expulsion (that is, matters relating to the official conduct of Members, officers, and employees), privilege of Members from arrest, their Speech or Debate immunity, and the protection of Congressional records (matters of constitutional separation of powers), all give rise to a question of the privileges of the House. Also, questions relating to the House's constitutional prerogatives in respect to originating revenue legislation and appropriations, with respect to impeachment and matters incidental thereto, to vetoed bills, including those claimed to have been 'pocket-vetoed', to its power to punish for contempt (whether of its own Members, of summoned witnesses or other persons), and to questions relating to legal challenges involving the prerogatives of the House, can all be raised by resolution without regard to a committee report or other privileged status being attached by standing rule or special order. Further, certain other actions which the two Houses may take under the Constitution are privileged for consideration, such as concurrent resolutions for adjournment sine die or to a day certain, and concurrent resolutions for joint sessions to receive messages from the President and to conduct the electoral count, because while requiring concurrence of both Houses, their consideration is essential to the constitutional functioning of the Congress as it prepares to interact with the Executive branch.

On the other hand, the ordinary rights and functions of the House under the Constitution to conduct business empowered by that document are exercised, in accordance with the rules, without precedence as matters of privilege. Thus neither the enumeration of legislative powers under Article I nor the prohibition in the seventh clause of section 9 of that Article against any withdrawal from the Treasury except by enactment of an appropriation renders a measure purporting to exercise or limit the exercise of those powers a question of the privilege of the House, because Rule IX is concerned not with the privileges of the Congress as a Legislative branch, but only with the privileges of the House as a House. It is not sufficient that a question arises from the Constitution or is one committed to the House thereunder. For example, a resolution to confirm the President's nomination of the Vice President, a duty committed to the House under the 25th Amendment, is not privileged for consideration but must await committee report and become a matter of business in the 'regular order'.

Assertion of constitutionally specified prerogatives of the House including the question of the vote required to pass a joint resolution extending the State ratification period of a proposed constitutional amendment have been held to present questions of privilege. Precedent establishes many additional matters of privilege which may interrupt ordinary business. They involve questions relating to the safety, dignity, and integrity (not merely 'fairness') of House proceedings, resignation of a Member from a committee, newspaper charges affecting the honour and dignity of the House, and the conduct of representatives of the press. Admission to and conduct on the floor of the House, the comfort and convenience of Members, the accuracy and propriety of reports in the Congressional Record, the protection and sanctity of House documents, and irregularities during the conduct of electronic votes can all give rise to questions of privilege.

Questions as to the propriety of the Chair in taking certain actions have given rise to questions of privilege where it has been alleged that the Chair has intentionally violated rules, practices, and customs, as for example holding a vote open far beyond the minimum time required in order to facilitate change in the outcome of the vote after the will of the House has been expressed. In the 110th Congress, the House adopted a resolution offered by the Minority Leader as a question of privilege establishing a select committee to investigate alleged voting irregularities by the Chair during the conduct of a specific electronic vote. The select committee filed a report with the House in September 2008.[1]

As discussed in the chapter on Ethics and Standards (page 541), Minority party leadership efforts to highlight an alleged 'culture of corruption' through misuse of Majority party power in the House are often implemented by raising questions of privilege charging improper administration of the rules and facilities of the House. In the early 1990s those matters included the misuse of the House Bank to facilitate Members' cheque-cashing, and of the House Post Office regarding misappropriation of postal allowances. Minority Members were able to successfully raise those questions to force the House to undertake investigations of institutional corruption. In 2005 and 2006 the Minority Leader similarly alleged improper voting durations and the improper change of the text of a conference report by unilateral action of the House and Senate Majority leadership after a conference report had been signed by the conferees but prior to its filing as the final document. On those latter occasions, the Majority leadership used the motion to table (kill) the resolution in order to prevent any debate thereon, but the record votes on the procedural motions to table were portrayed by press releases as representing sentiment regarding allegations of corrupt mismanagement. By way of contrast, in the 111th Congress a resolution creating a select committee to investigate the 'accuracy' of the Speaker's public statement and the Executive's response regarding classified briefings, but not alleging misconduct on her part impacting on the integrity of the House, was held not to give rise to a question of the privileges of the House. That ruling was appealed to obtain a record vote (see chapter on Scrutiny and Oversight at page 327).

Alleged improprieties in committee procedures have been denied privileged treatment in the House where the allegations fell short of accusation of deliberate misconduct, were addressable in committee, or were based merely on committee inaction or on political considerations. Allegations of deliberate violation of House rules by committee chairmen have, however, been held to constitute questions of privilege, because they are matters of ethics and official conduct where deliberate intent is a factor. On one recent occasion, a committee chairman's action in unilaterally releasing subpoenaed material prior to a collegial determination of secret status—as required by a committee rule—was proposed to be 'disapproved' in a resolution (laid on the table) raising a question of privilege suggesting deliberate disregard of committee rules in conducting an investigation. Other recent examples include complaints of a chairman's conduct of a committee markup, a chairman's improper dismissal of Standards Committee non-partisan staff, a denial of a Minority day of committee hearings, and the withholding of committee records from Minority members. The proliferation of such questions of privilege relating to procedural integrity in committees is consistent with Minority party public allegations of deliberate mismanagement.

The privileges of the House include questions relating to the comfort, convenience, and safety of Members and employees, including matters relating to proper attire on the floor and structural and fire safety deficiencies in the Capitol.

However, a motion to amend the rules of the House does not present a question of privilege, nor does a resolution affecting a change in the interpretation of standing rules or orders. Accordingly, a question of privilege may not be invoked to prescribe a special order of business for the House, for otherwise any Member would be able to attach privilege to a legislative measure merely by alleging impact on the dignity of the House based on political perceptions of House action or inaction. Speaker Gillett in a landmark ruling given on 6 May 1921[2] (which has been relied on by the Chair in several recent rulings) stated:

This whole question of constitutional privilege being superior to the rules of the House is a subject which the Chair has for many years considered and thought unreasonable. It seems to the Chair that where the Constitution ordered the House to do a thing, the Constitution still gives the House the right to make its own rules and do it at such time and in such manner as it may choose. And it is a strained construction to say that because the Constitution gives a mandate that a thing shall be done, it therefore follows that any Member can insist that it shall be brought up at some particular time and in the particular way which he chooses. If there is a Constitutional mandate, the House ought by its rules to provide for the proper enforcement of that mandate, but it is still a question for the House how and when and under what procedure it shall be done...

Prior to Speaker Gillett's ruling, Speaker Reed in 1898 had also ruled that the ordinary rights and functions of the House under the Constitution are exercised in accordance with the rules, without precedence as matters of privilege. He reasoned on that occasion that there are general powers conferred upon Congress:

the power to declare war, the power to legislate for the general welfare, and a series of other enumerated powers. No man up to this date has for an instant pretended or suggested that because the Congress has the right to pass laws upon certain topics, proposals for those laws become questions of privilege...and that those propositions in regard to war, or about recognition or any of those subjects which may or may not be within our purview, do not become questions of privilege at all because we have a right to pass upon them, because that would make everything a question of privilege and end by making nothing a question of privilege.

These precedents were cited in response to several attempts by the Minority party in the House to equate political inaction on Appropriation measures financing the operation of government departments (resulting in a partial government 'shutdown') with a matter impacting on the dignity and integrity of House proceedings.

The clause of the rule giving questions of privilege precedence over all other questions except a motion to adjourn is a recognition of a well-established principle that such a question supersedes the consideration of a matter already pending or scheduled to be considered, and must be first disposed of. As the business of the House began to increase it was found necessary to give certain important matters a precedence by rule, and such matters are called 'privileged questions', but as they relate merely to the order of business under the rules, they are to be distinguished from matters which relate to the integrity or constitutional functioning of the House itself. Several matters enjoy privileged status deriving both from precedent—regardless of a committee report—and from the rule conferring privilege on certain committees to file reports 'at any time'. These include reports from the Committee on House Administration on election contests and from the Committee on Standards of Official Conduct on the conduct of Members, officers, or employees.

Certain matters of business arising under provisions of the Constitution mandatory in nature, such as bills providing for census or apportionment and once held to constitute a matter of privilege merely because enactment was required by the basic law, have been held not to present such questions in modern practice, since they have no higher basis for privilege than the requirement that they be enacted by both Houses. Other mandatory functions of each House separately, for example to organize, elect its officers, consider vetoed bills, impeachments, and matters relating to the count of a specific electoral vote go more basically to the separate constitutionally mandated functions of each House, some with a necessity to avoid delay, and thus assume the status of privilege. Other requirements, such as the confirmation of a nomination to fill a Vice Presidential vacancy or the declaration of war have been considered not to constitute questions of privilege, under the rationale first expressed in Speaker Reed's and Speaker Gillett's rulings.

Charges of illegality or impropriety in official House functioning can give rise to questions of privilege if they extend beyond general political criticism of the Congress such as mere inactivity, and focus instead on alleged criminal or unethical activity, whether or not specific Members are named.

Charges made off the floor against specific Members often have been made the basis of a question of 'personal privilege', where under Rule IX the responding Member, by citing press accounts of his own alleged official misconduct or impropriety, may be recognized ahead of other business in either House to address the matter in his defence with no resolution being offered or voted on. This priority to respond to charges against a Member's official conduct does not extend, however, to general allegations of a 'culture of corruption' levelled against the leadership of the Majority party and carried in the press. A back-bench Member cannot suggest that he is unfairly tarnished by general press allegations of corruption where he has not been identified.

Personal allegations against specific Members spoken in debate, however, are not permitted to be collaterally challenged as questions of House or personal privilege at a subsequent time, being governed instead by the provisions of clause 4 of Rule XVII which provide that a Member may not be held to answer a call to order, and may not be subject to the censure of the House therefore, if further debate or other business has intervened from the moment of utterance. A subsequent press account of such improper debate, whether or not the debate had been ruled out of order, or any other charge against the integrity, official conduct, or reputation of a Member in the press or anywhere outside the Chamber, may be responded to as a question of personal privilege, with the offended Member being permitted up to one hour to refute the charges. The rationale for this distinction is that improper debate must be challenged immediately upon utterance, with the offending Member called to order, and the offended Member should not be permitted to subsequently use the debate as grounds for personal privilege in order to prolong the matter, unless based on a subsequent republication thereof. Notwithstanding this rule, a question of privilege censuring a Member for disorderly debate (a personal reference to the President), was held to be in order in 2007 where the resolution also alleged ethical misconduct bringing discredit to the House (see also Procedural Basics at page 192).

While Senate precedents reflect the importance of questions of personal privilege, where individual Senators are recognized to debate press accounts relating to their official conduct, there is no Senate rule comparable to House Rule IX with respect to the priority of questions of privilege which require action by the Senate. Senators are better able to bring matters to the immediate attention of the Senate for votes than are House Members in their Chamber. Individual Senators are not constrained by a rule of germaneness, thereby enabling them to bring any matter, including matters of institutional importance pertaining to the rights, integrity, and dignity of the Senate, to the immediate attention of the Senate for a vote. The Senate has not found it necessary to codify as a rule the myriad precedents which establish the privilege of certain business as matters which are eligible for immediate consideration and need not lie over for a day. The Senate Procedure Manual indicates thirty matters which by precedent constitute 'privileged business', listed alphabetically and ranging from adjournment resolutions, to amendments between the Houses, censure resolutions, cloture petitions, conference reports, credentials, personal privilege, and to vetoes. It is not in order upon request of a Senator to lay before the Senate a resolution as a privileged matter, a motion being necessary to proceed to its consideration. Likewise in the House, the question of consideration may be raised against any resolution presented as a question of privilege, and so consideration is not assured, absent a preliminary affirmative vote if the question of consideration is raised.

In the UK, the most striking—though far from the most significant—characteristic of parliamentary privilege is its antiquity. The earliest privilege case mentioned in Erskine May's *Parliamentary Practice* dates from the 1290s. The claim to possess special rights began as the insecure reaction of an aspirant institution in pre-modern times. Long after the Houses—but especially the Commons—successfully asserted their political authority, however, extravagantly broad claims continued to be made. Parliament was complainant, jury and judge, and the justice meted out by the 'law of Parliament' was often capricious and intolerant. The past—even the hallowed term 'privilege'—is often an obstacle to an appreciation of the present continuing need to protect Parliament from attacks as potentially damaging as royal absolutism in past centuries.

In the preceding and the present century privilege is no longer deployed to assuage the *amour propre* of individual Lords or Members, but to allow them freely to discharge their public duties. The House of Commons has taken a significant step to recognize this. In 1977 the Commons agreed to exercise its penal jurisdiction as sparingly as possible, and only when essential for protection against obstruction and substantial interference with the performance of its functions.

Though in many respects (not least the underlying aims) the parliamentary and Congressional systems overlap, there is a substantial practical area where, as sketched above, privilege is formally engaged in Congress but is not in terms relevant in Parliament, or the common end is achieved in a different way. In the absence of demands made on Parliament by a written Constitution—to count electoral votes, for example—and in the light of government control of the time of the House of Commons at least, no items of business at Westminster enjoy the formal status of a privileged question ousting other business, except so far as the raising of a complaint of a breach of privilege may be given precedence by the Speaker if he or she is satisfied that it is proper to do so (see page 500). There are however many issues understood as privileged matters in Washington which Lords or Members would raise at Westminster not as a matter of privilege but on a point of order, seeking immediate resolution but in practice often serving only to air the grievance. Motions critical of the Chair or raising issues of impropriety in the conduct of business are likewise not matters of privilege, but when they are tabled they are customarily disposed of at the earliest reasonable opportunity, if only to clear the air. The potential disadvantages of not having done so in the context of the resignation of Mr Speaker Martin in May 2009 are mentioned at page 36.

There are circumstances which may give rise to questions of privilege in Congress, which once would have done so also in the Commons but which nowadays are suffered in silence. A sustained personal press campaign against an individual Member would probably fall into that category. Charges of misuse of Commons facilities are, if serious, considered by the Committee on Standards and Privileges, but are not usually considered closely cognate to 'classical' privilege. Matters affecting the 'comfort and convenience' of Members (see page 479) are frequently aired but would not be given precedence as matters of privilege, being more likely to surface as points of order or querulous interventions at Business Questions. Over all considerations regarding the scope of the privilege of Parliament lies the shadow of the need to connect the act complained of with significant injury—or potential injury—to 'proceedings in Parliament'. Without that connection, privilege will not usually be engaged. Later paragraphs will show how central that concept is to modern parliamentary privilege.

The two legislatures share the concept of 'privilege' in the context of matters of their own constitutions (though at Westminster the disciplining of Members does not fall into that category) and in that of the peculiar powers or status of one House with respect to the other.

Contested issues of privilege usually arise in connection with proceedings in the Commons. The Lords enjoy the same privileges, but have much less frequently encountered the need (or expressed the desire) to assert them.

Particular privileges

Freedom of speech

At the heart of parliamentary privilege at Westminster, in the present as in the past, is the assurance, claimed for the Commons by the Speaker and conceded by the Sovereign at the opening of every Parliament, that no Member will be brought to account in the courts for what he or she says in the House.

The protection is—for the time being (see pages 487–8)—absolute. Statements which the Lord or Member making them knows to be false are protected as fully as if they were truth. This is however no cover for irresponsibility. Members or others found to have lied to the House are open to censure by the House, including expulsion if they are Members of the Commons. Members are politically responsible to those who elected them, and so far as order is concerned, they are subject to the House itself through the occupant of the Chair. The Speaker frequently reminds Members of their responsibility not to abuse their freedom, but within the rules of debate it remains a decision for individual Members whether the public interest requires them to use their privilege to indict those they believe to be wrongdoers. For example, in the course of a Question in the upper House, a Lord named an individual he alleged was concerned in a case of a kind where the courts do not normally permit identification,[3] and no legal action could be mounted against him.

Protection from the interference of a court is also all-embracing. If the line is breached at any point, every intervention in debate is put at risk because it can never be guaranteed that what is about to be said will not attract legal retribution. There are ways of modifying the absolute nature of the protection of freedom of speech in some legislatures. A number permit those who consider themselves to have been unjustly criticized in proceedings to insert a rebuttal in the official record. Others modify the completeness of the protection afforded to legislators in debate. The Commons has rejected the first option and the second is likely to share the same fate. The House tacitly prefers to rely on its customary intolerance of Members who abuse those who cannot defend themselves.

The Houses' privilege of free speech will not assist those who in the media report on parliamentary proceedings: their protection comes from statute and common law. An action for libel will not prevail against a fair and accurate report of a debate, published without malice. A few interesting conundrums remain. Suppose a Member speaking in the Chamber discloses some name or fact contrary to official secrets legislation or to the no-publicity order of a court. Privilege will be adequate protection for the Member against legal action, but is the broadcasting authority which transmits the words liable? The Joint Committee on Parliamentary Privilege thought a newspaper would not have the protection of common law in such circumstances.[4] Yet why should the media be prevented from carrying matter which anyone can read in Hansard? A solution, presumably in legislative form, was required, now all the more urgently because of the recent granting of 'super-injunctions' which debar the media from reporting what was said in Parliament and inhibit them even from mentioning the existence of the injunction. In marked contrast to the dilemma presented under UK law by the possibility of injunctive (even super-injunctive) prior restraint involving the republication of the libellous matter, in the United States the First Amendment would likely prevent such injunctive prior restraint from being imposed by a court. A super-injunction preventing even the mention of the existence of an injunction as in the UK would be constitutionally prohibited under the freedom of the press guarantee in the First Amendment. Also, any publication intent upon repeating the 'libel' would be well advised to refer to 'informed sources' for attribution.

The fundamentals of parliamentary claims to freedom of speech are crystallized in (but do not derive from) Article IX of the Bill of Rights 1689:

> The freedom of speech and debates or proceedings in Parliament ought not to be impeached or questioned in any court or place out of Parliament.

Most privileges stem from the common law of Parliament: the Bill of Rights however is statute law, so that the shots in the central matter of freedom of speech are called not by the Houses but by the courts. For centuries, the courts delivered judgements which rested on the deep conventions of the unwritten constitution, usually giving primacy to the collective interest in parliamentary freedom over the competing rights of individuals. From about the middle of the twentieth century, however, the courts began to rest their conclusions on the Bill of Rights, and the outcome has often been much less favourable to the Houses. Furthermore, over the past twenty-five years or so, the courts have attempted to resolve conflict between the general law's 'absolutes'—human rights or freedom of information for instance—and the ancient, often undefined but sweeping claims of the legislature. They have most frequently done so by interpreting the generalities of Article IX of the Bill of Rights.

Article IX shelters only remarks made in the course of 'proceedings in Parliament'. Not everything uttered by a Lord or Member within the Palace of Westminster is a proceeding. Speaking in the Chamber or in committee, voting, tabling motions or Questions, all these are undoubtedly activities for which a Lord or Member is not answerable in the courts of law. Practice is less clear where preparation for any of these is concerned. Much would depend on how far the proceeding for which the preparation was being made could be identified, how obvious the link between the preparation and the intended action, and how close in practice the connection between the Member and the preparatory activity. The only occasion when the matter was specifically considered in Parliament was in 1938–9 when a select committee endorsed the principle that certain action preparatory to a proceeding might enjoy a similar protection, but the committee's report and the House's agreement were tied fairly closely to the circumstances of the particular case.

The line between what is protected as a 'proceeding in Parliament' and what is not is drawn tightly rather than loosely. The House of Commons decided in 1957—initially by a tiny majority against a committee recommendation, but the practice is now hallowed—that Members' letters to and from constituents or to public bodies on behalf of constituents do not enjoy parliamentary privilege. A great proportion of a Member's daily work is therefore not covered. A Question tabled is protected: its alternative, a letter to the responsible minister, is not. The US Supreme Court, by contrast, has laid down that all activities which are 'an integral part of the deliberative and communicative processes by which Members participate in committee and House proceedings' are within the sphere of privilege[5]—a much wider protection.

Doubts have occasionally been expressed whether the prohibition on 'impeaching or questioning' in Article IX is effective only if someone is put in legal jeopardy for what has been said, or whether the phrase has a wider significance. In a landmark case in 1995, the Privy Council rejected the limited view. Going beyond Article IX to the principles of comity in the relationship between the courts and the Houses, the leading judge said that parties could not allege anything said or done in a House was inspired by improper motives or was untrue or misleading.[6]

The protection conferred by Article IX was at the heart of the objections to what is now the Parliamentary Standards Act, introduced after the expenses crisis in 2009 (see page 523). The constitutional difficulties to which the situation gave rise were many and complex. The completeness of the protection which the Bill of Rights affords is critical. It was difficult to devise independent disciplinary authorities and procedures, standing outside Parliament, which could investigate the actions of Members of the Commons and do so without directly or indirectly (for example by judicial review being permitted to extend beyond the exercise of the statutory functions) setting aside Article IX. The bill as introduced set aside Article IX if it would have prevented the Authority or the Commissioner proposed to be set up from carrying out any of their functions, and would have admitted evidence based on proceedings in Parliament in actions against Members for offences under the bill. As the Clerk of the House put it in a submission to the Justice Committee, these provisions 'could have a chilling effect on freedom of speech of Members and of witnesses before committees and would hamper the ability of House officials to give advice to Members'. The offending clause was in the event defeated on the floor of the House of Commons, and the Lords inserted a provision (subsequently agreed by the Commons) that nothing in the Act was to be construed by any court in the UK as affecting Article IX. The improvement was appreciable but not entirely conclusive. It remains after all for the courts and not the Houses to decide what is a proceeding in Parliament, and the possibility of such matters reaching European courts was regarded as remote but not completely out of the question.

The House of Commons in 1980 made permanent its agreement that reference might be made in court to parliamentary papers—Hansard, committee papers, and the like— provided the protection of the Bill of Rights was not breached. The intention was to permit parties to prove facts in court by use of privileged material, so long as they did not try to draw inferences from the facts. Initially the courts took a conservative view of what was permissible. It was decided in 1983 that Hansard could not be used to support a ground for relief in proceedings for judicial review in respect of something occurring outside Parliament. The Australian Parliamentary Privilege Act 1987—privilege law in Australia is very similar to that of the UK—does three things. It outlaws proceedings in court which question or rely on the good faith of proceedings in Parliament. It makes illegal the questioning in court of the motives, intentions, or good faith of those participating in proceedings in Parliament. And it prohibits absolutely the drawing or inviting the drawing of inferences or conclusions wholly or partly from proceedings. The Privy Council in the 1995 case mentioned above declared that the Australian statute contained the true principle to be applied.

Subsequently however, a judge in the High Court declined to treat the Australian statute as a rule of English law so far as concerned the prohibition on the drawing of inferences from proceedings in Parliament, which did not involve allegations of impropriety, inadequacy, or inaccuracy. Later judgements accordingly seem to outlaw only references in court to proceedings in Parliament where it is sought to prove that Parliament had been misled by inaccurate, improper, or untrue statements.[7] The Privy Council in 2007, citing judicial review and other cases and the report of the Joint Committee on Parliamentary Privilege, allowed a party in court to rely on evidence of what a minister said in Parliament to indicate what was in fact his motivation in taking certain actions outside Parliament.[8] The original conservative stance has altered: but it is to be hoped for the future that the judges will be quick to suppress arguments that alleged shortcomings of policy must imply improper motives at the time the policy was announced in Parliament.

Because many Commonwealth Parliaments share in some degree the Westminster heritage of privilege, decisions handed down in courts very far away have become of concern at Westminster, and judgements delivered elsewhere may come to affect British parliamentary privilege.

Comments were made in the New Zealand House of Representatives in 1997 about an individual who was not a Member of the House, which might have been defamatory if made elsewhere. When interviewed by the media on what had been said, the Member did not repeat the remarks he made but replied that he 'did not resile' from what he said in the House. Wellington and Westminster share with Washington the understanding that a Member who repeats outside the House what he said in the Chamber is on his own if challenged: in that sense privilege is an institutional and not a personal protection.

But did such a simple acknowledgement of the original protected statement amount to an actionable repetition? The Member failed to persuade the courts in New Zealand that no cause for action could be found which did not question words spoken in Parliament. When the matter came to the Privy Council, they took the view that there was an unbroken line from the words in the media back to the comment in Parliament. Using the Parliamentary record only to establish what it was that the Member was not resiling from, was not, so the court thought, 'impeaching or questioning'.[9] The logic surely runs the other way—'not to resile' from a statement may attract a sanction only if the statement itself was objectionable, and in this instance it was not for the court to make such a judgement on a proceeding in Parliament.

If such a case arises in the UK, the courts will no doubt find the New Zealand precedent persuasive, notwithstanding its chilling effect on public debate. Members interviewed on television may be faced with a split-second choice between the prospect of an action for defamation if they stand by words spoken by them on the floor or equivocation, with its associated political damage. Worse, any Member will inevitably hesitate over the terms of a proposed speech on the floor, and the purpose of protecting freedom of speech will be utterly defeated. The Privy Council's advice that Members must be circumspect when interviewed about statements in the House is hardly a credible substitute for the clear protection which parliamentarians have traditionally enjoyed. It is hard to see how any of this respects parliamentary freedom or facilitates legitimate political exchanges.[10]

Freedom of speech in Parliament may be affected not only by Commonwealth cases but by the decisions of courts established under treaties to which the UK is a party, whose decisions may well turn out more revolutionary than anything emanating from British judges. In a case which reached the European Court of Human Rights, a complainant alleged that her human rights had been infringed by the nature of a Member's references to her by name (including her address) and her children in the course of a debate in the Commons on municipal housing policy. Her rights had been breached, she said, since she had no access to a court of law to contest the allegations relating to herself and her family made in the course of the debate.

The Court in Strasbourg decided that the immunity enjoyed by the Member on the occasion of making these remarks pursued the legitimate aim of protecting free speech in Parliament. Furthermore, the immunity available to the UK Parliament was narrower than in many other parts of Europe, and there was no disproportionate restriction on access to a court since parliamentary immunity in the UK 'was consistent with and reflected generally recognised rules within member-states of the Council of Europe and the European Union'. Those in the complainant's situation could petition the House to secure a retraction; deliberately misleading statements might be punishable by Parliament as a contempt; and the Speaker of each of the UK Houses exercised a general control over debates.[11]

Though the outcome of that case was, in parliamentary eyes, satisfactory, witnessing freedom of debate being tried at the bar of a court beyond the jurisdiction was uncomfortable. The presiding judge wanted some way to be found of reconciling free speech in Parliament with individual rights, and there was a dissenting opinion that the present balance between the two was wrong and should be altered. As was acutely observed in a recent judgement in the Court of Appeal, the Strasbourg Court operates within the framework of an international treaty and considers the position of the State as a whole. UK domestic courts operate within the framework of national law and British constitutional principles.[12] It is far from clear what effect future decisions of the former may have on UK parliamentary privilege.

Both Houses at Westminster will protect the freedom of speech of witnesses before their committees. They must not be threatened as a result of evidence given. It is impossible to be certain how prevalent abuse is in this area. In 2004, the Commons Committee on Standards and Privileges found that the suspension of a lady from a statutory Board appeared to derive in part from evidence she had given to a select committee, and that therefore an act of contempt had been committed, even though there was no malicious intent.[13] A departmentally related committee has expressed disquiet about pressure which they suspected might have been felt by potential witnesses who feared their research aid might suffer from giving evidence.

Freedom of speech provisions in the US Constitution understandably began from much the same place as the encapsulation of parliamentary freedom. Article I, clause 6 of the Constitution shields Members of the House and Senators from questioning in any other place for any Speech or Debate in either House. This protection was approved at the Constitutional Convention without discussion and without opposition. The language was derived from Article V of the Articles of Confederation: 'Freedom of speech and debate in Congress shall not be impeached or questioned in any court, or place out of Congress', which in turn was taken from the English Bill of Rights of 1689 (see above). This language reflected the culmination of a history of conflict between the Commons and Tudor and Stuart monarchs during which successive monarchs utilized the criminal and civil law to suppress and intimidate critical legislators. As explained by Madison in Federalist no. 48, 'the Legislative privilege, protecting against possible prosecution by an unfriendly Executive and conviction by a hostile judiciary, is one manifestation of the "practical security" for ensuring the independence of the legislature'.

While the Speech or Debate clause has English roots, it has however been interpreted in light of the American constitutional scheme of separation of powers in that, unlike the British Parliament, the Congress is not the supreme sovereign authority but a coordinate branch, the independence of which must be balanced with the prerogatives of the other branches.

The first Supreme Court decision that addressed the Speech or Debate Clause held that the privilege should be read broadly, to include not only 'words spoken in debate' but anything generally done in a session of the House by one of its Members in relation to the business before it' (*Kilbourn v Thompson* 103 US 168, 204 (1880)). When the clause applies, it is an absolute privilege, and the question becomes whether the actions of a Member fall within the sphere of legitimate legislative activity.

A brief overview of Supreme Court jurisprudence in the area of speech or debate protection since Kilbourn is appropriate to establish the context for litigation testing the validity of an FBI search warrant of a sitting Member's Congressional office (for which cf. the remarks on a parallel UK case at page 494). The Court of Appeals for the District of Columbia Circuit in the case of *Brown and Williamson v Williams* 62 F 3d 408 (1995) accurately recites the background legal principles of that jurisprudence and is quoted here at length;

The clause confers on Members of Congress immunity for all actions within the legislative sphere, even though their conduct, if performed in other than legislative contexts, would in itself be unconstitutional or otherwise contrary to criminal or civil statutes...The purpose of the protection is to insure that the legislative function the Constitution allocates to Congress may be performed independently, without regard to the distractions of private civil litigation or the perils of criminal prosecution...The clause does not, for example, prevent the criminal prosecution of Members of Congress for misconduct, even if somehow connected with their performance of official responsibilities...Malfeasance by a Member does not fall within the legislative sphere simply because it is associated with congressional duties. As the Supreme Court explained in allowing a bribery prosecution to go forward in *United States v. Brewster*, 408 U.S. 501 (1972) where the prosecution established a prima facie case without relying on the Member's constitutionally protected legislative speech as evidence, the constitutional protection for acts within the legislative sphere does not extend to all conduct relating to the legislative process, but only to those activities that are clearly a part of the legislative—the due functioning of the process.

This formulation, of course, implies that the judiciary cannot avoid determining what are the outer limits of legitimate legislative process. The Clause applies in civil cases as well as criminal prosecutions. Although the Clause was not born primarily of a desire to avoid private suits, it was designed to prevent intimidation by the Executive and accountability before a possibly hostile Judiciary. The Clause states that Members shall not be called to account 'in any other place'—not just a criminal court. The prohibition of civil actions is consistent, moreover, with the objective of preserving legislative independence. A private civil action, whether for an injunction or damages, creates a distraction and forces Members to divert their time, energy, and attention from their legislative tasks to defend the litigation. Private civil actions also may be used to delay and disrupt the legislative function. Moreover, whether a criminal action is instituted by the Executive branch, or a civil action is brought by private parties, judicial power is still brought to bear on Members of Congress and legislative independence is imperilled. As with criminal prosecutions, however, the privilege only bars civil suits when the action complained of falls within the legislative sphere. For example, although a Congressman cannot be sued for defamatory statements made on the House or Senate floor, the Supreme Court in *Hutchinson v Proxmire* 443 US 111 (1979) established that he has no claim to immunity for a libel action based on his subsequent republication of those statements outside Congress; those later expressions are not part of the legislative process. The privilege also permits Congress to conduct investigations and obtain information without interference from the courts, at least when those activities are performed in a procedurally regular fashion. A corollary to this right to pursue investigations is Congress's privilege to use materials in its possession without judicial interference. In this context, the privilege operates to insulate materials held by Congress from claims based on actions or occurrences other than Congress's present use. The law is clear that even though material comes to a legislative committee by means that are unlawful or otherwise subject to judicial inquiry the subsequent use of the documents by the committee staff in the course of official business is privileged legislative activity. Although Members and (more likely) their agents can be held accountable for illegal seizures, that does not affect Congress's privilege to use illegally seized materials, so long as that use is consistent with legislative purposes.

Legislative employees acting under orders of the House are not necessarily protected under the Speech or Debate clause from judicial inquiry into the constitutionality of their actions if those actions are not properly legislative in nature. An aide of a Senator or Representative is, however, protected when performing legislative acts which would be protected by the Member himself, and there is no distinction between Members of a committee and its counsel insofar as absolute immunity under the clause is provided for the issuance of a subpoena pursuant to legitimate legislative inquiry.

The Speech or Debate clause does not protect transmittal of allegedly defamatory material issued in press releases and newsletters by a Senator, as neither is essential to the deliberative process of the Senate (see *Hutchinson v Proxmire* supra). A complaint against an officer of the House relating to the dismissal of an official reporter of debates has been held non-justiciable on the basis that her duties were directly related to the due function of the legislative process in *Browning v Clark* 789 F 2d 923 (DC Cir 1986). There is no distinction between the members of a Senate subcommittee and its chief counsel insofar as complete immunity is provide for the issuance of a subpoena pursuant to legitimate legislative inquiry (*Eastland v US Servicemen's Fund* 421 US 491 (1975)). Members and their staffs are given immunity for dissemination of a Congressional report (*Doe v McMillan* 412 US 306 (1973)). There is no protection for 'political' or 'representational' activities because they are not 'an integral part of the deliberative and communicative processes' by which Members participate in legislative activities. The clause protects certain contacts by Members with the Executive branch, such as investigations and hearings related to legislative oversight of the Executive, but does not protect others, such as assisting constituents in securing government contracts and making appointments with government agencies (*United States v McDade* 28 F 3d 283 (3rd Cir 1994)).

In *United States v Helstoski* 442 US 477 (1979) the Supreme Court discussed the extent of waiver of the protection by Members or by either House, assuming that a waiver were possible. A Member's conduct in testifying before a grand jury and voluntarily producing documentary evidence of legislative acts was not an explicit waiver by the Member nor was Congress's enactment of the official bribery statute an institutional waiver of the privilege, as it was not accompanied by an explicit and unequivocal expression of legislative intent to be a waiver. It cannot be assumed that either House could waive the privilege over the objections of the individual Member who sought its protection (cf. page 490).

In current contexts this background has taken on particular relevance where judicial subpoenas or search warrants for legislative materials in the possession of individual Members or of committees are issued. The fact that in the United States no search warrant had ever (until May 2006) been served to permit Executive branch search of a Member's office indicates the importance of establishing new precedent in this area. The absence of such attempts beyond subpoena to gain possession of materials within the possession of either House or of its Members in their offices underscores the respect which the Speech or Debate clause has traditionally commanded in the Executive and Judicial branches. This was all brought into question when in May 2006 the Department of Justice obtained a search warrant signed by a Federal judge to seize all the records of a sitting Member from his office in furtherance of a criminal investigation of that Member which had already disclosed potentially incriminating activity and had resulted in the conviction of alleged co-conspirators. The search warrant had been obtained without informing the Member of the House that the search would take place, thereby denying the Member the ability to review those documents which he might allege bore a Speech or Debate immunity from disclosure. The judge signed the warrant because he was convinced that a 'filter team' of FBI executive branch agents not connected with the investigation would separately evaluate the seized documents for legislative content, even though the Member and the House could not call legislative documents to the court's attention during the seizure. A stay of enforcement of this search warrant was subsequently granted by a Federal appeals court to permit the Member to review seized materials for legislative relevancy in order to claim immunity through ex parte particularized examination by the judge who signed the warrant. In July 2007 that same Federal appeals court unanimously ruled in favour of Rep. Jefferson in *United States v Rayburn House Office Building Room 2113*, 497 F 3d 654 (DC Cir 2007) cert denied 128 S Ct 1738 (2009), holding that the search was a violation of the Speech or Debate clause with respect to those records which are legislative in nature. The trial judge whose ruling was thereby overturned would continue to oversee the return to Rep. Jefferson of those documents found to be legislative in nature. The Supreme Court by denial of certiorari declined to review this decision, affirming an important protection to Members of Congress and to the independence of the legislative branch, signalling that the Executive branch through its prosecutorial agents is not able to unilaterally require disclosure of a Member's documents even with a search warrant signed by a judge until there has been a judicial determination, rather than an executive 'filter team' determination, that they are not legislative in nature. The decision is also an affirmation that the Speech or Debate protection extends to efforts to force initial disclosure of legislative material for inspection, and is not merely a constraint against its use in court proceedings.

Former Rep. Jefferson was convicted by a jury (he was re-elected in a run-off election to the subsequent Congress prior to the indictment but defeated for re-election to the next Congress) for violation of a Federal bribery statute (although not the Foreign Corrupt Practices Act) committed by a public official, defined to include a Member of Congress. The Speech or Debate privilege, which constitutionally inures to the protection of Members of Congress to prevent the disclosure of legislative activity which might also constitute an element of the crime of bribery or conspiracy, proved not to be an obstacle, as other non-legislative evidence formed the basis of a successful prosecution. Prosecutorial use of compulsory process—subpoenas, search warrants, and by wire taps[14]—by law-enforcement officials against Members or entities of Congress in an effort to uncover criminal activity, thus has its constitutional limits as prosecutors and the public become aware of alleged corruption by Members. In the Brewster case, the Supreme Court permitted the prosecution of a Senator to go forward while curtailing the admissibility of certain legislative activity under the Speech or Debate clause as evidence of a bribe.

Also at this writing, a former Representative (Renzi, Ariz.) has been indicted in Federal court for felony corruption for accepting money while in office in return for a legislative act. Important to the prosecution may be the introduction of wire tap evidence relating to legislative acts concerning a public–private land exchange enacted into law, in return for compensation indirectly inuring to the Member's benefit. Dismissal motions based on Speech or Debate protection have been filed and will be presented to the 9th

Circuit Court of Appeals following the trial judge's ruling, and further highlight the question of the ability of law-enforcement officers to uncover and prosecute public corruption based on seized wire-tap evidence, where Speech or Debate defences might be claimed by the Member.

Another question of the privileges of either House as it relates to documents of the Congress (rather than documents of individual Members) is addressed in much the same way as subpoenas addressed to individual Members, although its rationale is based more generally on the doctrine of separation of powers under the Constitution than on a specified privilege inuring to the particular Member under clause 6 of Article I. This issue is discussed in greater detail in the chapter on The Four Houses at page 109. For the purpose of this chapter, however, it is correct to assume as affirmed by a Federal appellate court in 2007 in *United States v Rayburn House Office Building Room 2113* supra resulting from issuance of a search warrant of a Member's office, and in *US v Jefferson* 546 F 3d 300 (4th Cir 2008), cert denied, 129 S Ct 2383 (2009), regarding grand jury testimony, that Speech or Debate protection covers documentary as well as testimonial compulsory production of legislative matter.

Freedom from arrest

Thomas Jefferson commented in 1800 in his *Manual* that 'the privileges of Members of Parliament, from small and obscure beginnings, have been advancing for centuries with a firm and never yielding pace...'. It was probably from this view of the encroaching character of privilege that the framers of the US Constitution, in their care to provide that the laws should bind equally on all, especially believed that 'those who make them shall not exempt themselves from their operation'. Article I, section 6 of the Constitution establishes two aspects of privilege for Members of Congress as follows: 'They shall in all cases, except treason, felony and breach of the peace, be privileged from arrest during their attendance at the session of their respective Houses, and in going to and return from the same, and for any speech or debate in either House, they shall not be questioned in any other place.' It is well established that the Clause provides Members of Congress with two distinct privileges. With respect to arrest, the clause itself serves to greatly limit the extent of the privilege to the point where it has been held not to apply to arrests of Members in any criminal case. Thus this privilege can only be invoked in cases not covered by the exceptions, as where there may be an arrest for delinquency in connection with a civil proceeding. The purpose of this clause is to maximize Members' presence at sessions of Congress, not to be disrupted by service of process in civil or criminal proceedings requiring their presence as a witness, or in civil cases as a defendant. It is clear, however, that 'the constitutional freedom from arrest does not exempt Members of Congress from the operation of the ordinary criminal laws...indeed implicit in the narrow scope of the privilege of freedom from arrest is, as Jefferson noted, the judgment that legislators ought not to stand above the law they create but ought generally to be bound by it as are ordinary citizens'.[15]

The Member may waive his privilege from arrest in order to appear as a witness even during a session of either House, with the acquiescence of the House concerned. The privilege inures to the House as much as to the individual Member, in order to prevent judicial or administrative disruption of legislative sessions and to better maintain quorums. The purpose of Rule VIII is to provide general authority to House Members to comply with a judicial or administrative subpoena or judicial order directing appearances as witnesses, without the necessity of a House vote in each case. Prior to the adoption of that rule of general applicability in the 97th Congress, the House would authorize a Member's response to a subpoena by adopting a resolution on a case-by-case basis considered as questions of privilege of the House. Where the Member wishes to assert the privilege from arrest via non-compliance with a subpoena, a question of privilege still may be raised to address the response of the House to a subpoena in any particular case. In all cases, the Member, officer, or employee receiving the subpoena informs the House through the Speaker, and the Member seeks legal guidance from the Office of General Counsel as to whether response to the subpoena is constitutionally consistent with the privileges of the House.

The Senate has no comparable rule to House Rule VIII, preferring to address each receipt of a subpoena by a Senator on an ad hoc basis by separate resolution as the House did prior to adoption of the rule in the 97th Congress, usually by authorizing the subpoenaed Senator to appear when the Senate was not in session.

The position in respect of freedom from arrest at Westminster is very similar, though it should be added that select committees in 1967 and 1999 recommended the abandonment of the privilege, since its scope is limited (as in Congress) to civil process, and a change in the law in 1870 made civil arrests very rare. A criminal act committed by a Member on the other hand has always exposed the culprit to arrest and prosecution in the ordinary courts as it would any other subject, even if the alleged crime took place in the precincts of the Palace of Westminster while either House was sitting. The Palace of Westminster is not a sanctuary. Indeed there is a case in 1815 where a Member vainly tried to avoid arrest by taking his place on the front bench of the House of Commons, on a day on which the House was to sit, though prayers had not been read. When in 1986 the Attorney General applied to the courts for an order restraining the showing of a film within the precincts of the Palace on grounds of national security, the judge declined to grant the injunction because the matter was within the control of the House authorities: and the Speaker then banned the showing. When the Privileges Committee came to consider the issue, they concluded that the courts had ample jurisdiction to grant an injunction (breach of which would be a contempt of the court, even if committed by the action of a Member within the Palace) and that the fact that the film was intended to be shown in the precincts gave those responsible no privileged protection.[16]

When a Lord or Member has been arrested on a criminal charge, the arresting authority must inform the relevant House.

A recent high-profile case involving police action within the Palace of Westminster in connection with allegations that Mr Damian Green MP had improper possession of protected government papers was initially referred to a committee nominated by the Speaker. In the meantime, it emerged that no charges were to be brought against the Member and the Speaker ruled that a warrant would always be required before the police might search a Member's office in the Palace of Westminster or have access to his or her papers. (An American case to which these events bear a distinct resemblance is discussed at pages 491–2.) Eventually, a select committee was set up, the members of which were nominated by the House in the usual way, to review the internal processes for granting permission for a search of Members' offices, including the privilege aspects. The committee has the difficult task of reconciling the absolute of Members' answerability before the criminal law with, first, the practical considerations which attend police action within the premises of the legislature and the politically sensitive nature of that action and, second, the competing absolute of protection of 'proceedings in Parliament'. There is however cognate Canadian and Australian as well as US experience to draw on.

Members are not obliged to answer subpoenas to give evidence on any matter in civil or criminal courts, though they may do so if they wish. The reason for this exemption is (as it is in Washington) the priority of their service to the legislature (in UK terms the High Court of Parliament) over attendance at other tribunals. The Joint Committee on Parliamentary Privilege, recognizing that courts are used to accommodating the needs of witnesses with special responsibilities, sensibly recommended the abandonment of the privilege, together with the requirement that no subpoena be issued in respect of a Lord or a Member without judicial sanction, to avoid vexatious summons.[17] This recommendation, in common with others, has not been implemented.

Contempt

Not every improper challenge to parliamentary authority is an offence against one of the fundamental privileges of Parliament, and so the British Houses claim a power to judge and punish contempts. Contempts are an undefined and unlimited type of action which have the effect of obstructing in the performance of their public duties Lords, Members, or those who serve or assist Parliament.

For a number of years, the most frequent example of contempt—which has still not been successfully tackled[18]—was improper advance release of select committee reports. Contempt may range from deliberately misleading or disrupting a committee, intimidating or trying to bribe a Lord or Member, or threatening to retaliate against a witness before a committee for what he or she has said there. Resisting an order of either House, for example to appear before a select committee, would result in the offender being held in contempt, as would a deliberate refusal to answer a proper question (see page 368). Contempt is thus an elastic concept, clearly susceptible of unreasonable extension, and in modern times the Commons has come to realize that the outer bulwarks of this part of the jurisdiction are no longer defensible. Abusive comments which might in the past have led to a complaint by an infuriated Member are now part of legitimate political exchange, or are simply ignored (and to all intents and purposes use of contempt jurisdiction against abusive contempts has been abandoned altogether in Australia). Nevertheless, though it is unlikely (alas!) that we will ever see again the editor of a national newspaper being rebuked at the bar, the need for some kind of quasi-legal protection against prolonged media campaigns of vilification or deliberate misrepresentation remains worth considering.

In another context, a recent incursion into the Commons Chamber by demonstrators, which brought about a suspension of proceedings, was by any standards a serious contempt. The House might have chosen to imprison the offenders without further ado: there would have been ample precedent for such action. But in the twenty-first century it would have been at best a very risky course to take, bearing in mind the elapse of time since the last committal and the likely public response. The offenders were proceeded against in the courts for public order offences. Such a decision was understandable and unavoidable, given the absence of a modern means of self-protection and the fragility of the traditional weapons, but subjecting the proceedings of the House to the scrutiny of a court in whatever context is always risky in terms of Article IX.

The Joint Committee on Parliamentary Privilege recommended that Westminster contempt jurisdiction should be codified, as it is in Australia,[19] to make it understandable to all. In fact, the justification for codifying goes wider than that. The Joint Committee itself concluded that 'contempt is a serious matter'.[20] If it has been established—as is surely the case—that traditional weapons are insufficient to protect Parliament, then a fighting retreat to defensible positions necessarily based on statute is essential.

When Executive officials or private persons refuse to comply with a Congressional request to appear before either House or their committees, to respond to questions, or to produce documents, one of the instruments of legislative coercion is the power to hold such persons in contempt. Although the legislative power of contempt is not expressly provided for in the Constitution and exists as an implied power, as early as 1821 the Supreme Court in *Anderson v Dunn* 19 US 204 (1821) recognized that without this power the legislative branch would be 'exposed to every indignity and interruption that rudeness, caprice, or even conspiracy may mediate against it'. As a power of self-preservation, a means and not an end, the inherent power does not—as distinct from the parallel power in Parliament (see above)—extend to infliction of punishment.

Of course, disruptive disturbance of Congressional proceedings can be contemptuous, and is constrained both by the two Houses' inherent power to respond to the disruption in order to remove and detain the individual, and by statutes criminalizing such behaviour occurring in the Congressional precincts. Criminal statutes proscribing disruptive or perjurious behaviour by witnesses include laws making it a felony to give perjurious testimony before a Congressional committee[21] and to corruptly influence, obstruct, or impede 'due and proper' Congressional inquiries.[22] These laws, together with the contempt statute[23] enable prosecution in Federal court of witnesses and others inhibiting Congress in its conduct of oversight or of any other proper committee proceeding, and indicate Congressional willingness to enact criminal laws enabling Executive branch prosecutors to bring cases in Federal court rather than assert Congressional sovereignty and handle the case internally.

With respect to contempt in response to compulsory service of process, Congress considered it necessary in 1857 to enact a statute creating a misdemeanour criminal offence for a subpoenaed witness before either House to refuse to testify or produce documents—the procedure utilized most frequently since that time where the Justice Department has cooperated in bringing the prosecution. While either House may exercise its inherent power to commit for contempt by detaining the witness in the custody of the Sergeant at Arms, it is a cumbersome time-consuming procedure involving a trial at the bar of the House not utilized since the 1930s.

In addition, the Senate, but not the House, is armed with a statutory procedure enabling it by adoption of a privileged resolution to begin a civil contempt proceeding in court by directing the Senate legal counsel to bring an action in Federal court to compel a witness to comply with the subpoena of a Senate committee, or to seek any other declaratory or injunctive relief on behalf of the Senate as so recommended by a vote of two-thirds of Joint Senate Leadership group or by majority vote of the Senate.

On 14 February 2008, the House for the first time adopted a resolution permitting the initiation of Federal proceedings seeking declaratory or injunctive relief for civil contempt similar to the existing statutory mechanism currently available to the Senate, by authorizing House Counsel to make application to a court. On that occasion it appeared that the Department of Justice would not prosecute a criminal certification of contempt against Presidential advisers asserting 'Executive Privilege'. Prior to that occasion, the House had never empowered its Counsel to seek declaratory or injunctive civil relief in court. The House has long abandoned its inherent contempt power (to detain the witness in its precincts) in favour of the criminal certification process, but where the Justice Department, despite the mandatory language of the statute, is reluctant to prosecute Executive branch officials found in contempt, another judicial remedy becomes necessary. In the above-mentioned 2008 civil action, a Federal district judge ruled in Committee on the Judiciary, *US House of Representatives v Harriet Miers, et al*[24] on 31 July 2008 that two former assistants to the President could not invoke a claim of Executive Privilege and refuse even to appear or produce documents in response to a valid committee subpoena, but rather would be required to respond and then to assert claims of Executive Privilege on an ad hoc basis before the committee. That court order was stayed by a Federal appeals court which assumed the mootness of the case at the end of the 110th Congress unless initiated anew in the next Congress by issuance of a new subpoena.[25] The re-initiation of those subpoenas and of that civil litigation was authorized on the opening day of the next Congress as a separate order in the rules package. The question of the extent to which a new administration would protect blanket claims of Executive Privilege on behalf of a former President was tentatively resolved by an agreement reached on 4 March 2009 that the two subpoenaed witnesses would respond in executive session hearings and could make ad hoc claims of Executive Privilege claims on behalf of a former President at that time, to be then evaluated by the Judiciary Committee.

Under the contempt statute, wrongful refusal to comply with a Congressional subpoena in either House is made punishable by a fine of up to $1,000 and imprisonment for up to one year. A committee may vote to seek a contempt citation against the recalcitrant witness. In its report to the House, the committee must properly document its jurisdiction over the matter being investigated and must have a proper quorum in voting to report. The statute directs that the US Attorney to whom the certification of contempt is made 'shall' bring the matter to the grand jury in the jurisdiction where the recalcitrant conduct occurred. The statute goes on to direct the Speaker or President pro tempore of the Senate to themselves certify contempts reported from committees when the Houses are not in session, having finally adjourned for the Congress. That interim authority has been construed by one Court of Appeals panel in 1966 to give those presiding officers discretion on behalf of their respective Houses to review the matter before certification, despite language directing that they 'shall' certify to the US Attorney. The House has been well advised to avoid such unilateral certification again and to await return for a vote of the full House.

Various Supreme Court and courts of appeals decisions have established the following rules: the question which the witness refused to answer must be 'pertinent to the question under inquiry', that is, it must relate to a legislative purpose that Congress may constitutionally entertain and must fall within the grant of authority made by the respective House to a duly authorized committee. The committee has a burden to explain to the witness that a question is pertinent and that despite the witness's objection, the committee demands an answer. In the prosecutions under the statute, constitutional claims and other objections to House investigatory procedures may be raised by way of defence. The witness defendant must be accorded all the rights guaranteed to defendants in all other criminal cases. All elements of the offence, including wilfulness, must be proved beyond a reasonable doubt. The courts have been reluctant to interfere with the statutory scheme and have not considered cases brought by recalcitrant witnesses seeking declaratory or injunctive relief. During committee proceedings, where a report to the House is contemplated, a witness's defence, including objections based on relevance, attorney–client privilege, self-incrimination, or Executive Privilege, may be considered separately by the committee or may merge into a vote on reporting the contempt to the House, and then may be debated in the House and subsequently asserted in any misdemeanour criminal prosecution.

In the 97th Congress, the House adopted resolutions[26] following the failure of officials of the Executive branch to submit Executive branch documents to a House subcommittee pursuant to a subpoena. This was the first occasion on which the House cited a cabinet level Executive branch official for contempt. On several prior occasions from 1975 to 1981, the House had threatened to hold Executive officials in contempt for refusing to cooperate with Congressional committees, but in each case the committees obtained access to the requested documents before the House voted on the resolution following a committee report.

In 1998 the House Committee on Government Reform reported a contempt resolution to the House regarding Attorney General Janet Reno's refusal to supply internal documents in her possession that had urged her to appoint an independent counsel in a campaign finance investigation of the Clinton White House.[27] When negotiations between the committee and the Attorney General to permit committee review of redacted documents failed, the Committee voted to cite her for contempt. The report was never called up in the House, however, during the remainder of the 105th Congress. The utilization of the statutory contempt approach by the House, had it been successful, would have placed the appropriate US Attorney in a conflicted situation requiring him to present the contempt of his boss, the Attorney General, to a grand jury for misdemeanour prosecution. As a demonstration of this reluctance, in 2008 the Attorney General announced his refusal to prosecute a similar contempt against Presidential advisers who were claiming Executive Privilege on the President's behalf, resulting in the civil action initiated by the House previously described.

Bradshaw and Pring cite Erskine May's *Parliamentary Practice*[28] to describe the power of each House of Parliament to protect its privileges and punish their violation as 'akin in nature and origin to the powers possessed by the courts of justice to punish for contempt'. They point out that while the House of Commons has dealt with contempts falling clearly within the field of its own privilege such as a witness's wilful misleading of a committee, or the refusal of a witness to answer or produce documents, the Commons had in the past travelled beyond the strict boundaries of its privileges and proceeded against speeches or writings in public prints or journals which reflected on the House or on individual Members in their official capacity. The justification has been a perceived diminution of the respect in which the House is held and a lowering of its authority, thus tending to obstruct its effective working (citing a 1957 case where the Speaker reprimanded a news editor at the bar of the House for misleading allegations of improper conduct by certain Members). Bradshaw and Pring point out that at this juncture the American practice parts company from the British tradition of the Commons' punishment of persons whose actions or allegations denigrate its authority. In the United States, while a Member can himself raise and debate a question of personal privilege relating to outside allegations of his own official misconduct, the House and Senate will not go further to vote on the matter or to arrest and either punish or attempt to coerce the contemptuous accuser. Thomas Jefferson in his *Manual* suggests the rationale for Congress not having so expanded its inherent contempt power to this extent. The fact that the British Parliament and many State legislatures all possessed the inherent power to punish suggested to some that it be presumed to be the prerogative of either House of Congress. Others point out that the punitive authorities in those bodies emanated from express provisions of law, and that the absence of express empowerment in the Constitution to punish for contempt suggests that Congress can only 'make all laws necessary and proper for carrying into execution the powers vested by the Constitution in them'. Thus until such a law was passed, as it eventually was in 1857, the Congress was limited in dealing with contempts only so far as necessary to protect its exercise of legislative authority expressly granted by the Constitution. Absent the statute, Congress was empowered to prevent acts which inherently prevent or obstruct the discharge of legislative duty and to compel the doing of those things which are essential to the performance of legislative function. While the Supreme Court in *Jurney v McCracken* 294 US 125 (1935) upheld the authority of the Senate to exercise its inherent contempt authority against a recalcitrant witness, neither House has exercised such since 1935, aware that the matter would immediately go before the courts under a writ of habeas corpus and preferring instead to utilize statutory procedures.[29] As Bradshaw and Pring go on to say: 'Both Parliament and Congress enjoy broadly the same privileges (from arrest and speech or debate), but in Parliament a further protection resides in each House, to arrest a person and punish him for contempt, regardless of whether the contemptuous conduct inhibited the direct performance of the legislative function or merely had the effect of bringing the body into public disrepute.' The exercise of that inherent power to punish for contempt has, in modern British practice, been limited to situations where the House 'is satisfied that to do so is essential in order to provide reasonable protection for the House, its Members or its officers from such ir obstruction or attempt at or threat of obstruction as is causing, or is likely to cause, substantial interference with the performance of their respective functions'. Bradshaw and Pring's conclusion—that in Parliament as in Congress, there is a growing tendency to lean upon the protection of privilege as little as possible, and to exercise with restraint their considerable powers against public criticism of their membership and activities—seems just as accurate today. Constant depictions of a 'culture of corruption in Congress' throughout the media have become imbedded in the public mind to the degree that assertions of constitutional privilege might further incur the wrath of that same voting public. A recent manifestation of this bipartisan leadership reticence to properly present assertions of privilege can be seen in a reluctance to question the constitutionality of an FBI warrant for the search of the office of a Representative (for which there is an analogy in recent events in the House of Commons, see page 494). The political fear that assertions of privilege as a protection of Legislative branch independence will be interpreted by the public as placing institutional prerogatives or individual Members 'above the law' should not distract either House from proper assertions of the constitutional and precedential importance of privilege. It is particularly when difficult cases arise, including recent examples of improper Executive branch searches and wire taps of Legislative branch precincts and of its Members, that each House must forcefully assert its proper privilege.

Other segments of this work will suggest that overly broad assertions of executive power or privilege in derogation of Congressional oversight responsibility, for example, the issuance of 'signing statements' asserting that the President will not enforce a portion of a law he has just signed into law, 'Commander-in-Chief' prerogatives, and other 'Executive Privilege' claims, all pose similar threats to Congressional prerogatives under the separation of powers envisioned by the Framers.

Complaints, judgments, and penalties

In Congress, a Member raises a question of the privileges of the House in the form of a resolution. Pursuant to Rule IX as amended in 1993, all Members except the Majority and Minority Leaders must first notify the House that they will raise a question of privilege, including the form of the resolution. The Speaker then schedules consideration of the matter at any time within his discretion within the next two legislative days. The notice requirement was inserted to prevent surprise and filibuster by resolutions offered as questions of privilege. The exception for the party leaders and for questions based on a prerogative of the House to originate revenue measures reflect the importance to be attached to immediate consideration without a two-day delay, where time is of the essence or top leadership priority is invoked.

A complaint of breach of privilege or the commission of an act amounting to contempt is, in the Commons,[30] made to the Speaker in writing. Until about forty years ago, Members were free to raise points of privilege in the same way as points of order. As a result, many so-called complaints were bogus, simply fired off by Members frustrated at not catching the Speaker's eye at Question Time. Nowadays, complaints are far fewer and more likely to be soundly based. The Speaker considers privately whether it would be right to give a Member making a written complaint precedence over the day's business so that he or she may move to refer the complaint to the Committee of Standards and Privileges. If he does not think it right, the matter, as far as privilege is concerned, is at an end. If the complaint is considered one on which the House needs to decide whether to send it to Committee, the Member will be allowed to make the appropriate motion, and the House's decision will follow. In effect, the Speaker sieves out unmeritorious complaints and those where the act complained of is not capable of being a breach of privilege or a contempt, and it is for the House to decide whether or not to take up those which pass that preliminary test. The Committee on Standards and Privileges will then hear any case referred to it, taking evidence from witnesses and making up its collective mind on whether the complaint should be upheld, and if so what the punishment should be. A report is made to the House, which finally decides what is to be done. For the most part, the House does not overturn the Committee's conclusions.

When a sanction is appropriate, the emptiness of the parliamentary arsenal is all too apparent, particularly if the offender is a non-Member (see page 368). In truth, the adequacy of penalties to enforce the Houses' right to protection began to fail more than a century ago. Imprisonment at the order of the Houses gradually ceased to be credible. The last imprisonment was ordered by the Commons in 1880. There is sufficient unclearness over whether the Commons has power to impose fines to close off that option too, at any rate without clarifying legislation, which might well not command public support. (The Lords' power to fine is more securely based, but has not been employed for two centuries—though it is worth recalling in that context that the New Zealand House recently imposed a fine after a gap of more than a century.) Admonition of non-Members at the bar, in earlier years powerful parliamentary theatre, is unlikely to carry sufficient opprobrium in the twenty-first century.[31]

So far as Members of either House are concerned, suspending or even expelling a Member of the Commons remain available sanctions. The last instance of expulsion is however half a century in the past, and the muddle that would inevitably follow a direct appeal by an expelled Member to the European Court of Human Rights hardly bears contemplation.[32] Admonition by the Speaker in the Chair or (more usually) censure in a motion are less severe but may remain unpleasant shadows over future careers. Expulsion is not possible in the Lords, their Lordships sitting by right of a writ of summons from Her Majesty, but suspension from the service of the House—a sentence unknown since 1642—has been judged compatible with the writ of summons, and the sentence was imposed on two Lords in 2009. The Prime Minister has promised legislation to clarify the powers of the Lords in regard to disciplinary sanctions, and so the two Houses may in future draw closer together in this matter.

Even if adequate sanctions were readily available, it is understandably no longer acceptable for one of the Houses to act as judge and jury on alleged breaches of parliamentary (but not always criminal) law or contempts, whether by Members or non-Members. Indeed, the modern Houses at Westminster have no machinery to undertake such a task, even if public opinion thought they should. At the same time, to devolve responsibility on any other authority risks allowing that body to sit in judgement on the sovereign legislature. Where an offence committed against the Houses is also a criminal offence and is proceeded against in the courts, the court may find it necessary, in order to do justice, to inquire rather deeper into 'proceedings in Parliament' than will sit easily with the Bill of Rights. The Joint Committee on Parliamentary Privilege proposed concurrent jurisdiction of Parliament and the High Court.[33] It may be the only way round these difficulties, but again, no legislation to make the change has been introduced, though the Joint Committee reported nearly a decade ago.

The privilege of Parliament is part of and not a derogation from the law of the land. As the general law has entered more areas of life and more detailed circumstances, the law of privilege has remained vague, buttressed by antique cases. The courts are no longer as deferential as they sometimes were a century ago. Individuals enjoy more rights at law and parliamentary defences are tested along with others. No clear consensus exists about the purposes privilege serves and where its boundaries should be, so that the benefits it might deliver are sometimes not sought. In those circumstances there may be no alternative—as the Joint Committee on Parliamentary Privilege itself pointed out[34]—to permitting the judges to determine many of the boundaries of privilege. The areas which are subject to judicial determination in that way however are those which happen to reach the courts, not necessarily those in greatest need of further thought. The Joint Committee's report was a first step towards redressing the balance, giving Parliament and government together an opportunity to prepare a coherent, modern, and above all statutory definition of parliamentary privilege. There will certainly be problems, but if much of privilege remains fixed in the nineteenth century (and earlier) it will be a poor protection for a twenty-first-century Parliament.

Congress, Parliament, and the statute law

It is important in contrasting the British and US approaches to Members' behaviour that the notion of absolute sovereignty of Parliament has to date prevented Parliament from enacting law which specifically criminalizes certain official misbehaviour by its Members and renders them subject to investigation and prosecution by other branches of government. Parliament prefers instead to investigate its own Members' official activities. Congress was not free to take that approach, since the privilege of Members from arrest in clause 6 of Article I was confined to civil cases. This exception left both Congress and State legislatures free as a matter of constitutional law to statutorily criminalize official misconduct which constituted a felony. The separate Speech or Debate protection remains, of course, an obstacle to prosecution or indeed to any other questioning in Federal or State courts, or in any other place, of Members with respect to legislative activity. In a constitutional system based on separation of powers among the three branches of government, this clause is a cornerstone in uniquely protecting Legislative branch independence. The courts, however, as ultimate interpreters of the Constitution under Article III, remain the final determiners of what conduct or material constitutes protected legislative activity under that clause in a particular case or controversy. This role of the judiciary has recently been affirmed on appeal in the Jefferson case involving materials seized by search warrant (page 492).

If a Federal judge were left free to merely accept the Executive branch's interpretation of the legislative nature of seized or wire-tapped material, with no input from the affected Member or from counsel in that Member's House, then the Speech or Debate Clause protection could be severely emasculated. The precedent would be set for the first time in US history that a search warrant or wire tap may permit the seizure of legislative materials from a Member or from a committee, in order to discover whether criminal activity has occurred or is even being separately investigated by that committee or its members. There must be—and *mutatis mutandis* the prescription applies to Parliament as well—a proper protocol permitting the court to evaluate any claim of privilege the Member might make with respect to specific documents or conversations before they are seized by the Executive branch. Otherwise the precedent would stand that legislative documents which are evidence of a crime, even a crime committed by a department of the Executive branch, are by definition not privileged and may be seized and removed from legislative custody.

The application of the Speech or Debate Clause in the context of employment decisions made by Members of Congress must also be examined. The relevant question is: is a decision to terminate the services of a Congressional employee based on alleged discriminatory motives and otherwise actionable under the Congressional Accountability Act of 1995 (the CAA), which for the first time applied Federal anti-discrimination statutes to Congressional employees, nevertheless non-justiciable under a Speech or Debate immunity defence based on the Member's assertion that the performance of the employee's duties complained of was a part of his (the Member's) legislative function and therefore not questionable in another place?

Until 2006 most of the jurisprudence on this question emanated from the Court of Appeals for the District of Columbia Circuit, but cases in that and in other circuits had drawn inconsistent conclusions over the extent to which a speech or debate immunity defence could be asserted by the defendant Member in litigation involving personnel decisions. While Supreme Court cases had given guidance on the extent to which the clause protected legislative activity, they did not go directly to the question of whether employment decisions made by Members relating to employees engaged in legislative work could be questioned either under common law, or after 1995 under the CAA. In 2006, the DC Court of Appeals consolidated two discrimination lawsuits brought by former employees of a Representative and of a Senator, respectively, against their employing 'offices' as required by the CAA. In both cases, the court permitted the cases to proceed to hearings on the merits of whether in fact discriminatory employment actions (based on race, gender, or medical condition) had taken place regarding employees who did in fact perform legislative duties for the Member. The court overturned the rationale of a 1986 case from its own circuit (*Browning v Clerk* 789 F 2d 923 (1986)) which held that the Speech or Debate Clause immunizes Members from suits challenging personnel actions concerning employees 'whose duties were directly related to the due functioning of the legislative process', in part because that rationale conflicted with the case of *Bastien v Office of Senator Ben Nighthorse Campbell* 390 F 3d 1301 (10th Cir 2004), which held that judicial review of a Senator's discriminatory personnel decision is only barred when the plaintiff's claim 'questions the conduct of official Senate legislative business'. The Court in the consolidated cases realized that the question of whether a Member's personal office can invoke the Speech or Debate Clause on the Member's behalf as defending a 'legislative act', or whether personnel decisions are always 'administrative' acts, was indeed perplexing. It concluded that the rationale in Browning was overly simplistic, that an employee's duties are too crude a proxy for protected activity since based on the presumption that a personnel decision with regard to an employee whose duties are directly related to the due function of the legislative process is 'always an integral part of the deliberative and communicative processes'. Thus the court rejected the holding in *Browning* that personnel decisions regarding legislative employees inherently implicate Speech or Debate, ruling that an employee's duties are not relevant; rather what is relevant is the reason the personnel action was taken against the employee. The court cited examples of legislative employees' conduct which, while 'related' to the legislative process, was not 'part of' the due functioning of the legislative process, for example, a termination of a legislative employee based on budget cutbacks, employee tardiness, etc. The court also rejected the notion that employees who prepare newsletters to constituents or speeches to be made outside Congress are acting in furtherance of the Members' legislative 'goals', against whom termination actions are therefore legislative acts which cannot be questioned, suggesting instead that such duties are 'political' and not legislative and therefore not protected. In holding that the plaintiffs were able to plead prima facie cases under the CAA without violating the Speech or Debate Clause, it did not mean that the clause in no way hinders their discrimination suits. While the suits are not precluded altogether, the Clause still protects Members from inquiry into legislative acts or the motivation for actual performance of legislative acts, and suits under the CAA must then proceed to fact finding where the defendant Member must provide evidence of a legitimate non-discriminatory reason for the discharge. To invoke the Speech or Debate Clause as a defence, the employing office should include with this evidence an affidavit from an individual eligible to invoke it recounting facts sufficient to show that the challenged personnel decision was taken because of the plaintiff's poor performance of conduct protected by the Speech or Debate Clause. The trial court must then determine whether the reason given for the firing by the Member was the true reason. In many cases the plaintiff would not be able to disprove the Member's assertion without drawing into question the legislative acts and motivations of the Member, and any such inquiry would be barred by the Clause, causing the action to be dismissed.

For the moment the applicable case law serves to further strengthen the Speech or Debate immunity defence for Members by applying the Clause to pre-emptive claims of immunity in the first instance and not merely to testimonial privilege against demands for verbal evidence in subsequent court proceedings.

At this writing a corollary area of jurisprudence has emerged interpreting the Federal Employees Liability Reform and Tort Compensation Act of 1988[35] (which was extended at that time to cover the Legislative and Judicial branches in addition to the Executive branch) to immunize Members whose defamatory statements outside the Congress were found to be within the scope of their employment and were thus barred from challenge where the United States (the Justice Department) declined to waive its sovereign immunity asserted on the Member's behalf. The cases have liberally construed the 'scope of employment' immunity to include a number of defamatory statements arguably related to the business of the House where remarks were made to the media to explain or enhance the Member's position or effectiveness as a legislator—an ordinary and natural incident of his job.[36] The most important case in this area is *Wuterich v Murtha*[37] involving a defamation action against a Member for press comments made against US military personnel in Iraq, where that Member's deposition to determine scope of employment is being sought (cf. pages 487–8 for the potentially very different position in the UK).

A final area of Speech or Debate uncertainty involves conflicting DC Circuit Court of Appeals cases regarding the extent to which a sitting Member under investigation in his House's Ethics Committee can assert a privilege against compulsory disclosure of his testimony to the Executive branch criminal investigators, *Ray v Proxmire* 581 F 2d 998 (1978) (cf. *US v Rose* 28 F 3d 181 (1994)). The question of whether a Member's own testimony in defence of an internal House or Senate investigation constitutes a legislative activity deserving Speech or Debate immunity merits subsequent examination if those cases are reconciled in that circuit.

At this writing, a Federal Appeals court panel has upheld a Member's Speech or Debate claim that his testimony before the House Committee on Standards of Official Conduct was legislative activity protected from disclosure to a grand jury (*United States v Feeney* Slip Op. 08-3056 (2009)), thereby upholding *Ray* and urging review of *Rose*.

In the UK, Parliament's privileges and its contempt jurisdiction are in addition to the more amorphous concept of exclusive cognizance. This is the principle that Parliament has the sole right to judge what is said or done within its walls in the exercise of its proper functions. Parliament must be free, for example, to determine what its procedures should be without interference from the judiciary (though it is true that there are a handful of statutes which prescribe how Parliament should act in certain circumstances). Parliament has the right, in the last resort, to compel evidence from individuals and bodies on which its judgements and those of its committees will rest. The House of Commons continues to decide whether Members are qualified to sit and vote, although the courts now determine whether a Member has been duly elected. If a Member is expelled, he or she has no recourse to the courts—or not, at any rate, to date.

In 1883, a Member was elected to the House of Commons who, being an atheist, declined to take the oath, as he was statutorily required to do before taking his seat. After a complex struggle, the House made an order restraining the would-be Member from taking the oath until he gave certain undertakings. The Member appealed to the courts to declare the House's order ultra vires and void. The courts decided that they had no jurisdiction to interfere, because the House's order related to its internal management, over which it had exclusive jurisdiction,[38] notwithstanding the relevant statutes. The conclusion was widely stated—

> the House of Commons is not subject to the control of...[the] court in the administration of that part of the statute law which has relation to its own internal proceedings...Even if that interpretation should be erroneous [the] court has no power to interfere with it...

Much that goes on in Parliament and its committees could not have been foreseen by the judges who determined the great cases of the nineteenth century, let alone the legislators of 1689. Both society and the scope of the law have since become much more complex, and the expansion of parliamentary staff and facilities has followed. Nowadays, the line around exclusive cognizance is often difficult to draw: the boundary is not tidy. As the Joint Committee on Parliamentary Privilege observed in 1999 'there is a need to distinguish between activities of the House which call for protection...and those which do not',[39] and in any case exclusive cognizance protects the Houses and not their members individually. It was ruled by a court as relatively recently as 1934 that the House of Commons could ignore the general law about the provision of alcoholic liquor,[40]but the judgement has since been criticized as exempting those who make the law from its effects on far too broad a front.

Some modern statutes explicitly bind Parliament. Where there is no such provision, for example in management, employment law, health and safety, the law of contract, food hygiene, and many other areas, both Houses in fact voluntarily comply with the law's demands. Article IX—the equivalent of the Speech or Debate clause (see above)—is pleaded neither by the Houses nor by their Members, and the 1934 precedent has not been extended beyond the immediate area of its application. Some regularization of the situation seems sensible. The Joint Committee on Parliamentary Privilege proposed that exclusive cognizance should be tied more tightly to proceedings in Parliament and that otherwise Acts should apply to the Houses unless it is expressly provided that they should not.[41] It seems a clear and logical position but here as elsewhere nothing has been done to implement the recommendation.

Impeachment

Impeachment is a proceeding of British origin. In the United States, it is a constitutional remedy, outlined in Articles I and II of the Constitution, addressed to serious offences against the system of government. It is the first step in a remedial process, that of removal from public office and possible disqualification from holding further office under the United States. The purpose of impeachment is not personal punishment. Rather its function is primarily to maintain government integrity. Hamilton in Federalist no. 65 describes the subject of jurisdiction of impeachment as 'those offences which proceed from the misconduct of public men, or in other words from the abuse or violation of some public trust. They are of a nature which may with peculiar propriety be denominated political, as they relate chiefly to injuries done immediately to the society itself.'

The Founding Fathers assigned the accusatory and trial functions uniquely to the House and Senate, respectively, in order to obtain a balance of power among the three branches in the process of removal from Federal office. As between the functions of each elected House, Hamilton in Federalist no. 66 describes the rationale as 'avoiding the inconvenience of making the same persons both accusers and judges, and guarding against the danger of persecution from the prevalence of a fractious spirit in either of those branches. As the concurrence of two-thirds of the Senate will be necessary to a condemnation, the security to innocence will be as complete as itself can desire.' Thus the power of impeachment is bifurcated by the Constitution. The House is given 'the sole power of Impeachment' and the Senate is given 'the sole Power to try all Impeachments'. Impeachments may be brought against the President, Vice President, and all civil Officers of the United States, but not against a private citizen who holds no public Federal office. The term civil officers is broad enough to include all officers of the United States who hold their appointment from the Federal government, whether their duties be executive, administrative, or judicial (and not merely to those whose nominations are subject to Senate confirmation). Military officers are not subject to impeachment since they are subject to disciplinary measures according to military codes enacted by Congress. An impeachable officer remains subject to impeachment even after his resignation, since a potential sanction includes not only removal but a disqualification from holding any other office under the United States. As a practical matter, however, the resignation of an official about to be impeached generally puts an end to impeachment proceedings because the primary objective—removal from office—has been accomplished. This was the case in the impeachment proceedings brought against President Nixon in 1974 following the decision of the House Committee on the Judiciary to report to the House Articles of Impeachment, where further proceedings were discontinued.

Ironically, while the British impeachment tradition was the model for the Constitution, it is in the United States, and no longer in the United Kingdom, where the process of impeachment remains relevant. Impeachments have commonly involved charges of misconduct incompatible with the official position of the office holder. This conduct falls into three broad categories: (1) abusing or exceeding the lawful powers of the office; (2) behaving officially or personally in a manner grossly incompatible with the office; and (3) using the power of the office for an improper purpose or for personal gain. The prevalent view is that the term 'misdemeanours' describes not merely criminal conduct but also acts which while not criminal, adversely affect the public interest. Historical evidence establishes that the phrase 'high crimes and misdemeanours', which over a period of centuries evolved into the British standard of impeachable conduct, had a distinctive meaning and referred to a category of offences that subverted the system of government.

Impeachment proceedings have been initiated in the United States Congress more than sixty times. Seventeen of these cases resulted in impeachment by the House: President Andrew Johnson in 1868, Secretary of War William W. Belknap in 1876, Senator William Blount in 1797 (his impeachment was subsequently determined inappropriate by the Senate—Senate removal by expulsion being the only available remedy, as a Senator is not a civil officer the Constitution), President William J. Clinton in 1998, and thirteen Federal judges, most recently on 19 June 2009. At this writing, only seven impeachments have led to Senate convictions, all of them Federal judges. The House and Senate chose to discontinue the trial of a House impeachment of a Federal judge in 2009 when the impeached judge resigned and was no longer a civil officer. Of the sixteen impeachments voted on by the House since 1789, at least eleven involved one or more allegations that did not charge a violation of criminal law.

An impeachment is initiated by a written accusation called an Article of Impeachment, which states the offence charged, the equivalent of an indictment in an ordinary criminal proceeding. It takes the form of a resolution introduced through the hopper or presented on the floor as a question of privilege. Under the modern practice, an impeachment process is normally instituted by the House by the adoption of a resolution calling for a Judiciary Committee investigation of charges against the officer in question. This committee may, after investigation, recommend the dismissal of charges or it may recommend impeachment.

In the 105th Congress in 1998, an Independent Counsel appointed by the Attorney General transmitted to the House pursuant to law a communication containing thirty-six boxes of evidence of possible impeachable offences (perjury and obstruction of justice before a grand jury) by President William J. Clinton. On the day after the materials were received by the Sergeant at Arms, the House adopted a privileged resolution reported from the Committee on Rules referring the communication to the Committee on the Judiciary, printing a portion of the materials and ordering the remainder printed at the end of two weeks unless otherwise determined by that committee. Non-committee members' access to the communication was restricted, and committee meetings and hearings on the communication were closed to the public and to non-committee members. The House decided without reviewing the material to immediately make public a summary prepared by the Independent Counsel, and presumed that the remainder would be public within a short time unless the committee voted to the contrary. By that resolution, the House varied standing rules otherwise permitting non-committee member access to executive session files, by denying it altogether. Subsequent information received by the Judiciary Committee from the Independent Counsel alleging other prior sexual misconduct by the President (which was not covered by the resolution) was, however, made available to non-committee members as executive session documents prior to the vote on Articles of Impeachment, potentially influencing their votes beyond the authorized scope of the investigation. This ultra vires action demonstrated the developing partisan nature of the controversy.

Judiciary Committee impeachment investigations are governed not only by standing House rules governing committee investigative and hearing procedures, but also by ad hoc rules and special procedures adopted by the House and by the committee for the inquiry. A unique aspect of this additional rule-making capacity is the ability of the Judiciary Committee which is conducting the investigation, as well as the Committee on Rules which originally authorized the investigation, to recommend to the House, as questions of privilege, additional rules and procedures. In no other context does an investigating committee other than the Committee on Rules have the authority to bring new rules changes to the immediate attention of the House. This unique ability is based on precedents which acknowledge the constitutional importance of impeachment proceedings and the need to conduct them expeditiously when the investigating committee itself seeks the approval of the House. Such proposals incidental to impeachment emanating from the Judiciary Committee include authorities to issue depositions and conduct interrogatories conferred on committee staff, and funding for the investigation. The resolutions authorizing the Committee on the Judiciary to investigate President Nixon and President Clinton in 1973 and in 1998 were virtually identical in form and reflected the importance of precedent in establishing consistent procedures regardless of party majorities.

In both of those Presidential impeachment investigations, as in all modern judicial impeachments, the accused was permitted to testify, present witnesses, cross-examine witnesses, and be represented by counsel. In the Presidential proceedings, the accused President was represented by counsel in all these respects and did not appear personally.

Because a resolution impeaching an Officer has a unique status under the Constitution—the House being given the sole power of impeachment and the remedy toward removal from office needing to be unencumbered by other standing rules—such a resolution reported from the Judiciary Committee may be considered immediately and is not subject to a three-day report layover requirement. Also, individual Members rising to a question of the privileges of the House may immediately propose to impeach an Officer of the United States. On several recent occasions,[42] the same Member served notice of his intention to impeach Vice President Richard Cheney or President George W. Bush by announcing to the House the full text of his resolution containing Articles of Impeachment. That Member was recognized to call up the resolutions as a question of privilege. The Majority Leader then moved to refer the resolutions to the Committee on the Judiciary. Those motions prevented debate on the resolution itself. They demonstrate the importance conferred upon impeachment resolutions as questions of privilege, forcing the House to immediately act on the motion of any individual Member. Together with resolutions to punish Members for disorderly behaviour, the constitutional impeachment prerogative carries with it the potential for immediate consideration, unlike other legislative prerogatives which merely empower the House to enact legislation but which do not carry with them the potential need for immediate consideration outside the ordinary application of the standing rules.

An amendment to an impeachment resolution providing instead for the censure of the accused official was held not germane, since it has no separate constitutionally contemplated status under separation of powers, no privileged status as an original proposition, and has as its fundamental purpose the punishment of the official as a condemnation of conduct, rather than as a remedy toward potential removal from office. This rationale was the basis of the Chair's ruling on 19 December 1998 that censure of the President was not germane to impeachment, a ruling that was sustained on appeal. The House Majority leadership, aware that the impeachment resolution could come directly to the floor as a question of privilege without being first made in order by a special order of business reported from the Committee on Rules, did not allow that committee's Majority members to permit a motion to censure to be offered as a non-germane amendment or as a motion to recommit through a waiver of points of order. Thus those Members seeking a record vote on the issue of censure chose to appeal the Chair's ruling on the question of germaneness of censure as an alternative to impeachment when it was offered as a general motion to recommit without the benefit of a waiver. The question was technically on the propriety of the Chair's ruling of non-germaneness, and not on the merits of censure. Had that alternative motion been offered in the form that 'the impeachment was not warranted', rather than as a censure, the alternative would have been germane and in order, as there existed precedent for the Judiciary Committee's filing privileged reports to that effect.

The Founding Fathers adopted the phrase 'high crimes and misdemeanours' from the British as a term which had been in use for over 400 years in Parliament. Some of those impeachments involved treason, others high crimes and high misdemeanours, both statutory offences and non-statutory offences involving abuse of official power or trust. The time when the offences were committed is a factor to be taken into consideration. In 1973 the House declined to take any action on a request by the Vice President (Agnew) for an investigation into allegations of impeachable offences, where they were not committed during his term of office and were pending before the courts. In the Independent Counsel investigation of President Clinton, some of the alleged sexual misconduct took place while he was in office, while other allegations involved his prior public service as governor. The impeachable offences alleged—perjury and obstruction of justice—were during his term as President while under oath before a Federal grand jury. Ultimately the decision whether to impeach is a political one, albeit based on precedent involving legal principles, since the deciding body—the House of Representatives—even in the capacity as accuser, acts as a political institution seeking the remedy of removal.

In 1974, the grounds for invoking the impeachment power against President Nixon involved charges arising out of a 1972 break-in at the Democratic National Headquarters in the Watergate Office Building in Washington, DC. The Committee on the Judiciary recommended to the House three Articles of Impeachment, charging him with abuse of his Presidential powers, obstruction of justice, and contempt of Congress. Before the full House voted on these articles, President Nixon resigned and thereby terminated further action on the issue, although the articles were submitted to and accepted by the House by adoption of a resolution of 'acceptance' considered under suspension of the rules rather than as a privileged resolution of impeachment.

Since Federal judges hold office 'during good behaviour', it has been suggested that misbehaviour properly defines the bounds of 'high crimes and misdemeanours' and constitutes an independent standard for impeachment of judges. The more modern view, however, is that the 'good behaviour' clause more aptly describes judicial tenure and does not constitute a standard for impeachability, but merely means that judges hold office for life unless they are removed under the 'high crimes and misdemeanours' provision of the Constitution.

While an impeachment may proceed only when Congress is in session and an incomplete impeachment proceeding in the House must be reinstituted anew in the subsequent Congress, an impeachment trial may begin or resume in the Senate in the subsequent Congress so long as the previous House had voted the Articles and transmitted them to the Senate. The subsequent House reappoints its managers whose terms have expired with the last Congress to prosecute the impeachment. In that sense the continuity of the impeachment proceedings between Congresses is not self-enforcing, and a vote in the House, while not again on the Articles of Impeachment, is necessary to continue proceedings. This precedent was established in the British Parliament when Warren Hastings was impeached by the House of Commons in 1790 and tried by the House of Lords in the next Parliament in 1791. This was mirrored in Congress in the judicial impeachment of Judge Alcee Hastings in 1988–9, and of President Clinton in 1998–9.[43]

As the sole power to try impeachments is vested in the Senate, the Senate resolves itself into a court for the trial. It is the only way in which the Senate exercises judicial power, and in this capacity is the equivalent of the entire House of Lords sitting as a court. The President of the Senate (the Vice President) presides over the trial, except in the case of the impeachment of the President or the Vice President, in which case the Chief Justice of the Supreme Court presides, to avoid the obvious conflict of interest. Upon organization of the Senate as a court, the House managers appear to present the resolution and articles of impeachment simultaneously, and the trial commences. The evidence against the accused is first presented by the House managers. During the Clinton impeachment, the House appointed thirteen managers (all Majority party Members), each of whom presented a portion of the evidence for the House. Evidence in defence is then presented by the accused through counsel, and the concluding evidence is presented by the House managers. The accused is permitted to testify in answer to the charges. Counsel are permitted to appear to argue on preliminary and interlocutory questions, to deliver opening and final arguments, to submit motions, and to present evidence and examine and cross-examine witnesses. Throughout the Clinton trial the Senate disposed of a variety of motions and resolutions by majority vote, including rejection of a motion to dismiss the trial, adoption of motions to consider certain proceedings in executive session, issuance of subpoenas for depositions of three witnesses, admission of miscellaneous documents into the trial record, a request that the President appear at a deposition, and a motion to permit House managers to admit transcripts and videotapes of oral depositions into evidence. President Clinton did not appear personally during his trial in the Senate but did attend a sworn televised deposition.

Under the Constitution, a two-thirds vote of Senators present is required to convict the accused on an article of impeachment, as each article is voted on separately under Senate rules by the yeas and nays. No vote on removal is required following conviction, since removal follows automatically under the Constitution. However, any further judgement of disqualification from holding future office requires a majority vote if it is presented by the House as a further sanction in the Articles of Impeachment. By votes of

45:55 and 50:50 respectively, the Senate on 12 February 1999 adjudged President Clinton not guilty on each of the two Articles of Impeachment.

The preliminary use of a Senate committee for hearings in judicial impeachment proceedings has been held not to violate any constitutional rights or offend fundamental notions of justice, so long as the entire Senate votes on each Article of Impeachment against the judge involved. The Senate's denial of an impeached Federal judge's motion for a hearing before the full Senate, which had accorded him the opportunity to present and cross-examine witnesses before a twelve-member committee of the Senate, and to argue both personally and by counsel before the full Senate, was held not to constitute a justiciable controversy and was dismissed by the Supreme Court in *Nixon v United States* 506 US 224 (1993).

In the UK, despite a flurry of political interest recently, the doomsday weapon of impeachment, though not formally abandoned, is (at any rate in its traditional form) neither a credible nor a practical parliamentary weapon and has not been so for many years. Its formal abandonment was recommended by a Commons committee forty years ago. Reviving classical impeachment in the UK defies all logic. It was a medieval means of removing the protection given to a royal servant whom the Commons found objectionable but could not otherwise persuade the Crown to dismiss. Ministerial responsibility to the House is the modern means of tackling that problem. There being no formal separation of powers on the US model, if the character of the action brought against a public officer is political, so ought to be its disposal, without quasi-legal trappings. Moreover, the prospect of a universally elected Commons solemnly seeking a political judgement from an unelected or partially elected Lords, using forms dusted off from the last impeachment in 1805, is absurd. Impeachment in Britain is dead and will rise from its grave—if ever it does—only in political circumstances which cannot now be envisaged, and certainly in a form different from that which it previously assumed. These considerations alone may be sufficient barriers against its resurrection.

Parliamentary privilege under pressure

Much that is antique about privilege law in the UK has silently expired over the years, as circumstances changed (though press comment remains too often at the simplistic level which characterizes it as 'dusty precedent since Magna Carta'). Equally, in recent times there have been thoroughgoing changes in the scope of privilege, mostly driven by the courts.

One of the most important of these happened in 1993 when in *Pepper v Hart* the Law Lords set aside the very old rule that debates in Parliament ought not to be cited in court as an aid to the construction of the Acts which were shaped by the debates.[44] The rule was a sensible way of preventing the judges from pronouncing on matters currently under debate in Parliament—a kind of separation of powers—but the judges in 1993 took the view that in limited circumstances reference in court to debates would not amount to the kind of 'questioning' of parliamentary discussion which the Bill of Rights prohibits. They contended that relaxing the rule would reinforce and not undermine Parliament. It is fair to say that that decision did not mark an entirely new departure, nor did what followed it amount to a revolution in itself. The Joint Committee on Parliamentary Privilege found the consequences of the ruling 'benign...unobjectionable', particularly where judicial review of government decisions was before a court, provided there was no general weakening of the prohibition in Article IX.[45] Nevertheless, the sluices had been opened and a rising tide soon forced them even wider.

In 2003 the Law Lords had to reverse a decision of the Court of Appeal which allowed the parliamentary record to be used not simply as a means of determining what a statute was intended to mean but whether that meaning could be reconciled with (in this case) the European Convention on Human Rights.[46] In other words, the Court of Appeal had passed from using words spoken in debate to find out the intended meaning of an apparently obscure statutory text to measuring against an external standard the acceptability of Parliament's reasons for legislating in the way it did. Indeed, the absence of reasons given for the legislation as it passed through Parliament was treated by the court as a factor making it more difficult to justify (not simply penetrate to the meaning of) parliamentary judgements. For a time, the Law Lords' rejoinder stemmed judicial inroads on to parliamentary ground. It was submitted that 'the exercise on which the Court of Appeal engaged is not an appropriate exercise for a court',[47] and the Law Lords seem to have taken the point. As a result, the pendulum has swung back a little. The original 1993 decision is now seen as being 'currently under something of a judicial cloud'.[48] It is now held to do no more than prevent the executive from using an unclear statute in a manner broader than it had claimed to Parliament was its intention.

The doctrine that an Act of Parliament can be assailed in the courts was described by one of the Law Lords in 1974 as 'dangerous and impermissible...When an enactment is passed, there is finality, unless or until it is amended or repealed...'.[49] Though perhaps rarely so crisply expressed, the principle was ancient. In 2005, however, the issue presented itself in an unusual aspect, and it was argued in court that the Hunting Act 2004 was invalid, because the Parliament Act 1949, under the accelerating provisions of which the 2004 Act was passed, was itself invalid. The 1949 Act amended the original Parliament Act of 1911 to reduce the delay involved in enacting law by the will of the Commons alone (see page 64). The question was whether the 1949 Act, passed under the procedures of the 1911 Act, and therefore without the consent of the Lords, could amend these procedures. Had a delegated authority—the Commons—improperly enlarged the sphere of its own delegation or was the 1949 Act no more than a new way of enacting law without the agreement of the Lords?[50]

The outcome was in no sense a revolution. The High Court, the Court of Appeal, and the House of Lords all accepted that the 1949 Act made a valid amendment to the 1911 Act. The interest of the case really derives from the background to the central issue. Were the courts right to accept jurisdiction at all? On one view, they were asked to determine the validity of an Act of Parliament; on another, they were simply called on to interpret the 1911 Act. But even if the matter were approached by the second route, was it possible to avoid examination of proceedings in Parliament in 1911 or 1949?

The Attorney General took no point on justiciability in the High Court. The Court of Appeal concluded that the case was no ordinary one turning on a point of statutory interpretation, but they asserted that they would not be adjudicating on what occurred in Parliament. In the event, however, the Court of Appeal freely entered territory long denied to the judiciary. The judges used quotations from parliamentary debates to elucidate not the words but the aims of the Parliament Acts, not impeaching or questioning but arguably extending *Pepper v Hart*. They quoted speeches of Commons backbenchers (and the Leader of the Opposition) in the distant past on an amendment not in the event made. They drew specific conclusions on what 'either House understood' at the beginning of last century. Non-ministerial Members speaking in 1949 were cited in support of the conclusion the court came to.[51]

The Law Lords were more cautious than the court below about encroaching on the Parliamentary sphere.[52] They recognized 'some sense of strangeness at the exercise which [they had]...been invited to undertake...These proceedings are highly unusual...somewhat surprising.'[53] They concluded that the matter was one of statutory interpretation, but explicitly refrained from examining in any detail the parliamentary career of the 1911 Bill, limiting themselves to what was formally done by both Houses in expressing views in resolutions and making or rejecting amendments. There being no obscurity or ambiguity in the statute which the court was interpreting, use of *Pepper v Hart*—which would have opened ministerial observations in debate (but no more) to scrutiny—was impermissible. The reassuring conclusion was that the 1949 Act and the Act of 2004 were both of full legal effect.

Less reassuring were the observations made by some of the Law Lords in the course of arriving at the court's unanimous conclusions. For example, it was asserted that parliamentary supremacy was

> a construct of the common law. The judges created this principle. If that is so, it is not unthinkable that circumstances could arise where the courts may have to qualify a principle established on a different hypothesis of constitutionalism.

Were there to be an attempt to abolish judicial review or the ordinary role of the courts, the new Supreme Court might (it was argued) have to

> consider whether this is a constitutional fundamental which even a sovereign Parliament acting at the behest of a complaisant House of Commons cannot abolish.[54]

As a matter of historical fact, of course, judicial interpretation of common law did not create the principle of parliamentary sovereignty. The revolutionary events of 1689 did that, and sovereignty has since remained where it then settled—with the Crown in Parliament. Were judicial sabre rattling to continue in the Supreme Court, a clear and coherent parliamentary rejoinder would be advisable. Since the suggestion by the Lords Committee on the Constitutional Reform Bill that there should be a joint committee to act as a bridge between legislature and judiciary[55] was not taken up, perhaps this responsibility might fall either to the Commons Justice Committee which regularly meets members of the judiciary or to the Lords Committee on the Constitution.

Judicial tanks again rolled across the parliamentary lawn in 2005 when a former minister was permitted to be cross-examined in court in order to establish whether what he told a select committee was truthful.[56] The judge in his summing-up apologized to the House for not having intervened to stop this line of questioning,[57] and the minister's conduct was referred to the Committee on Standards and Privileges, which came to its own conclusions on the issue.[58]

For all the antiquity and elasticity of Parliamentary privilege, situations may still arise which are novel and awkward to deal with. The Defamation Act 1996 allowed an individual Lord or Member, in certain kinds of proceedings and within limits, to waive the protection of Article IX. The genesis of the Act was a particularly hard case, where a Member found it impossible to argue in court that a press article about him was defamatory, because he was debarred from submitting to the judgement of the court certain proceedings in Parliament which he believed would advance his case. As usual, a hard case made bad law. Privilege belongs to the House, not to an individual Member, and it is illogical to permit the latter to abandon it without the consent of the former. Besides, what is to happen if two Members are involved in an action to which the Defamation Act is relevant, and one waives his privilege and the other does not? The Joint Committee on Parliamentary Privilege concluded that the Act 'created indefensible anomalies of its own which should not be allowed to continue',[59] but it remains unrepealed and the issues which it highlighted are still unsolved.[60]

Notes

1. H Rep 110–885.
2. *Cannon's Precedents*, vol vi, sect 48.
3. HL Deb (2005–6) 685 c 868.
4. 1998–9 HL 43-I, HC 214-I para 364. Whether the Houses should impose on themselves some kind of self-denying ordinance in these circumstances is discussed at paras 203–16 of the report, but the Joint Committee could not see any practicable means of doing so.
5. *Gravel v US* (408 US 606 at 625 (1972)).
6. *Prebble v Television New Zealand Ltd* [1995] 1 AC 337.
7. [1995] 1 AC 321; *Bradley and Others v Secretary of State for Work and Pensions* [2007] EWHC 242 (Admin); and *OGC v Information Commissioner*, HM Attorney General intervening on behalf of the Speaker [2008] EWHC 737 (Admin).
8. *Toussaint v Attorney General of St Vincent and the Grenadines* [2007] UKPC 28: HL 43-I, HC 214-I session 1998–9 para 49.
9. *Jennings v Buchanan (New Zealand)* [2004] UKPC 36.
10. The New Zealand Parliamentary Privileges Committee has responded by recommending that the law of New Zealand should be amended to provide that 'no person may incur criminal or civil liability for making any oral or written statement that affirms, adopts or endorses words written or spoken in proceedings in Parliament, where the oral or written statement would not, but for the proceedings in Parliament, give rise to...liability'. A committee in the Western Australian Parliament came to much the same conclusion. A parallel change in UK law is surely advisable.
11. *A v United Kingdom 2002* (European Court of Human Rights 35373/97).
12. *Wilson v Wychavon District Council* [2007] EWCA 52 at 38.
13. Fifth Report 2003–4 HC 447.
14. By contrast, the British Prime Minister gave an undertaking in 1966 that the telephones of Members of the House of Commons were not to be tapped, and that if the policy changed a statement would be made to the House. No such statement has been made.
15. T. Jefferson, *Manual of Parliamentary Practice*, S Doc 92-1 (1971), 437.
16. First Report 1986–7 HC 365 paras 17 and 30.
17. 1998–9 HL 43-I, HC 214-I paras 331–3.

18. Standards and Privileges Committee Twentieth Report 2007–8 HC 1212, and Special Report of the Culture, Media and Sport Committee 2008–9 HC 333.

19. Australian legislation in 1987 not only defined contempt but abandoned the power to proceed against contempts which are simply defamatory or critical, unless these views were expressed in the presence of the House or a Committee.

20. 1998–9 HL 43-I, HC 214-I para 280.

21. 18 USC 1621.

22. 18 USC 1505.

23. 2 USC 193.

24. Civil Action No 08-0409.

25. See *House Committee on Judiciary v Miers and Bolton*, Civil Action No 08-5357 (DC Cir, 6 October 2008).

26. H Rep 97–968; H Rep 97–898.

27. H Rep 105–728.

28. 18th edn (1971), 112.

29. *Deschler's Precedents*, chapter 15, section 17, at p 139.

30. Most of the disciplinary cases arose in the Commons. Informal self-regulation prevails in the upper House so that, as the Joint Committee on Parliamentary Privilege observed (1998–9 HL 43-I, HC 214-I0 para 286), the Lords has not investigated or punished a contempt for a century.

31. Indeed, the effect may have been fading in the mid-eighteenth century, when (it is said) a Jacobite, having received the Speaker's reproof kneeling at the bar, got up and ostentatiously dusting off his breeches audibly muttered 'Damned dirty House'—and no one was ever made to kneel again!

32. The Maltese House of Representatives was found to have breached the European Convention of Human Rights when two Members who were criticized by a magazine participated in proceedings which found the editor guilty of contempt (*Demicoli v Malta* (1992) 14 EHHR 47).

33. 1998–9 HL 43-I, HC 214-I paras 304–14.

34. Ibid, para 26.

35. 28 USC section 2679.

36. *Williams v United States* 71 F 3d 502 (5th Cir 1995).

37. Case no 2006cv01366, DC Cir.

38. *Bradlaugh v Gosset* [1883–4] 12 QBD 278–86; and see Erskine May's *Parliamentary Practice*, ed Sir William McKay (23rd edn, 2004), 188.

39. 1998–9 HL 43-I, HC 214-I, para 246.

40. *R v Graham Campbell ex p Herbert* [1935] 1 KBD 594.

41. 1998–9 HL 43-I, HC 214-I, para 251.

42. H Res 799, 6 November 2007; H Res 1258, 11 June 2008; and H Res 1345, 15 July 2008.

43. In 1998, the Clerk of the Journals in the House of Commons, James Hastings, transmitted copies of the Journal of the 1790 Warren Hastings impeachment to the House of Representatives Parliamentarian in order to document British precedent in this area at a time when attorneys for President Clinton were arguing that the House would have to re-impeach in the next (106th) Congress before the Senate could try the impeachment. As a further irony, Rep. Alcee Hastings, while removed from his judicial office by impeachment in 1989, was subsequently elected to the House of Representatives from a district in Florida where he continued to serve (not having been specifically disqualified by that impeachment from holding further public office). Just prior to the vote in the House on the impeachment of President Clinton, he offered an unsuccessful resolution to impeach Independent Counsel Kenneth Starr, the officer appointed by the Attorney General who submitted the impeachment evidence (grand jury testimony) to the House.

44. *Pepper (Inspector of Taxes) v Hart* [1993] 1 AC 593.

45. 1998–9 HL 43-I HC 214-I paras 45–55.

46. *Wilson and Others v Secretary of State for Trade and Industry (Appellant)* [2003] UKHL 40.

47. 1998–9 HL 43-I, HC 214-I para 53; and see also para 67. Despite the generally helpful thrust of their judgement, however, the Law Lords opined that it would be going too far to say that there are no circumstances where use may properly be made of the Official Report to answer the question whether legislation is compatible with rights under the Convention (UKHL 40 paras 116 and 142).

48. *Jackson and Others v HM Attorney General* [2005] UKHL 56 para 65.

49. *Pickin v British Railways Board* [1974] AC 788–90.
50. [2005] UKHL 56.
51. [2005] EWCA Civ 126 paras 24, 72, 79–87, 92.
52. [2005] UKHL 56.
53. Ibid, paras 27, 49, and 181.
54. Ibid, paras 102, 105. Another Law Lord added that it was no longer true to say that Parliament's freedom to legislate was unqualified.
55. 2003–4 HL 125-I para 420.
56. *The Times* 15 July 2005, p 12.
57. *Weir and Others v Secretary of State for Transport and Others* [2005] EWHC 2192 at 242.
58. Sixth Report 2005–6 HC 854.
59. 1998–9 HL 43-I, HC 214-I para 69. The Committee also suggested a way round the problem of conflict between the demands of justice and the protection of Lords and Members in their Parliamentary duties.
60. In addition to the several refences in this chapter to the Report of the Joint Committee on Parliamentary Privilege, it should be noted that written and oral evidence given by both of the authors of this work on 2 and 16 December 1997 and on 17 February 1998 respectively was included in HL 43-II and HC 214-II in volume 2 (oral evidence).

11

Ethics and Standards

From the beginning to the 1990s

The framers of the US Constitution contemplated that the Legislative branch, conceived to be the most predominant among the three separated branches of the Federal government, be enabled to scrutinize the behaviour of its Members. James Madison, in the Federalist no. 51, stated the perceived need as follows:

> If men were angels, no government would be necessary. If angels were to govern men, neither external nor internal controls on government would be necessary. In framing a government which is to be administered by men over men, the great difficulty lies in this: you must first enable the government to control the governed; and in the next place oblige it to control itself. A dependence on the people is, no doubt, the primary control on the government; but experience has taught mankind the necessity of auxiliary precautions.

Whether those auxiliary precautions should be solely internal to each House, or should involve other branches of government and independent entities in order to avoid real or perceived conflicts of interest inherent in self-discipline becomes part of the focus of this segment on ethics (and presents a particularly compelling contrast with the House of Commons' establishment of an independent Commissioner for Standards).

From the beginning of the existence of the Congress of the United States in 1789, the Constitution has in Article I, section 5, clause 2 empowered each House to 'punish its Members for disorderly behaviour, and, with the concurrence of two-thirds, expel a Member'. The House also adopted a rule in the first Congress to the effect that each Member shall be present and shall vote 'unless he has a direct personal or pecuniary interest in the event of such question'. Despite the constitutional mandate that each House police the conduct of its Members, for the first 175 years of Congress's existence, neither House determined the need for a systematized approach toward disclosure and discipline. The first recorded instance of the House attempting to take disciplinary action against a Member occurred in 1798, when a Member spat upon another during a vote. A letter of apology was sent. Nevertheless the

Committee of the Whole heard the evidence and recommended expulsion which fell two votes short of the two-thirds majority necessary. From the first Congress until 1967, the House undertook disciplinary action against Members over twenty-five times, with no standardized approach. The offences ranged from duelling to inserting obscene material in the Record. Some cases were handled directly on the House floor without Committee action, others through the creation of select investigative committees. A similar pattern emerges from a review of Senate precedents over that time period.

It was not until 1964 in the Senate and 1967 in the House of Representatives, that the two Houses established codes of official conduct, rules for financial disclosure and permanent committee mechanisms for the consideration and disposition of allegations of improper conduct by Members, officers, and employees. Thus for at least 175 years the two Houses chose not to require disclosures of 'interests' (beyond leaving it to each Member to determine whether he was 'immediately and particularly interested' in the outcome of a vote) and to respond to charges of improper official conduct in an ad hoc fashion, without having established guidelines for official conduct or financial disclosure. Up to that time the two Houses chose to establish temporary select investigative committees only as particular situations arose. More basically, 'for nearly two centuries, a simple and informal code of behaviour existed. Prevailing norms of general decency served as the chief determinants of proper legislative conduct. For most of its history, Congress has chosen to deal, on a case-by-case basis, only with the most obvious acts of wrongdoing, those clearly inconsistent with the trust and duty of a Member.'[1]

Publicity and the test of re-election were considered the major forms of redress for unethical behaviour in Congress. Then Speaker Sam Rayburn is credited with espousing the dominant view in Congress that the ethics of a Member should be judged not by his peers, but by the voters. That position has been analysed as having been based upon a combination of historical precedent, fear of partisan motivations, and a need to operate in an atmosphere of mutual respect, resulting in an unwritten norm of tolerance of conduct and characterized by a distaste for self-discipline in each House.

It is not mere coincidence that Congress's internal scrutiny capability materialized in the 1960s in response to the evolution of the job of Member of Congress as a full-time professional occupation. The fact that Congress had taken to meeting throughout the year and that Members established separate residency in the seat of government, rather than merely travelling to the District of Columbia as part-time legislators, inevitably increased pressures toward higher compensation for those positions and toward the potential for conflicts of interest between the roles of public legislator and income earner/private citizen.

In the mid-1940s concerns began to be voiced over the lack of specific standards of conduct and public financial disclosure requirements for the three branches of government, including criticism of Members' supplementing their salaries with income from speeches and other outside activities. Hearings were held in the Senate in the 1950s which established momentum toward broadly stated ethical standards for all government officials. In 1958 the Congress adopted a ten-point general Code of Ethics for Government for officials and employees.[2] While that code was in the form of a concurrent resolution and not therefore legally binding on subsequent Congresses or on the other branches of government, the standards expressed therein remain accepted rules of official conduct to this day, endorsed by subsequent reports from Congressional ethics committees and expected to be observed in all three branches.

Concerns over the lack of specific Congressional standards of conduct and enforcement mechanisms increased in the 1960s in the wake of ethical misconduct allegations against Secretary to the Senate Majority Bobby Baker, and against Representative Adam Clayton Powell, with widespread media coverage bringing a greater degree of public attention to the issue of Congressional ethics than theretofore. As a result of the Baker scandal and earlier publicized misconduct by Senator Joseph McCarthy during hearings he conducted in the 1950s (reported on by a select committee in 1954 and resulting in his censure by the Senate), the Senate Select Committee on Standards and Conduct was created in 1964.

During hearings before the Joint Committee on the Organization of Congress in 1965, the need for House and Senate codes of conduct, financial disclosure regulations, and ethics committees in both Houses was recognized, and that Joint Committee called for the creation of a House Committee on Standards, the Senate having already created a select committee the previous year. The House responded initially by creating a select committee on Standards and Conduct in 1966 which was empowered to recommend additional House rules or regulations on standards of conduct and to report by majority vote violations of law to proper law enforcement officials. In 1968, the select committee became a standing committee with new jurisdiction to investigate the conduct of Members, officers, and employees, and the Code of Official Conduct and rules on financial disclosure were adopted for the first time, to be subsequently revised on several occasions. Since their creation, these committees have been vested by their respective Houses with investigative, adjudicative, and advisory functions consistent with the self-discipline requirement imposed by Article I of the Constitution on each House. The creation of ethics committees reflected a need for systematizing House and Senate responses to questions of official misconduct and to Members' insistence upon a reliable internal source of information about potential conflicts of interest and about other ethical dilemmas which they faced.

This need in the House was particularly exhibited in the Adam Powell exclusion case. The House had at the beginning of the 90th Congress in 1967 established a select committee to investigate his alleged misconduct as a Member and as chairman of a committee in the prior Congress, and his avoidance of State court processes. The House had precluded his taking the oath of office pending that investigation. Upon the select committee's report[3] two months later, the House rejected its recommendations of seating, censure, fine, and loss of committee seniority by adopting instead an amendment excluding Rep.-elect Powell from membership in that Congress. While the Speaker advised the House that only a majority vote was required to adopt the amendment to the resolution recommended by the select committee, his ruling suggested that the House could by majority vote exclude a Member-elect from membership in the House although he met the constitutional qualifications of age, citizenship, and residency. The Speaker technically avoided responding directly to the question of whether the resolution as amended by the substitute would be treated as a de facto expulsion, even though in the form of an exclusion. The power of exclusion by majority vote is derived from the right of each House under Article I to determine the elections and qualifications of its Members, whereas the power of expulsion by two-thirds vote derives from each House's constitutional authority to discipline its Members for disorderly behaviour. Thus the resolution was regarded by the House (following an 1870 precedent cited by proponents of exclusion and relied upon by the Speaker, wherein a Member was excluded from the 41st Congress on the ground that he had sold appointments to the Military Academy), as an exclusion, although the final vote reflected adoption by more than two-thirds of the Members voting on the resolution, 307 yeas to 116 nays as amended by the substitute which had been adopted 248 yeas to 176 nays. Two years later the Supreme Court in *Powell v McCormack*, 395 US 486 (1969) reversed two lower court rulings and determined that the House could not validly refuse to seat a Member-elect who possessed the requisite qualifications for office, but rather must treat the matter as punishment by expulsion requiring a two-thirds vote for adoption. The fact that the House had adopted the exclusion resolution as amended by more than a two-thirds vote was immaterial since Speaker John W. McCormack had interpreted the action to merely require a majority vote. This case should be seen as a watershed event in the history of the House, to a great extent motivating and not merely coincidental to the establishment of a permanent ethics committee. The need for a systematized bipartisan response to allegations of Member misconduct and the inadequacy of select committee utilizations became apparent in the wake of Rep. Powell's disclosed official misconduct in a prior Congress and the public concern arising from the Supreme Court decision. (For a further discussion of exclusion/expulsion, see page 127.)

Nine Senators and twenty-two Representatives have been censured as a punishment for wrongdoing, ranging from assault to obstruction of the legislative process, to financial and sexual misconduct. In addition, eight Representatives have been reprimanded by the entire House since 1976, when this punishment was first used as a sanction considered less severe than censure. Adoption by the House of the Standards Committee report recommending reprimand constitutes the imposition of that punishment, while the censure of a Member normally involves the Speaker's reading the committee's findings and imposing the censure on the Member, who is required to stand in the well of the House. Suspensions from the House for specified periods of time have not been a contemplated punishment for disorderly—including unethical—behaviour, although early Senate precedents indicate temporary suspensions of Senators while in contempt of the Senate,[4] since the loss of the right to vote on the days of suspension has been considered to present a significant constitutional issue of deprivation of constituent representation short of an expulsion by a two-thirds vote[5] (for which see page 191). Thus since 1975 the House Code of Conduct has merely admonished Members convicted of felony crimes that they 'should' not vote in the House until the presumption of innocence is reinstated or until re-elected. This admonition against voting in the House does not amount to a suspension since not mandatory, and should be contrasted with procedures in the House of Commons permitting the Speaker to suspend Members for disorderly behaviour or the House to ban a Member from its precincts upon being 'named' by the Chair.

In the Senate since 1964 the committee has considered allegations involving thirty-five Senators, all but three of which occurred after 1977. One Senator has been censured in that period and two were denounced (a lesser form of censure) for financial misconduct. One Senator was admonished for acceptance of and failure to disclose prohibited gifts; one Senator was rebuked by the ethics committee for improper acceptance of gifts; and one Senator was reprimanded by the committee in the 'Keating Five' case involving a savings and loan association investigation. Four other Senators in that case were criticized in written statements from the committee for having given the appearance of acting improperly. In the remaining cases, complaints were either dismissed or no disciplinary or official action was taken.

Under the Senate Ethics Committee's rules, it has the authority to 'reprimand' or 'admonish' Senators without formal Senate action, while in the House reprimands are voted by the House upon recommendation from the committee.

In the House of Representatives, the Committee on Standards of Official Conduct has also noted infractions which it concluded did not merit sanctions by the House in the form of admonitions or letters of reproval to Members (including three Members in the 108th Congress in a matter involving improper pressure brought to bear on one of those Members—promising campaign finance assistance to his son—in an effort to change his vote on the House floor). The same committee subsequently admonished the Member who had filed the ethics complaint against one of the Members previously admonished (the Majority Leader) for having filed an overly broad allegation containing innuendo and allegations of criminal behaviour beyond factual bounds.

At least twenty-two Members of the House have resigned after court convictions, after inquiries were initiated by the Committee, or after charges were brought to the attention of the committee but before House action could be completed. In each case, the Member's departure has ended the House investigation, as the committee and the House do not have jurisdiction over the discipline of former Members. In the 109th Congress, four Majority party Members resigned before committee action was initiated; one (the Majority Leader) having denied guilt in a State felony indictment, two having pleaded guilty to bribery and conspiracy, and the fourth having had inappropriate homosexual electronic communication with current and former employees (House pages). In the latter case, the Standards Committee retained jurisdiction over those sitting Members and current House employees who were potentially implicated in an alleged cover up of the offensive activity, and filed an investigative subcommittee report. The full committee and the House took no action but the report was tacitly accepted despite that inaction.

In addition, the Committee on Standards of Official Conduct has been directed to conduct investigations of conduct not initially involving specified individual Members, where their identities are not immediately known, such as allegations of improper alterations of House documents or improper political solicitations, and allegations of improper overdrafts from the House 'bank' and improper operations of the House Post Office. The Committee deferred an investigation of the Post Office matter in 1992 pending an investigation by the Department of Justice. Prosecutions and convictions of some former Members resulted from these Executive branch investigations.

In the Senate, other investigations have covered special car-leasing arrangements for Senators, the introduction of legislation favourable to Chinese seamen, alleged illegal contributions from an oil company, alleged Korean influence peddling, the unauthorized disclosure of classified information relating to the Senate's consideration of a treaty, and several discrimination issues. No disciplinary action was taken in any of these cases.

From the time of the creation of the Committee on Standards of Official Conduct in 1968 to the present, the ethics process and standards of conduct in the House have been restructured several times, and the recommendations leading to the first four of those changes have come from separate bipartisan ad hoc advisory groups. In 1976 the

Commission on Administrative Review was established and directed to make recommendations to the House. In 1977 this resulted in changes in House rules governing financial disclosure, outside earned income, acceptance of gifts, unofficial office accounts, franking (mailing) privileges, and travel. The Commission also suggested the creation of a select committee with legislative jurisdiction in these areas.

In 1977 the House created a select committee on Ethics, to provide guidelines and interpretations concerning House ethics rules. During its two-year existence, the select committee issued thirteen formal Advisory Opinions, and at the conclusion of the filing of its final report its records were transferred to the standing committee on Standards of Official Conduct.

Corrupt or similarly improper behaviour in Parliament on the part of Lords, Members, and others was for centuries an offence only against Parliament. Breaches of what amounted to a code of honour might be punished as contempts or—in the second half of the last century—condemned as 'behaviour falling below the standard the House of Commons was entitled to expect' of its Members. Sanctions against offenders might reach those who offered as well as those who accepted improper gifts. A resolution of the Commons of 1695 proclaimed that 'the offer of money or other advantage to any Member of Parliament for the promoting of any matter whatsoever, depending or to be transacted in Parliament, is a high crime and misdemeanour'. The Houses were certainly unaccountable, but the Commons was no cosy club. The offender's contemporaries, who best understood the temptations as well as the limits of acceptability, were not necessarily over-indulgent judges. The House has expelled a Speaker for taking bribes to forward the progress of a private bill. Nevertheless, the number of cases was not large—and those recorded are overwhelmingly in the Commons and not the Lords—and, as in Washington, there was no settled method of dealing with them.

So far as concerns votes on matters where Members might have a personal financial interest, prohibitive rulings in the Commons date from the early nineteenth century, though doubtless the practice was improper long before then. There is however only one instance, now a century old and more, in which Members voted and then had their votes disallowed because they had a direct and separate personal interest on the matter of public policy under decision.

One of the fundamental transatlantic differences—and for the UK one of the main difficulties in dealing with inappropriate behaviour in financial matters—is that Parliament does not discharge its responsibilities within the framework of a written constitution which externally defines the right of the judiciary in certain circumstances to sit in judgement on Members of the legislature for deeds done in the course of their legislative duties. In ethical as in other areas of alleged misconduct, trial and judgement were for the offender's fellow Members and not for any other court or authority. This was not part of some elaborate scheme of institutional self-preservation. Parliamentary privilege did not and does not put Lords and Members[6] above the law; privilege protects Parliament so that it may serve the people. Any extra-parliamentary authority with the power to constrain parliamentarians from acting and speaking freely while engaged in 'proceedings in Parliament' or to deliver sanctions against them for having done so does not so much damage the individuals aimed at as it does the people of whose Parliament they are members. As the then Leader of the House told the Committee on Standards of Public Life in 2002:

> This is not some arcane or self-serving point...it is a fundamental principle of our parliamentary democracy, and an essential right of the British public, that no external agency may constrain the freedom of speech of elected MPs or the conduct of their proceedings.

The principle came under severe strain in the aftermath of the expenses crisis in the spring of 2009 (see page 530). On the one hand, both government and Parliament were agreed that control of parliamentary allowances and scrutiny of claims should be taken out of the hands of Members of the Commons and given to a specially constituted extra-parliamentary Authority with defined statutory powers. On the other, those whose actions might fall within the view of such an Authority were, in aspects other than financial, still protected by the privilege enshrined in the Bill of Rights 1689. Criticism centred on the contention that the two spheres were not adequately kept separate by the bill. Following amendments in the Lords, many of these difficult issues were resolved (see pages 486–7).

The Nineties and after: problems and solutions

Parliament

In the UK, the 1990s witnessed a very thoroughgoing revision of the procedures for dealing with allegations of improper behaviour, devising new institutions which (it was hoped) would simultaneously carry credibility with the public while respecting parliamentary rights. The sequence of events began in 1991 with committal proceedings against a Member on a common law charge of bribery for actions alleged to have been done not as part of 'proceedings in Parliament' (in respect of which Article IX of the Bill of Rights would have been a complete protection) but in his capacity as constituency Member. The action was unprecedented in any UK jurisdiction (though not elsewhere). It was argued that a Member of Parliament was not a public officer and so could not be guilty of common law corruption, and also that impropriety of this kind, if it had occurred, should be tried by the House and not the courts. The trial judge decided that it would be a common law offence for a Member of Parliament to accept a bribe. On the facts, however, he directed to the jury to find the Member's co-defendants not guilty. The Crown did not offer any evidence against the Member and he was acquitted.

Next, in 1994, allegations were made that certain Members had accepted payment for the tabling of parliamentary questions. The Committee of Privileges found that the conduct of two of the Members fell short of the standard the House was entitled to expect and a third had acted unwisely. The House suspended and reprimanded the two Members whose actions had attracted the more damaging conclusions. As stated below, one of the outcomes of the case was the setting in motion of a thoroughgoing process of scrutiny of the standard of ethics prevailing in public life as a whole, including Parliament.

The temperature in the media and among the public had now risen appreciably, and change was put in hand. An issue first raised by a Royal Commission in 1976 lay at the heart of any solution: should Members of Parliament be amenable to the common law if they were unwise enough to accept bribes to affect them in the discharge of their parliamentary duties? Though no one could produce any compelling evidence that instances of parliamentary corruption were rife and there were no known cases of an allegedly corrupt Member escaping prosecution through the loophole of Article IX of the Bill of Rights, the official Committee on Standards in Public Life thought the matter should be clarified by the Law Commission. The parliamentary Joint Committee on Parliamentary Privilege recommended that parliamentarians should be subject to the criminal law relating to bribery; evidence of words or actions in Parliament should be admissible in courts hearing such charges, notwithstanding the inroad such a change would make on Article IX (see page 484). The Lords Committee on the Constitution agreed. A draft Bill brought forward in 2003 proposed that Members should be within the scope of the statutory offence of corruption, and that if in proceedings against a Member accused of such actions evidence of proceedings in Parliament was thought essential by the prosecuting authority, Article IX should not apply.

The Joint Committee which considered the draft Corruption Bill, like its predecessor on Parliamentary Privilege, preferred the matter to be dealt with in the much wider context of a Parliamentary Privilege Bill. So far, however, there has been no sign of that much-to-be-desired text. The Joint Committee on the Bill was wisely unsympathetic to the unexampled breadth of the government proposals. Lords and Members should be brought within new statutory corruption legislation, but Article IX should, they proposed, be waived only as to words spoken or acts performed by a person alleged to have committed a corruption offence 'as a Member of Parliament' in proceedings against that person for that offence, or in proceedings arising out of the same facts. The Bill was not proceeded with. At the end of 2005 the government brought forward a Consultation Paper seeking a basis for progress, in particular agreeing to what the Joint Committee suggested. In March 2009, another draft bill appeared, containing provisions stipulating that Article IX should not prevent any words spoken in proceedings in Parliament (or any other conduct forming part of such proceedings) from being admitted in a court which tried a Member or a related person for a bribery offence. 'Related person' meant someone against whom charges are laid arising out of the same facts.

Of course a corrupt parliamentarian should not be able to shelter behind a rule of law which confers a unique status on Parliament at large in the general public interest. On the other hand, the furore in spring 2009 over Members' expenses claims should not obscure the fact that policing of parliamentary standards has—as subsequent paragraphs will show—made great strides since the mid-1990s. There is at least an argument that the latest draft bill was a cure too drastic for a serious illness—corruption—of which there were few or no visible symptoms. Self-regulation of improper conduct in financial matters having however been substantially modified by the introduction of an external element (page 528), it would not be surprising if the battle for the absolute protection of Article IX and parliamentary trial of more serious charges were lost.

An official Committee was set up in 1994 by the then Prime Minister to examine current concerns about standard of conduct of all holders of public office, including their financial arrangements, with a view to recommending changes 'to ensure the highest standards of propriety in public life'. The following year, the Committee reported on the paid outside interests of Members, and that report in its turn was sent to a Commons select committee, broadly tasked to adapt the rules and procedures of the House to the official Committee's conclusions.

From the select committee's report flowed the major elements in the current system. A Register of Interests was introduced, intended

> to provide information of any pecuniary interest or other material benefit which a Member receives, which might reasonably be thought by others to influence his or her actions, speeches or votes in Parliament, or actions taken in his or her capacity as a Member, and any other information as the House may from time to time require.

A Code of Conduct for Members of the Commons was devised. A Commissioner for Standards was appointed, and the four-centuries-old Privileges Committee became the Committee on Standards and Privileges.

All the major elements in the current system will be subject to change when the Parliamentary Standards Act is brought into force. At the same time, it is reasonable to speculate that the outline, even if not the detail, of the soon-to-be-superseded arrangements will survive into the new regime, despite the radical change in organizational responsibility. There follows a sketch of the present situation, followed under each of the four headings by a brief account of the changes effected by the Act.

The Register of Members' Financial Interests has been managed so as to provide continuously updated information on the pecuniary interests or other material benefit—broken down into ten categories—which might be thought to influence Members' conduct in Parliament or contributions to debate.[7] These categories cover remunerated employment, office or profession, personal services to clients which arise out of membership of the House, financial sponsorship amounting to more than £1,000 from a single source, gifts, overseas visits paid for by third parties, large shareholdings, and land yielding substantial income. Even if a Member enjoys no financial benefit from an otherwise prohibited source, he or she must register an interest which falls within the main purposes of the Register. The Register has been compiled by the Commissioner's office, on the basis of returns by Members. A printed Register has been published annually and an updated web-based version every two sitting weeks.

There have been many alterations since the beginning of the Register (see above) as experience has dictated how clarity may be improved without loss of rigour. Partners were added to spouses as third parties whose interests demanded registration in appropriate cases. Rules inhibiting Members in their contributions to debate were relaxed, as the impact of the associated interests or connections were reassessed. Since the spring of 2009, Members have been under an obligation in respect of directorships, remunerated employment, and services to clients to give the Registrar details of the precise amount of each individual payment received, the nature of the work performed and the number of hours worked, and the name of the person making the payment. The previous limitation that declaration had to be made only when an interest derived from or arose out of membership of the House has been jettisoned. There will now be complete transparency so far as non-parliamentary paid employment is concerned.

The Parliamentary Standards Act provides that the Code of Conduct to be drawn up by the Authority created under the Act must require Members to register financial information in a Register maintained by the Authority. Though no details are given in the Act itself, the Code when drafted must be approved by the Commons, so that the House will have a limited input into its requirements. What is to be the future of the other registers—for lobbyists, Members' staff and certain others—is uncertain. For the time being it seems they will remain the responsibility of the House's Standards Commissioner, though power exists in the Act for them to be transferred to that of the new Authority.

Secondly, a Code of Conduct was agreed by the House of Commons in 1996. A revised version was published in 2005. Its prescriptions for public and parliamentary but not private and personal life are in general terms, and rely in part on the principles of conduct identified as critical by the Committee on Standards in Public Life—selflessness, integrity, objectivity, accountability, openness, honesty, and leadership. When personal and public interests clash, the former should give way to the latter. The Code as a whole was intended to be a 'framework within which acceptable conduct should be judged'. Breach of the Code amounts to a broad verdict of 'conduct unbecoming'. Members are 'at all times [to] conduct themselves in a manner which will tend to maintain and strengthen the public's trust and confidence in the integrity of Parliament, and never undertake any action which would bring the House of Commons or its Members generally into disrepute'.

The Code of Conduct under the new Act, on the drafting of which the Speaker, the Leader of the House, the Standards and Privileges Committee, and Members at large are to be consulted, will presumably supersede the financial aspects of the present Code, leaving the remainder untouched. As will be the case with the registers (above), the outcome will at least initially be a more complex system than before.

Accompanying the present Code is a more detailed Guide to the Rules governing the Conduct of Members, substantially revised in March 2009 to relieve Members from the responsibility under House rules of reporting to the Registrar and also (under statute) to the Electoral Commission, with whose reporting limits House rules have generally been aligned. Neither the Code nor the Guide read like statute. The Guide explains that the reporting requirement covers not only gifts given gratis but those available at a cost below that at which they are generally available to the public. Even if specific gifts are below the threshold, where the cumulative value of all such from the same source in a calendar year exceeds the critical 1 per cent, all need to be registered. Tickets for sporting or cultural events received by another person together with or on behalf of the Member should be registered as if they had been received by the Member. Shareholdings must be declared if they amount to more than 15 per cent of the issued share capital of a company. Land and property (other than in connection with a Member's residence) must be declared if the income therefrom is more than the official parliamentary salary. Details must be given of overseas visits where the cost was met by a person or authority other than the Member or HM government.

Lobbying for reward or consideration is absolutely prohibited when the benefit sought is to accrue exclusively to a person or body from whom the Member receives or expects to receive benefit (the advocacy rule). Previous draconian restrictions on when Members with registrable interests might or might not initiate proceedings have been eased, but the Standards Committee said that it would consider it a 'very serious breach of the rules' if there was failure to register or declare an interest closely relevant to a matter initiated by the relevant Member.

Declaration of interests in debate, for the benefit of the Member's colleagues and the public, should be made in such a way as to allow the nature of the interest to be understood. They must go beyond the demands of the Register, taking into account past, present, and future expectations. There are means of identifying registered interests against Members' names on the House's printed papers when they give notices of motions or other business.

Third, a Parliamentary Commissioner for Standards was first appointed by the House of Commons in 1995, following the report of the select committee on Standards in Public Life. Following disputes which arose at the end of the term of office of the second Commissioner in 2001, the Standards and Privileges Committee, the House of Commons Commission, and the House accepted the suggestion of a non-renewable term for the Commissioner, to be fixed at five years. Only a resolution of the House following a report from the Committee could end the Commissioner's term of office before then.

However detailed and well thought out may be the details of registration and its policing, their achievements will be less than they might be if the culture of the institution and the attitudes of those subject to regulation do not reinforce the intention of the rules. To that important end, the Commissioner's office has given much attention, especially at the beginning of a new Parliament, to promulgating and explaining the values of the regulatory regime. The Commissioner does not investigate possible wrongdoing on his or her own initiative: a complaint must first be received. Anyone may submit a complaint, and there is no pre-authorization process linked to Members of the House. Concern at the way a complaint might be taken up in the press immediately it had been received by the Commissioner so that the Member complained of was equally speedily tried and condemned by the media was met by changes in the Commissioner's procedure.

Not all complaints are well founded, sufficiently specific, or within the Commissioner's power to investigate. If they raise issues of political views or complain about constituency casework, they are not relevant to the Commissioner's responsibilities. A number regularly fail because they do not name a specific Member. Some, having surmounted these hurdles, are winnowed out at the preliminary stage. Details are to be found in Table 11.1 in the Annex.

In the case of those complaints which appear to have merit, it is the task of the Commissioner to report to the Committee the facts as they appear after investigation and to offer a conclusion on whether, on these facts, the Code of Conduct has been breached.

The Commissioner has no independent power to compel the attendance of witnesses sub poena, though the Committee on Standards in Public Life and successive Commissioners thought that the office should have such authority. The change has not however been felt appropriate, first because the Committee—which itself has the power—has expressed its willingness to use it in cooperation with the investigations of the Commissioner, and because to devolve the power of a committee on an officer of the House would require primary legislation, which presumably must await any much broader statutory revision of parliamentary privilege. Reports of the Commissioner are not published on his own authority, but annexed to those of the Committee. It is therefore entirely clear on what basis the Commissioner has reached his conclusions, and what view the Committee has formed of his advice. Differences of opinion, and there have been differences, are not concealed. For these and reasons mentioned later, it would be hard for a government or any other authority effectively to influence the outcome of a complaint, either before the Committee or before the House.

The Parliamentary Standards Act provides for the appointment of an independent Commissioner for Parliamentary Investigations. The Commissioner will be appointed by Her Majesty on an Address by the House of Commons, having been selected by the Speaker with the agreement of a Speaker's Committee (see page 143). There is to be a fixed term of up to five years, and the Commissioner will be paid and resourced by the Authority created by the Act. He or she will investigate alleged irregularities in payment of allowances and failure to comply with the code of conduct relating to financial interests under procedures laid down by the Parliamentary Standards Authority. In appropriate cases, the new Commissioner will report his findings directly to the Standards and Privileges Committee. The continuing role of the Parliamentary Commissioner for Standards, an officer of the House of Commons, will presumably extend only to non-financial aspects of the propriety of a Member's conduct.

Finally, the Commons Committee on Standards and Privileges, which currently oversees the Commissioner and the Guide, is in most respects a select committee like any other. There are ten Members nominated by the House. Unlike any other committee, however, there has been since May 2004 no government majority. The Committee also possesses two unique powers—to order the attendance of any Member on its own authority without invoking that of the House, and to refuse to allow proceedings to which the public are admitted to be broadcast. When a complaint involving incorrect or defective reporting of a Member's registrable interests or 'other aspects of the propriety of a Member's conduct' reached the Committee, accompanied by the Commissioner's report on the complaint, the Committee usually proceeded to hear written and oral evidence from those principally concerned, and reported its decisions to the House, with whom the final word remains. Since much of this sensitive part of the Committee's work is quasi-legal, the three government law officers who are Members of the House may attend to give advice, but not to make motions or vote. Speaker's Counsel, an official of the House, is also available to help.

The Standards Committee's work comprised a steady stream of regulatory cases. (A breakdown is at Table 11.2 in the Annex.) The nature of the complaints has varied over time. Initially, the prevailing concern was that questions were being asked in return for considerations. Next, Members were accused of not registering interests, and after that that parliamentary allowances were being abused. In 2007–8, many cases which came before the Committee related to the newly introduced Communications Allowance, intended to allow Members to communicate proactively with their constituents in parliamentary but not party-political or campaigning issues. No fewer than nine inquiries of the Committee concerned charges that it had been used improperly, and the Commissioner assisted in clarifying the boundaries.[8] The Commissioner was recently given power to investigate misuse of facilities, and in that context problems arose over allegations that the House dining rooms had been used to entertain visitors with party advantage in mind. An area of particular sensitivity, and one where the rules at Westminster were more relaxed than in Washington, has recently been the employment by Members of those who are related to them by blood or marriage. Until relatively recently, the furthest that the Rules demanded was that Members should ask themselves certain questions before deciding to employ a relative. Following a high-profile case in 2008, however, there was a general acceptance that rules would have to be tightened and procedures made more transparent. Of the options available, the Standards and Privileges Committee chose a compulsory entry in the Register of Members' Financial Interests giving the name of the employee, his or her relationship to the employing Member, and the nature of the employment, 'where the terms of the employment might be influenced by virtue of the existence of a personal relationship to the parties'.[9] (See also page 145.)

At the end of the process, the Committee might recommend that a Member should apologize in and to the House for whatever fault had been found. The apology was offered—no doubt not the easiest of interventions—the Register was altered if necessary, and the matter was formally at an end. In other cases, the House, on the recommendation of the Standards and Privileges Committee, suspended the Member for a specified period during which he or she was not entitled to receive salary. The periods of suspension have varied from three days to a month. (See Table 11.3 in the Annex.)

The Committee operates in a non-partisan way. Its chairman is by convention a senior Member of the Opposition party. There is no written requirement that this should be so. The Committee itself would have liked one, but the government preferred to rely on informal agreement between the parties.

Accusations of political partisanship have been made, though they are not common. The chairman of the Standards Committee told the House in 2002–3:[10]

> My firm view is that when Members enter Committee room 13, they leave behind ... their party affiliations. A fly on the wall would find it impossible to deduce party affiliations from the contributions that Members make. It is a matter of considerable pride to me that our key decisions are always unanimous.

This robust defence of impartiality across the political divide is amply borne out by the facts. Between 2000–1 and the summer of 2008, the Committee made forty-eight reports into complaints against one or more Members. A number of those against whom complaints came before the Committee were ministers (including the Deputy Prime Minister), two were Leaders of the Opposition, and there was one report into the Conduct of Mr Speaker.[11] Only one report in that period (which in the event did not involve a frontbencher) was other than unanimous. Even where the Commissioner's conclusions were not wholly accepted by the Committee—the Eighth Report of the Committee on Standards in Public Life in 2002 pointed to 'a handful' of cases over the previous three years where they did not reach the same conclusion and there has been one since then—there is no evidence of political bias. Although nearly all the Members complained of in the disagreed cases were ministers or Leader of the Opposition, the members of the Committee were unanimous in the conclusion they reached. It seems a conclusive answer to charges of systemic party bias.

Insulating the Committee from external pressure in the shape of informal personal lobbying was identified by the Committee on Standards in Public Life as an important factor in the preservation of its impartial status. The Standards and Privileges Committee in 2003 had no evidence that lobbying had been in practice a serious problem. The Code of Conduct expressly forbids lobbying the Committee 'in a manner calculated or intended to influence their consideration of a complaint' of a breach of the Code (see page 526). Allied to that injunction is another imposing a duty on Members to cooperate with the Commissioner in his or her investigations. There have been instances where the Committee has had occasion to condemn (for example) a refusal to answer further questions from the Commissioner as not in accordance with the duty of accountability under the Code. The current Code now includes an explicit requirement that Members should cooperate, at all stages, with any investigation into their conduct by or under the authority of the House.

Under the new dispensation, it seems likely that the Committee would dispose of disciplinary cases based on the findings of the new Commissioner in much the same way as it did before the enactment of the Parliamentary Standards Act.

In the Lords, there was until 1995 no specific rule on personal interests. Lords spoke always on their personal honour. A decision to speak or vote where a financial or other personal concern might be involved was a matter for individual decision. In that year, a resolution of the House codified the practice about personal honour, and added that Lords should never accept financial inducements as an incentive or reward for exercising parliamentary influence. No Commissioner was appointed to accompany the change, but a Register was established, in which qualifying interests had to be declared, and allegations of failure to abide by the rules or to register interests were matters for the Committee for Privileges.

Towards the end of 2000, the Committee on Standards in Public Life[12] recommended that the Lords should agree a Code based on the existing canons for Lords' behaviour and on the same broad principles on which the Commons Code rests. Registration of all relevant interests (which had previously been in part voluntary) should become mandatory. In 2001, the Lords agreed such a Code. Complaints of non-compliance may be considered by the subcommittee on Lords Interests appointed by the Committee for Privileges. In any investigation, Lords are entitled to safeguards as rigorous as those in the courts or in the disciplinary codes of public bodies. There is a right of appeal from the subcommittee to the full committee, and the latter makes a report to the House. The arrangements in the Lords came into play in early 2009, when certain charges of accepting cash in return for action in their capacity as legislators were levelled against four Lords. Not only the climate of regulation but the inability, short of statute, to expel any Lord found to have acted improperly came under criticism. The matter was referred to the Interests subcommittee and the Privileges Committee was tasked to review the Code of Conduct, the consultancy rules, and the position regarding sanctions if an offence were to be proved. The Committee for Privileges cleared one of the Lords, invited another (whom they judged had demonstrated an inappropriate attitude to the rules regarding conduct) to make a personal statement to the House, and concluded that the remaining two Lords had failed to act on their personal honour in breach of the Code of Conduct. The Committee invited the House to suspend the two Lords from the service of the House until the end of the session.[13]

At Westminster, there is a clear lack of the deployment of the ethics sword in a wider 'culture of corruption' by which Washington is troubled. There is less party political pressure on the system itself in the UK than in the USA, and the rules are consequently more stable. On the other hand, Congress has been spared the trauma of the parliamentary expenses crisis in the spring of 2009, from which came substantial modification (at least) of the power of self-regulation, the consequences of which will take many years to tease out. Perhaps the best advice to both Houses of Parliament was given by the third President of the United States, who was quoted in the Lords debate on the report of the

Committee for Privileges: 'When a man assumes a public trust, he should consider himself as public property.'[14]

Congress

In 1989 a bipartisan Task Force on Ethics was established in the House of Representatives to conduct a comprehensive review of the rules concerning gifts, honoraria, outside earned income, financial disclosure, and the use of official resources, as well as issues relating to ethics committee procedures. An important motivation for enactment of these reforms was the cost-of-living-driven need for salary adjustments for Members and other senior government officials, an end only politically attainable with the inclusion of certain trade-offs. The final report of that bipartisan task force was enacted into law as the Ethics Reform Act of 1989 and included a total ban on honoraria, revisions to the outside earned income limits, new post-employment restrictions, changes in gift and travel limits, and financial disclosure revisions. The Act also accomplished procedural changes affecting the Committee on Standards of Official Conduct—its size, time limits for investigations of alleged violations, and bifurcation of the investigative and adjudicative functions of the committee.

Much of the work of the Committee on Standards of Official Conduct is advisory and is done by an Office of Advice and Education, created by the Ethics Reform Act of 1989 and in existence since 1991 to provide information and guidance to Members, officers, and employees of the House. This advisory role is intended to provide information in advance of contemplated conduct which, if undertaken, would either violate a specific standard of conduct prohibited by rule or law, or might not at all times reflect creditably upon the House, that is, would constitute an appearance of impropriety.

In 1992 the House Committee on Standards of Official Conduct published the *House Ethics Manual* (republished in 2008), which contained the history of ethics changes in the House and a compilation of statutes and codes of conduct applicable to the official conduct of Members, officers, and employees of the House. A similar history of the evolution of the ethics process in the Senate is contained in the *Senate Ethics Manual* (2003).

In 1997 the House leadership created an informal bipartisan Ethics Reform Task Force which was mandated to review the entire House ethics process. After a seven-month study, the House adopted with amendments that task force's recommendations, including the elimination of the ability of private citizens to file complaints against Members and staff with the Committee on Standards of Official Conduct. Instead the rules now require that complaints only be filed by Members or by private citizens but after a Member certifies that the information is submitted in good faith and warrants consideration by the committee. Of course, informal allegations of misconduct may always be called to the attention of the committee.

In the House, the party caucuses confer certain privileges on some of their members by virtue of seniority or other selections to leadership or committee positions of influence. Since the ethics process has been formalized in the latter part of the twentieth century, caucus rules have been amended to provide sanctions against party members who derive such positions from nominations of the caucus. Under both Republican and

Democratic party caucus rules, Members elected by the party to House leadership positions or to chairmanships or ranking Minority positions on committees or subcommittees are required to temporarily 'step aside' upon felony indictment for any crime in Federal or State court. Conviction for such felonies or censure by the House based on that conduct result in removal from those positions by the House upon recommendation of the respective party caucus. Acquittal, dismissal of the charges, or their reduction to a misdemeanour level restore the presumption of innocence and reinstate that Member to the committee position in question.

All committee assignments derive under House rules from party conference or caucus recommendations, and either caucus may vote at any time to 'remove' a Member which it had nominated from a committee, even prior to an indictment, regardless of an automatic step-aside of a chairman or ranking Minority member, where adverse publicity or political reality so dictate. In 2006, the Democratic Caucus voted to recommend removal of Rep. William Jefferson from the Committee on Ways and Means and was then able to bring a removal resolution to the floor for immediate consideration as a privileged disciplinary matter.

In that regard, in 2005 House Majority Leader Tom DeLay was indicted by a State of Texas grand jury on felony counts of raising and funnelling ('laundering') illegal corporate campaign contributions through a political action committee on which he served as an adviser to State legislative candidates. Mr DeLay announced his temporary resignation as Majority Leader to the Republican Conference pursuant to a conference rule. No conference action of removal or acceptance was required. He was then temporarily replaced by the Majority Whip, the next highest-ranking Member elected by the conference. That temporary election was announced to the House by the Chair of the party conference. Before the beginning of the second session of the 109th Congress, Mr DeLay announced to the Republican Conference his permanent resignation as Majority Leader, based not merely on the pendency of the State criminal indictment but also upon guilty pleas of lobbyists admitting corrupt associations with his former staff. This resignation triggered elections within the party Conference of a new Majority Leader.

No automatic Standards Committee investigation is triggered by the operation of this party caucus rule. House rules regarding the initiation of ethics complaints were impacted by a complaint filed by a 'lame duck' (defeated) Member in the preceding Congress alleging some of the same facts as contained in these felony indictments of the former Majority Leader. At the beginning of the 109th Congress and in advance of these grand jury indictments, House rules were twice amended upon partisan Majority recommendation to address the automatic referral of a complaint, once filed, to an investigative subcommittee should the ethics committee be evenly split on the issue of whether to investigate. The fear within the Majority party caucus that the 'presumption of innocence' until proven guilty would be shifted, at least in public opinion, upon automatic referral of a complaint to an investigative subcommittee after forty-five days of bipartisan inaction, gave way after several months of severe press criticism to the realization that the rule requiring such automatic referral (which had been repealed) should be reinstated.

The 109th Congress in the year 2005 marked a significant departure from the bipartisan nature of all ethics rules changes prior to that time, as the partisan origin of the new rules was a major factor leading to their repeal shortly thereafter. The basic recurring uncertainty of the status and application of House ethics rules in the 109th Congress revealed that periodic bipartisan institutional review of process is to be preferred to partisan imposition of rules changes. In the 109th Congress, the reluctance of the Standards Committee to properly organize itself where Majority votes of the evenly divided panel were necessary, when viewed in the context of the pendency in State court of charges brought against a prominent member of one party, symbolized concerns about the ability of the House of Representatives to effectively assume its constitutional duty. In the 110th Congress, with a new House Majority, a partisan vote established an Office of Congressional Ethics on 11 March 2008. The origin of this change resulted from the inability of a bipartisan task force to recommend a proper formula for preliminary investigations of alleged improper conduct which could be forwarded to the evenly divided Standards Committee. That committee had not publicly initiated its own investigations, and the acrimonious debate on that occasion revealed the personal animosities which, even under rules requiring confidentiality, had diminished its effectiveness. The future effectiveness of the outside Office of Congressional Ethics will remain an important case study of the advisability of partisan changes in ethics rules. The irony of a partisan vote to create a non-partisan entity (under pressure from the press and public interest groups) to improve the effectiveness of a bipartisan standing committee, demonstrates the perception of the need to repair the ethics process in the House. (See also page 543.)

The fact that both parties have acknowledged the political potency of ethics issues as party strategies in advance of new elections, based upon past successes over fifteen years in bringing down prominent leaders as well as rank-and-file Members in the opposing party, and upon actual shifts of party majorities, suggests that this pattern of recrimination and leadership denigration will continue. Indeed in the 110th Congress the Minority Leader offered several resolutions as questions of privilege censuring the conduct of the Chairman of the Committee on Ways and Means even prior to a committee investigation for various financial irregularities. The potency of this strategy ('the culture of corruption') had an obvious impact on the changing of party majorities in the House in the 2006 elections. The unwillingness of the Standards Committee to undertake an investigation of the former Majority Leader while he remained a Member of the House until his resignation was some indication of the institutional non-viability of the ethics process and of the inability of the House to investigate its own Members and staff. The decision of the Standards Committee at the end of the 109th Congress to investigate the matter of the electronic messaging of sexually explicit messages on the eve of a Congressional election, had given some renewed credibility to the ability and willingness of a bipartisan Standards Committee to perform its proper function. While the allegations do not appear to have been politically initiated by the Minority party claiming 'a culture of corruption', but rather by that Member's own resignation belatedly forced by the Speaker and Majority party leaders, it was yet another recent example of the politicization of the ethical problems of one Member into allegations of mismanagement by the Majority party of the House. In the Foley case, the Minority member of the bipartisan oversight entity of the Page Program had not been notified of the allegations, and only the Majority party chairman of the Page Board took initial action to confront the offending Member without notifying the Standards Committee. This lapse was rebuked by the Standards Committee in its investigative subcommittee report.

The foregoing review of the history of the ethics process in the House (and the cited references to comparable efforts in the Senate) through 2008 indicates that both Houses have continuously refined and reorganized their internal review procedures since their inception in the 1960s in response to internal ad hoc reviews. Those internal steps were in turn inspired by media and other public scrutiny and served on at least one occasion as a trade-off in rationalization of Members' salary increase demands. In 1989 a political decision to increase Members'salary compensation came at the expense of new restrictions imposed on outside earned income, and disclosure of levels and sources of outside unearned income. As pressures for salary adjustments in the face of cost of living increases have emanated from within Congress, media and public interest group scrutiny has resulted in demands that Congress refocus on revisions of its ethical standards and on outside income availability. This is an acknowledgment of the full-time nature of a Member's office as well as political justification of the salary increases. The recent partisan changes in internal ethics rules have led to unforeseen consequences in the House. The Senate has continued to examine its ethics standards in a more bipartisan manner and has twice rejected establishment of an outside entity to forward complaints to its Ethics Committee, either out of deference to the effectiveness of that committee or because of the insular nature of that body.

Beyond the centuries-old British practice governing declaration of interests in debate (see page 522), and the House of Representatives rule since its inception precluding Members from voting where there is a direct personal or pecuniary interest, the responses of both systems toward internal self-regulation mechanisms have been similarly recent. This has been the inevitable result of the evolution of the role of legislators as full-time professionals. These internalized efforts at self-regulation must be measured against the utilization of independent external authority, be they 'commissioners' or 'independent counsel' working in cooperation with internal investigative committees or relying upon other branches of government to separately investigate and prosecute official misconduct in the courts.

While in the House of Commons the creation of a Commissioner of Standards working with and reporting to the select committee on Standards and Privileges has been institutionalized in recent years (see page 527), in the House of Representatives and in the Senate decisions on whether ethics committees should employ the services of outside ('independent') counsel have been ad hoc in nature and have depended upon the high-profile status of the Member (respondent) being investigated. Only recently has the House and its Committee on Standards of Official Conduct codified the committee's own ability to retain outside counsel by a majority affirmative vote.[15]

Critics have suggested that both committees have been unnecessarily reluctant since their creation to investigate and to discipline colleagues. However, discipline within each House of Congress is not the sole remedy toward the punishment of improper behaviour. Provisions have existed in House and Senate rules since the creation of the permanent ethics committees which permit them (with the approval of the House or by a two-thirds committee vote, or in the Senate by majority committee vote) to refer to appropriate Federal or State law enforcement authorities any substantial evidence of violation of a law applicable to official conduct which may have been disclosed in a committee investigation. In fact, several of the criminal laws of the United States enacted even prior to the creation of an ethics system in Congress specifically address corrupt conduct by public officials, including Members of Congress, and reflect the acknowledgement that under the United States system of separation of powers, Congress may enact rules and law enabling the other branches of government to be involved in the investigation and prosecution of misconduct so long as not violative of Members' constitutional privilege against being questioned in another place for Speech or Debate (legislative activity)—contrast with Parliament's reluctance to enact law specifically applicable to parliamentary misconduct to permit prosecution in the courts.

Congressional internal ethics enforcement has been increasingly linked over recent years to the public's perception of wrongdoing. Conflicts of interest have been defined as the 'grey area' between activities which are unmistakably appropriate and those which are clearly illegal. Currently rules and laws defining and regulating conflicts of interest have been supplemented to extend to the 'appearance of impropriety'. Under this test, commentators suggest that it is no defence that the act is legal, but whether in the mind of a reasonable observer an inference of wrongdoing is created. The Code of Official Conduct in the House embodies this standard of `appearance of impropriety' by requiring conduct which at all times reflects creditably on the House and which adheres to the spirit and the letter of the rules of the House and its committees. An attempt at the beginning of the 109th Congress by the Majority party caucus to remove this 'appearance' standard and to retain only the prohibition against conduct which violated a specific law or rule was not pursued following intensive Minority party, media, and public-interest group criticism and pressure.[16]

In 1997 the House by unanimous consent imposed a formal moratorium on filing or processing ethics complaints and on raising certain questions of privilege with respect to official conduct, in the expectation that a bipartisan ethics task force would recommend rules changes relating to the ethics process. The moratorium terminated just prior to House adoption of the recommendations of the task force with certain amendments.[17] This formal order of the House is to be distinguished from so-called 'moratoria' or unwritten understandings negotiated by party leaders with respect to filings by sitting Members of ethics complaints in a particularly partisan atmosphere. Standards Committee rules restrict filing of ethics complaints within sixty days of an election of a sitting Member, in order to minimize the politicization of complaints on the eve of an election. To date, this threat of retribution at the party level and Members' tacit declinations to file complaints may still reflect a remnant of Speaker Sam Rayburn's observation in the 1950s that traditionally in the House both parties respect the need for some level of tolerance. However, there has followed the re-emergence of ethics challenges, to be waged through the press, through filed complaints, and through ad hoc challenges as questions of privilege in plenary session focused on Majority leadership conduct. Both parties currently ponder recent successes in prior Congresses using ethics allegations in criticism of a Majority party which is managing the House.

In the 108th Congress, there was press speculation that a bipartisan informal 'moratorium' had been arranged by party leaders to avoid a proliferation of politically motivated charges and counter-charges filed by Members of both parties leading up to the 2004 election (allegations of substantial misconduct in the form of complaints to be filed by Members were, critics argued, being suppressed under this leadership-negotiated understanding). It was temporarily disrupted by an ethics complaint filed near the end of that Congress against the Majority Leader by a Minority Member, coinciding with pendency of a judicial proceeding prompting the Standards Committee deferral of a concurrent investigation, until his subsequent resignation from the House mooted committee jurisdiction altogether. A further investigation of that and other allegations involving the Majority Leader (improper acceptance of gifts from a lobbyist) could have been re-instituted by the Standards Committee in the subsequent Congress but for his resignation. Also, the staying power of any informal moratorium against filing of other complaints may have been temporarily minimized in light of the success of Minority party allegations of corruption within the Majority leadership—a public issue leading up to the election. The election in 2006 secured a new House Majority for the first time in twelve years, and the 'culture of corruption' theme was one of several decisive issues in the campaign. Nevertheless the return of an informal 'moratorium' on ethics complaints again became the subject of press speculation in 2007–8, leading to renewed demands for establishment of an outside Office of Congressional Ethics to conduct preliminary investigations, in order to reinvigorate the ethics process.[18]

This dilemma is not entirely unique to the House, as in the Senate conflict of interest (stock ownership in companies affected by pending legislation) charges against the Majority Leader in the 108th Congress were pursued by the Securities and Exchange Commission, and were characterized as Majority party 'corruption' highlighted as a campaign issue by the Minority party. From joint public statements by the Minority Leaders of the House and Senate, it is clear that this matter was not confined as a campaign issue to either House alone. Unlike the House, however, the Senate has not viewed its ethics process as dysfunctional.

Also, whenever a criminal investigation by prosecutors or another committee's oversight investigation into improper lobbying activity develops credible evidence of corrupt conduct potentially involving a 'quid pro quo' for legislative activity by a Member or employee in return for financial campaign contributions or personal gifts, that matter may become the basis of a complaint or an ethics committee-initiated investigation. It may no longer be possible to avoid a separate House or Senate ethics inquiry where the implicated Member, officer, or employee has not resigned so as to terminate the committee's jurisdiction. (Former UK Members of Parliament may be charged with offences involving parliamentary standards. The Standards and Privileges Committee looked into a complaint against one former Member who by then was a member of the House of Lords; and there are other cases. No sanction of course can be levied in such cases.)

In an era of extraordinary political contributions to legislators' campaign funds, together with legislators' agreeing to perform legislative acts favoured by special lobbying interests, the question of a 'quid pro quo'—a financial contribution in return for a legislative favour—and the necessary nexus in terms of corrupt intent in order to establish an ethics or criminal violation, remain a recurring issue in the press and in the public mind. Also, the perception of corruption besmirching the reputations of Members of Congress has translated into 'reform' efforts begun in the 109th Congress to address special-interest access and influence. The House in the 110th Congress adopted several rules limiting Member and staff access to gifts, meals, and travel offered by lobbyists. The solution to this problem and its impact on the credibility of elected public officials (given the ever-increasing costs of waging successful political campaigns), and on time available to Members to address public issues through oversight and legislation, is a central challenge confronting the contemporary American body politic. Whether campaign finance reform—to limit the costs of pursuit of public office—will become inextricably linked to the need to eliminate corrupt influences on Members and staff in Congress remains to be resolved.

Revelations in 2006 of a lobbyist's admitted criminal behaviour brought new attention to the activities of lobbyists, an increasing number of whom are former Members or former staff with special access. The manifest impact of those charges on the party's Majority to Minority status in part resulted from increased public awareness of the insidious effects of money in politics. The role of Congressional staff who have received gifts from lobbyists and have then entered private sector employment arranged by those lobbyists focused additional attention on the inordinate degree of influence certain staff are permitted to exert in policy formulation in responses to special-interest concerns. The so-called 'K Street Project', whereby Majority Congressional leaders have openly importuned lobbyist firms to hire former Congressional staff, under pressure to employ Majority party persons, who will in turn have special access to Majority Members of Congress and who will then participate in fund-raising efforts on their behalf, was rationalized as a reaction to the forty-year accumulation of lobbyists' influence under a different Majority party. Following the 2006 election shifting majority control, Members' threats of official retaliation against private firms that hire employees who do not share the Members' partisan political affiliation—'K Street Project'—were specifically made a violation of the Code of Conduct in the House. Nevertheless, this practice highlights the inexorable connection between two constitutionally protected interests—the right of citizens to petition Congress for redress of grievances (and to compensate those who do so on their behalf), and the restriction in the 1st Amendment on Congress against passing any law restricting freedom of speech (the spending of funds for campaigns), and the influence of money in furtherance of both protected activities. For further discussion of Speech or Debate constitutional protection against release of Member's testimony before Ethics Committee, see Chapter 10 on Privileges and Contempt at page 504.

Approaches to the issue of lobbyists' influence in the immediate wake of the 2006 lobbying scandal included House rules changes further restricting former Members' access to the floor and to the Members' gymnasium, and a requirement for the public listing of 'earmarks' added in conference to spending and tax bills (see pages 282, 538). Approaches requiring statutory enactment (to regulate outside persons) finalized in the 110th Congress included restrictions in law extending from one year to two the time before which former Members and Congressional staff may register as lobbyists, and further restrictions on campaign contributions.

Other rule changes in the House at the beginning of the 110th Congress—totally banning lobbyist gifts (previously permitted if valued under $50), meals and private travel (including access to corporate jets, except to one-day events connected to official duties) provided to Members, requiring pre-certification of permissible travel by the Standards Committee, prohibiting the trading of earmarks for votes, requiring Members to disclose their earmark requests and certify that they and their spouses have no personal financial interest in the request—were adopted as prohibitions on Member and staff behaviour, and did not require statutory enactment. Separate Senate consideration of comparable rules changes was in the context of legislation[19] designed to regulate both internal Senate and external lobbyist behaviour. It enabled the Senate to consolidate internal and external regulation into one vehicle and to avoid separate consideration and clotures.

Also, House rule changes further requiring identification in accompanying reports of earmarks in Appropriation, tariff and tax bills providing funding for specific projects or benefits for ten or fewer persons, and permitting a separate vote where points of order are waived against this publication requirement were adopted in the House in the 110th Congress as recommended by the Majority party and supported by a bipartisan vote. Ironically, as the House imposed additional constraints on its Members through the Code of Conduct to separate them from lobbyists' influence by banning gifts, meals, and certain travel, and to disclose permitted activity, the result may be greater lobbyist attendance at legitimate fund-raising events to compensate for diminished special access, with the result that lobbyist contributions to campaigns will proliferate even further and will intersect even more readily with discussions of policy. The publication of this work will never coincide with the finality of legislative efforts aimed at addressing such conduct, as the remaining permissible influence of money in politics will transcend such attempts and will remain constitutionally protected.

This discussion reveals the political and constitutional significance of matters of Members' official misconduct, both in terms of pressures on and within the House to punish its Members for disorderly behaviour and, as a matter of separation of powers, in terms of the extent to which each House may forgo or share its sovereign responsibility under the Constitution to permit other forums, Federal or State, to investigate and prosecute sitting Members. It also reveals the basic dilemma which emanates from the 1st Amendment to the Constitution, namely that 'Congress shall make no law abridging the right of the people to petition the Government for a redress of grievances'. If the people cannot be denied the right of petition to the Legislative and Executive branches of government, it follows that they cannot be denied the right to compensate for their services those who petition or 'lobby' on their behalf, and that those who are compensated for their lobbying activities must be assured access to public officials to present their petitions.

Members of Congress, unless immunized by the Speech or Debate Clause of the Constitution, are subject to the same penalties under the criminal laws as are all other citizens. (The same is true of Members of Parliament, unless the activities at issue are covered by Article IX of the Bill of Rights; see page 486.) In addition to the rules of the House and Senate pertaining to official conduct of sitting Members, officers, and employees, the Federal criminal code (beyond provisions governing campaign activities described earlier in this chapter) addresses their conduct generically as public officials with respect to bribery, claims against the government, and public officials' actions as agents of foreign principals. The violations of such statutes may be considered by the ethics committees in recommending disciplinary actions to either House, but any discipline that either House invokes for a violation of such a statute is separate and distinct from sanctions that may be sought by law enforcement officials at the Federal or State level. Criminal prosecution may precede or follow committee investigation or House action in response to the same misconduct, and may proceed despite that respondent's resignation from the House or Senate. Criminal investigation by the Executive branch may even be initiated by a law mandating a specific inquiry. In 2008 the two Houses took the extraordinary step of directing by law the Justice Department to investigate the circumstances of a House Member's alleged involvement in a previous Congress in an improper change in an enrolled bill to benefit a campaign contributor, despite uncertainty as to whether the Standards Committee was already conducting an inquiry into the matter (see page 461).

Under current House rules, the Standards Committee may not investigate an alleged violation of a law, rule, regulation, or standard of conduct that was not in effect at the time of the alleged violation, or that occurred before the third previous Congress, unless such matters were directly related to an alleged violation that occurred in a more recent Congress. The question whether the offence was known to the offending Member's constituency at the time of his election may be relevant, as for example where conduct which had apparently been known to a constituency which continually elected the Member arguably militated against a punishment by the House for such prior misconduct. Expulsion thus far has been applied only with respect to offences occurring during terms of office (past or current) and not to action taken before their election to Congress.

Other rules applicable to the official conduct of Members in addition to the Code of Conduct (Rule XXIII) govern financial disclosure, the receipt of earned income, gifts and honoraria, and address the use of campaign funds, discrimination in employment, and use of mailings and stationery. Members are prohibited from retaining anyone under their payroll authority who does not perform duties commensurate with the compensation. The False Claims Act, which imposes liability on persons making claims against the government, prohibits a Member from authorizing salary payments if he knows such payments are for someone not doing official work, including false travel vouchers (for a parallel in the UK where statute law was not however involved, see page 528). Sexual harassment has been found to be a form of discrimination in employment prohibited by the Code of Conduct. Personal use of or failure to report receipt of campaign funds has likewise been found to be a violation.

A House rule places restrictions upon the amount of outside earned income for personal services a Member, officer, or employee may receive, limiting the aggregate amount to 15 per cent of annual Congressional salary per calendar year, but not applying to funds that are essentially a return on equity. This rule was imposed as an acknowledgement that covered positions are full-time public-service jobs demanding separation from time-conflicting employment for compensation.

In conjunction with this limitation on outside earned income, Members are also subject to various restrictions relating to their professional affiliations. House Members, for example, may not practise a profession for compensation that involves a fiduciary relationship, except for the practice of medicine. In 2005 the Senate voted that a Senator who had been a House Member and had practised medicine for compensation under that exception, was inhibited by Senate rules which provide no such explicit exception, such professional services being considered an improper distraction from full-time attention to the position of Senator.

Receipt of copyright royalties must first be approved by the Ethics Committee as coming under usual and customary contractual terms, and honoraria styled as 'royalties' accepted from special-interest groups for the sale of an authored book come within the limits on honoraria.

Acceptance of a gift is permitted only if it has an individual value of less than $50 and a cumulative value from any one source in the calendar year of less than $100. The value of perishable food sent to an office is allocated among the individual recipients and not to the Member. A Member has been censured for receiving gifts of money in the form of cheques marked 'loans' from a person with a direct interest in legislation before Congress.

Representatives and Senators are also prohibited from accepting honoraria, and payments to charity in lieu of honoraria are strictly limited by amount ($2000) and may not be received by a charity in which they have a beneficial interest.

Title I of the Ethics in Government Act of 1978, incorporated by reference as a standing rule (XXVI) of the House, requires Members, officers, and certain employees of the House (paid above a certain level) to file a publicly available annual Financial Disclosure Statement, as a way of assuring transparency in reporting of gifts, honoraria, and sources of outside earned and unearned income.

As further evidence of the recent imposition of partisan ethics rules changes, at the beginning of the 109th Congress the House, without bipartisan agreement, changed the rule which from 1997 to 2004 automatically referred a complaint to an investigative subcommittee of the Standards Committee after forty-five days, where both the chairman and ranking Minority member of the committee could not agree on the referral. Instead, under the new rule the complaint would not go forward to the investigative subcommittee unless both agreed on that referral or the committee or House voted by majority vote to initiate an investigation. Assuming the bipartisan composition of the committee as five Members from each party, at least one Member from the other party would be required to vote in favour of an investigation to present a six to four result in favour of going forward with an investigative subcommittee. This controversial change was premised on the assertion that a Member whose official conduct had been the subject of a filed complaint would suffer potentially irreparable political damage once the complaint was automatically forwarded to an investigative subcommittee in the event of a stalemate, that is, that Member would be 'hung out to dry' at least in public opinion, in disregard of a presumption of innocence. In the wake of the former Majority Leader's experience, that reversal of the presumption of innocence symbolized by the mere initiation of an investigation became the mantra for the Majority in support of the rule change. The rule change was short-lived, as the Majority leadership was accused of changing the rule to shield its own leader, resulting in repeal of the new rule a few months later. Following several months in 2005 when the Standards Committee was unable to organize and appoint staff due to tied votes within the committee, and amid much press attention which resonated with the public, the Committee on Rules reported and the House overwhelmingly adopted a privileged resolution repealing those rule changes and reverting to the rules of the prior Congress.[20] It remained to the Standards Committee to appoint staff, including counsel, by a bipartisan majority vote, in compliance with House rules requiring all House committees to collegially appoint staff by a vote of the committee. After further delay, some staff appointments were accomplished by a bipartisan vote (necessary under House rules since a majority vote on an evenly divided committee requires bipartisanship) but only after assurances that the committee's staff director would not be a partisan employee.

Since the 1980s, when Speaker Jim Wright's alleged improper receipt of royalties and other misuse of funds were revealed to the Standards Committee in 1989, forcing his resignation, political advantage is sought to be gained by raising issues of official Member misconduct. The Member most responsible for the instigation of those charges, Rep. Newt Gingrich of Georgia, parlayed that success and subsequent revelations of mismanagement by House leadership of the House Bank and Post Office in the early 1990s into achievement of the first majority in the House for his party (and the Speakership for himself) in forty years. The desire for retribution sparked by this tactic in the other party led to scrutiny of his own official conduct as Speaker (utilizing non-profit educational entities for partisan purposes and misleading the Standards Committee investigating that charge), and to his reprimand by a special Ethics Committee and the House four years later.[21] The political successes gained by the pursuit of such allegations of improper conduct lodged against high-ranking Members, including Speakers from each political party, have impacted on the diminishing importance of traditions of collegiality and mutual respect among Members.[22] A party strategy of personal recrimination in order to demonstrate the 'corruption' of opposing party leaderships has publicly emerged and has been regularized both inside and outside the House in debates, press statements and in fund-raising efforts. This has impacted on the willingness of both leaderships and all Members to conduct business in a civil, if not bipartisan, manner. With the ultimate political composition of the House at stake every two years, given the exceedingly close partisan majorities in each Congress since 1994, there resulted constant party fund-raising and reapportionment activity to maintain or reverse those narrow majorities, just as utilization of the ethics process to render additional incumbents vulnerable on election day has proliferated. Ethics complaints can be initiated not only by the complaint-filing process but also spontaneously as questions of privilege on the floor of the House by any Member. Thus the elements of surprise and resulting partisan publicity (while constituting expressions of legitimate institutional concern) have been additional unsettling factors leading to mutual distrust and recriminations among Members. The Minority Leaders of both parties have on several occasions offered resolutions as questions of privilege challenging the ethical propriety of actions taken by leaders of the Majority party, including charges of improper voting in the House and actions by prominent committee chairs.

At the end of the 108th Congress, the Committee on Standards of Official Conduct reported letters of admonition which found several manifestations of questionable official conduct by the Majority Leader. His perceived unwillingness to express adequate contrition for these activities, in the view of the Minority Leader, prompted her to rise in the House to a question of privilege to present without notice a resolution requesting the Committee to conduct a further investigation with the assistance of an independent counsel. While this unusual challenge to the propriety of a party leader's conduct by the opposition leader was not immediately successful, it symbolized the level of recrimination which can be utilized without advance notice when a Member, especially a party leader, feels particularly aggrieved. The Minority Leader renewed that procedural tactic without notice several times following the short-lived rule changes in the 109th Congress to allege the unfairness of those rules coupled with the intentional violation of House staffing rules by the new Standards Committee Chairman (unilateral dismissal of committee staff without a vote of the Committee, pending its reorganization). Those questions of privilege were also unsuccessful, but the Minority's insistence upon traditional bipartisan consultation in effecting ethics rule changes, coupled with allegations of intentional disobedience of current rules, enabled those issues to be immediately brought to the attention of the House and the public.

In the 109th Congress the Minority party's criticism of the Majority leadership's mismanagement of the legislative business of the House, including the conduct of electronic votes and the preparation of conference reports, has similarly given rise to questions of privilege based on allegations of deliberate violations of the Code of Conduct (clause 2 of Rule XXIV requiring that all Members adhere to the spirit and letter of the rules of the House). It has not been mere coincidence that all these votes have been coordinated with public relations efforts in the Congressional districts of some Members considered as vulnerable, to portray tacit support for a systemic institutional 'corruption' for having cast party-line votes on behalf of the Majority leadership. A more complete discussion of privilege as questions of the integrity and dignity of House proceedings appears in the chapter on Privilege and Contempt (see page 480).

In addition to concerns that the ethics process tends to become politicized by Members on the eve of elections, an often-repeated criticism from outside public interest groups has focused on the rule change in 1997 which required private citizens desiring to file a complaint with the committee to have a Member of the House certify in writing that the information is submitted in good faith and warrants consideration the committee. Private citizens or groups are thereby denied separate standing to file complaints, which must be examined by the committee. Combining this action with the now repealed step taken in 2005 to inhibit the automatic referral of a complaint to an investigative subcommittee, there had resulted media and public interest outcries against the increasing difficulty of initiation of ethics investigations.

Another standing rule imposes a term limit on the chairman of the Committee on Standards of Official Conduct to two Congresses and overall service on that committee to four consecutive Congresses. Press and outside public interest groups' insistence that the incumbent be returned as chairman, based on his demonstrated independence in examining the conduct of the Majority Leader, brought intensive political pressure on the Majority party to waive the term-limit rule. That waiver was not forthcoming. Another Majority party Member was elected chairman of the Standards Committee, and two other Majority Members replaced sitting Majority Members who, though their terms on the committee had not been exhausted, were perceived by the Majority leadership as too aggressive in their examination in the prior Congress of the conduct of the Majority Leader. Moreover, their new replacements had both substantially contributed to the legal defence fund of the Majority Leader (established to defray expenses incurred in subsequent investigations). The appearance of a conflict of interest, if not an actual conflict, could not have been more obvious, and led to successful demands for recusals in advance of possible further investigation of the Majority Leader.

As partisan and public focus on Members' conduct and on the ethics process intensified in the House in the 109th Congress and particularly as the traditional bipartisan review of ethics rules and organization of the Standards Committee and resulting investigations of individual Members foundered, some urged the establishment of a nonpartisan office comprising former Members or judges to examine complaints against sitting Members and current staff. This approach, while compelling in its effort to depoliticize the investigative process and while gaining new credibility in the wake of recent corrupt activity, arguably diminished the mandate of Article I, section 5 of the Constitution that 'each House may punish its Members for disorderly behavior'. Some argued that a delegation of that essential responsibility, even if limited to a preliminary or advisory role, and while consistent with the establishment of an independent Commissioner of Standards in the House of Commons, could, if implemented in lieu of a Standards Committee determination to initiate an investigation, be properly viewed as an abdication of a constitutionally prescribed responsibility.

The suggestion was made that a statutory approach must be utilized to create an outside entity consisting of non-Members, as internal rule changes within either body would not provide sufficient authority. In the 110th Congress, the Speaker and the Minority Leader announced the informal creation of a bipartisan task force of eight Members (four from each party) to examine whether the House should establish an independent investigative body to enforce House ethics rules, and to report its recommendations back to leadership by 1 May 2007. The task force's ultimate recommendation became partisan, as Minority Members did not wish to accord the Speaker a political victory and claimed to prefer reform within the Standards Committee itself (see page 533).

The resolution adopted in the 110th Congress on 11 March 2008 was recommended only by Majority party Members from the bipartisan feasibility task force. It established an Office of Congressional Ethics within the House, composed of non-Members who could not be registered lobbyists, to conduct preliminary investigations and to bring certain complaints to the attention of the Standards Committee. The Rules Committee sent that partisan recommendation to the floor for an up-or-down vote. Debate on that resolution focused on the question of including non-Members in the investigative process leading to discipline. It was the first time in the history of the House that non-Members comprised a House entity. Notwithstanding the partisan origin of the proposal, and the public nature of the Office's recommendations which could impact on the presumption of innocence prior to any Standards Committee investigation, the House established the Office as a free-standing resolution for the duration of the 110th Congress. The Senate had twice rejected a statutory approach on amendments to lobbying reform bills by decisive majorities in the 109th and 110th Congresses necessitating separate internal House action. In the Senate, the fact that outside complaints can be filed with its Select Committee on Ethics militated against that course of action.

James Madison in the Federalist Papers no. 51 acknowledged the need for the Legislative branch to be authorized by the Constitution to establish 'auxiliary precautions' as part of the obligation of each branch of the government to control itself. To that end, Article I authorizes each House to punish its Members for disorderly behaviour. This is not stated as a 'sole' authority (as is impeachment) but as an ultimate authority. There is no restriction against the creation of auxiliary entities to enable each House to better perform that function. Several States have successfully established commissions with ethics fact-finding, educational, and even disciplinary functions separate from and in addition to those of their legislatures.

The political reality of incumbent and institutional self-preservation partially explains Congressional reluctance to put in place these investigative entities beyond enforcement of the criminal code. In the modern context the mere publicity of an impending investigation 'hangs the potential respondent out to dry' and tends to reverse the presumption of innocence in the public mind. Some argue that while the Constitution requires each House to discipline its Members for disorderly behaviour, in performing that responsibility each House is also being asked to judge itself as an institution (a body of men and women), to determine whether the norms of acceptable behaviour applicable to that institution have been violated in the context of examination of the behaviour of a particular Member as compared to the behaviour of other Members. The Latin expression *nemo esse iudex in sua causa potest*—no one should be the judge in his own cause—raises the question whether either House is judging itself when it disciplines its Members.

Whether it becomes a conflict of interest for either House to discipline its Members when in so doing it puts its institutional norms themselves on trial, becomes a focus of reform efforts, premised on the acknowledgement that in political institutions Members depend on one another for their success. When the Member being judged argues that 'everyone does it', political pressures are brought to bear on the judges themselves to evaluate comparative conduct, and thus the integrity of the institution. To relieve the perception of this self-discipline arrangement as an inevitable conflict of interest in a political institution, the establishment of an independent fact-finding entity was adopted by the House as a compromise. A primary obstacle within the Congress remains the perception of the impact of such findings on a premature reversal of the presumption of innocence. Six non-Member commissioners were appointed, but the operation of the commission awaited re-establishment in the next Congress. There remained a tacit fear of partisan complaints being filed, and the inevitable publicity flowing from such filing, despite a general awareness that the Standards Committee itself had become dysfunctional.

In the 111th Congress, even as the Office of Congressional Ethics became operative, the Committee on Standards of Official Conduct was reconstituted, restaffed, and voted to investigate complaints filed against prominent Majority Members. They included allegations raised as questions of privilege (and referred by the Committee to the House) of tax evasion, lack of financial disclosure, and of quid pro quo 'earmarking' and other favoured legislative treatment in return for campaign contributions. In fact, a committee chairman publicly requested the Standards Committee to initiate an investigation of his own conduct once the allegations were known. The Minority was predictably continuing the 'culture of corruption' strategy utilized by the preceding Minority in an attempt to influence public opinion and election outcomes. Tensions between the new Office and the Standards Committee regarding the initiation of investigations emerged soon after their coexistence.

A reluctance to expose prominent and influential colleagues to political and personal criticism in advance of the completion of an investigation has to some extent given way in the wake of a majority-changing election, to a new acceptance of some institutional reform to avoid an adverse reflection on all incumbents. It is this political reality in an era of partisan use of ethics issues as an instrument for gaining majority control which became the basis for creation of the independent office to initiate internal investigations of Members' conduct. The propensity for radical and immediate reforms in the ethics area—such as an immediate complete ban on the acceptance of lobbyists' gifts by Members and employees imposed in 1995 (only to be relaxed several years later and then to be reimposed in 2007), suggests that at times the House has acted before it fully comprehended the impact of those changes on Members' conduct.

The success of the creation of a Commissioner for Standards in Public Life in the UK in minimizing ethics lapses has been suggested as a model in the USA. The greatest difference between the two political systems in this regard is the greater importance of campaign contributions as an incumbent protection in the USA compared with the UK. Any institutional safeguard beyond increased disclosure, having the ultimate tendency of lessening the availability of campaign money, is more likely to be resisted, especially where the factors of limited campaign periods, non-reliance on special-interest travel arrangements for Members to fund-raising events, and lower costs of televised campaigns which characterize the British election system are compared with the burgeoning impact of those factors in Congressional politics.

Where a Congress has finally adjourned so as to prevent plenary disposition of reports from the Ethics Committees, those Committees may nevertheless continue to deliberate ethics complaints against current Members and staff and may suggest sanctions against offending Members until the constitutional end of term (noon on 3 January). At the end of the 109th Congress, the House Standards Committee, through its chairman and ranking member acting jointly, criticized the conduct of two sitting Members (one of whom was not re-elected to the succeeding Congress) who had accepted improper gifts of travel expenses from a convicted lobbyist. While the House was not in session to vote to sanction those Members, and while the Committee has no delegated unilateral authority to impose fines as a punishment, the sanctions recommended by the Committee included reimbursement by those respondents for the costs of the improper travel which had occurred in the previous Congress. Those reimbursements were voluntarily made. Thus the Committee's recommendations, even if filed at a time when the House has adjourned, carry the weight of sanctions if accepted by the respondent Member.

In December 2006 while the 'lame-duck' final session of the 109th Congress was still in session, the investigative subcommittee of the House Standards Committee found that several sitting Members and then current employees, including the Speaker, had not been shown to have committed any specific violation of the Code of Conduct. No Member raised a question of the privileges of the House to collaterally question this subcommittee report. Nevertheless, the report recited findings and conclusions relating to the conduct of the sitting Members and staff over which it retained jurisdiction, in effect a judgement which, while not constituting a finding of specific violation, represented a rebuke of the credibility, inaction, and inattention of the persons under investigation.

The last two efforts in the House to adopt ethics reforms were the result of proposals which emanated solely from the Majority party, and not from bipartisan task forces or the Standards Committee itself. The first such effort, at the beginning of the 109th Congress, proved to be a failure because it was motivated by a partisan desire to minimize the Standards Committee's jurisdiction over a party leader, and was repealed several months later. By contrast, the more recent effort addressing gift and travel restrictions was adopted by almost unanimous bipartisan votes, even though incorporated as part of an opening day rules package recommended by a new Majority party. These latter changes were not perceived to foster partisan advantage, but rather to have been in response to excesses and abuses which had prominently impacted the previous Congressional elections. Nevertheless they contained 'loopholes' (akin to gaps in campaign finance laws) which continued to permit travel financed by companies hiring lobbyists to attend fundraising events if those events were combined with some legislative activity. The resulting scramble for advisory opinions from the Standards Committee as to the propriety of contemplated activity has consumed much of the time of the Committee.[23]

Notes

1. Richard Baker, Senate Historian, 'The History of Congressional Ethics', in B. Jennings and D. Callahan, *Representation and Responsibility: Exploring Legislative Ethics* (1985), 4.
2. W. H. Brown and Charles Johnson (eds), *House Practice* (2003), chapter 25, sect 8.

3. H Rept 90-27.
4. *Hinds' Precedents*, vol ii, sects 1141–2.
5. *Deschler's Precedents*, vol iii, sect 15.
6. Joint Committee on Parliamentary Privilege 1998–9 HL 43-II HC 214-II, p 233 and Qq 887 ff.
7. Unlike Congress, parliamentary standards requirements do not explicitly include staff, though there are separate registers for lobby journalists, Members' staff, and officers of informal parliamentary groupings with industrial (or similar) and country interests.
8. Annual Report of the Commissioner for Standards 2007–8 HC 797 (2007–8).
9. Seventh Report HC 436 (2007–8).
10. HC Deb (2002–3) 407 c 1246.
11. Ninth Report HC 559 (2007–8). The report concerned an allegation that the Speaker's use of publicly funded taxis might not have been in accordance with the Code of Conduct and associated rules. The Commissioner dismissed the complaint and the Committee endorsed both that decision and the grounds on which it was made.
12. Seventh Report, November 2000, Cm 4903.
13. The Committee for Privileges broke new ground in concluding (against the advice of the Attorney General) that there was a basis for suspension of Lords who sat by virtue of receipt of a writ of summons (First Report 2008–9 HL 87). The details of the recommendations in respect of the four Lords in question are to be found in the Second Report, HL 88-I.
14. HL Deb (2008–9) 710 c 1407.
15. House Rules and Manual 806a and Committee on Standards of Official Conduct Rule 6.
16. The Code of Ethics for Government Service likewise embraces this standard of appearance of impropriety by 'restricting favors or benefits under circumstances that might be construed by reasonable persons as influencing the performance of his governmental duties'.
17. H Res 168, 18 September 1997.
18. H Res 895, 11 March 2008.
19. PL 110-81.
20. H Res 240, 27 April 2005.
21. H.Res.31, Jan.21, 1997; H.Rept.105–1. In Boehner v. McDermott, 484 F3d 573 (D.C.Cir. 2007), the unauthorized redistribution (release to the press) of materials in possession of the Standards Committee (a tape of an illegally intercepted telephone conversation released by a member of that committee regarding the investigation of Speaker Gingrich), became the subject of a successful civil action filed for damages brought by a sitting Member (who had participated in the taped conversation). This was the first example of a successful (indeed any) law suit for monetary damages brought by a Member (in 1998, the year following House punishment of the Speaker) against another sitting Member. The defendant Member's claim of First Amendent freedom of speech protection was unavailing, as the release was in violation of Federal law and of a House and committee rule requiring confidentiality.
22. Unfounded Minority Member allegations that the Speaker and Majority Leader had exhibited religious bias in their nomination of a Chaplain took recriminations to a further level of personal and institutional non-collegiality on 23 March 2000 (Cong Rec 106 pages 3477–82), resulting in the Speaker's interim appointment (authorized by law) of the House's first Roman Catholic Chaplain, in order to defuse the situation. The Chaplain was subsequently elected by the House at the beginning of the next (107th) Congress.
23. The disparity in the length of treatment given the two legislatures in this chapter reflects the more accelerated politicization of the ethics process in the US Congress than in Parliament.

12

Conclusion

The extent and pace of procedural change in the US Congress have been appreciable, and have been greatly accelerated in the time frame covered by the authors. On 20 May 2004 a letter of resignation from the Parliamentarian was read to the House of Representatives, in part as follows;

> One need only refer to the prefaces of *Hinds'*, *Cannon's* and *Deschler's* precedents to gain a sense of the procedural evolution in the House for the first 190 years of the Republic and then compare with that documented history the nature and pace of more recent changes to understand the enormity of contemporary developments. Along the way, important matters of separation of powers and continuity of government have occupied high-profile status requiring the attention of my office. Numerous incremental changes have considerably altered the procedural landscape during my career. Examples include increased turnover in membership, committee seniority status, budgetary discipline, appropriations practices, an ethics process, televised proceedings, multiplicity of committee jurisdictions, oversight and authorization prerequisites, the impact of changing Senate practices, disposition of matters in conference, review of Executive actions, authorities to recess, to postpone and cluster votes and consolidate amendments, an issue-specific super-majority vote requirement, electronic capabilities, committee report availabilities, the five-minute rule and other special rule variations, and the interaction between traditional spontaneity of the House's proceedings and trends toward relative predictability of time constraints and issues presented.

These and more recent trends symbolize the diminution of traditions of transparency, fairness, and deliberative capacity which have characterized the House of Representatives for most of its procedural history. The more important, urgent, costly, and complex a measure to be considered in the House, the less time Members are given to scrutinize the measure to be voted upon and the greater the departure from the protections of standing rules. The time and attention given to the drafting of major legislation is adversely impacted by the leadership's rush to floor scheduling which often trumps thorough preparation of the work product. This is accomplished by the most important rule of the

House, that which empowers the Committee on Rules to recommend and the House to adopt virtually overnight ad hoc waivers of points of order in avoidance of those standing rules and traditions. This 'inverse ratio' axiom has increasingly been demonstrated in contemporary Congresses regardless of the Majority party setting the agenda, and despite the protestations of these changing majorities when in the minority.

Analysis of Senate practice and precedent has shown the profound differences and complexities of that body as part of a truly bicameral legislature under a constitutional system of separated and limited powers. The purpose has been to demonstrate the contrast between a majoritarian House of Representatives where the rules and agenda are developed by groups of Members to assure expedited consideration, often by ad hoc waivers of standing rules which might otherwise prolong consideration and enhance individual and Minority Members' options, and a far more individual Member-driven Senate, where the Minority and indeed each Senator exert great influence by the utilization of unanimous consent (sometimes premised upon tacit agreements on unrelated matters) and leverage assured by super-majority invocation of cloture to permit the consideration of most major measures.

This dichotomy is one illustration of the differences between the two parliamentary systems. Other comparisons have demonstrated, despite the common origins described in Thomas Jefferson's *Manual*, the evolution of the two lower Houses into vastly different institutions nowhere better symbolized than in the contrasting roles of their Speakers. The Commons Speaker's duty to enforce Standing Orders or ad hoc rules such as programme orders is not in practice inconsistent with his or her effective representation of the collective interests of the back benches, even though these rules were made by the House on the proposal of a government majority. Debate on legislation at Westminster has never been so restricted either by Standing Orders or by the kind of strict management of specific debates such as may be reported from the Rules Committee in the House of Representatives.

Looking at causes of difference beyond the purely institutional, many choices offer themselves. It may be that in the later twentieth century both American Houses were for so long under the control of the same party (the Democrats controlled the House for forty consecutive years between 1955 and 1995, and the Senate between 1954 and 1981) that when the Republicans gained control their frustration had been so great and their agenda was so pressing that they felt justified in cutting legislative corners. When control changed again, it was difficult for the Democrats to turn the clock back. In the UK since 1950, while a Conservative government has been in power for thirty-five years in aggregate against Labour's twenty-three, and the most recent Conservative period in office was an unbroken eighteen years, a sense of a regular (if less frequent) swing of the pendulum remains.

A two-year mandate in Washington as opposed to an effectively four-year term at Westminster puts a premium on securing re-election—a task beginning the day of election—and ensuring that it is adequately funded, and may well make the securing of political advantage by personal denunciation of opponents a more attractive option than courtesy across the centre aisle. There remains in the Commons an unspoken sense that political warfare has its limits, that the winner ought not to take all. One of the ministers in the new Labour government in 1945—Labour had been out of office since 1931—once incautiously stated 'We are the masters now.' The remark was denounced by his political opponents for decades afterwards as the unacceptable arrogance of triumphalism. Of course elected governments on both sides of the Atlantic must get their legislative way, but only after submitting themselves with as good a grace as they can manage to the scrutiny of the four Houses, in the context of rules which—to mix the metaphor—hold the ring and do not load the dice.

Annex of Tables

Note: in several of the following Tables, S signifies a short session of Parliament, usually before a General Election and L a long session, usually following a General Election

Table 2.1 European scrutiny: documents and debates

	Total number of documents considered by the scrutiny committee	Recommended for debate on the floor of the House	Recommended for debate in European Committee
2003–4	1,294	3	52
2004–5 (S)	251	4	23
2005–6 (L)	1,405	10	80
2006–7	999	5	71
2007–8	886	2	50

Table 3.1 UK Parties and the Speakership 1945–2009

Speaker	Party of origin	Party in power when elected and re-elected	
Clifton Brown	Conservative	1. Coalition	2. Labour
Morrison	Conservative	1. Conservative	2. Conservative
Hylton-Foster	Conservative	1. Conservative	2. Labour
King	Labour	1. Labour	2. Conservative
Selwyn Lloyd	Conservative	1. Conservative	2. Labour 3. Labour
Thomas	Labour	1. Labour	2. Conservative
Weatherill	Conservative	1. Conservative	2. Conservative
Boothroyd	Labour	1. Conservative	2. Labour
Martin	Labour	1. Labour	2. Labour

Table 3.2 Westminster Hall

Session	Number of days on which sittings took place in Westminster Hall	Number of hours of sitting in Westminster Hall	Westminster Hall sittings as a proportion of hours of sitting in the Chamber (%)
2003–4	103	408	30
2004–5 (S)	39	154	23
2005–6 (L)	136	532	34
2006–7	41	355	32
2007–8	110	469	32.75

Table 3.3 Major differences between the House of Representatives and the Senate

The House has a shorter term of office (2 years) compared with the Senate's longer term (6 years);
The House adheres closely to procedural rules on floor activity, while the Senate operates mostly by unanimous consent;
House Members have a narrower constituency, while the Senators have a larger, more varied constituency;
The House originates all revenue (and general appropriation) bills, while the Senate has sole power to ratify treaties and advise and consent to Presidential nominations;
House Members are policy specialists while Senators are policy generalists;
The House has less media and press coverage than the Senate;
Power is less evenly distributed among Members in the House than in the Senate;
Membership in the House is less 'prestigious' than in the Senate;
The House is more expeditious in floor debate than is the Senate;
The House enforces a strict requirement for the germaneness of amendments while the Senate (with limited exceptions) has no germaneness rule for amendments:
House Members rely less on staff than do Senators:
There is more partisanship in the House than in the Senate;
The House has strict limits on debate while the Senate permits unlimited debate; and
House methods of operation stress majority rule while Senate traditions and practices stress minority rights.

Note: Table from Oleszek, *Congressional Procedures and the Policy Process* (7th edn, 2007) at page 25.

Table 3.4 Party allegiances in the Lords, December 2008

Labour	214
Conservatives	198
Liberal Democrat	74
Cross-bench	206
Other	14

Table 3.5 Government defeats in the Lords

F/Y	No. of government defeats	Government defeats as a proportion of all divisions on government business (%)
2003–4	87	36
2004–5	67	43
2005–6	32	33
2006–7	43	34
2007–8	29	24

Note: Of the defeats in 2007–8, the government reversed all but seven.

Table 4.1 Population and representation

	Recent population (million)	Members in lower House
United Kingdom	59	646
France	64	577
Germany	82	612
Italy	59	630
United States	293	435

Table 4.2 UK: electorates and seats

	Total electorate	Average electorate	Seats
England	36,963, 545	70,006	528
Scotland	3,851,290	65,276	59
Wales	2,231,880	55,797	40
N Ireland	1,148,009	63,778	18
UK	44,251,545	68,501	646

Table 4.3 UK: general election major party campaign expenditure 2005 (£m)

	England	Scotland	Wales
Conservative	15.7	1.3	0.8
Labour	15.2	1.6	1
Liberal Democrat	3.6	0.4	0.26

Table 5.1 Sitting days in Parliament

Financial year	Lords	Commons
2003–4	165	151
2004–5	152	151
2005–6	132	134
2006–7	164	164

Table 5.2 Average daily lengths of sitting in both Houses of Parliament

	Lords (FY)	Commons (session)
2003–4	7 hours 9 minutes	7 hours 45 minutes
2004–5	7 hours 13 minutes	8 hours 14 minutes
2005–6	6 hours 39 minutes	7 hours 56 minutes
2006–7	6 hours 43 minutes	7 hours 40 minutes

Note: The average daily length of sitting in the Commons in session 2007–8 was 7 hours 55 minutes.

Table 5.3 Sitting days in Congress

109th Congress 2005–6 1st session:
House in session 140 days, 1,067 hours; and Senate in session 154 days.

109th Congress 2005–6 2nd session:
House in session 101 days, 850 hours; and Senate in session 125 days.

110th Congress 2007–8 1st session:
House in session 164 days, 1,477 hours; and Senate in session 164 days.

110th Congress 2007–8 2nd session:
House in session 118 days, 890 hours; and Senate in session 183 days (many pro forma to prevent recess appointments).

Further statistical data covering the past fifty years considered too lengthy for inclusion at this point may be found at http://www.gpoaccess.gov. Click on 'Congressional Calendars', then click on 'Final Calendars', then search for 'statistical recapitulation'.

Statistical Recapitulation and Comparison: First Session, One Hundred Tenth Congress; First Session, One Hundred Ninth Congress; First Session, One Hundred Eighth Congress; First Session, One Hundred Seventh Congress; First Session, One Hundred Sixth Congress.

House of Representatives

	First Session, One Hundred Tenth Congress	First Session, One Hundred Ninth Congress	First Session, One Hundred Eighth Congress	First Session, One Hundred Seventh Congress	First Session, One Hundred Sixth Congress
Convened	Jan. 4, 2007	Jan. 4, 2005	Jan. 3, 2003	Jan. 3, 2001	Jan. 6, 1999
Adjourned	Dec. 19, 2007	Dec. 22, 2005	Dec. 8, 2003	Dec. 20, 2001	Dec. 22, 1999
Calendar days in session	167	143	138	146	138
Legislative days in session	164	140	133	142	137
Bills introduced	4,930	4,653	3,700	3,610	3,517
Joint resolutions introduced	75	75	83	81	85
Simple resolutions introduced	911	645	485	329	400
Concurrent resolutions introduced	278	330	348	298	239
Total bills and resolutions	6,194	5,703	4,616	4,318	4,241
Public laws:					
Approved	179	169	198	136	170
Over veto	1	0	0	0	0
Without approval	0	0	0	0	0
Total, public laws	180	169	198	136	170
Private laws	0	0	0	1	3
Grand total, public and private laws	180	169	198	137	173

	First Session, One Hundred Tenth Congress	First Session, One Hundred Ninth Congress	First Session, One Hundred Eighth Congress	First Session, One Hundred Seventh Congress	First Session, One Hundred Sixth Congress
Committee reports:					
Union calendar	301	184	224	([1]) 196	260
House calendar	174	141	139	118	164
Private calendar	0	1	1	3	8
Conference reports	12	20	24	21	26
Special reports	8	10	6	9	12
Not assigned to a calendar	12	8	11	6	18
Total	507	364	405	353	488
Reported bills acted upon:					
Union calendar	257	120	161	164	205
House calendar	168	111	123	113	159
Private calendar	0	1	1	2	6
Conference reports	12	20	24	21	26
Special reports	0	0	0	0	0
Total acted upon	437	252	309	300	396
Special reports, conference reports, reported bills pending, and not assigned	70	112	96	53	92
Total reported	507	364	405	353	488
Resolutions agreed to:					
Simple	453	262	221	175	213
House concurrent	94	88	77	91	70
Senate concurrent	9	11	8	9	6
Total agreed to	556	361	306	275	289

[1]Total reflects one measure discharged from the Union Calendar. (19–61)

Statistical Recapitulation and Comparison: Second Session, One Hundred Tenth Congress; Second Session, One Hundred Ninth Congress; Second Session, One Hundred Eighth Congress; Second Session, One Hundred Seventh Congress; Second Session, One Hundred Sixth Congress.

House of Representatives

	Second Session, One Hundred Tenth Congress	Second Session, One Hundred Ninth Congress	Second Session, One Hundred Eighth Congress	Second Session, One Hundred Seventh Congress	Second Session, One Hundred Sixth Congress
Convened	Jan. 3, 2008	Jan. 3, 2006	Jan. 20, 2004	Jan. 23, 2002	Jan. 24, 2000
Adjourned	Jan. 3, 2009	Dec. 9, 2006	Dec. 7, 2004	Dec. 22, 2002	Dec. 15, 2000
Calendar days in session	119	104	110	126	138
Legislative days in session	119	101	110	123	135
Bills introduced	2,410	1,783	1,731	2,157	2,164
Joint resolutions introduced	26	27	32	44	49
Simple resolutions introduced	624	465	390	287	280
Concurrent resolutions introduced	165	174	184	223	208
Total bills and resolutions	3,225	2,449	2,337	2,711	2,701
Public laws:					
Approved	277	313	300	241	410
Over veto	3	0	0	0	0
Without approval	0	0	0	0	0
Total, public laws	280	313	200	241	410
Private laws	0	1	6	5	21
Grand total, public and private laws	280	314	306	246	431
Committee reports:					
Union calendar	277	221	241	268	304
House calendar	111	111	119	122	163
Private calendar	5	1	5	6	21
Conference reports	4	9	15	16	27
Special reports	28	34	24	34	40
Not assigned to a calendar	10	12	9	12	13
Total	435	388	413	458	568
Reported bills acted upon:					
Union calendar	215	152	170	168	218
House calendar	111	90	93	420	458
Private calendar	4	1	4	6	22
Conference reports	4	9	15	15	27
Special reports	0	0	0	0	0
Total acted upon	334	252	282	309	425

	Second Session, One Hundred Tenth Congress	Second Session, One Hundred Ninth Congress	Second Session, One Hundred Eighth Congress	Second Session, One Hundred Seventh Congress	Second Session, One Hundred Sixth Congress
Special reports, conference reports, reported bills pending, and not assigned	101	136	131	149	143
Total reported	435	388	413	458	568
Resolutions agreed to:					
Simple	369	213	211	169	18180
House concurrent	94	78	88	84	27
Senate concurrent	6	9	15	10	
Total agreed to	469	300	314	263	288

(19–62)

Statistical Recapitulation and Comparison: One Hundred Tenth Congress; One Hundred Ninth Congress; One Hundred Eighth Congress; One Hundred Seventh Congress; One Hundred Sixth Congress.

House of Representatives

	One Hundred Tenth Congress	One Hundred Ninth Congress	One Hundred Eighth Congress	One Hundred Seventh Congress	One Hundred Sixth Congress
Convened	Jan. 4, 2007	Jan. 4, 2005	Jan. 7, 2003	Jan. 3, 2001	Jan. 6, 1999
Adjourned	Dec. 3, 2009	Dec. 9, 2006	Dec. 7, 2004	Nov. 22, 2002	Dec. 15, 2000
Calendar days in session	286	247	248	272	276
Legislative days in session	283	241	243	265	272
Bills introduced	7,340	6,436	5,431	5,767	5,681
Joint resolutions introduced	101	102	115	125	134
Simple resolutions introduced	1,535	1,110	875	616	680
Concurrent resolutions introduced	443	504	532	521	447
Total bills and resolutions	9,419	8,152	6,953	7,029	6,942
Public laws:					
Approved	456	482	498	377	580
Over veto	4	0	0	0	0
Without approval	0	0	0	0	0
Total, public laws	460	482	498	377	580

(*continued*)

	One Hundred Tenth Congress	One Hundred Ninth Congress	One Hundred Eighth Congress	One Hundred Seventh Congress	One Hundred Sixth Congress
Private laws	0	1	6	6	24
Grand total, public and private laws	460	483	504	383	604
Committee reports:					
Union calendar	578	405	465	464	564
House calendar	285	252	258	240	327
Private calendar	5	2	6	9	29
Conference reports	16	29	39	37	53
Special reports	36	44	30	43	52
Not assigned to a calendar	22	20	20	18	31
Total[1]	942	752	818	811	1,056
Reported bills acted upon:					
Union calendar	472	272	331	332	423
House calendar	279	201	216	233	317
Private calendar	4	2	5	5	28
Conference reports	16	29	39	36	53
Special reports	0	0	0	0	0
Total acted upon	771	504	591	609	821
Special reports, conference reports, reported bills pending, and not assigned	171	248	227	202	235
Total reported	942	752	818	811	1,056
Resolutions agreed to:					
Simple	822	475	432	344	394
House concurrent	188	166	165	175	150
Senate concurrent	15	20	23	19	33
Total agreed to	1,025	661	620	538	577

[1]Total reflects one measure discharged from the Union Calendar and subsequently reassigned to it. (19–63)

Comparative Statement, Work of the Fifty-Second to the One Hundred Tenth Congress, Inclusive, House of Representatives

Congress	Number of bills	Number of reports	Public laws	Private laws	Total laws
Fifty-second	10,623	2,613	398	324	722
Fifty-third	8,987	1,982	463	248	711
Fifty-fourth	10,378	3,080	384	564	948
Fifty-fifth	12,223	2,364	429	1,044	1,473
Fifty-sixth	14,339	3,006	443	1,498	1,941
Fifty-seventh	17,560	3,919	470	2,311	2,781
Fifty-eighth	19,209	4,904	574	3,467	4,041

Congress	Number of bills	Number of reports	Public laws	Private laws	Total laws
Fifty-ninth	25,897	8,174	692	6,248	6,940
Sixtieth	28,440	2,300	350	234	584
Sixty-first	33,015	2,302	525	285	810
Sixty-second	28,870	1,628	530	186	716
Sixty-third	21,616	1,513	417	283	700
Sixty-fourth	21,104	1,637	458	226	684
Sixty-fifth	16,239	1,187	404	104	508
Sixty-sixth	16,170	1,420	470	124	594
Sixty-seventh	14,475	1,763	655	276	931
Sixty-eighth	12,474	1,652	707	289	996
Sixty-ninth	17,415	2,319	808	537	1,423
Seventieth	17,334	2,821	1,145	577	1,722
Seventy-first	17,373	2,946	1,009	515	1,524
Seventy-second	14,799	2,201	516	327	843
Seventy-third	9,968	2,066	540	436	976
Seventy-fourth	13,026	3,087	985	737	1,722
Seventy-fifth	10,940	2,785	919	840	1,759
Seventy-sixth	10,735	3,113	1,005	657	1,662
Seventy-seventh	7,869	2,748	850	635	1,485
Seventy-eighth	5,628	2,099	568	589	1,157
Seventy-ninth	7,239	2,728	733	892	1,625
Eightieth	7,163	2,479	906	457	1,363
Eighty-first	9,944	3,254	921	1,103	2,024
Eighty-second	8,568	2,519	594	1,023	1,617
Eighty-third	10,288	2,685	781	1,002	1,783
Eighty-fourth	12,467	2,974	1,028	893	1,921
Eighty-fifth	13,876	2,719	936	784	1,720
Eighty-sixth	13,304	2,238	800	492	1,292
Eighty-seventh	13,420	2,571	885	684	1,569
Eighty-eighth	12,829	1,947	666	360	1,026
Eighty-ninth	18,552	2,349	810	473	1,283
Ninetieth	20,587	1,985	640	362	1,002
Ninety-first	20,015	1,808	695	246	941
Ninety-second	17,230	1,637	607	161	768
Ninety-third	17,690	1,668	651	123	774
Ninety-fourth	15,863	1,793	588	141	729
Ninety-fifth	14,414	1,843	633	170	803
Ninety-sixth	8,456	1,567	613	123	736
Ninety-seventh	7,458	1,013	473	56	529
Ninety-eighth	6,442	1,199	623	54	677
Ninety-ninth	5,743	1,045	664	24	688
One Hundredth	5,585	1,135	713	48	761
One Hundred First	5,977	1,026	650	16	666
One Hundred Second	6,212	1,102	590	20	610
One Hundred Third	5,310	894	465	8	473
One Hundred Fourth	4,344	887	333	4	337
One Hundred Fifth	4,874	851	394	10	404
One Hundred Sixth	5,681	1,056	580	24	604
One Hundred Seventh	5,767	811	377	6	383
One Hundred Eighth	5,431	818	498	6	504
One Hundred Ninth	6,436	752	482	1	483
One Hundred Tenth	7,340	942	460	0	460

Table 7.1 Questions for oral answer in the Commons

Session	On the Order Paper	Answered orally	Percentage answered orally
2003–4	3,687	2,060	55.9
2004–5(S)	1,438	848	58.8
2005–6(L)	5,353	2,712	50.7
2006–7	3,776	1,775	47
2007–8	5,151	2,645	53

Table 7.2 Departments answering in the first week after the Christmas adjournment 2008–9

Monday 12 January 2009	Defence
Tuesday 13 January 2009	Foreign & Commonwealth
Wednesday 14 January 2009	Duchy of Lancaster: Prime Minister
Thursday 15 January 2009	Environment, Food and Rural Affairs

Table 7.3 Number of Questions not answered

	On the Order of Business for oral answer	Not answered orally
Monday 26 January 2009		
Children, Schools & Families	25	16
Tuesday 27 January 2009		
Transport	19	13
Wednesday 28 January 2009		
Wales	13	8
Prime Minister	14	see below
Thursday 29 January 2009		
Innovation Universities & Science	23	14
Monday 2 February 2009		
Work & Pensions	24	15
Tuesday 3 February 2009		
Justice	23	13
Wednesday 4 February 2009		
Scotland	15	11
Prime Minister	15	see below
Thursday 5 February 2009		
Business, Enterprise & Regulatory Reform	19	14

Note: The Questions to the Prime Minister being all in the same form—'if he will list his official engagements'—the total not answered orally for lack of time is not relevant.

Table 7.4 Topical questions

	Number answered	Number of Members intervening
Monday 26 January 2009 Children, Schools and Families	7	12
Tuesday 27 January 2009 Transport	7	8
Thursday 29 January 2009 Innovation, Universities & Skills	9	11
Monday 2 February 2009 Work and Pensions	6	15
Tuesday 3 February 2009 Justice	10	16
Thursday 5 February 2009 Business, Enterprise & 　Regulatory Reform	8	8

Note: The last column includes the original questioner but not frontbenchers on either side.

Table 7.5 Urgent questions

Session	Allowed
2003–4	12
2004–5 (S)	4
2005–6 (L)	14
2006–7	9
2007–8	4

Table 7.6 Questions for written answer

Session	Sessional total	Daily average
2003–4	54,875	350
2004–5(S)	22,292	343
2005–6(L)	95,041	457
2006–7	57,825	396
2007–8	73,357	444

Table 8.1 Numbers of select committees and Members

Session	Number of select and joint committees, including subcommittees	Number of Members serving on them
1977–8	41	244
1978–9 (S)	37	222
2005–6 (L)	48	382
2006–7	48	364
2007–8	50	326

Note: Number of committees excludes those dealing with the guillotining of bills and private business.

Table 8.2 Select and Joint Committee meetings

Session	Number of formal meetings
1977–8	552
1978–9 (S)	261
2004–5 (S)	577
2005–6 (L)	1,500
2006–7	1,096
2007–8	1,204

Table 9.1 Bills in the Commons

	Total public bills bills introduced or brought from the Lords	Of which govt bills	Percentage of govt bills enacted
2003–4	131	36	91.5[a]
2004–5 (S)	88	32	65.6[b]
2005–6 (L)	179	58	94[c]
2006–7	131	34	88[d]
2007–8	138	30	90[e]

[a]Three government bills were suspended until the following session.
[b]Of the eleven government bills which did not receive the Royal Assent, proceedings on one were suspended until the following session; and the remainder fell when Parliament was prorogued with a view to the following general election.
[c]Three government bills were suspended until the following session. The success rate of government bills would be even higher if these bills were counted with those enacted in the session in which they originated.
[d]One government bill was rejected by the Lords and three were suspended until the following session.
[e]Two government bills were suspended until the following session.

Table 9.2 Private Members' bills in the Commons

	Total private Members' bills introduced or brought from Lords	Of which enacted	Percentage of private Members' bills enacted
2003–4	95	5	5.26
2004–5 (S)	56	0	0
2005–6 (L)	118	3	2.46
2006–7	97	3	3
2007–8	106	3	2.8

Table 9.3 Committee of the whole House: Commons

Session	Number of bills in Committee of the whole House	Days on which Committee of the whole House sat
2003–4	3	5
2004–5 (S)	7	9
2005–6 (L)	8	14
2006–7	8	9
2007–8	6	18

Table 9.4 Programme motions

Session	Number of government bills programmed at all or some stages in the Commons	Percentage programmed
2003–4	28 out of 35	80
2004–5 (S)	18 out of 29	62
2005–6 (L)	44 out of 52	86
2006–7	24 out of 28	86
2007–8	23 out of 28	82

Note: Consolidated Fund bills are not taken into consideration in reckoning the total of government bills.

Table 9.5 Draft Bills

Session	Draft bills
1997–8	3
1999–2000	6
2000–1	2
2001–2	7
2002–3	9
2003–4	12
2004–5	5
2005–6	3
2006–7	4
2007–8	6

Table 9.6 Carry-over of bills between sessions

Session	No. of Government bills introduced into the Commons	No. of bills carried over to the following session
2003–4	25	3
2004–5 (S)	25	1
2005–6 (L)	42	3
2006–7	24	3
2007–8	22	2

Note: One hybrid bill—that is, a bill brought in by the Government affecting private rights in the manner of a private bill—figures in each of the sessions 2004–5, 2005–6, and 2006–7.

Table 11.1 Parliament: Standards Complaints which do not proceed

	2002–3	2003–4	2004–5	2005–6	2006–7	2007–8
All complaints	67	152	137	133	214	248
Not proceeded with	28	82	76	106	95	155
Failed at preliminary stage	10	6	15	15	11	29

Source: Annual Report of the Commissioner for Standards 2007–8 HC 797.

Table 11.2 Parliament: Standards Committee and Members

	2002–3	2003–4	2004–5	2005–6	2006–7	2007–8
All complaints	67	152	137	133	214	248
Complaints investigated	11	7	27	8	70	42
Commissioner's Memoranda to Committee regarding Members	10	6	21	0	53	15

Source: Seventh Report from the Committee on Standards and Privileges 2007–8 HC 436.

Table 11.3 Parliament: Members suspended on the recommendation of the Standards Committee

Session	Number of Members
2001–2	2
2002–3	2
2004–5	1
2005–6	–
2006–7	1
2007–8	1

Index

Where appropriate, the following key is used to identify the House or Houses to which an index entry refers. Many parenthetical cross-references are used, partially to overcome the asymmetry in indexing.

US *Congress*   HR *House of Representatives*   S *Senate*
P *Parliament*   HC *House of Commons*   HL *House of Lords*